Inside
CorelDRAW! 5

Fifth Edition

Dan Gray
Steve Bain
Gary Bouton
Jim Boyce
John Faunce
Ed Fleiss
Sue Plummley
Ken Reeder
June Reeder
Cheri Robinson
William Schneider
John Shanley

NRP
NEW RIDERS
PUBLISHING

New Riders Publishing, Indianapolis, Indiana

Inside CorelDRAW! 5, Fifth Edition

By Dan Gray et al

Published by:
New Riders Publishing
201 West 103rd Street
Indianapolis, IN 46290 USA

Printed in the United States of America 1 2 3 4 5 6 7 8 9 0

```
***CIP data available upon request***
```

Warning and Disclaimer

This book is designed to provide information about the CorelDRAW! computer program. Every effort has been made to make this book as complete and as accurate as possible, but no warranty or fitness is implied.

The information is provided on an "as is" basis. The author and New Riders Publishing shall have neither liability nor responsibility to any person or entity with respect to any loss or damages arising from the information contained in this book or from the use of the disks or programs that may accompany it.

Publisher	Lloyd J. Short
Associate Publisher	Tim Huddleston
Product Development Manager	Rob Tidrow
Marketing Manager	Ray Robinson
Director of Special Projects	Cheri Robinson
Managing Editor	Matthew Morrill

 The text in this book is printed on recycled paper.

About the Authors

Dan Gray is a journeyman graphics artist who has been involved in both traditional and electronic publishing for more than 12 years. Dan's electronic publishing experience includes stints at the drawing board, in the darkroom, in systems management, and with personal computers. Dan has worked on dozens of publications including The Princeton Packet and Women's Wear Daily. He is the author of Inside CorelDRAW!, a perennial bestseller. Dan currently is a Graphics Systems Analyst for the Continental Corporation and uses both Windows and Macintosh platforms to publish a wide range of periodicals. Readers are invited to contact Dan through CompuServe. His CIS number is 71210,667.

Steve Bain is an accomplished artist and free-lance graphics designer in Vancouver, Canada. His editorial writing, photography, and graphics illustration work appear regularly in *Corel Magazine*, *The Desktop Journal* (National Association of Desktop Publishers), and *Corelation Magazine*. He devotes much of his technical expertise to graphical and multimedia software development, digital color technology consulting, and digital color prepress system management. Steve is on Corel's Corporate Advisory Council and participates in its technical beta-testing program. He was a top-prize winner in Corel's 1993 World Art Competition for technical illustration, and earned an Award of Excellence for graphical presentation. Readers are invited to contact Steve through CompuServe. His CIS number is 72623,1233.

Gary Bouton is owner of Exclamat!ons, a company that "polishes rough ideas." He spends time training clients in the digital equivalents of traditional media as they produce electronic presentations, desktop publishing work, logos, graphics, and collateral materials. Gary has written several books for New Riders Publishing including, *CorelDRAW! for Beginners*, *Inside Adobe Photoshop for Windows*, and *Adobe Photoshop NOW!*. Gary has been in advertising for the past 20 years. He was a winner in the CorelDRAW! World Design Contest for the past two years, and has received international awards for *NewsBytes*, a local users group newsletter of which he is editor.

Jim Boyce is a Contributing Editor of Windows Magazine and a regular contributor to CADENCE Magazine and other computer publications. He has been involved with computers since the late 70s and has used computers in one way or another as a structural designer, production planner, systems manager, programmer, and college instructor. He has a wide range of experience in the DOS, Windows, and UNIX environments. Jim is the author and co-author of numerous books published by New Riders Publishing.

John Faunce discovered an interest in computers in the early 60s. He has built, sold, programmed, taught, and used PCs. He worked for Travelers Insurance Company operating UNIVAC mainframes, and then later worked for IBM as a systems programmer. He left the computer industry in 1975 only to return in 1985.

Ed Fleiss is a Technology Sales Manager for Marcus Computer Services, Inc., an integration firm specializing in the graphics industry. He also is a contributing editor of *Computer Pictures Magazine*. Ed has served as Director and Treasurer for International Digital Imaging Association since its inception in 1990. He resides on Long Island with his wife and daughter.

Sue Plummley is owner of Humble Opinions, a consulting firm that provides software training as well as network consultation and installation. Sue is author of *Inside Adobe Illustrator Version 4 for Windows* from New Riders Publishing and has written and co-authored several books for Que Corp.

Ken Reeder is co-owner with his wife, June, of Ideas to Images, a graphics training and consulting business. Ken has been a writer and trainer for the past three years. He also has traveled nationwide giving printing and publishing seminars. Ken has worked in advertising and as a communications manager.

June Reeder is co-owner with her husband, Ken, of Ideas to Images, a graphics training and consulting business. She has been a writer and trainer for the past five years. June has traveled nationwide giving printing and publishing seminars and worked as a product development specialist, writing, directing, and producing computer training videos.

Cheri Robinson is Director of Special Projects for New Riders Publishing, and specializes in Windows graphics and desktop publishing topics and electronic publishing. She has developed several New Riders graphics titles including Inside Adobe Photoshop for Windows, CorelDRAW! for Beginners, New Riders' Official Internet Yellow Pages, and CorelDRAW! Special Effects. Cheri also co-authored The Fonts Coach for New Riders. Before coming to Macmillan Publishing, she was a graphics designer for a monthly trade magazine.

William Schneider has degrees in both engineering and fine arts from Ohio University. After spending 10 years working as an engineer, he left the field to pursue a career in fine art photography. He has written for *Corel Magazine* and *Corelation*, and authored several books. His illustrations have appeared in books such as *CorelDRAW! Special Effects, Looking Good with CorelDRAW!*, and *Using CorelDRAW! 4*. William also has worked as a technical editor for New Riders Publishing. He currently teaches photography and desktop publishing at Ohio University's School of Visual Communication.

John Shanley is president of Phoenix Creative Graphics, a Somerset, New Jersey graphics design firm. He is a traditionally trained designer and illustrator who has worked in the graphics art and advertising field since 1975. John has used CorelDRAW! since version 1. You can contact John through CompuServe. His CIS number is 76535,3443.

Trademark Acknowledgments

All terms mentioned in this book that are known to be trademarks or service marks have been appropriately capitalized. New Riders Publishing cannot attest to the accuracy of this information. Use of a term in this book should not be regarded as affecting the validity of any trademark or service mark. CorelDRAW! is a registered copyright of Corel Systems Corporation.

Product Director
CHERI ROBINSON

Production Editors
LISA WILSON
CLIFF SHUBS

Editors
AMY BEZEK
LAURA FREY
PETER KUHNS
JOHN SLEEVA
STEVE WEISS

Technical Editor
GIUSEPPE DeBELLIS

Acquisitions Coordinator
STACEY BEHELER

Editorial Assistant
KAREN OPAL

Publisher's Assistant
MELISSA LYNCH

Cover Designer
JEAN BISESI

Book Designer
ROGER S. MORGAN

Graphics Image Specialists
CLINT LAHNEN
TIM MONTGOMERY
DENNIS SHEEHAN
SUSAN VANDEWALLE

Production Imprint Manager
JULI COOK

Production Imprint Team Leader
KATY BODENMILLER

Production Analysts
DENNIS CLAY HAGER
MARY BETH WAKEFIELD

Production Team
NICK ANDERSON
CHERYL CAMERON
STEPH DAVIS
MIKE DIETSCH
TERRI EDWARDS
ROB FALCO
KIMBERLY K. HANNEL
ANGELA P. JUDY
AYANNA LACEY
STEPHANIE J. McCOMB
MICHELLE MITCHELL
WENDY OTT
SHELLY PALMA
CHAD POORE
CASEY PRICE
SUSAN SHEPARD
MARCELLA THOMPSON
SCOTT TULLIS

Indexers
BRONT DAVIS
JOHNNA VANHOOSE

Acknowledgments

Once upon a time, *Inside CorelDRAW!* was a cool little book about a great little illustration program. Over the years, both this book and CorelDRAW! have grown to astounding proportions. All of this would have not been possible without the help of many fine people over the years.

To my fellow New Riders—Rusty Gesner, Kevin Coleman, Margaret Berson, Cheri Robinson, Stacey Beheler, Lisa Wilson, Cliff Shubs, and Tim Huddleston—this is no easy business we're in, but together, we've had a great ride.

At Corel Corporation, merci beaucoup to Vivi Nichol, Rus Miller, Fiona Rochester, Kelly Grieg, Bill Cullen, and everyone else who has been so helpful during the course of this book.

This book has been written by designers, for designers. Many thanks to all of my contributing authors, without whom this monstrous project would have never been put to bed: Ken and June Reeder for the Chart chapters; William Schneider for the Trace chapter; John Shanley for the Show and Move chapters; Ed Fleiss for the Paint chapter; John Faunce for the Mosaic chapter; Gary Bouton for the fonts chapters and the fonts appendix; Steve Bain for the color and system calibration, Windows controls, filters, reproduction, and service bureaus chapters, and part of the printing chapter; and finally, Cheri Robinson, at the bottom of the ninth inning, for the installation appendix. And a tip of the hat to Giuseppe DeBellis for his sharp technical editing.

The awesome CD-ROM that accompanies this book is the result of many months of phone tag and late night faxes. In particular, many thanks to John Halloran, Anthony Jackson, Bill Davis, Virginia Schmitz, and everyone else who returned my calls and came through with such great stuff!

My deepest gratitude to Gary Cartright for his humor, insight, and for teaching me (way back in 1990) the right way to engineer an electronic illustration.

Debbie, Allie, and Colton, you still deserve the most thanks of all.

Contents at a Glance

Table of Contents

Introduction

CorelDRAW! 5 continues to be the premiere Windows graphics package. The program has an intuitive interface that makes it easy to learn, but tricky to master. When you master CorelDRAW!, however, you can create publication-quality artwork on your PC, a domain formerly ruled by the Macintosh.

With version 5, you truly have in hand the total desktop publishing solution. This graphics suite of products enables you to create beautiful illustrations, professional advertising, brochures, annual reports, and to integrate your work into almost any other program.

CorelDRAW!, the cornerstone program in the package, is an object-oriented drawing program. In many ways, it is more similar to computer-aided design (CAD) programs—such as AutoCAD—than it is to many PC-based graphics programs. CorelDRAW! may seem akin to paint programs with its CorelPHOTO-PAINT! module, but the differences are clear. Paint programs use bitmapped graphics and give the illusion of painting on canvas or working with pencils. Although you draw in both genres, the process of producing an image in CorelDRAW! is more like building a collage.

Vector-based (rather than bitmapped) programs such as CorelDRAW! are the electronic artist's tool of choice for print media. The two major benefits of an object-oriented drawing program are precision and flexibility. Because you define objects with vector coordinates—think of it as working with mathematical equations—you can operate with output-device and resolution independence.

Who Should Read This Book

This book is written for anyone who uses CorelDRAW! or its associated modules and for newcomers to the program. Users can include:

✔ New and entry-level computer artists. Whether you currently use a computer graphics program or are new to computer graphics, this book eases the transition by getting you up to speed quickly.

✔ Users upgrading to version 5 from previous versions of CorelDRAW!. Release 5 offers many new features and time-saving shortcuts. This book spotlights the differences so that you quickly learn the new features.

How This Book Is Organized

Inside CorelDRAW! 5, 5th Edition is divided into six parts, which present a logical progression of information for inexperienced as well as seasoned CorelDRAW! users.

Part One: The Basics

In Part One, you start with the simplest of maneuvers and progress through the essentials of creating basic artwork. You also learn to manipulate the lines within your drawings.

Part Two: Putting CorelDRAW! To Work

You learn the basics of typography in the second part and how to perform some basic manipulations on type to create interesting typographical effects. You also learn to use the outline and fill features along with CorelDRAW!'s outstanding color management options. You learn some tips on creating advanced drawings and how to print your work.

Part Three: Using Corel's Modules

Part Three discusses the other modules that accompany version 5. You learn to design and create charts with CorelCHART!. You also learn proper scanning techniques and how you can incorporate photographs into your Draw creations by using CorelTRACE!. You create an animation sequence with CorelMOVE! and use CorelSHOW! to make a presentation.

Part Four: Advanced Topics

Part Four emphasizes the advanced topics that can really cause problems for the computer artist. You learn how to manage color and system calibration so that your end product looks like the product you designed. You learn to create your own font and to customize other fonts. Working to get good output from your service bureau is presented, as well as dealing with large files.

Part Five: Hardware Concerns

CorelDRAW! is an extremely powerful and large program that requires special considerations concerning system performance. This part concentrates on the additions you can make to your system to enhance CorelDRAW!'s performance.

Part Six: Appendixes

The appendixes include information on installing CorelDRAW!, keyboard shortcuts, a clip-art compendium, design tips, and more.

Using This Book

Inside CorelDRAW! 5, 5th Edition is a tutorial reference meant for you to use as you are sitting at the computer. You will find that the immediate visual feedback you get provides a most effective means of learning.

This book is neither a substitute for, nor a restatement of, the program's documentation. It was written as a learning tool and a reference. The CorelDRAW! reference manual and online help, along with other material from Corel, are as necessary as this book.

Exercise Syntax and Conventions

You also need to understand how the exercises are presented. The exercises are organized in a straightforward manner so that they are easy to follow and to use as a reference. The exercises are set apart from the rest of the text and are set up in a two-column format. You will find commands and instructions in the left column. Letters that are underlined on the screen are shown in bold text. Characters that you must type also appear in bold text. Each exercises's right column contains comments that correspond to the operations.

Many of the exercises are tied to text or drawings that you will find on the accompanying CD. This technique cuts your learning time by trimming the time required to create drawings or type text.

A Book for All Learning Styles

Inside CorelDRAW! 5, 5th Edition is a book that will work for you no matter what your learning style is. The book contains the following highlighted text:

Tip. Tips highlight special features, shortcuts, or other information that enhances your use of CorelDRAW!.

On the Disc. This icon points out the hands-on sample material that is found on the accompanying CD.

Note. Notes present extra information you should find useful, but which complements the discussion at hand, instead of being a direct part of it.

Stop. A Stop tells you when a procedure may be dangerous. They instruct you on how to avoid data loss, or describe the steps you can take to remedy the situation.

New To Version 5. Highlights features new to version 5.

Conventions Used in This Book

Most New Riders books use similar conventions to help you distinguish between various elements of the software, Windows, and sample data.

This means that once you purchase a New Riders Publishing book, you'll find it easier to use all the other books. Before you look ahead, you should spend a moment examining these conventions:

- ✔ Key combinations appear in the following formats:

  Key1+Key2: When you see a plus sign between key names, you should hold down the first key as you press the second key. Then release both keys.

- ✔ Windows programs underline one letter in all menus, menu items, and most dialog box options. For example, the File menu is displayed on screen as File.

  The underlined letter indicates which letter you can type to choose that command or option.

- ✔ Text you type is in **boldface**. This applies to individual letters and numbers, as well as text strings. This convention, however, does not apply to command keys, such as Enter, Esc, or Ctrl.

- ✔ New terms appear in *italic*.

New Riders Publishing

The staff of New Riders Publishing is committed to bringing you the very best in computer reference material. Each New Riders book is the result of months of work by authors and staff, who research and refine the information contained within its covers.

As part of this commitment to you, the NRP reader, New Riders invites your input. Please let us know if you enjoy the book, if you have trouble with the information and examples presented, or if you have a suggestion for the next edition.

Please note, though: New Riders staff cannot serve as a technical resource for CorelDRAW! or for related questions about software- or hardware-related problems. Please refer to the documentation that accompanies CorelDRAW! or to the applications' Help systems.

If you have a question or comment about any New Riders book, there are several ways to contact New Riders Publishing. We will respond to as many readers as we can. Your name, address, or phone number will never become part of a mailing list or be used for any purpose other than to help us continue to bring you the best books possible. You can write us at the following address:

New Riders Publishing
Attn: Associate Publisher
201 W. 103rd Street
Indianapolis, IN 46290

If you prefer, you can fax New Riders Publishing at (317) 581-4670.

You can send electronic mail to New Riders from a variety of sources. NRP maintains several mailboxes organized by topic area. Mail in these mailboxes will be forwarded to the staff member who is best able to address your concerns. Substitute the appropriate mailbox name from the list below when addressing your e-mail. The mailboxes are as follows:

ADMIN	Comments and complaints for NRP's Publisher
APPS	Word, Excel, WordPerfect, other office applications
ACQ	Book proposal inquiries by potential authors
CAD	AutoCAD, 3D Studio, AutoSketch, and CAD products
DATABASE	Access, dBASE, Paradox, and other database products
GRAPHICS	CorelDRAW!, Photoshop, and other graphics products
INTERNET	Internet
NETWORK	NetWare, LANtastic, and other network-related topics
OS	MS-DOS, OS/2, all OS except UNIX and Windows
UNIX	UNIX
WINDOWS	Microsoft Windows (all versions)
OTHER	Anything that doesn't fit the above categories

If you use an MHS e-mail system that routes through CompuServe, send your messages to:

mailbox @ NEWRIDER

To send NRP mail from CompuServe, use the following address:

MHS: *mailbox* @ NEWRIDER

To send mail from the Internet, use the following address format:

mailbox@newrider.mhs.compuserve.com

NRP is an imprint of Macmillan Computer Publishing. To obtain a catalog or information or to purchase any Macmillan Computer Publishing book, call (800) 428-5331.

Thank you for selecting *Inside CorelDRAW! 5, Fifth Edition*!

Part One

The Basics

Chapter Snapshot

Before you embark on a voyage, you should always check your bearings. In this case, if you expect to chart a course to electronic design nirvana, you need to understand CorelDRAW!'s operating basics. In this chapter, you learn to do the following:

- ✔ Open, close, save, and create new files

- ✔ Manipulate objects by moving, scaling, stretching, mirroring, and rotating

- ✔ Undo and redo changes

- ✔ Get a better view with the Zoom tool

- ✔ Adjust page setup and paper size

- ✔ Print files

If you don't know your port from your starboard, you are bound for trouble. These CorelDRAW! basics help to keep you out of dangerous waters. Get ready to shove off!

CHAPTER

Getting Up and Running

To function efficiently within the CorelDRAW! environment, you need to know how to handle all the basics. Even if you are familiar with the program's basic operation, you should look through this chapter. You are bound to pick up a hint or two along the way.

This chapter lays the foundation on which you build in the following chapters. To begin, you learn to start CorelDRAW! and open an existing Draw file. (Throughout this book, the name "CorelDRAW!" is often shortened to just "Draw.") After you open the file, you learn to use features such as Select, Move, Size and Stretch, Rotate, and Zoom features. Finally, you learn to save your file, open a new file, adjust the page setup, and import clip art.

As you move through the exercises, you learn the ways in which CorelDRAW! clusters multiple functions within a single tool. This organization runs throughout the program and is crucial to Draw's functionality.

The tutorial exercises in this book are written with the assumption that your hard disk is drive C and that your floppy disk is inserted in drive A. If your computer is set up differently, substitute your own drive letters as appropriate. The book assumes that you are using CorelDRAW! version 5.0.

You should have a basic knowledge of Microsoft Windows and be familiar with buttons, windows, scroll bars, and so on. If not, check the documentation that comes with the Windows program.

Getting Rolling with DeLook Design

In the imaginary village of Seaside, Joe DeLook has loaded CorelDRAW! on his PC's hard disk, and he is ready to take the plunge into the world of electronic art.

It is well past closing time on Friday afternoon, and everyone has left except for Joe. Rather than sitting with his buddies at the Beached Whale Brew Pub, Joe is sitting at his PC. While he'd rather be out having a cold one, Joe is intent on learning to use CorelDRAW!.

Joe has little experience with personal computers, but he has a solid background in graphics design. Although the PC has been in the studio for a few months, it has been used mostly for bookkeeping—not design work. Sitting at the PC, Joe has been aimlessly flipping through the book of symbol and clip-art libraries that came with the CorelDRAW! package. Leafing through the transportation section, he sees many fabulous cars, but none strikes his current fancy. Thankfully, a rendering of his favorite auto du jour—the Dodge Stealth—is featured on the CD-ROM that came with this book. Joe notes that the file is called STLTH50B.CDR, and he decides to see if he can load it into Draw. Before you begin, make sure that CorelDRAW! is properly installed. The installation process is easy to follow, although it can take some time to install the full program. The installation procedure includes options that enable you to install the program and its associated files according to your preferences. You can, for instance, choose which fonts to install, or whether to install the clip-art files or, if you have a scanner, you can select to install the appropriate driver, enabling you to scan pictures directly into Draw. For more information on installing CorelDRAW!, refer to Appendix A.

To perform many of the exercises in this book, you need to have the clip art handy. For best results, load pre-existing artwork (such as commercial clip art or a file you have created and saved on floppy disk) onto your computer's hard disk while you are outside the CorelDRAW! program. Although you can load your clip art into an existing subdirectory, the best advice is to create subdirectories of your own. These can be organized by subject, project, client, dates, or whatever scheme may suit your needs.

You can find most of Draw's clip art on the CD-ROM discs. A number of clip-art files and symbols, however, are loaded when you install Draw from the distribution disks.

Before you begin image manipulation, you must get Draw up and running—a very easy task. The CorelDRAW! icon should be located in the Corel Graphics window group. To start CorelDRAW!, double-click on the CorelDRAW! icon. If this icon is not present on your screen, double-click on CORELDRW.EXE in the File Manager to load Draw. The opening screen greets you, and a clean page appears.

Understanding the CorelDRAW! Screen

Now that Draw is up and running on your computer, take a look around and familiarize yourself with your on-screen surroundings. This won't take long, but it will help you to become comfortable with the program. You don't want to be running at full throttle before you realize that you don't know how to steer the ship!

Over the years, CorelDRAW! has garnered much attention regarding its user interface (UI). Truth be told, the current configuration still harkens back to the original design, though it has been filled with geegaws and the current rages in UI (user interface) design, including the ubiquitous button bar and roll-up menus.

Figure 1.1 is a handy map showing an annotated view of what's what in Corel-land. At the top of the screen, you'll find the standard issue Windows pull-down menu bar. To the left of the screen, the Toolbox provides access to all of Draw's tools. Just below the menu bar, CorelDRAW! 5.0's brand-new button bar offers access to 21 often-used functions. The on-screen palette and status line are found at the bottom of the screen.

A lot of effort has gone into the user interface (UI). You have great control over how the screen looks, because it is highly user-configurable through a number of settings on the View menu. More custom controls can be found in the Preferences menu located in the Special pull-down menu.

Using Menus

Anyone who has spent more than an afternoon with Windows knows how a pull-down menu works. Clicking on a word in the menu bar (or using the keyboard shortcut) displays or "drops" a selection menu. Once this happens, you can click on or "select" any of the items on the menu that are not grayed out. An item is grayed out when that choice is unavailable (for any of a number of reasons). Selecting from a pull-down menu might summon a dialog box, a roll-up menu, switch a selection on or off, or perform a specific function.

Figure 1.1
A guide to Draw's on-screen real estate or screen design.

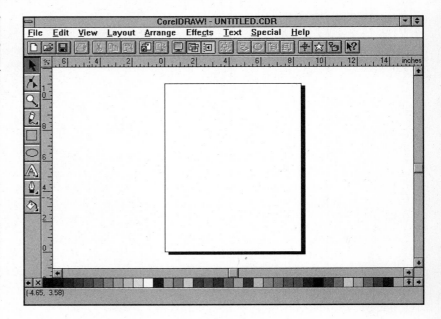

CorelDRAW!'s menu bar offers nine menu choices: File, Edit, View, Layout, Arrange, Effects, Text, Special, and Help. To use a keyboard shortcut (also called a hot key) to access any one of these menus, hold down the Alt key as you press the highlighted letter. Through menus comes the ability to perform a variety of functions, as well as configure your workspace.

The menus follow standard Windows conventions (see fig. 1.2). Hence, you see a check mark to the left of a selection that is currently "on" (or activated). Likewise, an arrow to the right of a selection means that there are additional choices that relate to that selection. An underscored, bolded letter indicates the keyboard shortcut to access that selection while the menu is active. A function key or keyboard combination, which is shown next to the item on the menu, denotes the keyboard shortcut for that function for use when the menu is not active.

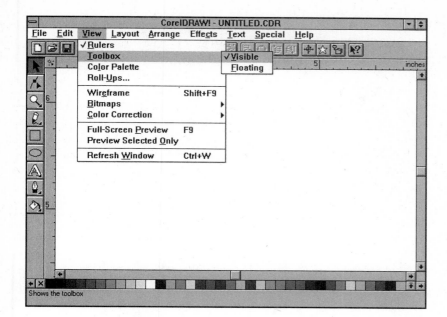

Figure 1.2
The annotated
View menu.

Introducing the Toolbox

Much of what you do in CorelDRAW! centers upon which tool you have selected
from Draw's Toolbox. (Figure 1.3 shows a cute version of the Toolbox.) To select a
tool, simply click on its respective icon. Each tool that is marked with a triangle in
its lower right corner (Zoom, Pencil, Text, Outline, and Fill) has a fly-out menu,
offering additional functionality. Clicking directly on a triangle accesses the fly-out
menu. As you work through this book, you learn about each tool in depth.

In version 5.0, Corel has refined its Toolbox, if ever so slightly. The
Toolbox is now customizable; you can have it float freely or be moored
at the left side of screen. You can also hide the Toolbox. These options
are controlled from the View menu.

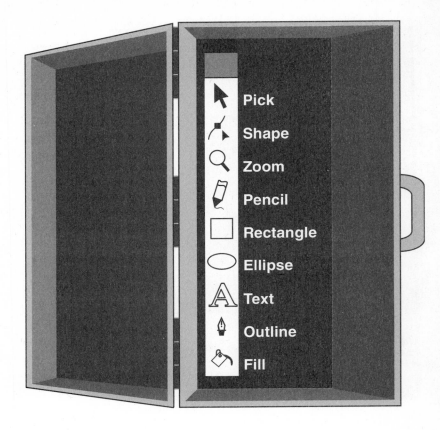

Figure 1.3
The
CorelDRAW!
Toolbox.

Pick

Shape

Zoom

Pencil

Rectangle

Ellipse

Text

Outline

Fill

Introducing the Button Bar

5.0

Button bars have gained great notoriety with the recent crop of feature-laden, Windows-based word processors. Not surprisingly, Corel has followed the user interface lemmings into the button-bar craze. However, to their credit, they created a group of buttons that should make sense to the average CorelDRAW! user. If you become confused about which button performs what function, all you need to do is pass the cursor over that button, and the Status Line will report the button's purpose.

Some buttons perform a function, such as import or export, while others switch between modes, as in Wireframe or Snap to Guidelines. In addition, there are buttons to access the Transform, Symbol, or Mosaic roll-up menus. Figure 1.4 provides a handy annotated look at the button bar.

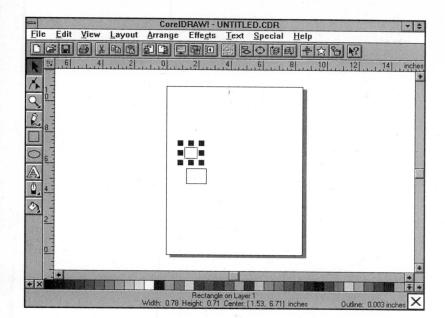

Figure 1.4
The annotated
Button Bar.

Understanding the Printable Page

CorelDRAW! uses what has been commonly referred to as a "pasteboard metaphor," which owes its name to the bad old days when you actually had to cut-and-paste things onto a page by hand, rather than click and drag things around electronically. The old-fashioned pasteboard encompassed more than the printed page itself, as does the CorelDRAW! screen. You have plenty of room to fiddle with things off the page, before dropping them into final position on the page.

When you look at the center of the Draw screen, you see what will be your printed page, highlighted by a gray drop shadow (refer to figure 1.1). Whatever you intend to print must be on this page. The limitations of your output device, however, determine how much of the image actually prints. Different printers have different margins from top-to-bottom and from side-to-side. Since it is a bit early to get into specifics in this chapter, you might want to jump ahead to Chapter 11, "Basic Printing Techniques," and Chapter 26, "Understanding CorelDRAW! Filters," for in-depth information on printing.

Using Dialog Boxes

Dialog boxes display on the screen immediately after you click on certain menu selections. For example, clicking on the Preferences selection (found on the Special Menu) summons the Preferences dialog box. This particular dialog box is an example of an index-tabbed dialog box, which allows you to flip through choices as easily as flipping though an index-tabbed file folder. Other dialog boxes come up as queries when the program asks you to make a specific decision. As a general rule, every dialog box includes at least an "OK" and a "Cancel" button. Clicking on OK implements whatever settings you have made in the dialog box, while clicking on Cancel ignores any changes you may have made.

Dialog boxes are advantageous in a number of ways. Primarily, they offer greater depth of settings than could be chosen through pull-down menus alone. Well-implemented dialog boxes enable you to move through various settings—without resorting to using a mouse or other pointing device—by pressing the Tab key (and Shift+Tab to move in reverse) along with the cursor keys. Experienced users know that keeping a hand on the keyboard is faster than "mousing around."

Previous versions of CorelDRAW! were chock full of dialog boxes. While Corel's engineers have not yet eliminated all of Draw's dialog boxes, a number of them have metamorphosed into roll-up menus, to mixed reviews.

Using Roll-Up Menus

What's the difference between a dialog box and a roll-up menu, you ask? That's easy. When you use a dialog box, you summon it and use it, and when you choose OK or Cancel, it automatically goes away. A roll-up menu, on the other hand, is persistent. Once you click on Apply, the roll-up stays on screen, hogging both real estate and system resources. Roll-ups do not go away until you put them away. Historically, you could bring up a roll-up menu through either a keyboard shortcut or a menu selection, and this is still the case.

Thoughtfully, the engineers have endowed CorelDRAW! 5.0 with a number of new roll-up management features. These are (ironically) accessed through a Roll-Up dialog box, which is summoned through the View menu. Through this new Roll-Up dialog box, you have the option to select which roll-up menus are visible and rolled down, both in your current session and upon program start up.

Although they might look spiffy, you should be forewarned. Because roll-up menus use up so much space, both on-screen and in memory, try to do your work with as few roll-up menus on-screen as necessary. Running CorelDRAW! with too many roll-up menus present prevents you from running other applications concurrently. Also, keeping them rolled out does not help gain back the Windows resources that are vital for Draw to run fast and smooth.

Now that you have the program running and have gotten a quick run down of the CorelDRAW! environment, you are ready to open a file. If you have had the chance to look at Draw's *Symbol and Clip-Art Libraries* booklet, you know that Draw comes with a bounty of clip-art files from a variety of manufacturers. These files offer a good sampling of what is available in the commercial clip-art marketplace. If you do not have the CorelDRAW! 5.0 CD-ROM handy, don't fret. For the purposes of this exercise, you will be opening a file from the CD-ROM that came with this book.

Opening an Existing File

The Open Drawing dialog box provides a powerful interface for searching, previewing, and loading artwork. When you work through the following steps and load the Stealth file that comes with this book, you see that you can easily choose files by name or by face. As you scroll through the clip-art files, click once on the file name; the preview window displays a thumbnail view (a small preview of the image) of the file's contents.

Like many other dialog boxes, the Open Drawing dialog box expands when you click on the <u>O</u>ptions button—the dialog box nearly doubles in size, as well as functionality. The <u>S</u>ort by feature enables you to sort files by file name or file creation date. You can do keyword searches and review notes without using the Mosaic utility program. You can even find files using the keyword search to search all directories. Access to Mosaic is now available through a speedy roll-up menu from within CorelDRAW!

As you open the Stealth file in the following exercise, notice the features hidden behind the Options button.

Opening a Clip-Art File

Click on <u>F</u>ile	The File menu appears
Click on <u>O</u>pen	The Open Drawing dialog box appears (see fig. 1.1)

continues

continued

Most likely, the directory that first appears is not the one you want. The Open Drawing dialog box, like other CorelDRAW! dialog boxes, remembers where you left it. You need to switch to the correct directory, library, and file type.

Change the directory to F:\ICD5-ART\CDR (where "F:" is your CD-ROM drive)

Click on **O**ptions	The dialog box expands
Click on STLTH50B.CDR	A Stealth appears in the preview window
Click on OK	The STLTH50B.CDR file opens
If a Conflicting Styles dialog box appears, click No	The STLTH50B.CDR file opens

If you prefer, you can forgo clicking on OK and simply double-click on the file name to open the file.

Figure 1.5
The Open
Drawing dialog
box.

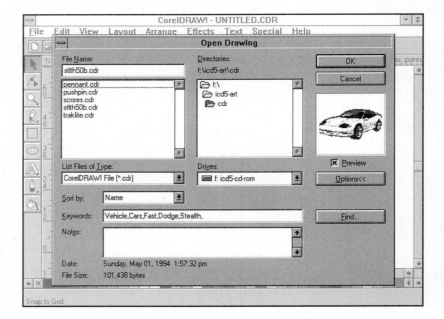

The two basic reasons to preload your clip art are speed and safety. Loading a file directly into Draw from a floppy disk is slow and can take more than three times as long as loading from your hard disk. A good feature of CD-ROMs is that they are secure (you can't overwrite or delete a file), but they are also quite slow. Loading times vary with your computer's speed and the type of your disk drives.

Avoid working with a clip-art file on its original floppy disk—if you ruin the file, you have no way to get it back to its original form. Always work with a backup.

As a shortcut procedure, you can press Ctrl+O to open a file.

Of course, the size of your hard disk is a major factor in deciding where to keep your clip-art files and libraries. If your hard disk has plenty of room, keep the clip-art files there. You shouldn't have to worry about backing up any clip-art that comes on CD-ROM.

You can load a file directly from a floppy disk into Draw, but if you preload it, you safeguard your original disks. Preloading is a good habit to get into. If Draw already is running, switch to the Windows File Manager to copy files to your hard disk before you use the File, Open command.

Full-Color or Wireframe Mode

When you open the Stealth file, it appears on your computer screen in either Full-Color or Wireframe mode. CorelDRAW! 5.0 provides full-color editing capabilities. Many electronic artists prefer Full-Color mode editing, but this convenience can take its toll on system performance—particularly on complex images. Wireframe editing is faster and, in many cases, dramatically so. For this reason, you will find yourself working in both editing modes. To switch between Full-Color and Wireframe editing, use the View menu, the Shift+F9 keyboard shortcut, or click on the Wireframe button on the Button Bar. If this feature is going to be used often, and to get a speedier response, you can designate the right mouse button to do so. Just go in the Preferences dialog box in the Special menu and, in the general folder, select the mouse action to be full screen preview. Now, by clicking the right mouse button, you will be able to switch swiftly between wireframe and full color.

In the following exercises, you work in Full-Color mode. A check mark next to the word Wireframe on the View menu indicates that Draw is in Wireframe mode (see fig. 1.6). If a check mark appears, click on Wireframe to remove the check mark and change to Full-Color mode.

Tip Press Shift+F9 to switch between Full-Color and Wireframe editing.

Figure 1.6
The **D**isplay
menu with
Wir**e**frame
selected.

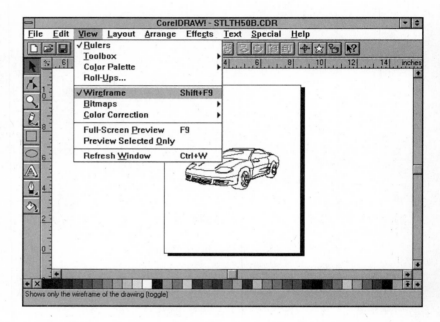

Now that the Stealth file is loaded, start exploring Draw. You should see a stunning white Dodge Stealth on a dark blue background. In the next few pages, you perform some basic functions on the sportscar. The following is a "Pick tool primer" that shows you Draw's interface at it's best.

CorelDRAW! is unique in that the Pick (or selection) tool allows you to implement a number of functions that other drawing programs (for example, Adobe Illustrator) break up between specific tools. This reason alone (and not the marketing flash and sizzle) is why many professional illustrators choose CorelDRAW! over the competition.

Selecting an Object

When you place your pointer on the Stealth and click, you see eight black boxes surrounding the car. These boxes are called *handles*. They indicate that the Stealth is selected. The black box handles designate that the object is in Stretch/Scale mode. An object must be selected before you can manipulate it.

Start out by moving the Stealth around the page. When you click and drag, be sure to position the cursor on the selected object. In Wireframe mode, the Pick tool's tip must touch one of the lines in the selected object. If you don't click directly on a selected line, you deselect the object and have to reselect it. In Full-Color mode, however, you can simply click anywhere on an object to select it.

As you drag the mouse up while holding down the left button, notice that a dashed outline box appears (see fig. 1.7). The cursor turns into a four-headed arrow, indicating that you are in the Move mode. Don't be surprised when the image of the Stealth does not appear to move while you are dragging. After you release the mouse button, the original Stealth disappears and the image appears in its new position.

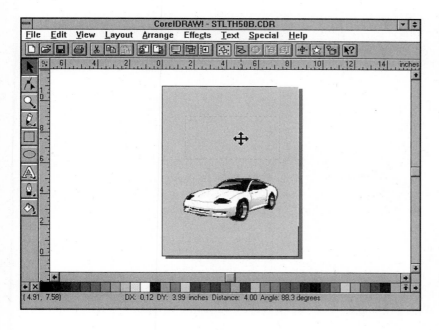

Figure 1.7
The Status Line changes as you move the selected object.

You can set Draw to display an object when moving by configuring the View/ Moving Objects section of the Preferences dialog box. Doing so yields a skeleton frame preview when moving a selected object, regardless of whether you are in Wireframe or Full-Color edit mode.

Moving an Object

As you move the image around, watch the numbers change on the Status Line at the bottom of the window. If you do not see a Status Line, it has been turned off.

The Basics

Pull down the Special menu, click Preferences, then click the View tab. Look at the Status Line section. An X next to Show Status Line indicates that the Status Line is operational. If no check mark appears, click on Show Status Line now. You also have the choice of placing the Status Line at either the Top or Bottom of the screen, along with a Small Size and Show Menu & Tool Help options.

Selecting and Moving the Stealth

Click on the Stealth	The eight handles appear
Drag the Stealth upward	The handles disappear and a dashed outline box appears
Drag the box to top of the page	
Release the mouse button	The image reassembles itself in its new position

It might take a few moments for your computer to reassemble the image. Notice that it redraws object by object. After you become more familiar with Draw, you might want to dissect the Stealth to learn how it was built.

Simple images redisplay much faster than complex images. As with loading files, your hard disk type affects the speed at which Draw operates. A fast hard disk, an accelerated graphics card, and a fast computer—with a speedy 80486 or Pentium processor—greatly improve Draw's operating speed. If you never wanted a faster computer before, you might after you spend a few hours working with complex graphics.

During the process of moving an object, the Status Line shows you four things: cursor coordinates, object position, distance, and angle. The *cursor coordinates* (shown in parentheses) tell you the exact position of the cursor relative to the horizontal and vertical rulers. The numbers denoted by *dx:* and *dy:* refer to the amount of horizontal and vertical distance, respectively, that you have moved the object from its original position. *Distance* also is a linear measurement, denoting the amount of diagonal movement. *Angle* refers to the number of degrees of movement.

As you discover in subsequent exercises, the Status Line has different gauges to record different functions. As you perform your own screen maneuvers, keep an eye on the Status Line.

Stretching an Object

Stretching an object affects only the width or the height of the object. This distorts the object's shape. To stretch an object, you must pull on the correct handle. Stretching is controlled by any one of the four center handles at an object's top, sides, or bottom.

The top or bottom handles make the object taller or shorter. The side handles make the object wider or thinner. As you stretch an object, it is anchored to the side opposite the one you are dragging.

Stretching the Stealth

Watch the Status Line as you stretch the Stealth. The status line reports the percentage of stretch.

Click on the Stealth	The eight handles appear
Place the cursor on the bottom center handle	The cursor arrow becomes a +
Drag the bottom center handle down	The handles are replaced by a blue box
Release the mouse button at the bottom of the page	A tall Stealth appears (see fig. 1.8)

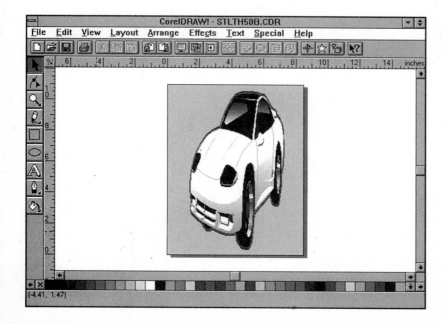

Figure 1.8
A tall Stealth.

Fixing a Mistake

Every artist needs an eraser to fix those occasional "Oops!" situations. Draw's eraser is the <u>U</u>ndo command in the <u>E</u>dit menu. Before you do anything else to your graphic, give <u>U</u>ndo a try.

Using Undo and Redo

The eight handles still should be around the Stealth graphic.

Click on <u>E</u>dit, *select* <u>U</u>ndo	The car returns to its original proportions
Click on <u>E</u>dit, *select* <u>R</u>edo	Returns the graphic to its pre-undo state
Click on <u>E</u>dit, *select* <u>U</u>ndo	The car is restored to its original proportions

Tip   Press Alt+Backspace to invoke the Undo command. Press Alt+Enter to invoke the Redo command

If you want, try stretching the car with its top and side handles. Return the car to its original state by using <u>U</u>ndo after each move. CorelDRAW! 5.0 allows up to 99 levels of <u>U</u>ndo, meaning you can "erase" up to 99 of your last steps. You can specify the number of levels of <u>U</u>ndo in the Preferences dialog box. However, for high <u>U</u>ndo level settings, you need plenty of RAM memory.

Stretching versus Scaling

If you are working with realistically rendered, finished graphics, you might need to *scale* (enlarge or reduce in size) them without distortion. In most cases, you want to scale the picture proportionally rather than stretching it disproportionately.

When you scale an object, it is done *proportionally*—the width and length of an object are enlarged or reduced in direct proportion to each other, maintaining their width-to-length aspect ratio.

When you pulled on the bottom handle of the Stealth, the image was scaled anamorphically; you enlarged (or reduced) the vertical (or horizontal) length (or width) without altering the other axis. This action is *asymmetrical* or *anamorphic scaling.* Draw simply refers to it as *stretching.*

Enlarge the Stealth by scaling it proportionally. As you do the next exercise, watch the Status Line. It tells you by what percentage you are reducing or enlarging the selected object.

Scaling the Stealth Proportionally

Click on the Stealth	The eight handles appear
Put the cursor on the bottom right handle	The cursor becomes a +
Drag the bottom right handle down and right	Handles are replaced by a blue dashed box that expands as you pull down
Release the mouse button	A large Stealth appears at the bottom of the page

In figure 1.9, the drawing is enlarged far beyond the CorelDRAW! page. If you try to print right now, only the part of the drawing actually in the page area (defined by the shadowed box) prints.

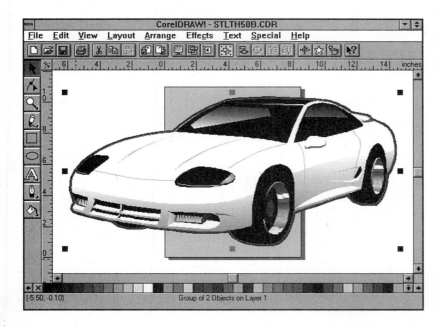

Figure 1.9
A big, proportional Stealth.

Sizing and Scaling Options

Draw includes options that can make your sizing and scaling more efficient: scaling a copy, exponential scaling, scaling from the center point, and creating a mirrored copy. Three options involve pressing a key while you drag the selected object's handles. You can use all four options in combination or in unison.

Leaving an Original

The first option uses a simple dragging procedure. Simply click the right mouse button or press + on the numeric keyboard as you drag, scale, stretch, or mirror to create a new object and to leave the original untouched.

Scaling a Copy

The first option enables you to create a new object without altering the original. If you press and release + during the stretching or scaling operation, Draw creates a new object and leaves the original object untouched. (You must use the + key on the numeric keypad, not the one on the top line of the standard keyboard.) You also can use + to duplicate an object while dragging. Clicking the right mouse button yields the same results.

If you press + as you pull on any of the handles, the Status Line reports the stretching or scaling percentage and includes the words Leave Original.

Exponential Scaling

The second option enables you to scale objects exponentially. By holding down Ctrl, you can scale in 100-percent increments. This feature makes it easy to make an object exactly twice as large as the original.

Scaling from the Center Point

You might have noticed that until now, the selected object has been stretched or scaled from its sides or corners. The third option makes it possible to stretch or scale from an object's center point. By holding down Shift, you can stretch or scale from the middle of a selected object.

Creating a Mirrored Image

The fourth and final option enables you to *reverse*, or flip over, an object. Draw refers to this action as *mirroring*. By pulling the bottom handles over the top handles or the left side handles over the right side handles (or vice versa in both cases), you can create a mirrored version of the original object. In addition to simply changing orientation, the mirroring process can be very useful when you want to create cast shadows and similar effects.

In the following exercise, practice the stretching, scaling, and mirroring options on the Stealth.

Using the Stretch/Scale Options

Press + as you drag the bottom right handle down and right	The new car is scaled; the original remains untouched

Caution: Press and release the + key quickly, or you create more than one copy.

Press Del	Removes the new image

Now scale the Stealth in 100-percent increments:

Press Ctrl as you drag the bottom right handle down and right	
Release the mouse button and then Ctrl	The image is scaled in 100-percent increments
Press Del	Removes the new image

Next, combine the commands and leave the original while scaling in 100-percent increments:

Hold down Ctrl, press and release the + key as you drag the bottom right handle down and right	
Release the mouse button, then Ctrl	
Press Del	Removes the new image

Finish this exercise with a mirror and leave the original.

Press and release the + key as you drag the top left handle down; release the mouse button	A mirrored Stealth appears
Press Del	Removes the new image

Remember that if you press and release + as you move, stretch, scale, or mirror, Draw creates a new object and leaves the original untouched. If you hold down Ctrl, Draw enables you to stretch, scale, or mirror in 100-percent increments. If you hold down Shift, Draw stretches, scales, or mirrors from an object's center point. You can mirror the object by dragging a handle across the opposite side of an object. You can mirror in any direction, but you must drag the handle over the opposite side.

The modifiers Ctrl, Shift, and + commonly are used in combination. Take the time to try a few maneuvers on your own.

Rotating an Object

You can rotate objects as well as size them. To rotate an object, you must select an object twice to display the Rotate/Skew handles. If the object already is selected, just click on it again. The black box handles turn into double-headed arrows. The object now is ready to be rotated or skewed. Each time you click on an already selected object, you switch between the two types of handles.

As you begin to rotate the Stealth, notice that the cursor turns into a rotation symbol. When you rotate the Stealth, remember to watch the Status Line, which tells you the amount of rotation in degrees. This reading is important, because you see only the dashed box.

To rotate an object precisely, it helps to specify the number of degrees of rotation. A protractor can serve as a handy guide.

Rotating the Stealth

Click on the Stealth	The eight handles appear
Click on the Stealth again	Arrows replace the handles
Position the cursor over the bottom right handle	The cursor arrow becomes a +
Drag the bottom right handle up and left	Arrow handles are replaced by a blue dashed box. The Status Line shows the amount of rotation in degrees
Release the mouse button at the top	A rotated sports car of the page appears
Choose <u>U</u>ndo	Back on all four wheels

Look at the center of the selected Stealth. A small circle with a dot should be in the center of the Stealth. This dot marks the *center of rotation*; it controls the point around which the object rotates. The first time you invoke the Rotate/Skew handles on an object, the center of rotation is horizontally and vertically centered on the object. You can change the center of rotation by moving the marker (see fig. 1.10).

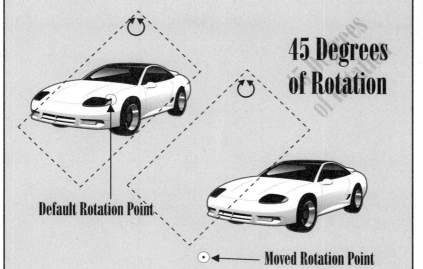

Figure 1.10
The default and moved rotation point.

The center of rotation can be hard to see if the screen is not zoomed in. However, the program enables you to select and move the center of rotation even if you cannot see it! The center of rotation's default position is the absolute center of the selected object. In this case, it is located in the middle of the Stealth's door. As you move the cursor over the center of rotation, the pointer tool turns into a + symbol, letting you know that the center of rotation is selectable. You then can click and drag it to a new location. After you move an object's center of rotation, Draw 5.0 "remembers" where you left it.

Changing the Rotation Point

Click on the Stealth	The eight handles appear
Click on the Stealth again	Arrows replace the handles
Position the cursor over the center of rotation	
Drag the center of rotation below and to the left of the Stealth	The rotation point moves
Now rotate the Stealth again.	The sports car rotates on its nose rather than its center.

continues

continued

Position the cursor over the bottom right handle	The cursor's pointer becomes a +
Drag the bottom right handle up and left	Arrow handles are replaced by a blue dashed box. The Status Line shows the amount of rotation in degrees
Release the mouse button at the top of the page	A rotated Stealth appears
Click on <u>U</u>ndo	The car is back on all four wheels

In addition to having control over the rotation point, you also can use + and Ctrl while rotating objects. The + key works as it does when scaling, leaving an untouched original behind. These features are useful if you want to build things such as spokes on a wheel or blades on a propeller.

If you want to make multiple rotations within a given point, and after you rotate the object and duplicate it by pressing the + key, you can hold down Ctrl and press R, and you will repeat the rotation. Press R several times and you will obtain a spiral effect of that object.

Using Ctrl as you rotate offers yet another advantage. Rotating with Ctrl pressed *constrains* movement to 15-degree increments with Draw's default setting (this increment can be changed in the Preferences dialog box found in the <u>S</u>pecial pull-down menu). Once again, this function can be useful for building objects that spiral from a given point.

Zooming In with the Zoom Tool

Use the Zoom tool to get a good look at the precision work involved in the Stealth drawing. This feature enables you to magnify your view (hence the magnifying glass icon), giving you ultimate control over your precision work. Zoom works in typical Draw fashion with its features clustered in a single tool.

Using Zoom

Follow these steps to zoom in:

Click on the Zoom tool	The Zoom fly-out menu appears (see fig. 1.11)
Click on the + tool *button*	The cursor is now a Zoom tool

Click the mouse button and drag across the front wheel	The blue dashed marquee appears
Release the mouse button	The screen displays a magnified view of the front wheel

Follow these steps to zoom out:

Click on the Zoom tool	The Zoom fly-out menu appears
Click on the - tool button	The view returns to its prior state

The Basics

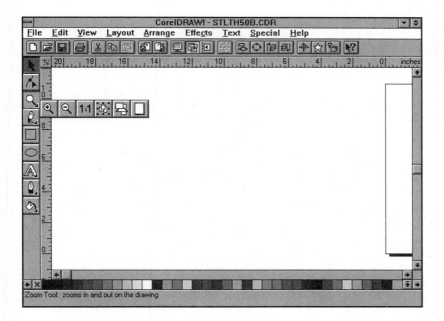

Figure 1.11
An annotated Zoom fly-out menu.

Besides the +/- Zoom tools, the other functions available on the Zoom menu are Actual Size (the 1:1 icon), which provides a close-to-actual-size view; Zoom to Selected (represented by three polygons surrounded by selection handles), which zooms to fit the selected items; Fit in Window (denoted by another peculiar group of polygons), which displays every item on the page and surrounding pasteboard; and a Full Page view (represented by an icon that looks like a page), which enables you to view the entire printable page.

Table 1.1
Zoom Tool Icons

Icon	Name	Definition
1:1	Actual Size	Provides a close-to-actual-size view
	Zoom to Selected	Zooms to fit the selected items
	Fit to Window	Displays every item on the page and surrounding pasteboard
	Full Page View	Enables you to view the entire printable page

Tip Two convenient shortcuts can be used with the Zoom tool. To quickly zoom in, just press F2, and the cursor changes to the Zoom In tool, enabling you to immediately marquee a selected area. To zoom out, press F3.

Saving Files

Although the process of saving files might seem obvious, you can save files two different ways: <u>S</u>ave or Save <u>A</u>s. Using the wrong option at the wrong time can wipe out a file.

If you look at the title bar at the top of your screen, notice that it reads COREL DRAW - STLTH50B.CDR. This line tells you that you are running the CorelDRAW! program and that your current file is STLTH50B.CDR. If you use the <u>S</u>ave command now to save the current screen, you overwrite the original file that you loaded at the beginning of the session (assuming the file came from something other than a CD-ROM).

The Save As Command

To maintain the originally loaded file, save the current version using the Save <u>A</u>s command. The program then enables you to name the new file. If you enter the same name as a file already stored on your computer, the program asks if you want to overwrite the old file.

To save your current version with a new name without writing over the previous version, you must use Save <u>A</u>s.

Using the Save As Command

Click on <u>F</u>ile	The File menu appears
Click on Save <u>A</u>s	The Save Drawing dialog box appears (see fig. 1.12)
Type **HOTCAR** *and press Enter*	A new file is saved as HOTCAR.CDR. The title bar reads CORELDRAW - HOTCAR.CDR

The Save Command

The Save Drawing dialog box enables you to save information along with a file, which can make it easier to organize, retrieve, exchange, and catalog your work. The Save Drawing dialog box has fields for keywords (which you can use to search through files by client, for example) and notes (which can be handy for job-specific reminders, such as production information, print-runs, or even phone numbers).

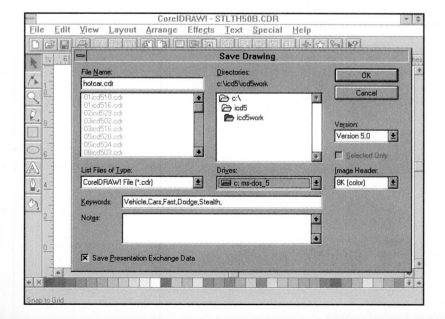

Figure 1.12
The Save Drawing dialog box.

The Save Drawing As dialog box's Image Header option gives you a number of choices for previewing thumbnails. You have your choice of None, 1 KB (monochrome), 2 KB (monochrome), 4 KB (color), and 8 KB (color). The higher the Image Header setting, the larger the file.

If you are working with someone who has an earlier version of Draw, you can save files as either a version 4.0 or 3.0 format. You must choose these options for backwards compatibility. Unfortunately, CorelDRAW! 5.0 cannot save files as 2.*x* format files. In the event you need to save a 5.0 file in 2.*x* format, you must save it first as a 3.0 file, then open that file in Draw 3.0 and save it as a 2.*x* file.

When you are constructing a drawing, get into the habit of saving your files frequently. You can do this simply by pressing Ctrl+S without using the mouse or menus. If you want to save using the mouse, access the **F**ile menu's **S**ave command. When you save a new drawing for the first time, Ctrl+S accesses the Save **A**s dialog box.

Saving your files frequently is a good habit. Try to save after every involved maneuver. This step limits your exposure to disaster. The longer you go between saves, the more time it takes for you to re-create your work in case of a computer crash or power failure.

CorelDRAW! version 2.0 introduced Timed AutoBackup. This convenient feature periodically saves files automatically. The program is shipped with a default Save File setting of 10 minutes. Draw 5.0 allows you to change this setting from within the program (earlier versions required that you edit an INI file). By altering the Preferences/Advanced dialog box, you can change the AutoBackup frequency to your liking. A setting of 0 disables Timed AutoBackup.

As added insurance, Draw has another backup feature. Each time you save a file, the program saves the current version with a CDR extension and automatically saves the earlier version with a BAK file extension. Should you accidentally overwrite a file, you easily can go back to the BAK file. Simply go to File Manager and rename the BAK file with a CDR extension, and you are back in business.

Opening a New File

In this section, you learn how to open a new file, work with the Page Setup dialog box, and import files. Once again, these steps are basic program functions that you should be familiar with before you proceed to more complex subjects.

You already learned to open and save an existing file. Draw uses the file extension CDR when it saves drawing files. Each Draw file must use the CDR extension, otherwise, the program does not recognize the file as a CorelDRAW! file.

To use a clip-art file stored in a format other than CDR, you must import the file. *Importing* converts the file from its native format to Draw's internal format. CorelDRAW! supports many popular image file formats. (See Chapter 3, "Editing and Manipulating," for a list of file formats that Draw can import.)

Creating a New File

To open a blank page and begin a new drawing, use the File, New option. Creating a new file is similar to opening an existing file. If an unsaved file is on the screen, the Save Changes dialog box asks whether you want to save your work. Respond appropriately to this query and the subsequent Save Drawing dialog box (if you are actually saving a file).

Alternately, you can click on the New File button at the far left of the button bar. It's the button with an icon of a blank page.

Press Ctrl+N to create a new file.

Opening a New File

Click on File	The File menu appears
Click on New	A blank file, UNTITLED.CDR, appears

You now have a blank page on your screen, but it might not be the properly sized page for your drawing. To change the page specifications, use the Page Setup dialog box found in the Layout menu.

Get into the habit of defining your desired page setup before you begin composing your images. Otherwise, you might need to make changes to your image mid-stream to accommodate a new page size or orientation.

Using Page Setup/Paper Size

Draw's default mode presents you with an 8 1/2×11-inch page in portrait orientation each time you open a new file. This arrangement suits most people most of the time. Certain projects, however, require paper sizes other than 8 1/2×11 inches. They also might require a different orientation. Use the Page Setup dialog box (see fig. 1.13) to set the desired page size and orientation to suit the situation. Double-click on a page border to access the Page Setup dialog box.

Figure 1.13
The Page Setup
dialog box.

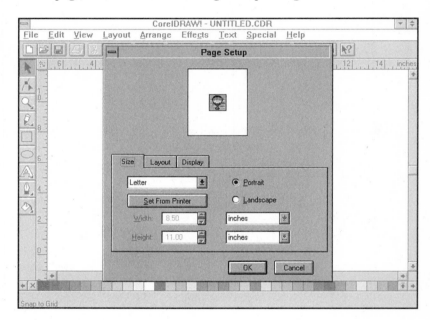

Understanding Page Orientation

Page orientation is an either/or choice, offering a portrait or a landscape orientation. *Portrait* (vertical or tall) and *landscape* (horizontal or wide) refer to the way a page is laid out, both on your screen and as it is output from your printer. Think of a page with portrait orientation as standing up (like you might paint a portrait of someone) and a page with landscape orientation as lying on its side (like you might draw a picture of a landscape). Once you call up the Page Setup dialog box and start fiddling around with the settings, you get a visual representation of what all this means. The Page Setup dialog box is highly interactive and provides instant feedback to your specifications. To start, change the orientation from portrait to landscape.

Changing the Page Orientation

Click on Layout	The Layout menu appears
Click on Page Setup	The Page Setup dialog box appears

Letter size is selected, and the Portrait button is highlighted. The Width and Height are dimmed but read 8.50 and 11.00, respectively.

Click on Landscape	The Width and Height entries are still dimmed, but have reversed themselves, and now read 11.00 and 8.50, respectively
Click on OK	

Look at the page on your screen. You have changed it from a letter-sized (8 1/2×11 inches) portrait page to a letter-sized landscape page.

Changing Paper Size

Although the majority of work you do in Draw can be accomplished with the standard letter page size, sometimes you will need something larger or smaller. Fortunately, Draw enables you to change paper sizes as needed.

The Paper Size section of the Page Setup dialog box offers 18 predefined paper sizes (including envelopes). You can choose the Custom option to specify paper size up to a maximum of 30 inches by 30 inches. You also can change the measurement units from inches to centimeters, picas, or points. You can probably get away with using the letter, legal (8 1/2×14), and tabloid (11×17) sizes for most of your work. On certain occasions, you do need the flexibility that the Custom option provides.

Changing the Paper Size to Legal

Click on Layout	The Layout menu appears
Click on Page Setup	The Page Setup dialog box appears. Letter size is selected, and the Portrait button is highlighted
Roll down, click on Legal	The Width and Height entries are still dimmed, but now read 8.50 and 14.00, respectively
Click on OK	

The page on your screen should now be a legal-sized portrait page. Try changing back to different paper sizes by calling up the Page Setup dialog box and clicking on the various predefined choices.

The predefined paper sizes (in inches) are shown in table 1.2.

Table 1.2
Predefined Paper Sizes (in inches except where noted)

Paper Size	Horizontal	Vertical
Letter	8.50	11.00
Legal	8.50	14.00
Tabloid	11.00	17.00
Slide	7.33	11.00
Statement	5.50	8.50
Executive	7.25	10.50
Fanfold	11.00	14.88
A3	297.03mm	420.01mm
A4	210.01mm	297.03mm
A5	148.03mm	210.01mm
B4	249.99mm	354.00mm
B5	182.02mm	257.00mm
Envelope #9	8.88	3.38
Envelope #10	9.5	4.13
Envelope #11	10.38	4.50
Envelope #12	11.00	4.00
Envelope #14	11.50	5.00
Envelope Monarch	7.50	3.88

Sometimes you want to use the Paper Size's Custom option instead of choosing a predefined size. For example, imagine that you are designing a wedding invitation with a finished size of 4.25×5.50 inches. You could lay out the piece on any of the predefined paper sizes, but that is not the smartest nor fastest way to go. Instead, choose Custom. CorelDRAW! creates crop marks for you when you go to print—you don't have to create them manually. When Custom is selected, the Width and Height edit boxes become active (black) instead of inactive (gray) so that you can enter the dimensions you want.

To change the Width and Height entries, highlight the current entry in the edit box and type in a new size or use the scroll window buttons to roll through the size options.

After you click on Custom, press Tab to move your cursor to the Width edit box. The current size is highlighted, enabling you to type in the new size immediately. After you enter the new size, two more tabs bring you to the Height edit box.

Changing to a Custom Page Size

Click on Layout	The Layout menu appears
Click on Page Setup	The Page Setup dialog box appears

The Portrait and letter buttons should be lit. The width and height entries are dimmed. (If they are not, do not worry—you are changing to a custom size anyway.)

Roll all the way down, click on Custom	The width and height entries are now active
Tab to the Width *entry*	A black bar appears over the entry
Type **4.25**	Changes the width of the page
Tab to the Height *entry*	A black bar appears over the entry
Type **5.5**	Changes the height of the page
Click on OK	

The page on your screen should now be 4 1/4 inches wide and 5 1/2 inches tall. Go ahead and experiment with different paper sizes by using the Custom paper size option. When you are finished, reset the paper size to Letter and the orientation to Portrait.

You can access other features within the Page Setup dialog box by clicking on the Layout or Display tabs. Layout provides a number of specialized page layouts for the creation of booklets and cards. Display enables you to set up facing pages (starting with either a left- or right-hand page), change the paper color, show the page border, and add a page frame.

Paper color affects only the on-screen representation of your image and does not print from any output device. This simulates how an image would look on different colored paper stock. It is also quite useful when designing images that will be screen printed on different colored T-shirts, and the like. Remember how the Stealth came in on a blue background? Try setting different paper colors for different on-screen effects. Set it back to white when you are done.

Printing

The final thing you need to do in this chapter is print out the Stealth. If the sports car is not on screen, go ahead and open the file again. When you are ready, you can go about printing your file. Although the Print dialog box might look big and scary at first, all you have to do for now is click on OK. The subject of printing is covered in depth in Chapters 11 and 26.

Producing output is CorelDRAW!'s reason for existence. A pretty screen file does no good if you cannot print it. Furthermore, you cannot tell what a piece really looks like until it rolls off the printer.

You can access the Print function in one of three ways. The first is through the **F**ile menu. But it is far easier to use either the shortcut, Ctrl+P, or to click on the Print Button on the Button Bar. The keyboard shortcut (along with Ctrl+S for Save) will eventually become an automatic keystroke for you. Your brain will think "print," and your fingers will press Ctrl+P.

Printing the Stealth

Click on **F**ile	The File menu appears
Click on **P**rint	The Print File dialog box appears
Click on OK	The file is sent to the printer

Try to get in the habit of saving your file with Ctrl+S before you walk away from your PC. Although the program always asks whether you want to save your file before you quit, and the program has Timed AutoBackup, it is still a good idea to save as frequently as possible. Always save a file before you print it. You will be covered if your system "hangs" while printing.

Quitting

You have one last thing to do before you take a break. You must learn how to quit the Draw program. You can quit in one of two ways, either from the File menu or by pressing Alt+F4.

If you have an unsaved file on your screen when you quit, the program first asks if you want to save the file. Pay attention to this dialog box—it can save you a lot of work!

Quitting CorelDRAW!

Click on File   The File menu appears

Click on Quit

If you have a file on your screen that you want to save, save it now.

Chapter Snapshot

Got your bearings? Now, it's time to set sail and create some simple artwork with CorelDRAW! To do so, you will need to know how to use the program's object-oriented drawing tools. In this chapter, you will create a simple illustration and learn to do the following:

✔ Draw straight and curved lines freehand with the Pen tool

✔ Select and delete objects

✔ Create ellipses, circles, rectangles, and squares

✔ Gain complete control over objects with the Transform roll-up menu

✔ Use both Grid and Guidelines to position objects

✔ Outline and fill objects

✔ Set a few simple lines of type

The project in this chapter provides an easy introduction to the basics of vector-based illustration. Once you have learned these fundamental drawing skills, you will be ready for more complicated challenges.

CHAPTER

Creating and Drawing

I n the last chapter, you learned about some of the Draw basics. Chapter 1, "Getting Up and Running," covered the essential file functions: opening, saving, and printing. You also learned to select, move, scale, and rotate an object. Along the way, you found out how to set up a page and how to use Zoom and Preview. What you did not learn was how to draw with CorelDRAW!. That is what this chapter is all about.

You will begin this chapter with an overview of how to use the drawing tools and specific functions. Then, it's time to put that knowledge to good use as you open up Draw's toolbox and use it to create your first project, a letterhead.

As you experiment with Draw's various tools, you see that most of them do double duty. First, you use the Pencil tool, noting how you can use it to draw either straight or curved lines. Next, you use the Ellipse tool to produce perfect circles and ovals, and you find that the Rectangle tool works in much the same way. For more precision, you set up and use the grid. A trip through the multi-faceted Transform Roll-Up Menu will give you complete control over object size, placement and orientation. You use the Group and Intersection functions and learn the basics of Outline and Fill to finish the drawing. Finally, a quick look at the Text tool gives you a chance to complete your first project.

Designing DeLook's First Project

On Saturday morning, Joe DeLook is at it again. Today, he is determined to conquer Draw's design tools. He promised to create a letterhead for his girlfriend, Katie, for her construction business.

Joe needs a really cool design, along with a line or two of type. This letterhead has to look great; he's out to prove to a skeptical Katie that his investment in computer gear was well worth the price. With a fresh pot of coffee in the galley, Joe sets sail into the uncharted waters of electronic design.

Drawing with the Mouse

If you have never drawn anything with a mouse, you are not in for a treat. Free-hand drawing with a mouse is like filleting a fish with a chain saw. It is not a pretty sight. Some excellent alternatives to the mouse are available; the most notable among them is the graphics tablet.

After you have used a graphics tablet, you will not want to go back to using a mouse. You might choose to purchase and use a tablet; for clarity's sake, however, this book still refers to it as a mouse.

This chapter begins with a blank page in CorelDRAW!. It soon fills up with all kinds of wonderful shapes and doodles. Your pages might become overly doodle-filled, but don't worry—you also learn how easy it is to remove unwanted objects.

Bitmap versus Vector

Draw is a vector-based drawing program, not a bit-mapped paint program. While the differences between paint and draw programs were briefly covered in the introduction to this book, this subject has some fuzzy lines. The latest version of CorelDRAW!—and new breed paint programs such as Live Image, Altimira Composer, Fractal Design Painter X2, Fauve Matisse, and yes, even Photo-Paint—blurs those lines even further.

Vector drawing programs should be used for situations where you want your artwork to print reliably across a variety of printers, with resolution independence. Bit-maps are always tied to their internal resolution as well as the resolution of the output device. With a vector illustration—such as a logo design—you will have fidelity between your desktop laser printer and your service bureau's imagesetter. A bit-mapped scan, however, will look drastically different, depending upon where you print it. The optimal way to work with bit-maps is to always keep the final output resolution in mind. With a vector illustration, the output resolution is not nearly as important.

Traditional paint programs operate on a strictly bit-by-bit basis, while draw programs—such as CorelDRAW!, Adobe Illustrator, and Aldus FreeHand—operate using vector coordinates. When you create a piece of artwork in a vector program, you have the ability to rework that image by rearranging the objects. Trying to do the same in a traditional paint program is far more difficult, if not impossible, depending on the image.

Amazingly, the aforementioned new breed of paint programs have added vector-object and layering capabilities, giving you the ability to cut up your canvas into editable elements. You will learn more about the power of object-based bit-map image composition in the Photo-Paint chapters, in part four of this book.

Using the Pencil Tool

The drawing tool to start with is the Pencil tool. The Pencil tool can draw straight lines or curved objects, depending on how you use it. Producing an image with CorelDRAW! is akin to building a collage; you assemble your drawings by using different shapes. Keep this philosophy in mind as you plan your drawings.

The Pencil tool has two drawing modes: Freehand and Bézier. Each mode has its place, but for the purposes of these next exercises, use the Freehand mode. The Bézier mode is explored in the next chapter, after you understand how Bézier curves work.

Drawing Straight Lines (Open Path)

The Pencil tool can draw either straight or curved lines. You begin by drawing some straight lines, then you connect them to build closed-path objects. As you draw, watch the status line; it tells you some important information.

The technique used to draw straight lines is quite simple. It consists of a position, a click, a second position, and a second click. As you move the cursor around the page, the status line informs you of the dx: and dy: change in position, distance (length), the angle of the line segment you are drawing, and the line segment's starting and ending points. The dx: and dy: entries are Cartesian coordinates for horizontal and vertical position, respectively.

Drawing a Straight Line

Click on the Pencil tool

The cursor becomes a +

Click the mouse button near the top of the page

A line appears, with a node where you clicked; the status line becomes active

Move the cursor to bottom of the page

The line pivots around its node

Click the mouse button

This action creates a line with a node at each end (see fig. 2.1)

Try this a few times to get the feel of it.

Tip

Press Ctrl+J to access the Preferences dialog box. You can use two methods to draw a diagonal line.

Figure 2.1
A single line.

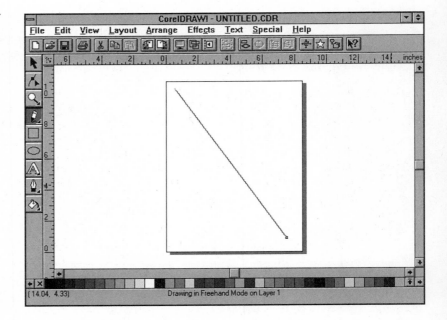

You can use two methods to draw a diagonal line. As you have probably seen, you can use the preceding technique to draw a diagonal line at any angle. In addition, you can constrain the angle to 15-degree increments by holding down Ctrl as you draw the line. Try drawing a few constrained-angle lines by using Ctrl. (You must release the mouse button before you release Ctrl.) You can adjust the constrain increment to your liking by changing the Constrain Angle option in the Preferences dialog box. You can access the Preferences dialog box from the Special menu or by using the Ctrl+J shortcut.

The lines you have just drawn are *open paths.* Although they can be outlined, they cannot be filled with any color or pattern. *Closed-path* objects are constructed from groups of connected lines, and they can be filled (more on this later).

Drawing Straight Lines (Closed Path)

An open path is like a lobster trap with an open lid. To keep the lobsters in the trap, you must close the lid. Closing an open path is like shutting the lid on a lobster trap. How do you close this open path? You play a simple game of connect the dots. The dots are called *nodes.*

You can connect the dots and close the path in several ways. The first method is to draw a line segment from one node to another. The simplest way to do this is by drawing one line with two nodes, then starting the second line directly from one of the first line's nodes.

Connecting Straight Lines

Draw a single horizontal line segment:

Click on the last node drawn

A new line segment is initiated, connected to the node

Move the cursor up and to the left

Click the mouse button

A second line segment is drawn, connected to the first line segment

Now two line segments are connected.

Objects other than ovals or circles usually consist of at least three segments. As you do this next exercise, you create a closed path to see a variation on the last exercise. The Pencil tool immediately starts a new line segment with the same node when you double-click rather than single-click.

Closing a Path

Click on the Pencil tool	The cursor becomes a + with a gap in the center
Click the mouse button at the bottom left of the page	
Move the cursor to the right	A line appears Maintain a 0-degree angle (use the Ctrl key)
Double-click the mouse button	Creates a line with nodes at each end, and a new line segment is started
Move the cursor up and to the left	
When you reach a 135-degree angle, double-click the mouse button	A connected diagonal line is drawn, and a new line segment starts.
Position the cursor over the initial node	
Click the mouse button	A triangular closed path is created (see fig. 2.2)

Figure 2.2
Connected lines.

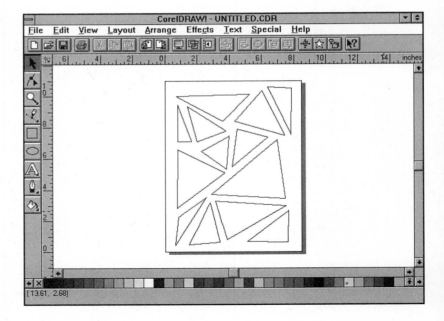

Snapping to Nodes Using AutoJoin

If you cannot seem to get those pesky little lines to connect, you can try an easier way to get them to snap to each other. A feature called *AutoJoin* controls the Pencil tool's "magnetic" node-connection range.

AutoJoin settings are altered at the Curves index tab in the Preferences dialog box, which you access from the Special menu. In this dialog box, scroll buttons enable you to set AutoJoin in a range from 1 (lowest) to 10 (highest). AutoJoin's default setting is 5. The lower the settings are, the more difficult it is to connect nodes. Reserve those settings for intricate work where lines need to be close without touching. The maximum setting of 10 greatly facilitates node-connection—you can almost feel the pencil snapping to the node. But be careful—it can snap when you do not intend it to. A high setting can give you haphazard autojoining.

Right now, use a few different AutoJoin settings to draw polygons.

Connecting Lines Using Different AutoJoin Settings

Click on Special	The Special menu appears
Click on Preferences	The Preferences dialog box appears
Click on the Curves *index tab*	The Curves Preferences appear
Set AutoJoin *to* 1	
Click on OK	
Click on OK again	

With AutoJoin set at 1, you might find it difficult to connect lines, but keep trying.

Click on the Pencil tool

Draw a single line segment

Click on the last node

Draw a second connected line segment

Draw a few more connected line segments to close the path

Now make it easier. Set AutoJoin to an ultra-sticky 10. Feel the cursor's magnetic attraction.

Click on Special	
Click on Preferences	The Preferences dialog box appears

continues

continued

Click on the Curves *index tab*	The Curves Preferences appear
Set AutoJoin *to* 10	
Click on OK	
Click on OK again	
Draw a single line segment	
Click on the last node	
Draw a second connected line segment	
Draw a few more connected line segments to close the path	

Return AutoJoin to its default setting of 5 and try just a few more.

Click on Special	
Click on Preferences	The Preferences dialog box appears
Click on the Curves *index tab*	The Curves Preferences appear
Set AutoJoin *to* 5	
Click on OK	
Click on OK again	
Draw a single line segment	
Click on the last node	
Draw a second connected line segment	

Draw a few more connected line segments to close the path.

In addition to AutoJoin settings, the Preferences dialog box offers many choices to help make your life with Draw a pleasant experience. Shortly, you learn about one of those: freehand tracking.

After all that, you should understand how to draw a closed path by connecting the nodes. Although you have been working with straight lines, the concept of connecting nodes works with curved lines as well.

The Basics

By now, your screen is probably full of triangles and other assorted polygons. Take some time to clean up the screen by deleting some of the objects. You can do this in a variety of ways.

Deleting Objects

The simplest way to delete an object is to select it with the Pick tool, and then delete it by pressing the Del key on your keyboard. You can use at least three other ways, however, to rid your screen of unwanted objects. This section takes a look at all four procedures:

✔ Click/Delete

✔ Shift-Click/Delete

✔ Marquee/Delete

✔ Select All/Delete

Deleting a Triangle (Click/Delete)

You should have plenty of lines (open paths) and triangles (closed paths) on the screen from the last exercise. If you do not have any, create a few.

Click on the Pick tool	The pointer is activated
Click on the triangle you want to delete	The handles appear, the triangle is selected
Press Del	The triangle is deleted

If you did not really want to delete the object, you can get it back by choosing Undo from the Edit menu (or by pressing Alt+Backspace).

Tip

Press Tab to select the next object.

Draw provides a way to select objects without using the mouse at all. With the Pick tool selected, you can cycle through objects by pressing Tab. CorelDRAW! refers to this wonderful feature as *Select Next.* You also can select objects in reverse order by pressing Shift and Tab at the same time.

Tip   Press Shift+Tab to select the previous object.

Try this timesaver right now. You should have plenty of objects on the screen to tab through.

Tabbing through Objects on the Screen

Click on the Pick tool	Activates the pointer
Click on a polygon	Selects the polygon
Press Tab	Selects the next object
Press Tab again	Selects the next object
Press Tab again	Selects the next object

If you want, try reversing through the objects by pressing Shift+Tab.

Sometimes you want to remove several objects at a time. The next three procedures enable you to delete a number of objects selectively. By shift+clicking (holding down Shift while clicking the left mouse button), for example, you can select several objects at a time. Watch the status line for the number of objects selected.

Selectively Deleting Several Lines

Click on the Pick tool	Activates the pointer
Click on the first object you want to delete	The handles appear; the object is selected
Shift+click on the next object to delete	The handles expand to include both objects; the status line indicates two objects have been selected on layer 1
Shift+click on the other object to delete	The handles continue to expand to include all selected lines; the status line shows the number of lines selected
Shift+click on one of the selected objects	Deselects the line; the status line reflects the selection
Press Del	The selected lines are deleted

A variation on the last select/delete is the marquee select/delete. Marquee-selecting is like throwing out a big net.

Using the Marquee To Delete

If you have run out of lines or triangles to delete, draw some more. Then take the following steps to delete them:

Click on the Pick tool	Activates the pointer
Position the cursor above and to the left of the lines to be deleted	
Drag the cursor below and to the right of the lines to be deleted	A blue dashed box appears around the lines
Release the mouse button	Handles appear that surround all the selected lines; the status line reflects the total number of objects selected
Shift+click on a selected object	Deselects the object
Press Del	The objects are deleted

If you want to erase all the objects on your page, the following exercise shows you the slickest way to do it.

Deleting All Objects

Click on the Pick tool	Activates the pointer
Click on <u>E</u>dit	The Edit menu appears
Click on Select <u>A</u>ll	Selects all objects
Press Del	Deletes all objects

Tip   Press Alt+E, then A, then Del to delete all objects.

By learning to delete multiple objects, you also have learned the principles behind selecting multiple objects. You soon see that you can use the shift+click, marquee-select, and select-all techniques to apply fills, outlines, and transformations on groups of objects.

Now that you have finished playing Search and Destroy, you can start filling up the screen with doodles again. Take your mouse in hand and get ready to draw some curves.

Drawing Curves Freehand

As mentioned earlier, the Pencil tool can create curved lines as well as straight ones. Like straight lines, curved lines can be open or closed paths. You can create closed paths composed entirely of curves or in combination with straight lines. In this section, use the Pencil tool to draw curves and create some simple clouds.

The more you work with Draw, the more you realize that the curves you draw using a mouse do not always turn out exactly the way you envisioned them. This fact is largely due to the imprecise drawing capabilities of the common mouse. A mouse can be a difficult tool to use for freehand drawing.

Nevertheless, try drawing some simple curves. Most likely, they do not look all that great at close inspection. Fear not. Through a process known as tweaking, you can refine your curves to a more suitable form. The actual process of tweaking is covered in Chapter 3.

The technique to use when you want to draw curved lines is different from the one to use when drawing straight lines. Drawing curved lines requires a click-and-drag technique. Hold the left mouse button down while drawing your curve. When you release the mouse button, CorelDRAW! takes a few seconds to plot your curve. When it is done, nodes appear along the path of the line. Once you have drawn a curved line, you will notice that the status line will read: Curve on Layer 1 Open Path. This message means that the selected object is not a closed path and cannot be filled. The status line will also specify the number of nodes contained in the line.

If you do not like the way your object looks while you are in the midst of drawing, you can erase part of it without starting from scratch. Press the Shift key as you draw a curved line to "back up" and erase the line. When you release Shift, you resume drawing.

 Tip   Press Shift as you draw to back up and erase.

In the next exercise, you will draw a curved closed path (see fig. 2.3). To close the path, you need to end your line on top of the node where you began the line. This procedure is almost like creating the triangular closed path, except this time you are working with curves. When you have finished drawing and your nodes are plotted, the status line should read Curve on Layer 1.

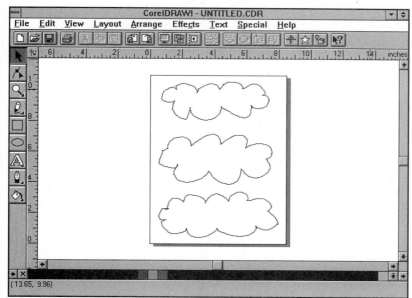

Figure 2.3
Clouds.

When working in Full-Color mode (as opposed to Wireframe mode), you see the immediate results of closing a path—the object is filled with the default fill. If, however, No Fill is the default, you might not notice a difference. If you are not sure whether the object is filled, just remember that the status line always tells you if it is an open or closed path.

Drawing a Curved Closed Path

Click on the Pencil tool

Drag the mouse in curving a cloud shape   A cloud shape is drawn

*Bring the cursor back to where
the line began*

Release the mouse button   After a few moments, nodes are
added to the cloud

If the status line reads Open Path, you did not close the path. (It can be tricky!) If you have an open path, try the exercise again. It might take a few tries for you to get your path closed.

What if you have drawn the ultimate cloud but failed to create a closed path? You can very simply join the nodes and close the path. In the next exercise, you use a new menu: the Node Edit menu. Node Edit is introduced here; Chapter 3 covers this feature in more detail.

This next exercise is similar to the last, except that you should try *not* to connect the end nodes when you lay down the drawing.

Leave plenty of room between the first and last nodes.

Closing an Open Path

Click on the Pencil tool

Drag the mouse in a curving cloud shape

*Bring the cursor back almost to
where the line began*

Release the mouse button

After a few moments, nodes are added to the cloud (see fig. 2.4); the status line should read Curve on Layer 1 Open Path. Number of Nodes: *X* (where *X* is the number of nodes).

Click on the Shape tool

The status line should read Curve: *X* nodes (where *X* is the number of nodes).

*Shift+click on the first and last
nodes*

Release the mouse button

The selected nodes turn black; the status line reads 2 selected nodes.

Double-click on a selected node   The Node Edit Roll-Up menu appears
(see fig. 2.5)

*Click on the button on the right
side of the minus symbol*

The status line reads First node of a closed curve (see fig. 2.6).

Click on Pick tool

The status line reads Curve on Layer 1 Number of Nodes: *X*.

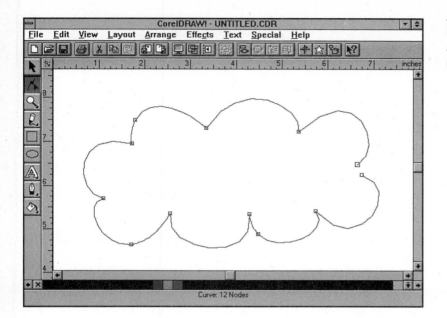

Figure 2.4
A curve (open
path).

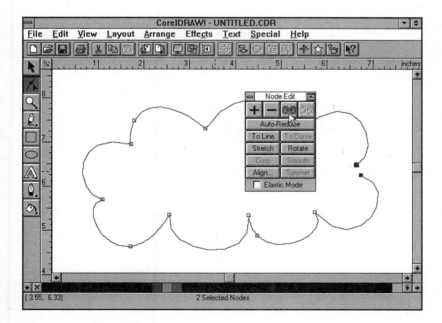

Figure 2.5
The Node Edit
Roll-Up menu.

Figure 2.6
A curve (closed path).

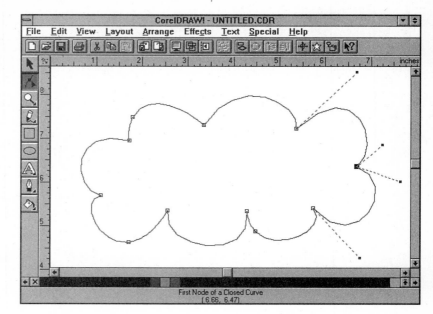

You have joined the first and last nodes of an open path by using Node Edit to form a closed path. If you were not successful in creating a closed path, you might have selected more than two nodes. Only two nodes can be joined. Deselect the nodes and try again. You also can try marquee-selecting instead of shift-clicking.

Drawing Smooth Lines

Do your lines seem really jagged or, conversely, far too smooth? If so, you can change a setting in the Preferences dialog box, which you access from the <u>S</u>pecial menu, to alter the precision that the program uses when it converts mouse movements to Bézier curves. CorelDRAW! refers to this function as *Freehand Tracking*.

Like AutoJoin, Freehand Tracking can be set in a range from 1 (lowest) to 10 (highest). The default setting is 5. Lower settings enable the program to follow the line with far more precision, but can render too many nodes and give the line a jagged appearance. High settings give the line fewer nodes and a smoother curve, but with a corresponding loss of precision. Figure 2.7 illustrates what different Freehand Tracking settings can do for your freehand drawings. Try drawing a few more clouds.

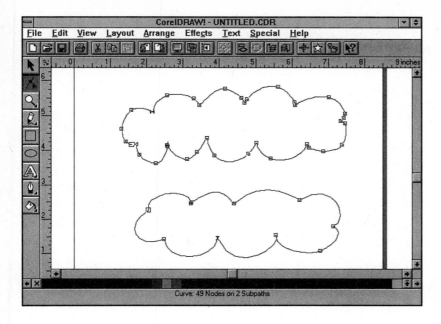

Figure 2.7
Jagged and
smooth clouds.

The Basics

Adjusting Freehand Tracking

Click on Special	The Special menu appears
Click on Preferences	The Preferences dialog box appears
Click on the Curves index tab	The Curves Preferences appear
Set Freehand Tracking *to* 1	
Click on OK	
Click on OK again	

With the Freehand Tracking set at 1, you get more precision, more nodes, and more jaggedness.

Click on the Pencil tool

Draw a cloud

That looks a bit rough. Smooth out your technique by setting Freehand Tracking to 10. You should experience a reduced number of nodes as shown in figure 2.8.

Click on Special	The Special menu appears
Click on Preferences	The Preferences dialog box appears

continues

continued

Click on the Curves index tab	The Curves Preferences appear
Set Freehand Tracking *to* 10	
Click on OK	
Click on OK again	
Draw a cloud	

Return Freehand Tracking to its default setting of 5 and try one more setting.

Click on Special	The Special menu appears
Click on Preferences	The Preferences dialog box appears
Click on the Curves index tab	The Curves Preferences appear
Set Freehand Tracking *to* 5	
Click on OK	
Click on OK again	
Draw a cloud	

Now is a good time to practice drawing with the Pencil tool. You might find it difficult to draw with precision, but have no fear—you can tweak those curves soon enough.

Draw several clouds. (Imagine that a storm front is moving in!) Delete all the clouds you are less than happy with and save your three favorite. Drag them to the top of the page—you are going to use them in your first drawing!

At this point, save your drawing. Use the file name CLOUDS.CDR. If you cannot recall how to save a file, refer to Chapter 1.

Drawing Ellipses and Rectangles

The Ellipse and Rectangle tools are as straightforward as you could hope a pair of drawing tools to be. Anyone who has ever tangled with mechanical compasses, plastic templates, and technical pens will be ecstatic over the Ellipse tool's ease of use. In fact, you probably will hang up your compass, put away your templates, and clean your pens for the last time, abandoning them in favor of working exclusively with CorelDRAW!'s superior electronic versions. You do not need to worry about ink splats or smudge marks. If you draw something the wrong size or shape, simply undo it and try again!

By using these tools in conjunction with Draw's Snap To Grid and Guidelines features (both of which are covered shortly), as well as the program's rulers, you can draw ellipses and rectangles of precise proportions. If the rulers are not already showing on your screen, select Show **R**ulers from the **V**iew menu.

The Ellipse and Rectangle tools offer flexibility that even the largest collection of templates and technical pens could not hope to match. While you are drawing these objects, look to the status line for immediate feedback.

The Ellipse Tool

The Ellipse tool works in one of two modes to produce either ovals or circles. By clicking and dragging, you can draw ovals of infinitely variable proportions. To draw a perfect circle, hold down Ctrl as you click and drag. You can draw an ellipse or a circle from its center point by holding down the Shift key. Figure 2.8 shows some samples of what you might draw. Remember to watch the status line as you draw—it shows the ellipse's exact height and width as well as the starting, ending, and center points.

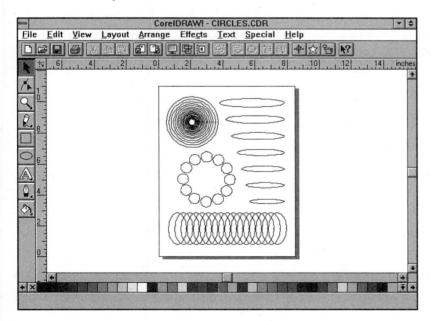

Figure 2.8
A variety of circles and ellipses.

Drawing Ovals and Circles

Click on the Ellipse tool	Changes cursor into a +
Click and drag the cursor diagonally	An oval grows as you move the cursor
Release the mouse button	An oval is drawn

That was too easy. Now try a circle. With the Ellipse tool still selected, take the following steps:

Press Ctrl as you click and drag the cursor	A circle grows as you move the cursor
Release the mouse button, then release Ctrl	A circle is drawn

Now draw an ellipse from its center point.

Press Shift as you click and drag the cursor from its center point	An ellipse grows as you move the cursor
Release the mouse button, then release Shift	An ellipse is drawn

Try drawing a few more ovals and circles. When you are finished, delete them by using one of the methods described earlier in this chapter. Try using both Ctrl and Shift to draw a circle from its center point. Attempt to draw to exact proportions, using the status line. After you complete an object and release the mouse button, the status line displays the dimensions and the page position of its center point.

The Rectangle Tool

The Rectangle tool works just like the Ellipse tool; it creates either rectangles or squares (see fig. 2.9). By clicking and dragging, you can draw a rectangle of infinitely variable proportions. To draw a perfect square, hold down Ctrl as you draw. If you want to draw from a center point, hold down Shift.

Drawing Rectangles and Squares

Click on the Rectangle tool	The cursor changes to a +
Drag the cursor diagonally	A rectangle grows as you move the cursor; the status line shows the width and height of the rectangle
Release the mouse button	A rectangle is drawn

Now that you have drawn a rectangle, draw a square. With the Rectangle tool still selected, take the following steps:

Press Ctrl as you click and drag   A square grows as you move the
the cursor   cursor

Release the mouse button,   A square is drawn
then release Ctrl

Next, draw a rectangle from its center point:

Press Shift as you click and drag   A rectangle grows from its center-
the cursor   point as you move the cursor

Release the mouse button,   A rectangle is drawn
then release Shift

I

The Basics

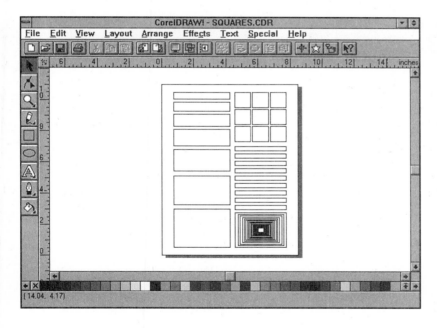

Figure 2.9
A variety of
squares and
rectangles.

As you have seen, the Ellipse and Rectangle tools originate (or pull) objects from their corners or from a center point depending on whether you press Shift. If you want, try drawing a few more ellipses, circles, rectangles, and squares using different combinations until you are comfortable with the tools. When you are done, delete them to clear the page.

Putting Outline and Fill to Work

The Outline and Fill tools affect the way an object appears, rather than its shape. *Outline* refers to the line surrounding an object. You invoke it by clicking on the Outline icon found in the toolbox (it looks like an old-fashioned pen nib). *Fill* is just that—a tool for filling, in much the same manner as you might fill a pie crust. Selecting different fills is like choosing different pie fillings. Fill is invoked by clicking on the icon that looks like a paint can, also found in the toolbox.

CorelDRAW! has amazing outline and fill capabilities. The program gives you the power of color, fountain, fractal texture, pattern, lens, and PostScript fills. Although this chapter only touches the surface, later chapters of the book go into depth on the subject. You see the various methods that Draw provides for selecting outlines and fills: fly-out menus, roll-up menus, and the on-screen color palette (at the bottom of the screen). You use only the fly-out menus for the exercises in this chapter.

In the default mode, new objects have an outline of None and a 100-percent black fill. You can alter the Fill and Outline attributes for objects before you create them by clicking on the Fill or Outline tool while no objects are selected. When you see the New Object Uniform Fill dialog box, click on OK to change the defaults. You should make sure that you have the same defaults as this exercise by resetting them now.

The dialog box offers three options: Graphic, Artistic Text, and Paragraph Text. In this exercise, you set the default for Graphic.

Setting New Fill and Outline Defaults

You should begin this exercise with a few rectangles (or other objects) on screen. With no objects selected, take the following steps:

Click on the Fill tool	The Fill fly-out menu appears
Click on Black	The Uniform Fill dialog box appears
Click on Graphic	
Click on OK	The Fill default is reset
Click on the Outline tool	The Outline fly-out menu appears (see fig. 2.10)
Click on None (X)	The Outline Pen dialog box appears
Click on All Objects	
Click on OK	The Outline default is reset

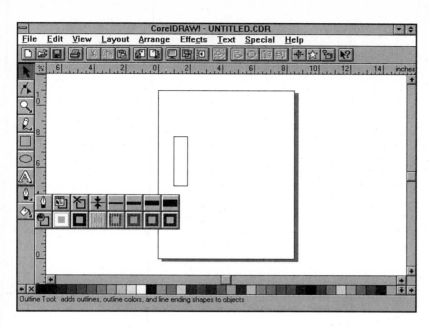

Figure 2.10
The Outline
fly-out menu.

You might have noticed that No Fill is denoted by a simple X, while No Outline is represented by a box interesected by an X. The icons can get rather interesting when language is removed! In the next step, you outline every object on your screen with a hairline. The Hairline icon is unique; it consists of two vertical arrows pointing at a thin segment.

Changing the Outline

Click on the Pick tool	
Click on Edit	The Edit menu appears
Click on Select All	Handles appear around all objects
Click on the Outline tool	The Outline fly-out menu appears
Click on Hairline	All objects have a hairline outline

If you are in Full-Color mode (not Wireframe), you probably cannot distinguish the difference (all objects are still black), but the objects now are outlined with a hairline rule. After the next step, you can see the hairline rule. While all objects are still selected, you are going to fill them with white.

After you change the fill to White, the different outline weights become readily visible. Apply the various rule weights to the drawing to get an idea of how they look.

Changing Fills

With all objects still selected, take the following steps:

Click on the Fill tool	The Fill fly-out menu appears (see fig. 2.11)
Click on White	All objects are filled with white

Figure 2.11
The Fill fly-out menu.

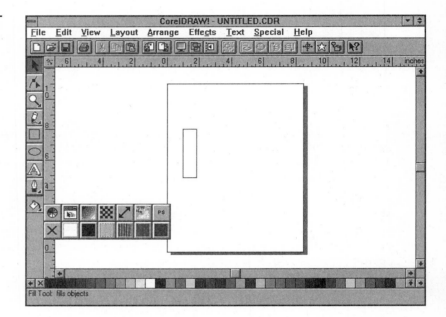

Your full-color screen is starting to look like your wireframe screen—you have a wireframe rendering of a wireframe! Do something about that now.

Deselect the objects by clicking on a blank area of the screen. Now you can select individual objects or a number of objects. Then fill the objects with a tint of your choice. Notice that the left side of the status line reports on the fill (or outline) type—as you pass the cursor over each color/tint on the fly-out menu or the on-screen palette—before you select it. Once the fill (or outline) has been assigned, the right side of the status line provides a full report on each object.

Selectively Changing Fills

Click on a blank area of the screen	Objects are deselected
Marquee-select an object	
Click on the Fill tool	The Fill fly-out menu appears
Click on 50% black	The status line shows the object filled with 50-percent gray
Click on another object	The object is selected
Click on the Fill tool	The Fill fly-out menu appears
Click on 10% black	The status line shows the object is filled with 10-percent gray
Try a few more!	

Continue setting different outlines and fills. Try using lighter or darker fills and try the different outline weights and tints. The fly-out menus provide you with quick access to only a few of the often-used tints.

As mentioned, CorelDRAW! offers far more outline choices and a wealth of fill possibilities. While the fly-out menus take care of your immediate needs, in subsequent chapters, you learn about on-screen palettes, roll-ups, calligraphic pens, fountain fills, pattern fills, and other marvelous features. For now, however, the fly-out menus offer a quick and easy way to build your images.

The Transform Dialog Box

When you played around with the Stealth in the first chapter, you learned how to move objects around and rotate them by acting directly upon them with the Pick tool. Those methods work great for changes you need to make quickly, where precision may be a secondary concern. Should you crave accuracy, however, you really must learn about CorelDRAW! 5.0's multi-faceted Transform roll-up menu. This handy device gives you complete control over an object (or group of objects) with regard to position, rotation, scale, size, and skew.

The Basics

You switch the Transform roll-up menu between its five different modes by clicking on the appropriate button at the top of the menu. At the center right side of the menu, you will find another button which toggles the menu between half mast and fully unfurled modes. When the entire menu is visible, you have the option of assigning a specific pivot point (other than the object center default). By changing an object's pivot point, you can control the location from which the object is positioned, rotated, scaled, sized, or skewed.

Like other roll-up menus, your changes do not take place until the appropriate Apply button has been clicked. The Transform roll-up menu allows you to either apply alterations to an existing object, or to apply the changes to a (new) duplicate object

Transform: Position

This feature allows you to precisely move an object (or any number of selected objects). The Position function will move objects in one of two ways, either in absolute or relative terms. With Relative Position unchecked, the transformation will take place at the page coordinates specified. Selecting Relative Position allows you to reposition the object with regard to the selected pivot point.

Unfortunately, CorelDRAW! 5.0 does not have a true step-and-repeat function. However, the exercise at the end of this chapter will show you a quick step-and-repeat workaround using a combination of the Transform Position roll-up menu and the Repeat command.

Transform: Rotation

If you need to rotate an object with any precision (other than what is specified in your Preferences-Constrain Angle setting), you will want to use the Transform roll-up menu's Rotation feature. This feature allows you to specify object rotation to within a tenth of a degree. It also gives you the ability to alter the Center of Rotation down to the thousandth of an inch.

Whether you are creating the spokes on a ship's wheel, the petals on a cactus flower, or spiny arms of a starfish, the rotation feature is an invaluable feature.

Transform: Scale

You will want to use the Scale feature to scale an object to an exact proportion, or when you need to mirror an object either horizontally or vertically (or both). The roll-up menu allows you to scale either proportionally or anamorphically. However, the Scale function does have a glaring omission; there is no easy way to calculate scaling percentages.

While CorelDRAW! 5.0 does not include a proportional calculator, you will find CubitMeister—the Windows DTPer's answer to a dream—on the CD-ROM that accompanies this book. Developed by one of the co-authors, you will soon find that this shareware program is perhaps the coolest little utility that a serious Windows-based graphic artist can own. Although this may seem like a shameless plug, you will quickly see the worth in CubitMeister. Give it a roll!

Transform: Size

In Response to user requests, Corel added a Transform (to exact) Size feature in version 5.0. This wonderful addition allows you to now specify an object's size without requiring you to calculate a scaling percentage. This is a capability that Draw had long been lacking. One can only hope that the next release will add the capability to create an object—such as a rectangle or ellipse—in a specific size, without the extra step of resizing.

Transform: Skew

When you apply Skew to an object, you impart a leaning look to it. Think of it as pushing an object's shape around, while either a horizontal or vertical axis remains anchored. You can use this tilting to create rudimentary cast shadows or a sort of pseudo-perspective. Perhaps you need to over italicize a typeface, or even lean it backwards... if so, Skew's for you!

The Skew function of the Transform Roll-Up menu allows you to apply either horizontal or vertical skew (or both) with accuracy to the tenth of a degree.

Using the Grid and Guidelines for Precision

You easily can make your objects fit a particular size by using CorelDRAW!'s grid and guidelines. The *grid* forces the cursor to snap to a predefined spacing pattern. You also can place *guidelines* at specific points on the page; these guidelines exhibit similar magnetic snap qualities. If you are familiar with Aldus PageMaker, you should find these features similar to PageMaker's Snap To Rulers and Snap To Guidelines options.

Draw's Grid & Scale Setup dialog box controls the horizontal and vertical Grid Frequency and the Grid Origin point. It also enables you to display the grid on the screen. If you have the grid set for a high frequency, the screen display does not show all the grid intersection points unless you magnify the drawing. The closer in you zoom, the more detailed the grid display becomes.

The variable options provided by the Grid & Scale Setup dialog box make setting up such (formerly difficult) tasks as business forms that require 1/10-inch horizontal spacing and 1/6-inch vertical spacing a snap! While Drawing Scale functions are not covered in this early chapter, you will find coverage on the subject in Chapter 9, "Advanced Drawing Techniques."

Note   Double-click on a ruler to access the Grid & Scale Setup dialog box.

The Grid and Guideline functions include layering controls, with both grid and guidelines placed on their own individual layers. Setup dialog boxes for both the grid and guidelines are accessed through either the Layout menu or the Layers Roll-Up window. Additionally, the Layers Roll-Up window allows you control over grid and guideline (non-printing) colors.

The Layers function is covered in depth in Chapters 3 and 9.

Begin by setting up a simple grid. You use the guidelines shortly.

Setting Up the Grid

Click on Layout	The Layout menu appears
Click on Grid & Scale Setup	The Grid & Scale Setup dialog box appears
At Grid Frequency, do the following:	
Adjust the Grid Frequency to 6 per inch	
Click on the Horizontal units *edit box, adjust to inches*	Sets the unit of measurement
Repeat for Vertical units	
Click on Horizontal Grid Frequency, *adjust to 6.00*	Sets the number of grid points per unit
Repeat for Vertical frequency	
Click on Show Grid	Designates that the feature is active; if the item already is checked, do not click on it—you will turn off the feature

Click on Snap to Grid	Designates that the feature is active; if the item already is checked, do not click on it— you will turn off the feature
Click on OK	

If you do not happen to be in the Grid & Scale Setup dialog box, you can use the Ctrl+Y shortcut to turn on and off Snap to Grid.

Always set the units before you set the frequency, because Draw automatically adjusts the frequency to the new units.

Now that you have turned on the grid, take a look at what it does. When the grid is turned on, the cursor snaps to the defined grid intersection points like a magnet snaps to a refrigerator. You can set the Grid Frequency to a maximum of 72 units per inch, conveniently echoing the number of points per inch. Current grid settings are saved with your drawings.

Press Ctrl+Y to turn the grid on and off.

Grid Origin enables you to place the grid's zero point anywhere on your page or pasteboard. You can change this setting with numerical precision by using the Grid Setup dialog box or change it visually by clicking on the ruler intersection point and dragging it to the new origin. You might want to set the zero point at the upper left hand corner of the page, for example.

Double-click on the rulers to access the Grid & Scale Set Up dialog box.

Aligning Objects to the Grid

For the last series of exercises, set up a coarse grid with six grid lines per inch. This setup translates to one grid line per pica. This size grid helps you develop a nice looking deck. You build the deck larger than its finished size and reduce it later.

Before you start this next section, try drawing a few rectangles with the grid on. Pull the rectangle out to the right, to the left, up, and down. Notice how the grid feature enables you to position your beginning and ending points precisely. It does not let you place a node at anything other than a grid intersection point.

After you are comfortable with the way the grid works, start the exercise. It is important to watch the status line when sizing your rectangles.

Katie's Construction Letterhead Project

Now that you have a basic understanding of what you need to accomplish your first project, it's time to get to work. You will be creating a letterhead for Katie's Construction Company, Seaside's foremost specialist in bulkheads, piers, and deck work. This exercise will utilize many of the tools and functions that you learned about earlier in this chapter.

Katie has a great idea for her company's letterhead, and Joe is pretty sure that he has the perfect solution in mind, as well. Both agree that the artwork should involve decking, water, and all the relevant information, including address and phone number. They want it to have an architectural and contemporary look, which Joe feels can be portrayed through both the artwork itself, as well as through his choice of typeface.

Building a Deck Using the Grid

The grid should be set according to the last exercise, with six grid lines to the inch.

Click on the Rectangle tool

To the left side of the page, do the following:

Drag the mouse down and to the right to form a rectangle	Make the rectangle .083 inch wide by five inches high
Release the mouse button	The status line reads Rectangle on Layer 1

This rectangle forms the first plank of the deck. Notice that you can draw a rectangle to the left or the right, and up or down.

Position the cursor just to the right of bottom right node of the rectangle	
Drag the cursor up and to the right to form a new rectangle 0.83 inch wide by 5 inches high	Creates a new rectangle
Release the mouse button	The status line reads Rectangle on Layer 1

Are you looking at the two rectangles and wondering how you are going to turn this into a deck? This is where you start to have fun. The two rectangles should be approximately 0.17 inch apart from each other. Go ahead and adjust them as necessary before you start the next sequence.

Sneaky Step-and-Repeats

A step-and-repeat is when you duplicate an image a number of times on a printed page, evenly spaced so that you may gain efficiency in your print run. While such page layout programs as Quark Xpress and Aldus PageMaker include the capability to perform automated step-and-repeats, CorelDRAW! 5.0 does not offer the same convenience.

Once you are done with the following exercise, you will have ten rectangles, spaced with 0.17 inch between each. You will have to do a little fancy keyboarding, however. The Transform Position roll-up menu suffers from short-term memory loss, and resets its position each time you click Apply (or Apply To Duplicate for that matter). This annoying trait prevents you form performing an automated step-and-repeat directly from the roll-up. Fear not; the following exercise will demonstrate a little workaround for creating accurate step-and-repeats.

Creating a Step-and-Repeat

Click on the Pick tool	
Click on the right rectangle	The right rectangle is selected
On the button bar:	
Click the Transform button	The Transform Roll-Up menu appears
On the Transform Roll-Up:	
Click the Position button	The roll-up configures into Position mode

continues

continued

Click Relative Position

Change Horizontal to 1.000 inches (see figure 2.12)

Click Apply To Duplicate   The third rectangle is duplicated, 1.000 inch to the right

Now it is time to get tricky with the Repeat function (Ctrl+R). This will replicate the last function performed and, in this case, will allow you to step-and-repeat seven more rectangles.

Press Ctrl+R   The fourth rectangle is duplicated, 1.000 inch to the right

Press Ctrl+R six more times   You now have ten equally spaced rectangles!

Drag a marquee around all ten rectangles

Press Ctrl+G   Groups the rectangles (see fig. 2.13)

Figure 2.12
Using the Transform Position Roll-Up to duplicate and position a plank

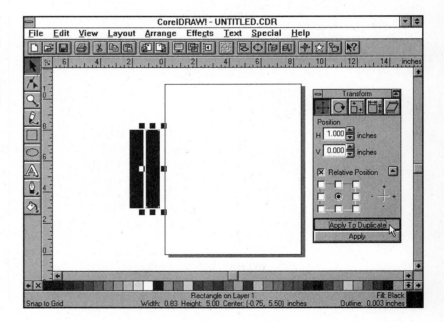

Using Skew

In addition to the complete control provided via the Transform roll-up menu, Skew can also be invoked directly from the object. Double-click on an object to display the Rotate/Skew handles. These handles are the same ones you used to turn the Stealth on end in the first chapter—yet another example of CorelDRAW!'s tool-clustering philosophy.

This next step gives your deck some semblance of perspective. You will press the Control key to constrain your skew to the default 15 degree increments.

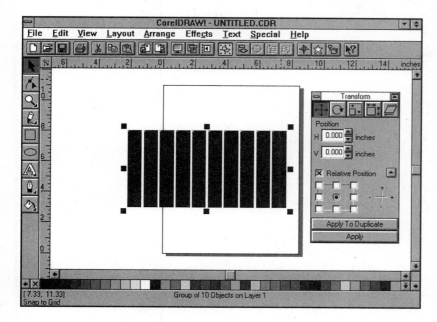

Figure 2.13
Ten equally spaced planks.

Skewing the Deck

Click on the Pick tool

Double-click on the deck   The Rotate/Skew handles appear

Position the cursor on the top center handle   The cursor becomes a + two-headed arrow

Hold down Ctrl, and drag the cursor to the right   The cursor is replaced by a skew symbol and a blue dashed skew box appears; the status line reports on the number of degrees of horizontal skew

Position the cursor for approximately –45 degrees of skew

Release the mouse button, then the Ctrl key   The deck is skewed 45 degrees horizontally

continues

continued

Now, instead of skewing the deck once again (but this time vertically), you can undo the skew, and try a combination horizontal/vertical skew.

Press Ctrl-Z   Undoes the skew

On the Transform Roll-Up menu:

Change H to –45.0 degrees,
Change V to –25.0 degrees

Click on Apply   Skews the deck both horizontally
                                                                 and vertically (see fig. 2.14)

Figure 2.14
The 10 planks
after being
skewed.

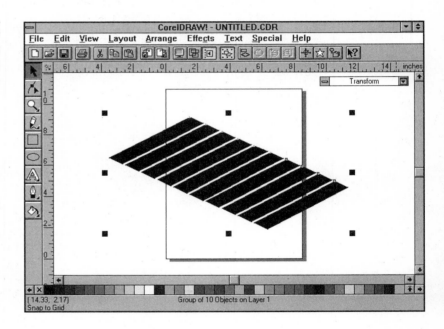

You can skew any object or piece of text. As you've seen, just like Rotate, you can constrain a skew angle by pressing Ctrl, but the Transform roll-up menu offers you the most flexibility. Be careful not to overdo the skew on typography, however; just because Draw enables you to make any typeface oblique does not mean that you should. The chapter on Special Type Effects includes some dramatic shadow treatments that you can add to your type designs using the skew function.

Figure 2.14 shows something that is beginning to resemble a deck. If the roll-up window is in your way, remember that you can quickly roll it up or down by clicking on the button at the top right of the menu.

Pulling in the Guidelines

Earlier, you read a little bit about Draw's guideline feature. Take a moment to draw guidelines to position your artwork on the page. Because Island Printing (Joe DeLook's cousin, actually) usually asks for lots of gripper space and good-sized margins, draw half-inch horizontal and vertical guidelines.

You can lay down guidelines in CorelDRAW! very easily. If you are familiar with Aldus PageMaker, this procedure is old hat. Position your cursor over a ruler (horizontal ruler for horizontal guidelines, vertical ruler for vertical guidelines) click, and drag your guideline into position.

Dragging Guidelines

If the rulers are not showing on your screen, activate them by clicking on Show **R**ulers on the **V**iew menu.

Position the cursor over the horizontal ruler

Drag the guideline 0.5 inch from the top of the page

Position the cursor over the horizontal ruler

Drag the guideline 3.0 inches from the top of the page

Position the cursor over the vertical ruler

Drag the guideline 0.5 inch from the left side of the page

Position the cursor over the vertical ruler

Drag the guideline 0.5 inch from the right side of the page

You easily can tell whether a guideline is in the exact position. Draw provides a convenient dialog box to handle it. By selecting G**u**idelines Setup, in the **L**ayout menu, you display the Guidelines dialog box, in which you can check a guideline's position and change it if necessary.

The Guidelines function is even more functional in version 5.0. The dialog box enables you to move, add, and delete guidelines, and in addition to toggling between horizontal and vertical guidelines, displays a comprehensive list of all guidelines. Corel has also added a much requested Delete All button!

After the dialog box opens, try changing the horizontal (gripper) guideline to three-quarters of an inch (10.25) and then set it back to half an inch (10.50). In the next section, with a few more steps, you size the deck down to fit the space allocated to the letterhead design.

Sizing with Precision, the Rotation Is Your Decision!

Instead of interactively sizing the deck, as you did with the Stealth, this time you will use the Transform roll-up menu to crunch the drawing down to a specific size. This next step gets the deck almost to the exact proportions you will need to finish the letterhead. You will have to rotate the deck to get it to look just right.

Sizing and Rotating the Deck using the Transform Roll-Up

Click on the Pick tool

Click on the deck The deck is selected

On the Transform Roll-Up menu:

Click the Size button
Change H *to 8.0 inches*
Change V *to 4.0 inches*

Click on Apply The deck is sized (see fig. 2.15)

The deck isn't quite perfect. You need to rotate it approximately 10 degrees counter-clockwise.

On the Transform Roll-Up menu:

Click the Rotate button
Change degrees to 10.0

Click on Apply   The deck is rotated

Drag the deck over to match
figure 2.16

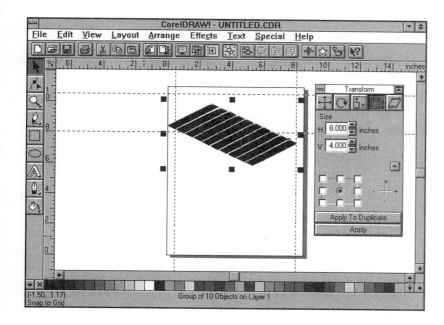

Figure 2.15
The deck gets
sized down.

You are making great progress. The letterhead is coming together, and with a few moves you will soon be amazed! The next thing that you will have to do is draw a rectangle to meet the guidelines. Then, you will use the intersection function to saw off the decking that you don't need.

Intersection is a great feature that allows you to create a new object from the intersection of two objects. You cannot intersect a group however, so this exercise begins with ungrouping the deck, before combining it into one object so that it may be intersected with the rectangle.

Pay Close Attention at the Intersection

Click on the Pick tool

Click on the deck   The deck is selected

Press Ctrl+U   Ungroups the deck

Click Arrange   The Arrange menu appears

continues

continued

Click **C**ombine	Combines the deck
Click on the Rectangle tool	
Click and drag a rectangle to meet the guidelines	
Click on the Pick tool	
Marquee-select the deck and rectangle	The deck and rectangle are selected
Click **A**rrange	The Arrange menu appears
Click **I**ntersection	The intersected deck object is created
Click the rectangle	The rectangle is selected
Press Del	Deletes the rectangle
Click the part of the deck that is below the guideline	The deck is selected
Press Del	Deletes the deck

Only the intersected deck remains! (see fig. 2.17).

Figure 2.16
The deck in
position.

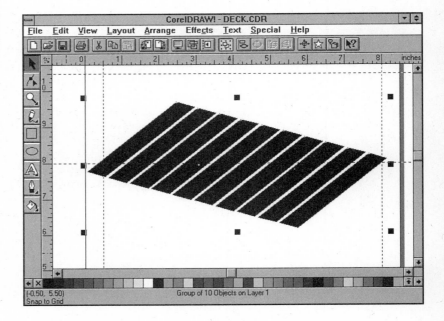

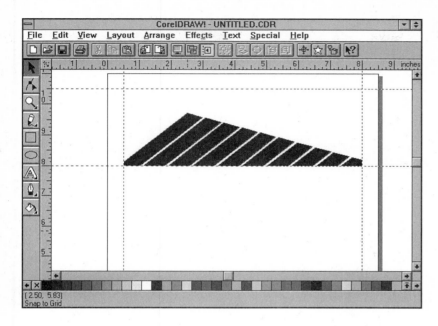

Figure 2.17
The intersected deck.

Now that you have completed that tricky section, you will change the deck's outline and fill before you use a shortcut that you picked up in the last chapter, Drag-Duplicate, to create a drop shadow for the deck. Because the grid is still on, you easily can place the duplicate precisely 0.17 of an inch to the left of the original. Remember to press + from the numeric keypad to make a duplicate and leave the original object untouched.

Tint, Drag-Duplicate, and Tint Again

Click on the Pick tool

Click on the deck   The deck is selected

Click Fill tool   The fill fly-out menu appears

Click 70% Black   The deck (shadow) is filled with
                                             70% black

Click Outline tool   The outline fly-out menu appears

Click No Outline   The deck has no outline

Click on the deck,
press "+" on the numeric keypad,
hold down Ctrl and drag the
deck 0.17 inch to the left

continues

continued

Release mouse button and then release Ctrl	A duplicate deck is created
Click Fill tool	The fill fly-out menu appears
Click 30% Black	The deck (surface) is filled with 30% black
Drag a marquee around both the deck-objects	Both decks are selected
Press Ctrl+G	Groups the deck

Stretch (shrink) the middle left handle to meet the leftmost guideline (see fig. 2.18).

Figure 2.18
The finished deck.

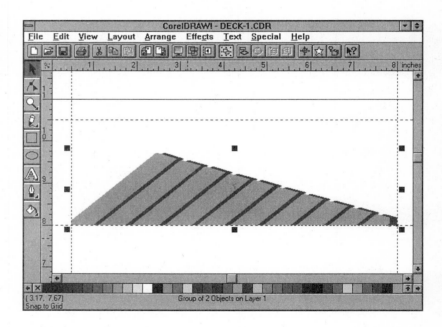

Now that you have the deck together, save your drawing if you have not already done so. Remember, the more often you save, the less work you have to redo in the event of a power failure or file mishap.

Now that you have completed the preceding exercises, you should be getting a good feel for using the grid as well as the Rectangle tool. Although the grid is very convenient, it can make things difficult at times. Items drawn without the grid on do not always snap to the grid easily after you enable it.

Tip   Press Shift+F9 to switch between Wireframe and Full-Color editing modes. Press F9 to enable Full-Screen Preview.

If, up until now, you have been working with CorelDRAW!'s Wireframe, rather than Full-Color editing mode, turn on the Full-Color mode by pressing Shift+F9.

Working in Wireframe mode speeds up your computer's screen display. It cuts down on the number of computations the processor must perform, and that can make a large difference in the time it takes to display a drawing. On complex projects, work with the wireframes and pop in and out of Full-Color mode only as needed. Draw also provides a Full-Screen Preview; simply press F9. For now, however, you may amuse yourself by switching between Full-Color and Wireframe modes.

You will really notice the speed hit that your system takes when you add the fractal texture fill in the next exercise. The texture fills look really cool, but certainly do take their time to come up to the screen.

Jump into Fractal Texture Fills

One of the most delicious features introduced in CorelDRAW! version 4.0, Fractal Texture Fills, is just as yummy in version 5.0. These algorithmically derived bit-map fills are full of surprises and photo-realistic effects. You will use one of the "Swimming Pool" fills to put some water under your deck.

There are countless variations to Draw's fractals. You can amuse yourself (and waste your bosses' payroll) for hours on end. Thankfully, there are a number of preset fills that offer point-and-shoot convenience, although you can tweak these until the wee hours, should you have the inclination.

You will start by creating a rectangle, which you will send to back and assign the Swimming Pool fill. Then, you will add another rectangle and get ready to add some type to finish Katie's letterhead.

Send to Back and Take the Fractal Plunge

Click on the Rectangle tool

Click and drag a rectangle   A rectangle is created, covering
to meet the guidelines   the deck

continues

The Basics

continued

You can adjust this by arranging the objects in your drawing with the To Front and To Back commands. These commands can be implemented from the button bar, through keyboard shortcuts, or via the Order submenu of the Arrange menu. For more information on arranging your work, refer to the next chapter.

Press Shift-PgDn	To send the rectangle to the back
Click Fill tool	The fill fly-out menu appears
Click Fractal Texture Fill	The Texture Fill dialog box appears
At Texture List:	
Roll down, click Swimming pool1	(see fig. 2.19)
Click on OK	The rectangle is assigned the swimming pool1 texture fill

Once you get a look at the fill, you may want to go in and tweak it a bit. Lowering the Brightness to -10% should provide a slightly darker surface, with less reflection. Adjust to suit your tastes.

Click and drag a rectangle at the right side of the letterhead, with a width of 0.67 inch and a height of 2.50 inches. Give it a black fill, and no outline.

Next, you get a quick preview of the Text tool.

Setting Type with the Text Tool

Typography, the craft of setting type, is made possible through one of CorelDRAW's most enabling features, the Text tool. You learn more about typesetting later on. For now, you finish setting up Katie's letterhead. Draw's Text tool is easy to spot on the toolbox; it is represented by the letter A.

Draw 5.0 ships with a bounty of over 800 typefaces. From this motherlode, Joe DeLook has chosen the ITC Enviro typeface for the letterhead, as it imparts an architectural feel upon the design. You may or may not have Enviro loaded. If not, feel free to substitute another typeface of your choice. For more information on dealing with all those fonts, check out the chapter on Font Management Techniques, in Part IV of this book.

Setting Type for Katie's Letterhead

Click on the Text tool	The cursor becomes a +
Click on the top of the page	The Text I bar appears

Type **Katie's Construction**	The type appears
Click on the Pick tool	
Click on Te**x**t	The Text menu appears
Click on Text **R**oll-Up	The Text Roll-Up menu appears
At the Text Roll-Up menu:	
Select 36 *points from the Size field, roll down, click on* Enviro	
Click on **A**pply	The text changes to the Enviro typeface
Click on the Text tool	The cursor becomes a +
Click on the top of the page	The Text I bar appears
Type **14th and the Boulevard, Seaside**	The type appears
Click on the Pick tool	
At the Text Roll-Up menu:	
Select 18 *from the Size field*	
Click on Enviro	
Click on Right Align	
Click on **A**pply	The text changes to 18 point Enviro
Click on the Text tool	The text I bar appears
Type **555-1234**	
Click on the Pick tool	

You now should have three blocks of text: the words "Katie's Construction" and the phone number, both in 36-point Enviro, along with the address in 18-point Enviro. Assign all three text elements a white fill and drag them into position. You may want to do some fiddling with type sizes to make things work just right. Try using the Text roll-up menu to precisely adjust the typesize.

Add guidelines as needed to help you properly align the different type elements. Your finished letterhead should look suitably impressive. Congratulations—you have completed your first project! Remember to save your file.

Chapter Snapshot

Now that you've set sail, you must learn to navigate the tricky waters of importing files, node editing, grouping, and basic layering. Successful object-oriented artwork follows a carefully plotted course. In this chapter, you learn to do the following:

✔ Import vector-based clip art

✔ Import bitmaps from your scans or stock photographs

✔ Identify, change, add, remove, and edit various types of nodes

✔ Draw with precision in Bézier curve mode

✔ Implement simple layering techniques with the Group function

✔ Arrange and position objects with the Align command

Node-level object editing is essential for precise work, as are simple object grouping and layering. Once you have completed this chapter, you will be able to navigate your way through a CorelDRAW! file with a steady hand.

CHAPTER

Editing and Manipulating

This chapter has three basic purposes: to enlighten you on the basics of importing files, to illustrate the finer points of nodes, and to help you understand the principles of grouping and layering your work. The concepts and practices in this chapter are a bit more complex than what was previously covered, but the end result of all this work—a series of postcards you create—is worth the effort.

CorelDRAW! enables you to create compositions that incorporate artwork from many sources. You may need to use your own scanned photographs, scanned clip art, text, or logos supplied by a client. These files will come to you in a variety of formats. Draw has the capability to incorporate these many images by importing all the most popular graphic and text file formats.

In Chapter 2, "Creating and Drawing," you learned to lay down the lines that you will soon be refining. You might think, "But my drawing is perfect—what do I have to change?" Plenty. If you begin to look at your work with a critical eye (and the Zoom tool), you will soon see the shortcomings of drawing with a mouse. You are going to use CorelDRAW!'s Shape tool to fine-tune your drawing.

The Importance of Object Editing

As with any creative work, you cannot expect to create excellence in an instant. Inspiration strikes with speed, but true perfection can only be accomplished through diligent attention to detail. Beauty takes time.

When you were drawing with the Pencil tool, you probably noticed that CorelDRAW! added little boxes to your curved lines. These boxes were positioned at distinct changes in the line's direction. These boxes are what CorelDRAW! refers to as *nodes*, and they are the key to producing high-quality images.

A good portion of this chapter discusses manipulating nodes and their control points. For many people, working with nodes is the most difficult CorelDRAW! function to understand. Although you can create drawings without ever using the Shape tool, its proper use separates the expert CorelDRAW! user from the amateur.

Understanding the concepts behind nodes and control points can help you perform more efficiently and produce work of a higher caliber. You must, therefore, not only sit through this little discourse but also spend time learning through doing. Consider yourself warned. You might need some practice before you become proficient with the Shape tool.

Just as important as grasping the idea of node manipulation is understanding the concepts behind building your work in a series of logical layers and groups. The ability to build structured pieces is the mark of the journeyman electronic artist. Simply looking good does not cut it; your pieces must be functional.

Again, it is a good idea to remember that you are assembling an electronic collage of shapes. Those shapes are of many different tints, colors, textures, and patterns. They have other shapes—filled with other tints, colors, textures, and patterns—"glued" on their surfaces. Planning the construction of your imagery takes time. The more thought you put into building your collage, the easier it is for you to go back and edit it.

One of the awful truths of commercial art is that the client often asks the artist to alter work that the artist feels is, for all intents and purposes, finished. The artwork could be very difficult, if not impossible, to alter. Conventional artists have been frustrated by this for years. Imagine Michelangelo at the Sistine chapel: "It is beautiful, Michelangelo, my son, but maybe the angel should be looking to his left instead of his right, and perhaps you could add a cherub or two in the corner?"

This scenario might have thrown the old master into a fit, but it illustrates the advantages of creating electronic artwork. Your images are reworkable. You do not have to start a piece over from scratch should your clients decide they want a different color scheme or an extra angel.

To accommodate changes, however, you must plan for them. You must build your collage in a way that accommodates easy editing. You must be able to import files, edit lines, and group objects to make a "working" drawing. CorelDRAW! provides the tools. To be effective, you must learn how best to use them.

Importing Artwork

When you import an artwork file into your image, CorelDRAW! uses an *import filter* to convert the artwork into Draw's internal format. You, or the person who installed CorelDRAW! on your computer, chose the import filters when the program was installed. If you find that you need to install additional import or export filters, you can use the install program to load the filter(s) at any time. See Appendix A for information on the installation process.

CorelDRAW! can import a wide range of graphics file formats, which is extremely helpful because most commercial clip art is not available in CDR format. Corel is constantly adding to the list—even more options might be available by the time you read this than are listed here. If you need to import a file in a format other than one of the following formats, you can use a third-party conversion utility or check in Corel's CompuServe forum (GO COREL) to see if a new import filter is available. Table 3.1 is a list of graphics file formats supported by CorelDRAW!'s import feature as of this writing.

Table 3.1
Import Formats for Graphic Files

Format	Extension(s)
AutoCAD	DXF
CompuServe (Bitmaps)	GIF
Computer Graphics Metafile	CGM
CorelCHART	CCH
CorelDRAW	CDR
Corel Presentation Exchange	CMX
CorelTRACE	EPS
Rich Text Format	RTF

continues

Table 3.1, Continued
Import Formats for Graphic Files

Format	Extension(s)
Microsoft Word for Windows	DOC
Excel for Windows	XLS
ASCII Text	TXT
AMI Professional 2.0, 3.0	SAM
PostScript (Interpreted)	EPS, PS
EPS (Placeable)	EPS, PS, AI
GEM	GEM
Hewlett-Packard (HPGL)	PLT
IBM PIF (GDF)	PIF
Illustrator 1.1, 88, 3.0	AI, EPS
JPEG (Bitmap)	JPG, JFF, JFT, CMP
Kodak Photo-CD	PCD
Lotus PIC	PIC
Macintosh (PICT)	PCT
Micrographx 2.x, 3.x	DRW
PC Paintbrush (Bitmaps)	PCX, PCC
Scitex CT (Bitmaps)	CT, SCT
Targa (Bitmaps)	TGA, VDA, ICB, VST
TIFF 5.0 (Bitmaps)	TIF, SEP, CPT
Windows Bitmaps	BMP, DIB, RLE
Windows Metafiles	WMF
WordPerfect Graphic	WPG

Notice that Draw's native CDR format is included in the list. Why would you want to import a file that you can open directly? An excellent example comes to mind. Imagine that you are producing an advertisement. You have finished the layout and have set all the type. Now you want to place a piece of electronic clip art (that you or another artist has created) into the file. Because CorelDRAW! 5.0 cannot have more than one open drawing at a time, importing artwork is the best way to assemble pieces from a number of different files and sources.

You can import many files into one drawing. Be advised, however, that the more complex a file is, the more time it takes to print and the more room it takes up on your hard disk. A file that has had multiple files imported into it saves as one (large) file.

Although most of the clip art supplied with CorelDRAW! version 5.0 is now in the new Corel Presentation Exchange (CMX) format, most commercial clip art is not. Appendix D, "Clip Art Compendium," features a list of companies that sell a wide variety of electronic illustrations in various formats. If you are looking for more clip art, the first place you should look is on the CD-ROM discs that come with CorelDRAW! 5.0. You will find an abundance of clip art (over 22,000 images). Of course, you need a CD-ROM drive to access it. CD-ROM drive prices have dropped dramatically and might not be as expensive as you expect. Low-end CD-ROM drives, from off-brand manufacturers, can be purchased for approximately $100.

The CD-ROM that accompanies this book contains a large variety of images from third-party vendors, as well as the authors' own files. There are sample textures, photographs, and clip art in a variety of formats. In this chapter, you will import and use a number of files from the *Inside CorelDRAW! 5.0 CD-ROM*.

The Basics of Importing Vector-Based Artwork

As you can see from table 3.1, CorelDRAW! can import files from a wide variety of formats. The vast majority of commercial clip art is available in Adobe Illustrator (AI) files, in either a 1.1, 88, or 3.0 format. This format does not support fountain fills, but it provides the common denominator to transfer images between the most popular drawing packages, as well as between various computer platforms.

Other vector formats are either not as widely supported or have severe limitations. The Windows Metafile Format (WMF) includes fountain fill information, but it generally is not supported on other platforms, nor is most commercial clip art available in this format. The Computer Graphics Metafile (CGM) was fairly popular at the dawn of the PC-based graphics revolution, but is considered passé due to its lack of any curve information. CGM files can only contain straight lines, not curves. In a CGM file, curves are created by using a multitude of eenie-weenie little straight lines. This shortcoming very quickly becomes apparent when you scale a CGM file up in size.

In the next exercise, you will import a little EPS file from the *Inside CorelDRAW! 5, Fifth Edition CD-ROM.* This file originally was created in Adobe Illustrator 4.0. Substitute the appropriate drive letter for your CD-ROM drive. When you import a file, you can initiate the procedure from either the File menu or by clicking on the Import File button on the button bar.

Importing an Adobe Illustrator File

Click on File	The File menu appears
Click on Import	The Import dialog box appears (see fig. 3.1)
At List Files of Type *roll down, click on* Adobe Illustrator 1.1, 88, 3.0 (*.ai, *.eps)	
Change the directory to F:\ICD5-ART\EPS *(where F: is the letter of your CD-ROM drive)*	
Double-click on DECOMPAS.EPS	A compass assembles on-screen

Figure 3.1
The Import dialog box for importing files.

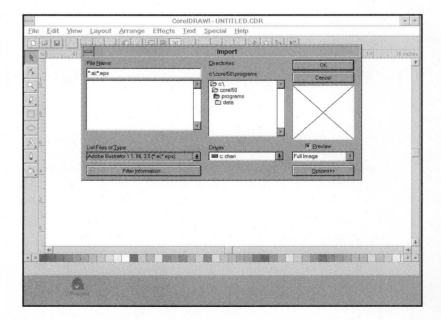

The Import File dialog box provides you with a variety of information about art files before you import them, including an image preview. By clicking on the Options button, you can expand the dialog box to display file statistics, such as file date, size, and format. You also have the option of sorting files by name or date. In addition, the Import File dialog box enables you to reduce the size of a piece of artwork when you import it, through the use of the AutoReduce function. If you know that the artwork you are importing is going to be too large, you can compensate for it before you click on OK.

Now that you have imported the compass, you can manipulate it within CorelDRAW! just as if it had originally been created there (see fig. 3.2). You are free to scale it, stretch it, skew it, and assign different fills, outlines, and special effects. Try a few of these maneuvers right now. You will be using the compass later as you help Joe DeLook complete a project that ties together the many principles illustrated by this chapter. Because you have the basic idea of vector imports, it is time to move on to the subject of importing bitmaps.

Figure 3.2
The compass and a few variations thereof.

A Little Bit about Bitmaps

Draw is a vector-based drawing program rather than a bitmapped paint program, but it does a nice job of importing bitmapped images from other sources and can even be used to export bitmaps of its own. This chapter discusses the different types of bitmaps that you can use within the Draw environment. CorelDRAW! version 3.0 introduced CorelPHOTOPAINT!, a powerful bitmapped paint program. The dramatically improved PhotoPaint 5.0 is covered later in this book in Chapter 19, "Using CorelPHOTOPAINT!."

Unlike object-oriented images, a bitmapped image is rasterized—that is, imaged dot by dot. Each pixel on-screen corresponds to a single dot on the output image.

A bitmapped image can be considered a grid of pixels or a matrix of dots. As you can see in figure 3.3, the individual dots in a bitmap matrix can be on (in black or in a variety of colors or grays) or off (white).

Figure 3.3
A close look at a bitmap.

Bitmapped images can come from a variety of sources. These sources include scanned images, original paint-type graphics (such as those you create and export from PhotoPaint!), electronic stock photographs, and clip art. You can, in fact, import a limitless variety of images into Draw, whether they begin as electronic files or printed originals.

In addition, you can incorporate "screen shots" or screen dumps into Draw images. In fact, many of the graphics in this book were reproduced in this way. Screen shots are especially useful for producing software documentation or promotional materials. Although New Riders Publishing uses a dedicated screen-capture program, for light duty you can use the Corel screen-capture utility, CCapture, supplied with CorelDRAW! 5.0.

Scanners

A *scanner* transfers a printed image or piece of artwork into a computer program. Scanners transform analog artwork into digital data through a process known as *digitizing*. Scanners are available in a variety of sizes and styles, from hand-held scanners at the low end to serious, "heavy-metal" drum scanners at the high end. In the past, very few shops combined six-figure scanners with CorelDRAW!, but times are changing. With PhotoPaint bundled in the Draw package, Corel users have the ability to alter 24-bit images.

Today, many people buy scanners in the $200 to $2,000 range. Some of these scanners are limited in image quality, but they have come a long way in a short time. Line art and grayscale scanning are commonplace. As computers grow faster, more powerful, and less expensive, expect to see a corresponding increase in scanning accuracy and resolution.

One of the most interesting developments in scanner technology is the advent of drum scanners in the $30,000 to $40,000 range. Entries from DS America, Optronics, Scanview, and Howtek are changing the way people work with color. Instead of relying on outside suppliers, designers can create high-caliber scans at their desktops. Quality four-color work, however, has never been a poor (or an unskilled) player's game. It takes serious commitment, skill, and expertise to create realistic full-color scans. It might be subjective, but there is no replacement for having an "eye."

Joe DeLook used a desktop scanner to digitize the image that you are about to import into Draw. The image looked nice, but was not of optimal quality. Consequently, after he had scanned the image, he took the time to touch it up, and he even played a bit with the color balance.

This time, before you import the file, be sure to look around in the File Import dialog box. Click on the **P**review button and watch as a thumbnail display appears. Click on the **O**ptions button and take note of all the file information that the dialog box supplies (see fig. 3.4). Version 5.0 offers bitmap import filters that even let you crop or resample images as they are being imported into CorelDRAW!.

Importing a Bitmap (BMP) File

Click on **F**ile	The File menu appears
Click on **I**mport	The Import dialog box appears
At List Files of **T**ype, *roll down, click on* Windows Bitmap (*.BMP;*.DIB;*.RLE)	
Change the directory to F:\ICD5-ART\BMP (remember: F: is the letter of your CD-ROM drive)	
Double-click on DEMARINA.BMP	The marina appears

Figure 3.4
The expanded
Import dialog
box.

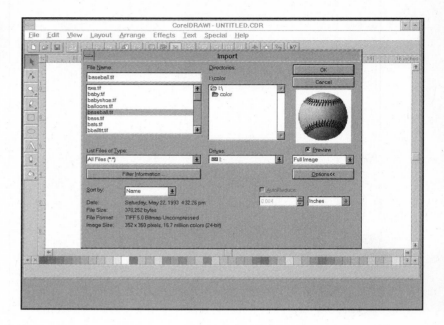

How does Joe DeLook's marina shot appear on your system? It all depends on how your system is configured. If you have a lame 16-color video card, the picture will look awful, and for a good reason—you need a new video card! You are doing yourself a disservice if you are running at less than 256 colors. At 256 colors, the image is noticeably dithered and just bearable (see fig. 3.5). Bitmaps look good only if you are running a decent video card, with 65K or more colors. At a full 24-bit (16.7 million colors), the marina should look almost photographic.

CorelDRAW! 5.0 includes an advanced Color Manager to match more closely your screen preview to your printed output. Part IV, "Advanced Topics," includes a chapter on managing color and system calibration.

Within CorelDRAW!, bitmapped objects behave differently from vector objects. Bitmaps are so large in file size—they can negatively affect screen redrawing performance—the program gives you a number of ways to change screen display. If you want to view your bitmaps in full color, you can use the View menu to choose either Standard or High Resolution mode. However, switching between these two modes makes a difference only if you are running a video driver with greater than 256-color display.

Figure 3.5
Joe's Marina Shot, imported and displayed at 256 colors.

You can, of course, change to Wireframe view; this yields either a wireframe box containing a very crude gray and white image or a simple unfilled bounding box, depending on whether you have chosen to make your bitmaps **V**isible. Should you rotate a bitmap in visible Wireframe mode, however, the screen will display a gray box with a white rectangle in what was originally the top left corner of the bitmap. Click on the Wireframe button on the button bar (or choose **W**ireframe from the **V**iew menu) to switch to Wireframe mode. Then try rotating the bitmap. Figure 3.6 displays a pair of visible bitmaps, side by side, displaying upright and rotated orientations.

A Scanning Caveat

You must be careful with the images you scan. It is too easy to break the law by using images that belong to another person or organization. The "copyright police" might not come knocking on the door, but a little professional courtesy goes a long way. Never use an image for which you do not have authorization. Failure to respect the ownership of an image could land you in court, facing a stiff penalty.

If a client should ask to include an image of, say, a popular cartoon character, *do not* do this without obtaining the proper authorization from the copyright owner. In many cases, you can easily contact the licensee, pay a fee, and avoid the legal ramifications. It's your responsibility to know where the image came from and who owns the reproduction rights.

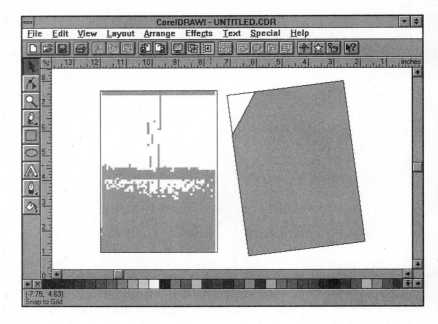

It's time to move on from the subject of importing artwork to one of the finer points of object-oriented vector illustration.

Drawing with Bézier Curves

CorelDRAW! uses a device called the *Bézier curve* to generate smooth, resolution-independent objects. Bézier curves are produced by a mathematical formula that governs the shape of a line. Don't worry: you don't have to get out your scientific calculator to complete a drawing—CorelDRAW! does the math for you.

One Bézier curve requires two nodes, each with its own control point(s), to complete the equation. The *node* is the hub from which the control points radiate. *Control points* are the mechanisms that govern the trajectory of a line segment. People have described the on-screen appearance of a node and its control points as looking "like a box with two knitting needles sticking out of it," a "bug with antennae," or even "the world's smallest voodoo doll." The last description echoes the way you might feel about nodes and control points after you spend a frustrating session wrestling with them.

Segments are the lines between the nodes. They form the edges of objects and can be curved or straight. A curved segment requires a control point at each end. Straight lines, however, have no control points. A node has a corresponding control point for each curved segment that radiates from it.

If a node is the first node of an open path, it can have only one control point. If it looks as if it has more, you probably have two selected nodes sitting on top of each other.

When editing Bézier curves, you have two options for changing the line segments you've drawn: you can either work with the nodes that exist or you can add additional nodes. You can affect the shape of a line segment in four basic ways without adding a node. The first method is to move the node. Repositioning the node affects the position at which the control points do their work. Because a line segment is governed by the nodes at either end, as one node is moved, it affects the relationship between both nodes. When you move a node, the shapes of the line segments on both sides of that node are altered.

If you do not want to move the node, you have three alternatives. The second approach is to change the node type. As you will soon see, different node types enable you to create curved or straight line segments. You specify the node type by using the Node Roll-Up menu. CorelDRAW! 4.0 introduced a third way to change a line's shape. You now can use the Shape tool to click and drag on the line. This new method feels like you are tugging on a garden hose; the nodes remain anchored, but the line segment moves freely.

The fourth and final method of altering the shape of a line segment is through control-point positioning. This process is the most involved of the three, and it is the one in which you do the heaviest tweaking. When you reposition a node's control points, you change the mathematical equation that defines the corresponding line segment. The power of Bézier curves lies in numbers. One Bézier curve is not of much use; linking Bézier curves to form paths fully exploits their potential.

Of course, you can always add a new node to an existing line segment. Adding a new node splits one line segment into two and enables you to make radical changes to either line.

At this point, review the various methods for drawing lines. Chapter 2 covered these techniques in depth; if you have any questions beyond that which is reviewed here, check back a few pages.

Here are a few basics:

✔ Click for single straight lines.

✔ Double-click for connected straight lines.

✔ Hold the Ctrl key to constrain straight lines to 15-degree increments (default setting).

The default setting can be changed in the Special, Preferences dialog box.

✔ When drawing curved lines, remember to hold down the left mouse button until you are finished drawing the line.

✔ If you want to erase a portion of a curved line (while drawing), hold down the Shift key and "back over" the offending portion of the line.

Selecting Node Types

CorelDRAW! supports three types of curved nodes: smooth, symmetrical, and cusp. When you execute a freehand drawing or import a traced object, CorelDRAW! (or CorelTRACE!) takes its best guess at which type of node is needed. On many occasions, the program does not make the right choice. (What do you want, a program that does all the work for you?) You should make the ultimate decision because you are the artist. Take the information that the program gives you and alter it as you see fit.

Drawing Some Curves

Before you read a formal explanation of the different node types, try drawing some curves. Attempt to draw a squid—an appropriately curved undersea creature. Try working in Wireframe mode to get a better view of the nodes' control points.

Tip Press Shift+F9 to switch between Wireframe and Full-Color editing modes.

You do not need a prompted exercise; just click on the Pencil tool and start drawing. It will probably take a few tries to draw a squid you are happy with. Do not worry about making it perfect the first time. You can alter the curves later and improve its appearance.

After you have drawn a nice-looking squid, as shown in figure 3.7, select it with the Shape tool. Notice that your squid has many nodes spread along the path that outlines its body. These nodes are a means for you to change the shape of your drawing.

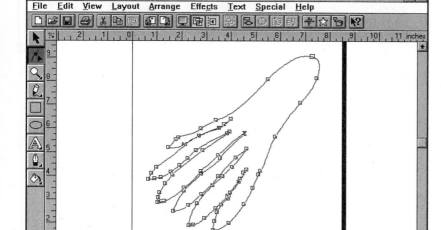

Figure 3.7
A squid.

The Basics

Select a node and try dragging it around. Watch what happens to the curves as you move the node. The node's control points become active after the node is selected. The control points are the squares at the ends of the dashed lines. Try pulling on the different control points and take note of the way the control points alter the shape of the line.

Don't worry about changing the shape of a line. If you don't like the result, you can always go back to its original form by using the <u>U</u>ndo command in the <u>F</u>ile menu.

As you select different nodes, you see that they do not all act the same. Also notice that a selected node's type appears in the status line. The next few sections discuss CorelDRAW!'s assortment of curved and line nodes. To change between node types, you must use the Node Roll-Up menu.

Smooth Nodes

In a *smooth* node, the control points and the node itself are in a straight line (see fig. 3.8). Pull up on one node, and the other goes down. The control points and the node are linearly linked. Think of a spinning propeller on a seaplane. The blades always spin in the same direction, be it clockwise or counterclockwise. Unlike a propeller, however, the control points in a smooth node do not have to be the same distance from the node. The farther away a control point is from the node, the larger the curve.

Figure 3.8
A smooth node.

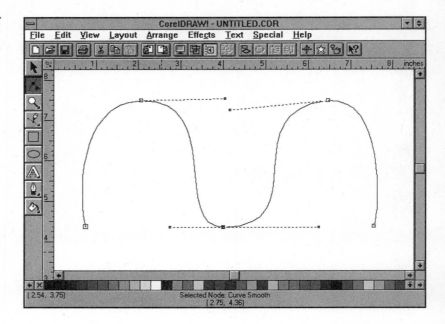

Symmetrical Nodes

The *symmetrical* node takes the smooth node's propeller analogy a bit further. Not only are the control points and node linearly linked, the control points are of equal distance from the node. Moving one control point affects the other control point, resulting in exactly the same curve on each side of the node.

Symmetrical nodes are, in effect, smooth nodes with equidistant control points (see fig. 3.9).

Cusp Nodes

Cusp nodes are very different from smooth and symmetrical nodes. In a *cusp* node, the control points operate independently of each other (see fig. 3.10). One side of the curve can be affected without altering the other side. A cusp node is used where there is a radical change in direction or a severe angle. You can compare cusp-node control points to a set of rabbit-ear antennae on a television set. To pick up different stations, you adjust each antenna individually. To manipulate a curve, you move the control point corresponding to that curve.

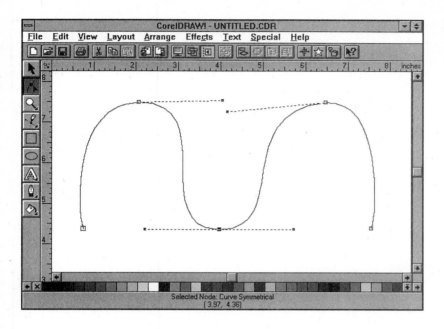

Figure 3.9
A symmetrical node.

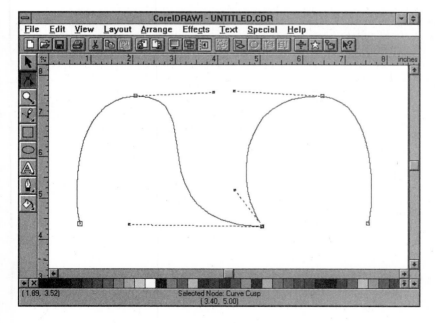

Figure 3.10
A cusp node.

Line Nodes

Line nodes are not as flexible as curve nodes. Where a line meets a line, you must have a cusp node. Two straight lines cannot be connected with a smooth node or a symmetrical node. On the other hand, when a line meets a curve, you can have either a cusp or a smooth node (see fig. 3.11). Because they do not curve, straight line segments do not have control points. Objects often are made up of both curved and straight line segments. A node with a straight line segment on one side and a curved line segment on the other has only one control point.

Figure 3.11
A smooth node where a line meets a curve.

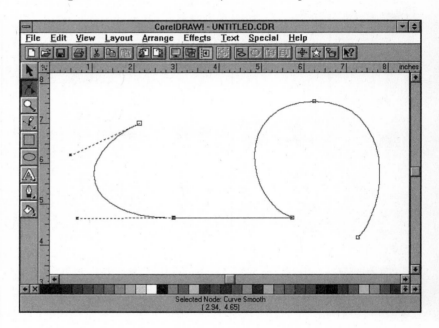

Now it is time to put you to work. You are going to clean up the squid you just drew, using the Shape tool. Before you begin cleaning the aquatic creature, save the file as SQUID.CDR by either clicking on Save (from the File menu) or by clicking on the Save button (it looks like a floppy disk) on the Ribbon Bar.

Editing Nodes

Click on the Zoom tool	The Zoom fly-out menu appears
Click on the + tool	
Marquee-select the squid	Zooms in on the squid
Click on the Shape tool	The cursor becomes the Shape tool
Click on the squid	The squid's nodes appear (see fig. 3.7)

According to the status line, the squid in figure 3.7 has 74 nodes—far more than necessary for this basic object. Your squid can have many more (or less) nodes. The first thing you are going to do is remove some of the excess nodes by simply selecting each node and deleting it with the Del key. You can also left-click on the minus sign symbol located in the Node Edit Roll-Up menu.

Later in this chapter, you learn how to eliminate the excess nodes with only one mouse click using the Auto-Reduce command.

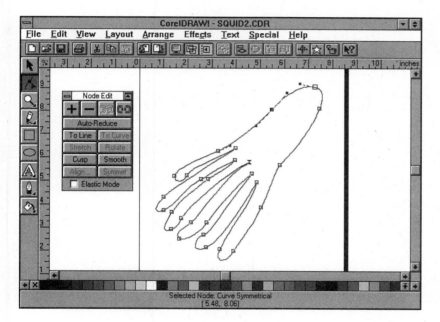

Figure 3.12
A pruned squid!

The Basics

If you marquee-select your squid, notice that curved nodes are denoted by small black boxes. Line nodes show as larger outlined boxes. The first node of a closed curve is always a large, black box when selected. Your squid drawing should consist of mostly curved nodes. Prune a few extra nodes (see fig. 3.12). As you do, watch the status line; it reads Selected node: Curve Cusp, or Smooth or Symmetrical, depending on what type of node is selected.

Removing an Extra Node

Click on an extra node The node turns black

Press Del The node is deleted

You have two other ways to delete a node. After you select a node, you can click on Delete from the Edit menu or from the Node Edit Roll-Up menu to accomplish the same thing. You also can add nodes—that is covered in the next section.

To access the Node Edit menu, double-click on a node.

CorelDRAW! enables you to work with more than one node at a time. Remove a pair of nodes by selecting them with a marquee and then deleting them. Another way to select more than one node at a time is to hold down Shift as you click on the nodes you want to select.

After you finish selecting and deleting nodes and you have grown tired of squid pruning, move on to working with (rather than simply deleting) the remaining nodes.

Begin by selecting a node. Click and drag that node to a new location. Watch how the node's control point (or points) moves with the node. The curves change, governed by the relationship between neighboring nodes.

When you click on a node, the control points for that point—as well as the relevant control points of all related nodes—become active. These "knitting needles" bend and flex their respective curve segments according to the conventions of their node type.

Now change a curve by dragging it. This editing method is a quick and easy way to reach outline-editing nirvana. As you drag the line around, watch the control points reposition themselves. Try clicking at different locations on the line. Notice how the selected location affects the way the curve is altered.

Before you get into an exercise, you should begin to get the feel of nodes and control points. Just tweak those nodes until it seems familiar. Push and pull on the different control points; tug on the curves like you are bringing in the lines.

If a line segment goes whacko after you delete a node, fear not; a quick fix is available. Select the wayward line, then click on To Line on the Node Edit Roll-Up. This changes the whacko curve into a straight line. Click on the (now straight) line again, then on To Curve. Finally, tweak the control points until the curve is back in shape.

I

The Basics

As you get further and further into tweaking your squid, you begin to understand the differences between the types of nodes. You see that the control points in a cusp curve operate independently of each other. And you see the similarity and differences between smooth and symmetrical curves.

Adding Nodes to an Object

In this next exercise, you build a cloud from scratch. Start by drawing an ellipse and use Convert To Curves to enable access to the object. Then, use Add (+) from the Node Edit menu to add four extra points.

CorelDRAW! does not allow manipulation of nodes in an ellipse, rectangle, or text without first using Convert To Curves. If you try to use the Shape tool on a "normal" ellipse or circle, CorelDRAW! turns the object into an arc or pie wedge (this technique is covered in Chapter 5). Using the Shape tool on a rectangle renders a rounded-corner rectangle (which you learn more about later in this chapter).

After an object has been converted to curves, you can perform some amazing maneuvers. By the time you finish this exercise, you will have more than a hint of what the Convert To Curves command enables you to do.

To get started, set up your grid so that there are six lines per inch. Then use this setup to build some perfectly cartoony clouds. Convert To Curves adds three nodes to the oval (it starts with one). If you click on each node, you find that they are all symmetrical curves.

Turning the Ellipse into a Cloud

Click on **L**ayout

Click on G**r**id & Scale Setup

Set the **H**orizontal *and* **V**ertical Grid
Frequency *prompts to* **6.00** *per inch*

Make sure that S**n**ap to Grid *is selected*

Click on OK

Click on the Ellipse tool

Draw an oval; make it 1.5 *inches high
by* 5.5 *inches wide*

Click on **A**rrange   The Arrange menu appears

Click on Con**v**ert To Curves   Three nodes are added to the oval

continues

continued

Click on the Shape tool

Marquee-select all four nodes
(see fig. 3.13)

Double-click on a node	The Node Edit Roll-Up menu appears
Click on +	Four new nodes are added (see fig. 3.14)
At the Node Edit Roll-Up menu, *click on* **Cusp**	All nodes are now cusp nodes
Click on the screen	The cloud is deselected
Click on a node	The node is selected
Pull control points from object *at a 90-degree angle*	Curves grow out from the object
Continue pulling out control points	A cloud forms (see fig. 3.15)

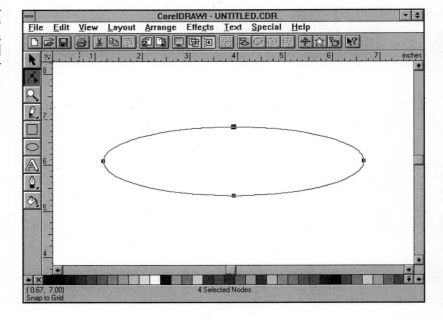

Figure 3.13
An oval that has been converted to curves (four nodes).

Tip

You can use a particularly helpful shortcut in place of Marquee-select to select all the nodes of an object. Press and hold down Ctrl+Shift, then click on any of the nodes forming the object.

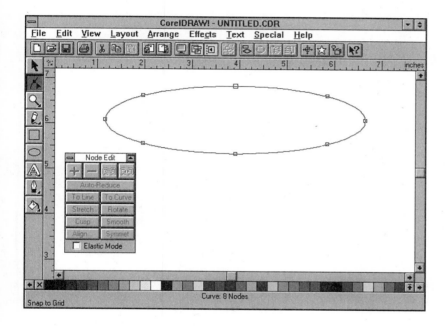

Figure 3.14
An oval with eight nodes.

The Node Edit Roll-Up menu provides a simple way to change node types. To display the menu initially, double-click on a selected node (the roll-up remains on-screen until you put it away). In this roll-up menu, you can choose line or curve nodes—the latter in cusp, smooth, or symmetrical variations. The menu also enables you to break or join a path and add or delete a node.

As you have seen, cusp nodes are capable of severely changing direction. See what happens when you change all the nodes to smooth or symmetrical curves. Remember, you can immediately undo any wayward actions with Ctrl-Z or Alt-Backspace.

In version 4.0, Corel significantly enhanced the node-editing features over previous versions. You can rotate, skew, scale, and stretch selected curve segments. In addition, you can edit nodes in either Standard or Elastic mode. When you use Elastic mode, you notice a subtle difference in the way groups of nodes react as you move them around (think of a rubber band). In Standard mode, all the nodes move in locked-in harmony. In Elastic mode, however, the nodes move in springy relation to the node you are dragging.

Figure 3.15
The finished
cloud.

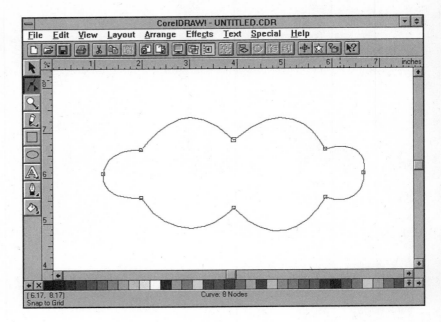

Nodes and Tracing

Generally speaking, you should use as few nodes in your objects as possible. The more nodes in an object, the larger your files. With the increase in file size also comes a loss of speed, both in screen display and in printing time. Less is more. An autotraced or freehand-rendered image often includes far more nodes than necessary to portray the object accurately. If you notice an excessive amount of jaggedness, you probably have a bunch of untweaked cusp nodes. For this reason, use cusp nodes sparingly—only where you must.

CorelDRAW! 4.0 also introduced a fabulous node-editing time saver: Auto-Reduce. Like a diet plan that helps you shed unwanted pounds, Auto-Reduce kills off needless nodes with just one click. To Auto-Reduce, use the Shape tool to select the object (or portion of an object) that you want to trim down. Then press the Auto-Reduce button on the Node Edit Roll-Up menu. Excess nodes are instantly removed. It's like eating a huge lobster dinner (with gobs of drawn butter, of course) and waking up the next morning to find that you have actually lost five pounds!

Node Tips

Here are a few other things you should know about nodes:

✔ You can constrain the movement of a node or control point by using the grid. In addition, pressing and holding down Ctrl while moving a node or control point restricts the action to either vertical or horizontal movement.

✔ You can easily add a node at a specific point. With the Shape tool, click on the spot where you want to add the new node. At the Node Edit Roll-Up menu, simply click on +. A node is added at the exact coordinates on which you clicked. To add nodes with pinpoint precision, remember to use Draw's Snap To Guidelines. Drag out a set of horizontal and vertical guidelines, adjust them for dead-on accuracy, and go! Take the time to try this technique on one of your clouds.

✔ If a /control point is hidden beneath a node, you can easily dig it out. First, make sure the node is deselected. Press and hold down Shift, then drag the control point from underneath the node.

Do not worry if you still feel uncomfortable with nodes. It takes time. The best way to learn is practice, practice, practice. After you are finished with your node tweaking, remember to save your work. In the next section, you start with a clean screen. As you get further along in the book, you see how important it is to create lean, mean objects with a minimum of nodes. An extra node is a wasted node.

Drawing in Bézier Curve Mode

CorelDRAW! enables you to draw directly in Bézier curve mode. This might seem like torture for some, but others welcome the extreme precision and flexibility this feature offers.

Learning to draw in Bézier mode helps you understand the way the curves function. No substitute for practice exists when it comes to mastering the skill of working with Bézier curves. Practice is essential if you want to be successful with object-oriented graphics programs such as CorelDRAW!, Adobe Illustrator, Aldus Freehand, and Deneba Canvas.

To work in Bézier mode rather than in Freehand mode, you select a variant of the Pencil tool. When you click on the Pencil tool, hold down the left mouse button and drag downward and to the right to access the Pencil fly-out menu. Click on the second icon to get into Bézier mode.

When you click on the Pencil tool, the status line reports Drawing in Bézier Mode. When you draw straight lines in Bézier mode, you might not notice any differences between it and Freehand mode. Drawing curves in Bézier mode, however, is quite different from drawing curves in Freehand mode.

When drawing curves, consider how the curve exits and enters its starting and ending nodes (respectively). Think of threading a line through a series of fish hooks. The line segments form your fishing line and the nodes are the hooks. The direction you pull the line through the hook affects the first half of the arc. Likewise, the direction you thread the line into the next hook (node) affects the second half of the arc. Figure 3.16 shows three Bézier curve drawing techniques.

Figure 3.16
Point and shoot
Bézier curves.

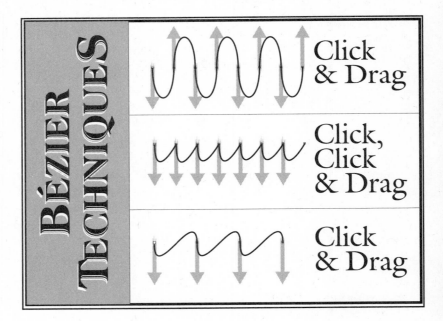

In practice, it goes something like this: if you click-and-drag away from the first node in one direction, then click-and-drag (placing the second node) in the opposite direction, you draw a one-bump curve. However, if you click-and-drag away from the first node in one direction, then click-and-drag (placing the second node) in the same direction, you draw a two-bump curve.

Try working in Bézier mode. Start by laying down a few straight lines to form a triangle. Afterward, move on to the curves. For the straight lines, you can turn on the grid (by pressing Ctrl+Y) for precision, but you may want to turn it off (by pressing Ctrl+Y again) when you draw your curves.

Drawing in Bézier Mode

First, draw a triangle with straight lines:

Press Ctrl+Y	Turns on the grid
Click on the Pencil tool, drag down and to the right	The Pencil fly-out menu appears
Click on the Bézier icon	The cursor becomes a +
Click on the page	The first node is placed
Click two inches to the right of first node	A two-inch line is drawn
Click one inch to the left and one inch above second node	A one-inch line is drawn
Click on the first node	A triangle is formed

Now try some curves. When you first click, the curve's starting node appears. As you drag, two control points pull away from the node in opposite directions. Remember: the curve is drawn in the direction you pull away from the starting node until the apogee, where it then is drawn in the direction you thread through the ending node.

Press Ctrl+Y	Turns off the grid
Place the cursor at the curve's starting point	
Click and drag down	Node and control points appear
Release the mouse button	Node and control points remain on-screen

Now position the end of the curve segment, and draw the curve. Draw a one-bump curve to begin. Watch how the curve is altered as you drag.

Place the cursor at the curve's ending point	
Click and drag upward	The end node, control points, and line segment appear
Release the mouse button	A line segment is drawn, and the end node and control points remain on-screen

Draw a few more connected curves. Then try pulling in the same direction for both the starting and ending nodes. You see the curves change into two-bump segments.

To draw cusp nodes, you need a little more patience and a bit more skill. The technique consists of a double-click on each end node and a control-point position for each segment. Double-click, position; double-click, position; double-click, position—not quite as tough as learning to waltz in junior high! Try drawing a few clouds this way. Give yourself plenty of time; soon you will be laying down Béziers with precision!

> **Tip**   To begin drawing a new object, press the spacebar twice. (This shortcut works in Freehand and Bézier mode.) This deselects any active objects or nodes and reselects the Pencil tool.

At this point, save your drawing and open a new file.

Planning a Layering Strategy

Layering and arranging your work is like shuffling a deck of cards. You can stack the deck in your favor by assembling your image so that it can be easily manipulated.

Except for the most rudimentary drawings, all your drawings should contain groups. Only the most quick-and-dirty scribbles, with a minimum of objects, should not be grouped.

Complex work requires careful planning and execution. Thankfully, CorelDRAW! has a sophisticated layering function. In addition to layer control, Draw can arrange the order of objects through the use of five basic commands: To Front, To Back, Forward One, Back One, and Reverse Order. This command set works well, especially when used in conjunction with layer control.

You can extend the versatility of these commands by using two other commands from the <u>A</u>rrange menu: <u>G</u>roup and <u>C</u>ombine.

By building groups of objects, you take the first step toward forming an effective layering strategy. A complex drawing should not consist of hundreds of individual objects. It should be broken down into as few groups or layers as practical.

If you do not arrange your work properly, you will spend far too much time reworking the composition when the time comes to make changes. And you *will* make changes, like it or not.

Although it can take more time initially, grouping and layering saves time in the long run. Similar objects should be strategically combined to take advantage of like features, such as outline and fill. Likewise, objects or combined objects should be arranged into layer-specific groups.

The spots on a leopard and the stripes on a zebra are excellent examples of objects that might be grouped, if not combined. If they are exactly alike and on the same layer, combine them. If they are all on the same layer, but not necessarily alike, group them. You can group combined objects with other objects. You cannot, however, combine objects and maintain individual attributes.

As you get further on in the book, you delve into the subject of layering and grouping in depth. In the next exercise, you see that with strategic grouping, you can rearrange your drawings at will.

A Lonely Saturday Night at DeLook Design

What is Joe DeLook doing? It is Saturday night, and he is still sitting at his desk, working with CorelDRAW!. That is what owning your own business will do for you. Joe would rather be with his buddies in the back room of the Tiki Bar for the regular Saturday night poker game. He would even settle for playing blackjack in Atlantic City and donating his money to Donald Trump. But here he is.

Joe has cards on his mind. Not just playing cards, but postcards! The Seaside Town Council has commissioned him to create a series of postcards for the sleepy little beach town. Joe is psyched about the project, but has promised himself that he will only work for an hour or so before he cuts out. Determined though he is to finish the postcard project, Joe is itching to lose some money to his pals.

There are three postcards in the collection. You might remember the first image— the marina at sunset—that you imported in the beginning of this chapter. Joe has two additional pictures: a dune-and-surf beach shot and a great flock of flamingos from the Seaside Municipal Bird Sanctuary.

Building a set of postcards and shuffling them helps illustrate the concept of grouping and layering your work. In this exercise, you help Joe create the three postcards to learn to arrange objects without resorting to using CorelDRAW!'s Layers Roll-Up menu.

To make your computer respond faster, make sure Wireframe mode is active. You can sneak a peak at the real thing at any time by turning on full-color mode again. Although each postcard will be 4×6 inches, you will begin the following exercise by setting the page layout to a tabloid size page. This size will allow you to work as if you were ganging the postcards for the printing press. Afterward, you will adjust the grid settings to 6 grid lines per inch.

Tip   To access the Page Layout dialog box, double-click on the edge of the page.

Setting up the Postcard's Page Layout

Double-click on the edge of the page   The Page Setup dialog box appears

Click on Tabloid

Click on OK   The page layout is changed to tabloid

Click on Layout   The Layout menu appears

Click on Grid & Scale Setup   The Grid & Scale dialog box appears

Set the Horizontal *and* Vertical *Grid Frequency prompts to* **6.00** *per inch*

Make sure Snap to Grid *is checked*

Click on OK

Now that the page is properly set up, you can import the first postcard image. Actually, if you have been following the chapter, you are re-importing the marina image that you imported earlier. To do so, follow the same procedure here that you did in the earlier section.

After you have imported the marina image, you learn how to crop a bitmap to size using the Shape tool. The marina shot is purposely too large so that you can learn how (and why) to crop an image. When you look at the top of the picture, you will see a black band that should not print. The Shape tool enables you to remove the unwanted black edge from the image.

Cropping a Bitmap with the Shape Tool

Click on File   The File menu appears

Click on Import   The Import dialog box appears

At the List Files of Type *roll down, click on* Windows Bitmap (*.BMP; *.DIB; *.RLE)

Change the directory to F:\ICD5-ART\BMP (F: is the drive letter of your CD-ROM)

Double-click on DEMARINA.BMP   The marina appears

The marina is too large for the page! That is a good thing because you need to crop the black bar at the top of the image, as well as trim a little on the left and right sides. But first, you need to draw four guidelines:

*Click on the horizontal ruler
and drag a guideline eight inches from
the bottom of the page*

*Click on the horizontal ruler and drag
a guideline 14 inches from the bottom
of the page*

*Click on the vertical ruler and drag a
guideline one inch from the left side
of the page*

*Click on the vertical ruler and drag a
guideline five inches from the left side
of the page*

*Click and drag the bottom edge of the
marina image to the bottom guideline*

Press Ctrl+Y to turn off the grid

Click on Layout   The Layout menu appears

Deselect Snap to Guidelines
if it is selected

*Center the marina horizontally
on the guidelines (see fig. 3.17)*

Click on the Shape tool

Click on Layout   The Layout menu appears

Reselect Snap to Guidelines

Click on the edge of the marina bitmap   The marina bitmap is selected

*Drag the bitmap edges in so that they
approximately meet the guidelines
(see fig. 3.18)*

Figure 3.17
Before the crop.

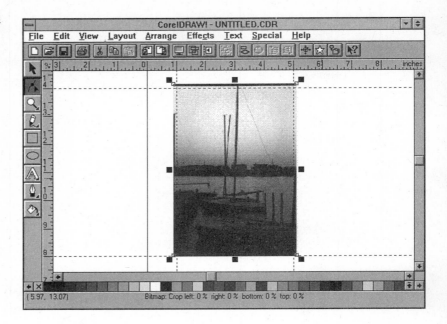

Figure 3.18
After the crop.

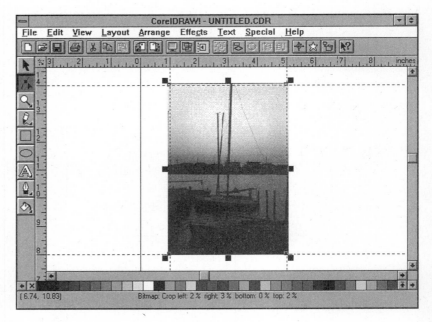

Draw has always given you the ability to crop bitmaps with the Shape tool. However, most pros will tell you that you should do your bitmap cropping in a program such as CorelPHOTO-PAINT or Adobe Photoshop. Conventional wisdom says to import the smallest file possible, with just the image you need, at the proper resolution for your intended output device. This is good advice because the image area you crop out (with the Shape tool) remains in the file, needlessly taking up disk storage space and adding to output times, regardless of whether the area is cropped out with the Shape tool.

CorelDRAW! 5.0 includes a wonderful new cropping and resampling function within the bitmap import filters. This function enables you to crop or resample a file precisely while it imports. By cropping on import, you can cut down your CDR file sizes dramatically, slashing storage requirements and theoretically reducing output times. Resampling enables you to import bitmaps at exactly the correct dpi for imagesetting, laser, or Fiery printing.

In the next exercise, you will use the import-cropping function when you bring in the flamingo picture.

Cropping a Bitmap on Import

Click on **F**ile	The File menu appears
Click on **I**mport	The Import dialog box appears
At List Files of **T**ype, *roll down, click on* Windows Bitmap (*.BMP;*.DIB;*.RLE)	
Change the directory to F:\CD5-ART\BMP (F: is the drive letter of your CD-ROM)	
Click on FLAMINGO.BMP	
At Full Image, roll down, click on Crop	
Click on OK	The Crop Image dialog box appears (see fig. 3.19)

There isn't much to crop. Set the **W**idth and **H**eight to 4 and 6 inches, respectively. (Notice how the image size decreases when you crop the image.)

Click on OK	The cropped flamingos appear
Click and drag the marina image off to the right	
Press Ctrl+Y to turn off the grid	
Click on **L**ayout	The Layout menu appears

continues

continued

Deselect Snap to Guidelines *if it is selected*

Center the flamingos horizontally
and vertically on the guidelines

With the two images side-by-side, it looks as if the Crop Image dialog box did a more precise job than the Shape tool, even if the status line indicates that both images are exactly the same size!

Figure 3.19
The bitmap
import Crop
Image dialog
box.

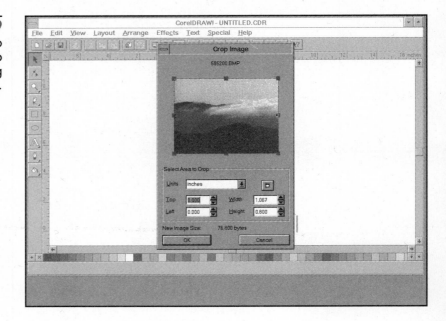

The bright pink flamingos should be jumping off your screen, if flamingos were prone to jumping, that is! These laid-back birds are really more of the sauntering type.

Now that you have the first two images on-screen, you can import the third image—the dune shot—without the aid of a prompted exercise. Just follow the steps in the last exercise, but substitute the file name DEBEACH.BMP. This image is a horizontal shot, a relaxing view of the breakers over one of Seaside's trademark dunes. After you have imported DEBEACH.BMP, you can delete the guidelines and drag the image down below the other two images (see fig. 3.20).

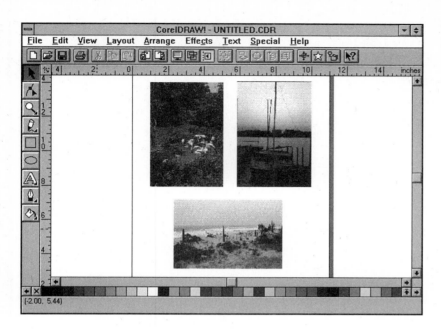

Figure 3.20
The imported
Seaside images.

CorelDRAW! 5.0 includes a handy little method for removing all the guidelines in one fell swoop. This had been one of the most requested features by users of previous versions of the program, and its inclusion in version 5.0 is a welcome addition.

Delete All Guidelines

Click on Layout	The Layout menu appears
Click on Guidelines Setup	The Guidelines Setup menu appears
Click on Horizontal Guidelines	
Click on Delete All	The Horizontal Guidelines are deleted
Click on Vertical Guidelines	
Click on Delete All	The Vertical Guidelines are deleted
Click on OK *(see fig. 3.21)*	

Figure 3.21
The Guidelines
Setup dialog
box.

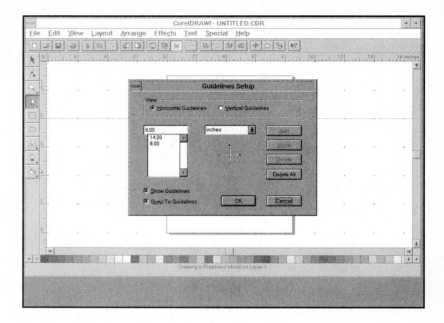

With all the images on-screen, your system might be getting a bit sluggish. Everyone's machine is different, but in general, the more RAM your machine has, and the more free disk space, the happier you and your machine will be. Take the time to save your working file as POSTCRD1.CDR. This file might be as large as six megabytes, so make sure you have enough room on your hard drive to store it.

Now you need to add some type and other embellishments to your postcard project. Each postcard needs a descriptive title to make it complete. This will be very basic typesetting; don't worry if you aren't familiar with all the intricacies of the Type tool. That will come soon enough! To finish off the marina postcard, you will also re-import the compass (AI) file.

CorelDRAW! 5.0 comes with over 800 typefaces. It is unlikely you loaded all the typefaces that are used in the following exercise. If you do not have a particular typeface loaded, feel free to substitute any typeface you feel looks "right" for that particular postcard. This is a rather subjective issue, and in this early chapter, you can certainly get away with a typographical crime or two! Try a different typeface for each of the postcards, and then try a few alternates as well.

Adding Type to the Postcards

Click on the Text tool	
Click on the page	The I bar appears
Type: **Evening Calm**	
Press Ctrl+spacebar	Changes to the Pick tool
Press Ctrl+F2	The Text Roll-Up menu appears
At the Text Roll Up: roll down, click on SloganD, *and change the size to* 48 points	
Click on Apply	The text specifications are applied
Press the spacebar	Changes to the Text tool
Click on the page	
Type: **Think Pink!**	
Press Ctrl+spacebar	Changes to the Pick tool
At the Text Roll Up: roll down, click on BrodyD, *and change the size to* 60 points	
Click on Apply	The text specifications are applied
Press the spacebar	Changes to the Text tool
Click on the page	
Type: **Hazy Daze**	
Press Ctrl+spacebar	Changes to the Pick tool
At the Text Roll Up: roll down, click on NevisonCasD, *and change the size to* 72 points	
Click on Apply	The text specifications are applied

Drag each piece of type to fit its respective postcard (see figs. 3.22, 3.23, and 3.24). Remember that different typefaces set differently. You might have to adjust the point sizes up or down, depending on the typefaces you actually use.

Figure 3.22
Evening Calm at
the Marina.

Figure 3.23
Flock 'O
Flamingos!

Figure 3.24
A Hazy Daze on
the beach.

Go ahead and assign different fills to the type. You can start with simple white type
for the marina and flamingos and good old black type for the dune shot. Then try
a few different grays and proceed to pick a few colors off the on-screen palette. The
flamingos scream out for hot-pink type, while the dune shot looks good with a dark
green that matches the dune grass.

With a simple line of type, you have turned each photograph into a cliché-laden
postcard! Each one is suitable for mailing back to the neighbors or coworkers, just
to rub in the fact that you are on vacation in paradise, and they are not. Joe
DeLook has achieved exactly what he set out to do. The town council will be
ecstatic!

Joe has decided to import the compass symbol so that it can be placed at the top
left corner of the marina postcard. You can use the procedure you learned at the
beginning of this chapter to import the compass. Once you have imported it, you
can size it to fit.

Grouping Objects

Before you go any further, it is important for you to group each postcard. Although each postcard consists of only two elements, if you do not group them at
this point, they will "fall apart" when you try moving them around. Grouping
"glues" objects together, although not permanently. You can always ungroup
objects.

Draw provides you with three ways to group objects. You can choose <u>G</u>roup from the <u>A</u>rrange menu, press Ctrl+G, or click on the Group button on the button bar. (Power users almost always use the keyboard shortcut Ctrl+G.)

Press Ctrl+G to group selected objects.

Go ahead and group each of the postcards. Use any or all of the three grouping methods.

Arranging Grouped Objects (or Shuffling the Deck)

You should now have three separate postcards: the Marina, the Dune Shot, and the Flamingo Farm—a fine trio of Seaside's greatest attractions. Drag the three postcards into a horizontal row, with space between them. Go ahead and turn on Full-Color editing (turn off Wireframe mode).

You should see three perfect, complete postcards in the preview mode (see fig. 3.25). If one of the cards seems to be missing type or other objects from its face, have no fear. The wayward object merely needs to be brought forward. Ungroup the postcard in question, deselect it, click on the unruly object(s), and select To <u>F</u>ront from the <u>A</u>rrange menu. When you are done, group the card again.

If you had to mess around with anything in the last paragraph, you got a head start on everyone else. You are about to shuffle the stack of postcards (in an abbreviated manner) using just three commands.

Start by rotating the dune postcard by 90 degrees. Then, proceed to shuffle them by dragging all three postcards on top of each other. Stack them perfectly by selecting them all, then pressing Ctrl+A (or click the Align button on the button bar) to access the Align dialog box, and using horizontal and vertical align (see fig. 3.26). You can also perfectly align your cards in the center of the page by clicking on Align to Center of Page. If you look at them in Full-Color mode or in a full-screen preview, only the top postcard should show. Deselect the stack of postcards.

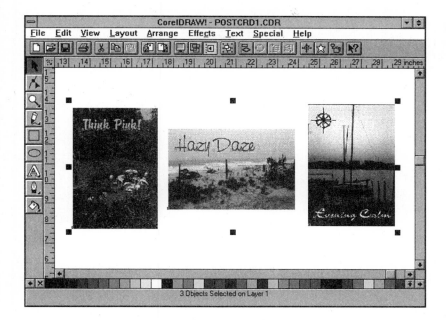

Figure 3.25
Paradise
defined.

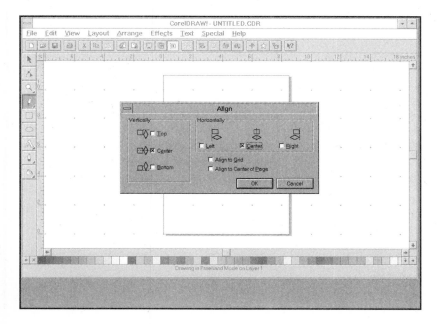

Figure 3.26
The Align dialog
box.

Cutting the Cards

Click on the top card	The top postcard is selected
Click on Arrange	The Arrange menu appears
Click on Order	The Order fly-out menu appears
Click on To Back	The top postcard is sent to back and the next postcard in the stack appears

As you learned earlier, Draw has five commands in its object-arranging lingo: To Front, To Back, Forward One, Back One, and Reverse Order. Now that you have seen what To Back does, try To Front.

One More Time

Click on Arrange	The Arrange menu appears
Click on Order	The Order fly-out menu appears
Click on To Front	The original top postcard reappears

That was easy. Try sending the postcards to back and front a few times. By using To Front and To Back, you can place an object on top of everything or underneath everything. You can access the To Front and To Back commands from either the Arrange/Order menu or from the button bar.

You can handle the in-between layers—those neither at the top nor bottom—by using Forward One and Back One. Reduce your work to as few logical levels as possible. Each level can contain many other levels and sublevels. Try rearranging the postcards by using Forward One and Back One. You can cycle through the postcards by using Tab or Shift+Tab.

The last object-arranging tool, Reverse Order, is the device that you often use for between-object work. Reverse Order works with two or more selected objects and transposes the sequence between them.

Start this next exercise by sliding the postcards out, as if you were fanning them out on a table. On each card, leave at least a half-inch vertical strip showing.

Switching Cards with Reverse Order

Shift-click on the top two cards	The top two cards are selected
Click on Arrange	The Arrange menu appears
Click on Order	The Order fly-out menu appears
Click on Reverse Order	The top two cards swap sequence

This simple example demonstrates the way the object-arranging command set works. Obviously, as you get more proficient with CorelDRAW! and your illustrations become more complex, it is increasingly important that you construct and arrange your work logically.

Using Layer Control

In response to many requests from the installed user base, CorelDRAW! version 3.0 introduced a full-blown layering structure. Layer control is handled through the Layers Roll-Up menu, which you can summon by using the keyboard shortcut Ctrl+F3 or by selecting Layers Roll-Up from the Layout menu.

Press Ctrl+F3 to access the Layers Roll-Up menu.

If you are accustomed to working with overlays on conventional mechanical artwork, you should feel right at home with the Layers Roll-Up. You can think of each layer as residing on its own individual acetate. The following example demonstrates when you might want to use layers in a drawing.

Suppose you want to use the postcards you just created in another drawing. This new drawing contains a number of elements, including a glass (filled with scotch on the rocks), a stack of casino chips, a patterned tablecloth, and perhaps an ashtray (can we add any other vices?). To simplify the composition of a complex drawing, you might want to place each object on its own layer. Furthermore, Draw enables you to name the layers as you want using up to 32 characters. You can call the tablecloth layer Tablecloth and the ashtray layer Ashtray.

As you delve further into more complex projects, you learn to handle layers with authority. After you have completed the project in Chapter 9, "Advanced Drawing Techniques," you should have a thorough understanding of the way Draw's layers work. For now, reflect on the project you just completed, in which you worked on just one layer. You need these skills whether your artwork requires the control afforded by the Layers Roll-Up menu or not.

Part Two

Putting CorelDRAW! To Work

Chapter Snapshot

It's time to get to work. But fear not, you won't have to swab the decks! These exercises step you through some typesetting basics. In this chapter, you create a flyer and learn to do the following:

✔ Identify common typographical conventions

✔ Set, condense, and alter headline type with the Artistic tool

✔ Take charge of your type with the Text Roll-Up menu

✔ Add symbols with CorelDRAW!'s Symbol Roll-Up menu

✔ Import text for use with the Paragraph Text tool

CorelDRAW!'s text-creation tools are quite powerful, although they do have their share of drawbacks and eccentricities. Understanding the intricacies of the Text tool can save you from running aground at deadline time.

CHAPTER

Basic Typography

With the drawing basics out of the way, you can move on to working with type. By this point, you should be familiar with the CorelDRAW! interface. Earlier chapters led through exercises that briefly involved the Text tool. This chapter shows you ways in which you can use CorelDRAW!'s Text tool in the real world to produce flyers, T-shirts, advertisements, 35mm slides, and more.

In this chapter, you use the Text tool to produce a simple menu. It isn't very complex, but it serves its purpose. The menu begins as a simple piece and builds in complexity. It was designed to ease you into the craft of setting type using Draw.

Those of you who bought CorelDRAW! to set fancy type will spend much of your time using the Text tool. Therefore, you must have a thorough understanding of the tool and its features. The Text tool packs a lot of power in a simple guise.

How Does CorelDRAW! Treat Text?

Draw's Text tool can operate in one of two modes: Artistic (headline) text or Paragraph text. This chapter introduces both modes. The Text tool operates in a logical manner (like the other implements in Draw's toolbox) in that it has a consistent look and feel.

The way the Artistic Text and Paragraph Text tools work are analogous. The exercises in this chapter illustrate these similarities by leading you through the use of the Artistic Text tool for much of the following exercise. You then add a bit of embellishment with the Symbol Text tool and finish by using the Paragraph Text tool in a two-column layout.

The Text tool's user interface is similar to that of many other drawing packages. Type size and face are specified by using scroll bars and edit boxes. Type weights (normal, bold, italic, and bold italic), where available, are selected by using the text-entry windows buttons. In addition, you can select ragged left, ragged right, centered, unaligned, and fully justified margins.

Implementing CorelDRAW!'s numerous text options can be perplexing to the novice and the professional. Specifically, the superfluous duplication of controls between the Text Roll-Up menu and the Character Attributes dialog box can be confusing. You can use either method to specify type, but the Character Attributes dialog box is a much-modified holdover from the earliest version of the program.

Type Sizes

In Draw, you can freely specify type point sizes as large as 2,160 points or as small as 0.7 point, in tenth-of-a-point increments. This flexibility is a boon to the typographer whose clients continually ask for type to be set "to fit." After you have set a block of type, you can scale type proportionally or anamorphically just as you can any other object.

 Be careful when using a 300 dpi laser printer: the legibility of type smaller than 6 points is severely impaired. On a high-resolution imagesetter such as the Lino L/300, however, do not worry about this restriction—the L/300 is capable of imaging at 2,540 dpi. Newer, high-end imagesetters from Linotype-Hell, Scitex, and other manufacturers can print at even higher resolutions.

Typefaces

You will never run out of typefaces; CorelDRAW! 5.0 ships with dozens of immediately accessible typefaces in TrueType format. The CD-ROM version of Draw features over 800 fonts (in both PostScript and TrueType formats). If you need a font not supplied with the program, it is no more than a phone call—and a credit-card charge—away. With more than 10,000 fonts available in the PostScript format, your design choices are governed only by your financial resources.

CorelDRAW!'s *font load* (the total list of all fonts) has grown in quality and quantity over the years. In the past, when you looked at Draw's font list, some unfamiliar names appeared. The bizarre names referred to typefaces you may have already been familiar with. Corel had to name standard typefaces with curious names to avoid stepping on anyone's copyright.

For some obscure reason, the laws protect typeface names, but not designs. This unfair practice only serves to punish type designers who spend inordinate amounts of time creating and perfecting new typeface designs. However, the Bitstream fonts added in version 4 and the URW fonts added in version 5 are of a much higher quality. Generally, the (oddly named) CorelDRAW! typefaces were inferior to the original designs. If you are a professional designer or typographer and need additional fonts, you might want to purchase the authentic font from its original foundry.

Version 5.0 features a greatly improved font library, in quantity as well as quality, with the addition of many new scripts and display faces. The Bitstream fonts taken on in version 4.0 were a quantum leap in caliber over earlier versions. Although the more than 820 fonts supplied with CorelDRAW! 5.0 provide an instant type library, it still is possible that your favorite faces are not included. The newest, freshest faces are available from a number of sources. Check out Chapter 10, "You're the Designer," for more information on obtaining fonts.

Other Type Specifications

Type specifications other than point size, typeface, and alignment are set with the Character Attributes dialog box. You can access this dialog box in one of three ways: press Ctrl+T, or through buttons on the Edit Text dialog box or Text Roll-Up menus. Use the Character Attributes dialog box to specify character, word, and line, as well as (in Paragraph text) before and after paragraph spacing. Typographers usually refer to these settings as *tracking, word spacing, leading* (pronounced "ledding"), and *paragraph spacing*, respectively.

CorelDRAW! 5.0 offers another improvement over earlier versions: you can specify line and paragraph spacing in either relative (based on a percentage of point size) or absolute (such as 12-point type on 14-point leading) terms. Absolute settings are the typographer's choice for Paragraph Text (and in many cases, Artistic Text) because different typefaces set in distinctly different sizes. Copperplate will set at approximately 80 percent of the height of Galliard, for example.

These text-spacing settings, along with settings available in the Character Attributes dialog box, make setting type with CorelDRAW! a breeze. The clients make the job tough.

PostScript or TrueType?

Both PostScript and TrueType are vector-based type formats, but there are differences. The former is revolutionary technology; the latter is reactionary.

Adobe PostScript fonts and the PostScript Page Description language spawned the desktop-publishing revolution. Since the mid 1980s, PostScript has become the standard of the printing and publishing industries. PostScript provides true platform and printer independence.

TrueType was a reaction to PostScript, brought on by the odd couple of Apple and Microsoft. These two arch enemies sought to break Adobe's high licensing fees. TrueType is now integrated into both the Macintosh system and Microsoft Windows.

When CorelDRAW! 3.0 and Windows 3.1 were introduced, a new dilemma for electronic artists and desktop publishers emerged. Earlier versions of Draw used only proprietary WFN fonts, but both of these programs changed, and added PostScript and TrueType fonts. Like all contemporary Windows applications, CorelDRAW! 5.0 continues to enable you to use either PostScript or TrueType (although WFN fonts are still used for symbols). You have to decide which font format you want to use.

Although version 5.0 provides over 820 fonts in both formats, only a small portion of the TrueType fonts are loaded automatically from the distribution floppy disks. The vast majority of the fonts—both TrueType and PostScript—are on CD-ROM. You must use the Adobe Type Manager (ATM) control panel to load the PostScript fonts from the CD-ROM. If you want to load the TrueType faces, you can use either the Windows Fonts control panel or Corel's font installation program.

See Chapter 23, "Font Management Techniques," for complete details on installing or uninstalling fonts.

Managing all those fonts is a real chore. The more fonts you have loaded on your system at any one time, the slower Windows loads and runs. The best commercial solution to the font dilemma is Ares Software's FontMinder. You find more information on FontMinder in Chapter 23.

Which font format should you choose? It all depends on who you are, what you do, and where your images are ultimately printed. Because Windows 3.1 integrates TrueType so tightly, many offices use TrueType. If your work is printed on a laser printer and run on an office copier, TrueType is fine.

Professional graphic designers, typographers, and publishers should stick with PostScript. If your files are printed on a high-resolution imagesetter, your service bureau will probably want nothing but PostScript files and fonts. The same is true for files handed up to a high-end prepress system at a color trade shop or large printer. If your work goes to an Agfa, Lino, or Scitex system, save yourself some hassle and stick with PostScript.

It's not a matter of typographical snobbery. Service bureaus have a large inventory and large investments in PostScript fonts. In addition, files made with TrueType fonts take longer to output on an imagesetter. Many times, TrueType fonts misprint or cause other anomalies. Many service bureaus therefore refuse to run files with TrueType fonts.

Creating a Menu

If you have been in the graphic arts field for a while, you know that rush jobs are the norm, as are last-minute changes. With that in mind and just for fun (?), hang a deadline over your head while you work through the example in this chapter.

Although you are working through the exercises in this chapter just for kicks, the sample menu you create is an excellent example of life of the graphic artist. It seems that clients can never stop in to see the typesetter until the job is already a week late. This chapter should give you an idea of how CorelDRAW! can be put to work in the real world.

Speaking of the (almost) real world, stop in at DeLook Design and see what Joe and the crew are up to. Monday morning has arrived. Joe has learned some CorelDRAW! essentials over the weekend, and he is anxious to put them to work.

DeLook Design has just landed a new client—The Neon Newt, a popular Seaside nightspot. The Newt is more than just a bar; their sandwiches are famous for miles around, and you can order their tasty delectables until four in the morning!

The Neon Newt's proprietor, Fast Freddie (who also owns a local used car lot) has actually come up with an interesting idea (and a sufficient budget) for the menu.

He will be springing for a four-color menu jacket, with the inside tastefully done in two colors on attractive paper stock. Freddie has come a long way since he first started working with Joe DeLook, doing flyers for his used car lot!

This is exactly the type of work that DeLook Design likes to take in—a challenging project and a client that pays on delivery! Freddie has that wad of bills out and is willing to cover Joe's troubles, as long as Joe can whip up the inside of the menu in an hour or so. Considering that the rent is due, and Joe is a bit short, he agrees to do a presto-chango slam design! He and Freddie agree that they will just concentrate on the guts of the menu for now. The cover will come later (see Chapter 6, "Special Type Effects").

Freddie hands over a napkin on which he has scrawled his basic information (see fig. 4.1). With a qualifying "Think you can handle that in an hour? I'm going over to The Newt for an early lunch," Freddie heads out the door. Joe doesn't even have time to roll up his sleeves. He fires up CorelDRAW! and goes to work. Looking at Freddie's napkin layout, Joe sees he doesn't have time to prepare any intricate graphics, just good, solid design.

Figure 4.1
Napkins make the best layout paper!

The Anatomy of the Menu

The inside of the menu consists of two 8 1/2 × 11-inch pages. The left page is just a few lines of type, with the Neon Newt's motto, philosophy, and address. The right page is the establishment's short but tasty menu. Freddie wants to promote the Newt's reputation as "A Great Place To Meet," as well as inform his patrons of his scrumptious grub.

In this menu, limit the number of typefaces. In practice, you find that fewer typefaces make committing typographic hara-kiri less likely. This menu might not win any awards, but it will be readable and do its job. Joe will not have time for all the niceties, but who ever saw a pretty menu from a bar in Seaside anyway?

One of CorelDRAW!'s greatest features is its excellent typographical screen representation. Although not perfect, it is about as good as you are going to get without Display PostScript. The screen quality is good enough that you can specify typefaces on the computer itself, rather than on a layout sheet. If a block of type is too big at 60 points, you can see it immediately and reduce the point size before you run a copy from the printer.

Without wasting any more time, open a new file and get down to work. In the Page Setup dialog box, specify a portrait letter page. When you choose a letter-sized page (or any other predetermined page size), the horizontal and vertical settings boxes are grayed out. Custom is the only page size option that enables you to make changes to the horizontal and vertical dimensions.

When you go into the Page Setup dialog box, click on the Display tab to make a couple of additional settings. For the purposes of this project, you need to configure the dialog box for Facing Pages, starting with Left First. This step ensures you have a proper designer's spread on which to work. A *designer's spread* simply enables you to work in facing pages.

Setting Up the Page Layout and Grid

Click on File	The File menu appears
Click on New	A new page appears
Click on Layout	The Layout menu appears
Click on Page Setup	The Page Setup dialog box appears
Click on Letter	Sets up letter-sized page
Click on Portrait	Sets page to portrait orientation
Click on the Display tab	
Click on Facing Pages	
Click on Left First	
Click on OK	A new page appears

continues

continued

Click on Layout   The Layout menu appears

Click on Grid & Scale Setup   The Grid and Scale Setup dialog box appears

At Grid Frequency, *change both settings to* per pica

At Horizontal, *type* **1**

At Vertical, *type* **1**

Make sure that Snap To Grid *is selected*

Click on OK

Adding and Deleting Pages

CorelDRAW! 5.0 enables you to have multiple pages (up to 998) in a file. For the purposes of this exercise, you only need to add one page. Now that you have your page layout set up, add the second page. You can access the Insert Page dialog box (see fig. 4.2) from the Layout menu, through the keyboard shortcuts, PageUp and PageDown, or with the + button at the bottom-left of the drawing window.

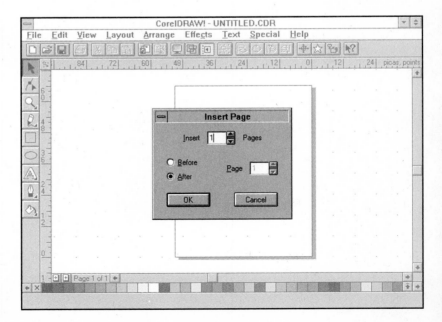

Figure 4.2
The Insert Page dialog box.

The Insert Page dialog box enables you to add a page (or pages) before or after a specific page. In other words, you can selectively expand your files. In the next chapter you will learn more about multiple-page documents. For now, this two-page job will help ease you into things.

Adding a Page to a File

Press PgDn   The Insert Page dialog box appears

At Insert Pages, *type* 1

Click on After

Click on OK   A new page is added

Way too easy, wasn't it? Try adding additional pages. This will give you the opportunity to learn how to delete pages. Deleting pages is just as easy as adding them: access the Delete Page dialog box (see fig. 4.3) from the Layout menu. The Delete Page dialog box enables you to delete pages or ranges of pages selectively.

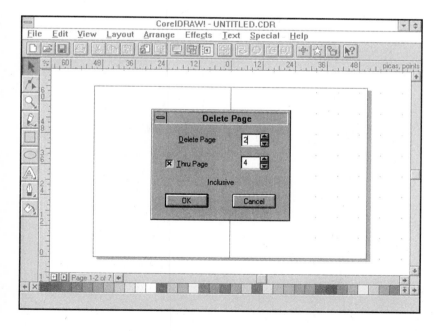

Figure 4.3
The Delete Page dialog box.

Unfortunately, the Delete Page dialog box does not give you another chance to change your mind before it deletes material. Unlike PageMaker (for example), there are no friendly "Do You Really Want To Delete This Page" messages; after you click on OK, the program immediately deletes the specified page(s). However, you can always use the Undo command to undelete a page, if necessary. Try deleting some pages and restoring them with undelete.

When working with multiple-page documents, you can flip from page to page by clicking on the little arrow button at the bottom of the drawing window or by choosing **G**o To Page from the **L**ayout menu. The little arrow button moves you from page to page or from spread to spread, depending on whether you have **F**acing Pages chosen in the **P**age Setup/Display dialog box. The **G**o To Page dialog box gives you more control and enables you to jump to a specific page. If you work on short documents, the little arrow button is better for moving around. Use the **G**o To Page dialog box only if you are working with a large number of pages.

Using the Artistic Text Tool

The preceding chapters gave you a taste of using the Text tool. Now you really start setting type. In the next exercise, you use many of the settings in the Character Attributes dialog box (see fig. 4.4). Take a moment to learn about the various text specifications.

Figure 4.4
The Character
Attributes dialog
box.

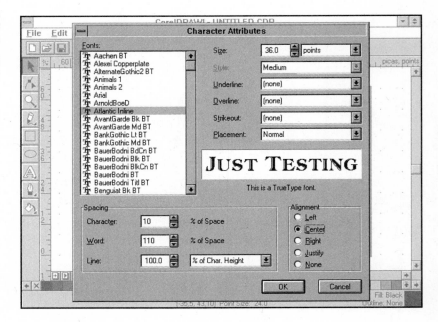

The Character Attributes dialog box enables you to set the following specifications:

✔ **Character spacing (or tracking).** This specification controls the space between all characters in a text block. Do not confuse character spacing with kerning, which affects only the space between two specific characters. Tracking influences the overall "color," or density, of the type on the page. You will find that a slightly negative number works best in everything but body copy sizes. In most cases, you should tighten up headlines to maintain readability, but avoid tightening up body copy (which might actually benefit from a bit of positive or "opened up" character spacing in the smallest type sizes).

✔ **Word spacing.** This specification governs the space between words. The factory default setting (of 100 percent) might be too wide for display-type purposes. At times, you might find yourself adjusting this specification to a value of 70 percent or less.

✔ **Line spacing.** This specification, more commonly referred to as *leading*, affects the space between lines of type in a text block. Most type is set with a slightly positive leading (more than 100 percent of the size of the typeface). A value slightly larger than 100 leaves white space between the lines of text. Negative leading (less than 100 percent) is used in special cases, such as when type is set in capital letters. Care must be taken when setting uppercase and lowercase type with negative leading to avoid crashing ascenders and descenders. CorelDRAW! 5.0 enables you to specify leading as either a percentage of character height or in absolute points.

✔ **Alignment.** This specification determines how a block of text is set, either Left, Center, Right, Justified, or with no alignment. You may refer to these specifications as *quad left, quad center,* and *quad right*; or perhaps, *flush left/ragged right, ragged center,* and *ragged left/flush right.*

You can control tracking and leading interactively, in addition to entering precise measurements in the Character Attributes dialog box. When you click in a text block with the Shape tool, character- and line-spacing control arrows appear left of and below the text block. Although this method is easy to use with Artistic Text, it can be difficult to use with Paragraph Text.

Tip   Press F8 for the Artistic Text tool.

Putting CorelDRAW! to Work

The exercise is broken down between the two menu pages. You will begin on the first (left-hand) page. The Artistic Text tool will be used to create a few blocks of text and then you will drag-and-drop from the Symbol Roll-Up menu to add the Neon Newt's namesake. The exercise uses the following fonts:

Eras Light

IceAgeD

Van Dijk

First load these fonts, then proceed with the exercise.

If the fonts are not loaded, follow the applicable procedure for loading them as outlined in Chapter 24, "Font Management Techniques." You also can substitute your own font choices for the suggested fonts. Be advised that if you choose to pick your own fonts, the text might not fall as planned, and consequently, you might have to tweak point size and leading.

IceAge is used throughout this menu and is a trendy typewriter-ish font. It has a fuzzy outline and a funky feel. Fast Freddie will appreciate the impact of this typeface.

As mentioned earlier, the Text tool has two different modes: Artistic Text and Paragraph Text. Figure 4.5 illustrates their icons. To complete the next series of exercises, you will have to be in Artistic Text mode. To switch between modes, you can use the following keyboard shortcuts: F8 for Artistic Text mode or Shift+F8 for Paragraph Text mode. Of course, you can also choose each tool directly from the Toolbox; clicking on the little arrow at the bottom right of the currently active icon will pop out the fly-out menu.

Figure 4.5
The Artistic Text and Paragraph Text icons.

As you work through the exercises, take the time to cover all the specifications to ascertain that the type is correct. Make sure you use every dialog box.

Setting Type with the Artistic Text Tool

Click on the Text tool	The cursor becomes a +
Click on the page	The Text I bar appears

Type the following and press Enter after every line except the last one:

We believe in good, honest
value and a great atmosphere.
Seaside's famous Neon Newt ...
Where you can't afford
not to have a good time!

Press Ctrl+spacebar	The Pick tool is selected
Press Ctrl+T	The Character Attributes dialog box appears

Make sure that you have points selected

At Si<u>z</u>e, *enter* **24**

At <u>F</u>onts, *roll down and click on* IceAgeD

Click on <u>C</u>enter

At <u>C</u>haracter, *enter* **6**

At <u>W</u>ord, *enter* **90**

At <u>L</u>ine, *select points, then enter* **33**

Click on OK	The type is set according to your specifications

Use the Pick tool to drag the block of type to the center of the page and eyeball it into position (see fig. 4.6).

You should have an 24-point IceAge motto, set centered on 33-point leading. The word and character spacing should be fairly open to work with the fuzzy IceAge typeface.

On second thought, it looks like 24 points is just a bit too large. Bring the size down to 18 points. Although you can attempt to scale down the text by eye, do it with precision. Go back into the Character Attributes dialog box to adjust the point size accurately.

Figure 4.6
Type in position.

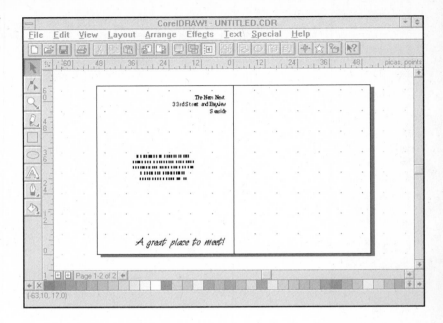

Figure 4.6
Type in position.

Adjusting the Point Size

With the text still selected, take the following steps:

Press Ctrl+T	The Character Attributes dialog box appears
At Si̱ e, enter **18**	
Click on OK	The type is reset according to your specifications

---

When you use the Text tool in this next exercise, notice that all previously entered type specs are gone. CorelDRAW! 5.0 (unlike versions prior to version 4.0) requires that you plug in the specs from scratch. Although the program now supports Styles, you do not need them for this simple exercise. Styles are, however, covered a bit later.

Press Ctrl+T for the Character Attributes dialog box.

Setting the Second Block of Text

Click on the Text tool	The cursor becomes a +
Click on the page	The Text I bar appears

*Type the following and press Enter after
every line except the last one:*

The Neon Newt
33rd Street and Bayview
Seaside

Press Ctrl+spacebar	The Pick tool is selected
Press Ctrl+T	The Character Attributes dialog box appears
Make sure that you have points selected	
At S<u>i</u>*e, enter* **24**	
At <u>F</u>*onts, roll down and click on* Van Dijk	
Click on <u>R</u>*ight*	
At <u>L</u>*ine, select points, then enter* **22**	
Click on OK	The type is set according to your specifications

Use the Pick tool to drag the block of type to the top of the page and eyeball it into position
(refer back to fig. 4.6).

Notice that this last block of type was set with reverse leading (where the leading is
a lower number of points than the point size). This is not always possible. You can
get away with reverse leading or setting solid (where the leading is the same
number of points as is the point size) when you are setting text in all caps, when
there are no or very few descenders, or when the typeface allows. In this case, there
is only one descender, and it tucks in nicely.

There is just one more block of type to set on this page—the tagline at the bottom
of the page. This block is set in 48-point Van Dijk.

Setting the Tagline

Click on the Text tool	The cursor becomes a +
Click on the page	The Text I bar appears

continues

Putting CorelDRAW! To Work

continued

Type the following:

A great place to meet!

Press Ctrl+spacebar	The Pick tool is selected
Press Ctrl+T	The Character Attributes dialog box appears
Make sure that you have points selected	
At Si_ze, *enter* **24**	
At _Fonts, *roll down and click on* Van Dijk	
Click on _Right	
Click on OK	The type is set according to your specifications

Use the Pick tool to drag the block of type to the bottom of the page and eyeball it into position (refer back to fig. 4.6).

If you look back at figure 4.6, you notice that the typefaces might not display correctly when zoomed out while working in full-color editing mode. Don't worry; this is normal and is actually there to help speed up your screen display. When you zoom in, things will look as they should. You can adjust the size at which CorelDRAW! starts *greeking* text, through adjustments made in the Preferences/ Text dialog box. The _Greek Text Below setting governs the number of pixels at which the program will display a greek, rather than the real thing.

The page might look a bit barren at this point. You will be fixing that momentarily. In the next short exercise, you will use the Symbol Roll-Up menu to add the Neon Newt's namesake to the page.

Using Symbols

In addition to Artistic and Paragraph Text tools, Draw also includes a wonderful device for adding special symbol characters. The Symbol Roll-Up menu enables you to drag and drop objects onto your artwork. With all the type set for the first page of the menu, it is time to finish it off by adding a pair of symbols with the Symbol Roll-Up.

The Symbol Roll-Up Menu

The Symbol Roll-Up is a fast way to place rudimentary art—objects that are more icon-like than lifelike—into a file. CorelDRAW! comes with thousands of black-and-white symbols at no additional cost. The program also enables you to export images and create your own personal symbol library. You soon see the advantages of using and creating symbols.

There are three ways to access the Symbol Roll-Up: you can click on the button bar (the Symbol button is denoted by a star), select Symbols Roll-Up from the Special menu, or Press Ctrl+F11. The Symbols Roll-Up menu provides you with dozens of symbol libraries. To scroll through an individual symbol library, click on the up and down arrows at the bottom of the roll-up menu.

The Symbols Roll-Up menu asks you to make three choices. First, you must select the library you want to use. Then you select the size of the symbol you are placing. Finally, you select and place a symbol by clicking on it and dragging it onto the page. This is known as drag-and-drop symbol placement. When you click on a symbol, notice that the symbol number appears at the # entry window; alternatively, you can type the symbol number directly into the entry window.

After the symbol is on the page, you can scale, stretch, rotate, skew, or mutate it as you would any other object. Symbols can be assigned different fills and can be extruded, blended, enveloped, or manipulated in whatever manner you can imagine. Just be careful with the effects you choose; assigning a fountain fill, texture fill, or lens to a complex symbol (with many nodes) might be the kiss of death at print time!

Symbols can be either TrueType or Corel WFN fonts. Take note that symbols are different from special characters (which will be discussed in the next chapter on advanced typography). The symbol libraries that come with CorelDRAW! 5.0 are listed here.

Animals1	Animals2
Arrows1	Electronics
Arrows2	Festive

Awards	Food
Balloons	Furniture
Borders1	GeographicSymbols
Borders2	HomePlanning
Boxes	HomePlanning2
Buildings	Household
Bullets1	Hygiene
Bullets2	Kidnap
Bullets3	LandscapePlanning
Business&Government	Landmarks
Charting	Medicine
Clocks	Military
CommonBullets	MilitaryID
Computers	MorseCode
Music	Sports&Hobbies
MusicalSymbols	SportsFigures
NauticalFlags	Stars1
OfficePlanning	Stars2
People	Symbol
Plants	SymbolProp BT
Science	Technology

Semaphore	Tools
Shapes1	Tracks
Shapes2	Transportation
Signs	Weather
SignLanguage	Wingdings
Space	Zapf Dingbats BT

Remember that when a roll-up menu is on-screen, you can move it around at will. The Symbol Roll-Up is no exception. When you want to get a roll-up out of the way, simply click on its up arrow to make the menu spring up and close like a window shade. Another click drops the menu down again.

Placing Symbols

Press Ctrl+F11	The Symbols Roll-Up menu appears
Roll down, click on Animals1	The Animals1 symbols appear

Remember, you can select a symbol in one of two ways: click on the symbol in the sample window or type the symbol number directly into the text box.

At #, type **77**	A newt is highlighted in the sample window
At Size*, type* **24,0**	
Drag-and-drop the newt onto the page	A 24-pica newt is drawn (see fig. 4.7).

Click the Symbol Roll-Up button to get the menu out of the way.

The newt looks pretty cool, but you need to make some adjustments to the little critter. Now that you have the newt on the page, you will use the Align dialog box to center it—along with the motto—to the center of the page, and then you will scale it up to fill the width of the page. As you scale the newt up, you will hold down the Shift key to scale from center, so that the little amphibian remains correctly positioned as well as precisely scaled to fit the width of the page.

Figure 4.7
A 24-pica newt,
ready to be
centered and
scaled up.

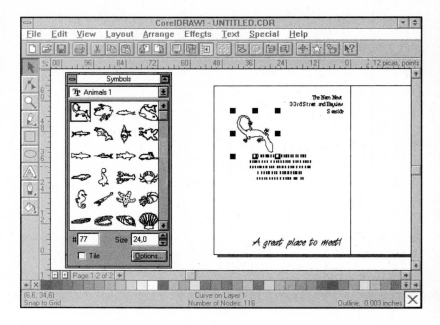

Centering to the Page and Scaling the Newt

Choose the Pick tool

Select the newt and the motto	The Status Line reads: 2 Objects Selected on Layer 1
Press Ctrl+A	The Align dialog box appears
Click on Align to Center of **P**age	Both Vertically and Horizontally Center are automatically selected
Click on OK	The newt and the motto are centered to the page
Shift+click on the motto	Only the newt remains selected

Click and drag a corner handle, while holding down the Shift key to scale from center. Drag
the handle out to the edge of the page. Now that's a big newt (see fig. 4.8)!

Just as Joe DeLook finishes scaling up the newt, Fast Freddie walks in with a huge
grin. Joe's stomach is churning, but the page looks pretty good, considering…. All
that's left to be done with this page is to send the newt to the back, change its tint,
and make a printout (see fig. 4.9).

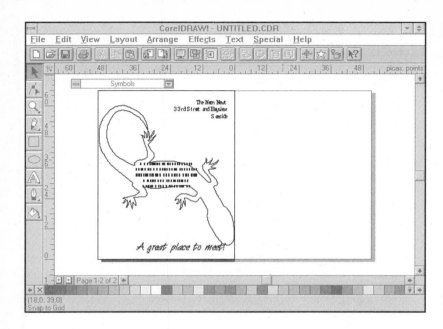

Putting CorelDRAW! To Work

Figure 4.8
The scaled-up and centered newt.

Centering to the Page and Scaling the Newt

With the newt selected:

Left-click 20% gray *from the on-screen palette*

The newt has a 20% gray fill

Right-click No Outline (X) *from the on-screen palette*

The newt has no outline

Click the Send to Back *button from the Button Bar*

The newt is sent back

The page is done (see fig. 4.9)!

Save the file as **NNMENU-1.CDR**

"That's it!" exclaims Freddie as the page rolls out of the laser printer. "That looks great," he continues, "I can hardly wait to see the rest of the menu. Hurry up, I don't have much time to get this to the Seaside Print Shop before they close!" With that acclamation and impetus, Joe has no choice other than to plunge forward and finish.

Figure 4.9
The first page of
the menu.

You begin the second page of the menu by setting a bunch of headlines with the Artistic Text tool, and tweaking them with the Text Roll-Up menu. You proceed to use the Paragraph Text tool to add the menu items, after you have imported the text file from the CD-ROM that accompanies this book.

Quick Changes with the Text Roll-Up Menu

The Text Roll-Up menu is great for making quick changes to blocks of type and can be a wonderful convenience. To access the Text Roll-Up menu, select the Text **R**oll-Up option from the Te**x**t menu or use the Ctrl+F2 keyboard shortcut.

The Text Roll-Up menu offers instant access to a number of text attributes, including typeface, size, and justification. You can set type in bold or italic with one click. More involved type specifications require that you dig deeper. You can summon the Character Attributes dialog box or click on the Frame button to display the Frame dialog box (for Paragraph text only).

As you've seen in the exercises earlier in this chapter, the Character Attributes dialog box is used to apply type specifications, such as character, word, and line spacing. In addition, the Character Attributes dialog box enables you to set text as superscript or subscript, and apply different underline, overline, and strikeout settings.

The Character Attributes dialog box acts differently, depending on whether you have selected text with the Pick or Shape tool. When you choose type with the Shape tool, the Character Attributes dialog box enables you to make changes to horizontal or vertical shift and character angle. You will see exactly how this works when you set some superior figures later on in this chapter.

Getting back to the Text Roll-Up menu, you can use it in two ways to make changes to text already on-screen. The first is to select a block of text with the Pick tool, and then use the Text Roll-Up menu to make changes to the entire block. The second method is to use the Text tool to click and drag over a range of text, and then make changes in much the same way that you make changes with the Character Attributes dialog box: by affecting only a selected range. Remember that you can access selected character specifications only if text has been selected with the Text tool rather than the Pick tool.

After you finish the menu exercise in this chapter, you can try using the Text Roll-Up menu to set the menu in a variety of typefaces. It is easy to select a block of type, choose a typeface, and click on Apply to make the changes. When you are finished experimenting, set the type back to its original specs.

Choosing between the Character Attributes dialog box and the Text Roll-Up menu can be a tough decision. Although your choice depends on personal preferences, only the Character Attributes dialog box offers full control. Corel's Text Roll-Up menu is vastly inferior to the excellent text-control panels in both Aldus PageMaker and QuarkXPress. Perhaps they will take a long look at the controls offered by those two DTP heavyweights.

You will begin working on the second (right-hand) page of the menu by dragging in a few vertical guidelines to help align the text. Then you will add the text, and use the Text Roll-Up to apply the character settings. As you roll through the typefaces, you will see a handy sample on the Text Roll-Up's fly-out (see fig. 4.10).

Figure 4.10
Fly-outs help to
specify typeface.

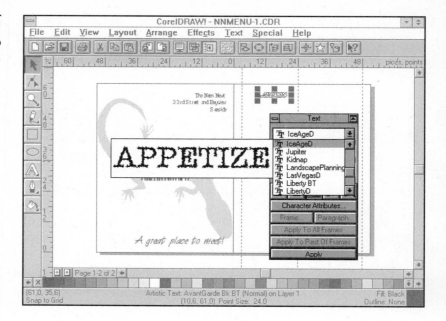

Dragging in Guidelines and Setting the Headlines

Click on the Vertical Ruler and drag out three vertical guidelines. Place them at 3, 24, and 48 picas.

Click on the Text tool	The cursor becomes a +
Click on the page	The Text I bar appears
Type **APPETIZERS**	
Press Ctrl+spacebar	The Pick tool is selected
Press Ctrl+F2	The Text Roll-Up menu appears
Make sure that you have points selected	
Enter **48**	
Roll down, click on IceAgeD	
Click on the Flush Right *button*	
Click on Apply	The type is set according to your specifications

Use the Pick tool to drag the block of type to the top-left corner of the page and eyeball it into position (see fig. 4.11).

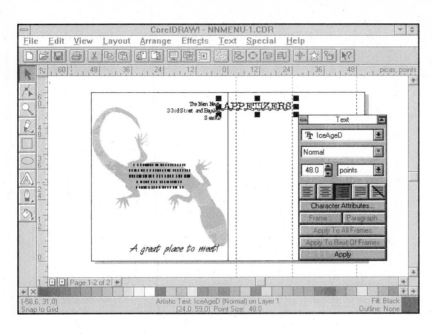

Figure 4.11
The first
headline in
position.

Uh-oh. The headline looks just a little bit too large. Try setting different point sizes with the Text Roll-Up menu. You will find that 40 points is just about right. When you are done applying different settings, set it back to 48 points. In a few moments, you will be using a little trick to make this headline fit the specified width. But first, you must go ahead and set the remainder of the headlines. You will set each as a separate block of type so that you have complete control over how they are spaced out. To create a series of separate text blocks, you will switch between the Text and Pick tools with the Ctrl+spacebar shortcut. Then, the Copy Attributes From feature will be used to assign the type specifications.

Save Time by Copying Text Attributes

The Copy Attributes From feature is another great time-saver. With just a few clicks, you can copy an object's outline style, outline color, fill, and character attributes, or any combination thereof. In the next exercise, you use this feature to assign the character attributes from the first headline. You also see how the Repeat function can help you speed things up even more.

When you use the Copy Attributes From feature, the dialog box enables you to choose the attributes that you want to copy (see fig. 4.12). After you click on OK, an arrow appears. Simply click on the object from which you want to copy the attributes; in this case, it is the word APPETIZERS.

Figure 4.12
The Copy
Attributes
dialog box.

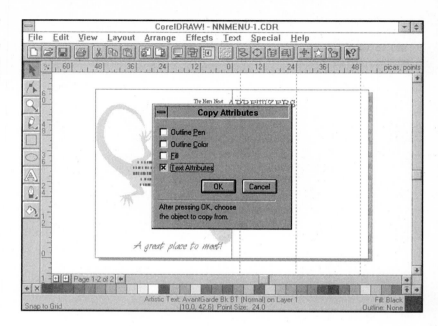

Setting the Second Headline Using Copy Attributes From

Click on the page	Removes the focus from APPETIZERS
Press Ctrl+spacebar	The Text tool is selected; the cursor becomes a +
Click on the page	The Text I bar appears
Type **SOUPS**	
Press Ctrl+spacebar	The Pick tool is selected
Press Alt+E	The Edit menu appears
Press F	The Copy Attributes dialog box appears
Click on Text Attributes	
Click on OK	The Copy Attributes From arrow appears (see fig. 4.13)
Click on APPETIZERS	The Attributes are copied to SOUPS

Use the Pick tool to drag SOUPS to the top left corner of the page, just below APPETIZERS.

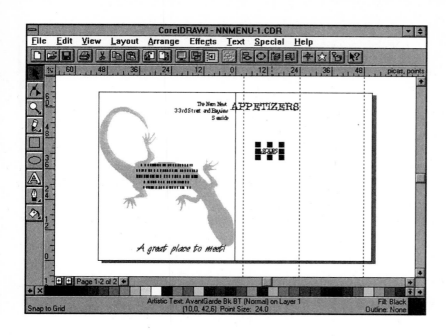

Figure 4.13
The Copy
Attributes From
arrow.

Presto-chango! The attributes were copied from APPETIZERS to SOUPS in a flash. In the next exercise, you set the remainder of the headlines, and then use the combination of Copy Attributes From and Repeat to copy the specifications.

Setting the Rest of the Headlines Using Repeat

Click on the page	Removes the focus from SOUPS
Click on the Text tool	The cursor becomes a +
Click on the page	The Text I bar appears
Type **SALADS**	
Press Ctrl+spacebar	The Pick tool is selected
Click on the page	Removes the focus from SALADS
Press Ctrl+spacebar	The Text tool is selected; the cursor becomes a +
Click on the page	The Text I bar appears
Type **SIDE ORDERS**	
Press Ctrl+spacebar	The Pick tool is selected

continues

continued

Click on the page	Removes the focus from SIDE ORDERS
Press Ctrl+spacebar	The Text tool is selected, the cursor becomes a +
Click on the page	The Text I bar appears
Type **SANDWICHES**	
Press Ctrl+spacebar	The Pick tool is selected
Click on the page	Removes the focus from SANDWICHES
Press Ctrl+spacebar	The Text tool is selected, the cursor becomes a +
Click on the page	The Text I bar appears
Type **DESSERTS**	
Press Ctrl+spacebar	The Pick tool is selected
Click on the page	Removes the focus from DESSERTS
Press Ctrl+spacebar	The Text tool is selected, the cursor becomes a +
Click on the page	The Text I bar appears
Type **BEVERAGES**	
Press Ctrl+spacebar	The Pick tool is selected
Press Alt+E	The Edit menu appears
Press F	The Copy Attributes dialog box appears; Text Attributes should still be selected
Click on OK	The Copy Attributes From arrow appears
Click on APPETIZERS	The Attributes are copied to BEVERAGES
Click on DESSERTS	
Press Ctrl+R	The Attributes are copied to DESSERTS
Click on SANDWICHES	
Press Ctrl+R	The Attributes are copied to SANDWICHES
Click on SIDE ORDERS	
Press Ctrl+R	The Attributes are copied to SIDE ORDERS

Click on SALADS

Press Ctrl+R   The Attributes are copied to SALADS

Use the Pick tool to position the headlines roughly as illustrated in figure 4.14. Save the file as **NNMENU-2.CDR**.

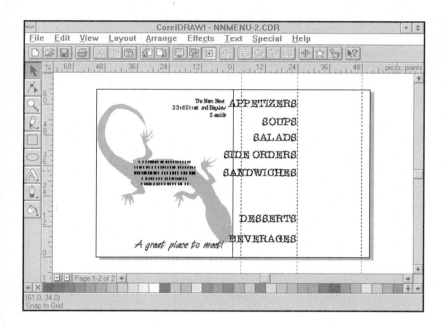

Figure 4.14
The headlines, roughly positioned.

The preceding exercise showed how useful the Repeat function can be, especially when used in conjunction with Copy Attributes From. In the next chapter, "Advanced Typograph," you will learn how to use Styles to apply type specifications with point-and-shoot ease. For now, however, you move on to another type trick—condensing type.

Condensing Type

As you can see in figure 4.14, the seven headlines are slightly too wide for their allocated space. Use the stretch function to scale the headlines anamorphically to fit the area. This action maintains the character heights as it condenses the widths.

The stretch function is a convenient CorelDRAW! feature, but it is often abused. Condensing type beyond a certain percentage reduces the type's legibility. It might fit on the page, but the reader might not be able to read it. Be very careful when you squeeze, extend, or squash type. Use the tricks you learn here with caution.

You will be right-aligning the seven headlines, grouping them, and then stretch-condensing the entire group. By grouping the headlines together, you ensure that they all are condensed by the same percentage. Once the headlines are condensed, you will ungroup them.

Grouping and Squeezing Text

Click on the Pick tool	
Select all the headline type	The status line reads: `7 objects selected`
Press Alt+A	The Arrange menu appears
Press A	The <u>A</u>lign dialog box appears
Click on <u>R</u>ight	
Click on OK	The 7 headlines are right aligned
Press Alt+A	The Arrange menu appears
Press G	The 7 headlines are grouped

Drag the right side of the selected group of headlines to the guideline at 24 picas horizontal. Drag the left-side center handle toward the center of the group; release the mouse button when you reach the guideline at 3 picas horizontal (approximately 75%), as shown in figure 4.15.

In one click-and-drag procedure, you condensed all seven headlines by exactly the same percentage, saving you much time and hassle. By now, you should be getting a feel for how to build and use groups. In the next section, you set up the menu prices and learn how to set superior figures.

Fast Freddie had a simple menu price structure for the Neon Newt. This is part of his overall philosophy. In short, appetizers are $5, soups are $3, salads are $4, side orders are $2, sandwiches are $6, desserts are $3, and beverages are $1. This will make it easy for you to set the prices. Go ahead and set each of these prices as a separate text block, in right-aligned, 72-point Van Dijk. After you have done that, drag them into position, as illustrated in figure 4.16, and save the file as **NNMENU-3.CDR.**

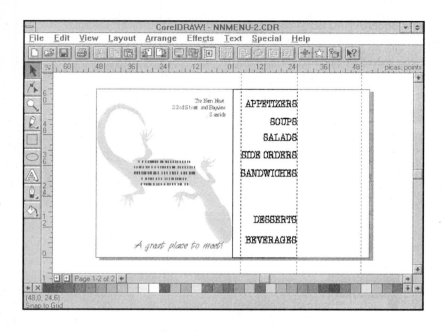

Figure 4.15
The condensed headlines.

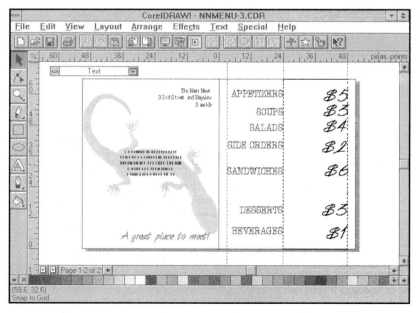

Figure 4.16
The prices before tweaking.

Setting Superior Characters

Now that the prices are in position, it's time to turn the dollar signs into superior figures with the Character Attributes dialog box. By choosing a specific character with the Shape tool (rather than the Pick or Text tool) you can make alterations in this handy dialog box that apply only to that selected character (or characters) in a text string. This feature enables you to use superior (superscript) and inferior (subscript) characters. It also enables you to change the typeface, size, and baseline of individual characters. In addition, the dialog box provides a precise method for character kerning and rotation.

Remember when you double-clicked on a selected object's node to display the Node Edit Roll-Up menu? When using the Shape tool, the Character Attributes dialog box is accessed in a similar manner by double-clicking on a selected text character's node (see fig. 4.17). If you are only kerning or shifting baselines, you need not use the dialog box. You can manually kern characters or shift individual baselines by dragging the characters by their nodes. You learn this in the next exercise when you drag a character.

Figure 4.17
The Character Attributes dialog box as accessed through the Shape tool.

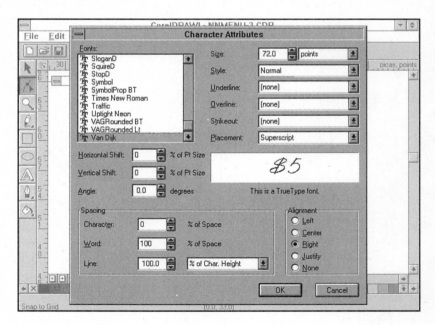

Creating a Superior Figure

Click on the Shape tool	
Click on $5	Nodes appear for the characters
Double-click on the $ *node*	The Character Attributes dialog box appears
At <u>P</u>lacement, *click on* Superscript	
Click on OK	The $ is now a superior figure
Drag the $ *node down and to the right*	The $ is now properly positioned
Double-click on the $ *node*	The Character Attributes dialog box appears

Take a look at the <u>H</u>orizontal and <u>V</u>ertical Shift percentages. They should be set at approximately 20 and -12, respectively.

Click on OK	The superior $ is properly positioned

If you set many advertisements that include price information, the superscript option comes in handy. The steps were necessary to align the superscript $ precisely to the imaginary line at the top of the caps. Your working style will dictate how much precision you need and to what degree you use the mouse or enter exact specifications.

Go ahead and use the preceding method to convert all of the dollar signs into superior figures. Van Dijk is such a swoopy typeface that you probably want to tweak each of the dollar signs to slightly different horizontal and vertical shift percentages (see fig. 4.18). After you finish tweaking, go ahead and save the file again, this time as **NNMENU-4.CDR**.

 The next step in the exercise is to import the menu text from the *Inside CorelDRAW! 5 Fifth Edition CD-ROM*. If you do not have a CD-ROM drive attached to your machine, ask a friend with a CD-ROM drive to copy the file onto a floppy disk.

Importing Text

Luckily for Joe, the first page of Freddie's menu had only a small amount of text on it. Joe is a two-finger typist; he could never have impressed Freddie so quickly if he had had to type a lot of characters. There is no reason to retype text that has already been typed in another program. You can import big blocks of text into Draw in a couple of ways.

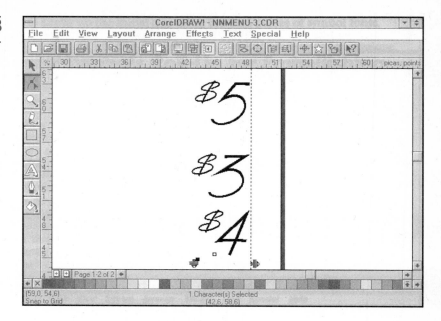

Why import text? Two simple reasons: to save time and trouble. By importing text, you eliminate the need to retype text that might already exist electronically. Unless you really enjoy typing (do you also like making your bed?), importing text saves loads of time, especially with large amounts of text. If you type, rewrite, and proofread large blocks of text before bringing them into Draw, you save time in the long run.

With your word processor, check your text's spelling and run it through a thesaurus. (Even though CorelDRAW! now contains both a spelling checker and thesaurus, they are not tools for wordsmiths.) Alternatively, you can scan in text or capture it from electronic mail—even from PC-Fax. You can bring in files from across the office network or across the world. Importing text enables you to concentrate on design, not keyboard skills. You might even do yourself a favor and let your clients do the typing on larger jobs. This method encourages workgroup computing: the designer designs, the writer writes, the proofreader proofreads.

If you have been using desktop publishing for a while, you probably have had to import text from a word processing program into a desktop publishing program like PageMaker. PageMaker has a large variety of text (and graphics) import filters that are similar in purpose to CorelDRAW!'s graphics import filters.

CorelDRAW! 5.0 contains numerous text import filters. Importing text is the best way to get lots of text into Draw. Alternatively, you can make use of the Windows

Clipboard and those old friends, the Cut, Copy, and Paste commands, but the Clipboard method is best for copying small chunks of text. The Clipboard method is covered first, before delving into the process of importing text with the text filters.

Bringing In Text with the Clipboard

One of the most functional features of the Windows environment is the capability to move items between two concurrently running programs by using the Clipboard. Never heard of the Clipboard? Whether you are aware of it, you have been using the Clipboard since you first started CorelDRAW!—or any other Windows program.

Every time you use the Cut, Copy, or Paste command, you access the Clipboard. When you cut or copy an object, it is placed onto the Clipboard. When you paste an object, it is taken from the Clipboard.

The Clipboard is like a shallow bucket; it can hold only one object or group of objects at a time. If you copy something to the Clipboard, it dumps itself out before another item (or group of items) can be poured in. Although the Clipboard can only be full or empty—whether with a block of text or a graphic—you can store Clipboard files. Check out your copy of the Windows documentation for more information on saving CLP files.

Windows comes with its own minor word processors, Windows Write and Notepad, which are both limited in function (Notepad even more so than Write). These programs have no built-in spelling checker or thesaurus, although you can always use Draw's built-in spelling checker and thesaurus. These small Windows programs do, however, provide a couple of ways to key text ultimately intended for inclusion in a CorelDRAW! file.

For best results, use a Windows-based word processing program such as Microsoft Word for Windows, Lotus Ami Professional, or WordPerfect for Windows. These programs allow a direct link to the Clipboard. Simply copy the block of text you need, switch to Draw, open the Text dialog box, and paste the block.

Importing Text

CorelDRAW! 5.0's text filters enable you to import text files from a variety of word processors and spreadsheets into Paragraph Text blocks. Using the text import filters, you can bring text files into Draw without having the originating application program on your system. Table 6.2 lists Draw's text import filters.

Table 6.2
CorelDRAW!'s Text Import Filters

Program	Versions	File Extension
Ami Professional	2.0, 3.0	SAM
Excel for Windows	3.0, 4.0	XLS
Lotus 1-2-3	1A, 2.0, 3.0	WK?
Lotus 1-2-3 for Windows	3.0	WK?
Microsoft Rich Text Format RTF		RTF
Microsoft Word	5.0, 5.5	DOC
Microsoft Word for Windows	1.0, 2.0, 6.0	DOC
Microsoft Word for Macintosh	4.0, 5.0	
ASCII text		TXT
WordPerfect	5.0, 5.1, 6.0	WP

In the next exercise, you bring in the menu choices, which were prepared in Word for Windows 2.0. If you do not have the Word for Windows import filter installed, you must do so before attempting to complete this exercise. To install the filter, use CorelDRAW! 5.0's Install program.

Importing text is a lot like importing graphics. For the most part, the import filters maintain the original document's formatting. When you import the menu, notice that it is already specified for the Eras typeface. Although the typesize is quite small, you change its typesize and line spacing.

Importing the Menu from a Word for Windows 2.0 file

Click on **F**ile	The File menu appears
Click on **I**mport	The Import window appears
Click on MS Word for Windows 2.*x*	The Import window configures as Word for Windows import

Move to your CD drive

At **D**irectories, *double-click on exercise*   The Exercise directory is selected

Roll down, double-click on MENU.DOC   The MENU.DOC file is imported

With the menu file successfully imported, go ahead and drag it roughly into position on the right-hand page, as illustrated in figure 4.19. Save the file as **NNMENU-5.CDR** before continuing.

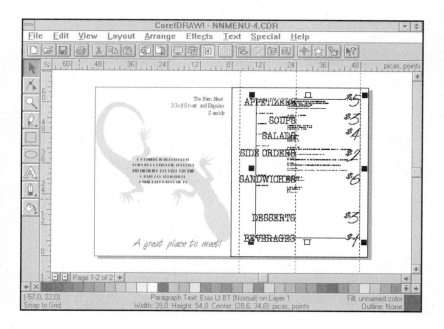

Figure 4.19
The menu as imported.

Using Paragraph Text

This chapter has made repeated references to Paragraph Text. *Paragraph Text* is body (or columnar) text. Think of a newspaper; Artistic Text is for headlines, and Paragraph Text is for body copy. Although it is highly unlikely that you would put yourself through the agony of publishing a newspaper with CorelDRAW! (it would do quite well in the advertising department), the newspaper is a good analogy to remember.

The Paragraph Text tool adds a new dimension to CorelDRAW!. If you produce brochures and other similar documents, you will welcome the flexibility that the Paragraph Text tool offers. The Paragraph Text tool builds on the basics of the

Artistic Text tool, embellishing it with the additional capabilities of columnar text, tabs, indents, and full justification.

Even though you can fully justify Paragraph Text, the results might be disappointing with narrow columns. If you have narrow columns, you will be much happier with the flush left/ragged right setting. Wider column measures enable the program more room for inter-word spacing.

You can use the Paragraph Text feature for many projects. Corel's engineers worked hard at improving the Paragraph Text feature in version 5.0. Although Draw might still seem slow to process Paragraph Text, it might be faster than shuffling between two separate programs. If your job contains only a few colors and is more text-based than illustration-based, you probably are better off using Ventura, PageMaker, or QuarkXPress for the text-heavy pages.

If your project involves lots and lots of color, it might be better to do the whole job in Draw. The idea behind CorelDRAW! is to generate plate-ready film, complete with traps. Although this is a lofty goal, it can save the experienced graphic artist money. For more information on trapping, see Chapter 11, "Basic Printing Techniques."

Thankfully, QuarkXPress and PageMaker 5.0 now can color separate placed graphics. These two programs are far better (and faster) tools for producing text-heavy documents, such as magazines and catalogs. Ultimately, the decision on which program to use and when to use it is yours.

The Paragraph Text Tool

The Paragraph Text tool is just as easy to use as most other Draw tools. If you understand how the Artistic Text tool works, then you have all the basics. The only important extras you need to know are how to access the tool, how to set up columns, and how to work with imported text files.

Now that you have the menu imported, it is time to learn about the workings of Paragraph Text. Since it was imported, you don't have to worry about creating the Paragraph Text box from scratch; the import filter did that for you. But when you go to create your own text boxes, you see that the Paragraph Text tool works in the same click-and-drag fashion as the Rectangle tool. Used in conjunction with snap-to-grid or guidelines, the Paragraph Text tool can lay down a text box of exact proportions. The status line reports the size of the paragraph text box as you draw it.

You can resize a Paragraph Text box after it is on the page; it can be stretched or scaled to fit. The concept of Paragraph Text boxes is very familiar to QuarkXPress users. You "pour" your text into the box after it is drawn. Like XPress or

PageMaker, if a box is too small for the text file you have imported, Draw will tell you that there is more text. Just look for the + at the bottom of the text box.

The Paragraph Dialog Box

The Paragraph dialog box contains many of the same controls as the Character Attributes dialog box. CorelDRAW! 5.0 enables you to draw a Paragraph Text box and immediately access the Paragraph Text dialog box (unlike version 3.0, which required that you first have a character in the text box before you could open the dialog box).

After you have the text on the page, you can change the specs with the Text Roll-Up menu. It enables you to access the full paragraph specifications, with tabs, indents, and bullets. You learn more about these advanced functions in the next chapter. In this next exercise, you simply apply typesize, character, and line spacing information.

Applying Paragraph Specifications

Click on Text	The Text menu appears
Click on Paragraph	The Paragraph dialog box appears
At Line, *select* Points	The dialog box configures itself for points
At Character, *type* **10**	
At Line, *type* **12**	
At Before Paragraph, *type* **12**	
Click on Left (see fig. 4.20)	
Click on OK	The paragraph specifications are altered
At the Text Roll-Up menu, change the point size to **10**	
Click on Apply To Frame	The typesize is altered

Now that the type is a little larger, you can see that the Word for Windows text file imported with its typeface and indents intact. Go ahead and reposition the text box, squeezing it to fit, as shown in figure 4.21. As you have seen, the Paragraph Text tool enables you to finesse imported text—a powerful, time-saving feature. Of course, you can always type your text directly into CorelDRAW!.

Figure 4.20
The Paragraph
dialog box.

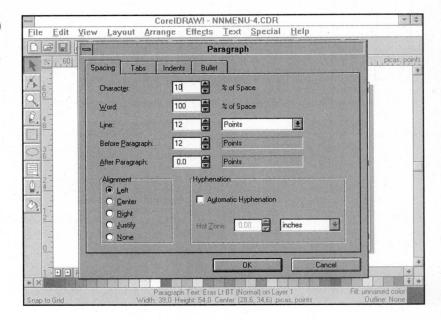

All text within a Paragraph Text block does not have to be of the same typeface and size; CorelDRAW! 5.0 enables you to alter individual characters within a paragraph. You can boldface or italicize certain words (although it may take more work to do it in Draw than it does in a word processor or page layout program).

Take the time now to go in and selectively change the kicker lines, such as "Just Trolling," to 24-point Van Dijk with the Text Roll-Up menu. Afterward, line things up with the guidelines and Align feature (see fig. 4.21), then save the file as **NNMENU-5.CDR**. Don't worry that things are not all that readable at this point! You are changing the fills to achieve a semi-interesting deconstructionist-wannabe look.

Joe DeLook is coming down to the wire as Fast Freddie once again bounces through the door. "That looks awesome, Joe!" he bellows. "Now can we make it a little more readable and change it into a two-color job?" Joe nods affirmatively and asks for a few more minutes. With a mad look of determination, Joe starts changing the fills of the different elements. He begins by adding page frames to both pages, and fills them with 10% PANTONE Blue 072. Then, he mirror-duplicates the newt, and gives it a 20% PANTONE Blue 072 fill. The headlines are also in the same color, but with a 30% tint, and the prices are given a 40% tint. He is still fiddling around with the different fills as Freddie blows the whistle (see fig. 4.22).

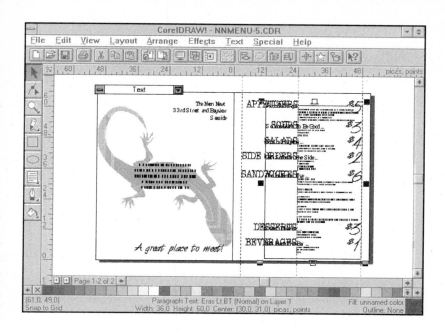

Figure 4.21
Align things with
the guidelines
and the Align
feature.

Figure 4.22
Everything in
position!

"Just in time to get it to the Seaside Print Shop before they close for lunch!" A big
grin washes over his face as he reaches for his wad of bills. "Say, we're gonna do
right well together, if you keep up that kind of work!" Joe grins back sheepishly,

shakes his hand, takes his money, and laughs like hell as soon as Freddie is up the block and out of earshot. The rent is paid. It is time to take a break before tackling the next chapter on advanced typography.

You now have seen that much of Draw's strength is in its text handling and links to other programs. After producing that first, simple menu, the program's typographical power should begin to become apparent. The exercise on importing text gives you an idea of how the program can be used in a workgroup environment.

Building an effective system composed of both computer and human factors is the key to success in electronic arts. For more information on putting together a selection of software and hardware, refer to Chapter 10, "You're the Designer."

Chapter Snapshot

Experienced desktop publishing and computer graphics professionals don't do anything by the rules, but instead create their own. This stubbornness in turn produces visually sumptuous pieces and exciting, provocative communication. If you are bored to tears with automated font settings and yawn at the latest "fad" font everyone is overusing these days, this chapter is for you. CorelDRAW! breaks all the typographical traditions with respect to setting headlines and text, because in addition to font properties, text you use with CorelDRAW! has graphical properties.

In this chapter, you:

✔ Use only two fonts to create a wealth of different graphical looks

✔ Use PhotoPaint to turn text into a graphic

✔ Create an ornamental cap from symbol sets

✔ Use the Envelope Roll-Up to create wrap-around text in a page layout

CHAPTER

Advanced Typography Techniques

Although CorelDRAW! comes with 830 high-quality display and text type-faces, it's obvious to most creative people that an inspired use of fonts in a design doesn't always come from a font's appearance. An amateur's layout frequently has a "graffiti" appearance because the fonts used bear no visually congruous element, and there's never any less than 20 fonts used in a single paragraph.

Okay, I'm exaggerating, but I've found that a good practice for CorelDRAW! users of all skill levels is to pare back the fonts used in a document to only one or two, make these fonts ones from traditional, plain families, and use your ingenuity to dress up the document. The results might startle you. You'll find yourself depending on your own inventiveness and using CorelDRAW!'s excellent graphical tools more than its excellent type handling tools. And the whole process can lead to a more integrated use of CorelDRAW! features, which in turn will make you a more accomplished designer.

Combining Typefaces

Combining typefaces within one document can add impact to your message. The Futura family is a gothic, sans serif design that's been used for over three decades in advertising and publishing. Part of its longevity is due to its lack of distinctive character; you can use it in a variety of design situations. CorelDRAW!'s power to reshape objects can transform Futura or any other font into a shape uniquely suited for your assignment.

Garamond is a little overused lately, but it still is more pleasant to view in a long paragraph than Times Roman variations. Garamond is a serif, Roman face, which means that unlike Futura, its stroke widths vary with each component of the characters (some are wider than others) and the ends of strokes are fluted, not right-angled.

The following sections give you a hands-on qualitative feel for how Futura and Garamond work together. You may feel more like a font-wealthy designer after the exercises.

This chapter takes you through the process of designing different graphical pieces. You'll recognize that "font abundance" is truly what you make it through your own inventiveness.

Designing a Page Layout

Page layouts are experiencing a renaissance with the present generation of digital designers, who challenge all but the most fundamental laws of good design. Ultra-wide paragraph text leading creates a flashy way to get a message across, and mixing typefaces that ostensibly don't mix produces powerful new styles in printed communication. But the function of headlines and body text will always serve to direct the reader's attention to important parts of a page. Font size and font selection can create a harmonious or dissonant design, depending on your intention.

In figure 5.1, a two column spread has been set in Futura Book BT (Bold) and GaramondNo4CyrTCYMed. The Futura Book BT (Bold) member of the Futura family is used as a subhead (smaller than an actual headline) at 18 points flush right, and Garamond is justified, 12 point size with 12 point leading (a little tighter than the conventional 120 percent of the point size).

The User's Guide
to Coping with System
Failures

Yesterday, I looked up to see what I believed to be an XT class PC hurtling out the window of a seven story apartment building. Apparently, people's emotions aren't keeping pace with technology. If you've ever had the desire to permanently end system failures this way, let's

re-think the measures that can be taken today to insure a better and more stable computer performance.

First, memory management is more important than ever with newer applications and systems. Since DOS addresses the first 640K of conventional memory, the order that programs and utilities are loaded into upper memory is also important, especially when using on-the-fly compression schemes for hard disks. The memory management should typically be loaded before disk compression, and this should be your first line in **CONFIG.SYS**. The reason for this is that a portion of disk compression is loaded high before the boot process, but the actual drivers are loaded after that. But nothing is loaded high until memory management is initialized, because there is no "high" until upper memory is visible.

A properly set up temp directory is another first step to a better functioning system. It doesn't really matter where the temp subdirectory resides, but if the hard disk partition where you set it up is uncompressed, your system will perform better and faster. **SET TEMP=X:\TMP** and **SET TEMP=X:\TEMP** are both necessary

Figure 5.1
Decide on a headline and a body text font for producing a page layout.

Tip

Note the tone that the two fonts create. It's serious and commands the words to be read. Choose your fonts to reflect the subject matter. There's nothing more laughable than an eviction notice set in Ad Lib or Kunstler Script; the letterforms suggest an occasion other than the one intended.

Using Different Weights and Styles

To further demonstrate the multiplicity of the Futura/Garamond teamwork, different weights and styles are used in the next exercise to convey a very different tone than you saw in the page layout.

Futura Extra Black BT is almost a design element disguised as a typeface, due to its hefty predominance on the page even when a few characters are set in it. And Garamond italic is a very elegant, almost ornamental member of the Garamond family. Using these two fonts together in an ad creates movement; the reader's eye will flutter continually from one graphical element to the other. This is good when you're trying to communicate an otherwise boring message.

In figure 5.2, the graphical and text elements might not be exciting, but the composition is. Futura Extra Black BT was stretched in CorelDRAW! to add further dynamic reading interest to the slogan.

Figure 5.2
Treat text as another compositional element in your design.

You've now seen two different tones presented to the viewer using the same families of fonts. This strongly suggests that Futura and Garamond have a place on your hard disk.

Kerning and Spacing Type

Often the tone or effect you want to create requires special spacing of the font you are using. Suppose that the law firm of Dent & Polk, for example, wants you to design its letterhead stationery. The desire is to convey the seriousness of its practice and create something that won't get lost in the paper shuffle on the desks of clients.

Once again, Futura XBlk BT and Garamond are used to create the logotype in the following exercise. To follow the exercise, you must have Futura XBlk BT, GaramondNo4CyrTCYMed, and GaramondNo4CyrTCYLig (Normal, Italic, Bold)

installed in your type manager. I recommend installing them from the CorelDRAW! CD as Type 1 fonts because they're an important, permanent part of a serious designer's collection.

Beginning a Logotype with Type

Open a New document in CorelDRAW!, then click on the Text tool, click an insertion point on the Printable page, and type **DENT**.

Press Ctrl+spacebar	Switches you to the Pick tool
Press Ctrl+T	Selects Te<u>x</u>t, <u>C</u>haracter Attributes
Choose Futura XBlk BT *from the list of available* <u>F</u>onts *on the* Character Attributes *menu and click on OK*	Specifies a dense weight of Futura
Click and drag on the lower right selection handle and pull in a 4 o'clock direction until the status line tells you the Artistic Text is about 100 points	

You can increase point size of Artistic Text by scaling it like any other CorelDRAW! object, or you can use the Si<u>z</u>e field in the Character Attributes menu.

Click on the Zoom tool, click on the Zoom In tool on the fly-out menu, then marquee zoom (click and diagonal drag) so that you have about 2 screen inches of Printable Page bordering the text selection	This provides you with a comfortable view of the selection, with plenty of room to add to the text
Click on the Shape tool, then press Ctrl *and click and drag the node that precedes the D toward the right so that it overlaps the E by about 1/8 ", as shown in figure 5.3*	The Ctrl key constrains movement of the selected character to a straight line, in the direction you first drag it

This is called manual kerning of letters.

Figure 5.3
Kern the letter
by selecting and
dragging the
node that
precedes it using
the Shape tool.

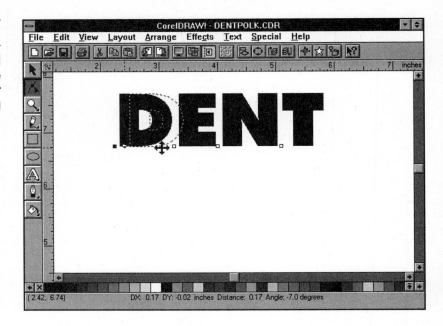

Don't hesitate when you Ctrl+click+drag a character with the Shape tool. CorelDRAW! is very sensitive to cursor movement, and if you don't make a decisive horizontal move after a character node has been selected, the character might disappear. CorelDRAW! understood that your first move was vertical because you made a slight mouse movement in a vertical direction, and your character is now somewhere out of view, most likely off the Printable Page.

To correct this problem, continue to hold the Ctrl key while dragging the cursor back and forth, still holding the character node with the Shape tool. The character should then reappear. If it still doesn't, immediately press Ctrl+Z to **E**dit, **U**ndo your last move, then Ctrl+click+drag the character again.

Kern the other characters so that each touch the other, with the exception of the E and the N; give these two about 1/16" space in between. Letterforms that have open sides, such as the E, become unreadable when closed by a following letterform that starts with a vertical stroke. Instead, leave a small space between them.

Next, the word POLK gets the same treatment as the DENT Artistic Text. The easiest way to make sure Dent's partner gets equal billing is to copy the DENT text, and backspace, then type the new text. Unfortunately, your fancy kerning work on the DENT text will vanish when you replace the DENT copy text with new characters because this is a temporary attribute.

Here's the quickest way to create the text element that uses the Futura Extra Black font in this logotype design.

Copying and Modifying Existing Text

Select the DENT Artistic Text, *then click and drag it so that the dotted boundary box clips the original text's bottom at about 1/8 screen inch*

Moving the text but not releasing the left mouse button is the first phase of creating and repositioning a copy of DENT

Right mouse click, then release both mouse buttons

Creates a duplicate below the DENT text, which hasn't moved at all

Click on the Text tool, as shown in figure 5.4

A blinking vertical insertion point appears at the end of the copy of the DENT text (this means that the text is selected in a text editing mode, and you can highlight or backspace over the text as you would in a word processing program)

Press the backspace key four times

Deletes the DENT text copy, and you can begin to type in the 100-point Futura XBlk BT font

Type **POLK**, *then press Ctrl+spacebar*

You have your new text entry, and the Pick tool is now active for repositioning the text

Click on the Wireframe View *button on the Ribbon Bar, then click and drag a vertical guideline to meet the vertical stroke in the "D" in DENT*

Sets up the Printable Page for exact aligning of the two words

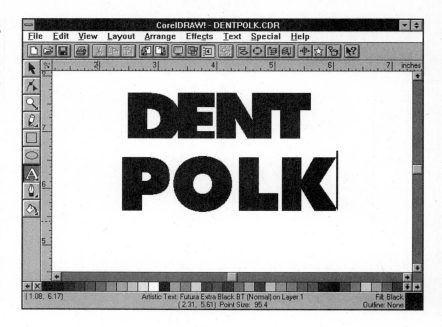

Don't use Snap-To Guidelines when trying to align different strings of Artistic Text. The boundary around Artistic Text usually is not the same as where the outline of a character lies; it's outside the Artistic Text a little. Therefore, you'll never be able to align the text precisely because a guideline will attach the selected text to the wrong position. Use the Nudge feature (the keyboard arrows) to align text or other objects precisely. Set the Nudge amount to a small amount, such as 0.007", under Special, Preferences.

Using the Shape tool, kern the characters in the word POLK the same way you did with DENT, then align the word to the left of DENT, as shown in figure 5.5.

Using Negative Space within a Design

It's time to place an ampersand between the two lawyers' names, but with kerning and leading as tight as it is now, there doesn't seem to be a convenient space. This is where the use of negative space comes to the rescue. The DENT and POLK lettering is so dense, parts of it can be easily used to reverse out an ampersand within the letterforms. Once again, Garamond can be used here to soften the oppressively overbearing DENTPOLK Futura text and add a touch of class to the logotype.

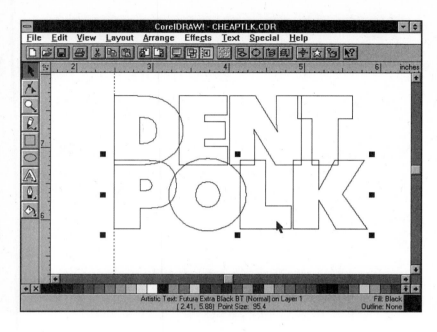

Figure 5.5
Overlapping
characters
integrate the
lettering into a
design element.

The following exercise shows how to get creative with a black-and-white logotype
design.

Using Negative Space within a Text Object

Using the (Artistic) Text tool,
click an insertion point in the
center of where the D in DENT
and P in POLK meet

*Type the **&** symbol, and then left*
mouse click on the white swatch
on the colors palette to make the
***&** white*

Switch back to Preview mode and
click on the Wireframe button
on the Ribbon Bar (or press
Shift+F9) so that you can
clearly see the
ampersand (see fig. 5.6)

The logotype is now shaping up, and you can easily view and edit the ampersand now.

continues

continued

Press Ctrl+spacebar to switch to the Pick tool, and reposition and resize the ampersand as your artistic sensibilities dictate

Figure 5.6
You can reverse text out of bold typefaces as part of a logotype design.

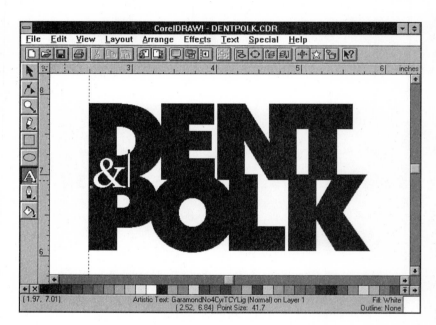

Customizing a Typeface

Dent and Polk presently have a nice logotype with punch, but the logotype fails to indicate their line of work. Dent and Polk could be physicians, but they probably wouldn't attract a lot of business with these names.

Personal Claims Attorneys is a rather long text string, and, if centered beneath the logotype, surely would require a small point size or additional lines of text. This is where condensed faces come into play in a lot of assignments. At this point, you have Garamond on your disk, but not Garamond Condensed. No problem if you remember that Artistic Text can be horizontally scaled (smushed) the same as any object in CorelDRAW!. Here's how to make some on-the-fly condensed type that'll finish off the logotype design.

Creating a Condensed Typeface

Press Ctrl+spacebar to activate the Pick tool, then click on a blank area of the Printable Page

Deselects all objects

If you were to select the Text tool again without deselecting, the ampersand would have an insertion point following it, eagerly awaiting more text string entries, and you don't want this.

Click on the Text tool, and click an insertion point below the DENT and POLK text

This is the area where you'll create a new text string.

Type **Personal Claims Attorneys**, *then press Ctrl+spacebar, Ctrl+T*

Adds the description of the lawyers to the logotype and selects the entire text string for modifying in the Character Attributes menu

Choose GaramondNo4CyrTCYMed from the list of Fonts, type **40** *in the points Size field, then click on OK*

Specifies a typeface size that's about 1/4 the total vertical height of the DENT and POLK type, making it legible

Reposition the text string so that it sits beneath DENT & POLK, flush left with the logotype

Puts the text string in position for some manual condensing

Click and drag the middle right selection handle to the left, until the dotted boundary box around the text is basically flush with the "K" in Polk, as shown in figure 5.7

Bolder text such as GaramondNo4CyrTCYMed will withstand "compression" and still maintain readability, unlike lighter weight fonts

Save the file and exit CorelDRAW!

Figure 5.7
Change the Y
scale of the
selected text to
about –50% of
its original width
to condense it.

Manually condensing a text string provides a simulation of a condensed face, but it is not exactly the same as using a manufacturer's condensed version of a font. Great care has been taken to optimize readability of different weights and faces.

Although this CorelDRAW! disproportionate scaling trick will work for short text strings, do not depend upon it for long paragraphs of text. Paragraph Text cannot be resized because it is displayed as text within a frame. The frame can be reshaped like any other CorelDRAW! object, but the text within is immutable.

Figure 5.8 features the finished logotype. It's clean, professional, a little silly, but again, variations on the Futura and Garamond theme provide a distinctive look because you know how to "work" type in CorelDRAW!.

The "Photographic" Treatment of Text

To conclude our adventures with the Garamond and Futura families, the next exercise shows how text can become so much a part of a design element, it becomes the graphic for which other text has to clarify.

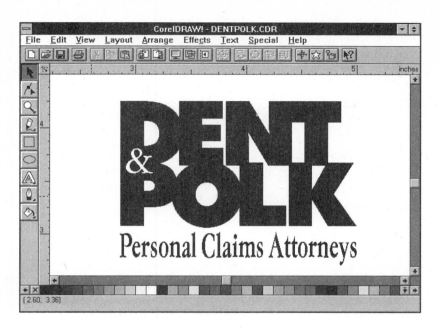

Figure 5.8
CorelDRAW!
treats Artistic
Text as a
graphical
element you can
edit with the Pick
tool.

CorelPHOTO-PAINT has a magnificent collection of effects filters. The one used in the next assignment is the motion blur. The author had the opportunity the other week to sit on his reading glasses, thus hindering their usefulness for reading, eating, and unlocking the front door utilities. After a quick drive (as a passenger) to the opticians', he was back in action and got to thinking about how PhotoPaint's motion blur effect could be used quite dramatically to advertise the need for a good optician.

In this next assignment, you'll use a logo from the *Inside CorelDRAW! 5, Fifth Edition CD-ROM*, CorelPHOTO-PAINT!, and Futura and Garamond to create an ad for some fictitious eye specialists. Here's how to make plain text a very unusual design element in a graphic.

Creating Blurred Text

Double-click on the   Launches the PhotoPaint application
CorelPHOTO-PAINT! icon in
the Corel Group in Program
Manager

continues

continued

If you chose not to install PhotoPaint in Corel Setup, you might want to install it now, or use the CLEAR___.TIF image on the *Inside CorelDRAW! Fifth Edition CD-ROM* later in this exercise, which was built using the steps that follow.

Choose <u>F</u>ile, <u>N</u>ew (Ctrl+N),   Displays the Open a New Image menu
or click on the New *button*
on PhotoPaint's Ribbon Bar

Choose Gray Scale *as the*
<u>C</u>olor Mode *from the drop-*
down list, select inches *as*
the <u>W</u>idth *and* <u>H</u>eight
increments, type **3** *in the*
<u>W</u>idth *field and* **2** *in the*
<u>H</u>eight *field, set the Resolution*
to 150 dpi *(pixels per inches),*
then click on OK

The preceding measurements are proportionate to the logo you'll be working with in this exercise. A resolution of 150 ensures the bitmap image reproduces well even to an imagesetting device.

Choose the Text tool, then
select Futura XBlk BT *from*
the Font drop-down list box,
set the Typesize to 45 points,
and click on the Center
Justified *button on the Text*
Ribbon Bar

The Ribbon Bars change according to which tool is active. These are the specs for the text to fit within the design you'll later finish in CorelDRAW!.

Click an insertion point in
the NEW-1.CPT window, then
type **CLEAR.** *Press Enter, type*
 SHARP. *Enter* **PRECISE.**

This is the text element to which you'll be applying an effect.

PhotoPaint offers no facility to adjust kerning and leading of text objects. If you want tighter leading in this assignment, try typing one line, then choose the <u>O</u>bject, <u>M</u>erge command (Ctrl+G). Then type a second line and click and drag the text with the Object Picker tool until it fits nicely beneath the first line. Then use the Merge command and repeat the process a third time.

When you're done typing, click on the Object Picker tool (the arrowhead cursor on the top of the toolbox)

Selects the text selection and it becomes an uneditable graphic

Choose O bject, M erge

The text selection becomes fused to the background image

Choose Effe c ts, Fancy, *then* Motion blur

Displays an options box with a preview window of the effect you've chosen

Click on the Up button (the top center of the nine in the *center of the* D *irection box), set the* S *peed to about* 30, *then click on* Apply

Sets the motion blur parameters for really messing up the text graphic; you can also click on the Preview button to see how the effect is applied prior to issuing the command

Choose F ile, Sa v e As, *then select* TIF Bitmap (*.TIF, *.SEP) *from the* Save Files as T ype *drop-down list, name the file CLEAR___.TIF, and save the file to a working directory that you've set up on your hard disk*

Saves the image, as shown in figure 5.9

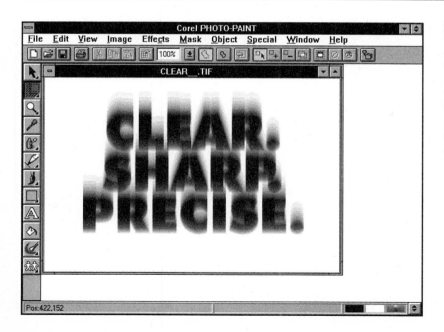

Figure 5.9
A text-as-graphic can be saved in the TIF format and used by other programs that can import or edit the file.

Working the Text-As-Graphic into a CorelDRAW! Design

Unlike PhotoPaint, CorelDRAW! can only edit imported graphics of the vector type. CorelDRAW! lacks the tools to edit or paint a bitmap image, but it still accepts and prints a TIF image format that's part of a CorelDRAW! design. In the next set of steps, you'll see how the transformed Futura text plays the role of an illustration for an ad. The weight of the font was extremely important for the purposes of blurring it; few other fonts could maintain legibility after being motion blurred, and the graphic must now serve both a design purpose and have some textual content.

Here's how to complete a design for an advertisement beginning with only the logo.

Making an Advertisement from a Logo

Launch CorelDRAW!, then open the OAKTREE.CDR file from the Inside CorelDRAW! Fifth Edition CD-ROM

This document has been prepared to work with the file size and dimensions of the CLEAR___.TIF image you created last.

Choose File, Import, *then choose* TIF bitmap (*.TIF, *.SEP) *from the* List Files of Type *drop-down list*

Displays all the TIF images located on the present directory and drive

Choose the appropriate Drives *and* Directory *listing from the drop-down lists, click on* CLEAR___.TIF, *then click on OK*

Readers who don't have a PhotoPaint creation at this point can use the CLEAR___.TIF image located on the *Inside CorelDRAW! Fifth Edition CD* in the CHAP05 subdirectory.

Either way, the TIF image is now being imported.

When the TIF image imports, click and drag it into position above the Oaktree Opticians logo so that it fits within the frame of the ad, leaving room beneath it

You'll add a snappy slogan next and need room in which to type it.

Click on the Artistic Text *tool,*
and place an insertion point at
the left of the advertisement frame

Type **Maybe it's time to see it like it is.**, *then press* Ctrl+spacebar, *and press* Ctrl+T	Enters the text, makes it the active selection, and displays the Character Attributes box
Choose GaramondNo4CyrTCYLig *as the Font, type* **11** *in the* Si*z*e field, *then click on OK*	Changes the text to an understated Garamond, which contrasts against the blurred text, as shown in figure 5.10

Figure 5.10
Do not adjust this page. There is nothing wrong with it.

Once again, Garamond and Futura are used for a different type of graphic design, and if you look at the past four examples, you'll see that the real difference is in the concept, and not necessarily having 800 billion fonts installed. Typography is a tool, and the best use of one is in combination with other CorelDRAW! tools.

II

Putting CorelDRAW! To Work

If you're sick and tired of pressing Alt+146 to get a typesetter's apostrophe, CorelDRAW! 5 has a new feature called Type Assist. To use it, choose <u>T</u>ext, Typ<u>e</u> Assist.

By checking the Change Straight quotes to Typographic Quotes box, quotation marks and apostrophes automatically convert to their extended character equivalent every time you type Paragraph or Artistic Text.

Creating a Storybook Initial Cap

CorelDRAW! now has many features that automate near-impossible tasks in previous versions. In fact, many users now are wondering what to do with all the new effects, tools, and Roll-Ups. Because this is a chapter about the creative use of fonts, it spends some quality time discussing the fine art of creating initial caps from available CorelDRAW! materials.

Initial caps are those oversized ornamental letters that kick off a paragraph in magazines and books. While CorelDRAW! serves up more than enough fancy and business fonts, very few foundries offer a collection of the storybook caps that begin every "Once upon a time..." story. The solution is to make your own, and this section shows you how. You'll create a layout of a children's story later in this chapter, so to get way ahead of the game, you'll design an ornamental "O" initial cap next.

The design begins with a square, reminiscent of the woodcuts that were used before the Guttenberg presses. Here's how to set up CorelDRAW!'s workspace for the grand adventure.

Setting Up the Storybook Cap Design

Choose the Zoom tool, then click on the Zoom In tool and marquee zoom to view about 5-by-4 (horizontal/vertical) screen inches of the Printable Page

This is your work area for an initial cap 2" in size

Click and drag guidelines from the rulers to make a 2" square on the Printable Page

If your rulers aren't visible, choose <u>V</u>iew, then check <u>R</u>ulers.

<table>
<tr><td>Click on the Snap-To Guidelines button on the Ribbon Bar</td><td>Everything you design now is guided to the Guidelines you've set up</td></tr>
<tr><td>Choose the Rectangle tool, then click and drag from the upper left to bottom right of the guidelines square</td><td></td></tr>
</table>

Your rectangle should be a perfect square. The guidelines forced your cursor movement to create this shape.

<table>
<tr><td>Choose Effe<u>c</u>ts, Co<u>n</u>tour Roll-Up (Ctrl+F9)</td><td>Displays the Contour Roll-Up in the Drawing Window</td></tr>
<tr><td>Click on the Inside radio button, then type .07 in the Offset inches field, and set the number of steps to 2</td><td>Creates a border inside the square, part of the design of the initial cap</td></tr>
<tr><td>Click on Apply</td><td>A group of Contours appear inside the square, which is now a Control Object, as shown in figure 5.11</td></tr>
</table>

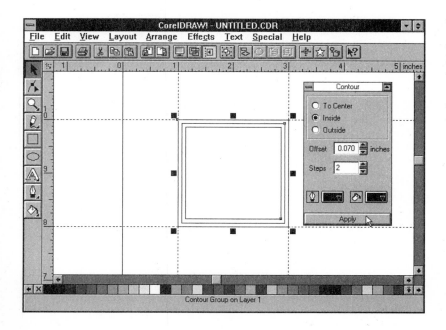

Figure 5.11
Contour effects can be applied to either the inside or outside of closed paths.

Breaking a Dynamic Contour Link

Like many of the effects in CorelDRAW!, a dynamic link is made between the "source" objects (Control Objects, according to the Status Line). This can be a good thing or bad thing on occasion. Now you want to break the link between the contour shapes and the original square so that they can be filled independent of one another to make a bordered box for the initial cap.

Here's how to break the links and create the background for the initial cap.

Giving Contour Shapes Independence

Select the Contour group, *not the control object, if it's not already selected*

Dynamic object links must be broken with the effects object selected, not the original shape.

Choose **A**rrange, **S**eparate	The contour group and control object are now free of one another, and the status line tells you that two objects are presently selected
Click on an empty area of Printable Page	Deselects the group
Click on the innermost shape, then click on the Group/Ungroup *button on the Ribbon Bar*	By default, Contours separated from the Control Object are grouped; clicking on the button on the Ribbon Bar toggles the grouped shapes to ungrouped
Click on an empty Drawing Window area	Deselects everything
Click on the innermost square, then left mouse click on the black swatch on the color palette, and right mouse click on the X	Fills the innermost square with black and removes its outline
Click on the original square, then Shift+click on the square directly inside of it	Additively selects the two objects
Choose **A**rrange, **C**ombine (Ctrl+L), *then left mouse click on the black swatch on the color palette, and right mouse click on the* X	Combines the selection to create a border around the innermost square, and you've filled it with black and removed its outline, as shown in figure 5.12

Click on the up arrow in the upper right of the Contour Roll-Up	Retracts the Contour Roll-Up to make way for more Drawing Window action

You'll use the Contour Roll-Up again later, so click and drag the retracted Roll-Up's Title bar to an out-of-the-way area, like in a Drawing Window corner.

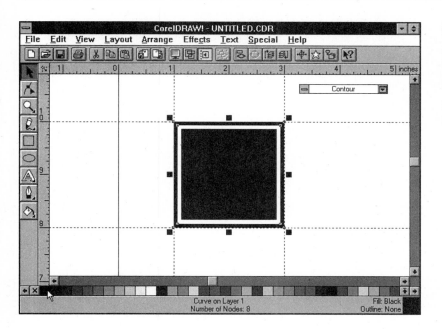

Figure 5.12
Closed paths inside of other paths become a "counter" when the two are combined.

Adding Embellishments to the Initial Cap Background

Craftspeople have slaved for centuries adding tiny filigree work to ornamental art, like on folding money, certificates, and high school rings. CorelDRAW! simplifies this painstaking task, and in the next set of steps, you'll see how to perform your own imitation filigree work to the initial cap. Will it be authentic? No, it's taken about 1,000 years of refining the art of embellishing text, but faking something is an art in and of itself.

Zapf Dingbats BT and Wingdings belong to the Pi or symbol set of font families. They're packed with ornamental goodies that, when properly placed and edited, serve very nicely as filigree work for the initial cap. Windows installed Wingdings and Zapf Dingbats should be part of your basic working set of fonts (Zapf is 8556x___.pfb and 8556x___.pfm in the Z subdirectory in case you'd like to add the Type 1 face to ATM).

Here's how to pretty up the initial cap using bits and pieces of symbol fonts.

Using the Symbols Roll-Up for Embellishing

Click on the Symbols Roll-Up *button on the Ribbon Bar (or press Ctrl+F11)*	Displays the Symbols Roll-Up
Choose Wingdings *from the categories drop-down list on the* Symbols Roll-Up	Special symbol fonts appear both as available system fonts and as sets on CorelDRAW!'s Symbols Roll-Up
Select symbol 203, either by typing this number in the # box or by scrolling down to find it	
Choose 1.75 inches for the size of the symbol, then click and drag the symbol onto the Printable Page, as shown in figure 5.13	The default size of the symbol, 2", would be too large to fit inside the innermost Contour shape
Left mouse click over the white swatch on the colors palette, then click and drag the symbol to the center of the bordered background	By default, symbol shapes have a hairline outline and no fill, so this makes the symbol visible against the black background
Right mouse click over the X on the color palette	Removes the black outline from the symbol
Click on the Save *button on the Ribbon Bar (or choose* F*ile, Save; Ctrl+S), then name the initial cap OH!.CDR*	
Roll down the Contour Roll-Up (*click on the down arrow, upper right corner*), *type* **0.05** *in the Offset box on the* Symbols Roll-Up, *then set the steps to 1*	Creates an inside contour to the Wingdings symbol making it appear a little more ornate
Click on Apply	Applies the effect, and you should now have an initial cap border background similar to that in figure 5.14

Putting CorelDRAW! To Work

Retract the Contour Roll-Up again to conserve screen space, but don't close it; you'll need some of the settings soon

Closing and re-opening Roll-Ups changes settings back to their defaults

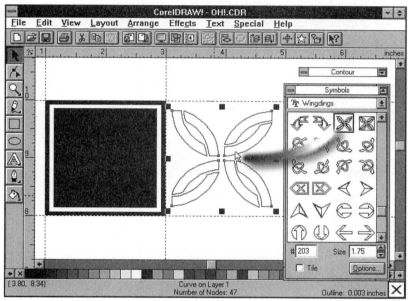

Figure 5.13
Click and drag a symbol from the Roll-Up to add the shape to your design.

Adding Other Symbols to the Background

This bordered background for the initial cap can't hold a candle against a genuine storybook cap at present. That's because the tenet held by engravers more than 500 years ago was, "Anything that's good in moderation becomes excellent in excess." We need to fill a few blank areas of the border, and here's where Wingdings again comes to the rescue.

Here's an easy, quick way to manually mirror a symbol so that it fills in twice the background area in almost the same time as performing this operation once.

Figure 5.14
Add a contrasting inner shape to a symbol using the Contour Roll-Up.

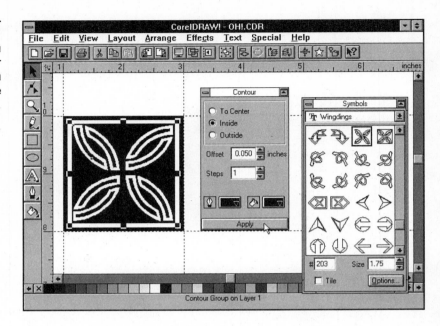

Assembling Symbol Components

On the Symbols Roll-Up, *set the Size option to* **.5** *inches, then select symbol* 208, *and drag it onto the Printable Page*

Adds a small symbol that fits in a number of areas of blank background at present, as shown in figure 5.15

Left click on the white swatch on the color palette

Fills the symbol copy with white so that it can be seen against the black background square

Click and drag the symbol to the 12 o'clock area inside the border

Reposition the symbol so that it fits compositionally in a vacant spot within the copy of symbol 203

Right mouse click over the X on the color palette

Removes the outline from the shape

Press Ctrl, then click and drag the top selection handle around the symbol straight down (don't release the mouse button yet, though)	Mirrors the selection, as shown in figure 5.16
Right mouse click, then release both mouse buttons	Duplicates the selection you've commanded CorelDRAW! to mirror
Click and drag the mirrored selection to a point where it fills the 6 o'clock space in the design	Creates an ornamental background that now has a little more action going on with it

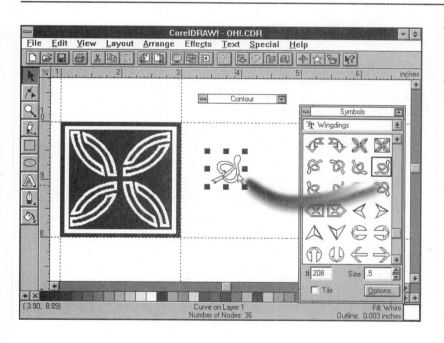

Figure 5.15
Controlling the size of a Symbol you copy saves resizing it later.

II

Putting CorelDRAW! To Work

Trimming a Fancy Border around the Background

New features to this version of CorelDRAW! are the Trim and Intersection commands. The Trim command treats one selection like a scissors and a different object like paper. In the next section, you'll use a symbol to trim the border around the square and make it more ornamental.

Figure 5.16
The Ctrl key
constrains
resizing
selections to
100%...
mirroring a
selection.

Here's how to play your cards right and use a club symbol from Zapf Dingbats BT to add visual interest to a plain border.

Clubbing a Border into Shape

Choose Zapf Dingbats BT
from the list of categories
on the Symbols Roll-Up

This collection of symbols features playing card symbols, ideal for Trim objects.

Type 1 *in the* Si**z**e *field*
of the Symbols Roll-Up,
then choose symbol 168 and
click and drag it onto the
Printable Page, as shown in
figure 5.17

This is the shape you'll use as the "scissors" shape with the Trim command

Press Alt+F7 *to display*
the Transform Roll-Up (or
choose Effe**c**ts, **T**ransform
Roll-Up)

This is the set of tools for precisely rotating, skewing, resizing, or moving a selected object. The club needs to be rotated, but manual rotation is imprecise.

Click on the Rotate button on the top of the Transform Roll-Up	Changes the Transform Roll-Up's options to those for rotating functions
Type **90** *(positive is counterclockwise) in the Angle of Rotation field, then click on* Apply	Turns the club on its left side with its leaves in a good aspect to use for trimming the square border, as shown in figure 5.18
Left click on the white swatch on the colors palette	Fills the club shape so that you can see what you're doing next
Click and drag the club so that it's half inside the right border of the initial cap background	

This is where the club is used to trim the background.

Press Ctrl and click+drag on the middle right selection handle of the club selection, then right mouse click before releasing the left mouse button	Horizontally duplicates a mirrored image of the club shape
Click and drag the duplicate club so that it half fills the 9 o'clock position on the background square	The left and right clubs appear symmetrical (see figure 5.19)
Hold the Shift key, click on the original club, then on the innermost background square	

There's an order to selecting the "scissors" and the "paper" objects before issuing the Trim command. The last object (the innermost square) is the paper.

Choose **A**rrange, **T**rim, *as shown in figure 5.19*	Removes the area from the rectangle where the club shapes overlap it
Deselect the three shapes by clicking on a blank area of the page, then click on each club shape and press the Delete key	Removes the clubs, and you can now see the carving they've done to the rectangle border

If you marquee select two or more objects rather than additively selecting them (using the Shift key), and then choose the Trim command, the bottom-most shape on the page is trimmed by the top-most shape.

Figure 5.17
Consider the "negative space" of a symbol as you'd subtract its geometry from a different shape using the Trim command.

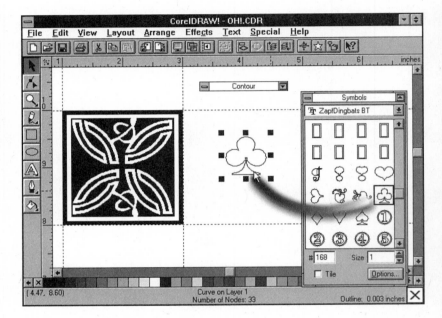

Adding the Initial to the Initial Cap

It's time to add a letter to the initial cap background. The letter "O" can be from any font family you choose, but for the purposes of this next exercise, go with a generic "O" from the Times New Roman family. It's a font that many will have installed, and there's a final trick or two you'll see next to dress up even the most common character.

Here's how to finish the initial cap "O" in preparation for an excursion into page layout with CorelDRAW!.

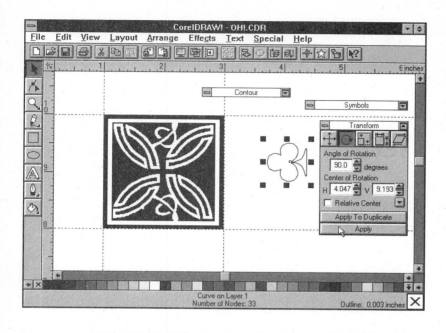

Figure 5.18
Precisely rotate a shape (or group of shapes) using the Transform Roll-Up.

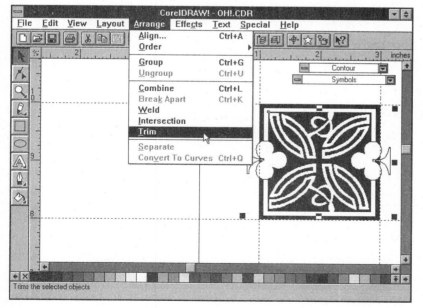

Figure 5.19
The Trim command subtracts the geometry of the first object(s) from the last one selected.

Adding a Character to the Initial Cap

Click on the Artistic Text tool, make an insertion point to the right of the initial cap background, then type an uppercase "O"

This is the letter you'll modify and add to the background collection of shapes.

Press Ctrl+spacebar, *then press* Ctrl+T

Switches you to the Pick tool, the "O" is selected, and the Character Attributes options box is displayed

Choose Times New Roman *(or any other face you think would be cool) from the* **F**onts *list, choose the* Bold **S**tyle *for the font from the drop-down list, then click on OK*

Changes the default font for the selection to Times New Roman and returns you to the Drawing Window, as shown in figure 5.20

Figure 5.20
Choose a bold font as the centerpiece for your initial cap design.

Click and drag on the lower right corner selection handle of the "O" in a 4 o'clock direction, stop when the status line tells you the "O" is about 177 points

There are 72 points in an inch, the innermost square is about 1.75", and was Windows Calculator popped over CorelDRAW! to figure this one out

Roll down the Contour Roll-Up, *click on the Fill button and choose white, set the Offset to* **0.05** *inches, leave the other settings as you last defined them, then click on* Apply

Creates an "open face" character, as shown in figure 5.21

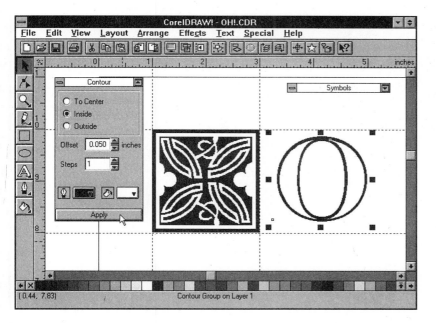

II

Putting CorelDRAW! To Work

Figure 5.21
A contour around the inside of the letterform makes the entire group stand off from the ornamental background.

Click and drag the selection inside of the background border so that it's centered on top of the other shapes

This is the final position for the contoured cap "O"

continues

continued

*Click a second time to put
the "O" in Rotate/Skew mode,
then drag a corner rotate
handle counterclockwise about
40°*

Creates a more asymmetrical
design, with a little more
character, as seen in figure 5.22

Figure 5.22
Rotate the "O" a
quarter turn to
make the initial
cap less static.

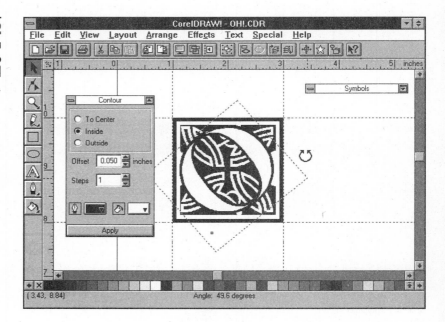

*To gild a lily (that's already
been chrome-plated, I believe),
set the Symbols Size to 1",
click and drag symbol #166 from
the Zapf Dingbats Symbols category,
then click on the white swatch on
the colors palette, and right
mouse click on the X*

This is called over-embellishing
a design

*Left click on the white swatch
on the color palette*

Gives the plum symbol a white fill

On the Contour *Roll-Up,* click
on the Outside *button, set
the Offset to* **0.04** *inches,
choose the black fill swatch
from the drop-down swatches,
then choose* Apply

Gives the plum symbol a heavy black
outline appearance

Click and drag the plum symbol
to the center of the "O"

You're done. Press Ctrl+S to save your work at this point. You've got yourself a beautiful initial cap for stories that begin with the letter O, as shown in figure 5.23.

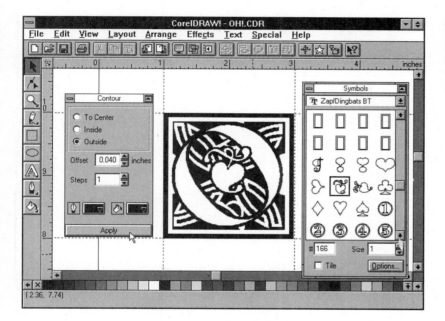

Figure 5.23
Now you need a story to go along with this initial cap.

Setting a Paragraph Text Story for the Initial Cap

Was this a setup, or what? Actually, knowing how to work with Paragraph Text is more important than with previous versions of CorelDRAW! because you can work almost as fast as you can in a word processor and definitely as fast as a desktop publishing application in CorelDRAW! 5. Corel Corporation has gone to great lengths to get its drawing program up to speed, and what used to be painstaking work is now a breeze if you know the ins and outs of designing with Paragraph Text.

First things first, though. Paragraph and Artistic Text both come into CorelDRAW! at a default font and font size, which is 24-point Avant Garde BT (unless you accidentally removed this font from your system). You can change what typeface and point size Paragraph Text imports in as the default font, and for good reason.

If you import text from your favorite word processing program into CorelDRAW!, it fills the page and continues to flow in linked text frames for as many pages as your imported story is. CorelDRAW!'s default frame for imported Paragraph Text has a 2" margin inside the page, and at 24 points, your imported text will flow to many more pages than you intend it to.

In the next exercise, you'll see how to change the default text for Paragraph Text. You can change it back, or to some other specification when you're done, but the important point here is that you have some control in CorelDRAW! over how text is directly entered onto the Printable page.

Here's how to set your default Paragraph Text.

Changing CorelDRAW!'s Default Text Settings

Launch CorelDRAW!, then without opening a new document or selecting a tool, press Ctrl+T

A special Character Attributes box pops up, as shown in figure 5.24, and prompts you for the defaults to use in the future for Paragraph and Artistic Text

Figure 5.24
When you have no text selected, the Character Attributes dialog box offers to change defaults for future use.

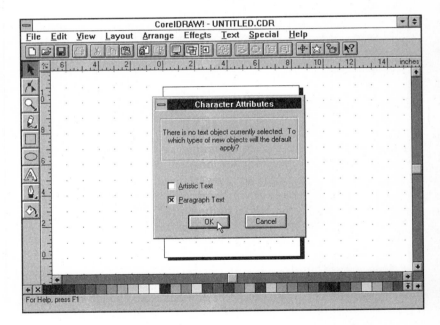

Leave the Paragraph Text box checked, then click on OK

It is recommended that you uncheck the Artistic Text box at this point. 24-point Avant Garde actually is okay to begin an Artistic Text string; generally display type is about this size in a finished ad or design. The dialog box leads to the Character Attributes options menu.

Select Times New Roman (TrueType or Type 1) *from the* Fonts *list,* *type* **12** *in the* Size *field, then click on OK as shown in figure 5.25*	Causes all unformatted text in the future to be imported as Times New Roman 12 point, unaligned

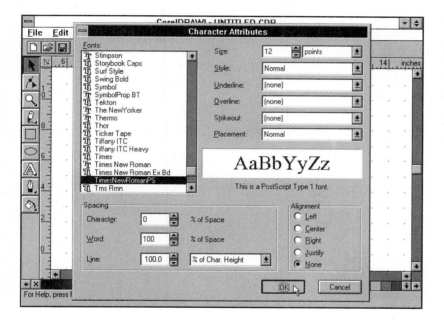

Figure 5.25
Any Paragraph Text you enter directly in the Drawing Window will be set in 12 pt. Times New Roman, too.

Try this experiment to see how the new Paragraph Text default works.

Choose File, Import, *then select* TESTGRAF.TXT *from the* Inside CorelDRAW! 5, Fifth Edition CD-ROM	Imports an ASCII text file with no typeface specified

Make sure you select the Unformatted Text (*.TXT) option in the List Files of Type drop-down list, and that the Directories list points at CHAP05 on the CD.

When the text imports, a frame will land in the center of the Printable Page, with the text inside it beginning in the upper left corner.

continues

continued

Choose the Pick tool and click and drag on the bottom handle of the Paragraph Text frame until it's about an inch beneath the text it contains	Paragraph frames for imported text will fill the Printable Page whether or not the frame is full of text; you're simply making the dimensions of the frame smaller, and this doesn't affect the text within it
Click and drag the right middle selection handle of the frame to the left until the status line displays that the frame of Paragraph Text is about 3" wide	Reshapes the Paragraph Text frame so that the rest of the page can be designed without tripping over the frame
Choose the Zoom tool, then click on the Fit In Window tool	Zooms into a very tight view of the Paragraph Text

Your own eyes and the status line confirm that this text is indeed Times New Roman. It's really small, and the experiment in changing text defaults in CorelDRAW! is a success, as shown in figure 5.26.

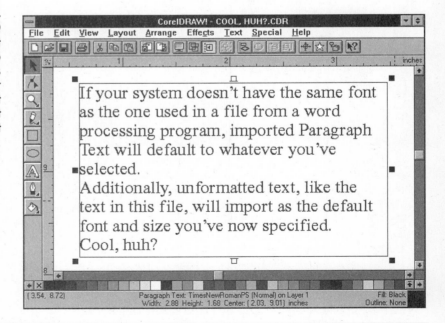

Figure 5.26
Imported text doesn't flow to additional pages when your default Paragraph Text is small in point size.

Working with Imported Paragraph Text

Unlike unformatted text, text that's attributed a style in many word processing programs retains most of its formatting when imported into CorelDRAW!. You might prefer to compose a story in a word processing program (or have a story someone gave you on disk), then import it into CorelDRAW! to complete a page design.

Paragraph Text can be as easy and quick to lay out in a full-page design using CorelDRAW! as using a desktop publishing application. The advantage CorelDRAW! has over DTP programs is that you can edit a CorelDRAW! graphic right on the page; DTP programs typically cannot edit imported graphics.

In the next exercise, you have a two-page spread with graphics. Your charge is to import a short story from a Word for Windows 6.0 document, add the initial cap you designed earlier to it, and use some of the design power in CorelDRAW! to wrap the text so that it flows around the graphics. Much of this assignment is set up for you. The HAPPYREC.CDR file on the *Inside CorelDRAW! Fifth Edition CD-ROM* has two layers; Layer 1 containing the graphics is locked so that nothing can come loose while you work. Guidelines have been laid out on the page, and the WinWord document has been formatted with the Windsor LtCn BT font from the CorelDRAW! CD. All you really need to do before digging into page layout is load the Windsor LtCn BT font either as a Type 1 or a TrueType onto your system.

0326a___.pfb and 0326a___.afm are the Type 1 DOS file names and tt0326m_.ttf is the TrueType DOS file name for Windsor Light Condensed BT in case you'd like to remove the font from your hard disk after this assignment.

In figure 5.27, you can see the document, The Happy Rectangle, as it's saved as a Word for Windows document. The type face, size, and justification have been defined in the document, and all these attributes will override CorelDRAW!'s default text fonts when the story is imported.

Figure 5.27
Formatted text
files carry
header
information
about the fonts
and styles used
that
CorelDRAW!
recognizes.

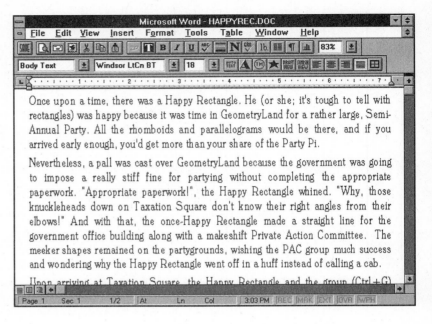

Here are the first steps toward creating a full-page spread in CorelDRAW!.

Importing a Text Document into CorelDRAW!

*Click on the Open button
on the Ribbon Bar (or
choose* <u>F</u>ile, <u>O</u>pen; Ctrl+O),
then click on the
HAPPYREC.CDR *file in the*
CHAP05 *subdirectory of
the* Inside CorelDRAW! 5,
Fifth Edition CD-ROM,
then click on OK

Opens a copy of the HAPPYREC.CDR
file in the Drawing Window,
as shown in figure 5.28

The current active layer is Layer 2. Layer 1 containing the graphics is locked. It's a good idea
to adopt this practice on your own CorelDRAW! page layouts.

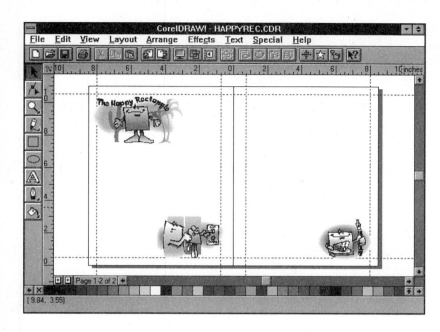

Figure 5.28
HAPPYREC.CDR
was laid out in
facing page
format by
choosing this
option from the
Layout, **P**age
Setup command.

II

Putting CorelDRAW! To Work

Choose **F***ile, Save* **A***s, then
save this copy to a location
on your hard disk*

This, too, is good practice. CorelDRAW! can't save to a read-only CD, and your file might get lost forever if there is a sudden system failure while you work.

Choose **F***ile,* **I***mport, then choose* MS Word for Windows 6.0 (*.DOC) *from the* List Files of **T***ype drop-down list, and choose CHAP05 as the directory on the* Inside CorelDRAW! 5, Fifth Edition CD-ROM *(see fig. 5.29); then click on* HAPPYREC.DOC *and click on OK*	CorelDRAW! imports the WinWord document

Figure 5.29
Choose from
many popular
word processing
formats in
CorelDRAW!'s
List Files of Type
drop-down for
importing.

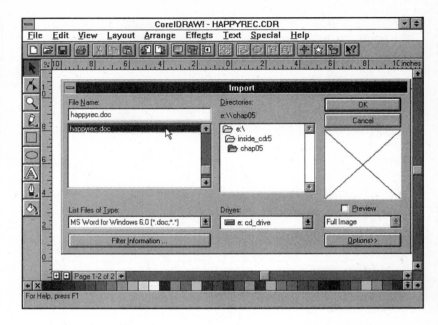

As you can see in figure 5.30, CorelDRAW! sort of dumps the text on the Printable
Page and flows the rest of the text onto as many pages as needed to accommodate
it.

Figure 5.30
Paragraph Text
imports in
frames whose
sizes don't
exactly match
the source
document for
margin width.

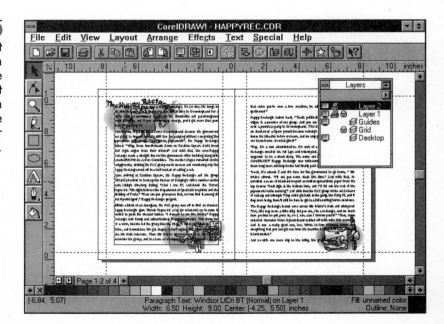

The problem here is not with the text; it's 18-point Windsor Condensed and will fit within the layout. But CorelDRAW! imports text to fill a frame that's smaller than the Printable page, and this calls for adjusting the frames in the next part of the exercise.

Resizing Paragraph Frames

You can use two techniques for reshaping the flow of Paragraph Text; the frame that holds the text can be resized using the Pick tool, and the Shape tool can be used along with the Envelope Roll-Up to custom design a container for the text. You can achieve many wonderful page layouts using the Shape tool and the Envelope effect, like sculpting a silhouette of a pyramid to hold a story about Egypt, or simply creating a border that runs around a graphic to make wrap-around text.

In the next exercise, you'll concentrate on simply getting the margins correct on the text and eliminating the extra pages CorelDRAW! has flowed the story to. Then you'll get to the fancy stuff.

Here's how to make the linked text frames conform to the guidelines set up on the layout:

Creating Refined Paragraph Text Margins

Click on the Snap To Guidelines *button on the Ribbon Bar (or choose* **L**ayout, Snap To Guideli̲nes)	Makes the Paragraph Text frames become attracted to the guidelines when you drag them near the guidelines
Click on the middle left selection handle on the left page text frame and drag toward the left guideline	The border is attracted to the guideline and snaps to it, increasing frame size. The text inside is not distorted in any way
Perform the preceding step with all remaining seven sides of the left and right frames	Increases the overall frame size to the extent that the story concludes on page 2, and pages 3 and 4 are now blank
Choose **L**ayout, **D**elete Page	A dialog box appears with fields for defining which pages you want to delete
Type **3** *in the* **D**elete Page *field and type* **4** *in the number field next to the* **T**hru Page *check box; make sure the check box is checked, then click on OK*	Deletes empty pages 3 and 4, and the Page controls at the bottom left of the Drawing Window disappear

Reshaping Paragraph Frames

Here comes the fun part. Paragraph frames can behave like any path in CorelDRAW! as long as you have an envelope assigned to it. You may have played with the various modes of Envelope in your CorelDRAW! adventures, but when you assign an Unconstrained mode to a Paragraph Text frame, the Shape tool can bend the frame like Silly Putty.

In the next exercise, you'll clear the text away from the title illustration area, and create some room for the fancy initial cap you created earlier. Here's how to change the properties of a Paragraph Text frame in CorelDRAW!.

Distorting a Paragraph Text Frame

Choose the Zoom tool, then click on the Zoom In tool, and marquee zoom into the upper left corner of the left page

Start at about −11" horizontal rule, then diagonal drag to about 6" vertical rule for a good view of the title illustration

Click on the left text frame border   Selects the frame

Press Ctrl+F7 (or choose Effe<u>c</u>ts, <u>E</u>nvelope Roll-Up)   Displays the Envelope Roll-Up

On the Envelope Roll-Up, *click on the Unconstrained mode button (the one that looks like the Shape tool icon), then choose* Add New   Adds a new envelope around the text frame

Double-click on the top of the frame envelope   Displays the Node Edit Roll-Up

Click on To Line *on the* Node Edit Roll-Up, *as shown in figure 5.31*   Turns the segment of the envelope between the nodes to straight properties; Unconstrained mode gives the text Envelope smooth curves between segments, which are harder to work with than straight lines

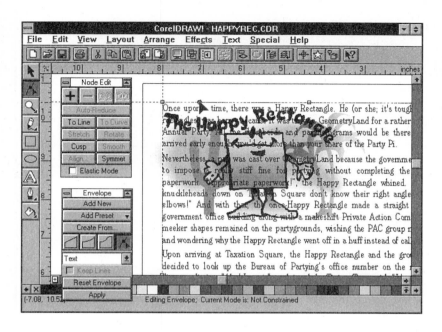

Figure 5.31
Unconstrained envelopes can be edited exactly like any other shape using the Shape tool and Node Edit Roll-Up.

Click on the upper left segment of the paragraph text envelope, then click on the To Line button on the Node Edit Roll-Up

Both segments nearest the title illustration are now straight lines

Click and drag the upper left corner node down and inward so that the dotted envelope preview doesn't surround the title illustration, then choose Apply *from the* Envelope Roll-Up

Changes the outline of the frame in which the Paragraph Text is held, as shown in figure 5.32

Figure 5.32
Click on Apply
to update the
changes you
make to the
envelope around
the Paragraph
Text.

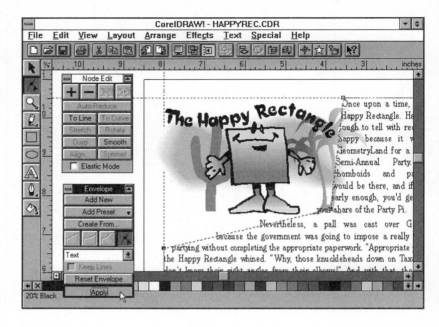

You'll notice that the options for enveloping the frames is automatically changed to Text on the Envelope Roll-Up whenever Paragraph Text is selected. You cannot change this, but you can change editing modes. Single Arc, Curved Arc, and so on are valid envelopes for Paragraph Text, but it is only with Unconstrained mode that you can take advantage of the Node Edit Roll-Up's powerful features.

Wrapping Text around a Graphic

This new custom border is in its early planning stages at the moment. In the next exercise, you'll bend it further to allow Paragraph Text to flow partially into the title illustration, then add a node to the envelope and make way for importing the fancy initial cap.

The design of the title illustration was meant to be partially obscured by text, and by doing the next steps, you'll add extra room for all the text to fit within the page margins. Whenever you wrap text, you lose space.

Here's how to allow some of the text to run over the illustration.

Increasing Text Space within the Envelope

Click on the envelope segment that now borders the text directly to the right of the illustration four text lines from the top, then press the + keypad key	Adds a node on the envelope outline
Click and drag the node at the bottom of the indented text about 1" to the left	This is the original envelope corner node that you dragged across the illustration in the last exercise
Click on the segment between the new node and the node that you just moved, as shown in figure 5.33	Selects the segment
Choose To Curve *on the* Node Edit Roll-Up	Changes the segment to curved properties
Click and drag on the segment in an 11 o'clock direction; stop before the envelope segment actually touches its hand	Arcs the segment toward the Happy Rectangle's right hand
Click on Apply *on the Envelope* Roll-Up	Updates changes made to the segment of envelope, and text now flows over the light-colored palm tree

Don't ever switch tools before applying a change to the envelope around Paragraph or Artistic Text. If you do, you'll lose the editing changes you've made to the envelope outline. Make it a practice to click on the Apply button after you've performed some fancy editing work.

Setting Spacing for Paragraph Text

Before adding the initial cap, it's a good idea to adjust the text within the frames. The initial cap will steal some space away from the layout design, and without getting the text as you want it to appear in the final layout, you'll be playing a guessing game with the layout with respect to how the text will flow.

Figure 5.33
Use the Node
Edit Roll-Up to
reassign
properties to
envelope outline
nodes and
segments.

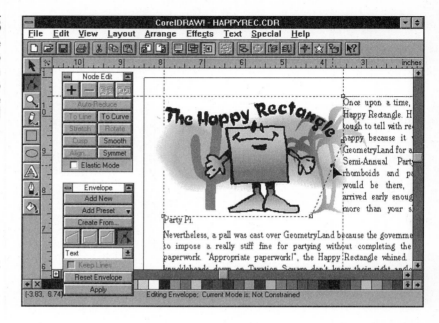

There's a dynamic link between Paragraph Text frames on the left and right pages; you take away text space from the left page, and text will flow to the right. Don't let CorelDRAW! add another "flow" page simply because the Paragraph Text isn't perfect yet.

CorelDRAW! picked up the before and after paragraph spacing as was originally defined in the Winword document. Also, the single column is justified, as was defined in HAPPYREC.DOC. But what's throwing the text off now is the hyphenation.

In the next exercise, you'll see how to add hyphenation to the Paragraph Text to make the lines as smooth and polished as magazine typesetting.

Fine-Tuning Paragraph Hyphenation

*Measure the word "Rectangle" in
the first paragraph against
the horizontal ruler*

"The" is a word fairly average in length within the story. It's about 3/4", right?

Double-click on the Text *tool*   Displays the Text Tool Roll-Up

*With the left Paragraph frame
selected, click on the* Paragraph
button on the Text Tool Roll-Up

Check the A̲u̲tomatic Hyphenation box, type .25 in the Hot Z̲one field, then click on OK (see fig. 5.34)

The word now hyphenates when it exceeds a quarter inch in length at the end of a line, a number arrived at by measuring a three-syllable word that's 3/4 inches. In combination with the Justified alignment, the story now flows from line to line with better word and character spacing.

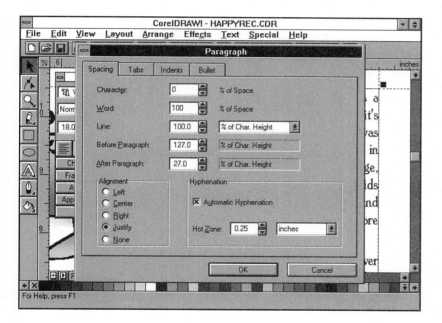

Figure 5.34
Automatic hyphenation breaks a word whose length exceeds the Hot Zone.

Tip Depending on the typeface used, you might want to adjust inter-word spacing within Paragraph Text in addition to activating Automatic Hyphenation. Bookman, for example, is an atypically wide font, and CorelDRAW!'s default value of 100% inter-word spacing is a little too loose for paragraphs set in this font. In this case, try setting the **W**ord spacing to 50% of space, then work your way up in increments of 5% until you feel the spacing is adequate.

Importing a Native File

Now that you're finished fine-tuning the Paragraph Text, it's time to place the initial cap you designed at the beginning of the first sentence. CorelDRAW! can import files in its native *.CDR format, which is an alternate to copying a design, then pasting it into a different document. Because CorelDRAW! can't have more than one file open at a time—it's not MDI (Multiple Document Interface)-enabled— this sometimes is the only way to assemble multiple design elements from different CorelDRAW! files.

In the next exercise, you'll notice one or two interesting things about importing CDR files into another document; the OH!.CDR initial cap design wasn't grouped, yet when it imports, CorelDRAW! automatically brings in the file contents grouped. Additionally, the grouped objects appear in the same spacial coordinates relative to the Printable Page from which it was designed. Because you're presently zoomed in to the top of the page, when the OH!.CDR design imports, it might not be immediately visible, depending on what area of the page you designed the initial cap.

Here's how to import and resize the initial cap for use in the page layout.

Adding a Cap to the Page Layout

Click on the Zoom *tool,*
then choose the Show Page *tool*
(the button on the far right of
the fly-out menu)

Displays the entire two-page layout, so that you can see the initial cap at whatever location it imports

Click on the Import File *button*
on the Ribbon Bar (or choose File,
Import), *then select*
CorelDRAW! (*.CDR) *from the* Import
Files of Type *drop-down list*

CorelDRAW! imports the contents of a file in its own native format

Select the location of OH!.CDR
from the Drives *and* Directory *lists,*
click on OH!.CDR, *then click on OK*
(see fig. 5.35)

If the Preview box is checked, it will slow your exit from the Import command box, but you'll see a low-resolution preview of whatever you want to import. This is handy sometimes if you've forgotten what's in a file you've saved.

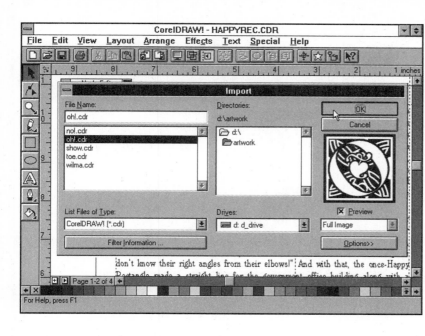

Putting CorelDRAW! To Work

Figure 5.35
You can preview a graphical (not text) file before you import it using the Import command.

Using the Pick tool, click and drag the imported initial cap up to the top of the left page, positioning it to the right of the title illustration, on top of the beginning of the first paragraph

This is where the initial cap will be located within the page layout

Choose the Zoom tool, then click on the Zoom In tool, and marquee zoom to the area where you positioned the initial cap

The cap was designed too large for this layout, but like every graphical element in CorelDRAW!, it can be scaled to size.

Click on the Snap To Guidelines button on the Ribbon Bar, then click and drag the initial cap upward

Snaps the initial cap to the guideline at the top of the page

Click and drag the lower right selection handle of the cap toward the center of the cap; stop when the dotted boundary reaches the fourth line of type in the paragraph

Scales the cap to about 55%, and the cap now becomes a drop cap indenting the first four lines of text, as shown in figure 5.36

continues

continued

Figure 5.36
Scale the initial
cap so that it
can indent the
first four lines of
Paragraph Text.

Indenting the Paragraph Text

The initial cap is in place within the layout, so it's time to further modify the envelope that surrounds the Paragraph Text frame to flow the text around the cap. Also, the story sports a redundant "O" now that the initial cap is in place. Here's how to finish the top half of the left page layout.

Making Way for the Initial Cap

Choose the Shape tool, click on the top envelope outline, about 1/16 of an inch to the right of the initial cap's right edge, then press the + key on your keyboard, or the one on the Node Edit Roll-Up	Adds a node to the envelope outline
Click on the segment between the two nodes on the envelope outline above the initial cap, then press the To Line *button on the* Node Edit Roll-Up	Turns the curved outline segment to a straight line

Click on the envelope node above the upper left corner of the initial cap, and drag it beneath the lower right corner of the cap, then click on Apply *on the* Envelope Roll-Up

Reshapes the envelope to wrap the text around the initial cap, as shown in figure 5.37

Figure 5.37
Apply changes whenever you've edited a node or segment that makes up an envelope.

Choose the Text *tool, then click an insertion point between the "O" and the "n" in "Once"*

An insertion point appears, and CorelDRAW!'s rulers change to Paragraph Text mode, telling you where tabs are in the selected text frame

Press the backspace key

Removes the redundant "O" from the story

As you can see in figure 5.38, the top of the left page looks pretty good now. Zooming out periodically helps you get an idea of how text is flowing and how the design is shaping up.

Don't work too hard on reshaping the envelope so that it looks perfect in its geometry. The purpose of the envelope around the text is to flow the text, and even though the frame might appear to border the text imperfectly, its functionality is more important than its appearance. Neither the frame nor the envelope are visible in the printed, finished document, so pay attention to how the text wraps rather than the appearance of the envelope and text frame.

Also, use guidelines to snap envelope nodes to specific locations. Guidelines don't print either.

Figure 5.38
The text will fill the page after it's been enveloped to flow around the remaining illustrations.

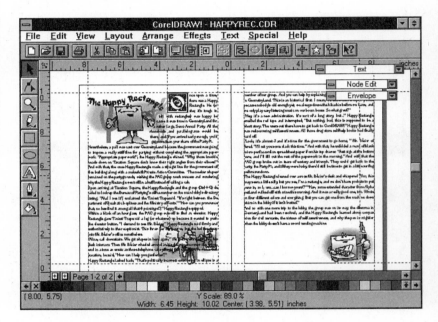

Creating a Custom Text Wrap

The remaining two illustrations need to intrude upon the Paragraph Text, and this is a perfect opportunity to refine your skills at reshaping the text envelope. In the next exercise, you'll create a shape that contours around the right-hand, left page illustration at the bottom. You'll see that a simple line around the drawing works beautifully, and there's really no need to create an elegant outline with many nodes to complete the task.

Additionally, you do not want to bend the envelope so that text flows around the top of the illustration. If you do, text will flow to the left and right above the illustration, and the single column of Paragraph Text will become harder to read where a line is split.

Here's how to make the text flow around the second illustration.

Editing around a Right-Hand Graphic

Scroll down to the bottom of the left page where the second illustration is located

With the Shape *tool, click on the bottom envelope segment to the left of the illustration, press the +key, then choose* To Line *on the* Node Edit Roll-Up

Adds a node, turns the bottom segment to a straight line, and is easier to manipulate

Click on the vertical envelope segment to the top right of the illustration, press the + key, then press To Line *on the* Node Edit Roll-Up

Adds a node, and the right segment between the new node and the corner becomes a straight line and is easier to work with, too (see fig. 5.39)

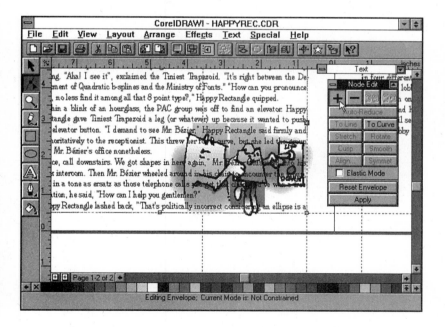

Figure 5.39
Add nodes that frame the illustration, and convert the segments in between to straight line envelope segments.

Click and drag the bottom right corner envelope node up and to the left of the illustration, then click on Apply *on the* Envelope Roll-Up

Flows the text around the illustration

It's okay if some of the text violates the illustration. You'll refine the envelope border next.

continues

continued

Click on the envelope segment above Happy Rectangle's left eyeball (his left, your right), then press the + key on the keypad	Adds a node to this segment of envelope
Click and drag the corner node above the upper left of the illustration	Contours the flow of text to wrap around the illustration
Click on the envelope segment to the left of the illustration, then press To Curve *on the* Node Edit Roll-Up	Changes the segment from a straight line to a curve
Click and drag the curve segment to the left so that the outline clears the illustration, then click on Apply *on the* Envelope Roll-Up	Creates an envelope area that flows text around the illustration, as shown in figure 5.40

Figure 5.40
Use the Node
Edit Roll-Up to
create a custom
shape that
Paragraph Text
flows around.

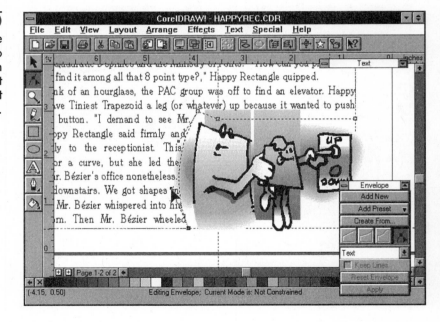

Finishing the Page Layout

If you keep a lookout from a full-page view every now and then, you'll notice that the Paragraph Text has flowed from the left page to the right. The right page is pretty full now, and by shaping the right Paragraph frame to flow around the bottom right page graphic, the text should end at the bottom of page 2.

In the next exercise, you'll learn a trick for keeping the left and right page ends at the same margin. It's called "playing with the envelope"; if the bottom right page comes out a line too short, you increase the wrap around the graphic to force the second-to-last text line to break prematurely. This adds a line to the bottom, and both pages will look perfectly set when printed in a book.

Here's how to finish the typesetting in the short story.

Creating a Flexible Text Wrap

Scroll to the bottom of page 2, then select the Paragraph frame and click on Add New *on the* Envelope Roll-Up

Although the left and right paragraph frames are linked, they are separate objects, and the right frame needs an envelope of its own

Click above the illustration on the right side of the envelope, press the + key, then click on Cusp *on the* Envelope Roll-Up

Adds a node to the envelope outline and gives a Cusp attribute to the node (by default, nodes added to unconstrained envelopes are smooth)

Click to the left of the illustration on the bottom of the envelope, press the + key, then click on Cusp *on the* Envelope Roll-Up

Adds a node to the envelope outline and gives a Cusp attribute to the node

Click on the corner envelope node and drag up and to the left so that it lies outside of the illustration, then click on Apply

Flows the text around the illustration

After the corner node has been repositioned, click on Smooth

Corner envelope nodes have Cusp attributes, and, by giving the repositioned node a Smooth attribute, the reshaped envelope creates a soft arc around the round-shaped illustration.

Click on the bottom envelope node, then click and drag on the control

Creates more room into which the point text may flow

Click on the right node, then click and drag on the control point

Refines the custom envelope so that the last word, "machine," in the story winds up on the last line

continues

Putting CorelDRAW! To Work

continued

Click and drag on the smooth node
until the bottom line of text is
occupied within the frame

When the bottom line has text in it,
you're done (see fig. 5.41)

Figure 5.41
Adjust the
nodes
surrounding the
graphic until the
Paragraph Text
flows to the
bottom line of
the frame.

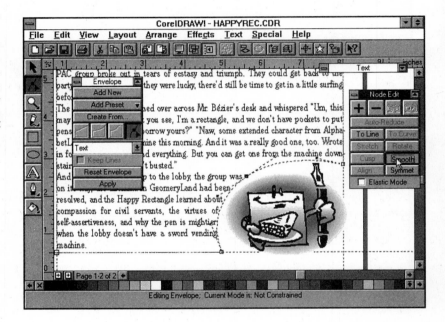

Adding a Storybook Ending to the Story

It's a convention in publishing to place a bullet at the end of a story, and storybook layouts are no exception. To complete the layout design, you'll add an ornamental bullet or two (or three) after the last word on the second page. It's easy, and also changes the "color" of the text on the page, balancing out the design, and delighting children who read the story (especially children who use CorelDRAW!).

Here's how to use the Symbols Roll-Up to add a graphic touch to a happy ending for the story.

A Plum of an Ending

Click on the Symbols Roll-Up *button on the Ribbon Bar (or choose* **S**pecial, Sym**b**ols Roll-Up; Ctrl+F11)

Displays the Symbols Roll-Up

Click on the Categories drop-down title, then select Zapf Dingbats BT

This is one of many symbol fonts commercially available that feature a typographic plum shape.

Type **167** *in the # field, then type* **.5** *in the inches field of the* Symbols Roll-Up

You also can scroll to find the plum shape. Half an inch is an arbitrary value; symbol sizes are relative and frequently inaccurate. Mathematicians and artists almost never mix.

Click and drag the plum shape onto the page, then left mouse click on the black swatch on the color palette, and right mouse click over the X

Gives the plum a black fill and removes the outline

Click and drag the plum to the right of the word "machine," and reposition it so that it's centered vertically to the word

This is the final position for the first of three plums

While holding the Ctrl key, click and drag the plum to the right, right mouse click, then release both mouse buttons

Duplicates and moves the first plum

By holding the CTRL key, you constrain the movement of the duplicate to a straight (in this instance horizontal) line, so plum 2 is aligned with the original.

Repeat the last step, so you have three aligned plums, as shown in figure 5.42

This concludes the page design

Congratulations! Wanna buy the rights to the story?

Tip

You'll notice in the last figure that the Symbols Roll-Up is sort of wider and squatter than its default size. You can re-proportion Roll-Ups to give more free space on your screen if you click and drag the borders in any direction. The Options and Preview window will realign to

II

Putting CorelDRAW! To Work

conform to the new shape, and you can scroll through the symbols quicker when there is only one row of previews.

Treat Roll-Ups like any other image window in any Windows application.

Figure 5.42
Duplicating and moving a symbol is quicker than pulling three copies from the Roll-Up and recoloring each one.

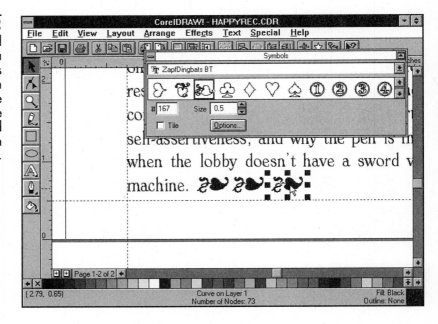

Choose File, Save As, and name the piece HAPPYEND.CDR. This will prevent you from overwriting this file if you decide to save the original CD file to your hard disk in the future.

As you can see, figure 5.43 shows the finished layout. Guidelines have been removed to show off the layout without any distracting elements.

Hopefully, you've been so pre-occupied in this chapter exploring the unique ways to treat text in CorelDRAW!, you haven't had the opportunity to miss playing with the other 800 fonts on CorelDRAW!'s CD! When words become art, and art is created from the inspired use of text, you then hold the vision of what electronic publishing can be at its best. If you think about it for a moment, this isn't really so much a chapter about fonts as it is about integrating elements of visual communication. CorelDRAW! excels at bringing all sorts of digital media to a common virtual canvas, and the techniques and facility with which you mix them up can be considered a tool of your trade as much as any filter, icon, or font.

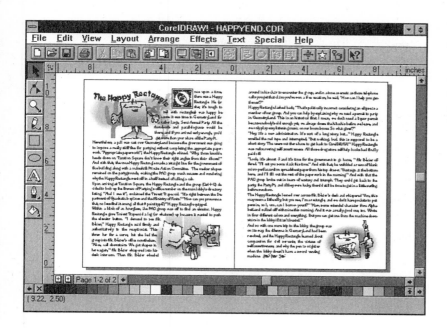

Figure 5.43
You're ready
now to give the
Brothers Grimm
a little
competition in
the marketplace.

Chapter Snapshot

Are your creative batteries worn down? Turn the pages for a creative jump-start and a review of various typographical pyrotechnics! In this chapter, you learn to do the following:

- ✔ Use a variety of drop shadow styles, including perspectives, knockouts, and embosses

- ✔ Give your type a glow with a neon effect and add depth with Tube Type

- ✔ Go wild with Punk Text

- ✔ Achieve a chiseled look with Bevel Text

- ✔ Get a heavy metal look with Chrome Type

- ✔ Take flight with Spin Type

- ✔ Create high-brow designs with Two-Tone and Letterspaced Type

- ✔ Cook up some tasty Bitmap Type Treats

- ✔ Experiment with Textured Type

What may be fresh to one graphics designer may be cliché to the next. Cast your net into these waters and pull out your catch—the design fish are running!

CHAPTER

Special Type Effects

R emember Felix the Cat, the cartoon feline with his bag of tricks? This
chapter is your equivalent to Felix's magic bag. When you run short of
ideas, turn to this chapter for an instant concept, a creative jump-start, or
a new way to solve a design dilemma.

The majority of this chapter is devoted to type effects. Some techniques might be
familiar to you, but others might not be obvious. Each effect is illustrated along
with a quick how-to exercise, providing a fun and easy way to perfect your technique. Most of the techniques are accomplished within Draw itself, but others have
been created with a combination of Draw and PhotoPaint.

If you are feeling a lack of creativity or technical prowess, the latest version of
CorelDRAW! helps you overcome your shortcomings. The program comes with a
wide range of preset options that enable you to create your own special designs.
Presets are fully covered in Chapter 10, "You're the Designer."

This chapter concludes by exploring backgrounds. Textures can come from a
variety of sources. By using a scanner and a bitmap paint program, you can
misappropriate any pattern from marble tile to spattered paint to achieve a unique
look. And in the vector world, you learn to create a zooming grid by using the
Perspective effect.

Exploring Advanced Typographical Effects

As you have seen in previous chapters, CorelDRAW! enables users to produce a slew of impressive tricks with type. Serious design power comes into play when you use those effects to create multifaceted pieces of artwork. Images that are exhaustively time-consuming, incredibly expensive, or almost technically impossible to create conventionally can be produced on time and under budget.

This section investigates a number of effects that are not one-click endeavors, but require a bit of savvy and technical skill. As you work through the type effects, you soon realize that many of these tricks can apply to objects other than text. Most of the examples in this section strive to conjure up illusions of depth, texture, or motion.

With a depth effect, you add a three-dimensional look to two-dimensional artwork. Draw enables you to add a prop to your work with effects like Extrude. Although CorelDRAW! 5.0's Extrude is capable of employing three light sources, you may still need to take the extrusion apart and apply different tints to each side of an object to effectively add depth to add the illusion of lighting angles. The concept of lighting angles figures strongly in creating bevel type, embossed type, and tube type. The artist must fool the beholder's eye into accepting different tints as different faces of a multidimensional object.

This chapter uses a handful of the many fonts you can find on CorelDRAW! 5.0's CD-ROM discs. If you do not have a CD-ROM drive, you can substitute similar fonts, although Draw's huge font load is all the justification you need to buy a CD-ROM drive!

Exploring Drop Shadow Variations

A *drop shadow* is a duplicate of an object filled with a different tint and placed behind the original object (see fig. 6.1). The fill can be lighter, darker, or a completely different color. The drop shadow is usually the first type embellishment discovered by neophyte desktop publishers who sometimes overuse it brutally. In experienced hands, a drop shadow is perfect for popping text off the page. When the drop shadow effect is correctly rendered, it makes type look as if it were magically suspended, floating above the page. Although drop shadows are commonly created with shades of gray, color adds more subtleties than shades of gray alone can portray. In color advertising or packaging, the drop shadow is almost a necessity.

Plain Vanilla

Figure 6.1
A standard drop
shadow effect.

Even though a plain vanilla drop shadow is hardly worth writing (or reading) about, a few variations are worth discussing. This section presents perspective shadows, knockout drops, and embossed type. A number of methods are available to create the drop shadow. CorelDRAW! enables you to use the Duplicate command (Ctrl+D), the Move command (with leave original), and Drag-duplicate. And don't forget that pressing the numeric + leaves a duplicate exactly on top of the original.

The Move and Duplicate commands offer the most accuracy. *Move* enables you to change the distance moved each time you use the Transform Roll-Up menu; you can change Duplicate's setting in the Preferences dialog box. When you work with a number of objects that all must have the same drop shadow, *Duplicate* is the most convenient choice.

If you are shadowing only one object, *drag-duplicating* (pressing the numeric + while dragging) is an excellent option. After the duplicate object is on the page, the Nudge function (when set at 0.01 inch or smaller) is the slickest way to reposition objects in fine increments. You can also duplicate an object by clicking on the right mouse button while you are dragging the object.

Creating Perspective Shadows

Figure 6.2 shows an example of a perspective shadow. The words are sitting on the horizon line, backlit by an offset radial fill. The foreground is a linear fountain fill with the fill angle set to flow from the focal point of the background. The perspective shadow completes the illusion by following the same imaginary light source.

Figure 6.2
The perspective
shadows effect.

The procedure to set a perspective shadow either behind or in front of a piece of type is simple. Contrary to popular belief, you can create a perspective shadow by using the Perspective effect rather than using the Skew function.

You begin this exercise by drawing a pair of rectangles to form the background and foreground of your graphic. Draw the first rectangle by using the Rectangle tool, and duplicate the second from it by using Ctrl+drag. Then add the type with its baseline resting on an imaginary horizon line. Pull a perspective shadow forward, and manipulate it using Skew. Finish by setting the fill of each object.

Creating a Perspective Shadow

Click on the Rectangle tool	The cursor changes into a +
Draw a rectangle 5 inches wide by 1 inch high	
Click on the Pick tool	
Drag the rectangle's top center handle down; hold down Ctrl and press +	
Release the mouse button when the X scale is (100%)	A duplicate rectangle is created

The two rectangles should butt against each other. This line forms the horizon.

Click on the Text tool	The cursor becomes a +
Click on the center of the top rectangle	The Text I bar appears
Type **LONG SHADOWS**	
Click on the Pick tool	
Press Ctrl+T	The Artistic Text dialog box appears

Change to 48-point Jupiter Normal	Changes the point size and face
Click on OK	A 48-point LONG SHADOWS appears
Drag the text to align its base with the adjacent sides of the two rectangles	Long Shadows is now aligned to the horizon line
Drag the text's top center handle down; hold down Ctrl, and press +	
Release the mouse button when the X scale mirrored is (100%)	A duplicate LONG SHADOW is created
Click on the mirrored LONG SHADOWS	The Rotate/Skew handles appear
Position the cursor on the center two-headed bottom arrow	The cursor becomes a +
Drag the cursor to the right	The cursor goes into Skewmode
Position the cursor for approximately 50 degrees of skew	
Release the mouse button	LONG SHADOWS has some pseudo-perspective
Click on LONG SHADOWS' base text	
Press Shift+PgUp	To bring the base type to the front
Click on E̲dit	The Edit menu appears
Click on Select A̲ll	The status line reads: 4 objects selected
At the on-screen palette, right-click on No Outline	

When everything is in place (see fig. 6.3), assign object fills. Give the perspective shadow a 60% black fill and the base type a black fill. Give the background (top rectangle) a radial fountain fill from 40% black to white. Use Center Offset to move the center, -50% in both x and y. The foreground (bottom rectangle) uses a linear fountain fill that runs from 60% black to 10% black at a 110-degree angle.

 Tip   Click the right mouse button as you drag to leave an original.

Figure 6.3
The long
shadows
wireframe.

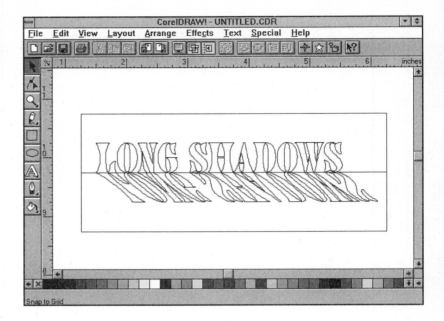

Notice that the shadows fill is set to be as dark as the darkest point of the foreground to ensure that it is, in fact, a shadow. Try setting the shadow to an intermediate tint (say, 40% black) for an interesting effect.

Creating Knockout Drops

No, knockout drops are not leftover barbiturates from a 1940s spy movie. *Knockout* refers to the white outline of the text that knocks (or drops) out of the drop shadow (see fig. 6.4). You can use this effect when printing a multiple color job in which the drop shadow is a different color from the type itself and the printer's specifications call for loose register. This method is one way to avoid problems with trapping (see Chapter 11, "Basic Printing Techniques").

This exercise is simple. Enlarge the size of the first letter in each word to give a small caps effect and reposition a number of characters to make the type follow a jumpy baseline. Notice that when you create knockout drops, you select **B**ehind Fill in the Outline Pen dialog box. This extra step prevents the outline from choking the fill, avoiding an undesirable result. The results of this exercise are shown in figure 6.5.

KNOCKOUT DROPS

Figure 6.4
The knockout drops effect.

Figure 6.5
Knockout drops wireframe.

Creating Knockout Drops

Click on the Text tool	The cursor becomes a +
Click on the page	The Text I bar appears
Type **KNOCKOUT**, *press Enter, type* **DROPS**	
Click on the Pick tool	

Press Ctrl+T	The Text dialog box appears
Change to 72-point Dom Casual BT	To change point size and face
Set Line Spacing to **80** *points*	
Click on OK	A 72-point KNOCKOUT DROPS appears
Click on 100% Black	Fills text
Right-click on White	Outlines text
Click on the Outline tool	Outline Pen fly-out menu appears
Click on the Outline Pen Options tool	Outline Pen dialog box appears
Click on <u>B</u>ehind Fill *and* <u>S</u>cale With Image	
Click on Rounded Corners *and* Rounded Line Caps	
At <u>W</u>idth, *enter* **4** points	
Click on OK	
Click on the Shape tool	
Drag a marquee around K and D	
Double-click on K's node	The Character Attributes dialog box appears
At Point Size, enter **100**	
At Vertical Shift, enter **-10**	
Click on OK	Initial caps are enlarged

Use the Shape tool to select and position individual characters to achieve a jumpy baseline:

Click on the Pick tool	
Drag KNOCKOUT DROPS *down and to the left, then press* +	
Release the mouse button when X and Y both are approximately -0.07	A duplicate KNOCKOUT DROPS is created

Assign a 20% black fill to the duplicate and preview. The drop shadow is in front of the base text. Use Shift+Page Down to send the drop shadow to the back.

Creating Embossed Text

Unlike standard drop shadows, which make type look as if it were floating above a page, embossed text makes type appear as if it were pressed into the page (see fig. 6.6). This effect is useful when rendering type that should look as if it were set in stone. CorelPHOTO-PAINT! and other bitmap paint programs can apply an embossed look to text or artwork with a built-in command. Vector-based CorelDRAW! offers a one-click solution. If you open the Preset Roll-up, found in the Special Menu, you find a Preset called EMBOSS. This effect was created by *Inside CorelDRAW!'s* technical editor, Giuseppe De Bellis.

Figure 6.6
The embossed text effect.

CorelDRAW! enables you to emulate embossed text by setting two drop shadows—one above and one below the base text. This provides the illusion of highlight and shadow. Although this solution is not the most elegant, it is effective and easy to accomplish. You can create interesting effects by setting the base type with the same tint or color as the background, or by carefully highlighting sections of the embossed text with slivers of tint, color, or fountain fill. If you work from a textured background, you can achieve a granite look, especially if you bring in a granite scan.

Creating Embossed Text

Click on the Rectangle tool	The cursor changes to a +
Draw a rectangle 5 1/4 inches wide by 1/2 inches high	
Click on 30% Black Fill	
Click on the Text tool	The cursor becomes a +
Click on the center of the rectangle	The Text I bar appears
Type **Emboss**	
Click on the Pick tool	
Press Ctrl+T	The Text dialog box appears

Change to 96-point ArnoldBoeD	Changes point size and face
Click on OK	A 96-point Emboss appears
Click on 30% Black	Fills base Emboss with 30% black
Drag Emboss, press +	
Release the mouse button when X and Y are approximately 0.02	A duplicate Emboss is created
Press Ctrl+R	Creates a third Emboss
Press Ctrl+PgDn	Sends the third Emboss back one layer
Click on White	Fills the highlight Emboss with white
Click on the leftmost Emboss	
Click on 50% Black	Fills the shadow emboss with 50% black
Drag a marquee around all three Embosses	
Press Ctrl+G	Groups Emboss
At on-screen palette, right-click on No Outline	The Embosses have no outline
Shift+click on the rectangle	The Emboss and the rectangle are selected
Click on Arrange	The Arrange menu appears
Click on Align	The Align dialog box appears
Click on Horizontal Center	
Click on Vertical Center	
Click on OK	The Emboss is centered in the rectangle (see fig. 6.7)

In the previous example, the lighting angle is set to come from the upper right corner of the page. To change the way the emboss is lit (altering the angle by 180 degrees), give the leftmost Emboss a 10% black tint, and the rightmost Emboss a 40% black tint.

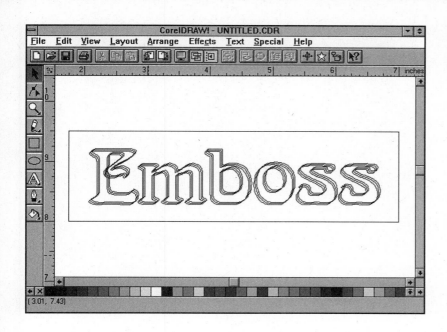

Figure 6.7
The emboss
wireframe.

Creating Neon Type

Neon signs are back in vogue. This part of American culture has made the jump from the real thing in Las Vegas and Times Square to hand-lettered signs, pickup trucks, and print advertising. CorelDRAW! makes it easy to create lettering with a neon look (see fig. 6.8). Such typography can work beautifully in black and white, spot, or process color. Certain typefaces work exceptionally well as neon type. One of the best faces to use is VAG Rounded; its rounded ends give the perfect tubular feel. For script faces, try Freestyle or Kaufmann. In general, use a face that is of equal weight throughout the letterform.

Building neon type with CorelDRAW! is not incredibly difficult, but it does take time, patience, and experimentation to get things perfect. The Outline Pen dialog box is essential when you create neon type. Be sure that you select Scale With Image, Rounded Corners, and Line Caps. This ensures that you can scale your neon type reliably and that it does not present any spiky outline surprises. Use the Blend effect, at its default setting of 20 steps, to create the illusion of neon.

Figure 6.8
Examples of
neon and tube
type.

 Tip For more information about using outlines and fills, see Chapter 7.

Back in the summertime paradise of Seaside, your hero, Joe DeLook, has just landed a design contract with his favorite waterfront bistro, The Neon Newt. The first project they want Joe to create is a full-color menu cover (see fig. 6.9). The cover depicts who else but Ned, namesake of The Neon Newt, and is lettered in their corporate typeface, VAG Rounded.

Joe decided on a simple design for the menu cover, which is to measure 6 inches by 8 inches. To begin the exercise, create a custom page with Page Frame.

Figure 6.9
The Neon Newt
menu cover.

Creating Neon Type

Click on F̲ile	The File menu appears
Click on N̲ew	A new page appears
Click on L̲ayout	The Layout menu appears
Click on P̲age Setup	The Page Setup dialog box appears
Roll down and click on C̲ustom	
At W̲idth, *enter* **6.0** inches	
At H̲eight, *enter* **8.0** inches	
Click on A̲dd Page Frame *(in the display section)*	
Click on OK	A 6-by-8-inch page is created with a page frame
Click on the page frame	
Click on the Fill tool	The Fill fly-out menu appears
Click on Uniform Fill	The Uniform Fill dialog box appears
Scroll down the Custom Palette and select Deep Navy Blue	
Click on OK	The Page Frame is filled with Deep Navy Blue

Drag the vertical ruler to create a guideline 0.5 inches from the left margin. Then drag the vertical ruler to create a guideline 0.5 inches from the right margin.

Click on the Text tool	The cursor becomes a +
Click on the page's top left corner	The Text I bar appears
Type **NEON**	
Click on the Pick tool	
Press Ctrl+T	The Artistic Text dialog box appears
Change to 96-point VAG Rounded BT	To change point size and face
Click on OK	A 96-point VAG Rounded NEON appears
At the on-screen palette, click on No Fill	
Click on the Outline tool	The Outline Pen fly-out menu appears
Click on Outline Color	The Outline Color dialog box appears

Scroll down the Custom Palette, and
select Deep Navy Blue

Click on OK   NEON is outlined with Deep Navy Blue

Click on the Outline tool   The Outline Pen fly-out menu appears

Click on Outline Pen Options   The Outline Pen dialog box appears

Click on <u>S</u>cale With Image

Click on Rounded Corners *and* Round Line Caps

At <u>W</u>idth, *enter* **0.222** inches

Click on OK   Base NEON has a fat outline, the same
                                       color as the background

Drag NEON *to butt against the left guideline*

Click on the Shape tool

Drag the letterspace arrow to the   NEON is letterspaced
right guideline

Click on the Pick tool

Drag NEON *to the bottom of the page*

Hold down Ctrl and press + (on the numeric keypad)

Release the mouse button   A duplicate NEON is created

Click on the Text tool   The Text I Bar appears

Backspace over NEON *and type* **NEWT**

Click on the Pick tool   NEWT is set in 96-point VAG Rounded

Now that you have set the type, get Ned the Newt. Use Draw's Symbol Library to summon the
slimy creature:

Click on <u>S</u>pecial   The Special menu appears

Click on Sym<u>b</u>ols Roll-Up   The Symbols Roll-Up menu appears

Click on Animals1

At Symbol #, *type* **77**   Selects Ned the Newt

At Size, *type* **8** *inches*   To change the size of Ned the Newt

Drag and drop Ned the Newt *onto the*   A big newt appears
page

At the on-screen palette, click on No Fill

Click on the Outline tool	The Outline Pen fly-out menu appears
Click on Outline Color	The Outline Color dialog box appears
Scroll down the Custom Palette, and select Grass Green	
Click on OK	Ned is outlined with Grass Green
Click on the Outline tool	The Outline Pen fly-out menu appears
Click on Outline Pen Options	The Outline Pen dialog box appears
Click on Scale With Image	
Click on Rounded Corners *and* Round Line Caps	
At Width, *enter* **0.167** inches	
Click on OK	

At this point, all the base elements are on the page. You need to create the highlight elements into which you will blend the base elements. CorelDRAW! has a handy one-button shortcut to place duplicates directly on top of their originals. You might remember pressing + while dragging an object to create a duplicate. You also can select any object and press + without moving the object to create a duplicate.

Click on NEON	
Press +	NEON is duplicated
Click on the Outline tool	The Outline Pen fly-out menu appears
Click on Hairline	
Click on the Outline tool	The Outline Pen fly-out menu appears
Click on Outline Color	The Outline Color dialog box appears
In the Custom Palette, select Magenta	
Click on OK	Highlight NEON is outlined with Magenta
Drag a marquee around both NEONs	Both NEONs are selected
Click on Effects	The Effects menu appears
Click on Blend Roll-Up	The Blend Roll-Up menu appears

Use the default settings of 20 Blend Steps and 0 degrees Rotation.

Click on Apply	NEON is blended (see fig. 6.10)

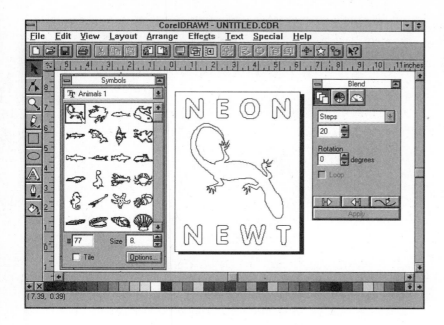

Figure 6.10
Creating the
Neon Newt
menu cover.

Now press F9 to see what you have done so far. Notice that the outline seems to fade into the background. If you recall, this effect was created by using the same color for both the background and the type's base outline. Repeat the last steps (duplicate outline, change outline width and color, then blend) to neonize the word NEWT. Then finish off Ned himself. Use a Turquoise Hairline for Ned's highlight. Notice how different Ned looks, as opposed to the type (refer to fig. 6.9). Ned appears to be popping off instead of fading into the background because of his base outline color.

Creating Tube Type

Tube type is similar in concept, execution, and appearance to neon type. Again, the Blend effect is used to create an illusion. But instead of a blend radiating outward, tube type grows inward to create a three-dimensional effect (see fig. 6.11). Think of gel toothpaste, silicon caulk, or the lettering on a birthday cake to get the gist of what tube type is all about.

Neon type gets its magic from blending two similar pieces of type with different outline widths and tints. Tube type, on the other hand, does not necessarily use an outline. It works its wonders with an object's shape and fill.

Figure 6.11
Tube type.

To create tube type, start with a flowing script like Freestyle. Take care of any character pair kerning, duplicate the text string, and drag the duplicate off to the side (you use this for a drop shadow). Give the original text string a black fill/no outline, convert it to curves, and break it apart. Recombine any multiple path characters (such as A, B, D, and so on). Then, working letter by letter, create a duplicate of each letter. Make sure that the duplicate is on the top, and use the Shape tool to create a character just a little bit shorter and narrower, but, more importantly, thinner than the original.

Fill the skinny character with a 10% gray highlight fill. Marquee-select the skinny character together with the original character, and use Blend to impart the illusion of depth.

Do not break the duplicate character apart to manipulate the individual paths! If you do, the blend does not work properly, and you go crazy trying to fix it.

Creating Tube Type

Instead of rendering an entire word of tube type, create only one letter: a 500-point Q. Working in large scale gives you greater precision in line placement, which is crucial in developing different lighting angles.

Click on the Text tool	The cursor becomes a +
Click on the center of the page	The Text I bar appears
Type **Q**	
Click on the Pick tool	

Press Ctrl+T	The Artistic Text dialog box appears
Change to 500-point FreestyleScrD	To change point size and face
Click on OK	A 500-point Freestyle Script Q appears
At the on-screen palette, right-click on No Outline	
Click on 100% Black	The Q is filled with 100% black, with no outline
Click on **A**rrange	The Arrange menu appears
Click on Con**v**ert To Curves	The Q is converted to curves
Press + on the numeric keypad	The Q is duplicated
Click on 10% Black	The Q is filled with 10% black
Click on the Shape tool	

Move individual nodes inward and adjust control points to form a skinny Q inside the original. Take your time and adjust the control points as needed, pushing the highlight to the top right of the letter (see fig. 6.12). Remember, you can use the Nudge feature to move selected nodes around or drag directly on a line. Do not break the duplicate character apart into its individual paths! Next, create the blend by using Draw's default (20-step) setting (see fig. 6.13).

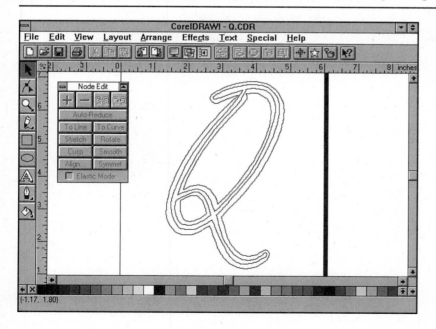

Figure 6.12
Before the blend.

Figure 6.13
After the blend.

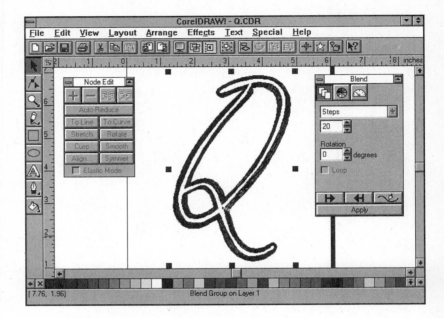

Creating the Blend

Click on the Pick tool	The skinny Q is selected
Shift+click on the original Q	Both Qs are selected
Click on Effects	The Effects menu appears
Click on **B**lend Roll-Up	The Blend Roll-Up menu appears

Use the default settings of 20 Blend Steps and 0 degrees Rotation.

Click on Apply	A 20-step blend appears

Go ahead and preview the tube type Q. If you are not happy with the way the lighting angle looks, delete the blend, tweak the skinny Q, and blend again.

Tip   Click on the numeric keypad's plus symbol (+) to duplicate any selected object.

To finish a piece of tube type, use the duplicate you made to set a drop shadow behind it; it will provide the extra oomph to pop the image off the printed page.

Tube type might seem like a long way to get the same effect as neon type, but it actually offers more. Although it takes more time and patience, tube type provides far more control over each individual character. It might take all afternoon to create a single line of words, but the results will be worth it.

Creating Punk Text

On occasion, you might need to use an informal typeface that looks as if it were hand-lettered. In these cases, you find that the standard-issue CorelDRAW! fonts do not fit the bill—until you pull a cheap trick out of the bag: punk text.

The name might conjure up visions of black leather and adolescent angst, but punk text is one of the best-kept secrets to create fast, easy, and distinctive display heads. Where would you use such unique typography? Anything that has to do with rock and roll, such as T-shirts, concert flyers, compact-disc and cassette-tape packaging, and band logos.

Using the Text Tool Method

You can create punk text quickly by using the Text tool. Plug in the type in your choice of base typeface; sans-serif faces like Bauhaus Heavy are good choices. Next, select the text and convert to curves. Switch to the Shape tool and drag a marquee around the entire text block. Double-click on any selected node to bring up the Node Edit Roll-Up menu, and change all the line segments to straight lines. There you go: punk text (see fig. 6.14).

Some characters fare better than others in the conversion process, as do certain typefaces. Angular characters, such as A, E, and F, might not change at all, and require artistic persuasion. Use the Shape tool to finesse the letterforms. Certain effects, such as using different colors/tints for each letter or rotating individual letters, require you to break apart and possibly recombine characters.

As a general rule, the more complex a face, the poorer a choice it is for creating punk text because the results often are unreadable. However, a face that already consists of purely straight lines—such as Machine—is not a candidate for conversion.

Figure 6.14
Punk type.

Tweaked Vogue Bold

RENFREW
ABCDEFGHIJKLM
NOPQRSTUVWXYZ

Hand-Altered: R

BAHAMAS
ABCDEFGHIJKLM
NOPQRSTUVWXYZ

Hand-Altered: B, C, E, G, O, R

OTTOWA
ABCDEFGHIJKLM
NOPQRSTUVWXYZ

If you create a punk face that you really like, you can always save it as a PostScript or TrueType typeface by using the Symbol/Typeface Export Filter. By doing this, you save even more time when you set type for the same account. After you do this, you can export the font for use with those few applications that can't use PostScript or TrueType by converting the font with Ares FontMinder.

After you have created your punk text, you can apply any CorelDRAW! treatment. Just remember that when you convert text to curves, you will not be able to edit it, so be sure to check for typos before converting to curves. To finish, try using punk text with drop shadows or knockout drops.

Using the Duplicate Method

Another quick way to create punk text is to duplicate a text string, drag the duplicate down the page, and change it to a completely different typeface. Then, use Blend to mutate between the two different typefaces. Zingo—instant punk text! The more blend steps you use, the more gradual the change. Separate the blend elements, ungroup the blend, and delete the iterations you don't need.

This technique surely leads you into uncharted typographical territory. Font creation has never been so immediate, not to mention random. Certainly, much of what you get with this technique is unreadable, but you are bound to create at least one usable style.

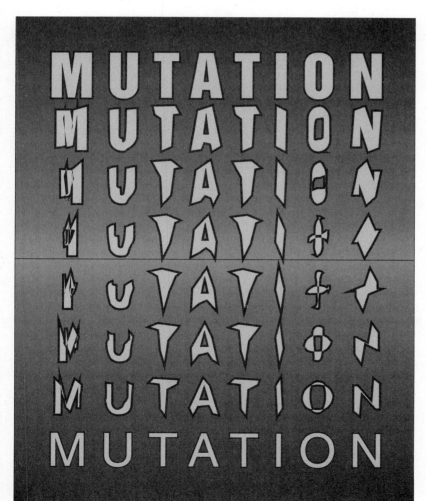

Figure 6.15
More mutant punk type, courtesy of the blend effect.

Creating Bevel Text

Have you ever wanted your type to appear as if it had beveled edges? By following this straightforward but exacting process, you can create multidimensional type like a pro. To bevel a piece of type, you must add facets to each side (see fig. 6.16). You accomplish this through the diligent use of the Pencil tool, snap-to guidelines, and the Pick tool.

Figure 6.16
The beveled text
effect.

The trick to maintaining your sanity when creating beveled type is to start with a typeface that has a minimum of curves. Machine is a good choice because it has no curves at all. You also can try beveling punk text for an ultra-custom look. If the face contains curves, expect to spend extra time getting the curves to work out properly.

When you bevel text, the idea is to create the illusion of depth. To do this, use different tints of gray or base color on each side of a character. With process colors, you can easily add different percentages of black to the base CMYK mix. Spot colors (or good old black) can be altered with different screen densities. If you want to get real tricky (and spend an additional amount of time), you could use fountain fills on each facet, altering colors, angles, and edge padding appropriately.

In the following exercise, you bevel just one character, an E, set in 600-point Machine. Like the previous tube type exercise, this illustrates the technique without becoming too cumbersome. Create the E with a full-beveled surface, as opposed to a flat surface with beveled edges, which you can try to create on your own. Use the approach illustrated here, along with a variation of the tube type technique, to apply a flat surface bevel (see fig. 6.17).

Figure 6.17
A slightly different bevel effect.

Creating Beveled Text

Click on the Text tool	The cursor becomes a +
Click on the center of the page	The Text I bar appears
Type **E**	
Click on the Pick tool	
Press Ctrl+T	The Artistic Text dialog box appears
Change to 600-point Machine	Changes point size and face
Click on OK	A 600-point Machine E appears
Click on **L**ayout	The Layout menu appears

Make sure that Snap-to Grid is off and Snap-to Guidelines is on.

Click on the Zoom tool	The Zoom fly-out menu appears
Click on +	
Marquee-select E	To zoom up on E
Click on the Pick tool	
Position the cursor over the vertical ruler	
Drag the guideline to the left edge of the E *and repeat for each vertical edge*	
Position the cursor over the horizontal ruler	
Drag the guideline to the top edge of the E *and repeat for each horizontal edge*	

Now that the edge guidelines are in, draw the center guidelines by using a sneaky little trick. You might recall back in Chapter 5 that you used nonprinting, guideline-layer ellipses to help balance your composition. This time, cut a few rectangles in half to determine the centerlines of the E. After the center guidelines are drawn, the rectangles are deleted (see fig. 6.18).

Figure 6.18
Beveling the E
on-screen.

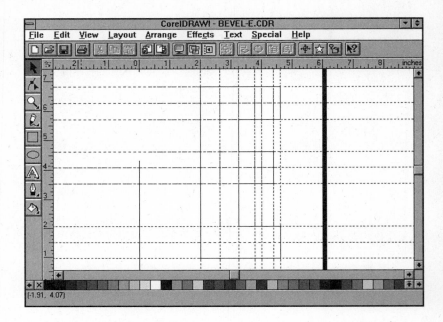

Drawing the Centerlines

Click on the Rectangle tool

Starting at the left side of the E, take the following steps:

*Click and drag a rectangle the width
of the E's downstroke*

Click on the Pick tool — The rectangle is selected

Click on Effe<u>c</u>ts — The Effects menu appears

Click on <u>S</u>tretch & Mirror — The Stretch & Mirror dialog box appears

At Horizontal, *type* **50**

Click on OK — The rectangle is half as wide

*Snap the rectangle to the leftmost
guideline*

*Position the cursor over the vertical
ruler*

Drag the guideline to the rectangle's right edge	A centerline is drawn
Click on the Rectangle tool	

Starting at the top of the E, take the following steps:

Drag a rectangle the depth of the E's top cross-stroke	
Click on the Pick tool	The rectangle is selected
Click on the T*ransform button*	The Transform Roll-Up menu appears
Click on Scale & Mirror	
At Vertical, *type* **50**	
Click on Apply	The rectangle is half as tall
Snap the rectangle to the uppermost guideline	
Position the cursor over the horizontal ruler	
Drag the guideline to the rectangle's bottom edge	A centerline is drawn

Use this procedure to draw centerlines throughout the E's cross-strokes. Drag two more vertical guidelines to denote the right side cross-stroke facets. Then delete the four boxes.

Click on the Pencil tool

Draw a series of three- and four-sided polygons to form the facets of the E (see fig. 6.19). Draw's Layer Control comes in handy on this project! This procedure is easiest if you create another layer for the facets and switch MultiLayer off.

Finish by assigning a fill to each of the facets. Use an 80% black fill for all the southsides, a 20% fill for all the northsides, a 60% fill for all the eastsides, and a 40% fill for the westside (see fig. 6.20). Experiment with and without object outlines.

Figure 6.19
The beveled E
wireframe.

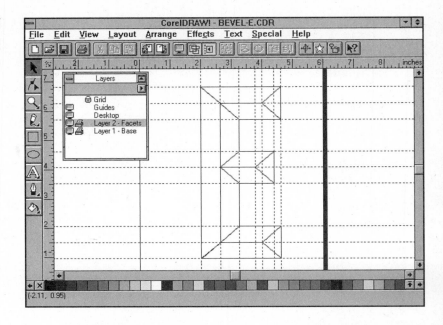

Figure 6.20
The beveled E in
full-color mode.

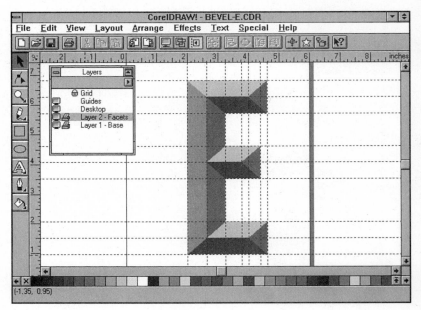

Creating Chrome Type

The chrome look is almost as overdone as the common drop shadow, but many desktop designers are asked to set type in this style. Chrome type takes time and effort to render; it is not a point-and-click affair. Well-executed chrome type looks as shiny as the emblems on a custom show car, but poorly constructed chrome type can be complex and time-consuming to print. You must consider two things: visual appeal and image engineering. If it looks great but does not print, you have not done your job. The same is true for the reverse scenario.

Hopefully, after working (and reading) through the rest of this book, you will understand how to work with fountain fills without choking your printer, or worse, your service bureau's imagesetter, which might result in overtime charges for intensive pages. The trick to creating chrome type that looks great and prints reliably is to construct the fountain fills as simple objects layered on top of the original type. Mindlessly fountain-filling large strings of type—as type—can needlessly tie up a printer's RIP. Your responsibility is to put your files together properly.

Traditionally, chrome type is rendered with an airbrush, but CorelDRAW! does not have an Airbrush tool so you must use a combination of methods. High-end chrome type is constructed by using both fountain fills and blends to achieve a metallic luster. Starbursts—glints of light—also can be built by using either a radial fountain fill or a blend between a fat and a skinny object, using a tube type-like methodology. When used sparingly, these sparkles add the finishing touch.

The method you are going to use makes heavy use of the Shape tool to break character outlines into smaller chunks. The chunks are then assigned different fountain fills, depending on their geographical location on the face of the character. At the very least, you might find that breaking a character into two chunks, upon a base character, provides a good foundation for building. The bottom edge of the fountain fill of the top chunk can fade into the base character; the top edge of the bottom chunk can contrast sharply with the base.

Once again, you create just one character—C—due to the complexity of the process. Good-looking chrome type takes a bit of effort and experimentation. To make your life easier, you can use Layer Control to orchestrate your drawing. When you are done with the letter C, try setting the rest of the word CHROME.

Creating Chrome Type

Click on the Text tool	The cursor becomes a +
Click on the center of the page	The Text I bar appears
Type **C**	
Click on the Pick tool	
Press Ctrl+T	The Text dialog box appears
Change to 500-point Aachen BT	Changes point size and face
Click on OK	A 500-point Aachen C appears
Click on L̲ayout	The Layout menu appears

Make sure that Snap-to Grid is off and that Snap-to Guidelines is on.

Click on the Zoom tool	The Zoom fly-out menu appears
Click on +	
Marquee-select the C	To zoom in on the C
Click on the Pick tool	
Position the cursor over the vertical ruler	
Drag the guideline to the left edge of the C's downstroke; repeat for the right edge of the C's downstroke	
Position the cursor over the horizontal ruler	
Drag the guideline to the bottom edge of the C's top serif; repeat for the top edge of the C's bottom serif	See figure 6.21
Press + on the numeric keypad	The C is duplicated
Press Ctrl+Q	The duplicate C is converted to curves
Click on the Shape tool	

At each of the two bottom leftmost guideline intersection points, take the following steps:

Double-click	The Node Edit Roll-Up menu appears
Click on +	A node is added

After the two extra nodes have been added, follow these steps:

Marquee-select all four nodes that fall on the guideline intersection points

At the Node Edit Roll-Up menu, follow these steps:

Click on **B**reak	The object is now four subpaths
Click on the page	Deselects the nodes
Click on the top left node (of the four)	The node is selected
Click on **D**elete	The line segment is deleted
Click on the top right node (of the three)	The node is selected
Click on **D**elete	The line segment is deleted

You now have an object with just two subpaths.

Click on **A**rrange	The Arrange menu appears
Click on Brea**k** Apart	The duplicate C is now two separate (open path) objects
Click on the page	Deselects the two objects
Click on the top half of the C	The top half of the C is selected
Click on the Pencil tool	The cursor becomes a +
Draw a line between the top half's two lower nodes	Closes the path
Click on the Pick tool	Deselects the Pencil Tool
Click on the bottom half of the C	Selects the C's bottom half
Click on the Pencil tool	The cursor becomes a +
Draw a line between the bottom half's two upper nodes	Closes the path (see fig. 6.22)
Click on **E**dit	The Edit menu appears
Click on Select **A**ll	All the objects are selected

At the on-screen palette, right-click on No Outline

You now have three separate objects: the original C, along with the top and bottom halves of the duplicate C. Give the original C a 10% black fill. Experiment with different linear fountain fills for the top and bottom halves of the duplicate C. Start with a 10% to 60% 90-degree fill for the top, and a 30% to 70% 90-degree fill for the bottom. Try adding a duplicate C, with an outline but no fill, and bring it to front. Then add a neon effect for a glowing result, as shown in figure 6.23. You can also use Custom fountain fills for more realistic effects. In addition, you can use CorelDRAW! 5.0's new PowerClips function to create great-looking chrome type.

Figure 6.21
The C with guidelines drawn.

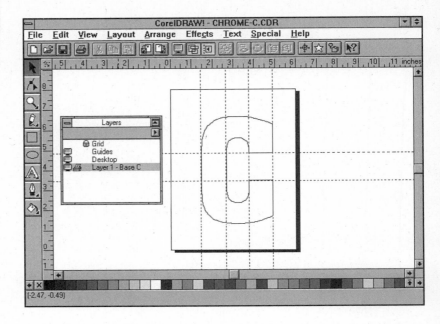

Figure 6.22
The finished C wireframe.

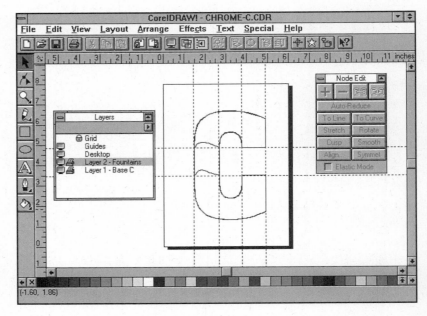

Figure 6.23
The chrome C
with a neon
effect.

Combining effects and techniques is one way to render distinctive, eye-catching artwork. Use the chrome, bevel, and neon effects together to yield impressive results. When used in combination with CorelDRAW!'s Extrude effect, you can achieve wonderful results.

The most realistic chrome type has images reflected on its surfaces. To achieve that degree of realism (without spending days trying to mimic the look), you need to use a real three-dimensional rendering package. In particular, use a rendering program that can implement *reflection maps*. Reflection maps, as their name implies, add a mirror-like effect to objects, creating a high degree of photo-realism. Visual Reality, from Visual Software, includes a powerful three-dimensional rendering program, Renderize Live. You can find information on Visual Reality in Chapter 9, "Advanced Drawing Techniques."

Creating Spin Type

Spin type often is seen in program manuals and advertisements, but gets little work in the real world. This effect can be used to add the illusion of motion or depth to an object (see fig. 6.24). Spin type is fast and easy to do. You can use one of two techniques: the Multiple Repeat-Rotate-Leave Original technique or the Blend effect. Each technique has advantages. If you are not sure how much rotation you want, try the Multiple Repeat-Rotate-Leave Original technique. If you want to change tint as the type rotates, use the Blend effect.

Figure 6.24
Spin type
created using
Multiple Repeat-
Rotate-Leave
Original.

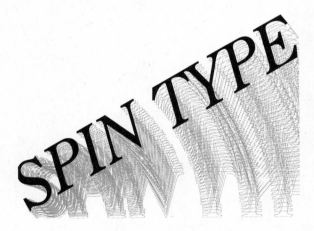

Remember in Chapter 1 when you rotated the Stealth? Now you are going to move the object's rotation point and use Rotate to rotate the piece of type one degree while leaving an original. Then, repeatedly using the keyboard shortcut, Ctrl+R, repeat the step, amazing yourself at how fast you can grow a piece of spin type!

Using the Multiple Repeat-Rotate-Leave Original Technique

Click on the Text tool	The cursor becomes a +
Click on the center of the page	The Text I bar appears
Type **SPIN TYPE**	
Click on the Pick tool	
Press Ctrl+T	The Text dialog box appears
Change to 48-point Century Oldstyle	To change point size and face
In the drop down Style *Field,* Select *Normal-Italic*	
Click on OK	A 48-point Century Oldstyle Italic SPIN TYPE appears
At the on-screen palette, click on No Fill, *right-click on* 30% black	
Click on SPIN TYPE	The Rotate arrows appear
Position the cursor over the center of rotation	
Drag the center of rotation below and to the left of SPIN TYPE	
Position the cursor over the top right handle	The cursor's pointer becomes a +
Drag the top right handle up and left	A blue dashed box replaces the arrow handles. The status line shows amount of rotation in degrees
Press +	The status line reads Leave Original
When Angle is 1.0 degree, release the mouse button	A duplicate SPIN TEXT is created, rotated 1.0 degree from the original
Press Ctrl+R	Repeats the procedure

Use Ctrl+R another 28 times, and give the last object no outline and a 100% black fill.

The Multiple Repeat-Rotate-Leave Original technique used to create spin type also is valuable when creating objects that radiate from a central point, such as petals on a flower or spokes on a wheel.

Next, try spinning a bit differently. This time, make use of the Blend effect to create your SPIN TYPE (see fig. 6.25). This next exercise uses the very first and last SPIN TYPEs you just created, so save the file if you want to hold onto it.

Figure 6.25
Spin type created using the Blend effect.

To begin, select and delete all but the very first and last SPIN TYPEs. When you have done that, proceed with the following steps:

Using the Blend Effect

Click on the bottom SPIN TYPE

At the on-screen palette, click on 10% black, *right-click on* No Outline

Click on the top SPIN TYPE

At the on-screen palette, click on 50% black, *right-click on* No Outline

Shift-click on the bottom SPIN TYPE	Both SPIN TYPEs are selected
Click on Effe**c**ts	The Effects menu appears
Click on **B**lend Roll-Up	The Blend Roll-Up menu appears
Click on Apply	A 20-step blend appears
Click on **A**rrange	The Arrange menu appears

Click on **S**eparate	The blend is separated
Click on the page	To deselect the blend
Click on the top SPIN TYPE	
Click on the Fill tool	The Fill fly-out menu appears
Click on 100% Black	
Press F9 to view the Blended Spin Type	

Notice how the Blend effect SPIN TYPE differs from the first technique. Of course, the outline and fill characteristics were set up differently, but it is more than that. See how the Blend effect text moves in a straight line? Now take a look at the Multiple Repeat-Rotate-Leave Original type; it moves in a gentle arc. Try each technique with different fills, outlines, and rotation percentages. To have the spin layer go in the opposite direction when using the Blend effect, select both originals and click on Reverse Order (on the **A**rrange menu, under **O**rder) before blending.

Creating Two-Tone Type

Have you ever had the need for a piece of type that is half positive (black letters on a white background) and the other half reversed (white letters on a black background)? CorelDRAW! provides a straightforward way to accomplish this effect (see fig. 6.26). By combining the text with an object, you can create two-tone type in a matter of mouse clicks.

Figure 6.26
Two-tone type.

This technique is so easy that it might bring tears to the eyes of any graphics designer who ever had to do it using the old reversal stats and a technical pen.

Remember, after you combine text with any other object, it is not editable. Always make a duplicate of the type and objects you are about to combine for safekeeping. Drag duplicates off to the side just in case you need to make an edit or adjust character kerning.

You also can easily add a spot color to the design by dragging a duplicate of the original shape behind the combined object. Change the tint/color of the duplicate object and send it behind the original.

Creating Two-Tone Type

Click on the Text tool	The cursor becomes a +
Click on the center of the page	The Text I bar appears
Type **TWO-TONE TYPE**	
Click on the Pick tool	
Press Ctrl+T	The Text dialog box appears
Change to 72-point Exotc350 DmBd BT, *then click on* **C**enter	To change the point size, face, and alignment
Click on OK	A 72-point TWO-TONE TYPE appears
Click on the Pencil tool	The cursor becomes a +
Draw a triangle taller than, but not as wide as, TWO-TONE TYPE	
Click on the Pick tool	
Shift-click on TWO-TONE TYPE	Both objects are selected
Press Ctrl+A	The Align dialog box appears
Click on Horizontal and Vertical **C**enter	
Click on OK	The objects are horizontally and vertically aligned
Press Ctrl+L	The objects are combined
At the on-screen palette, right-click on No Outline, *and click on* 100% Black	

Preview your work. If it does not look quite the way you want it, immediately undo the combination, then adjust the elements and recombine.

Creating Letterspaced Type

Letterspaced (or blown-out) type, also known as force-justified type, is a simple task with Draw's snap-to guidelines and interactive letterspacing. By dragging out a pair of vertical guidelines, you can adjust type to fit any width (see fig. 6.27). Set your type with the left side hitting the left guideline and switch to the Shape tool. Draw displays the type's interactive spacing controls. Drag the horizontal (intercharacter) marker to pull the type out to the desired width. To set interword space, press and hold down Ctrl while you drag.

D e L O O K   D E S I G N

Figure 6.27
Blown-out text.

S E A S I D E , U . S . A .   8 0 0 / 5 5 5 - 1 2 3 4

Creating Letterspaced Text

Position the cursor over the vertical ruler	
Drag the guideline to the left side of the page	
Position the cursor over the vertical ruler	
Drag the guideline four inches from the first guideline	
Click on the Text tool	The cursor becomes a +
Click on the left guideline	The Text I bar appears
Type **DeLOOK** *(use 3 or 4 spaces)* **DESIGN**	
Click on the Pick tool	
Press Ctrl+T	The Text dialog box appears
Change to 24-point Eras Light	Changes point size and face
Click on <u>N</u>one	Changes justification
Click on OK	A 24-point, Eras Light DeLOOK DESIGN appears
Click on the Shape tool	

Drag DeLOOK DESIGN's intercharacter marker to the right guideline and release the mouse button	DeLOOK DESIGN is letterspaced
Click on the Text tool	The cursor becomes a +
Click on the left guideline	The Text I bar appears
Type **SEASIDE, U.S.A.** *(use 3 spaces)* **800/555-1234**	
Click on the Pick tool	
Press Ctrl+T	The Text dialog box appears
Change to 12-point Eras Light	Changes point size and face
Click on OK	A 12-point, Eras Light "SEASIDE, U.S.A. 800/555-1234" appears
Click on the Shape tool	
Drag SEASIDE, U.S.A. 800/555-1234's *intercharacter marker to the right guideline and release the mouse button*	SEASIDE, U.S.A, 800/555-1234 is letterspaced (see fig. 6.28)

Figure 6.28
Force-justified
letterhead.

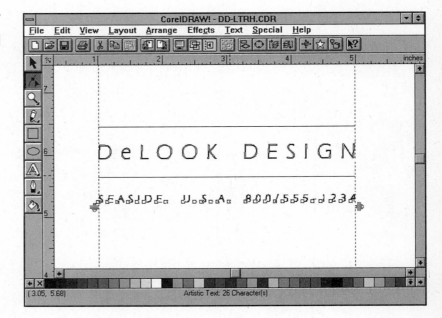

Creating Texture Type

You fooled around with texture text in Chapter 5, "Advanced Typography." Remember creating the Wave masked bitmap? You can use the same technique with a scanner to create some interesting texture type (see fig. 6.29). Of course, you can use bitmaps with type, without masking. When combined with beveled, embossed, or a carefully extruded technique, texture type can be even more striking (see fig. 6.30).

Figure 6.29
Texture type.

CorelDRAW!'s fractal texture fills are a wonderful source of textures. However, try not to overdo it with the fractal fills because your file sizes (and print times) can explode!

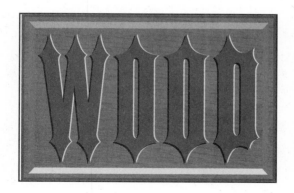

Figure 6.30
Texture type combined with other techniques.

Using CorelPHOTO-PAINT! To Create Type

You don't have to create special type effects using just CoreDRAW! alone; by making use of version 5.0's tight integration with PhotoPaint, you can accomplish some awesome effects. This section of the chapter assumes that you know how to apply filters within PhotoPaint, and instead of walking you through a bunch of tedious step-by-step exercises, it illustrates the wild looks you can get from applying various filters to black-and-white type. You can apply one filter or combine them for a more refined (not to mention bizarre) effect.

Much of the cutting-edge typographical design work you see today is accomplished in a similar manner—with Adobe Photoshop. This program is the de facto graphic arts standard for image editing. One of its most wonderful features is its ability to rasterize Adobe Illustrator (AI) files. You are in for a great treat because PhotoPaint Version 5.0 offers similar versatility!

PhotoPaint opens and rasterizes CorelDRAW! CDR files. This feature makes it easy to create your base type within Draw, then apply the wild effects in PhotoPaint, without having to tolerate PhotoPaint's far more limited Text tool. For the purposes of these exercises, when you open the CDR file, open it as a grayscale image (256 shades of gray) at 300 dpi. You can fool around with color type on your own after you learn the basics.

Applying the Diffuse Filter to Type

PhotoPaint's Diffuse filter can be used to create an interesting effect that runs from slightly blurry to three-dimensional, depending on the intensity of the filter's setting. The BlacklightD typeface is used here to illustrate the effect.

Using the Motion Blur Filter

Want to give your type a feeling of speed? Apply a Motion Blur filter. Whether you are creating advertising for a sports-car dealership or just need to imply movement or action, the Motion Blur filter gives your type a look that cruises anywhere from 20 to 200 miles per hour. These examples were prepared using the Benguiat Gothic Bold Italic typeface.

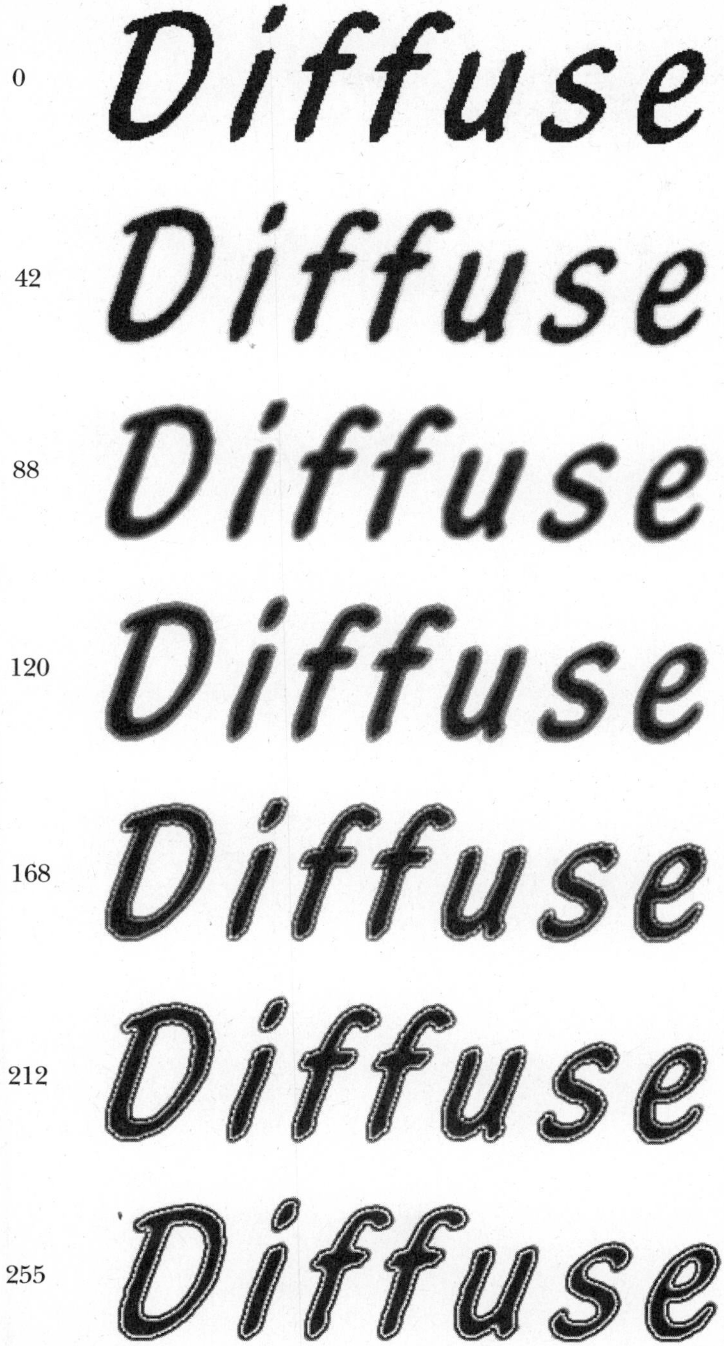

0 *Diffuse*

Figure 6.31
Various Diffuse
Filter settings.

42 *Diffuse*

88 *Diffuse*

120 *Diffuse*

168 *Diffuse*

212 *Diffuse*

255 *Diffuse*

Figure 6.32
Various motion
blur intensities.

MOTION BLUR 0

MOTION BLUR 8

MOTION BLUR 16

MOTION BLUR 24

MOTION BLUR 32

MOTION BLUR 40

 48

0

Figure 6.33
Around the clock
with motion blur
at a set speed
of 32.

3

4

5

6

7

8

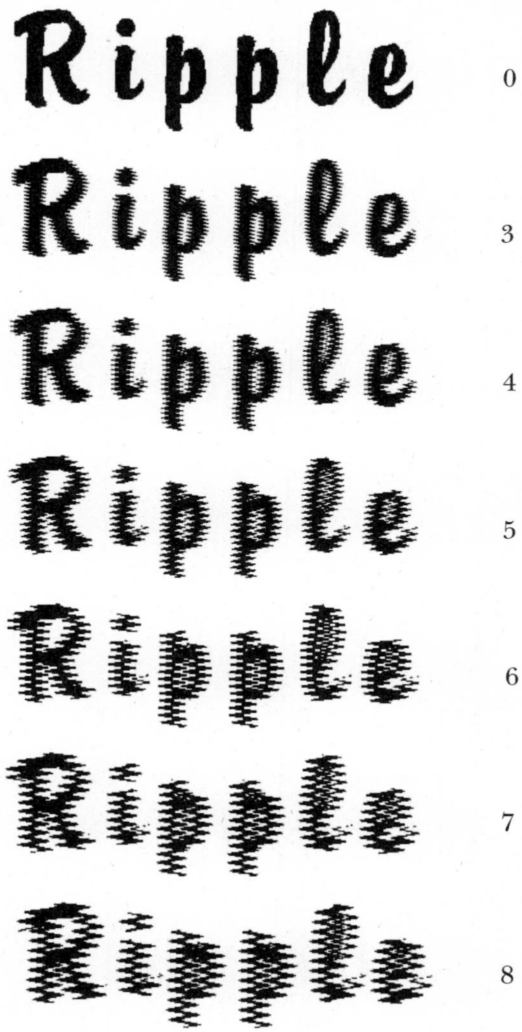

Figure 6.34
The Horizontal
Ripple filter at
identical periods
and amplitudes.

Ripple 0

Ripple 3

Ripple 4

Ripple 5

Ripple 6

Ripple 7

Ripple 8

Using the Ripple Filter

This is the perfect effect to portray seasickness. The Ripple filter really does a number, and this is best used with type only at low settings. Higher settings render the type totally illegible, although one never knows—this might be the effect you're after! This example uses the BrodyD typeface.

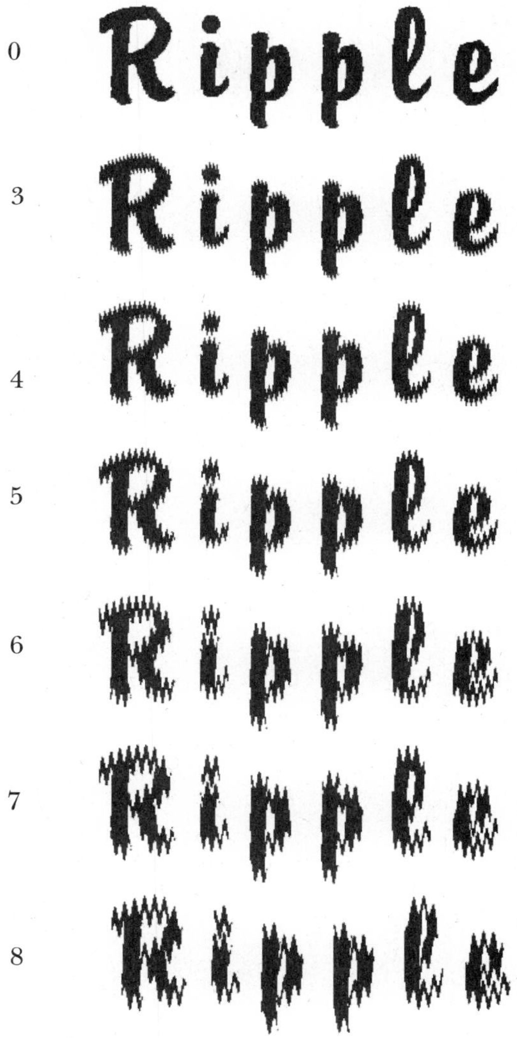

0

3

4

5

6

7

8

Figure 6.35
The Vertical
Ripple filter at
identical periods
and amplitudes.

Putting CorelDRAW! to Work

Figure 6.36
The Horizontal
and Vertical
Ripple filter at
identical periods
and amplitudes.

Using the Glass Block Filter

The Glass Block filter resembles looking through a wall of (what else!) glass blocks. To make this visual trick work, you need to create a piece of type that intrigues the eye so that the viewer is pulled into the illusion.

In this example, the Uptight Neon typeface is filled with a custom fountain fill that ping-pongs between shades of gray. The type is outlined with a fat, dark gray tone and placed behind the fill. The type is kerned so that it is tight, but (for the most part) not touching. This file will take a while to open in PhotoPaint. Be patient; the program must interpret a ton of information.

The image was softened before the glass block filter was applied.

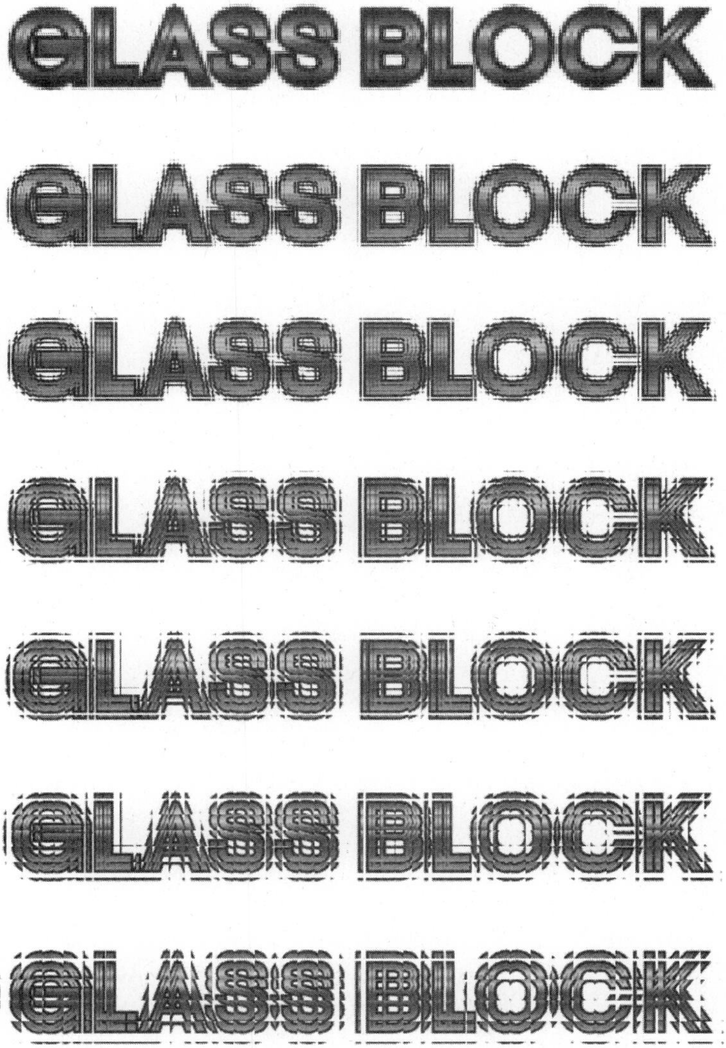

35

25

20

15

12

10

8

Figure 6.37
The Glass Block filter at identical horizontal and vertical settings.

II

Putting CorelDRAW! to Work

Using the Impressionist Filter

Just to confuse their users, Corel decided to name two very different filters with two very similar names. You can use the Impressionist filter for various type treatments. Do not confuse this filter with the Impressionism filter (what a difference an "m" makes!). In this example, the NevisonCasD typeface was used.

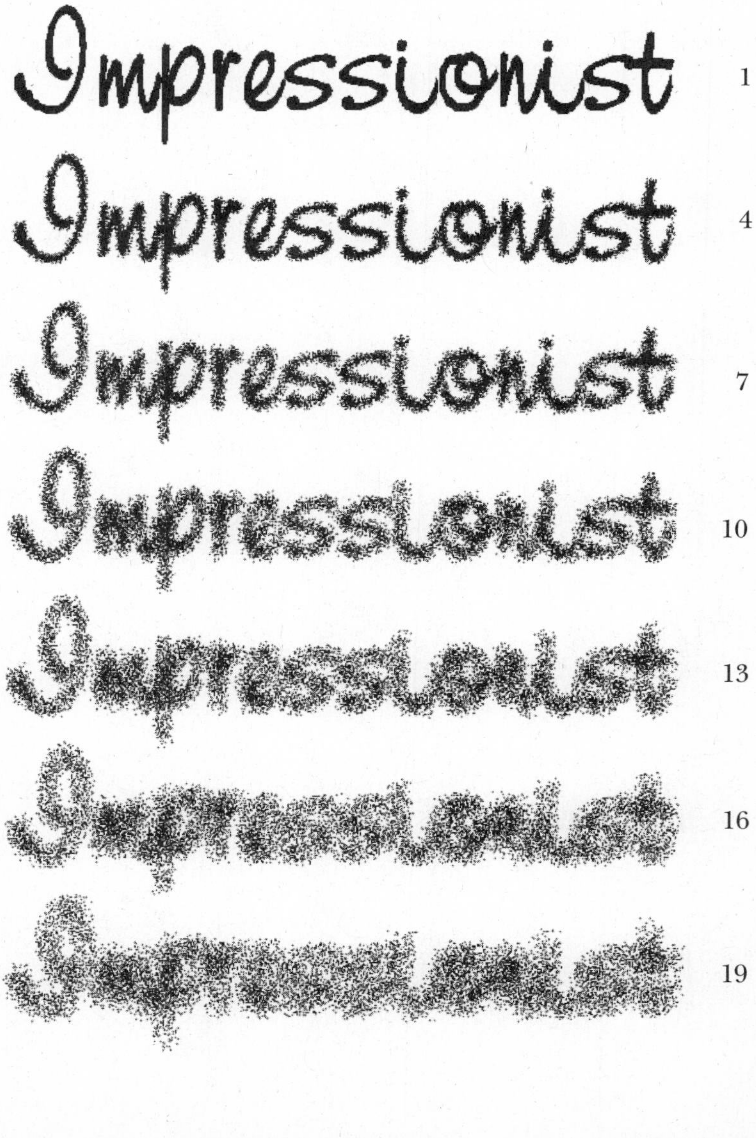

Figure 6.38
The Impressionist filter at identical horizontal and vertical settings.

Impressionist   1

Impressionist   4

Impressionist   7

Impressionist   10

Impressionist   13

Impressionist   16

Impressionist   19

Using the Lens Effect

CorelDRAW! 5.0's dramatic new Lens effect has some great typographical applications. You can create type that floats over anything and casts a realistic shadow (not a poor facsimile). The Lens effect is covered in depth in Chapter 9, "Advanced Drawing Techniques," but to whet your appetite, here are a pair of cool Typographical Lens treatments for your viewing pleasure (see figs. 6.39 and 6.40).

Figure 6.39
A Lens effect.

II

Putting CorelDRAW! to Work

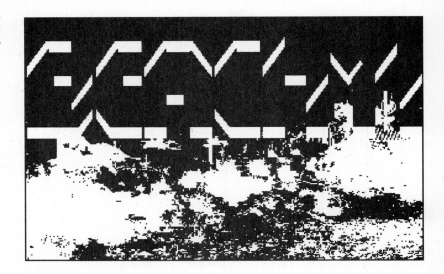

Figure 6.40
A Lens effect
drop shadow.

Exploring Backgrounds and Design Elements

As mentioned in the last section, bitmapped textures add visual impact to the artwork you create with CorelDRAW!. Many sources are available for bitmap images; you can use scanners to create images, or you can use paint programs such as CorelPHOTO-PAINT!, Fractal Design Painter, or Fauve Matisse, as well as high-end image retouching programs such as Adobe Photoshop or Aldus PhotoStyler. You will find a number of textures on the CorelDRAW! version 5.0 CD-ROM disc, as well as on the Inside CorelDRAW! CD-ROM disc. You also can find bitmap images in the public domain and from a variety of clip-art companies.

Using TIFF/PCX/BMP/GIF/TGA Textures

Some of the more popular textures are organic, such as marble, granite, and wood. A local tile or flooring store is an excellent source for marble patterns. Ask if you can borrow a few tiles to scan. When you return the tiles, bring your finished artwork with you. Although the store owners might be skeptical at first, you might end up with a new account after they see what you can do.

Non-organic textures, such as drybrush (see fig. 6.41) or splattered paint (see fig. 6.42), also are quite popular. The drybrush and splattered paint techniques that have been all the rage in recent years have their popular base in custom car paint jobs and their inspiration in the work of Jackson Pollock. Although CorelDRAW! does not enable you to create drybrush or splattered effects directly from within the program, you can easily import TIFF or PCX scans of conventional artwork. After the TIFF or PCX image has been imported into Draw, you have the full range of color and tints. In the process of colorizing black-and-white (1 bit) line art, the fill color affects the (white) background, and the outline color affects the (black) foreground.

Figure 6.41
A drybrush accent.

Figure 6.42
A splattered background with punk type.

II

Putting CorelDRAW! to Work

Figure 6.43
The Crumpled
Paper effect.

Figure 6.44
The Grid effect.

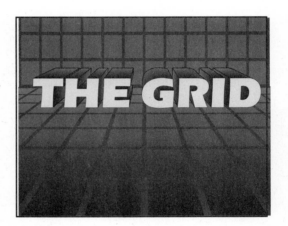

Crumpled paper is an interesting background that can be created quickly with a grayscale scanner. After being brought into CorelDRAW! as a TIFF, PCX, or BMP grayscale bitmap, crumpled paper can be assigned a fill of any color or tint you want, becoming an intriguing design element (see fig. 6.43). An even slicker trick is to set a piece of type, print it on laser paper, crumple the print, and scan.

The grid is one of the most overused graphics gimmicks in design. Nevertheless, you can easily create perspective grids with CorelDRAW!'s Perspective effect (see fig. 6.44). And when properly used with a tasteful fountain fill, the results can be so handsome that the viewer may forget that this effect has been done a zillion times before.

True innovation is hard to come by. In many cases, tried- and- true not only gets the job done, but leaves the client feeling comfortable with what you have designed. Like all the other design effects reviewed in this chapter, the grid is an iteration of what other artists have repeatedly created.

Do not be afraid to innovate. But don't kill yourself for a client who does not appreciate, expect, or truly want innovative work; it can be too frustrating to attempt to convince someone who has no artistic appreciation. Do not waste their time or yours; if they expect formula, give it to them.

In this chapter, you have learned the basics of special effects, from the ubiquitous drop shadow through neon and punk type. Through it all you should come away with the realization that beauty takes time (and work).

CorelDRAW! has many built-in effects, such as Extrude, Blend, and Lens. These magical implements can work wonders when used properly. But when an effect is used as an effect, without thought and overall design concept, you run the risk of losing focus. You can easily be caught up in the mechanics and technique (and fun) of creating a piece of electronic artwork and forget the real purpose of what you are doing.

Design should come first, not the computer. If you lose sight of your overall design concept, your finished product suffers. Use Draw's design power to your advantage. Do not let the constraints of the computer control your design.

You have a new set of brushes in your hands and a fresh canvas. Each time you approach a blank screen, you are faced with the same question that has faced artists since the beginning of time: How do I convey the message?

Chapter Snapshot

In a vector-based illustration, individual objects can be outlined and filled with colors or patterns. CorelDRAW! is no exception. It offers outlines and fills with color possibilities worthy of a tank of expensive tropical fish. In this chapter, you learn to do the following:

✔ Use both process and spot PANTONE colors

✔ Take control of the many outline pen options, such as width, style, corners, and color

✔ Create calligraphic pen shapes

✔ Identify PostScript screen types

✔ Assign (and alter) linear, radial, square, and conical fountain fills

✔ Apply PostScript texture fills, and two- and four-color pattern fills

The right outline and fill make a drawing work, but make your choices wisely; choosing the wrong type of outline or fill can send the wrong signal.

CHAPTER 7

Understanding Outline and Fill

I n the previous chapter, you learned about color basics. This chapter shows you how to apply color and how it relates to the many properties of the Outline and Fill tools, including fractal textures, fountains, and full- and two-color patterns. You also learn how to create, apply, and adjust the different types of patterns as you help Joe DeLook design a line of surfboards.

Preparing artwork for color printing—whether spot or process—is not something to be taken lightly. Each type of printing has its own peculiarities, and it is best to consult with professionals to ensure that your projects are successful. For more in-depth information on preparing your work for color printing, refer to Chapter 11, "Basic Printing Techniques," as well as Part IV of this book, where you will find more information on preparing your files for reproduction.

For now, this chapter moves on to the extended functions of the Outline tool, including the fundamentals of specifying color.

Using the Outline Tool

Draw offers a wide range of outline colors, widths, and shapes. Until now, you have worked with only the most immediate choices—those present on the Outline fly-out menu (see fig. 7.1). Although this menu offers enough options to render uncomplicated black-and-white drawings, you must go further into the menu structure to make use of color outlines.

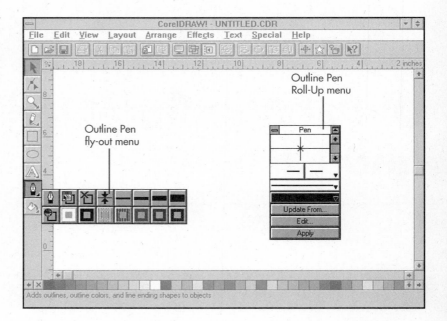

Figure 7.1
The Outline Pen
fly-out and roll-
up menus.

As your drawings become more complex and your familiarity with Draw increases, you learn that new possibilities are continually unfolding. The Outline tool provides versatility without being cumbersome. Its options are there if you need them, but are not a hindrance.

You can access the Outline dialog boxes from the Outline fly-out menu (or the Pen Roll-Up menu shown in fig. 7.1). Notice the two icons at the far left of the fly-out menu, in addition to the default line width and color choices. The upper icon, a pen nib, is a duplicate of the icon that opens the Outline fly-out menu; click on this icon to access the Outline Pen dialog box. The lower icon, which represents a color wheel, gives you access to the Outline Color dialog box; the icon next to the Outline Pen accesses the Pen Roll-Up menu.

Customizing the Outline Pen

The Outline tool is as versatile as a slew of calligraphy pens. Through the Outline Pen dialog box, you can control pen type and shape, color, corners, line caps, dashing, and arrowheads (see fig. 7.2). Options also are provided for placing the outline behind the fill and for scaling the outline with the image.

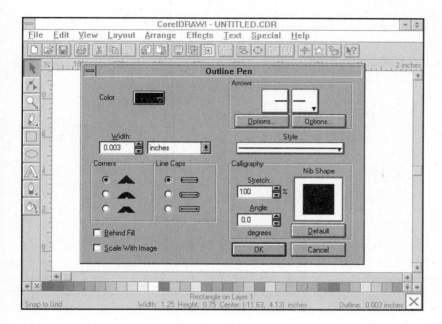

Figure 7.2
The Outline Pen dialog box.

II

Putting CorelDRAW! To Work

Style

Draw offers great flexibility with regard to dashed and dotted line styles. Right out of the box, you get 15 predefined line styles (in addition to solid lines) with the option of adding up to 25 more. To access dashed and dotted lines, click on the line under Style (to reach the Dashed and Dotted Line Styles pop-up menu, shown in fig. 7.3). Use the scroll bars to browse through the available line styles. To change a dashed line style into a dotted line style, select a short dash and click on the round Line Caps selection.

Figure 7.3
The Dashed and
Dotted Line
Styles menu.

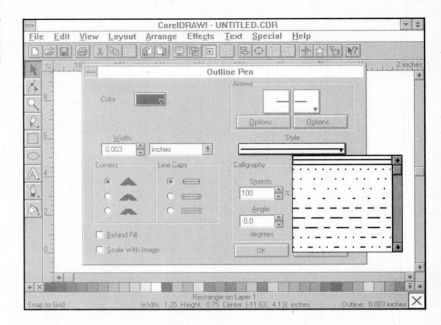

The dash sizes are scaled in direct proportion to the weight of the line specified. Hence, the thicker the line, the larger the dash pattern. The predefined line styles probably will not meet all your needs. To add your own custom variations of dashed lines, you must edit CORELDRW.DOT, a text file that describes line styles (see fig. 7.4). You can find CORELDRW.DOT in your CORELDRW\CUSTOM directory.

Editing the CORELDRW.DOT file might sound difficult, but is really easy. You need to use an ASCII text editor, such as Notepad, to do the job. Just remember to make a backup copy of CORELDRW.DOT before you edit the original.

Look at figure 7.4. Each line style is defined by a row of numbers, which includes the amount of elements (maximum of ten), the length of the dash, and the space between dashes. Dashed lines run in a continuous loop from left to right. One of the effects you can create with dashed lines is shown in figure 7.5.

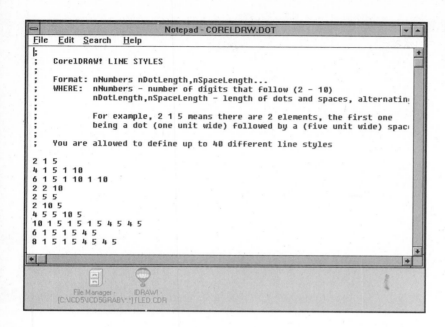

II

Putting CorelDRAW! To Work

Figure 7.4
CORELDRW.DOT.

Figure 7.5
A dashed
coupon border.

To create a line style, type the specifications for the new line style on a new line (after the existing group of line styles is the best place to start). If you want, you can bring your favorite styles to the top of the chart by using the cut-and-paste procedure. After you have altered CORELDRW.DOT, you must save the file and restart CorelDRAW! for the changes to take effect.

Behind Fill

The <u>B</u>ehind Fill option is useful when working with text. Outlines are always centered on the perimeter of an object. If <u>B</u>ehind Fill is enabled, the fill prints to the midpoint of the outline. If it is not enabled, the outline encroaches on the fill. The thicker the outline, the more important is this option. If you fail to use this option, the result can be unreadable or just plain ugly text (see fig. 7.6).

Figure 7.6
Use caution (and
Behind Fill) when
outlining text.

In other words, when <u>B</u>ehind Fill is enabled, the outline prints at half its weight because the outline's width is centered on an object's outline. The <u>B</u>ehind Fill option is definitely of interest when you attempt some rudimentary trapping in Chapter 11.

Scale with Image

The <u>S</u>cale With Image option is extremely important when creating artwork to be scaled or rotated. Suppose you create a logo at full-page size, then scale the logo to fit on letterheads and business cards. If <u>S</u>cale With Image is not used, the outline weight remains constant. The too-thick outline fills in the logo. The logo that looked good at full-page size turns into mud when reduced (see fig. 7.7).

II

Putting CorelDRAW! To Work

Figure 7.7
Scale With
Image logo.

Scale With Image
NOT Selected

Scale With Image
Selected

CorelDraw!'s Scale With Image is very different from Adobe Illustrator or Aldus Freehand. These two programs conveniently enable you to address line scaling at the time of stretching or scaling. Draw does not provide you with this convenience.

In addition to affecting line weight, Scale With Image also plays an important role when scaling or rotating objects that have been drawn with a calligraphic pen shape. Enabling this option ensures that the pen shape rotates with the image. If Scale With Image is not checked, the object rotates, but the pen stroke does not.

Corners

You have three options for line corners: miter, round, and bevel. The options are rather self-explanatory (see fig. 7.8). Miter extends the outer edges of the two meeting lines. To avoid corners in small angles that overshoot, you might need to adjust the miter limit upward. The miter limit setting is accessed from the Special, Preferences dialog box.

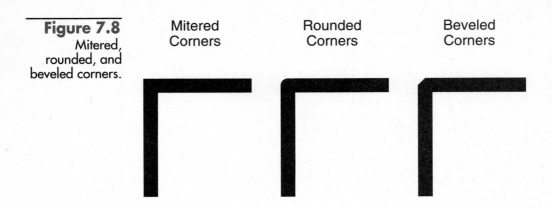

Figure 7.8
Mitered,
rounded, and
beveled corners.

Mitered Corners   Rounded Corners   Beveled Corners

Arrows

Draw comes with an array of arrowheads and other symbols necessary for technical illustrations. The program also enables you to create your own arrows and doodads (that is, anything you want). The Arrowhead pop-up menus shown in figure 7.9 are accessed by clicking on the starting (left) or ending (right) arrow buttons in the Outline Pen dialog box (see fig. 7.2). Use the scroll bars to browse through the arrowhead styles.

Figure 7.9
The Arrowhead
pop-up menu.

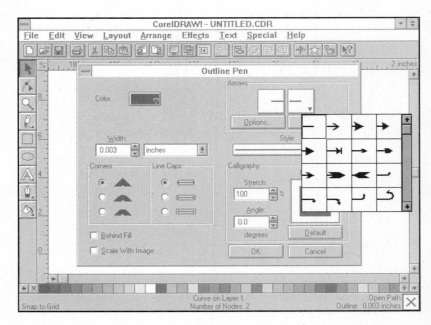

When you find the arrowhead you want, assign it by clicking the left mouse button. Choose an arrowhead from the left menu to place it at the start of the line; choose an arrowhead from the right menu to place it at the end of the line. To return a line to non-arrowhead form, click on the flat line (the first icon in the Options pop-up menu). To switch starting and ending arrowheads, click on the Options button and then on swap.

Designing a new arrowhead for the Arrowhead pop-up menu is an easy task. Simply select any object (including combined objects) and use the Special, Create Arrow command. Draw asks if you really want to create a new arrowhead before it stores it. Note that the outline and fill attributes do not carry over (for example, you cannot have a fountain-filled arrowhead); instead, these settings are governed by the outline color and weight. If you want an arrowhead with no fill, draw a combined doughnut object or break a closed path object by using the Node Edit Roll-Up menu.

The Arrowhead pop-up menu also enables you to delete or edit existing arrowheads. You can delete an arrowhead from the list simply by clicking on the arrowhead that you want to remove, and then clicking on Delete from the list in the Options pop-up menu.

To edit an existing arrowhead, click on Option, then on Edit. This summons the Arrowhead Editor (see fig. 7.10). The Arrowhead Editor enables you to stretch/scale, reorient, and position the arrowhead in relation to the line. Stretching and scaling an arrowhead works the same as stretching and scaling other objects in Draw, although the keyboard modifiers (such as Ctrl and Shift) have no effect. Side handles stretch; corner handles scale. Unfortunately, the editor has no Undo command within it (except for Cancel).

You cannot edit individual arrowhead nodes, but you can use them as snap-to points. By clicking and dragging on a node, that point becomes magnetic and is attracted to the guidelines. Reflect in X and Reflect in Y flip the arrowhead on the vertical or horizontal guideline, respectively.

Center in X and Center in Y center the arrowhead to those same guidelines (also respectively). 4X zoom zooms up by a factor of four.

Figure 7.10
The Arrowhead Editor dialog box.

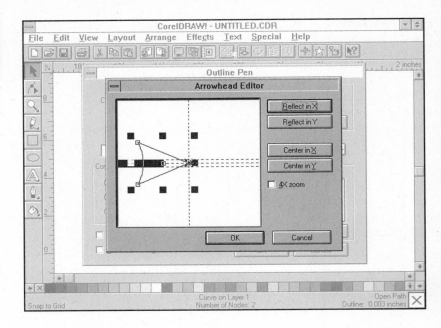

Figure 7.10
The Arrowhead Editor dialog box.

Line Caps

In addition to arrowheads, line caps have three options: butt, round, and square (see fig. 7.11). Line caps apply to both ends of a line unless, of course, you use an arrowhead on one or both ends of the line.

Figure 7.11
Line caps.

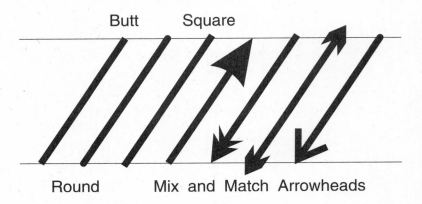

Butt   Square

Round   Mix and Match Arrowheads

Pen Shape (Calligraphic Pens)

The Pen Shape option gives flexibility to the pen width, shape, and angle. This feature is similar to snapping in a completely different pen nib with only a few clicks (see fig. 7.12). Show this feature to a calligrapher and watch him or her salivate!

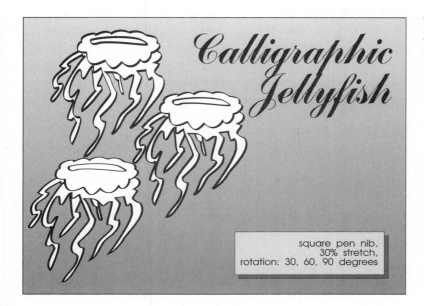

Figure 7.12
The calligraphic jellyfish.

Specifications are entered in typical Corellian fashion: <u>W</u>idth defines the size of the pen nib and can be specified in inches, centimeters, points, and picas, or fractional points. S<u>t</u>retch alters the actual shape of the pen, and <u>A</u>ngle rotates the pen upon its axis.

A standard 300 dpi laser printer outputs a line 1/300 inch in width; an imagesetter might be able to print lines 1/1270 or 1/2540 in width (possibly even thinner, depending on the model).

A subtle feature introduced in CorelDRAW! 3.0 was the interactive capability to define a calligraphic pen shape. Place your cursor in the Nib Shape window and click and drag around the window; the cursor becomes a plus sign (+). You can freely adjust both the stretch and angle of the pen nib without ever touching the keyboard or size buttons.

To get the feel of using different calligraphic pens, try signing your name, duplicating the signature, and assigning different outline pen attributes to the duplicates.

Signing Your Name with Different Pens

Click on the Pencil tool

Sign your name at the top of the page

Your signature probably looks pretty bad, especially if you used a mouse to do it. The creator of the illustration was lucky and had a cordless pen and graphics tablet (see fig. 7.13). In any case, feel free to tweak your signature by using the Shape tool. Try to get the signature to look at least vaguely as it should. You are going to duplicate the signature twice, ending with a total of three.

Figure 7.13
The signature of
John Q. Public.

Round Nib, 0.02 inches, 0% Angle, 100% Stretch

Square Nib, 0.03 inches, 40% Angle, 50% Stretch

Round Nib, 0.04 inches, 60% Angle, 20% Stretch

Duplicating the Signature

Select the Shape tool

Tweak the nodes as desired

Select the Pick tool

Marquee-click all the paths in the signature

Click on G*roup*   The signature is grouped

Click on **E**dit	The Edit menu appears
Click on **D**uplicate	Duplicates the signature
Drag the signature to the bottom of the page	
Click on **E**dit	
Click on **D**uplicate	The signature is duplicated again
Drag the new signature to the middle of the page	

To make life easier when you work with duplicating objects, remember that the keyboard shortcut for **D**uplicate is Ctrl-D.

You should have three signatures on the page. Now assign a different calligraphic pen type to each signature so that you can see the differences between the various pen nib shapes. At this point, make sure that the full-color editing is turned on (press Shift+F9 to switch it on or off).

Assigning a Pen Type

Select the Pick tool	
Click on the uppermost signature	The signature is selected
Select the Outline tool	The Outline fly-out menu appears
Click on the Outline Pen icon	The Outline Pen dialog box appears
Click on the round corners	The corners are selected
Change the pen width to **0.02** *inches*	
Change Angle *to* **0** *degrees*	
Change Stretch *to* **100** *percent*	
Click on OK	
Click on the middle signature	The signature is selected
Select the Outline tool	The Outline fly-out menu appears
Click on the Outline Pen icon	The Outline Pen dialog box appears
Click on the square corners	The corners are selected
Change the pen width to **0.03** *inches*	

continues

continued

Change Angle *to* **40** *degrees*

Change Stretch *to* **50** *percent*

Click on OK

Click on the lower signature   The signature is selected

Select the Outline tool   The Outline fly-out menu appears

Click on the Outline Pen icon   The Outline Pen dialog box appears

Click on the round corners   The corners are selected

Change the pen width to **0.04** *inches*

Change Angle *to* **60** *degrees*

Change Stretch *to* **20** *percent*

Click on OK

If you have a printer available, try printing the file to see the distinction between pen shapes. The differences in pen shape might not be obvious. In general, the larger the pen nib and the more extreme the stretch, the more apparent the pen shape becomes. The rectangular pen nib yields a harder, sharper edge; the rounded pen nib is softer and more flowing.

The Outline Pen Roll-Up Menu

Another time-saving menu is the Outline Pen Roll-Up menu (see fig. 7.14). This menu offers point-and-shoot convenience for line characteristics, including line width, arrows, line style, and outline pen color. In addition, the menu enables you to use Update From (which is the same as Copy Attributes From) to copy the characteristics of any other line, and it provides easy access to the Outline Pen dialog box (from the Edit button). Like other roll-up menus, you must remember to click on Apply to assign any changes!

Outline Colors

A full range of colors is available for outline use. These include spot as well as process color choices. To access the Outline Color palette (see fig. 7.15), click on the color palette-outline icon on the Outline Pen menu. When you get into color fills later in this chapter, you will see that this dialog box is similar to the Uniform Fill dialog box.

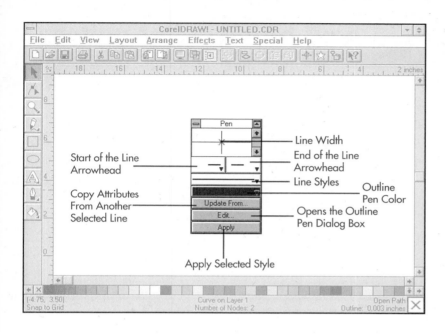

Figure 7.14
The Outline Pen
Roll-Up menu.

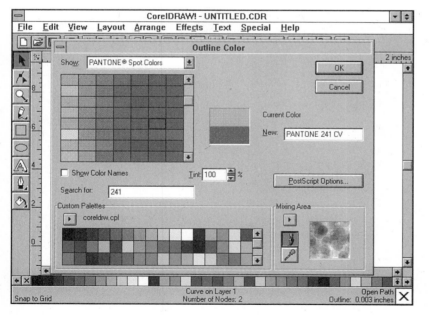

Figure 7.15
The Outline
Color dialog
box—PANTONE
Spot Color
mode.

When you click on the More button located below the color palette, the first option in the Outline Color dialog box is the choice of color specification method: CMYK, RGB, HSB, Grayscale, Uniform, FOCOLTONE, PANTONE Spot, PANTONE Process, or TRUMATCH. Look at the Show box and notice that CorelDRAW! 5.0 defaults to the CMYK Color Model. Click on the down arrow and choose a graphics color method according to your budget and the type of printing press on which the final project will be printed.

To select a color, just click on it. As you scroll through the different color choices, notice that Draw shows a color swatch and name for each selected color. Once again, use the on-screen color sample as a loose guide only; the sample is not accurate. To specify colors precisely, you must use an actual printed process (be it PANTONE, TRUMATCH, or FOCOLTONE) or spot PANTONE color guide.

Spot Color Outlines

If the graphic is to be reproduced using spot colors, click on PANTONE Spot Colors. Draw enables you to choose PANTONE colors, either visually from the palette or by name using the Search for: option.

Tip If you are working with a traditional printed swatch book, you can expedite your color specifications by using the Search for: option.

If you use the palette method, notice as you click on each color that its PANTONE number appears in the New color name box. You cannot specify directly by number in this box, but all inks are in sequential order. Need a PANTONE 288 blue? Scroll to the blues and start clicking while looking for 288 in the Color Name box. This is not the most direct method, but it works.

If you want to be dead sure about what you are selecting, you can specify by name. By clicking on Show Color Names, you can scroll through the ink colors numerically rather than visually. However, the fastest way to specify a PANTONE color is to use the Search for: option. Type the number into the field and voilà!

With spot colors, you can easily specify tint percentages, which can greatly extend the color range of a printed piece. Reds can yield pinks, dark blues can spawn lighter blues, and so on. When the file is output as color separations, each color's separation will include all the tints of a color, along with the color at full strength. To specify a Spot Color tint percentage, click on the up/down arrows at the % tint box, or type in the tint percentage directly.

You also can render a depth-filled black-and-white graphic by using the full range of grays made available on the Outline Color dialog box. Select the Show Grayscale command and specify the precise percentage of tint. This can lead to a far more realistic grayscale effect than you might get by simply specifying the default fills from the fly-out menu or the on-screen color palette.

PostScript Options

Draw enables those with PostScript printers to specify the PostScript screen type of any spot color outline. The subject of PostScript halftone screens is covered in the Fill tool section. Version 5.0 eliminates any worries you may have had about overprinting colors using this dialog box. Instead, you must specify overprints through each object's object menu.

Process-Color Outlines

If the graphic is to be printed on a four-color press, outline colors can be specified directly: in percentages of cyan, magenta, yellow, and black (CMYK) or by one of the other process color models.

Try using the custom palette. As you select different colors, notice that a descriptive name might pop up in the Color Name box. This is a nice touch that proves useful when you begin building your own colors. For instance, say you are illustrating a woman's face. You can mix specific colors for each tone, calling them by descriptive names such as ruby lips, ear lobe, nostril, rosy blush, and so on.

Process Color can be chosen by using one of a number of methods: CMYK (Cyan/Magenta/Yellow/Black), PANTONE Process Colors, FOCOLTONE, or TRUMATCH. This diversity can be confusing. You should try to use either PANTONE Process Color, FOCOLTONE, or TRUMATCH for four-color print work (along with a swatch book). RGB (Red/Green/Blue) and HSB (Hue/Saturation/Brightness) are common in the computer video world but not for print graphics. If you specify colors using either RGB or HSB, the colors are converted to CMYK values when the file is printed (although the conversion might not yield the result you expect).

Using the Fill Tool

Tapping into the Fill tool's capabilities is a little like sneaking into Grandma's jelly cupboard—there are so many delicious choices that it can be tough to decide on which one to use. Draw gives you enough choices so that you will not become bored with the same old flavors. Each one is a treat!

The Fill fly-out menu offers the default fills of black, white, 10-, 30-, 50-, and 70-percent tints, along with no fill. In addition, the menu gives you access to the Fill Roll-Up menu, Uniform Fill, Full- and Two-Color Pattern Fill, Fountain Fill, Fractal Texture Fill, and PostScript Texture Fill dialog boxes. Figure 7.16 illustrates this menu.

Figure 7.16
The Fill fly-out and roll-up menus.

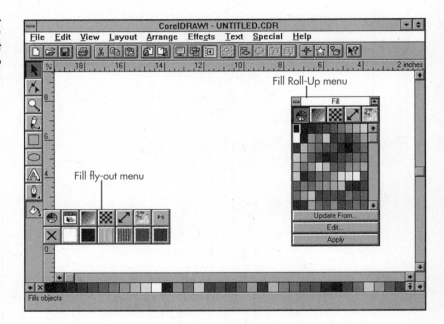

Uniform Fills

At the far left of the Fill fly-out menu, you see Uniform Fill, which is accessed through a color wheel icon. Click on the color wheel to summon the Uniform Fill dialog box.

This dialog box looks and functions exactly like the Outline Color dialog box. Again you are offered the choice of spot or process color. You can access various PostScript Options only if you have specified PANTONE Spot Colors.

PostScript Screens

An interesting feature of the Uniform Fill and Outline Color dialog boxes is the opportunity to specify different PostScript halftones and to set screen frequencies and angles (see fig. 7.17). This flexibility enables you to design artwork that uses a wide range of fill patterns.

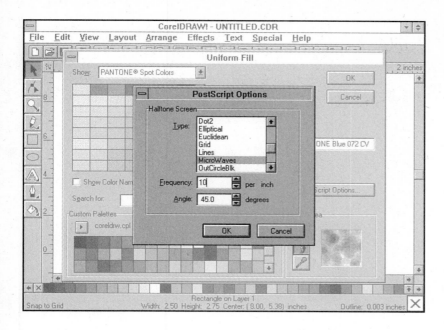

Figure 7.17
The PostScript Options dialog box.

Screen Types

The PostScript halftone screens are most enticing when used with screen frequencies of 30 per inch or less. With low frequencies, the different screen types become prominent and can be used to their best advantage. At higher screen frequencies, the eye loses focus on the patterns, resulting in the visual interpretation of gray rather than black-and-white lines.

PostScript halftone screen types include Default, Dot, Line, Diamond, Diamond2, Dot2, Elliptical, Euclidean, Grid, Lines, MicroWaves, OutCircleBlk, OutCircleWhi, Rhomboid, and Star. Figure. 7.18 illustrates the cool effects you can achieve with the different screen types at a low frequency (these are at 10 lpi). As demonstrated in the exercise at the end of this chapter, these low frequency custom screens look really wild when used on fountain-filled objects. Once again, as with the Outline color choices, you cannot specify the PostScript halftone screen when using process color.

Screen Frequency and Angle

Every halftone screen has a frequency and angle. The higher the quality of printing, the higher you should go with screen frequency. The finer the screen, the less noticeable it is to the naked eye. Newspapers customarily use halftone screens of 85 lines per inch; magazines use 110, 133, or even higher.

Figure 7.18
Examples of
PostScript
halftone screens.

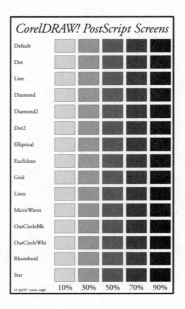

If you are outputting to a desktop laser printer, try not to specify more than 60 lines per inch. High-resolution imagesetters can commonly handle screens of 150 lines per inch. Screen angle becomes readily apparent at low-screen frequencies and also is an important part of process color separations.

Overprint

If you are preparing spot colors for printing, your printer (the person, not the machine) might need overprints or traps. Unlike earlier versions of CorelDRAW!, the Overprint option is no longer found in the PostScript Options dialog box. To assign a fill (or outline) overprint, you must do so through each object's *object menu*. Chapter 11, "Basic Printing Techniques," discusses this subject.

Fountain Fills

Fountain fill is one of Draw's most seductive features. Everyone has been (or will be) attracted to the smoothness this tool provides in blending one color to the next. This appealing characteristic can be used with either spot or process color.

CorelDRAW! version 4.0 featured greatly-enhanced fountain fill capabilities, and they were bolstered yet again in version 5.0 with the addition of square fountain fills. The program now provides four types of fountain fills (see fig. 7.19): linear, radial, square, and conical—which you can specify with the Fountain Fill dialog box (see fig. 7.20). *Linear* fountain fills start at one side of an object and migrate to the facing side. *Radial* fountain fills start at the outside edges of an object and radiate in a circular pattern, inward to the object's center point. *Square* fountain fills work much the same way as radial fountain fills, but are best put to use on rectangular objects. *Conical* fountain fills sweep around an object and are anchored by the object's center point.

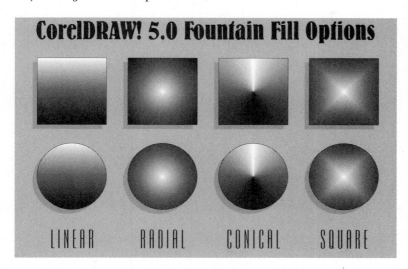

Figure 7.19
Linear, Radial, Square, and Conical fountain fills.

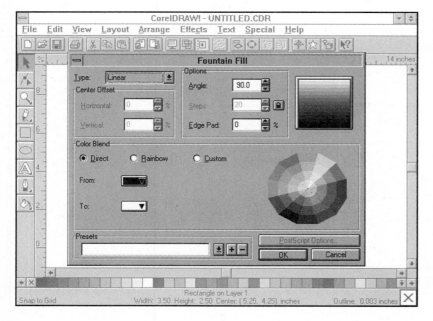

Figure 7.20
The Fountain Fill dialog box.

You can specify (and create) fountain fill presets. This gives you point-and-shoot control over fountains and ensures that you can assign accurate and consistent fills.

Linear Fountain Fills

Linear is the most common form of fountain fill. You have seen these fills plenty of times and have probably wondered how they were created. With CorelDRAW! 5.0, creating linear fountain fills is simple. In the next exercise, you set up a simple one-color linear fountain fill and try setting different fill angles (see fig. 7.21). Full-color editing should be on for this exercise. If it is not, press Shift+F9 to turn it on.

Figure 7.21
Linear fountain fills.

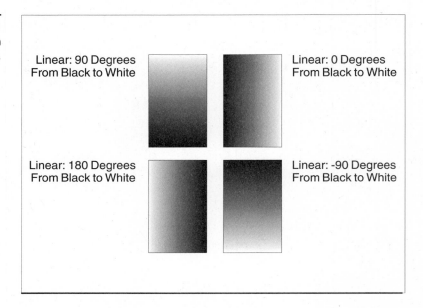

Linear: 90 Degrees
From Black to White

Linear: 0 Degrees
From Black to White

Linear: 180 Degrees
From Black to White

Linear: -90 Degrees
From Black to White

Experimenting with Linear Fountain Fills

Select the Rectangle tool

Hold down Ctrl and draw a three-inch square

Select the Fill tool — The Fill fly-out menu appears

Click on Fountain Fill gradient — The Fountain Fill icon looks like a vertical

The default fill should appear as follows: Linear; 90 degrees; From Black; To White. If these are not your settings, change them for the purposes of this exercise.

Click on OK — The square is fountain-filled

At 90 degrees, the square is filled from the bottom up. Change the direction of the fill.

Click on the Fill tool	The Fill fly-out menu appears
Click on Fountain Fill	The Fountain Fill dialog box appears
Change the angle to -90 degrees	
Click on OK	The square is fountain-filled

If you want, try setting the fill to 180 or 0 degrees.

The Fountain Fill dialog box offers a choice of Draw's full complement of colors and PostScript options. Colors can be freely specified using any color model. Clicking on More (accessed by clicking on a color to show a mini-palette) brings up a dialog box that looks remarkably like the Uniform Fill or Outline Color dialog boxes. These dialog boxes provide access to any possible color fountain fill. Click on **P**ostScript Options while in Spot Color mode to access PostScript halftone screens, which can add dramatic effects to fountain fills.

Edge Pad enables you to increase the fountain fill starting and ending color bands by up to 45 percent. Because fountain fills follow an object's bounding box, irregularly shaped objects can be persnickety; **E**dge Pad ensures that the starting/ ending fountain fill colors hit the edges of the object, rather than falling outside. You also can alter the specific number of steps (or bands) in a fountain fill by changing the **S**teps setting. To access **S**teps, you must first unlock it by clicking on the lock/unlock button.

CorelDRAW! version 3.0 introduced the capability to interactively alter linear fountain fill angles. Remember the way you changed the Calligraphic pen shape earlier in the chapter? You can change angles just as easily. Just click and drag in the fountain fill display window. Your cursor turns into a + sign, and a line appears, drawing itself from the middle of the window through the cursor to the edge of the window. As you drag around the window, notice the angle percentage changing. When you release the mouse button, the display window is redrawn with the angle you have specified. The easiest way to understand the way this procedure works is to click near the edge where you want the fountain fill to go.

Tip

If you hold down the Ctrl key while you are dragging the mouse in the Fountain Fill display, the angle will change in increments of 15 degrees (the default), enabling you to have more control over the fill.

II

Putting CorelDRAW! To Work

Radial or Square Fountain Fills

Now that you have seen the way a linear fountain fill works, try the radial and square fills. The Fountain Fill dialog box enables radial and square fountain fills that flow to the center of an object. The From color spec refers to the outside of the object. The To color spec refers to the inside of the object. No angles are involved. What if you want to have the radial or square fill offset to the top left corner? (See fig. 7.22.) Don't worry; you can achieve this effect in a few simple steps.

Figure 7.22
Centered and Offset Radial fountain fill.

Centered

Offset
(-22% Horizontal, 18% Vertical)

The easiest method of changing the lighting angle is to use the interactive click-and-drag technique. When you click in the radial or square fountain fill display window, crosshairs appear, enabling you to drag to any position you want. Alternatively, you can specify Center Offset in horizontal and vertical percentages. Positive values push the light source upward and to the right. Negative values push the light source downward and to the left. The radial and square fountain fills also enable you to use Edge Pad.

Follow the steps in this next exercise to fill the square you just drew with a radial fountain fill, then try different center offsets.

Altering the Lighting Angle of a Radial Fill

Click on the square	
Select the Fill tool	The Fill fly-out menu appears
Click on Fountain Fill	The Fountain Fill dialog box appears
Click on <u>R</u>adial	
Set Colors *as* From Black *and* To White	
Click on OK	
Click on <u>E</u>dit	The Edit menu appears
Click on <u>D</u>uplicate	The square is duplicated
Drag the duplicate square below the original	

Now that you have set the fill and made a duplicate, use Center Offset to change the lighting angle.

Click on the Fill tool	The Fill fly-out menu appears
Click on Fountain Fill	The Fountain Fill dialog box appears
At Horizontal: *type* **-25**	
At Vertical: *type* **25**	
Click on OK	The fountain fill is offset

The center of the radial fill should now be in the upper left corner of the square. Once you get the hang of it, you can alter the lighting angle with this method fairly easily. Go ahead and alter the center offset by using the interactive method, then try experimenting in a similar manner with square fountain fills.

Conical Fountain Fills

This spinning fountain fill was added to CorelDRAW! in version 4.0. Conical fountain fills are great for creating everything from a hubcap to a desert road at sunset. In a conical fill, the gradient spirals around a center point that you are free to move at will, either by entering precise Center Offset percentages in the Fountain Fill dialog box (see fig. 7.23) or by clicking and dragging around in the preview window.

Figure 7.23
Conical fountain
fill options in the
top left of the
Fountain Fill
dialog box.

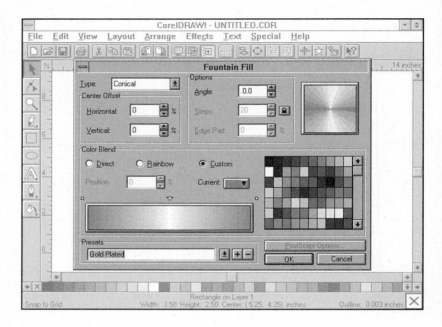

The Baby and Gold Plated fountain fill presets are two good examples of a conical fountain fill. Conical fountain fills really show their stuff when you use the Custom option (as you will see in the next section) to add a number of colors to the fountain. Try using a few conical fountain fills on your own.

Fountain Fill Options

Draw enables you to set a wide variety of fountain fill color options in addition to those already discussed. You can choose the type of blend: **D**irect, **R**ainbow, or **C**ustom. All the exercises thus far have been direct blends—from one specific color directly to another specific color. The **R**ainbow blend works differently. It enables you to spin around the color wheel—in a clockwise or counterclockwise direction—to yield a rainbow-like effect.

Perhaps most interesting is Draw's **C**ustom fountain fill option. With **D**irect blends, you can only go from one color to another color (or shade). The custom fountain fill feature gives you the capability to "ping-pong" a fountain fill between different colors or shades. In other words, you now can go from blue to red to blue, all in one fountain fill. If you look at the color plates, you see that the Gold Plated, Green Metallic, Orca, and Pink Neon Presets are examples of this effect.

To add more colors to a custom fountain fill, double-click on one of the little black squares at either end of the preview window, and a black triangle appears (see fig. 7.24). You then can drag it into position and assign a color to it by clicking on a color in the palette. Just remember that the black triangle is the active triangle. You can assign a new color to an existing blend point by selecting its triangle and clicking on a new color.

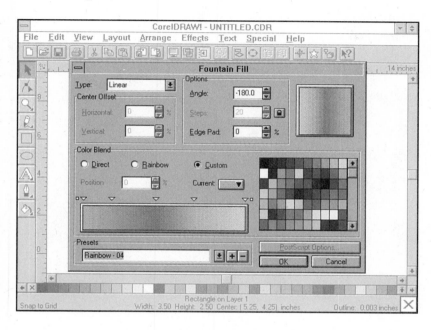

Figure 7.24
Custom fountain fill color options.

As you have read, CorelDRAW! enables you to create fountain fills with either spot or process colors. You cannot, however, have a fill that changes from a spot color to a process color. If you specify the first color as spot and the second as process, the first color is converted to process automatically.

Fountain fills can give a dimensional look to an illustration. Take care to limit the use of this feature. Fountain fills are quite demanding on the printer, and the use of too many fountain fills, or fountain-filling objects with many nodes, slows down your printer. Sometimes, using too many fountain fills or fountain-filling an object with too many nodes actually prevents a file from printing. The time for your preview screen to redraw also increases dramatically. Fountain-filling a rectangle is safe, but doing the same to an object with dozens of curved nodes is just asking for a long run on your printer's RIP. Of course, you could go out to lunch while you are waiting.

If a file full of fountain fills refuses to print, try replacing some of the fountain fills with solid color fills. Avoid rotating fountain-filled objects. Also try to minimize the number of nodes in any fountain-filled object. The trick is to construct the leanest file possible. The subject of building intricate illustrations is covered in Chapter 9, "Advanced Drawing Techniques."

PostScript Texture Fills

The PostScript texture fills are located under the button with the letters PS on the Fill fly-out menu. They are available only when printing on a PostScript output device. The 42 different characteristic fills can be individually altered to yield a seemingly limitless number of possibilities. Figure 7.25 shows some sample effects.

Figure 7.25
PostScript
texture fills.

To specify a PostScript texture fill, click on PS on the Fill fly-out menu. The PostScript Texture dialog box (see fig. 7.26) enables you to specify the type of fill and its parameters, which include Frequency, LineWidth, ForegroundGray, and BackgroundGray. Parameters depend on the fill being used. These parameters differentiate the many possibilities within each fill type.

The warning given on fountain fills holds doubly true for PostScript texture fills. They might look neat, but they can take a long time to print. These little critters (one is even called Reptiles) are an extreme drain on output device resources. If plans include using texture fills, be sure to allow plenty of time for the printer to image the file.

Hopefully, advances in PostScript technology and increases in printer speed will make these warnings a thing of the past. Only PostScript printers can print PostScript fills—yet another reason to recommend using one!

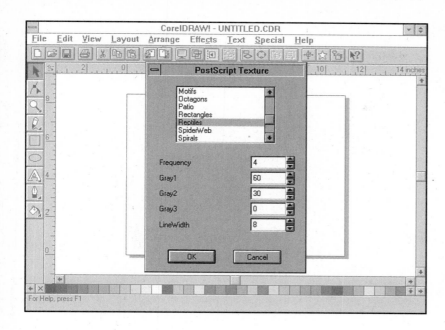

Figure 7.26
The PostScript Texture dialog box.

Two-Color Pattern Fills

Although CorelDRAW! is basically a vector-based illustration package, the program ships with a number of two-color bitmap patterns, and additional patterns are available from a variety of sources. Bitmaps can be imported from scanned images or created in CorelPHOTO-PAINT!, Windows Paintbrush, and other paint programs. Draw's Two-Color Pattern Editor can create new patterns or edit existing ones. The Special menu even has a Create Pattern option for creating bitmap (as well as vector) pattern fills from existing CorelDRAW! objects.

The Two-Color Pattern Fill icon (located on the Fill fly-out menu) looks like a tiny checkerboard. When you click on it the Two-Color Pattern dialog box (see fig. 7.27) appears. You can click on the preview pattern to access the pop-up menu and use the scroll bars to select a bitmap pattern visually. If you cannot find a pattern that you like, you can import or create a new one.

As its name implies, each two-color pattern fill can have only two colors: a foreground and a background. They are initially black and white (respectively), but they do not have to stay that way. You can use spot or process methods to colorize patterns, but you cannot mix process and spot colors in a pattern. Plan your color scheme carefully because you can use only two process or two spot colors. The dialog box includes a handy preview feature so that you can try applying different foreground and background colors without leaving the box. PostScript options provide control over PostScript screens (in spot-color mode only).

Figure 7.27
The Two-Color
Pattern dialog
box with pop-up
menu.

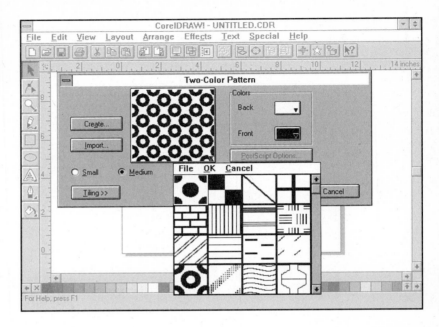

Figure 7.27
The Two-Color
Pattern dialog
box with pop-up
menu.

Pattern fills are based on the tile concept. Click on **T**iling to expand the dialog box and show tiling options (see fig. 7.28). The dialog box provides three default tile sizes: **S**mall, **M**edium, and **L**arge. You are free to resize tile width and height to suit your needs. Be careful not to stretch out or squish tiles too much. Remember, these are bitmaps that become jagged or blurred when removed from their original size and scale.

Patterns can be offset to compensate for discrepancies in object size the same way a tile man sets floor tile. If a pattern does not fit an object cleanly, you can use **X** and/or **Y** offsets to lay down the pattern precisely. You also have the option of using Row/Column Offset to stagger the pattern.

Working with matrix patterns takes some thought, but sometimes the best work happens by chance. Time spent here is worth the effort. You learn more about how patterns work through experimentation.

Two-color pattern fills are print time-consumers. Remember that each time you send a job to the printer, you are creating a print file. The more times a pattern is reproduced, the larger your print file becomes and, consequently, the longer the file takes to print. For this reason, patterns should be used with caution. The caveats that apply to fountain fills also apply here.

The Two-Color Pattern Editor works in three bitmap sizes and four pen sizes (see fig. 7.29). The Two-Color Pattern Editor is summoned by clicking on the Cre**a**te

button in the Two-Color Pattern dialog box. The Editor might remind you of
Windows Paintbrush in its Zoom Up mode. Click on a square with the left mouse
button to turn it black, and click with the right mouse button to turn it white.

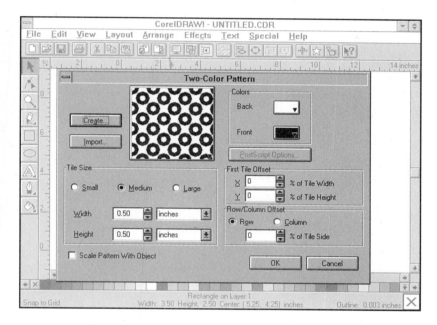

Figure 7.28
Two-Color
Pattern tiling
options.

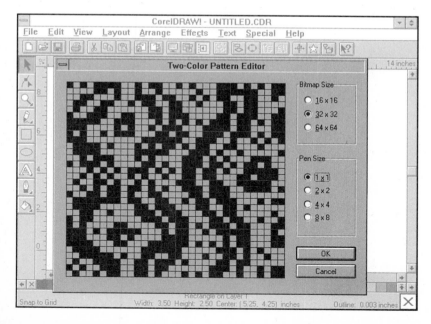

Figure 7.29
The Two-Color
Pattern Editor.

Full-Color Pattern Fills

Somewhere in between two-color patterns and PostScript textures lie full-color (or vector) patterns. Drawing from a little of both, full-color pattern fills can offer more flexibility than either of the aforementioned fills. However, full-color pattern fills succumb to the same print-time malady as other fancy fills. If you want to use them, be prepared to wait for the output.

Like two-color patterns, full-color pattern fills can be created from existing CorelDRAW! objects with the Create Pattern option on the Special menu. Unlike two-color patterns, however, you can use more than two colors or tints.

Full-color patterns are stored as files. When you choose a full-color pattern, you select a file from the Load Full-Color Pattern dialog box. Thankfully, a preview window enables you to check the different patterns one by one.

Like two-color patterns, you can control the tile size and offsets of full-color patterns, but you cannot alter the color of a full-color pattern through the Full-Color Pattern dialog box. To do so, you must edit the objects that the full-color pattern was based on and re-create the pattern.

Editing an existing full-color pattern fill is no more difficult than editing any other Draw file. To edit an existing full-color pattern fill, you open it, edit it, and then use Create Pattern (on the Special menu) to save it (see fig. 7.30). The trick is to use the PAT file extension in the Open Drawing dialog box in place of the CDR extension.

Figure 7.30
Loading a full-color pattern.

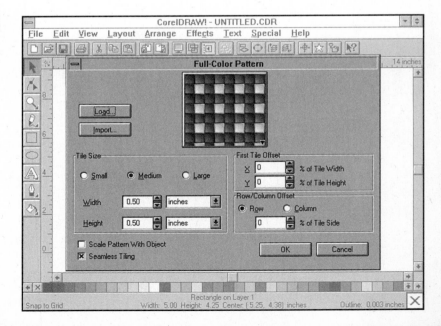

Unlike two-color patterns, full-color patterns can be resized without losing image quality. But once again, full-color patterns are tough on the printer. The more patterns you use, the longer you can expect to wait.

CorelDRAW! 5.0 ships with 65 full-color patterns, but there is always room for many more. As a special bonus, the *Inside CorelDRAW! 5, Fifth Edition CD-ROM* that accompanies this book contains 117 full-color pattern fills from Virginia Schmitz's Lovely Illusions collection. Virginia offers 400 additional full-color patterns for a small registration fee. Check the \goodies\patterns directory on the CD-ROM for the patterns, installation, and ordering information (in the file README1.TXT).

The Fill Roll-Up Menu

The Fill Roll-Up enables easy access to almost all of Draw's fills: uniform, fountain, two-, and full-color patterns (see fig. 7.31). In addition, it enables you to use the Update From feature (which is the same as Copy Style From) on any other fill, plus it can whisk you to the supporting fill dialog boxes (through the Edit button) to make more involved fill decisions. The Fill Roll-Up menu lacks one thing: You cannot access PostScript pattern fills (which must be accessed from the Fill fly-out menu).

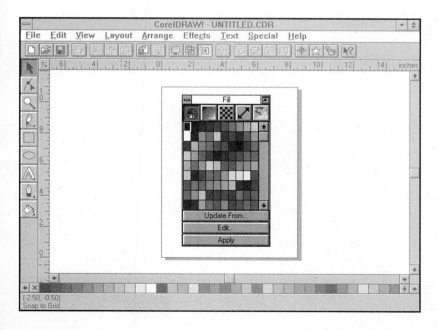

Figure 7.31
The Fill Roll-Up menu.

You can save plenty of time with the Fill Roll-Up menu. Assigning existing two- or full-color pattern fills (from their respective pop-up menus) is a breeze, as is altering fountain-fill characteristics.

You have just covered a lot of ground, including learning how to specify color outlines, fills, and patterns. In the next section, you are going to put that theory to work.

DeLook Design Creates a New Line of Boards for Rippin' Surfboards, Inc.

The crew at DeLook Design is elated. They have been selected by their favorite client, Rippin' Surfboards, Inc., to create the artwork for a new line of surfboards. It was not all that much of a surprise because the president and founder of the company is Joe DeLook's old surfing buddy, Rip Raster.

Rip wants a line of exciting board designs that will make surfers eager to part with their hard-earned cash. Rippin' Surfboards is thriving, but a constant flow of hot new designs is absolutely essential to their continued success. Rip is counting on DeLook Design to come up with magic.

Joe has promised Rip that he can put a few designs together in just a couple of days. With the deadline screaming toward the coastline like a killer Nor'easter, Joe conjures up his three sample designs, Tubular Dreams, The Rasterizer, and ShredZilla.

Surfboard Design Number One— Tubular Dreams

The first surfboard design, Tubular Dreams, is a chrome look that uses a fountain fill preset to achieve a great design. CorelDRAW! 5.0 added a large number of convenient new fountain fill presets that will make this exercise a breeze. You will be able to finish this board with a minimum of hassles, and, in just a few steps, you'll get tubed!

You start with a surfboard shape that is filled with color and patterns. You can create one yourself with the Ellipse tool, or you can load one from the *Inside CorelDRAW! 5, Fifth Edition* CD-ROM. The file is named BOARD.CDR and is found in the \EXERCISE\CH7 directory.

To create the surfboard shape yourself, first draw an ellipse. Then convert the ellipse to curves. Pull the left side of the ellipse slightly to the left, and open the curve on the opposite (right) side by pulling out on the symmetrical control points (see fig. 7.32).

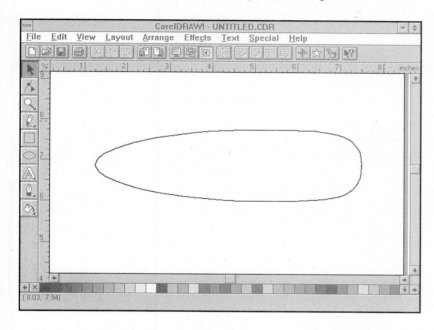

Figure 7.32
The empty surfboard.

Assigning a Fountain Fill Preset

With the surfboard selected:

Click on the Fill tool	The Fill fly-out menu appears
Click on Fountain Fill	The Fountain Fill dialog box appears
At Presets, roll down, click on Cylinder - 30	
At Angle, *set to* **45**	
Click on OK	The surfboard is tubular!

Try a few more Fountain Fill Presets. Then try altering the Presets to make your own tubular fountain fill.

You should avoid having too many color percentage entries in your custom fountain fills. The shipping version of CorelDRAW! 5.0 may hang up when assigning intricate custom fountain-fills. In cases such as the Tubular Dreams fill, you may want to create a group of adjacent fountain-filled rectangles, and then use the PowerClip function to paste the objects inside the container object (surfboard). Remember, however, that PowerClipping a number of fountain-filled objects will lead to increased print times.

Surfboard Design Number Two—The Rasterizer

The second surfboard design, Rip's namesake, Rasterizer, illustrates the effects that you can achieve with PostScript screening options. These options can be wonderful, but they are limited in that they are size dependent. When you set up the first design using the PostScript screening options, you must understand that the screen pattern is totally tied to the size you are printing. For the purposes of the mockup, the pattern works just fine, but when you actually go to create the final artwork, you will have to go through some gyrations.

Rip Raster is into some wild color combinations. Joe is out to accommodate him with the color scheme for The Rasterizer. He will use a bright combination of purple and green, with magenta highlights.

Creating Linear Fountain Fills with Custom PostScript Screens

Select the Fill tool	The Fill fly-out menu appears
Click on Fountain Fill	The Fountain Fill dialog box appears
At From*, click on* More	The Fountain Fill Color dialog box appears
At Sho<u>w</u>*, click* PANTONE Spot Color	
Select PANTONE Purple CV	
Click on OK	
At To*, click* More	The Fountain Fill Color dialog box appears
At Sho<u>w</u>*, click on* PANTONE Spot Color	
Select PANTONE 361	
Click on OK	
Click on <u>P</u>ostScript Options	The PostScript Options dialog box appears

At <u>T</u>ype:, *select* Line

Set <u>F</u>requency: *to* **10**

Click on OK

Click on OK again

The surfboard is set with a purple-to-green custom PostScript screen

If you have a PostScript printer, go ahead and print the Rasterizer. Try the Fountain Fill angle at a number of different settings. Then try a few more Custom PostScript Screens.

If you have a color PostScript printer, you are in luck. You can print a proof copy of the design in all its glory. If you have a regular PostScript laser printer, you can still print out separations—this helps you to see how the screens really look. If you don't have a PostScript printer (or interpreter), you are able to use only conventional halftone screens.

Remember the size dependency problems of custom PostScript halftone screens discussed earlier? You may have problems with conventional halftone screens. A problem arises when you go to resize objects that have been assigned these custom halftone screens. When you resize the object, the screen remains at its original frequency. This is a major bummer, although there is a workaround. What looks right at one size does not look right when resized because the screen is fixed to a certain frequency and, consequently, does not change with scaling percentages.

To create final artwork to the proper scale, you might have to print your mock-up version to a high resolution imagesetter so that you can scan in the print (also at high-resolution). Then, you have to go in and re-create the pattern, either through manual tracing, autotracing, or with CorelTRACE!. In effect, you are converting the PostScript halftone pattern into normal vector objects.

Surfboard Design Number Three—ShredZilla

The third surfboard design, ShredZilla, is filled with a lizard pattern. Joe will use a full-color pattern, filled with green interlocking lizards.

Assigning a Full-Color Pattern

Click on the Fill tool

The Fill fly-out menu appears

Click on Full-Color Pattern Fill

The Full-Color Pattern Fill dialog box appears

continues

continued

Click on Lo**a**d   The Load Full-Color Pattern dialog box
                                                            appears

Roll down, click on reptiles.pat

Click on OK

Click on **L**arge

Click on OK   ShredZilla is filled with reptiles

Try different patterns, sizes, and tiling options, and don't forget
Virginia Schmitz's Lovely Illusions full-color patterns on the *Inside
CorelDRAW! 5, Fifth Edition* CD-ROM!

Fractal Texture Fills

The addition of fractal texture fills was the most radical enhancement to
CorelDRAW! version 4.0. These awesome beauties are the coolest thing to come
out of Ottawa in ages! But what are fractal texture fills, you ask? Quite simply, they
are seemingly random textures borne out of millions of possibilities through
mathematical genius (and your careful selections within the Texture Fill dialog
box).

You might remember the water texture that you added to the letterhead, back in
Chapter 2, "Creating and Drawing." Perhaps you took the time to explore the
dialog box then. In any case, you are bound—sooner or later—to spend hours
fiddling with the many settings there, and then you are on your way to fractally-
generated texture-nirvana.

In addition to water-like textures, there are settings for everything from vegetation,
minerals, and marbles, to clouds and aerial photography.

Your role as an electronic artist is to help your clients get their messages across.
Whether the medium is print, slides, or even three-dimensional objects, Draw
enables you to do it right. The program's control over color, in both PANTONE
and process permutations, makes it an essential instrument in your quest for
artistic success.

As you move through the rest of this book, Draw's potential should become
increasingly obvious. It is up to you to harness that power, whether your field is
commercial art or somewhere within the fine arts.

Chapter Snapshot

In a vector-based illustration, individual objects can be outlined and filled with colors or patterns. CorelDRAW! is no exception. It offers extensive color possibilities. In this chapter, you learn the color basics as they relate to the graphic arts, and how to do the following:

✔ Use spot PANTONE colors

✔ Use CMYK process colors

✔ Create custom colors

✔ Work smart with custom color palettes

Color helps convey your message. However, make your choices wisely; the wrong color choice can send the wrong message.

CHAPTER 8

Understanding Color

A well-designed page can work in black-and-white or in color. Structure is what makes the difference. Of course, a poor choice of colors can ruin a design from a chromatic standpoint, but the mere inclusion of color cannot make up for poor design. A flashy paint job on a leaky hull will not keep the boat from sinking.

Because color printing can be expensive, the place to experiment with color is certainly not on the (traditional) printing press. Mistakes can be more than expensive; they can cost you your job or cause you to lose an account. Take precautions at every step and keep an eye on the meter. When you are working with color, the meter is always running. This book includes a good deal of additional information on avoiding the pitfalls of color printing (see Chapters 11 and 25).

This chapter covers the fundamentals of working with color, providing you with the basics for both spot and process colors. The only way to gain real experience with color is through trial and error. Like most subjects in the art world, learning through experience is mandatory. Understand the theory, then practice, practice, practice!

Using CorelDRAW! and Color

Color is described in one of two ways, depending on the medium. Printed color involves layering partially transparent inks onto opaque paper. The subsequent printed piece is an example of *subtractive color*, which subtracts wavelengths (colored inks) from white light (paper). When you are working with video screens or producing 35mm slides, projected color entails *additive color*.

Viewing and specifying color on a computer monitor can be difficult. The dilemma occurs because your monitor must display additive color images, but you may ultimately need subtractive color output. Many variables affect how colors appear when you are creating your artwork on-screen. The appearance of color on artwork at its intended destination, be it a printed piece or multimedia presentation, also can be affected. You may want to jump ahead to Part IV, "Advanced Topics," and read Chapter 21, "Managing Color and System Calibration."

CorelDRAW! has two different methods for specifying color when the artwork is destined for the printing press: spot and process. These terms refer to the two basic methods of reproducing color images on a printing press. *Spot color* is used when two or more specific colors are required for a print job. *Process color* is used to give the printed illusion of full color.

CorelDRAW! also provides two ways to specify color in additive terms. The Red-Green-Blue (RGB) and Hue-Saturation-Brightness (HSB) color models are most commonly used when creating projected images. These color models cannot be output to separate RGB or HSB printing plates because RGB and HSB printing presses are the graphic arts equivalent of pixie dust. Not to worry! Corel has you covered: if you happen to specify objects with either RGB or HSB values, Draw will convert these values to their process color equivalents when printing. This occurs as long as you plan to print with process colors!

For those who are just jumping into the world of printed color, the first place to start is with spot color, rather than process. It is wiser to wade into uncharted waters, rather than to dive in head first.

Understanding PANTONE Color

In most print shops, a scheme known as the *PANTONE Matching System* (PMS)—commonly referred to simply as PANTONE color—ensures that the final printed color correctly corresponds to the color specified by the designer. Quite simply, PANTONE is a recipe book for mixing printing inks. The pressperson follows a predefined recipe to cook up the correct color, the same way a cook prepares clam chowder.

When using the PANTONE system, an exact color is requested. The printed color should match the one chosen from the PANTONE color swatch book. A few colors come straight from the can, but most colors must be mixed from other colors.

This process should eliminate inconsistencies, but the system relies on the pressperson's ability to mix the specified inks accurately. If the ink is not meticulously mixed, the printed color will not match the requested color. If color printing is important to you, find a competent printer and stick with him or her.

Although CorelDRAW! does a good job with PANTONE color screen representations, do not, under any circumstances, trust the screen colors to be true. Buy a PANTONE book and use it to specify your colors accurately. Most graphic arts supply houses carry them. They are not cheap, but are well worth the investment.

Understanding Process Color

As opposed to PANTONE or spot color, process color mixes ink on the printed page, not before it is put on the press. Process color is commonly referred to as *four-color printing*, referring to the four colors of ink used: cyan, magenta, yellow, and black (CMYK). Each color has a separate printing plate and, when printed, the four colors are combined in different ratios to give the illusion of a full-color photograph. When you specify a color using the process color model, you can enter specific percentages of each of the four process colors, blending them to create a full spectrum of color.

How CorelDRAW! Handles Color

CorelDRAW! does an excellent job of creating either spot or process color separations. The power of the PostScript language enables you to send Draw files to a high-resolution imagesetter, where negatives can be produced. These negatives are then used to *burn* or make the printing plates. By imaging directly onto negative film, you are assured the highest-quality image possible. Much of the manual (and costly) preparation that you might have formerly encountered with color printing is eliminated.

You also can proof images on a color PostScript output device prior to sending out the files for separations. The best of these printers can print using either process or PANTONE color-simulating capabilities. Although (in most cases) they should not be used for final output, color printers can be helpful in the design process, enabling comps to be made in a short time frame. The Fiery/Canon Color Laser Copier is an exception. This device is perhaps the most significant advance in short-run color printing to occur in the past few years. It enables you to print your full-color CorelDRAW! (and other DTP) files directly, without going to film, plate, or printing press. Although the Fiery's quality cannot match that of a real four-color (or more) press and a good pressperson, you can achieve wonderful results at previously unheard-of prices.

Understanding Draw's Color-Selection Methods

Specifying color with CorelDRAW! might seem mystifying. The color selection choices are vast and the methods might not be instantly understood. The secret is in using the proper palette, which depends on the printing method you plan to use. The first choice is to specify either spot or process color. If you specify spot, your choices are simple; you are allowed to choose spot PANTONE colors either visually or by name.

If you are working with process color, your choices are far more varied. Draw enables you to specify process color from a number of methodologies. Choosing each method determines the layout of the Outline Color or Uniform Fill dialog boxes. For the purposes of this book, you deal with spot PANTONE and process CMYK color exclusively. CorelDRAW! 5.0's color models include the following:

CMYK (Cyan/Magenta/Yellow/Black)

RGB (Red/Green/Blue)

HSB (Hue/Saturation/Brightness)

Custom Palette

PANTONE Spot Colors

PANTONE Process Colors

FOCOLTONE Process Colors

TRUMATCH Process Colors

The Uniform Fill dialog boxes are versatile. You can specify a color with one color model (perhaps RGB), switch to another (CMYK), and retain a semblance of color integrity. With a quick click, the program converts any color into a CMYK, RGB, or HSB color. Draw does not, however, automatically convert any color into a PANTONE, FOCOLTONE, or TRUMATCH color. Color specification methods might seem odd at first, but you will soon become accustomed to them.

Once a year, Corel redesigns these color dialog boxes for each major release. The tradition continues with version 5.0 (see fig. 8.1). In 1994, CorelDRAW! introduced a 3D CYMK color space model. They have also added a color mixing area for you to test your colors before loading them into the dropper.

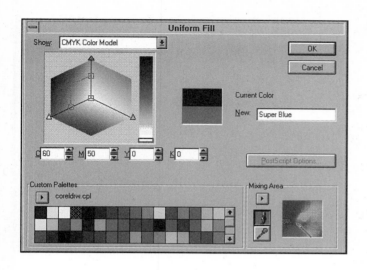

Figure 8.1
The new and improved CorelDRAW! 5.0 Uniform Fill Dialog Box.

II

Creating Custom Colors

A number of methods are available to choose from when it comes to creating your own custom CMYK colors. The most precise method is to enter specific percentages for Cyan, Magenta, Yellow, and Black. You can do this by either typing the numbers directly, or by clicking on the percentage up/down buttons. You can interactively create CMYK colors by clicking and dragging the CMYK handles around in the 3D color space, but this method can be more confusing than productive. Most intriguing, however, is the new color mixing area.

CorelDRAW! 5.0 took a cue from the paint programs that use similar color mixing areas. This new device lets you blend two colors together to create a number of variations. To add color to the mixing area, click the paintbrush button and choose a color from either the existing palette, the 3D color space, or dial one up through CMYK percentages. Then proceed to dabble in the mixing area until you achieve the desired color. Click the eyedropper button and move around the mixing area, clicking on different colors. Each time you click, the dialogue box will show the selected color in three ways: as CMYK percentages, in the 3D color space, and as the New color. After you have a "keeper" you can name it by typing the name in the New box. The color is then automatically loaded into the current palette.

Using Palettes to Your Advantage

Specifying colors in CorelDRAW! can be simplified through intelligent use of the on-screen color palette. The on-screen palette should be used whenever possible, in the same manner a painter loads paint onto his palette (see fig. 8.2). It enables you to load, arrange, and use only the specific colors in your artwork's color scheme. The palette is a great time-saver, but you must first understand how to specify and mix the colors.

Figure 8.2
The on-screen palette.

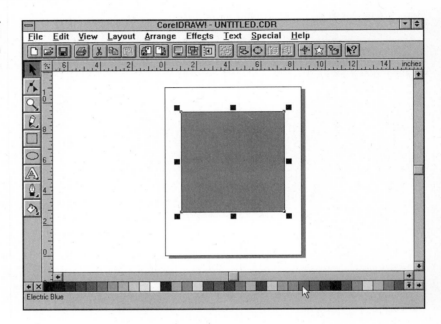

The on-screen color palette saves time by allowing you to specify an object's fill or outline color with one mouse click. With an object selected, position your cursor over any chosen color. As shown in figure 8.2, when you move your mouse over the on-screen palette, the status line reports on each color's name or CYMK percentages. Click with the left mouse button to fill; click with the right mouse button to outline. Instant colors!

There is even an easy on-screen way to remove an object's outline or fill. Select an object and click on the X button at the far left of the palette with your left mouse button to assign a fill of None, and click with your right mouse button to assign an outline of None (see fig. 8.3).

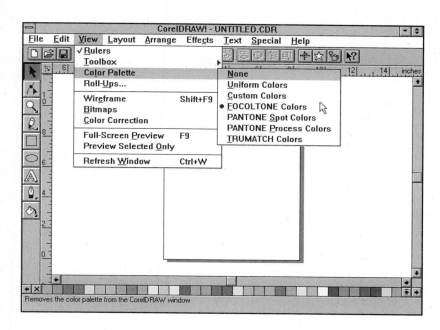

Figure 8.3
Palette choices.

The palette can be switched on or off from the <u>V</u>iew menu (see fig. 8.3). You can choose from PANTONE <u>S</u>pot Colors, PANTONE <u>P</u>rocess Colors, <u>F</u>OCOLTONE Process Colors, <u>T</u>RUMATCH Process Colors, <u>U</u>niform Colors, <u>C</u>ustom Colors, or no palette. To move through the on-screen color palette, use the left/right pair of scroll buttons. You can also expand the palette to view six full rows of color (see fig. 8.4) by clicking on the up arrow, just to the inside of the right palette scroll button. After you have chosen a color from the expanded on-screen palette, it will automatically revert to the original one-row mode.

When you start working on a piece of artwork, consider the color scheme. Decide whether the image will be constructed with spot or process colors (or both). In most cases, you will probably just use one of the standard palettes, including the expanded palette shown in figure 8.4. You have the option of building your own custom color palettes according to job specifications or personal preferences. CorelDRAW! will launch with the last used palette displayed. If you create a custom palette, you should save it as a CPL palette because palettes are not stored with your files.

Figure 8.4
The expanded
on-screen
palette.

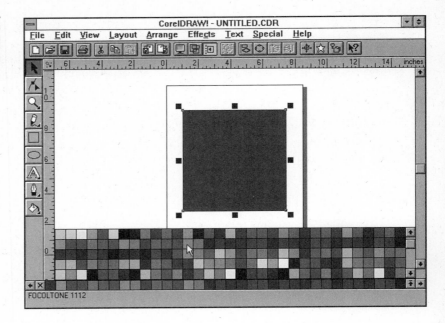

Palettes are infinitely customizable. You can load colors from many different color systems into one palette. This comes in handy when working with several color systems. Suppose, for example, you are working on a brochure that will be printed on a six-color press. In addition to process color, the brochure also has two PANTONE spot colors, to match a corporate logo. You can load the two PANTONE spot colors into a custom palette along with the applicable process colors. The process colors can come from any or all of the process color specification methods (FOCOLTONE, TRUMATCH, PANTONE process, or the do-it-yourself CMYK). You are free to mix and match colors from the different systems.

As your artwork evolves into the production stage, decide which colors you want to load onto your palette. After they have been loaded, you can arrange them to allow for enhanced productivity and to fit your own personal working style. When you create custom colors, they are added to the end of the custom palette.

You can make the most of the palette by reordering the colors so that those you use often are at the top of the list. To shuffle the colors around, go to the Uniform Fill dialog box. At the Custom Palette, click on and drag colors, positioning them to set up your palette in the order that best suits the artwork at hand. The order of the Uniform Fill dialog box Custom Palette matches the order of the on-screen custom palette.

Draw provides complete control over color. This chapter covered the basics of printed color, and its use as a powerful communications tool. Your role as an electronic artist is to help your clients get their messages across. Whether the medium is print, slides, or even three-dimensional objects, Draw enables you to do it right. The program's control over color, in both PANTONE and process permutations, makes it an essential instrument in your quest for artistic success.

As you move through the rest of this book, Draw's potential should become increasingly obvious. It is up to you to harness that power, whether your field is commercial art or fine arts.

Chapter Snapshot

Ready for the tough stuff? While Joe DeLook is dreaming, you get the chance to draw (excuse the pun) on your illustration skills as you create a mildly complex butterfly and learn to do the following:

✔ Build images that work by proper use of Combine and Group

✔ Use the Contour and Blend effects

✔ Weld objects together

✔ Create woodcut-like images with PowerLines

✔ Take precautions when working to avoid mishaps

✔ Use various techniques to speed up your work

✔ Add perspective to your drawings

✔ Learn about CorelDRAW! 5.0's new Intersection, Trim, and PowerClip features

Working with complex images requires a thorough knowledge of how the program functions. Creating successful (and editable) complex images is something that happens not by accident, but by design.

9

CHAPTER

Advanced Drawing Techniques

___

S o far, this book has covered most of the fundamentals of creating electronic artwork with CorelDRAW!. Along the way, it has stressed the proper way to assemble modular images so that you can easily alter and print them with confidence.

Those with an art background who use CorelDRAW! might have a distinct advantage, although such experience does not ensure success. An artist might make wondrous achievements with oil colors but fail to grasp Draw's theory. The vector-based, object-oriented environment might be daunting to those without the vision to use it to their benefit.

An artist whose training includes print-making, whether artistic or commercial, will be comfortable with Draw. Many of Draw's core principles also are found in the arts of serigraphy (screen printing) and lithography.

Success with Draw entails more than just drawing a pretty picture. The intent is to build working drawings—illustrations that have the flexibility to change at a moment's notice. To accomplish this goal, a drawing must not only be designed and rendered, it must be engineered.

Building Images That Work

No matter what the application, solid design is the key to success. A well-engineered building stands the test of time. A precisely crafted automobile handles impeccably. A well-thought-out computer program runs flawlessly. This last example is the key here because when you create an image with Draw, you are writing a computer program.

Draw (CDR) files are source code. Windows print drivers could be considered compilers. The files that Draw sends to the printer are object code. If a Draw file is not properly drawn, the resulting program will not run.

There is a right way and a wrong way to solve a problem, write a computer program, and execute a drawing. If a computer program functions, but is slow and difficult to use, it is a flop. If a Draw file fails to print or takes half a day to do so, it too is a failure.

What good is a drawing that you cannot print? A pretty picture on the screen does nothing for you at deadline time. Who do you blame for nonprinting images—the manufacturers of the program, the operating system, the description language, or the artist/operator responsible for using them?

No one should take the blame, but the artist should take the ultimate responsibility. Through in-depth working knowledge, the experienced Draw artist knows the program's limitations. He or she knows what the program can and cannot do. Pushing the design envelope should not be done at deadline time, or at least should be done only with extreme prudence.

A variety of concepts can help you build working images. The following pages cover many of the basic points necessary to achieve success with Draw.

Getting the Most from Combine and Group

The Combine and Group commands are significant players at Draw's cutting edge. While the inexperienced Draw user might see little use for these two commands, you must understand the difference between them. Combine is a function of systematic design, whereas Group is a function of composition convenience. Combine makes a huge difference in screen redraw and printing. Group is of great assistance in image construction. These two commands are similar, but far from the same.

Combine is one of the most important, yet least used, of Draw's command sets. It enables you to fuse objects so that they act as one. Although they are not physically connected, combined objects share the same outline and fill characteristics. Thoughtful use of Draw's Combine command can make it possible to print drawings that would regularly choke a printer. To effectively challenge Draw's frontiers, you first must become practiced in the proper use of Combine.

The following are some general guidelines for using the Combine command effectively:

✔ For maximum efficiency, try not to combine more than 20 to 25 objects at a clip. Larger combinations can cause problems at print time. Also, avoid combining complex, multinode objects.

✔ Combined files are well-designed files. They take up less space because file size is kept to a minimum. This consideration is important for conserving disk space, whether it is fixed or removable.

✔ By observing preview redraw, you easily can tell if a group of objects has been combined. Uncombined objects pop in, one by one. Combined objects pour down the screen—from top to bottom—in a fraction of the time.

Unlike Combine, Group does not affect screen redraws, file size, or print times. Group simply collects objects, acting mainly as an item of convenience. In the postcard exercise from Chapter 3, "Editing and Manipulating," you grouped clusters to make assembly easier.

In this chapter's exercises, you see how Group and Combine can simplify image manipulation, speed up screen preview, reduce file size, and help complex images to print with ease.

Keeping Things in Control with Layers

When your drawings start to get complex, CorelDRAW!'s Layer controls are essential to maintain order—not to mention your sanity. The Layers Roll-Up menu (which is accessed through the Layout menu or by the keyboard shortcut Ctrl+F3) is a powerful device, helping you create artwork that would otherwise be impossibly complicated, if not beyond the realm of sense entirely.

Layers are easy to work with after you understand the basics. You can have an endless number of layers, each with a distinctive name (of up to 32 alphanumeric characters). You can make individual layers invisible or nonprinting for the sake of clarity while working, previewing, or manipulating your drawing. Draw also provides the option to assign a color override that designates a specific color outline to all objects on a layer (in addition to making them transparent). Color override affects only the on-screen appearance while you are working in Wireframe view; it has no effect on output. You can lock layers so that you do not disturb them as you work with other layers.

Artists who render technical drawings will find using layers invaluable. In most basic drawings, you can do your artwork on one layer and the annotation on another. Corel might have taken a number of releases to include layer control, but now that it is here, make use of it!

Using Fountain Fills Properly

Using too many fountain fills is a sure way to choke an output device. If you are imaging a file with fountain fills and the file refuses to print, you have only one realistic option: get rid of some or all of those fountain fills. Of course, you can always increase curve flatness when printing, but that is another story (covered in Chapter 11, "Basic Printing Techniques").

Complexity for complexity's sake is pointless. Slapping layer upon layer of over-noded fountain-filled objects is an exercise in futility. If you really want to waste your (or your employer's) time, you can slap on as many as you want, but the ultimate result seldom is printable. If you have the latent desire to work your imagery to death, you should buy a canvas, a few brushes, and some oil paints.

The intent here is not to discourage the use of fountain fills. You must realize, however, that they can exceed the capabilities of the output device. Use them with great discretion. Additionally, try to avoid fountain-filling objects with a large number of nodes, such as strings of intricate type. This task can be extremely processor-intensive, and, at the very least, the output device can take hours to print the file.

Eliminating Excess Nodes

Like too many fountain fills, excessive nodes can choke a printer quickly. When executing a freehand drawing or tracing a bit-mapped file, Draw invariably lays down far too many nodes. The artist is responsible for stripping out the unnecessary nodes.

Tracing an image might yield a 100 nodes where two might suffice. The number of nodes created depends on the quality of the original and the user settings. Once again, the artist must rectify the situation. CorelDRAW! 5.0's Node Edit Roll-Up menu includes a marvelous auto-reduce function; using it saves you time and effort.

The fewer the nodes in a file, the smaller that file is and the faster it can be produced, both on the screen and at the output device. In short, file sizes, screen redraw, and print times improve if you eliminate excess nodes.

Some file types (such as CGM and WPG) are vector formats even though they contain line segments instead of Bézier curves. Any time a file is imported in either of these formats, it contains far more line segments than are necessary in CDR format. In addition, the object does not scale with the smoothness that one would expect from a Bézier-based object. When using imported CGM images, select and delete excess nodes before sending the images to a high-resolution output device.

Joe DeLook Takes an Early Lunch

A hungry Joe DeLook has cut out for an early lunch and some fishing. With his lunch bag and fishing gear in hand, he is ready for a few hours of relaxation. He reaches his favorite spot, throws in a line, and opens his lunch pail.

Although nothing seems to be biting today (save the mosquitoes), Joe welcomes the time out of the office. The quiet bay-front setting is calming relief from the pandemonium back in the studio. Joe's eyes briefly focus on a monarch butterfly, flitting from flower to flower, before he slips into a peaceful snooze.

Building a Working Drawing

You are going to use an exercise that greatly relies upon your creativity as well as your discipline. This next segment demonstrates the advantages of using Combine and Group in building a working drawing. You will draw a butterfly to illustrate some of the principles of complex work.

Because drawing a butterfly is a rather subjective thing, feel free to take off in a different direction from the monarch that is assembled here. If, after completing this exercise, you want to try another critter, by all means, do so.

A butterfly is used for this exercise because no hard and fast right or wrong exists. Who is going to know if the butterfly is not exact? Above all, have fun!

The butterfly exercise is broken down into eight separate steps. For clarity's sake, you work in Wireframe mode. You proceed in a methodical fashion, grouping each set of objects as you go along. Grouping makes it easy to move sections around the drawing, whereas Combine makes a big difference in preview speed. You finish one wing before you start combining objects. Draw does not enable you to combine grouped objects. Hence, you select each group, ungroup, and combine.

Before you actually draw your first object, set up the Outline Pen New Object default for a one-point outline. This step is a great time-saver, and it beats going back to the outline menu every time you need the same weight rule.

The first step consists of drawing the silhouette of the butterfly's left inner and outer wings. Figure 9.1 uses only four nodes; you might need a few more. The wings are filled with black and outlined with a one-point black rule.

Figure 9.1
The wing's
silhouette.

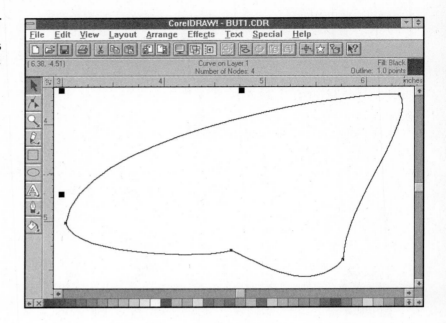

If you have problems creating closed path curves, check the AutoJoin setting in the Preferences/Curves dialog box accessed from the Special menu dialog box. Set AutoJoin to 10 to zap curves closed. You might want to experiment with different settings. Remember: 1 is the least likely to close, whereas 10 is the most likely.

Drawing the Silhouette

Set up the page for letter size, portrait orientation.

Select the Pick tool

Click on the Outline tool   The Outline fly-out menu appears

Click on Outline Pen   The Outline Pen for New Object dialog
                                                            box appears

Click on Graphic

Click on OK   The Outline Pen dialog box appears

Set <u>W</u>idth *to* 1.0 points	
Click on <u>S</u>cale With Image	
Click on OK	Sets the new object's default outline
Select the Pencil tool	
Draw the wing	
Select the Fill tool	The Fill fly-out menu appears
Click on Black	Fills the silhouette with black
Select the Shape tool	
Click on and delete the extra nodes	
Tweak the control points to achieve the proper shape	
Save the file as BUT1	

Beginning with the next section, you place colors on top of the silhouette. At this point, the file is about as compact as CorelDRAW! files get. This file measures in at 13,172 bytes, with an 8 KB color image header (but your file sizes might differ slightly). If you want to save as much disk space as possible, save your files with 1 KB monochrome image headers. (With a 1 KB header, the file is only 5980 bytes.)

The second step entails drawing nine large orange segments on the wing. All segments are filled with a uniform fill of 40-percent magenta and 100-percent yellow and outlined with a one-point rule of 60-percent magenta and 100-percent yellow. The segments are then grouped (see fig. 9.2).

After you open the Uniform Fill and Outline Color dialog boxes and configure them for Process Color CMYK mode, they stay that way. Each time you call one of these dialog boxes, it appears in the same mode as you last left it.

Figure 9.2
The wing begins
to develop.

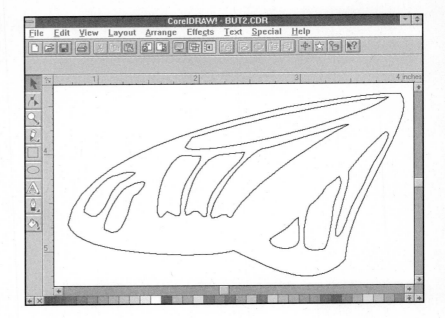

Adding the Nine Orange Segments

Take a look at the preceding illustration for an example of how the nine orange segments should look.

Click on the Pencil tool

Draw nine segments

Select the Shape tool

Delete the extra nodes. Don't forget to use AutoReduce, too! Tweak the control points to achieve the desired shapes.

Select the Pick tool

*Shift-click or marquee-
select all nine segments*

Click on **A**rrange	The Arrange menu appears
Click on **G**roup	Groups the segments

Select the Fill tool	The Fill fly-out menu appears
Click on Uniform Fill	The Uniform Fill dialog box appears
Select CMYK Color Model	The dialog box configures for process color

If the dialog box is in CMYK mode, leave it that way. If not, change it.

At <u>C</u>, *enter* **0**	
At <u>M</u>, *enter* **40**	
At <u>Y</u>, *enter* **100**	
At <u>K</u>, *enter* **0**	
Click on OK	The nine segments are filled
Select the Outline tool	The Outline fly-out menu appears
Click on the Outline Color icon	The Outline Color dialog box appears
Select CMYK Color Model	The dialog box configures for process color

If the dialog box is in CMYK mode, leave it that way. If not, change it.

At <u>C</u>, *enter* **0**	
At <u>M</u>, *enter* **60**	
At <u>Y</u>, *enter* **100**	
At <u>K</u>, *enter* **0**	
Click on OK	Outlines the nine segments in orange-red
Save the file as BUT2.CDR	

The wing is starting to develop, and the file size is growing: 17,258 bytes (with an 8 KB color image header).

Step three places 11 oval shapes near the leftmost section of the wing (see fig. 9.3). The ovals are grouped and then filled with 10-percent magenta and 100-percent yellow. They are outlined with a 1-point rule of 40-percent yellow.

II

Putting CorelDRAW! To Work

Figure 9.3
The wing gets
some spots.

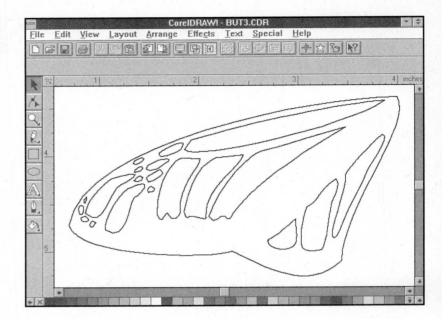

Placing the Oval Shapes

Select the Pencil tool

Draw 11 oval shapes

Select the Shape tool

Delete the extra nodes

Tweak the control points to achieve the proper shape.

Select the Pick tool

Shift-click or marquee-select all 11 ovals

Click on <u>A</u>rrange	The Arrange menu appears
Click on <u>G</u>roup	Groups the ovals
Select the Fill tool	The Fill fly-out menu appears
Click on the Uniform Fill icon	The Uniform Fill dialog box appears
At <u>C</u>, *enter* **0**	
At <u>M</u>, *enter* **10**	
At <u>Y</u>, *enter* **100**	
At <u>K</u>, *enter* **0**	

Click on OK	The 11 ovals are filled
Select the Outline tool	The Outline fly-out menu appears
Click on the Outline Color icon	The Outline Color dialog box appears
At <u>C</u>, enter **0**	
At <u>M</u>, enter **0**	
At <u>Y</u>, enter **40**	
At <u>K</u>, enter **0**	
Click on OK	Outlines the 11 ovals in bright yellow
Save the file as BUT3.CDR	

Figure 9.3 shows how the 11 oval shapes should look.

As the file grows in complexity, so do screen redraw times and file size. At this point, the file weighs in at 20,392 bytes. (Again, your file size might differ slightly.)

Step four adds 66 spots to the bottom of the wing. These spots are filled with 20-percent yellow, and outlined with a 1-point rule of 40-percent yellow. The spots are broken into three groups of 20, 23, and 23 items. The slickest way to accomplish this feat is to build one group and duplicate it. Then add or delete spots as needed.

Get Your Kicks with 66 (Spots)

Select the Ellipse tool

Draw approximately six ellipses

Instead of drawing a zillion spots, you use these six as a base. Use Rotate or Mirror with Leave Original, found on the Transform Roll-Up, to make each spot seem almost unique.

Click on the Pick tool	
Double-click on a spot	Displays Rotate/Skew handles
Use a corner handle to rotate the spot	
Press and release the + on the numeric keypad	The original remains in place
Release the mouse button	
Click on another spot	
Drag a side handle to the opposite side to mirror the spot	

Putting CorelDRAW! To Work

Press and release +	Leaves the original in place
Release the mouse button	

You should now have eight spots. Repeat the two techniques you just used to create 15 more spots. When you're done, group, fill, and outline the spots.

Select the Pick tool	
Shift-click or marquee-select all 23 spots	
Click on A̲rrange	The Arrange menu appears
Click on G̲roup	Groups the spots
Click on the Fill tool	The Fill fly-out menu appears
Click on the Uniform Fill icon	The Uniform Fill dialog box appears
At C̲, enter 0	
At M̲, enter 0	
At Y̲, enter 20	
At K̲, enter 0	
Click on OK	The 23 spots are filled
Select the Outline tool	The Outline fly-out menu appears
Click on the Outline Color icon	The Outline color dialog box appears
At C̲, enter 0	
At M̲, enter 0	
At Y̲, enter 40	
At K̲, enter 0	
Click on OK	Outlines the 23 spots in light yellow

Now, you need to duplicate the group of spots two times and drag the groups into position.

Press Ctrl+D	Duplicates the group of spots
Drag the new group into position	
Press Ctrl+D	Duplicates the group of spots
Drag the second new group into position	
Save the file as BUT4.CDR	

Figure 9.4 shows the 66 spots.

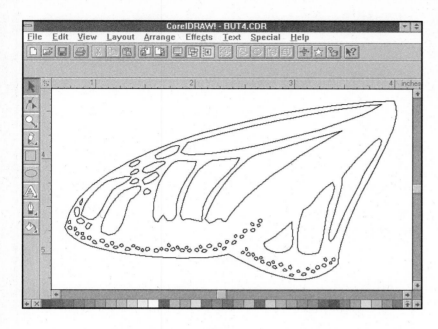

Figure 9.4
The wing gets
some more
spots.

The file is getting larger, and screen redraw should be taking longer and longer. At this point, the file size is 46,974 bytes.

In the fifth step, you combine your first objects—a large number of orange-red one-point rules. Outline them with 80-percent magenta and 100-percent yellow. These are open-path objects and can have no fill. After you're done, check your screen redraw time.

Adding and Combining Lines

Now you can combine the lines in two clusters.

Select the Pencil tool

Draw three or four straight lines in each of the orange segments

Draw a freehand line at the bottom of both the inner and outer wings

Select the Shape tool

Delete the extra nodes on the freehand lines

Select the Pick tool	
Shift-click on half the lines	
Click on <u>A</u>rrange	The Arrange menu appears
Click on <u>C</u>ombine	Combines the lines
Click on the page	Deselects the lines
Shift-click the remaining lines	
Click on <u>A</u>rrange	The Arrange menu appears
Click on <u>C</u>ombine	Combines the lines
Click on the first set of lines	
Select the Outline tool	The Outline fly-out menu appears
Click on the Outline Color icon	The Outline Color dialog box appears
At <u>C</u>, enter **0**	
At <u>M</u>, enter **100**	
At <u>Y</u>, enter **40**	
At <u>K</u>, enter **0**	
Click on OK	The lines are drawn in deep orange-red
Click on the second set of lines	
Click on <u>E</u>dit	The Edit menu appears
Click on Copy Attributes <u>F</u>rom	The Copy Attributes From dialog box appears
Click on Outline <u>C</u>olor	
Click on OK	An arrow appears
Click on the first set of lines	Outline color is copied

If you want, go in and change the straight line segments to curves. Tweak the control points to have the lines follow the dimensions of the orange segments.

Save the file as BUT5.CDR

With the addition of the combined lines, the file size has hardly grown. It is now 50,010 bytes. Figure 9.5 shows the on-screen results of this exercise.

In the sixth step, you combine everything of like fill and outline into assemblies of no more than 25 objects. This procedure considerably speeds up screen redraw time.

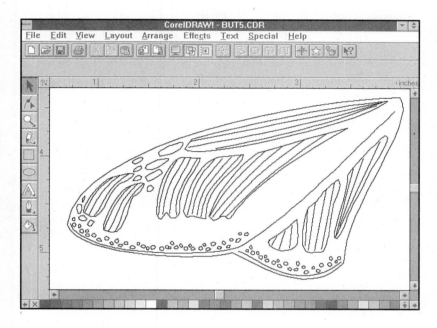

Figure 9.5
The wing gets lines.

Combining the Wing

The time has come to combine each cluster of objects. This procedure is made easier because you have grouped them along the way. The procedure in this case goes like this: select, ungroup, and combine—simple, clean, and effective.

Select the Pick tool

Click on an orange segment

Click on **A**rrange	The Arrange menu appears
Click on **U**ngroup	Ungroups the ovals
Click on **A**rrange	The Arrange menu appears
Click on **C**ombine	Combines the ovals

Click on a group of spots

Click on **A**rrange	The Arrange menu appears
Click on **U**ngroup	Ungroups the spots
Click on **A**rrange	The Arrange menu appears
Click on **C**ombine	Combines the spots

Repeat the procedure for the last two groups of spots.

Save the file as BUT6.CDR

Now you are seeing the fruits of your labor. Notice the speed at which the wing appears in Full-Color editing mode or in full-screen preview. The wireframe might look identical, but the redraw time tells the story. If you take a look at the file size, you see that it has dropped dramatically: from 50,010 to 23,564 bytes since you last checked. Saving the file with a 1 KB image header drops the file size to a modest 16,372 bytes.

The seventh step merely involves grouping and mirror/duplicating the first wing, and then dragging it into position and rotating it, if necessary. Next, you group the two wings together so that you can move the pair as one unit.

Duplicating and Positioning the Second Wing

Marquee-select the wing

Click on **A**rrange	The Arrange menu appears
Click on **G**roup	Groups the wing
Click on Effe**c**ts	The Effects menu appears
Click on **T**ransform Roll-Up	The Transform Roll-Up menu appears
Click on the Scale button	The roll-up changes to the Scale and Mirror function
Click on the Horizontal Mirror button	The button depresses
Click on Apply To Duplicate	Mirrors and duplicates the wing

Drag the new wing into position and rotate if necessary (see fig. 9.6).

Now to build the butterfly's body. You draw a silhouette body (in black) and use the contour effect to fill the body with a variety of tones. Contouring the original outline into a skinny highlight gives the body a more three-dimensional look. The different tones provide the illusion of lighting.

Before you build the body, construct the head, eyes, and antennae. Use the Pencil and Ellipse tools to build these, and remember to combine like objects.

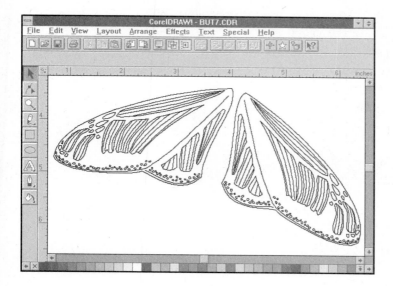

Figure 9.6
The wing gets mirrored and rotated.

Contour

The Contour effect—introduced in version 4.0—provides a way to create a number of distinctive fills. The Contour effect uses an algorithm to create concentric duplicates of an object. You can create these duplicates in one of three ways: to the center, to the inside, or to the outside. At its simplest, a contour resembles a blend. When taken to the extreme, however, a contour can yield stunning results. This concept is difficult to picture without a picture to refer to. Take a moment to look at figure 9.7 before you proceed; it illustrates the difference between the three different types of contours.

For both inside and outside contours, the Contour Roll-Up menu gives you control over the number of steps in the contour and the distance between the steps. The To Center Contour, on the other hand, contours directly to the center of the object and uses only the distance setting. (You cannot set the number of steps.) The three contouriffic sea horses (in fig. 9.7) were set with identical contour distance settings and outline widths. As you can see, both the inside and outside examples have seven concentric contours.

Like blends, you have the option of changing outline and fill colors of your contours. Similarly, contours are dynamically linked to the original object. If you make a change to the original object, the contour restructures to reflect the change.

Figure 9.7
Choose your contour: to center, outside, and inside.

To Center Outside Inside

Tip Press Ctrl+R to repeat the last function completed.

Contour is a processor-intensive operation. It might take a few minutes for your computer to complete the calculations—even on a fast computer! In the next exercise, you make the butterfly's body pop off the screen when you apply a contour (to center). Watch when you click to center—the Steps setting becomes inactive (grayed out).

Tip Perhaps you want to shrink (or enlarge) an object, but are not sure what the object's final size should be. Scale the object down (or up) by a small percentage, say 2 percent. Then, use the Ctrl+R shortcut to scale the object repeatedly down (or up) to the exact size. You also can use this technique to rotate objects.

Using Contour To Build the Butterfly's Body

Select the Pencil tool

Draw the silhouette of the body

Select the Fill tool — The Fill fly-out menu appears

Click on Black — The silhouette is filled with black

Draw a body section

Select the Shape tool

Reduce the number of nodes in the body section to about 11

Tweak the nodes as needed (see fig. 9.8)

Select the Fill tool — The Fill fly-out menu appears

Click on the Uniform Fill icon — The Uniform Fill dialog box appears

At <u>C</u>, *enter* **90**

At <u>M</u>, *enter* **40**

At <u>Y</u>, *enter* **0**

At <u>K</u>, *enter* **70**

At the on-screen color palette, click on No Outline

Click on Effe<u>c</u>ts — The Effects menu appears

Click on Co<u>n</u>tour — The Contour Roll-Up menu appears

Click on To Center — Steps grays out

At Offset, enter **0.01** *inches*

Click on the Contour Fill Color button — The Contour Fill Color fly-out menu appears

Click on Light Blue

Click on Apply *(see fig. 9.9)*

Press F9 to preview

The butterfly's body looks almost three-dimensional!

Marquee-select the butterfly's
body, head, and antennae

Drag the body into position
between the wings (see fig.
9.10)

Marquee-select the entire butterfly

Press Ctrl+G   Groups the entire butterfly

Save the file as BUT9.CDR

Figure 9.8
Ready to
contour.

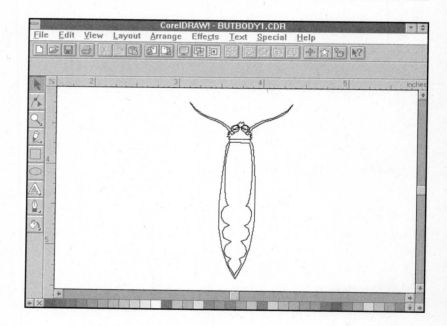

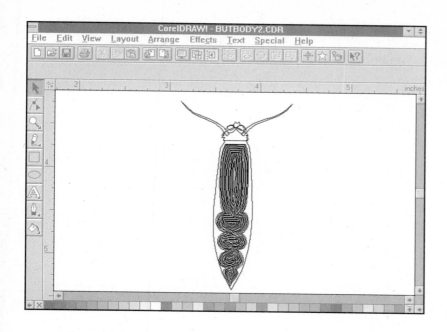

Figure 9.9
The contoured
butterfly body.

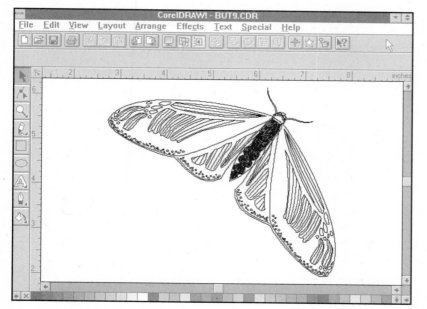

Figure 9.10
The finished
butterfly.

Contour does have some restrictions. You cannot contour groups of objects, nor can you use the Blend effect to blend contours into other objects, or fill them with bit maps. Although the application of contours might not be initially apparent, after a while you can come up with some really cool effects!

Now that the butterfly is complete, press F9 to view your handiwork in glorious full color. Watch how quickly the combined spots pour in and see how the butterfly's body seems to pop right off the screen. In the next exercise, you put the butterfly on its own layer, then create a setting for the butterfly to fly around in.

Put the Butterfly on Its Own Layer

Click on <u>L</u>ayout	The Layout menu appears
Click on <u>L</u>ayers Roll-Up	The Layers Roll-Up menu appears
Double-click on Layer 1	The Layer Options dialog box appears
In the <u>N</u>*ame box, type* **Foreground**	Changes the name of the layer
Click on OK	
Click on the Layers fly-out arrow	The Layers fly-out menu appears
Click on New	The New Layer dialog box appears
In the <u>N</u>*ame box, type* **Background**	Changes the name of the layer
Click on OK	
Click on the Layers fly-out arrow	The Layers fly-out menu appears
Deselect MultiLayer	

Before moving on to the next subject, take the time to print your butterfly. If you encounter any problems with printing, check out Chapter 11. Although the butterfly is not a hopelessly complex piece of art, it might tie up your printer for a while.

It's time to draw a world for the butterfly to live in! In the next section, you create some ferns by using both the Blend effect and the Weld function.

Blender Drinks for Everyone!

Joe DeLook is in the midst of a delirious dream, involving coconuts, blender drinks, and a giant talking lizard named Olaf. Perhaps he is obsessed with the animation that Chameleon Racing Boats had asked about (which you will create in Chapter 17, "The Basics of CorelMOVE!"), or maybe he's just really thirsty in his unconscious state. Whatever the case, now is a good time to dive into the Blend effect. Although it's not as refreshing as a frosty blender drink, it's a cool thing in its own right.

The Blend effect, which debuted in CorelDRAW! version 2.0, is a powerful drawing tool (see fig. 9.11). Using Blend, you can interpolate between two different objects. The outline color and width, fill, and object shape are melded. Blend has a wide variety of uses. You can, for instance, turn apples into oranges, dogs into cats, and purples into reds. In the last case, notice the functional overlap between the Blend effect, fountain fills, and contours.

CorelDRAW! version 3.0 featured great improvements of the Blend effect. Most importantly, blends were changed so that they became dynamic. Thus, after you have created a blend, you can make changes to the starting or ending objects, and the blend re-creates itself. The Blend effect was improved again in version 4.0 with the capability to fuse objects in a compound blend. Except for some cosmetic changes made to the roll-up, the Blend functions have remained the same for version 5.

Blend is accessed through its roll-up menu, which offers incredible control over a number of blend characteristics. In the following exercise, you use only a fraction of Blend's capabilities. The engineers put their efforts to good use on this one! Blend is one of Draw's nicest features.

In this next exercise, you create the basic parts of a fern—pinnules. You create one large pinnule and one small pinnule, and then use the Blend effect to create a number of intermediate pinnules, which form the pinna.

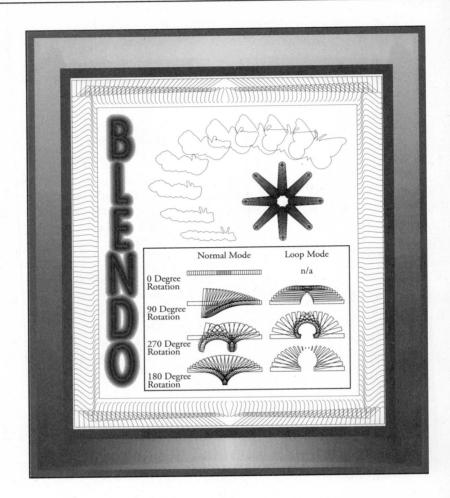

Using Blend To Create a Fern's Pinna

Select the Pencil tool

Draw a kidney-shaped object (a pinnule). Make sure it is a lean and mean object with only 4 nodes, then duplicate the pinnule while stretching it down to 30 percent of its original width (refer to figure 9.13).

Drag the smaller pinnule 3 inches from the original

Tweak the smaller pinnule so that it is almost round

Marquee-select both pinnules

Click on Effects	The Effects menu appears
Click on **B**lend Roll-Up	The Blend Roll-Up menu appears (see fig. 9.12)
At Steps, type **12**	
Click on Apply	Blends the pinnules (see fig. 9.13)

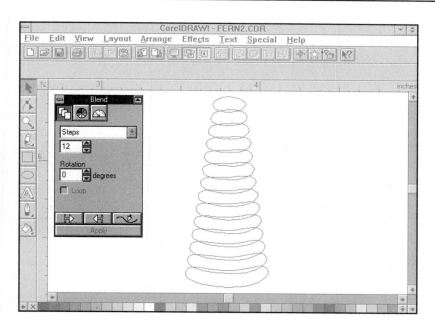

Figure 9.12
The **B**lend Roll-Up menu.

Notice that the blended segments are grouped together; you can easily delete them if they do not come out looking quite right. Of course, you can ungroup the blend and work with the individual objects, tweaking nodes and colors as you see fit.

Blend works on object shapes, fills, and outlines, but with some restrictions. You can blend between only two entities at a time, but these groups can include objects or multiple-path objects (refer back to figure 9.11). Blending between objects of different fills or outline colors has certain constraints, as outlined in table 9.1.

Figure 9.13
The pinna after blending.

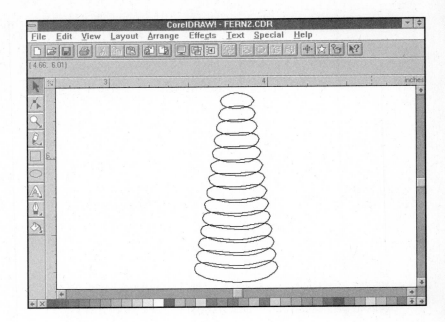

Table 9.1
Blend Characteristics

Starting/Ending Object Fill	Blend Objects Fill
No Fill/Any Fill	No Fill
Uniform/Linear Fountain	Uniform to Linear Fountain
Uniform/Radial Fountain	Radial Fountain
Radial Fountain/Linear Fountain	Radial Fountain
Two Fountains of Same Type	Similar Fountain
Uniform/Pattern	Uniform
Pattern/Any Fill	Other Fill
Two Patterns	Top Object's Pattern
Spot Color/Process Color	Process Color

Starting/Ending Object Fill	Blend Objects Fill
Two Different Spot Colors	Process Color
Two Tints of the Same Spot Color	Spot Color Tints

In addition to the blend fills mentioned earlier, you can set specific blend color attributes. By clicking on the Blend Roll-Up's color wheel, you are able to access an HSB color wheel. Clicking on Rainbow enables you to apply a rainbow effect—in a clockwise or counterclockwise direction—to your blend.

The Blend dialog box offers a variety of different effects. The first value you might enter is the number of blend steps. This value (from 1 to 999) governs the number of interpolating objects created between the starting and ending objects. Remember that the more objects you use, the smoother the blend; but file size (and print time) grows proportionately.

You can use rotation for some interesting arcing effects. Figure 9.11 shows settings for 270-, 180-, 90-, and 0-degree (clockwise) rotation. Using negative values rotates the objects in the opposite direction. In addition, you can pull out an object's center of rotation before blending to give the blend a twisting path.

Editing intermediate blend objects can yield some interesting results. Press Ctrl and double-click on any intermediate blend object, and you can alter that object's position, outline, fill, size, and shape. You can even get into some heavy node editing.

The position and number of nodes in each object affect the blend. By default, blends act upon the starting nodes of both objects. You can alter this setting by selecting Map Nodes. This option enables you to choose the nodes—in effect, temporarily reassigning the starting nodes—to achieve different blends.

Blending along a path became a reality in CorelDRAW! 3.0. You now can have a blend follow a specific, editable trail. When blending along a path, you have the option to use predefined spacing or a number of steps. A blend can follow the full path, or just a portion of it, with magnetic accuracy. You also can rotate the blend objects to follow the curve of a path.

Now that blending is interactive, you can move or otherwise alter a starting or ending blend object, and then watch the blend redraw. You even have the ability to reshape the blend path interactively. The blend objects instantly and precisely align themselves to the path.

Blend has many uses. The more you work with the effect, the more you find. In figure 9.11, a caterpillar was turned into a butterfly with seven intermediate steps. The butterfly came from Draw's symbols. It was duplicated and rearranged into a caterpillar shape with the Node Edit tool. By blending two objects with the same number of nodes, some of the bizarre effects that happen when blending two wildly different objects were avoided. Notice that the blend steps are always equally spaced; however, you can separate and ungroup the blend after its completion and space the interpolated objects as you see fit.

The neon effect on the word "Blendo" was easy to create. First, the word was set with a fat 10-percent outline. Then, the word was duplicated and centered on the original. The duplicate was given a 100-percent hairline outline. Eight blend steps were used between the two. Presto! Instant neon. For a step-by-step exercise in creating neon type, check out Chapter 6, "Special Type Effects."

Welding without Safety Glasses

The Weld function was introduced in CorelDRAW! 4.0. It works in a manner similar to Combine, with one important difference: it was designed to create one object from a number of overlapping objects. (Does that sound confusing?) After you work through the next little exercise, you will understand.

Weld works only on ungrouped objects. Because the blend you just created is attached twice—once to the starting and ending control objects, and once to itself—you first must go through the hassle of separating, and then ungrouping before you can proceed with your weld.

Welding the Pinna

Select the Pick tool	
Click on one of the blend pinnules	The blend group is selected
Click on Arrange	The Arrange menu appears
Click on Separate	Separates the blend
Deselect the group of pinnules	
Click on an intermediate pinnule	The group of 12 blended pinnules is selected
Press Ctrl+U	Ungroups the group

Marquee-select the complete
pinna (all 14 objects)

Click on <u>A</u>rrange   The Arrange menu appears

Click on <u>W</u>eld   The pinna is welded
                                             (see fig. 9.14)

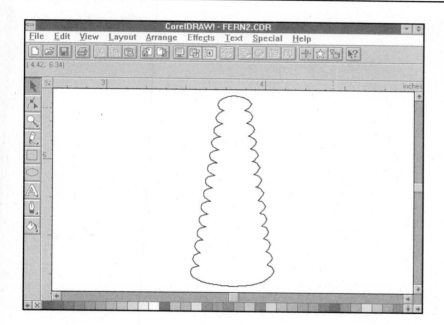

Figure 9.14
The welded
pinna.

Welding is essential if you want to create your own typefaces and symbol fonts with CorelDRAW! because neither PostScript type format enables you to overlap objects. Weld takes the drudgery out of combining and node-editing combined-path objects.

Now that you have one pinna, you can quickly and easily create the fern's frond, by duplicating, scaling, stretching, and mirroring a number of pinnas. Use the Envelope effect for more realism. You are on your own with this one (refer to figure 9.15).

To really finish off this drawing, you use PowerLines—another one of CorelDRAW!'s amazing features.

II

Putting CorelDRAW! To Work

Figure 9.15
The fern frond.

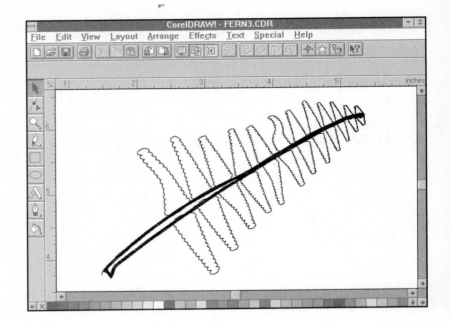

Be a Trendy Artist (or Just Draw Like One) by Using PowerLines!

Have you ever wanted to create electronic artwork that looked as if it were the computerized equivalent of a woodcut or linocut? Draw's PowerLine feature gives you the tools you need to render illustrations with a real electro-retro feel. CorelDRAW! 5.0 ships with 24 different PowerLines and gives you the option of creating your own personal PowerLines to boot. In addition to creating electronic illustrations that mimic traditional artwork, the PowerLine tool also is great for building design elements for distinctive logos.

PowerLines work with all pointing devices. But when coupled with a pressure-sensitive drawing tablet, such as the Wacom UD-1212 (reviewed in Chapter 10, "You're the Designer"), PowerLines gain a new dimension. With a pressure-sensitive pen, Draw uses the pressure input to build lines of variable thickness—the harder you press, the thicker the line.

In the following exercise, you add some more vegetation to your butterfly illustration, complementing the fern created in the last exercise. You do not have to be an artist extraordinaire to finish this one off. Just take your time and have some fun!

As you draw your first PowerLines, notice that the computer can take its time to display them. The more complex a PowerLine, the longer it takes to appear.

Drawing Clover with the Teardrop2 PowerLine

Click on Effects	The Effects menu appears
Click on PowerLine Roll-Up	The PowerLine Roll-Up menu appears
At the PowerLine Roll-Up, roll down and click on Teardrop2	
Set Max. Width *to* .75 inches	
Click on Apply *when drawing lines*	
Choose the Pencil tool	
Draw a line 1 inch long	Creates a cloverleaf

Draw two more leaves, but do not connect them to the first leaf. Drag them into position after they have been drawn. Use Snap to Objects so that the leaves touch each other. Go ahead and plant a whole field of clover (see fig. 9.16)!

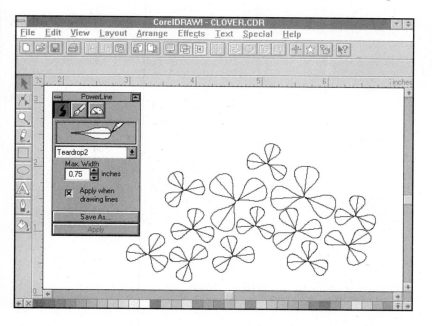

Figure 9.16
Rolling in clover with Teardrop2 PowerLine.

II

Putting CorelDRAW! To Work

You can change a PowerLine's style or attributes after it has been drawn. And, you can change a line that was not drawn as a PowerLine into a PowerLine. If you are obsessed with tweaking things, you'll have plenty to tweak! You can fiddle with a plethora of settings, in addition to the outline color and fill choices. Figure 9.17 illustrates the four faces of the PowerLine Roll-Up menu.

Figure 9.17
The four faces of
the PowerLine
Roll-Up menu.

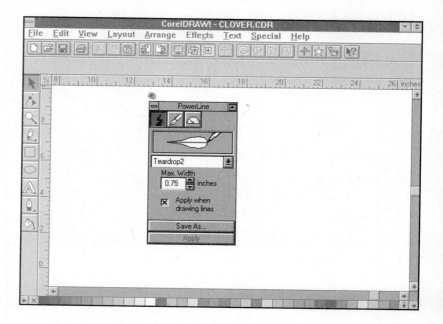

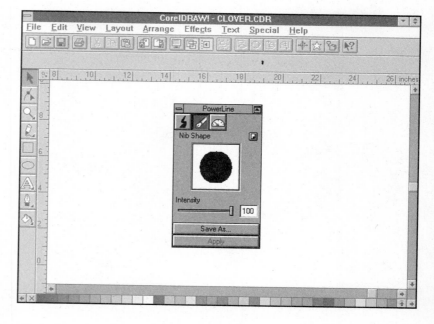

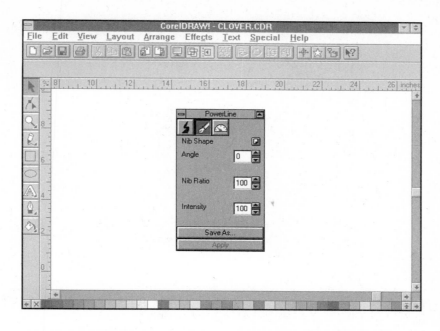

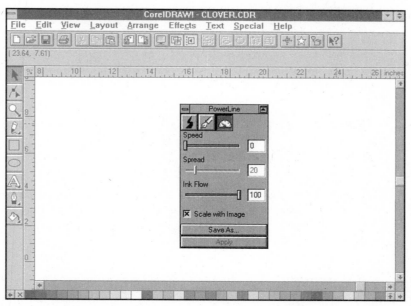

Now that you've got a nice collection of clover, try using the Woodcut3 and Bullet3 PowerLines to create even more vegetation. Don't forget to save your file frequently. In the next section, you learn more about the pragmatic approach to electronic artwork.

Preventing Problems

It would be tough to find an electronic artist, or any computer user, who has never lost a file—or at least a few hours of work—because of lackadaisical file management practices. Most people learn the hard way. For this reason, you must learn to follow proper file management techniques.

A few basic details should be kept in mind. Nothing earth-shattering here, just commonsense stuff. In fact, you have been using these techniques throughout this book and have done so rather extensively in this chapter.

Save Files Frequently

Once again, use the Save command to write working files to the hard disk at regular intervals. This procedure prevents file loss in the event of a power outage (barring a disk crash). It also provides a "super undo," for those occasions when the file gets really trashed through a series of unfortunate choices. With a saved file on hand, you merely reopen the file, relax, and get back to work.

Even though CorelDRAW! provides some protection in the form of the backup file, get into the habit of saving the file each time an intricate maneuver is performed. This step helps to thwart the gremlins.

In addition to simply saving files, you also can make multiple copies of intricate files (as you did with the butterfly). This step provides extra insurance in case a version gets trashed along the way. Number these files sequentially to make it easy to go back in and rework the file at any stage of completion.

CorelDRAW! version 2.0 introduced Timed AutoBackup. This feature is yet another mechanism for safeguarding work. Versions 2.0 through 4.0 required a change to the CORELDRW.INI file to adjust the backup interval. Thankfully, CorelDRAW 5.0 enables you to set the backup interval through the Preferences/Advanced dialog box (found on the Special menu).

Use Undo Immediately!

This next point also might seem obvious, but run through it one more time. Use Undo immediately after fouling up. Do not try to "fix" what has gone wrong. Do not touch anything else, be it an object or a tool.

The second that you say "oops," stop everything. Then, without delay, choose Edit, Undo, or use the keyboard shortcut Ctrl+Z, (the old Alt+backspace combination still works, also). This step ensures that Undo performs its function. Although CorelDRAW! 5.0 features multiple levels of Undo, failure to use Undo immediately might jeopardize the drawing. With the Undo level's default setting of 4, your drawings can quickly enter the land of no return. If your computer has plenty of RAM, consider devoting some of it to a higher number of Undo levels. You can set the Undo levels up to 99 in the Preferences dialog box.

Always Back Up Important Files!

The final preventive measure to mention is file backup. Most users have a tremendous amount of information stored on their systems' hard disks, and are unaware of the potential disaster that could befall them. Hard disks are like bank vaults—a great place for storing things, but if the disk should crash, it would be akin to throwing away the key to the vault. Salvaging data from a trashed hard disk can be tougher than breaking into a bank (or trying to resuscitate a failed savings and loan).

Fortunately (or is that luckily?), the author followed strict backup procedures while working on a previous edition of this book. Deep into the production process, one of the computers had a hard disk failure. Although it was a setback, it was not monumental. All important files had been backed up to floppies. A spare hard disk was slapped into the computer and all the software and data files were reloaded. In half a day, everything was once again running at full speed.

Which files should be backed up? All important CDR files, for starters. Imagine putting days, weeks, or even months into building a library of images, only to have them lost to a disk crash. There are disk utilities on the market that might enable the user to salvage files that would otherwise be lost. One of the most popular is the Norton Utilities. But keep in mind the words "*might* enable the user to salvage files."

Backing up important CDR files to floppy disks is an inexpensive way to safeguard against loss. Use the Windows File Manager on a regular basis to copy all pertinent files from the hard disk to floppies. If you can afford a tape backup, buy one (and use it). Tape drives are cheap insurance against disaster.

Preview Strategies

A lot of the material discussed in this chapter concerns operating efficiency. The time it takes to get things done is vital. Most people have grown up in a world that refuses to wait for anything, including the time it takes for computers to process information.

When building complex drawings, the screen redraw times can become quite substantial. It helps to keep in mind a few strategies that can cut down the waiting time. Of course, you could go out and get the fastest computer available and outfit it with a speedy hard disk and powerful graphics card, but no matter what, you will eventually find yourself (broke and) seeking something a little faster. The concepts you are about to learn work with any PC running CorelDRAW!.

The simplest advice is to work in Wireframe mode most of the time. This mode obviously cuts down on screen redraw time. You must determine what works best for you. When speed is the prime consideration, work with wireframes. When it is imperative to do full-color editing, press Shift+F9 and go for it!

If you like the biggest preview screen possible, then you should use true full-screen preview. By pressing F9, you instantly summon up a nice big preview, unencumbered by windows, toolboxes, and the like. The disadvantage is that you must return to editing mode to make any changes to the image.

 Tip Press Shift+F9 to switch between wireframe and full-color editing. Press F9 to invoke full-screen preview.

Interruptible Display

When you are working on a large file, screen redraws can get to be quite time-consuming. One way to speed things up is to use Interruptible Refresh. This feature enables you to perform a function before the screen has been completely redrawn. You can switch on and off this time-saving feature on the View section of the <u>P</u>references dialog box (in the <u>S</u>pecial menu).

Auto-Panning

Auto-panning was introduced in CorelDRAW! version 3.0, but PageMaker users should be quite familiar with the concept. With this feature enabled, the screen scrolls automatically when you drag an object past the Draw Window's border. You can switch on or off Auto-panning by means of the View section of the <u>P</u>references dialog box.

CorelDRAW! version 4.0 users may find that the Auto-panning feature takes a little effort to get reacquainted. In earlier versions, all you need to do is drag a screen element anywhere off the workspace to initiate the panning action. Version 5.0 requires more precise action by the user to start the Auto-panning feature. This is because "drag and drop" technology has been implemented in CorelDRAW! 5.0 and other applications, such as PhotoPaint and Mosaic. This means that Corel had to limit the area that recognizes the panning feature to just the inside edge of the scroll bars that surround the Drawing Window. If your cursor turns into a circle with a slash through it, you know that you have overshot the scroll bars.

Getting the Most from Layers

Among the Layer options, you might decide to make a layer invisible, or apply a color override. By hiding a complex layer, your screen redraws faster and your drawing is easier to work with. Assigning a color override can yield much the same result, without losing sight of those layers.

Preview Selected Only

This strategy involves using the Preview Selected **O**nly option, which is found on the **V**iew menu. It is useful when composing very complex drawings with a multitude of objects. Using this function speeds up preview redraw times enormously because the program displays only selected objects rather than the entire drawing.

This option also is useful for isolating objects. If an image contains a heap of objects, each indiscernible from the next, Preview Selected **O**nly often is instrumental in sorting things out. With this option on, merely click on or Tab through the objects until the correct one is located, and press F9 to preview.

Save Time by Programming Your Mouse

One last way to speed things up is to set up your mouse button to perform a frequent task. The Preferences dialog box provides the means to pop into six different modes instantly. You can set your right mouse button to summon 2×Zoom, Edit Text, Full Screen Preview, or Node Edit. These four shortcuts are the same as when introduced in version 4. CorelDRAW! 5.0 adds two more functions to the programmable mouse feature: Character and Edit Text. Character opens the Character Attributes dialog, and Edit Text opens a WYSIWYG editor that enables you to make changes to your text strings.

Tip

Clicking the right mouse button while dragging always leaves an original. This procedure has no effect on any of the programmable mouse functions.

It is obvious that Corel Systems truly listens to its user base. Many of the features that were incorporated into the latest incarnations of Draw were requested by users. If you have a feature request, be sure to let Corel know about it.

Joe Wakes Up

When you last left Joe DeLook, he was asleep at his favorite fishing spot. A sharp tug on the line has brought Joe back into the waking world, but, alas, the fish took the bait and swam off. Belatedly, Joe remembers the Beached Whale Brew Pub project that he was working on.

With only a few hours to deadline, Joe hustles back to the studio. The work is not too far from being finished, but he still must complete the comp of a proposed shopping bag design.

Adding Perspective

The Perspective effect was introduced in CorelDRAW! version 2.0 to great acclaim. This feature provides a means to apply one- and two-point perspective to any object (see figs. 9.18 and 9.19). If you are not familiar with perspective, briefly go over the theory basics presented here. If you are interested in learning more background information, consider taking a course in two-dimensional design.

Figure 9.18
One-point
perspective.

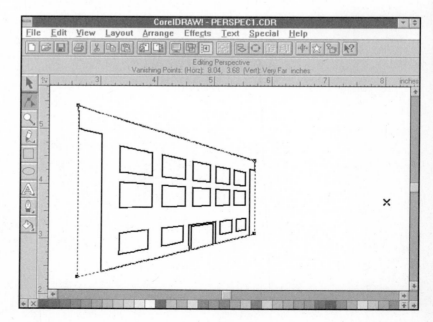

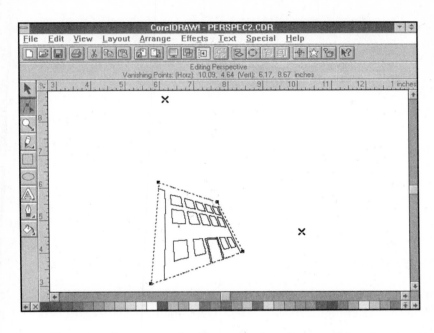

Figure 9.19
Two-point
perspective.

You can refer to many familiar examples when speaking about perspective. The most common might be the ubiquitous railroad tracks and telephone poles. Think how these objects fade off into the distance, shrinking to tiny spots on the horizon.

When working with perspective, two constants should always be kept in mind. You must have a horizon line and at least one vanishing point. The horizon line, as its name implies, is a horizontal "edge of the earth," whereas the vanishing point is the point of convergence on the horizon line. As objects get farther away, they grow vertically closer to the horizon line.

Remember that the horizon line is at eye level. If eye level is five feet and seven inches, so too is the horizon line. Consequently, any object that is at eye level—regardless of its location on the plane—hits the horizon line.

The best way to lay down a horizon line with CorelDRAW! is to drag in a horizontal guideline. Then, you can drag in a vertical guideline (or two) to set up your vanishing point(s). This method is especially handy when aligning the vanishing points of a number of objects.

Using the Perspective Effect

When you choose <u>A</u>dd Perspective (on the Effects menu), CorelDRAW! applies a bounding box to the object, and the cursor turns into the Shape tool. To alter one-point perspective, drag a corner handle. If you want to constrain the movement horizontally or vertically, hold down Ctrl. To affect the perspective on two opposite handles simultaneously, hold down both Ctrl and Shift; the handles move in opposite directions.

To alter two-point perspective, drag a corner handle toward (or away from) the object's center. Watch for a pair of X markers on the screen; these markers are the object's vanishing points. After they are on-screen, you might find it easier to change an object's perspective by dragging the object's vanishing points rather than on the object's handles.

Not too surprisingly, one-point perspective enables for one (usually horizontal) vanishing point, whereas two-point perspective affords two (vertical and horizontal) vanishing points. You can use the click-and-drag positioning technique on either variety.

You can use the perspective effect on a single object, a group of objects, or a number of (ungrouped) objects. But if you want to apply perspective to an illustration of a building with doors and windows, for example, you should group the objects on each "face." Otherwise, the perspective is applied to each object rather than to the objects as a whole, and you would have to adjust the perspective for each object (see fig. 9.20).

Figure 9.20
Remember to group before copying perspective!

Remember Copy Style From? You also can use Copy Perspective From. Select the object that you want to apply the perspective to and select Copy...Perspective From (on the Effects menu), and an arrow appears. Then click on the object from which you want to copy the perspective. Instant perspective! If you copy to a number of ungrouped objects, a separate perspective is applied to each object.

Right now, give the perspective effect a try. Take a version of the Beached Whale Brew Pub logo and see how it looks on a shopping bag (see fig. 9.21). This exercise should ease you into perspective. Draw a couple of rectangles and a couple of handles and set some type before you get around to applying perspective.

Figure 9.21
The Beached Whale Brew Pub shopping bag.

Using Perspective To Put the Logo on a Shopping Bag

Set the grid to an easy 2 per inch, and turn it on.

Select the Rectangle tool

Draw a rectangle 2 inches wide by 2 1/2 inches high

Click on 10% tint

Click on the Outline tool	The Outline fly-out menu appears
Click on the two-point rule	
Draw a second rectangle 1 inch wide by 2 1/2 inches high to the left and vertically aligned with the first rectangle	
Click on 30% tint	
Select the Outline tool	The Outline fly-out menu appears
Click on the two-point rule	
Drag the horizontal guideline down 1.5 inches below the top of the rectangles	This is your horizon line
Drag the vertical guideline over 1.5 inches from the left of the rectangles	This is your left vanishing point
Drag the vertical guideline over 2.5 inches from the right of the rectangles	This is your right vanishing point
Press Ctrl+Y	Turns off grid

Now, you set some text for the left side of the bag and draw a couple of handles.

Select the Text tool	The cursor turns into a +
Click on the inside of the left rectangle	The Text I bar appears
Type **A** *and press Enter*	
Type **WHALE** *and press Enter*	
Type **OF A** *and press Enter*	
Type **GOOD** *and press Enter*	
Type **BREW!**	
Press Ctrl+T	The Character Attributes dialog box appears
At Si̲ze, enter **24**	
Click on C̲enter	

After you import the logo into your design, drag the logo onto the front of the bag

Scale the logo to fit	See figure 9.24
Click on Effe<u>c</u>ts	The Effects menu appears
Click on Cop<u>y</u>	The Extended Copy menu appears
Click on <u>P</u>erspective From	An arrow appears
Click on the front of the bag	Copies the perspective

The logo might need to be resized after perspective has been added. Go ahead and resize as necessary. When you have it right, click on the Shape tool and reposition the vanishing point. Finish up by reshuffling the objects, and group when you are done. The final artwork should look similar to figure 9.25.

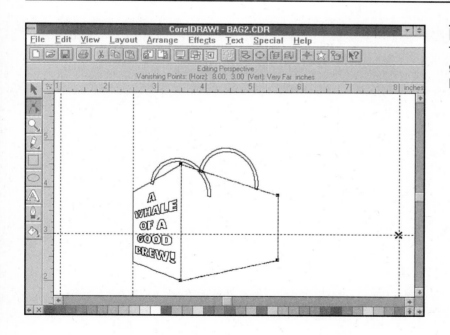

Figure 9.23
The bag gets some perspective.

Figure 9.24
Proper position
of logo before
copying
perspective.

Figure 9.25
The finished
shopping bag.

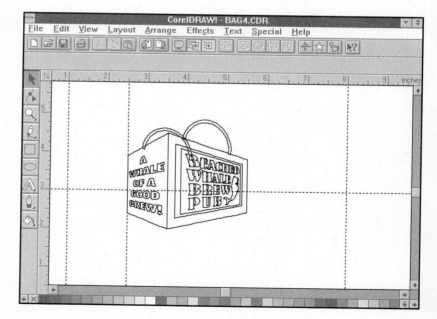

If an object's perspective gets out of hand, you can easily remove it with the <u>C</u>lear Perspective command. For objects with multiple perspectives, the command clears each perspective, one at a time. Clicking on <u>C</u>lear Transformations removes all perspectives (as well as envelopes) at once. Both commands are found under the Effe<u>c</u>ts menu.

Like the Envelope effect, text that has been given a perspective remains in an editable state. You can easily change the wording on a packaging mock-up (like your shopping bag) or on a billboard rendering.

CorelDRAW! 5.0's Cookie Cutters: Weld, Intersection, and Trim

In version 5.0, Corel introduced a pair of new path editing functions: Intersection and Trim. These two new features, when taken into account with the previously existing Weld and Combine commands, constitute a formidable group of path editors. They provide you with a number of new drawing techniques that greatly simplify the assembly of complex objects. Figure 9.26 illustrates the possibilities of each tool.

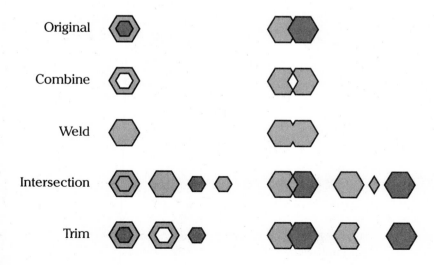

Slicing and Dicing with CorelDRAW! 5.0's Cool Cookie Cutters

Figure 9.26
The cookie cutters at work.

Original

Combine

Weld

Intersection

Trim

You can consider these commands as being similar in that they enable you to automate the creation of new objects (which have been based on existing objects), without forcing you into manual editing. Think back over the exercises you completed in the previous chapters. In Chapter 5, "Advanced Typography," you used the Combine function to reassemble the characters in the Beached Whale Brew Pub label. Earlier in this chapter, you used the Combine function again to combine many of the objects in the butterfly exercise, in addition to using the Weld function to create the fern. These exercises focused on the creation of new objects from existing objects. The difference between the functions of these commands centers upon how they treat overlapping objects.

Weld

Weld fuses objects together into one object. As shown in figure 9.26, you see that in each instance, the two objects are fused cleanly together, leaving one object. If you compare this to the Combine command, you are creating a similarly shaped object, but without the "doughnut hole" where the overlap was.

Intersection

The Intersection command creates a new object from the overlapping area between objects. Figure 9.26 illustrates how the original objects are left untouched. If you do your own trapping, you should find the Intersection command to be of great help when creating intricate traps.

Trim

Trim is where the cookie cutter analogy fits the best. When you apply the Trim command to two overlapping objects, the program cuts away the overlapping area. In the first column of figure 9.26, you will notice how Trim acts in a similar manner to Combine, while leaving the top object untouched. In the second column of the figure, notice how the top object takes a bite out of the bottom object.

CorelDRAW! 5.0's New PowerClip Function

The PowerClip feature introduced in version 5.0 arrived after years of repeated requests from hard-core CorelDRAW! users. PowerClips are Corel's version of *paste inside* — a feature which has been around in other drawing packages for ages. Now that Draw version 5.0 has the ability to paste objects inside other objects, you no longer need to use manually constructed clipping paths (as you did in previous versions of the program). In fact, the PowerClip feature does a good job of creating flexible clipping paths with negligible bloating in file size. Figure 9.27 shows some examples of PowerClips.

Figure 9.27
PowerClips.

PowerClips get their name from clipping paths. A *clipping path* can be thought of as a mask or a stencil in which only the open areas show through. The term is adapted from its corresponding function in conventional printmaking and airbrush work. The use of clipping paths is essential when creating complex illustrations.

When you create a PowerClip, the container (masking) object holds from one to many objects, including other PowerClips. You can nest up to five levels of PowerClips, although system performance will take a hit with each nested level. The objects contained in a PowerClip can be imported bit maps, text, or vector artwork. PowerClips are invaluable for creating texture type, as covered in Chapter 6, "Special Type Effects."

CorelDRAW! 5.0 is preset to automatically center PowerClips upon container objects. You can disable this pesky feature in the Preferences/General dialog box (accessed via the Special menu) by deselecting Auto-Center Place Inside. This allows you control over how the container object clips the fill. You should place the fill object behind the container object and fine tune its position before placing the object in the PowerClip container.

Chapter Snapshot

CorelDRAW! is not an island unto itself. The Windows desktop publishing market has matured and a plethora of program choices abound. Savvy Windows desktop publishing professionals pick the right tool for the task at hand. In this chapter, you learn to do the following:

✔ Upgrade your system for maximum potential

✔ Choose between various graphics programs, such as Adobe Photoshop, Fractal Design Painter, Adobe Illustrator, and Aldus FreeHand

✔ Jump into the third dimension with Visual Reality

✔ Make use of shareware programs

✔ Find more information on desktop publishing and design

✔ Use the on-line world for electronic artists

Staying on top of the ever-changing world of desktop publishing and design is no easy task. The information and sources contained here help you to keep afloat.

10

CHAPTER

You're the Designer

The competition for graphics design work has never been tougher. As of this writing, most designers have gone or are going electronic. Even now, you can find the obligatory Macintosh in a majority of professional design studios. You have seen the TV commercials. You read the magazine advertisements. You hear the hype: if you want to get into desktop publishing, you have to have a Mac. Well, it just is not true—certainly not today.

The information on the following pages should help round out your perception of Draw's place in the PC-based designer's studio. This chapter touches on the subject of Windows (with more coverage in Part IV of this book). You will learn what is important when it comes to setting up your electronic workshop and where you should and should not spend your money. In particular, this chapter covers hardware, as well as various programs and utilities, that can make your work easier and your life more bearable. This chapter also includes a list of publications and other sources to help you obtain further information about the publishing field.

This chapter is dedicated to those professionals who have decided on the PC platform for their desktop publishing work. It presents resources that can be instrumental in helping you achieve success. Professionals must keep abreast of the ever-changing industry. Graphics arts veterans can attest to the fact that systems go in and out with the seasons. Desktop publishers who feel a blind allegiance to any platform had better open their eyes.

When the next greatest system rolls along, well-heeled and far-sighted designers will jump from both ships. The rest will soon follow. Traditionally, Macintosh has ruled the desktop publishing market. In fact, it made the market, but now runs the risk of losing the market. Early versions of Windows held back the PC, but Windows 3.11 is faster and more stable. Although Macintosh still has the edge in many designers' eyes, the gap is much narrower than it was. All the major graphics arts applications—XPress, Photoshop, Illustrator, and FreeHand—have finally been ported to Windows.

PC-based desktop publishers have a few distinct advantages over their Macintosh-based brethren. Their hardware choices are greater. They are not tied to Apple for systems. They can buy PCs at competitive prices from countless manufacturers, thus lowering their overhead. Even the most staunch Mac users accept the fact that even with Apple's numerous price reductions, a comparably equipped PC still costs less than a Macintosh (although this may change as more PowerMacs enter the market).

PC-based desktop publishers can share files with a greater number of people because there are far more PCs in use than Macs. Since the introduction of Apple's Super Drive, however, Macs have become far more compatible. They can easily read from and write to PC disks. Score one for Apple—it's not so easy to read a Mac disk on a PC.

Finally, do not forget: you have CorelDRAW!. And while there have been rumblings of a Mac version of Draw for years, as of this writing it has all been vaporware.

Taking Charge

As the year 2000 approaches, graphics communications are playing an increasingly important role in society. Once upon a time, people outside the publishing field knew little about type and design; the savvy businessperson of today, however, looks at the subject with a discerning eye.

Concurrently, society has begun to demand instant gratification. Witness the success of fax machines and overnight delivery services. These devices and services are not new developments—both have been used by the publishing industry for years. Today's business world, in fact, accepts these privileges as undeniable realities.

In addition to bringing design to the forefront of everyday culture and paving the way for faxes and overnight mail, newspapers and magazines were some of the first heavy-duty computer terminal users. For the publishing industry, timeliness is everything. Business has borrowed heavily from the experiences of professional publishers.

In today's world, demanding business people have begun to expect overnight design magic as well. You can probably blame this partially on those computer commercials stating, "My department can do it." Although the computer has brought wonderful innovation to people's lives, it also has wrought havoc. People expect more from the designer, and they expect it faster. The aim of electronic artists is to stay competitive.

You are going into battle. Arm yourself. You need to become as cunning and shrewd as your competitors. You have to know what is out there and what works. You must form a strategy, yet be able to roll with the tide. Plenty of resources are available—it is up to you to use them.

Putting CorelDRAW! To Work

Working with Windows

Because CorelDRAW! is a Windows-based program, it makes sense to outfit your software library with other Windows-based programs. In other words, to achieve the full potential of the environment, equip your computer with the proper software.

Just what does that mean? Primarily, if you need a certain program to perform a particular function, you should choose a Windows-based program over a DOS- or other operating-system–based alternative. Rebooting your computer to change from program to program is not fun and is an incredible strain on productivity.

Although Windows 3.1 is far more forgiving and offers more alternatives than its earlier versions, it asks more from the machine on which it runs. Previous generations of PC programs were coded to run on the lowly 8088 processor. Windows programs are drawing the line between the power machine haves and have-nots.

Buying the Right Hardware

Windows eats up memory, both on the hard disk and in RAM. The first edition of this book (covering CorelDRAW! 1.2 published in 1990) was written and illustrated on a 10 MHz 80286 computer equipped with only a 20 MB hard disk and 2 MB of RAM. That machine couldn't run CorelDRAW! 5.0. Windows 3.1 must run on a more powerful computer equipped with a larger, faster hard disk and loads of RAM. Subsequent editions of this book were produced on a 33 MHz 386 with 16 MB of RAM and a 124 MB IDE drive—barely an entry-level machine by today's standards. The current edition came to life on a large number of machines, including a local bus 486/66 with 32 MB of RAM and a gigabyte of hard disk space (50 times the size of the disk in the original machine and still cramped!).

Historically, computers keep getting faster and cheaper. Prices drop as power rises—one of the lucky truths (at least for now) of the computer industry. Although prices for such commodities as memory chips tend to rise and fall due to market volatility, the general trend is toward more power for less money. A new machine costs no more (adjusting for inflation) than an older machine did just three years ago.

The best advice is to buy the fastest, most powerful computer you can afford. Do not take out a second mortgage to buy it, but do not try and save a few hundred dollars, either. The time you save is your own. This section discusses specific items you can upgrade to take full advantage of CorelDRAW! 5.0. You will learn that the dominant theme is: bigger, faster, and more expensive. If you want to go fast, you've got to pay for it.

Stock Up on System Memory

CorelDRAW! 5.0 asks for 8 MB of system memory, but you and your machine will be far happier with more. In fact, Corel recommends 16 MB. System memory is often referred to as *RAM* (random access memory), and an adequate supply is essential for memory-hungry graphics applications such as those found in Corel's suite. In practice, power users believe 16 MB is the minimum amount of memory you should have when dealing with big CDR files.

If you commonly work with large bitmap files in PhotoPaint or Adobe Photoshop, you will want far more RAM. Although your system might be set up with virtual memory (VM) by allocating a swap file, you still will take a performance hit. Maximizing the amount of RAM in your system will drastically speed up Photoshop's performance. Silicon will always be faster than hard drives. Professional-level desktop retouching stations commonly have 128 MB of RAM—and often double that.

Most computers come with their system memory loaded on SIMM (Single Inline Memory Module) chips—which are really just little circuit boards covered with memory chips. Most likely, your computer was delivered with either 4 or 8 MB of RAM, although it probably has the capacity to accept far more. SIMM chips come in 1, 2, 4, 8, 16, or even 32 MB varieties. They also come in various speeds—either 60, 70, or 80 nanoseconds.

Different computers have different RAM capacities. This depends on such variables as how many SIMM slots there are on the motherboard, as well as the type of SIMM slots. For example: a new machine may have only 4 SIMM slots on the motherboard, but may be capable of accepting up to 16 or 32 MB SIMM chips; an older machine may have 8 SIMM slots that will only accept 1, 2, 4, or 8 MB SIMMs. In general, the older a motherboard is, the less likely that it will accept the 16 or 32 MB SIMMs. That's why an older machine with 8 SIMM slots could only accept a maximum of 64 MB of RAM, whereas a new machine with 4 SIMM slots will accept up to 128 MB.

In addition, there may be restrictions to how you can add memory. Older machines tend to be less lenient than new machines. Commonly, you need to add chips in pairs or fill a bank of slots at the same time. When it is time for you to add memory to your machine, start by referring to the manual that came with it. Each computer is different—Compaq may do it one way, Dell another, and Gateway yet another—and there are even differences in product lines. If you can't find a definitive answer about your machine in its manual, you can always try the appropriate manufacturer's technical support line. Be sure to have your computer's serial number (check the back of the machine) at hand so that the customer service representative can accurately identify exactly what type of motherboard your machine has, and subsequently tell you what you can do to expand your system's memory.

SIMM chip prices tend to be volatile; the laws of supply and demand are definitely in effect. Often, vendors will not list prices for SIMM chips in a magazine advertisement, preferring instead to quote prices over the phone. This is because these prices can change considerably in a very short period of time. Recently, prices went berserk due to a fire in a Japanese manufacturing plant. The facility was a key source for one of the raw products necessary for the production of SIMM chips; the fire knocked the plant out of production, sending the price of SIMMs soaring. Prices eventually returned to normal, but this is a prime example of the fragility of the world's high-tech manufacturing community.

The bottom line—like many upgrade purchases—is to buy as much RAM as your wallet allows and your workload dictates. The more RAM you have installed, the more applications you can run concurrently, and the faster your computer will respond when handling large files.

Which Processor—80486, Pentium, PowerPC or ...?

You should not consider running CorelDRAW! 5.0 on anything less than a 80486-equipped computer. Whether you choose a fast 80486 or a Pentium is a decision best left to you. As of this writing, Pentium machines are just becoming commonplace, although the price difference between a Pentium-equipped machine and a fast 80486 machine is not justified in performance terms. If you have the money, go for the Pentium—just make sure that you have taken care of important issues like RAM, hard drives, and video.

Intel's Pentium has been blown away in certain speed tests by chips such as Motorola's PowerPC, Digital's Alpha (is 275 MHz fast enough?), and Silicon Graphics' MIPS. Because Windows NT is portable, you can expect Corel to have a version of Draw running at warp speed on these processors in the very near future, if not as you read this.

Intel is no longer the dominant factor that it was just a short time ago. The chip market is a big battleground, with plenty at stake. Intel has taken plenty of heat in recent years from such manufacturers as AMD and Cyrix. You can be sure to expect plenty more fireworks in the future.

Looking into Video Cards

When you talk about video cards, the first two considerations should be resolution (such as 640 × 480) and color depth (such as 24-bit, or 16.7 million colors). The amount of resolution and color depth is usually governed by the amount of video memory. The more memory your video card has, the greater the resolution and color depth can be.

If you are running CorelDRAW! 5.0 in 640 × 480 mode with 16 colors, you should give yourself a break. At the minimum, you should have 256 colors. Workable SuperVGA video cards can be had for less than $100, but the better cards will cost a bit more. Invest in a decent card and your eyes will thank you.

The resolution you run at should have a lot to do with the size of your video monitor; specifically, the larger your monitor, the higher the resolution should be. Running at 1024 × 768 on a small monitor is an exercise in futility. Things will be so small, you won't be able to see them. Give yourself a break, and use the right resolution for your monitor. As a general rule: 640 × 480 is fine for 14" monitors; use 800 × 600 for 15–16" monitors; 1024 × 768 for 17" monitors, and save the highest resolutions for the monster 20–21" screens.

One of the most essential items that comes with a brand new video card is its video driver—the program that makes the card operate at its full potential. You may encounter video driver problems with new cards and with new releases of major Windows versions. Obtaining the latest video drivers for your card is essential. Buying a name-brand video card is your best bet, but even a name brand can burn you.

When you purchase a video card, you are faced with myriad choices. Once again, the more video memory you get, the more resolution and color depth you can get, but it will cost more, too. Video speed is enhanced through the use of accelerator chips and coprocessors. Not surprisingly, the faster the card is, the more you can expect to pay. Today, the vast majority of the industry is pushing for accelerated Windows video. The fastest cards operate on either the VESA Local Bus standard or the Intel PCI standard. The card you choose must fit into the type of slot in your computer. Do not consider either of these types of cards if you do not have the proper slot on your motherboard.

If resolution, color depth, and video speed are not important to you, you can get away with your original video card. However, if you crave any (or all) of these features, you can expect to pay anywhere from $200 to $2,000. Don't get frightened by the high number. There are a good number of fast video cards available in the $300 range from vendors such as ATI, Diamond, Hercules, Orchid, and Number Nine.

During the writing of this book, over half a dozen video cards were used. But only one card stood out from the rest. The Number Nine GXE, level 14, VESA Local Bus card was exhaustively tested and found to be competent in handling anything that CorelDRAW! 5.0 could throw at it. The GXE series of cards comes in several configurations. The level 14 card tested was configured with 4 MB of VRAM, enabling True Color display (16.8 million) at 1024×768 resolution. While working at this resolution and color depth (with lesser cards) can significantly degrade the performance of Windows, the GXE is built for speed and handled the chore with ease.

As mentioned, the software side of a video subsystem is equally as important as the hardware aspect. The software drivers supplied with the Number Nine GXE video card proved to be superb. The dreaded video driver GPF was never seen. Not only has attention been given to optimize the core drivers to squeeze every nanosecond of speed out of Windows, but much thought was given to the included suite of software utilities which add significant features and ease-of-use to Number Nine cards. These utilities are collectively called the Hawkeye Feature Set. You can control resolution and color depth, hardware Zoom, monitor refresh rate, vertical and horizontal screen centering, cursor size and color, virtual screen size, power consumption reduction, color calibration and other functions right from the Hawkeye Group (which is automatically installed in Program Manager). You can even assign these functions to hotkeys or mouse buttons so they are instantly available for customization.

The GXE level 14 quickly is becoming a granddaddy in the video world. As this book was being completed, Number Nine released a completely new line of 64-bit graphics accelerator cards that significantly outperform the card tested. This new line of cards includes configurations to meet the requirements of every Windows user. And the best news is that the prices of these new cards are lower than ever. There are even greater things to come because Number Nine has released the first 128-bit graphics and multimedia processing chip. The video world is hot, and Number Nine is turning up the heat!

Video Monitors—How Big Is Too Big?

Installing a large monitor is one of the best productivity enhancements you can make. Once you have worked with a large monitor (19"–21") you will have a difficult time readjusting to smaller screens. Although you can expect to pay $2,000 or more for a large screen, it is an investment well worth the price for a busy production shop. The time you save by not scrolling, zooming, or fiddling with your display is enormous, and can easily outshadow the financial outlay.

When shopping for a large video monitor, look for a smaller dot pitch, a high refresh rate, and a maximum resolution of 1024 × 768 or 1280 × 1040. Be sure to outfit your computer with an adequate video card for the monitor you choose. You should coordinate these two purchases, if possible. If you have a good-sized budget, consider the video cards and monitors from SuperMatch—as the name implies, they make a great pair.

Sound Cards—Not Just for Playing Games Anymore

Sound Cards have taken the leap from computer game necessity to corporate necessity. Multimedia presentation software, such as CorelSHOW!, only begins to shine when it is coupled with effective audio. While SoundBlaster made the market, experts say the best sound cards come from Turtle Beach.

Once you've installed a decent sound card, don't be cheap with the speakers. Spend a few more dollars on a respectable speaker system. Some of the coolest systems available are from Acoustic Research.

Fixed Hard Drives—the Bigger (and Faster) the Better

As mentioned earlier, the first edition of this book was produced on a machine with a 20 MB hard drive. That's astounding, considering that 20 MB is absolutely nothing in today's terms. If you are purchasing a new machine, you should have a minimum of a 300 MB drive. If you are adding a drive to an existing machine, you may be pleasantly surprised; hard drives have dropped well below the magical $1 per megabyte figure.

Today, you have two basic choices when it comes to fixed hard drives. You can choose either an IDE or a SCSI drive (other drive types have fallen out of favor). Among SCSI drives, there are two types: SCSI and SCSI-2. If you are looking for a big fast drive of one gigabyte or larger, you probably want SCSI-2 drives exclusively. The bigger and faster you go, however, the more you can expect to pay.

It's up to you to ascertain whether your work requires a screaming-fast 8 millisecond, 2.4 gigabyte Seagate Barracuda SCSI drive, or a more affordable (and pedestrian, by comparison) 450 MB Western Digital IDE drive. The longer you work, the more you will crave that bigger, faster drive. Installing a speedy drive is one of the best performance modifications you can make.

A Removable Hard Drive Lets You Take It with You

One alternative to a huge fixed hard drive is to use a removable hard drive, such as a Bernoulli, Syquest, or Magneto-optical drive. These devices enable you to pop in multi-megabyte disk cartridges with the ease of floppy disks. Syquests are most common in the Macintosh world, but are generally acknowledged to be less secure than other storage methods. Magneto-optical disks are considered to be quite secure, but they tend to be on the expensive side initially; per megabyte costs are low, however.

Taking all this into consideration, the authors use a combination of storage methods, but rely heavily on a number of Iomega Bernoulli 150 MB drives. These devices enable you to move huge files around with ease. A Bernoulli Transportable outfitted with a parallel port interface enables you to move the drive from machine to machine with ease. The Bernoullis are legendary for their reliability, and they have a low initial and subsequent per-megabyte cost.

Removable drives are essential to designers that rely on service bureaus or high-tech printers. These disks are the medium used to move large files from the design studio to the service bureau. You can read more about service bureaus in Part IV of this book.

CD-ROM—What Are You Waiting For?

CD-ROM drives should be standard equipment. If your machine is not equipped with one, the good news is that by waiting, you will get yourself a faster drive at a lower price. CD-ROM drive prices have dropped dramatically in recent years. You should be able to install one for less than $200. Spending more money will get you a faster drive, but no CD-ROM is anywhere as fast as a hard drive.

Having access to a CD-ROM drive is essential for maximizing your investment in both CorelDRAW! 5.0 as well as this book. Be sure to get a drive that is capable of reading Kodak PhotoCDs. This technology will give you access to low cost image scanning without adding a scanner!

Back It Up

Often, users forget to back up their files, which leads to tragedy when a disk drive crashes or a file is accidentally misplaced. Having a backup file ensures that you can quickly and easily recover from such potentially disastrous situations. You can avoid losing your mind (and your job) by installing and using a tape backup drive.

It costs very little to buy yourself lots of protection. A 250 MB tape backup drive is incredibly inexpensive; you can be adequately covered for between $200 and $300. Tape backup drives have reached such affordable levels that you have to wonder why the computer manufacturers have not begun to offer them as standard equipment. DAT tape drives, capable of backing up 2 to 8 gigabytes of data, are more expensive, however.

Protect Your System with an Uninterruptible Power Supply

If you have a significant investment in computer equipment, you would be wise to spend a few more dollars for an uninterruptible power supply (UPS). In addition to surge suppression and line conditioning, the best of these devices provide a number of hours of backup battery power in case you experience a blackout. This gives you plenty of time to save your files and close everything down.

Even if you do not live in a community prone to power outages, you should purchase a decent UPS. Do not settle for a cheap $9.95 surge suppresser from the local discount store unless you have a $9.95 computer. It is your investment to protect. There are a number of brands and styles to choose from; American Power and Tripp Lite are two of the best known.

Scanners

Do you really need a scanner? Although having a scanner attached to your computer can be a time-saver, it is not imperative. If you do not have a scanner, you can always scan artwork on another machine and then transfer the file to your machine, either through a network (if so equipped) or through removable media.

A properly scanned, black-and-white line artwork file will usually fit on a floppy disk—even artwork that was scanned at high resolution. Smaller grayscale images may fit on a floppy as well. Larger grayscale images, and practically any 24-bit color scans, will not. In a serious shop, 40 MB (and up) color files are not uncommon—in fact, they are the norm. This is why you need to have a Syquest, Bernoulli, or Magneto-optical drive.

If you are lucky enough be in a networked environment, it makes good sense to set up one computer as a scanning workstation. Fill that machine with all the good stuff (huge, fast hard drive, lots of RAM, and a killer video card such as the SuperMatch Thunder) and let it handle all the scanning chores. This deploys your assets exactly where you need them.

 A few words of scanning wisdom: you must be careful about the images you scan. It is too easy to break the law by using images that belong to another person or organization. While the "copyright police" might not come knocking on the door, a little professional courtesy goes a long way. If a client asks you to include an image of a popular cartoon character, for example, do not do this without obtaining the proper authorization from the copyright owner. In many cases, you can easily contact the licensee, pay a fee, and avoid the legal ramifications.

Want to read more about scanning? Chapter 19, "Using CorelPHOTO-PAINT!," covers the hands-on aspects of scanning and image manipulation.

Digitizing Tablets

Electronic artists need precision and flexibility. Design concessions based on the limitations of hardware are a sad truth for many artists. Because mice, trackballs, and the like are not conducive to drawing in an intuitive manner, many a work has been compromised. It need not be that way.

An artist should be liberated, not imprisoned, by his tools. Imagine a paintbrush chained to a canvas, or a stick of charcoal wired to a sketch pad—not exactly an artistically stimulating thought. The computer and its peripherals should enable, not hinder, artistic creativity. Throughout the creation of this book, many input devices were tested, and it was agreed that for serious illustration work, you must put the mouse, its siblings, and its cousins on the shelf.

Putting CorelDRAW! To Work

Only one serious mouse alternative for electronic design exists: the digitizing (or graphics) tablet. Although a mouse might be inexpensive compared to a tablet, the mouse can never hope to offer the tablet's drawing precision. With a graphics tablet, freehand drawing becomes a genuine reality rather than a bad joke. Try a good tablet. The cost difference soon becomes meaningless. The proper tablet enables you to draw in a natural manner rather than in a clumsy tangle of mouse and cord.

These statements might invoke the ire of mouse loyalists. But if you spend some time working with a quality graphics tablet, you will come to the same conclusion; drawing with a mouse is like painting with a brick.

On the forefront of digitizing tablet manufacturers, Wacom, Inc. offers high-quality products at reasonable prices. Although less expensive graphics tablets are available, they offer far fewer amenities. All of Wacom's tablets are cordless, for example. No cords connect the *stylus* (pen) or *cursor* (puck) with the tablet itself, so the user can hold the pen or puck in the most natural manner possible. Cordlessness alone makes Wacom tablets specialized devices. There are few cordless tablets on the market, and certainly none with the same feel or features.

You can economize by purchasing a smaller (and less expensive) tablet. Wacom offers a full line of digitizing tablets, running from the compact 6-by-8-inch ArtZ to the monster 35-by-47-inch SD-013. For DTP work, a 12-by-12-inch UD-1212 tablet is the largest tablet you will need. Throughout the production of this book, the authors had the good fortune to work with both a Wacom ArtZ and a UD-1212, each equipped with cordless pens and pucks.

The tablets were a joy to work with and installation was a simple process. The tablets operated well with Windows 3.1, using Wacom's highly configurable Control Panel and Pen Windows drivers. WinTab drivers are also available, although they were not tested in the course of producing this book.

Wacom provides excellent product support. During the development cycle of CorelDRAW! 5.0, it became apparent that Wacom's existing Windows driver needed to be updated to accommodate Draw 5. Wacom's engineering team came through with a new driver within days. Throughout testing, the authors ran into only one drawback to the cordless design—it was easy to pick up the pen and forget where it was put down. To minimize this problem, Wacom offers an attractive desktop pen holder.

The quality-conscious yet budget-minded artist would be wise to look at Wacom's pressure-sensitive 6-by-8-inch ArtZ as a viable alternative to either a mouse or a full-sized tablet. The ArtZ provides, at an affordable price, many of the same features as its larger siblings.

CorelDRAW! 5.0 supports pressure-sensitivity through the PowerLine tool. Corel also boasts pressure support in PhotoPaint!. The number of PC-based programs that support pressure-sensitivity is on the rise. On the bitmap side, Adobe Photoshop, Image-In-Color, Fractal Design Painter, and Fauve Matisse do a fabulous job. In the vector world, Aldus FreeHand's pressure tool is wonderful, as is the implementation in Altsys Fontographer. The PC community has finally embraced pressure sensitivity.

Buying the Right Software

Windows users naturally are prejudiced toward Windows software. Programs that share a common graphical user interface (GUI) (in this case, Windows) operate intuitively and integrate with other programs that have been designed with the same interface. For example, why buy a word processing program that does not run in the Windows environment if you are already running Draw and, perhaps, PageMaker?

Although this is not the place to get into the Aldus PageMaker versus Quark Xpress versus Ventura Publisher argument, the marketplace as a whole tends to favor PageMaker, while the high-end magazine market is saturated with Xpress users. Ventura Publisher's market share had dropped dramatically to a fraction of its former position. Corel's recent acquisition of Ventura was viewed by many as a last gasp for the one-time king of PC-based desktop publishing. How the program fares in its latest incarnation remains to be seen. CorelVentura, as the product has been renamed, was not initially released with CorelDRAW! 5.0, although the company had every intention of doing so. Instead, Corel wisely chose to release the module at a later date, with early-bird purchasers receiving Ventura upon returning proof of purchase.

In this tumultuous industry, you constantly have to keep track of an ever-changing game. The ante is constantly being upped. More and more programs are being released in Windows-compatible format. As computers progress along the PC-GUI path, it is safe to say that Windows is becoming the norm.

Using Paint and Image Manipulation Programs

If you are reading this book, you probably already own one of the best object-oriented drawing packages available for the PC. You probably even use a page layout package or two. And even though Draw comes bundled with CorelPHOTO-PAINT!, you might want more firepower in the critical bitmapped paint arena.

Adobe Photoshop

There can be no question that Adobe Photoshop is the de facto standard of professional-level image-manipulation programs. Adobe rolled out Photoshop for Windows in the spring of 1993 to great acclaim, assuring it of an increased foothold on the market. Photoshop features plug-in filters that enable users to employ third-party software that extends the program's capabilities. Adobe also has allowed hardware developers to hook into the code, which has spawned a number of awesome video cards engineered to speed up specific Photoshop functions.

> Adobe Systems, Inc.
> 1585 Charleston Road
> P.O. Box 7900
> Mountain View, CA 94039-7900
> (415) 961-4400

Aldus PhotoStyler

Formerly marketed by U-Lead, PhotoStyler was one of the first high-end bitmap image-manipulation packages available for Windows. In the summer of 1991, Aldus acquired the rights to market PhotoStyler, and by fall had subsequently rebadged and repackaged the product with the Aldus label.

PhotoStyler provides all the serious tools that you need to retouch, enhance, and compose full-color images on your PC. The program can read and write files in a number of formats, including BMP, GIF, PCX, TGA, and TIF. In addition, it can write files in EPS format. Scanners from Epson, Nikon, and Microtek are supported, along with most popular printers.

A number of built-in filters provide an array of smoothing, sharpening, and spatial effects. In addition, the program allows user-definable filters for ultra-custom work. The ubiquitous illustration tools—airbrush, paintbrush, pencil, and eraser—are included as well. This program, however, is designed for pre-press work rather than image creation. PhotoStyler provides support for GCR (gray component replacement) and UCR (under color removal), essential tools for CMYK printing.

> Aldus Corporation
> 411 First Avenue South
> Seattle, WA 98104-2871
> (206) 628-2320

Fauve Matisse

Named for Henri Matisse and the Fauvist school of painting he inspired, this exotic program is indeed the "wild beast" of the paint programs. Fauve Matisse successfully emulates traditional painting techniques, such as watercolors, oils, charcoals, pastels, and pencils. It also provides pressure-sensitive tablet support. In many respects, the program offers what Fractal Design Painter does (with the Painter X2 extensions) at a fraction of the price.

Although you can certainly perform photo retouching with Matisse, its real forte is in image creation. The program enables users to use multiple floating objects and access standard Photoshop filters, such as Kai's Power Tools and Aldus Gallery Effects. In addition, it deals with text (TrueType only) as editable vectors, rather than rasterized images. This is a true artist's tool, although you don't have to be an artist to have a great time with Matisse.

 On the *Inside CorelDRAW! 5, Fifth Edition CD-ROM* that accompanies this book, you will find a complimentary copy of Fauve Matisse in Gray—the grayscale version of this hot new Windows-based paint program. Load it up and give it a whirl—you'll become an instant convert! Fauve Matisse supports TIF, TGA, BMP, GIF, JPEG, PCX, PICT, EPS, WMF, and WPG formats.

Fauve Software
875 Walnut Street, #320
Cary, NC 275111
(800) 898-ARTS
(919) 380-9933

Fractal Design Painter

Unlike other image manipulation programs, Fractal Design Painter was developed as a tool for the fine artist rather than the pre-press photo retoucher. Although the program can import images in a variety of file formats, you do not want to use it merely to remove dust and touch up scratches. Painter for Windows supports BMP, PCX, RIF, TGA, and TIF formats and is compatible with the Wacom tablet's pressure-sensitive pen.

When coupled with a Wacom tablet, Painter provides an environment so realistic that your nose might begin to twitch from the pastel dust and your eyes might water from the turpentine. Painter's toolbox includes chalk, charcoal, crayons, felt-tip markers, and other amazingly true-to-life implements. The program even has settings that enable artists to paint in the brushstrokes of Van Gogh and Seurat. The canvas also is changeable, giving artists the freedom to alter the tooth of the work surface.

You would have difficulty finding a forgotten tool. Image cloning is supported with a twist; cloned images can be rendered in a variety of media, turning a photographic image into something far more organic. Painter includes electronic tracing paper and friskets to protect the original copy. The X2 extensions add object-oriented image composition capabilities. This is one powerful program, and you need to load it on the most powerful machine you can muster. Fractal also offers a powerful grayscale image editing program called Sketcher that does not require as much computer power.

Fractal Design Corporation
101 Madeline Drive, Suite 204
Aptos, CA 95003
(408) 688-8800

Image-In-Color Professional

Minnesota-based Image-In Incorporated's Image-In Professional is positioned to go head-to-head with Adobe Photoshop and Aldus PhotoStyler, but is fighting a David-against-Goliath battle for the PC-image retouching crown. Image-In-Color was the first Windows program to support the Wacom pressure-sensitive tablet.

With color separation controls developed in cooperation with AGFA Compugraphic, such as GCR, UCR, press gain compensation, and three color-absorption settings, Image-In is going after the serious pre-press crowd. Color trade shops that have grudgingly accepted that the Mac is here to stay are in for a surprise. PC workstations are a whole lot more affordable.

Targeted at the high-end professional market, the program supports BMP, EPS, IMG, PICT, PCX, TGA, and TIF (including 6.0) formats, and can directly load Kodak Photo CD images. Color correction controls enable savvy users to create customized printer tone curves. A full range of more than 20 photographic filters is standard issue, as is the capability to create user-definable custom filters. The Wacom tablet's pressure-sensitive input is well-implemented in the program's painting tools, metering the flow of paint or density of a brushstroke.

Image-In Incorporated
406 East 79th Street
Minneapolis, MN 55420
(612) 888-3633
(800) 345-3540

Using Other Drawing Programs

You might ask yourself if there is any reason to use a drawing program other than
CorelDRAW!. There might be. For the most part, Draw does a fine job, but it does
fall short in a number of places. The program's four chief competitors are Adobe
Illustrator 5.5, Aldus FreeHand 4.0, Deneba Canvas 3.5, and Micrografx Designer
4.0. Rather than a feature-by-feature comparison, what follows are the strong points
of those programs.

Adobe Illustrator 5.5

The granddaddy of the PostScript illustration programs has been updated with
many new features. Adobe Illustrator has always been known for its accuracy and
output worthiness, but this latest release offers an improved interface, convenience, and a number of features that will make CorelDRAW! users envious. As in
version 4.0, two of the most convenient features are that you can open multiple
files (or versions of a file) at one time (Draw still cannot do this), and that the
charting tool is integrated into the program—it is not called as a separate module
(as is CorelCHART). Pressure-sensitive tablet users will be pleased to note that the
program now includes calligraphic brush features.

Illustrator continues to possess the utmost level of typographical refinement (to a
thousandth of an em). The program allows an infinite number of characters in a
text block and allows for hanging punctuation. The program now supports tabs, a
spell checker (with custom dictionary), as well as the capability to search and
replace by typeface. Unlike CorelDRAW!, text can be entered and edited directly
on a path. Adobe is also bundling Acrobat Exchange and Distiller with version 5.5.

With this latest version, Adobe has implemented a plug-in filter architecture, much
like that of Photoshop. This helps users stay on top of the latest developments with
plug-in tools from Adobe and third-party developers. The Pathfinder filters give
Illustrator users far more options than Corel's Combine/Weld/Intersect/Trim
commands. If you are a power user and have not looked at Illustrator in a while, it
is certainly worth looking into now.

Adobe Systems Inc.
1585 Charleston Road
P.O. Box 7900
Mountain View, CA 94039-7900
(415) 961-4400

Aldus FreeHand 4.0

Developed by Altsys—the folks who brought you Fontographer—Aldus FreeHand 4.0 provides a number of amenities. As with WinIllustrator, FreeHand offers support for color calibration. FreeHand offers powerful text handling and linking. Like CorelDRAW!, the program features style sheets and full control over paragraph specifications and tabs. The program also provides automatic-copyfitting to force text to fit to a specific width, through size, leading, and character spacing adjustments.

Much of the changes in FreeHand 4.0 have to do with the user interface. The program features drag-and-drop color selection with solid colors as well as with gradients. FreeHand's Inspector Palette is far more streamlined than Corel's combination of kludgy roll-up windows, without being an on-screen real estate (or system memory) hog. Aldus has done its work, and has listened closely to its user base. As an example, you can now have multiple page sizes within one document—a wonderful feature for designers that produce a variety of printed brochures.

As with version 3.0, one of FreeHand's most notable features is the program's support for pressure-sensitive drawing tablets. FreeHand was the first vector-based Windows drawing program to use pressure-sensitivity, and the implementation is quite impressive. When you use the pressure tool, the harder you press, the fatter your drawn object becomes.

Aldus Corporation
411 First Avenue South
Seattle, WA 98104-2871
(206) 628-2320

Deneba Canvas for Windows 3.5

Canvas offers a number of interesting features at a competitive price. Best known in the Macintosh world for excellent technical illustration features, Deneba brought its flagship product to Windows in 1993. Like FreeHand and Illustrator, Canvas offers excellent cross-platform support, which is imperative in environments where PCs and Macintoshes must coexist.

The program is built around a modular tool structure. Users can load tools at will, enabling them to customize Canvas to their particular situation. Deneba is extremely responsive to user requirements and has been known to develop specific tools according to the needs of its client base. A number of these tools provide capabilities not found in CorelDRAW! 5.0, such as the Parallel Line, Star, Polygon, Spiral, Concentric Circle, and Cube tools. In addition, bitmap editing is integrated into the program rather than as a separate module.

With CAD work and technical illustration as the bread and butter applications for Canvas, it should come as no surprise that the program excels at such necessities as autodimensioning. The SmartMouse feature provides automatic control over object alignment and angles. Deneba also offers free, unlimited technical support.

Deneba Software
7400 SW 87th Avenue
Miami, FL 33173
(305) 596-5644

Micrografx Designer 4.0

Prior to the arrival of CorelDRAW!, Micrografx Designer was the PC drawing program champ. Recent years have not been kind to the program's market share, but many of Designer's features still are enviable. Designer had a reputation for precision, but a difficult user interface (UI). This latest version was totally rewritten with an improved UI and a number of new features.

The most amazing addition to Designer 4.0 is the program's capability to create true three-dimensional objects. Unlike CorelDRAW! 5.0's pseudo-3D extrude effect, Designer's 3D tools enable you to instantly create real cubes or spheres. In addition, you can extrude a 2D object. And most impressively, you can use 3D Sweep to lathe a 2D object into 3D. None of the other leading vector-based illustration packages offer this 3D power; you have to begin looking at 3D rendering packages to get these capabilities.

Micrographx worked heavily on the program's text-handling capabilities. Text can be flowed within or around objects. Multiple column text is handled with ease, including complete control over vertical and forced horizontal justification.

Micrografx, Inc.
1303 Arapaho
Richardson, TX
(800) 733-3729

Breaking Into the Third Dimension with Visual Reality

For all of CorelDRAW!'s wonderful features, it is still strictly a two-dimensional drawing package. Even though Draw offers a (psuedo-) 3D extrude effect, it is far from being a true three-dimensional rendering program. Although there are a number of DOS-based 3D programs, such as Crystal Topas and Autodesk 3D

Studio, they have been slow to come to the Windows platform. Take note, however: the wait is over for Windows-based artists ready to take the 3D plunge.

Visual Reality is a suite of Windows programs designed for photo-realistic three-dimensional rendering and animation. It consists of five modules: Visual Model, Visual Font, Visual Image, the Visual Player, and Renderize Live, along with over 500 pre-built Visual 3D Clipart objects. In addition, the suite comes complete with a CD-ROM full of ImageCels textures and materials. Figure 10.1 is a photo-surrealitic image created with Visual Reality.

Figure 10.1
Samurai-driving
T-Rex terrorizes
Seaside,
courtesy of
Visual Reality.

Visual Model gives you the ability to create three-dimensional wireframe models. The toolbox features all the standard drawing tools you might expect, such as lines, curves, arcs, and polygons, as well as instant boxes, spheres, cylinders, and cones. In figure 10.2, you can see a T-Rex being modified in Visual Model.

The dinosaur was brought into the program from a CD-ROM supplied by Visual Software. The T-Rex was then ungrouped, and the bottom half of the beast was removed. If you take a look at figure 10.1, you can see why the poor critter had to have surgery: his feet would have stuck out the bottom of the 4 × 4 ... and this rendering is silly enough, as it is!

Figure 10.2
Visual Model is used to lop the T-Rex in half.

As you can see in figures 10.3 and 10.4, Visual Font enables users to create three-dimensional text using any TrueType font. The program provides complete flexibility with regard to extrusion and beveling. Extrusion depth and offsets are controlled through the Settings dialog box, while Bevel width and depth settings are handled in a separate dialog box.

Type can be set on multiple lines, and can be set flush left, flush right, or centered. Extruded type can be saved in two-dimensional or three-dimensional DXF format. Beveled faces are grouped separately from front, back, and side faces. Once a piece of three-dimensional type has been created, you can import it into Renderize Live and apply colors, textures, and materials on a group-by-group basis.

Visual Image is a lightning-fast, object-oriented bitmap image composition program. The program features most standard bitmap editing features, such as cutting, cropping, resizing, and image enhancement. It excels in its speed and ability to build composite collages, as well as in defining alpha channel mattes. In figure 10.5, you may recognize the flamingo and dune shots that you used to create the postcards early on in the book. Here, they are in the midst of being combined using Visual Image's excellent controls.

Figure 10.3
Visual Font
provides
complete control
over extrusions.

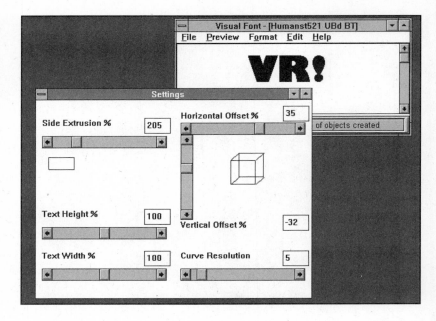

Figure 10.4
Visual Font also
provides
complete control
over text
beveling.

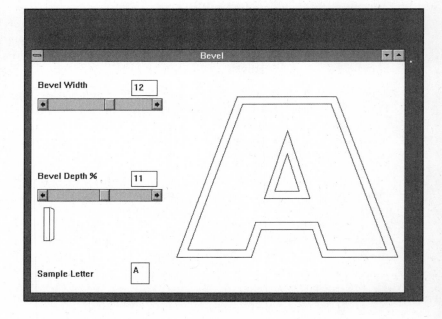

Figure 10.5
Building a
composite beach
scene in Visual
Image.

Once you have your objects and background ready, it's time to put together the entire scene (see fig. 10.1). Renderize Live is where you literally set the stage, combining input from the other modules. You build your scenes by arranging objects in a 3D space. Lighting and camera angles are fully supported, as are texture, bump, and reflection maps. Still images can be rendered as TGA, TIF, PCX, or BMP. Camera animations can be recorded as FLC or AVI format files.

The core of Visual Reality—Renderize Live—is a true 32-bit application that runs on a number of platforms (including Windows NT, on the screaming-fast 275 MHz Digital Alpha machines). The program has the performance, look, and feel of a high-end rendering workstation. If you want to create photo-realistic still images or animated flybys and walk-throughs in Windows, you need Visual Reality.

Visual Software, Inc.
21731 Ventura Boulevard, #310
Woodland Hills, CA 91364
(800) 669-7318
(818) 883-7900
Fax: (818) 593-3750

II

Putting CorelDRAW! To Work

Searching for Desktop Publishing Information

To get what you need to stay abreast of the desktop publishing field, you must know where to look. The fact that you are reading this book shows that you have a thirst for knowledge and an appetite for information. The stronger that craving is, the more successful you will be.

The design revolution that has taken place since the advent of the Apple Macintosh, Adobe PostScript, and Aldus PageMaker is staggering. The immediacy of desktop publishing is now available to far more designers at increasingly affordable prices. Programs and computers have become more powerful than previously thought possible. And the trend shows no sign of subsiding.

The huge retail industry that has sprung up around the personal computer market is, to a large extent, mail order-based and service-oriented. You do not need to drive out to the store and lose a few hours of valuable time. Just pick up the phone, dial a toll-free number, place an order for whatever you could possibly need, and receive it the next day in the overnight mail.

Your job is to find resources and make contacts. Discover which programs and outlets are reliable, and support them. To that end, this section presents a selection of interesting products and firms that can make a difference in your day-to-day operations.

Clip-Art Connection by Modem

For those of you who do not have the resources—whether talent or time—to create art in a pinch, Clip-Art Connection from Connect Software (a division of Adonis Corporation) offers an exciting and innovative service: on-line clip art. Just boot up Clip-Art Connection and search for a graphic by category or by publisher. After you find the correct image, use the built-in communications capabilities to access the on-line electronic clip-art database and download the art you need. The service runs 24 hours a day.

Clip-Art Connection enables users to preview the clip-art files by providing thumbnail images. The thumbnails are small, monochrome bitmaps for preview purposes only. Adonis states that there are over 29,000 thumbnails in its library from 17 top vendors. By keeping thumbnails on the user's local PC, communications charges are kept to a minimum. You do not need to buy complete clip-art collections just to get a single piece of art; per-piece rates can run on the high side, however. Adonis claims that the price usually ranges from about $1 to $25, although you can save money by not paying for any extra images that you will not use.

Although most subscribers to the service download and purchase individual files, you can also purchase complete collections. Although the complete collections are not downloadable—telephone costs and time factors make it prohibitive—Connect Software promises 48-hour shipping and competitive pricing.

Vendors include T/Maker, 3G Graphics, Studio Advertising Art, Metro Creative Graphics, ArtRight, Micrografx, ArtBeats, DreamMaker, Cartesia, and others. Payment is billed through most popular credit cards.

Connect Software
A Division of Adonis Corporation
6742 185th Avenue NE, Suite 150
Redmond, WA 98052
(800) 234-9497

Using Shareware

The personal computer shareware community is an oddity in today's society. Where else can you find people willing to give you their products without making you pay for them up-front? *Shareware* is software that is distributed free of charge, with a proviso: if you try it and like it, you buy it. If you do not like (or use) the program, you do need not to pay for it.

The entire premise is based on trust. The shareware developers trust that if you like the program, you will buy it. They have no marketing, distribution, or production costs to speak of other than the cost of living. The registration fees they ask are paltry in comparison to the utility of their programs.

This type of personal computer program can be a boon to the electronic artist on a budget. There are literally thousands of programs out there for the asking. You can find them on computer bulletin boards around the world.

The disk supplied with this book contains a collection of some of the best shareware programs for the Windows desktop publishing professional. Remember that shareware is try-before-you-buy. If you find that one or more of these programs fills your needs, make sure that you pay the registration fee(s).

PKZIP

One of the most wonderful shareware utilities available, PKZIP, compresses files for cost-effective telecomputing, archiving, and storage. If you transmit files by modem, PKZIP can save you big bucks in telephone costs and on-line charges. PKZIP is available on many bulletin boards, including its own. It is commonly distributed in a compressed, self-extracting EXE format. The program contains utilities for compressing, decompressing, password encryption, and more.

Table 10.1 shows the results of tests run on some typical files. The files that were compressed included a database file, a word processing file, a file in native CorelDRAW! format, and various exported (EPS, SDL, CGM) versions of the Draw file.

Table 10.1
Compressed File Sizes

Type of File	Original Size	PKZIPPED Size
CDR	2584	1273
EPS	18606	6098
CGM	48088	23816
SCD	48916	24684
Database	85504	32918
Word Processing	54423	17759

Depending on your modem speed, you can save the cost of registration in no time at all. PKZIP is a utility that no telecomputing electronic artist should be without!

> PKZIP
> PKWARE, Inc.
> 7545 N. Port Washington Road
> Glendale, WI 53217-3422
> (414) 352-3670
> BBS: (414) 352-7176
> Fax: (414) 352-3815

Code To Code

Bruce Robey, a type shop owner, programming professional, and university instructor based in Washington, D.C., offers two excellent shareware resources for typesetters and desktop publishers. The first of these two, Code To Code, is a typesetter/desktop publishing utility collection.

Using Code To Code, you can update typesetter/desktop publishing files without the hassle of reading through strings of obscure codes. A coded file, while fine for a typesetter experienced in editing around lengthy, intricate codes, can cause headaches for an editor who only wants to make text changes.

Although the program is not intended to be used with Draw, it certainly has a place in the desktop publishing arsenal. Hard-core Ventura users, as well as high-end typographers, will find Code To Code to be of great use for removing delimited codes. You also have the option of storing removed codes that can be stored in a separate file.

Code To Code is shareware and is available for an economical $29 registration fee. The latest version and printed documentation are available through registration directly from the author. Code To Code also is available on a free trial basis by downloading it as CTOC21.EXE from the CompuServe IBMAPP forum LIB 12. The program also is available through BIX, GENIE, and MAGNALINE, and from disk distributors across the country.

AlphaQuote

Bruce Robey's other offering, AlphaQuote, is a DOS-based typesetting and desktop publishing estimating and copyfitting program. The program was originally sold as commercial software and has been used by thousands of typesetters worldwide. AlphaQuote has been completely rewritten and re-released as shareware.

If you bill for your work, you will find AlphaQuote indispensable for estimating and copyfitting books, magazines, and newsletters. The menu-driven format is practical and easy to use. AlphaQuote Version 3.0 is available for $29. Interested parties might call for a registered version or download the shareware version from CompuServe, IBMAPP LIB 12 as AQ30.EXE.

> Code To Code 3.0
> AlphaQuote 3.0
> Bruce Robey
> AlphaBytes, Inc.
> 111 Eighth Street, S.E.
> Washington, D.C. 20003
> (202) 546-4119
> CompuServe ID: 71131,2734

Cubit Meister

After you start using Cubit Meister, you will never misplace your proportional sizing wheel again. Cubit Meister is an on-screen idiot wheel that painlessly computes reduction or enlargement percentages. In addition to providing you with fast, accurate sizing information, this handy program converts from one system of measurement to another.

Version 1.03 (included on the disk that accompanies this book) features a new three-dimensional look and can float on top of other active applications. Developed by graphic designer and *Inside CorelDRAW! 5, Fifth Edition* coauthor John Shanley, Cubit Meister provides essential functions for the Windows desktop publishing professional.

> Cubit Meister
> Phoenix Creative Graphics
> 5 Clyde Road, Suite 101
> Somerset, NJ 08873
> CompuServe ID: 76535,3443

FontSpec

Have you ever wanted to create a catalog of type specimen pages for your personal type library? FontSpec makes it easy. The program enables you to display TrueType or PostScript typefaces on-screen or on a printed page. You can create fully customized specimen pages, complete with header and footer information. FontSpec prints in your choice of single-column, two-column, or full-sheet samples. This neat little program is a great addition to your desktop publishing arsenal whether you have a small, one-person shop or a big design studio.

> FontSpec
> UniTech Corporation
> 2697 McKelvey Road
> Maryland Heights, MO 63043
> (314) 770-2770

SetDRAW

The INI file situation in CorelDRAW! version 4.0 can be a tough nut to crack. David Brickley created SetDRAW in order to tweak Draw's INI files without using Notepad (or other text editors). The program enables you to check or alter Draw's most pertinent settings in its five INI files (CORELDRW.INI, CORELAPP.INI, CORELPRN.INI, CORELFLT.INI, and CORELFNT.INI), and it does so with point-and-shoot ease. Not only is the utility simple to use, it is also very safety conscious—you can restore your INI original settings at any time. The program features help at every step, so there is seldom any need to refer to Corel's documentation.

SetDRAW is a very cool thing—the utility that Corel Corporation forgot to provide. For more information, see Chapter 22, "Customizing Windows Controls for System Performance," which covers fine-tuning your system.

SetDRAW
Shooting Brick Productions
P.O. Box 549
Moss Beach, CA 94038
(415) 728-0244

WinPSX

Downloading PostScript fonts to your PostScript printer can save valuable minutes at print time. WinPSX comes to the rescue. Costas Kitsos' Windows utility is a no-nonsense PostScript font downloader that deserves a place on your hard drive.

Many features make dealing with the Windows font situation a much more pleasant experience. By clicking on Show Font Name, for example, you can select fonts by their real names (rather than by those cryptic eight-character alphanumeric hieroglyphics that Bitstream is so fond of). The program also enables you to create job lists for batch downloading. WinPSX is freeware, but Costas asks that, "If you find WinPSX useful and enjoyable, please plant a tree." This one's worth a forest.

WinPSX
Costas Kitsos
P.O. Box 64943
Los Angeles, CA 90064
CompuServe ID: 73667,1755

WinZip

WinZip brings the convenience of Windows to the use of ZIP, LZH, and ARC files. It features an intuitive point-and-click interface for viewing, running, extracting, adding, deleting, and testing files in archives. Optional virus-scanning support is included.

The Windows 3.1 drag-and-drop interface is fully supported. You can drag-and-drop files from WinZip to other applications. WinZip extracts the files before it drops them on the target application. The target application treats the files as if they had been dropped by the File Manager. You also can drop archives on WinZip to open them, or drop files on WinZip to add them to the open archive.

WinZip includes built-in unzipping. It requires PKZIP to create ZIP files, and LHA, ARJ, and/or ARC to access files LZH, ARJ, and ARC files, respectively. WinZip is Association of Shareware Professionals (ASP) Shareware.

WinZip
Nico Mak
P.O. Box 919
Bristol, CT 06011-0919
CompuServe ID: 70056,241

The Association of Shareware Professionals

Just because a program is shareware does not necessarily mean that it comes as is and without software support. The Association of Shareware Professionals (ASP) was formed in 1987 to bolster the image and ensure the future of shareware as an ongoing alternative to conventional/commercial software.

ASP software developers must subscribe to a code of ethics and commit themselves to the concept of shareware. The association publishes a regularly updated catalog of programs, which includes file descriptions, locations, and registration fees. The ASP catalog is available in Library 8 of the CIS IBMJR forum, and must be extracted from ARC format using the shareware program ARC-E.COM.

Although the ASP does not review members' software for functionality or usefulness—its philosophy is to let the users try before they buy—the association does provide an ombudsman to deal with any post-registration disputes. However, the ombudsman cannot provide technical support for members' products.

Organizations such as the ASP have all your best interests in mind. The concept of shareware is simple, elegant, and fragile. Electronic artists must lend their support if it is to survive.

The Association of Shareware Professionals
P.O. Box 5786
Bellevue, WA 98006

Publications for Publishers

Information-hungry electronic artists have many avenues to pursue in their quest for knowledge. To stay on top of developments, it is important to have a variety of information resources. Many publications are available on the subject of graphics design, typography, and desktop publishing.

Aldus Magazine

Okay, okay, so this is a house organ, but it is still worth mentioning. This slick four-color publication—sent free to registered Aldus users—is a testament to what can be done at the high-end of desktop design. Although the first issues were a bit unpolished, *Aldus Magazine* has evolved into a fine publication.

The original and ambitious premise behind the bimonthly *Aldus Magazine* was to use a completely new design with each issue. These redesigns were potential nightmares for its designers, but tasty pickings for those of you who might be short on ideas. The magazine has since settled down to a consistent layout, but is still full of great design. Subscriptions are available for those folks who are not registered Aldus users.

> *Aldus Magazine*
> Aldus Corporation
> 411 First Avenue South
> Seattle, WA 98104-2871
> (206) 628-2321

Communication Arts

This is the real thing—a scrumptious contemporary museum of design, in printed form. *Communication Arts* first began publishing in 1959, consistently and reliably reporting on the ongoing explosion in the design world. A beautiful and expensive magazine, *Communication Arts* is published eight times a year, with four special issues: the Design Annual, the Photography Annual, the Advertising Annual, and the Illustration Annual. Certainly not for everyone, but an essential read for professional designers, art directors, and those that aspire to be.

> *Communication Arts*
> P.O. Box 10300
> Palo Alto, CA 94303-0807
> Fax: (415) 326-1648

Corellation

Corellation, the official magazine of the Association of Corel Artists & Designers (ACAD), is an independent publication produced by Draw-loving publishing professionals. Each issue is full of information that suits Draw artists of all levels. The magazine includes articles and how-to information for everyone from beginners through advanced users. The monthly magazine includes listings for training centers and service bureaus, along with product reviews and interviews.

Randy Tobin, *Corellation*'s editor/designer, does a fine job. The magazine is light and airy, making good use of editorial white space. Both design and content are of high caliber. This magazine is exceedingly well-printed for one of its type, making good use of spot varnishes and soy inks. Yearly subscriptions are bundled with a yearly membership in ACAD (a nonprofit group).

Association of Corel Artists & Designers
1309 Riverside Drive
Burbank, CA 91506

Electronic Publishing (formerly *TypeWorld*)

TypeWorld, founded in 1977, and until recently edited by the venerable (and opinionated) Frank Romano, is now known as *Electronic Publishing*, "the first and only newspaper for electronic publishing." Recently purchased by the PennWell Publishing Company, *Electronic Publishing* is published twice a month. Though not for the low-end desktop publisher, the newspaper provides pages upon pages of product information for service bureaus and electronic publishers. Chances are, a product hits the pages of *Electronic Publishing* before it hits the streets.

The newspaper also includes a good-sized classified section that lists equipment for sale, from low-end desktop stuff through six-figure high-dollar systems.

Electronic Publishing Editorial Offices
One Stiles Road
P.O. Box 170
Salem, NH 03079
(603) 898-2822

Flash Magazine

The diminutive *Flash Magazine* measures in at only 5.5-by-8.5-inches, but proves that age old adage about good things coming in small packages. Running under the tagline "Wild Ideas in Laser Printing," you will find a wide variety of articles targeted at the working desktop professional. Recent articles have featured such interesting phenomena as etching glass with a laser printer, book-on-demand binding, and how to build a padding press.

Flash focuses on cool things you can do with your laser printer. Much of this centers upon the use of transfer toners that enable you to transfer your printed pieces to T-shirts, wood, metal, and other materials. The magazine is an invaluable resource for guerrilla marketers and nonprofit groups alike. If you miss an issue, don't fret—the publisher also bundles the magazines into yearly *Flash Compendiums*.

Flash Magazine
RR 1 Box 2G
West Topsham, VT 05086-9988
Fax: (802) 439-6463
CIS: 73130,1734
waltervj@flashmag.com

U&lc

A true treasure, *U&lc* (which is proofreader's code for upper- and lowercase) bills itself as the international journal of type and graphic design. *U&lc* is a quarterly celebration of the typographer's craft. Within its large format, you are treated to design at its best, whether black and white, spot color, or process color. Each issue brings incredible spreads that beg the mind for thorough consideration. Typographic history is taught here, and it is taught quite well.

Published by the International Typeface Corporation and available for a nominal fee, *U&lc* is a resource that you should not be without.

> *U&lc*
> International Typeface Corporation
> 2 Hammarskjold Plaza
> New York, NY 10017
> (212) 371-0699

Using CompuServe Information Service (CIS)

Do you have a question that needs to be answered, and you cannot afford to spend the time or money to call Ottawa? Try CompuServe.

CompuServe is one of the most amazing resources in the computer world. It is a support network, offering you thousands of people who are ready to offer advice on whatever your computer problems might be.

Type up a note that covers the problem in your favorite word processor. Then save it as an ASCII file and upload it to either the Corel or DTP Forums. Within a day, sometimes even hours, you will get the answer you need without waiting on hold or spending big bucks on telephone calls. You've probably heard lots of mumbo-jumbo about the information superhighway. Well, this might not be that promise of nirvana, but it sure is a quick route to answering specific questions about Draw!

The Desktop Publishing Forum

The Desktop Publishing Forum (DTPFORUM) is the place where savvy desktoppers hang out to trade advice and talk shop. DTPFORUM includes the message board, with its winding threads of questions, answers, and conversations on topics ranging from desktop publishing issues to what is the best Canadian beer. In the libraries, you can find demo programs, fonts, clip-art samples, and more. Every Tuesday night at 9 p.m. (Eastern time), the DTPFORUM sponsors an on-line conference where desktop publishers can visit and trade information. To access this forum, type **GO DTPFORUM** at the CompuServe menu.

The Zenith Forum

The Zenith Forum (ZENITH FORUM) originally was created to support owners of Zenith Data Systems computers, most notably the Zenith portables. It has since grown to support portables in general, as well as Windows products. ZENITH FORUM is an excellent place to scour for shareware programs from graphics converters to Windows utilities.

For the convenience of forum members, an up-to-date catalog of library files is posted on the first of every month. It is always LIBSUM.EXE in the New Files Library (Library 1). This forum is especially sensitive to the needs of new CompuServe users and holds a beginners conference every Sunday night to give them live help. To get to the ZENITH FORUM, just type **GO ZENITH**.

The Corel Forum

In late spring 1992, Corel opened its own CompuServe forum. Just type **GO COREL**, and you'll be whisked to one of the most interesting forums on CIS. Here you can ask specific Draw-related questions and expect a prompt response from a number of folks (including many of the people responsible for this book) well-versed in the program's intricacies. You can even upload problem files, connect-time-free, for Corel's on-line sleuths. In addition to the message board, the Corel Forum includes libraries that contain bug-fixes, various CDR sample files, and a number of utilities.

> CompuServe Inc.
> 5000 Arlington Centre Boulevard
> Columbus, OH 43220

CorelDRAW! is but one of many weapons you can use in your electronic graphics arts arsenal. Thankfully, it does a tremendous job of integrating with many different packages. The trick is to know which packages to use and what to buy. The only way to do so is to stay current with the steady stream of information in this industry. You accomplish this feat not by keeping your ear to the ground, but by keeping your nose in the trades.

The resources presented in this chapter are a starting point. To be successful, you must be informed. The ultimate business weapon is knowledge. It is up to you to go out and get it.

Chapter Snapshot

A job isn't worth the paper you can't print it on. In other words, it's all too easy to create files that either will not print or that will image poorly. In this chapter, you learn to do the following:

- ✔ Access and configure the Print dialog box
- ✔ Use overprinting to create traps
- ✔ Avoid banding in grayscale and color PostScript fountain fills
- ✔ Turn your images into 35mm slides and posters
- ✔ Identify a quality service bureau
- ✔ Circumvent printing problems

CorelDRAW! can create some incredibly complex files, but it is your responsibility to see that these files will actually print. Adherence to the following recommendations will help to ensure your printing success.

CHAPTER

Basic Printing Techniques

W ith this new and improved version of CorelDRAW!, everyday printing has changed considerably and for the better. You have more control and more options to choose from, and the dialog boxes just don't look like they used to. For serious users, this chapter and the following (on advanced printing techniques) will be the meat-and-potatoes information.

This chapter takes you through all your everyday printing concerns and how to set them up exactly the way you need. In CorelDRAW! 5, you will see that the Print Options controls section has been greatly expanded to include almost every possible printing concern.

One word of advice, though. Be sure to at least skim Chapter 21, "Managing Color and System Calibration."

Nature of the Beast

Multitudes of printers are out there, and identifying the procedures for each would fill more pages than a set of encyclopedias. Once you have a basic understanding of the various printer types on the market and the principles under which they operate, the world of printing should seem much simpler.

If a final printed file is what you're after, it is extremely important to get to know the properties of the printer or printers you will be using. Printers are not just black boxes through which white paper goes in one end and text and pretty pictures come out the other. Don't just thumb through the manual hoping a head will suddenly poke out and tell you all you need to know. Read through the information thoroughly; chances are you'll find something you didn't know before.

It is important to know whether your printer is a PostScript or a Non-PostScript printer. These are the two basic types of printers and no matter which reproduction technology they use, they differ in how they handle the data that describes the information on your pages.

Find out if and how much rapid access memory (RAM) your printer has, and what its limitations are (maximum page size, resolution, colors). Four megabytes of RAM is suggested as a minimum for printers that perform heavy font downloading tasks. It wouldn't hurt to write down the model, serial number, and warranty expiration date for handy reference. What about the technical support number? Most manufacturers have a 1-800 number to call to get service or answers to technical questions.

Installing a Printer Driver from the Control Panel

Before you install a printer from the Control Panel you must have two important items. First, the PostScript Printer Driver (.PPD) if it's a PostScript printer you are installing. Second, the most recent Windows printer driver (PSCRIPT.DRV and PSCRIPT.HLP), version 3.56 or later. If your printer is non-PostScript, you will need the vendor-supplied printer driver (.DRV) for that particular non-PostScript printer.

If you aren't sure whether you are using the latest PostScript printer driver, this can be easily checked by following this procedure:

1. From Program Manager open the Main Windows group (see fig. 11.1) and double-click on Control Panel. The Control Panel window appears (see fig. 11.2).

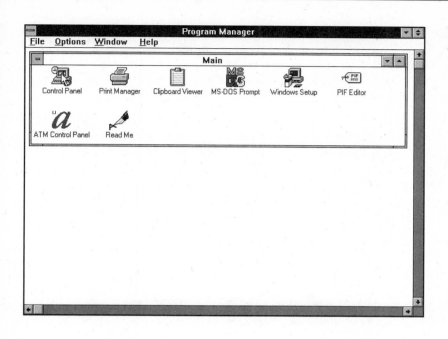

Figure 11.1
The Main
program group.

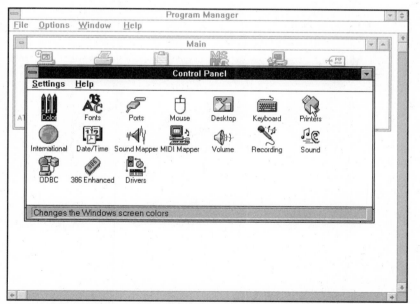

Figure 11.2
The Windows
Control Panel.

2. Double-click on the Printers icon to open the Printers dialog box (see fig. 11.3). Select any PostScript printer listed in the installed printers listing. If there are no printers installed, select a printer from the list supplied with Windows by clicking on <u>A</u>dd and selecting any of the Linotronic printers.

    After you select a printer, click on <u>I</u>nstall and the printer should appear in the list of installed printers. Windows prompts you to insert a disk with the updated driver on it (see fig. 11.4). Chances are you already have a copy of PSCRIPT.DRV on your system if you installed printers when you performed your original Windows install. Click on <u>B</u>rowse, locate the directory in C:\WINDOWS\SYSTEM, and click on OK (see fig. 11.5).

    Windows then has the information it needs for that particular printer.

Figure 11.3
Installing a printer.

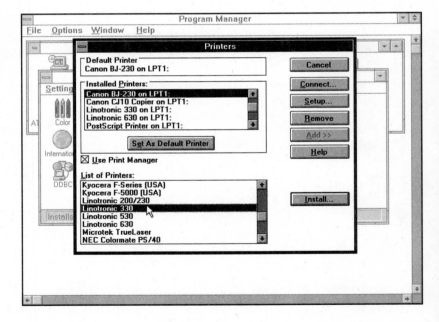

3. Now click on <u>S</u>etup to show more information about the printer (see fig. 11.6).

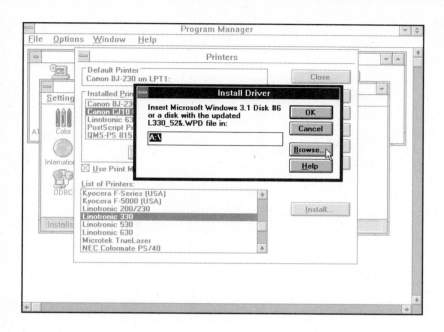

Figure 11.4
Installing the
print driver.

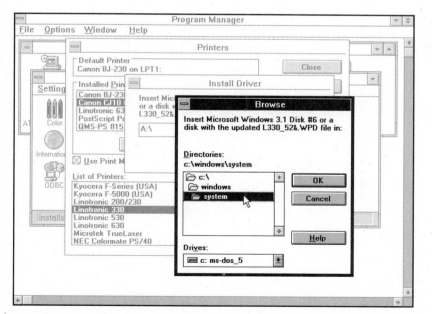

Figure 11.5
The Browse
dialog box.

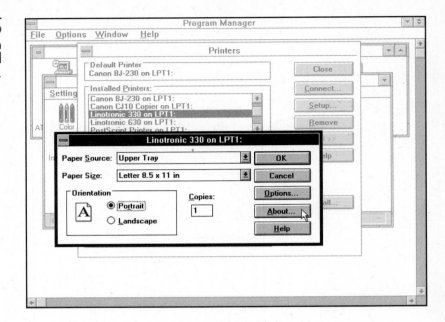

4. Click on About and the About window appears (see fig. 11.7).

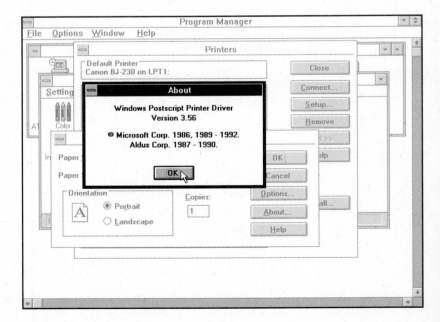

Windows displays dates and version numbers for the PSCRIPT.DRV installed on your system.

If you don't have a copy of the most recent PSCRIPT.DRV, contact your nearest Microsoft office, the dealer where you purchased the printer, or the printer manufacturer. Any of these should be willing to provide the latest driver. If you happen to have access to CompuServe, you can download the latest drivers from the Microsoft forum. Also, every printer driver imaginable is available through CompuServe's Microsoft Software Library (type GO MSL). CompuServe is a pay-by-use service.

Setting Up Your Page

You have many options to choose from to set up the page layout style of the work you create. The layout you choose, of course, depends on your specific work. You must consider the size of paper, the orientation of your illustration, and page numbering.

To set up your page, select Layout, Page Setup. CorelDRAW! displays the Page Setup dialog box (see fig. 11.8).

You also can display the Page Setup dialog box by double-clicking on the perimeter of your on-screen page.

The Page Setup dialog box is now split into three different areas: Size, Layout, and Display. Click on the tab of the area you want to change. Each tabbed area controls specific settings.

Figure 11.8
The Page Setup
dialog box.

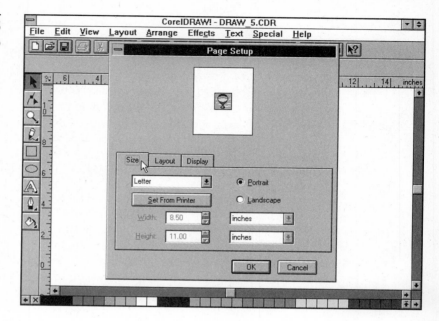

Selecting Size

Choose the dimensions of your paper in the Size box. The Size section enables you to:

- ✔ Set the page dimensions from the preset page sizes in the pull-down menu

- ✔ Select a custom page size (bottom of the list) and enter your own dimensions

- ✔ Set your page size from whatever your printer happens to be set up for at that particular moment

The page orientation can be set to Landscape or Portrait, and the dimensions for the custom page size can be entered in inches, millimeters, picas and points, or just points.

There are approximately 6 picas to an inch, 12 points to a pica, and 72 points to an inch.

Choosing a Layout

Layout is another ingenious automatic function of Page Setup, but is a little tricky to figure out at first, and will likely be one of the least-understood features in this area. Layout takes the page size and orientation of the print size you select and automatically divides it into little parts.

Imagine that you need to make tent cards for a presentation and are printing onto letter size landscape pages. The tent cards need to be letter-size and folded down the middle so that each name is right-side up. In the Size tab, select letter size, landscape, and in Layout, select tent card. Draw automatically splits the page in half and turns over the second page. CorelDRAW! also gives you a screen representation of each side of the tent card and lets you work on the second side right-side up. Draw also enables you to preview the finished page size after the calculations have been made and displays this information to the right of your selection.

The Layout section is dedicated to preformatting your printouts to enable output of your pages in the following signature formats:

- ✔ Full Page
- ✔ Book
- ✔ Booklet
- ✔ Tent Card
- ✔ Side-fold Card
- ✔ Top-fold Card

These formats are displayed in the preview window (see fig. 11.9). For instance, if you were to select the Top-fold Card option as the preview indicates, your pages would be set in position according to this preformatted layout: page one in the bottom right corner, page two above it, page three in the upper left corner (upside down), and page four in the bottom left corner (upside down). The page size you select to print to must also accommodate the page sizes you have selected in the Size dialog box. If you choose to use one of the preselected layouts, be sure to select this in the Layout section of the Print Options dialog box before printing.

Figure 11.9
The available
output formats.

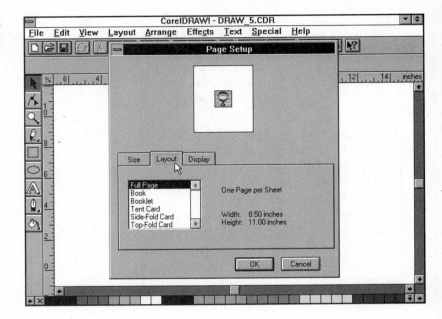

In **L**ayout, **P**age Setup the little balloons in the preview window indicate which direction each page is oriented.

Choosing Display

The Display section describes how the pages are laid out within CorelDRAW! according to the Layout selection. The Full Page, Book, and Booklet selections enable CorelDRAW! to show facing pages, but only Full Page and Book enable you to view the pages beginning on either the left or right page first. All selections allow the feature of controlling the page color and adding an automatic page frame (see fig. 11.10).

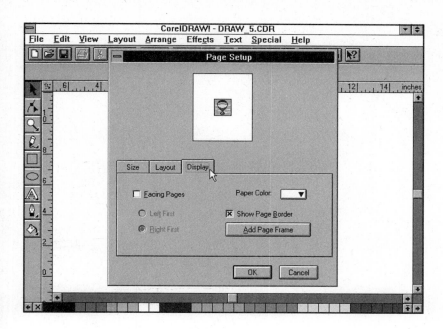

Figure 11.10
The Display
options.

II

Putting CorelDRAW! To Work

Printing Files

Printing in CorelDRAW! has taken on a new and different look since version 4. The user interface looks the same, but the way it works is a bit different. As mentioned earlier, creating a pretty picture or perfect layout is one thing, and printing it is another. Draw version 5 has many new controls and options for printing but also has many highly complex drawing capabilities that may not be the greatest if your printer can't handle highly complex printing.

Selecting a Printer

CorelDRAW! provides two methods for choosing a printer. The first is straightforward: select File, Print Setup, and the Print Setup dialog box is displayed (see fig. 11.11).

Within this dialog box, you want to choose the printer you will use from the list of printers installed on your system. You also will be able to set the printer's setup configuration by clicking on Setup. This might save some time before selecting the next method, but is basically a repeat of what you find in the File, Print dialog box.

The second way to select a printer is by selecting File, Print (or Ctrl+P). Figure 11.12 shows the Print dialog box, which provides access to all of the printing controls.

Figure 11.11
The Print Setup
dialog box.

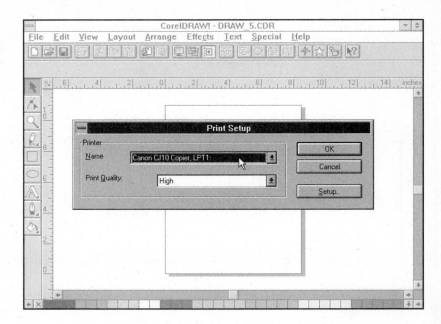

Figure 11.12
The Print dialog
box.

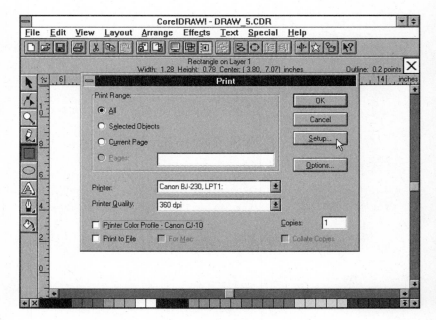

To the right of the dialog box, you find two buttons titled <u>S</u>etup and <u>O</u>ptions. The <u>S</u>etup button enables you to make changes to the chosen printer's setup (see fig. 11.13). The <u>O</u>ptions button lets you choose from a myriad of choices which determine how your file prints (see fig. 11.14). CorelDRAW! 5.0's Print Options dialog box is so huge that it gobbles up the entire screen on a 640×480 display! There are so many choices that Corel chose to use a tab metaphor to flip between the three Print Option modes (Layout, Separations, Options).

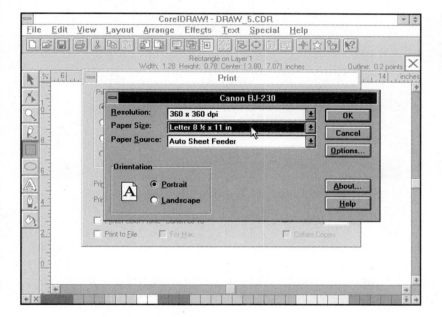

Figure 11.13
A dialog box for selecting options for your printer.

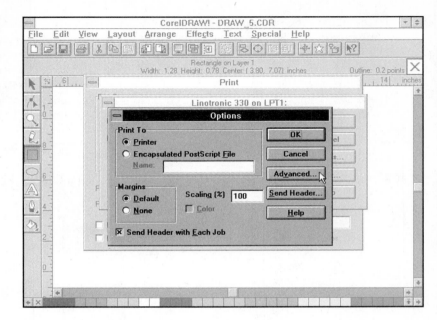

Figure 11.14
You can set further print options by selecting Setup in the Print Setup dialog box.

Printing Options

CorelDRAW!'s print savvy is controlled by the Print dialog box. Please note that this means the print options as they relate to a PostScript output device. Although Windows can drive plenty of non-PostScript devices, it is hardly worth using CorelDRAW! with anything but a true Adobe PostScript-licensed printer.

The one exception is a relatively inexpensive color inkjet printer, which can be a real convenience when used as a design tool. However, do not use an inkjet printer as a prepress proofing device for images that ultimately will be output as separations on a PostScript imagesetter. The continuity just is not there.

Take a look at the first choices that Draw gives you when printing files. To access the Print dialog box you have three choices: you can click the Printer button on the button bar, you can click on <u>F</u>ile and then select <u>P</u>rint, or you can simply press Ctrl+P.

The available options are as follow:

✔ **All.** As you've probably figured out, clicking <u>A</u>ll tells Draw that you want to print all the pages in a file.

✔ **Selected Objects.** This time-saving option is valuable when working with images that consist of many objects. It works in a similar manner to Preview Only Selected. In this mode, the printer outputs only those objects you have selected when you open the dialog box. If you want to print just one or a few objects without waiting for the printer to image all the objects, use Selected Objects.

✔ **Current Page.** Here's a convenient feature! It allows you to print only the page you are currently working on, without setting a range.

✔ **Pages.** If you want to print a page, or a number of pages, this box enables you to specify which pages to print. If you are printing a number of single pages, you must separate each page with a comma (for instance, 3,6,7,9). To print a number of consecutive pages, separate the starting and ending pages with a hyphen (for instance, 3-7). You can use these in combination as well (for instance, 1,3, 5-8). And in addition, you can print even pages (1~) or odd pages (2~).

✔ **Printer.** This box tells you for which printer Draw is composing its printer output. For a printer to be listed here, it must first be installed through the Windows Control Panel.

✔ **Printer Quality.** Certain printers have the capability to print at more than one dpi. This is most often true of imagesetters, but some high resolution desktop laser printers can toggle between different resolutions as well. Lowering the dpi will usually speed up printing.

✔ **Printer Color Profile.** Checking this box turns on Draw's color calibration printing routine. Check out Chapter 21, " Managing Color and System Calibration," in Part IV of this book for more information on color profiles.

✔ **Print To File.** Selecting Print To File causes Draw to create a PostScript file that you can download to an imagesetter from any other computer. If the other computer is a Mac, you should select the For Mac check box. This option removes a pair of control characters that Draw normally includes in PostScript files. These characters are filtered out by the printing ports on a PC. If you are printing to a Mac and do not select this option, these characters are passed on to the printer and end up generating a PostScript error, keeping the pages from imaging.

✔ **Copies.** Simply lets you select to print more than one copy of your image. Note that with version 4.0, this option didn't work correctly on all printers. The same may be true with version 5.0. If printing multiple copies takes a long time, it probably means that CorelDRAW! is sending the complete print job to the printer multiple times instead of sending a command to just print multiple copies. In this situation, you should select the Printer button and set the number of copies in the printer's setup dialog box.

✔ **Collate Copies.** Selecting this feature will collate the output from multiple page/multiple copy print jobs.

Layout Print Options

When you click on the Options button, the Print Options dialog box opens in Layout mode (see fig. 11.15). Notice the new button bar just below the page preview. This button bar gives you control over various options that are essential when running repro or negative film, and it stays at the bottom of the screen, regardless of which tab section of the Print Options dialog box is active. Table 11.1 shows each button, along with a brief explanation of its function.

Figure 11.15
Print Options—
Layout.

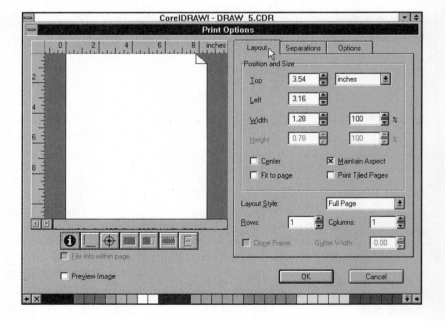

Table 11.1
Print Options Button Bar

Button Name	Description
	Prints file name, date, page number, color plate name, screen frequency, and color profile. This data is printed outside the image area unless you select File Info Within Page. If File Info Within Page is selected, this information might print over parts of your illustration, so be careful.
	A must for either repro or film. This option adds marks to the output image that tell the pressperson where the actual edges of the page should be if the page has to be trimmed from a larger sheet of paper.
	These "bull's-eye" marks are imperative for aligning the printed image on the press and are absolutely necessary for color printing.
	The calibration bar is a series of color swatches that print in the margin of the drawing. These swatches help you calibrate your monitor to the actual output colors and helps you to ensure color fidelity (see the chapter on color calibration in part IV).
	This selection prints a grid that shows the range of color from 1 to 100 for the current color separation plate. Lets you or your printer determine that the imagesetter is properly calibrated.
	Sets the PostScript output device to invert the file image, turning black to white and white to black. You need this option when imaging negatives that will be directly burned to the printing plates. Film negatives give the highest possible quality.
E	Switches between right reading and wrong reading film. The "E" refers to the emulsion of the film, as in "emulsion up" or "emulsion down."

To use any of the reference marks, such as cropmarks, registration marks, the color calibration bar, or the densitometer scale, you must be printing to a paper size that is larger than the page size of your drawing.

Underneath the button bar you see the File Info Within Page option. This selection only becomes active if the Info button is depressed; it prints the file information within the cropmarks, rather than outside. You are most likely to use this option when you are checking a file on your laser printer before sending it out for repro or film. Running a check on your files before sending them out to print is often referred to as *pre-flight* testing. Pre-flighting a file can save you many headaches; if you are going to send a file out for high-resolution output, you should get in the habit of test printing each plate to your laser printer.

To get a good look at where things are falling in the print area, click on Preview Image. After you have a preview, you can see whether you need to move the image. The Position and Size functions give you the capability to reposition the selected objects (as a group, not individually) on the page. You can move the image by typing new coordinates in the Top and Left entry areas of the dialog box. To move from page to page, use the little arrow buttons at the bottom left of the preview window.

CorelDRAW! 5.0 also introduced a new convention for scaling print images. Don't bother looking for anything that says "Scale," however. To resize the printed objects, type a percentage at the % box to the right of the Width box, making sure that Maintain Aspect is selected.

Layout Position and Size also presents the following selections:

✔ **Center.** As the name implies, this option centers the objects on the page.

✔ **Fit to Page.** This option is a subset of Scale. With one click, the oversized image is scaled up or down and centered to fit on the imageable area of the selected output page.

✔ **Maintain Aspect.** When this box is checked, the dialog box scales your image proportionally, maintaining the aspect ratio. Deselecting this selection enables you to stretch an image disproportionally.

✔ **Print Tiled Pages.** The Tile option prints an image larger than the output device's largest paper size. For example, when proofing a tabloid-sized image on a printer whose paper size is limited to 8 1/2 inches by 11 inches, click on Tile. The printer breaks the image up into pieces (or tiles), which then can be taped together for proofing.

Just below the Position and Size area, you see a number of choices that relate to Layout, including Layout Style, Rows, Columns, Clone Frame, and Gutter Width.

Separations Print Options

Clicking on the Separations tab brings up CorelDRAW!'s powerful separations options (see fig. 11.16). In this section, you can specify the settings for a variety of color separation needs.

✔ **Print Separations.** This option is used for color imaging. Each color used is broken into its own plate. If you are using process color, you get separate plates for cyan, magenta, yellow, and black. With spot color, each spot color used has its own plate, too. This option also works with a combination of spot and process colors, just in case you want to pay for that seven-color press. When Print Separations is selected, Draw automatically selects the Crop Marks, Registration Marks, and File Information buttons. You can turn off these options as required. Selecting Print Separations enables a number of functions, including Convert Spot Colors to CMYK, Use Custom Halftone, and Auto Trapping.

✔ **Convert Spot Colors to CMYK.** Checking this option converts your spot colors to CMYK process equivalents so that the job outputs as a four-color separation without additional spot color plates.

✔ **Use Custom Halftone.** Rather than using an output device's default halftoning, you often want to use specific settings, depending on a number of variables, such as paper stock, type of printing press, etc. With Use Custom Halftone selected, clicking the Edit button in the dialog box opens the Advanced Screening dialog box (see fig. 11.17) where you can change the Halftone Type, frequency, and angles to suit your needs. Underneath Screening Technologies, there are presets for a number of imagesetters, in particular, those from Linotype-Hell. Choosing a particular model allows you to then set the Resolution and Basic Screen.

Figure 11.16
CorelDRAW!'s
separation
options.

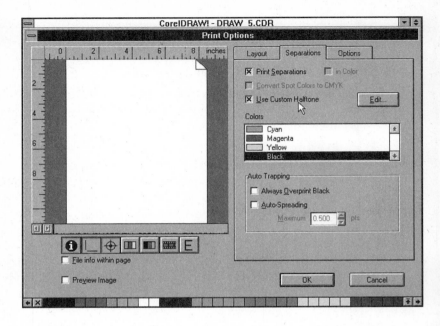

Figure 11.17
The Advanced
Screening dialog
box.

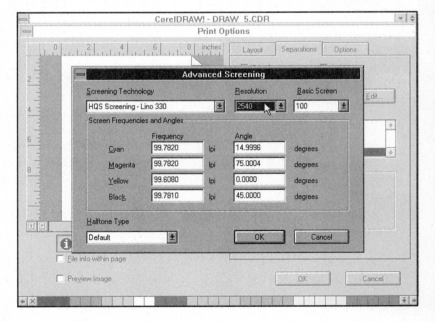

Avoid altering the CMYK Frequency and Screen settings. There are plenty of places to go astray here. If you don't quite know to what these options refer, you definitely do not want to change them. Only do so under direct instruction from your printer (again, the person, not the machine). Part IV of this book contains a wealth of information on setting your files up for your service bureau and printer.

CorelDRAW! 5.0 has a limited amount of automated trapping functions. While these may fit the bill for some folks, they do not offer the degree of control offered by the trapping functions of Quark Xpress. At the bottom of the Separations dialog box, you notice several Auto Trapping settings.

✔ **Always Overprint Black.** When this option is turned on, Draw automatically overprints anything that is 95-100% black.

✔ **Auto-Spreading.** Creates traps (spreads only) for objects that have no outline, have a uniform fill, and have not been set to overprint in the Object menu. You can set the spreading value from a minimum of .01 of a point to a maximum of 10 points.

While these Auto Trapping options provide an "easy" solution to trapping, discuss trapping issues with your printer first for best results. Your printer might want a set of negatives with no trapping (so the stripper can create the traps manually) or might ask for an Encapsulated PostScript (EPS) file that can be processed through a stand-alone trapping solution (such as Aldus TrapWise). Please refer to the section later in this chapter on manual trapping for more information on the trapping process.

Other Print Options

Corel's engineers named the third tab in the Print Options dialog box with a rather confusing name: Options. So when you read about this section of the dialog box, remember that it is the Print Options Options that you are reading about. The Options selections let you set a number of specifications including (see fig. 11.18):

✔ **Screen Frequency.** This option sets up the output device's halftone size for spot colors or composite color (screen frequency and angle for process color separations is controlled in the separations dialog box). Although the drop-down list has only a limited selection of screen frequencies, you can type in specific values. To ascertain the correct screen frequency to use, check with the printer (the person, not the machine) who ultimately will print the job. He should be able to give you complete specifications.

The Screen Frequency setting is overridden by any individual changes in the Outline or Fill PostScript screen options dialog boxes (for those objects only). Thus, you can use, for instance, a 110 screen for an entire image with the exception of the logo, which might require a special screen effect, such as a line pattern at 25 lpi. Please note that special screen effects do not rotate. If you rotate such a screened image, the lines do not rotate with the image. This might lead to some unexpected results if you print proofs on a PostScript laser printer in portrait mode, then print your final output on an imagesetter that rotates the page to print across the paper in the printer.

✔ **Set Flatness to.** *Flatness* governs the smoothness of curves in PostScript output files. The lower the setting, the smoother the curves (and the more difficult a file is to print). Complex objects sometimes can choke a printer. Raising the Flatness setting enables Draw to simplify the curves, making the file more palatable to PostScript printers. Printing to a high-resolution imagesetter can be more problematic than printing to a desktop laser printer because of printer memory constraints and the number of dots and points that the imagesetter has to manage. If you are finding that your files print OK on a 300 dpi PostScript printer, but fail on a 1200 dpi imagesetter, you can *lower* the flatness setting to 0.25 here when printing to the laser printer (don't forget to set it back to 1 for final output for the imagesetter). This simulates printing to the imagesetter and might give you warnings about problem files before going out to your service bureau. If you find that raising the flatness helps many of your drawings to print, you may find that you have to break large curves into smaller segments.

✔ **Auto Increase Flatness.** This option was introduced in CorelDRAW! 3.0. As indicated before, Draw makes it too easy to create overly complex images that can be trouble at print time. When you choose this option, Corel takes control of printing by setting up the PostScript file to automatically increment the flatness setting by 2 (relative to the initial flatness setting) up to 5 times each time the printer returns a Limitcheck error when processing a clipping path in a print job. If the PostScript object is still too complex to print, the printer will skip the object and go on to process the next object in the page description. One of the downsides of this feature, though, is that it has the potential to increase printing time greatly.

✔ **Fountain Steps.** The Fountain Steps option governs the number of stripes in a printed fountain fill. Low values print faster (with visible banding), and high values look smoother (and take longer to print). For high-resolution imagesetters, Corel recommends 128 for 1270 dpi, and 200 for 2540 dpi. Set this option to a lower number to speed up proof printing (at the expense of exaggerated banding in fountain fills).

✔ **Number of Points in Curves.** The Maximum setting governs curve smoothness. Early PostScript printers might have trouble printing complex images. If so, try lowering the value from the default setting of 1500. You can have a setting of anywhere from 100 to 200000. The smaller the number, the smaller the print file, and consequently, the more likely that it will print on a cranky old printer. Conversely, if you are after a really clean image and have the output device to handle it, the larger the number, the smoother the curve, and the larger the print file.

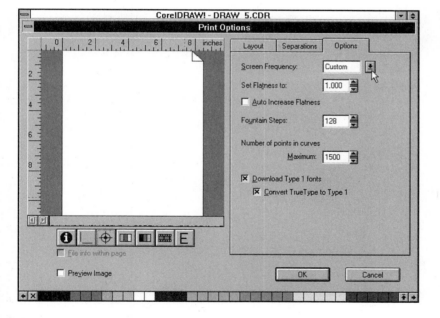

Figure 11.18
Print Options options.

The last two options in the Print Options Options dialog box have to do with fonts. Perhaps the single greatest change made to CorelDRAW! 5.0 is the adoption of standard font handling. The program now treats fonts as a proper graphics application should. Prior versions of the program had bizarre font handling characteristics, much to the dismay of the graphic arts world. Corel is to be commended for finally getting their font act together!

II

Putting CorelDRAW! To Work

The subjects of font management and working with service bureaus are covered in great depth in Part IV of this book, so rather than be redundant, there will be just a brief mention here.

✔ **Download Type 1 Fonts.** This is the one option that professional CorelDRAW! users have all been waiting for. If this box is checked, Draw downloads each PostScript font used in a job. If you are printing to file, it includes the font(s) in the print file. If your fonts are printer-resident, however, you can save time by not downloading the fonts.

✔ **Convert TrueType to Type 1.** If you use TrueType fonts and are sending files to a service bureau or printing to a PostScript laser in your office, you probably want to have this selected. Doing so converts the TrueType fonts into PostScript Type 1 fonts. This should reduce print file sizes and, consequently, reduce imagesetting time. If this box is left unchecked, CorelDRAW! sends down curve or bitmap information for your TrueType fonts, resulting in lower quality and increased imagesetting time. Regardless of this option, if you are sending any files to a high-resolution PostScript device, you really should be using PostScript fonts.

Part Three

Using Corel's Modules

Chapter Snapshot

This chapter introduces some of the charting terminology used in CorelCHART!. For instance, when creating a bar chart, it helps to know what a data series and category axis are. Because selecting the right chart type is key to effective charting, this chapter also examines the various chart types available in CorelCHART!. In this chapter, you will learn the following:

✔ Elements of a chart

✔ Types of charts that version 5 offers

✔ How to convey the right message by choosing the correct chart type

✔ How to open, start, and save a chart

Charting has truly changed the way we read and interpret data. The chart's power to inform, motivate, and persuade has made presentation graphics a part of contemporary culture. Due to its flexibility and attention to detail, CorelCHART! is an excellent choice for developing presentation graphics. Because graphics professionals like you are charged with the responsibility of developing them, it is important that you understand how CorelCHART! approaches the task of developing charts and graphs. As you will see in this chapter, CorelCHART! boasts incredible power and flexibility for producing an impressive range of chart types and styles.

CHAPTER

The Basics of CorelCHART!

Not long ago, if you wanted to "take a look at the figures," you actually had to read real numbers. Today, when someone examines the figures, frequently they don't see actual numbers; instead, they see charts and graphs. For years, charts and graphs were the domain of engineers, mathematicians, and accountants who toiled for ways to make their complex data comprehensible to their nontechnical coworkers. When the business world discovered them as a powerful way to show trends and statistics, chart popularity exploded.

Over the last few years, charts and graphs have gone through an evolution of sorts. What used to be called charts are now called info-graphics or presentation graphics. The key word is *graphics*, and that is where you come in. No longer are charts just visual representations of numbers. Charting has become an art form in its own right. For example, consider the little chart appearing each day on the front of *USA Today*. These quick, concise graphs provide readers with interesting tidbits in a visually entertaining way. Whether you're learning about the First Lady's cookie recipes or how much time people spend with their dogs, these graphs catch your eye and make you think. This is your charge as a developer of presentation graphics; first capture the viewer's attention, then quickly convey a message.

Creating Charts with CorelCHART!

As a graphics professional, you are in the business of creating visually impressive charts with that professional look so important in competitive business environments. The goal is more than to make the audience understand the figures and data; the goal is to knock their socks off. CorelCHART! is an application with the power to achieve this goal. It has the broad range of charting options, and the attention to detail that the pickiest of number-crunchers will admire. At the same time, design professionals will appreciate CorelCHART!'s capability to create stunning works of art. It's this artistic inclination that sets CorelCHART! apart from other charting applications.

CorelCHART! has powerful allies in CorelDRAW!, CorelPHOTO-PAINT!, CorelMOVE!, CorelSHOW!, and CorelVENTURA!, some of the other applications provided with CorelDRAW! 5.0. In many cases, if you can't create the graphic you need in CorelCHART!, you can produce it in Draw or PhotoPaint and then bring it into CorelCHART!. The movement and animation features of CorelMOVE! enable you to add energy to your presentations. And the wonderful transition effects in Show provide an excellent showcase for your presentation masterpieces.

Identifying Basic Chart Elements

As an artist or designer, you are well aware of the precious little time you have to grab the viewer's attention and communicate your message. Your chart must be easy to understand and interpret. Every element of your chart has a singular purpose: to assist the viewer in comprehending the chart's overall message. Therefore, to create effective charts and graphs in CorelCHART!, it's essential that you have an understanding of how CorelCHART! identifies and labels these chart elements.

Working with Chart Titles

Chart *titles* are some of the first things your audience sees. The title is normally displayed at the top of the chart and is usually the largest text element on the chart (see fig. 12.1). Titles set the visual tone for your chart, so make sure they state the point of each chart as vividly as possible. As with all chart text, the title should be kept at three to five words, with limited punctuation and limited use of words such as "and," "the," and "of."

The *subtitle* offers a more in-depth description of the chart message. The subtitle should reveal that which encourages further inspection of the chart. Subtitles normally are displayed just beneath the chart title and usually are the second largest text element on the chart.

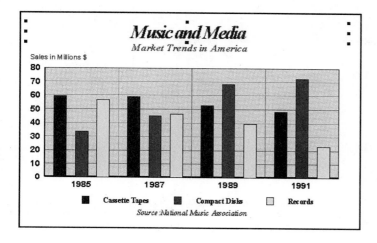

Figure 12.1
Chart titles catch the viewers' attention and inform them of the chart content.

Many of the charts you create will be filled with statistical data. It might be important that you provide supporting information about those statistics in a footnote. For instance, a footnote might tell us when the chart data was published or what organization originally compiled the statistics. Though footnotes typically are placed at the bottom of the chart, CorelCHART! places them just beneath the subtitle, but they can easily be moved as desired. Remember that footnotes should tell us something that we don't already know from viewing the chart.

Understanding Category and Data Axes

Most of the charts you create fall into one of two general categories: text or word charts, and numerically based charts, often called graphs. Because you can use CorelDRAW! to create text charts, CorelCHART! concentrates on numerical charting.

The lion's share of the graphs you will create will likely be XY charts. Included in this group are bar, area, line, scatter, and hi/lo charts. XY charts are composed of an X axis and a Y axis. An *axis* is a line that serves as a reference for plotting data in a graph.

The X axis, which CorelCHART! refers to as the *category axis*, shows the different groups of data that you want to graph. The Y axis, which CorelCHART! refers to as the *data axis*, serves as a reference for you to gauge the numerical value of what you are graphing. In figure 12.2, the category axis displays years, and the data axis displays the number of units sold. CorelCHART! refers to the bars that represent the data as *risers*.

Figure 12.2
XY charts use two axes to plot chart data.

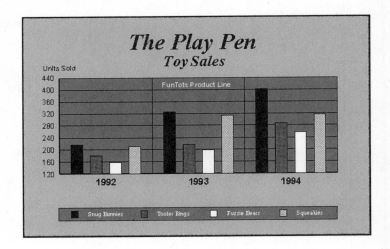

Understanding Data Groups and Data Series

The classifications along the Category axis, which in figure 12.3 are the months July, August, and September, are called *data groups*. For each data group in this example, there are four risers: one each for Frames, Paint, Brushes, and Canvas. Collectively, a set of similarly colored risers is called a *data series*. A data series enables you to gauge the quantity or value of an item over a specified period of time. For instance, the Data series for Frames enables you to gauge the number of frame sales for each of the three months.

Figure 12.3
The categories of data along the category axis are called data groups. The values for each set of data per category are data series.

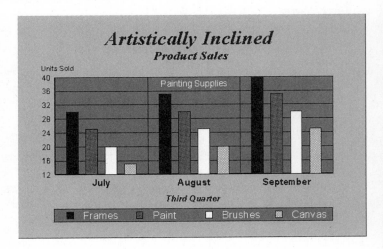

In some cases, you might want to include titles for the category and data axis. For instance, you might add a data axis title to inform the viewer that the values along the data axis represent the barrels of oil pumped or the revenue from the oil. The data along the category axis might also be rather ambiguous until you add a title. For instance, if you're using fiscal quarters along the category axis, a category axis title could impart the specific year to which the chart is referring.

Understanding Legends and Legend Markers

A *legend* identifies each data series much like the legend on a road map provides a guide to the colors and symbols on it. In figure 12.4, the legend informs the viewer which bars represent the specific scoring areas for the skaters. Legends are generally at the bottom of the screen and contains *legend markers*, the reference tags that identify each Data Series. Legends can be turned on or off in CorelCHART!, and formatted to display in a variety of ways.

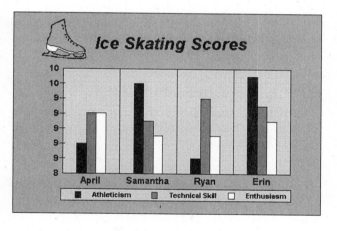

Figure 12.4
Legends are an integral part of communicating the chart data.

Understanding Grid Lines

The horizontal lines adjacent to each number on the data axis in figure 12.4 are the *data axis grid lines*. Those running vertically on the category axis are the *category axis grid lines*, and they help guide the eye from each series marker to the corresponding value or category on the axis. Grid lines help make a graph more readable, especially if the graph is very large. Be wary of too many grid lines because they can clutter up your chart. In CorelCHART!, you can turn on or off grid lines and adjust their width and style.

Choosing the Right Chart Type

The whole objective of your chart is to communicate an idea. Many charts fail to do this because they use the wrong chart type. It's important to learn not just how to create charts, but how to create *effective* charts. Data presented in the wrong chart type can become convoluted and might even project the wrong message. Before creating a chart, give serious thought to the best chart type for communicating your data.

CorelCHART! can create 16 basic chart types, most of which are available in a variety of formats. The chart type that best presents your data depends upon the types of relationships you are illustrating. The main chart type is selected when you first create the chart in CorelCHART!. From there, you can select one of the chart variations from the Gallery menu. Refer to Chapter 13, "Designing a Chart," for more information on creating new chart files.

Bar Charts

Bar charts are excellent for illustrating how numerical values compare with others. For instance, comparing the bars in figure 12.5 makes it easy to see that Alaska was the most popular cruise location for the past two years. Bar charts can be divided into two distinct groups: horizontal bars and vertical bars.

Figure 12.5
Bar charts facilitate comparisons between series of data.

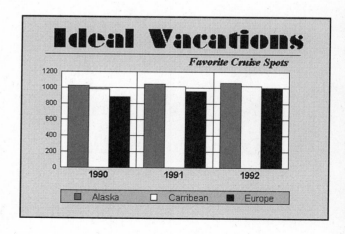

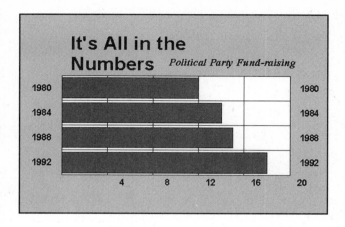

It's All in the Numbers

Political Party Fund-raising

Figure 12.6
Horizontal bar charts work well when expressing a limited number of data series per data group.

Vertical bar charts are for charts with more than one series of data or for illustration of how values change over time. Figure 12.5, for example, has three series of data (1990, 1991, and 1992) for each data group (Caribbean, Alaska, and so on).

Horizontal bar charts are scaled along the horizontal axis and are the most simple of the XY chart types. Optimally, they are used in situations with a limited number of data series per data group. In figure 12.6 for instance, the horizontal bars document only one series or bar per data group. Table 12.1 covers the available templates for bar charts.

II

Using Corel's Modules

Table 12.1
Types of Bar Charts

Chart Type	Description
Side-by-Side	Standard bar chart where bars are placed side-by-side along the category axis.
Stacked Bar	The bars in a data group are stacked on top of each other to represent the total value for a data group.

continues

Table 12.1, Continued
Types of Bar Charts

Chart Type	Description
Dual-Axis Side-by-Side	A second value or Y axis is placed on the chart. Some bars are plotted against a second data axis to compare series that use different units of measure or that exhibit a large disparity in magnitude.
Dual-Axis Stacked	Similar to Dual-Axis Side-by-Side, except bars are stacked on top of each other to represent the total value for a data group.
Bipolar Side-by-Side	Chart has two data axes, each starting at the center of the chart and increasing in value as they move outward, away from the center.
Bipolar Stacked	Similar to Bipolar Side-by-Side chart, except that the bars are placed on top of each other to represent the total value for a data group.
Percent	The percent chart displays values as a percentage of the total for a specific data group. The total value is represented as 100%, and the values in a given data group are shown as a percentage of the whole.

Line Charts

Select a line chart when you want to show trends or a change in data over a longer period of time. For instance, the line chart in figure 12.7 examines the ups and downs of truck sales over the last 12 months. Each point on the line marks a known occurrence, and the connection of these marks forms a line that emphasizes time flow and rate of change. Line charts are great when you need to plot multiple sets of data. If you have to plot the sales of VCR's over the last twenty years, for example, a line chart would be your best bet. Line charts, however, are not a good choice for a graph with multiple series. For example, if you have to plot the sales of VCR's, TVs, CD players, and Camcorders over the last two years, you would have better luck using a bar chart. Table 12.2 covers the available line chart templates.

Note Though CorelCHART! doesn't specifically state that it does a 3D line chart, the 3D Connect Series and the 3D Connect Group options in the **G**allery menu provide variations on 3D line charts with a third axis for depth.

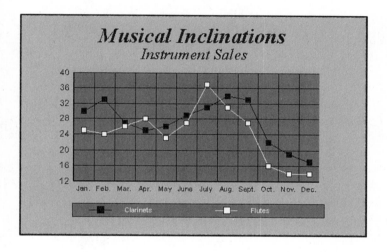

Figure 12.7
Line charts help
the viewer
analyze trends.

Table 12.2
Types of Line Charts

Chart Type	Description
Absolute	A basic line chart. The data points are connected by a line which stresses change between data groups.
Stacked	The lines for each data group are stacked to represent the total value for a data group. Stacked lines communicate the same basic information as traditional lines plus the contribution of the parts to a whole.

continues

Using Corel's Modules

Table 12.2
Types of Line Charts

Chart Type	Description
Bipolar Absolute	Chart has two data axes, each starting at the center of the chart and increasing in value as they move outward, away from the center.
Bipolar Stacked	The lines in each data group are treated cumulatively to represent the total value for a data group, but in a bipolar format.
Dual-Axis Absolute	A second value or Y axis is placed on the chart. Some lines are plotted against a second data axis to compare series that use different units of measure or that exhibit a large disparity in magnitude.
Dual-Axis Stacked	Similar to Dual-Axis Side-by-Side, except lines are stacked on top of each other to represent the total value for a data group.
Percent	The percent chart displays values as a percentage of the total for a specific data group. The total value is represented as 100%, and the values in a given data group are shown as a percentage of the whole.

Area Charts

Area charts are similar to line charts with one addition: the space defined by the line and the horizontal axis is filled in. The filled in area suggests volume or quantity. The area chart in figure 12.8 documents the dramatic fluctuations in electrical bills. Similar to bar charts, area charts can be either horizontal or vertical. You can place greater emphasis on the volume of the data by using 3D area charts. Table 1.3 covers the available area chart templates.

Although CorelCHART! doesn't specifically state that it does 3D area charts, the 3D Connect Series and the 3D Connect Group options in the Gallery menu provide variations on 3D area charts with a third axis for depth.

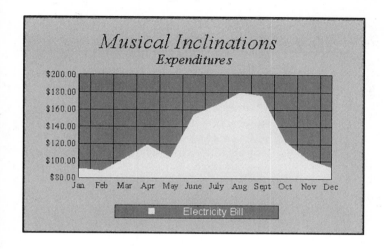

Figure 12.8
Area charts
emphasize
changes over
time.

Table 12.3
Types of Area Charts

Chart Type	Description
Absolute	This is a basic area chart. The data points are connected by a line that stresses change between data groups.
Stacked	The areas for each data group are stacked to represent the total value for a data group. Stacked areas communicate the contribution of the parts to a whole.
Bipolar Absolute	This chart has two data axes, each starting at the center of the chart and increasing in value as they move outward, away from the center.
Bipolar Stacked	The areas in each data group are treated cumulatively to represent the total value for a data group, but in a Bipolar format.

continues

Table 12.3, Continued
Types of Area Charts

Chart Type	Description
Dual-Axis Absolute	A second value or Y axis is placed on the chart. Some areas are plotted against a second data axis to compare series that use different units of measure or that exhibit a large disparity in magnitude.
Dual-Axis Stacked	Similar to Dual-Axis Side-by-Side, except areas are stacked on top of each other to represent the total value for a data group.
Percent	The percent chart displays values as a percentage of the total for a specific data group. The total value is represented as 100%, and the values in a given data group are shown as a percentage of the whole.

Pie Charts

Pie charts are about as simple as charting gets. Pies show proportions in relation to a whole. Pie charts are easily comprehended and are good for highlighting a significant element for comparison. For instance, the pie chart in figure 12.9 quickly informs the viewer that saxophones are the lowest selling instrument. By default, CorelCHART! creates three-dimensional pies. You can change the tilt and thickness of the pie to simulate a greater 3D effect or to have no dimension at all. Three-dimensional pies put more emphasis on the values on the front of the pie by simulating depth and volume. Table 12.4 covers the available pie chart templates.

Table 12.4
Types of Pie Charts

Chart Type	Description
Pie	This is the single pie format.

Chart Type	Description
Ring Pie	Pie is shaped like a ring with a hole in the center. The pie total is generally placed in the center of the ring.
Multiple Pies	Multiple pie charts to plot several data groups. Multiple pies can demonstrate several, related ideas at once.
Multiple Ring Pie	Multiple pie format, but with ring-shaped pies.
Multiple Proportional Pie	Multiple pie charts with all figures sized in relation to the other pies based on numerical volume. This option enables you to emphasize how pie totals (group data) have changed over time.
Multiple Proportional Ring Pies	Multiple proportional pies, but with ring shapes.

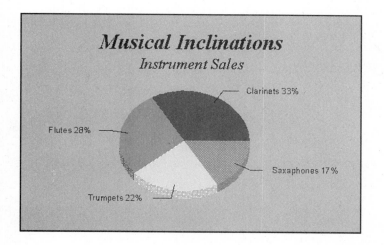

Figure 12.9
Pies show proportions in relation to a whole.

Scatter Charts

Scatter charts have two data axes, allowing you to show the correlation or relationship between the two sets of data. They are particularly useful for showing patterns or trends and for ascertaining how variables might show a relationship to one another. As illustrated in figure 12.10, for example, a scatter chart might be preferable to a line chart to compare income versus hours worked. Scatter charts are frequently accompanied by a regression line. The slope and placement of the line are calculated from the data to identify the trend of the data set. Table 1.5 covers the available scatter chart templates.

Figure 12.10

Scatter charts show the correlations or relationships between the sets of data.

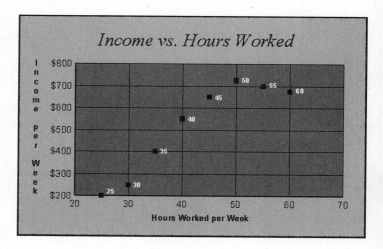

Table 12.5
Types of Scatter Charts

Chart Type	Description
Scatter	This is the fundamental scatter chart.
X-Y Dual Axis	A second value or Y axis is placed on the chart. Some areas are plotted against a second data axis to compare series that use different units of measure or that exhibit a large disparity in magnitude.
X-Y with Labels	Basic scatter chart, except each data point is accompanied by a label.
X-Y Dual Axis with Labels	Dual-axis scatter chart, but with labels for each data point.

Using High/Low/Open/Close Charts

High/low/open/close charts are used to express a range of values for a single item in a particular time period. These charts are most often used to display stock market information. High/Low/Open/Close charts are excellent for showing data that regularly fluctuates in a given time period, such as weather or currency exchange rates (see fig. 12.11). Table 12.6 covers the available high/low/open/close templates.

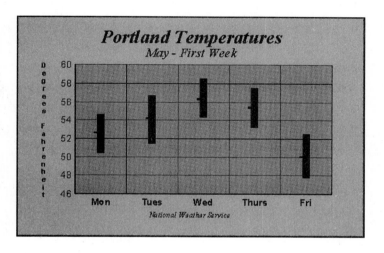

Figure 12.11
High/Low/Open/Close charts express a range of values in a particular time period.

Table 12.6
Types of High/Low/Open/Close Charts

Chart Type	Description
High/Low	Plots the high and the low values for a specific data group.
High/Low Dual-Axis	High/low chart with a two-data axes. Some values are plotted against a second data axis allowing you to compare series that use different units of measure or that exhibit a large disparity in magnitude.

continues

Table 12.6, Continued
Types of High/Low/Open/Close Charts

Chart Type	Description
High/Low/Open	Identical to the high/low chart, but with a third data point added to display the starting value for a specific data group.
High/Low/Open Dual Axes	High/low/open chart, but with two data axes.
High/Low/Open/Close	Identical to the high/low/open chart, but with a fourth data point added to display the closing value for a specific data group.
High/Low/Open/ Close Dual Axes	High/low/open/close chart, but with two data axes.

Spectral Maps

Spectral maps are best used to demonstrate the occurrence of an item with regard to a specific spatial relationship. A common use of a spectral map is to show population density. Spectral maps are unique because they exhibit value based on color intensity rather than numerical quantities (see fig. 12.12). Spectral maps have only one template.

Figure 12.12
Spectral maps demonstrate occurrences of a specific spatial relationship.

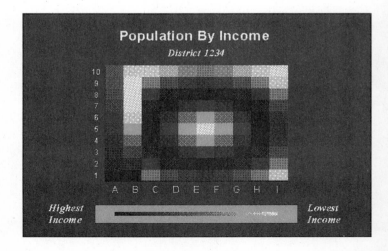

Histograms

Histograms show the frequency of values in a data group. The shape of a histogram exhibits a pattern of measurements in a way that reveals the individual values of each item. A good example of a histogram is a bell curve displaying test scores (see fig. 12.13). The curve plots the number of values that fall in a particular range of scores. Table 12.7 covers the available histogram chart templates.

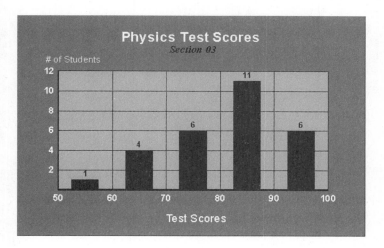

Figure 12.13
Histograms show the frequency of values in a data group.

Table 12.7
Types of Histograms Charts

Chart Type	Description
Vertical Histogram	A histogram where the bars are vertically oriented.
Horizontal Histogram	A histogram where the bars are horizontally oriented.

Table Charts

Table charts show the actual numbers in a ledger form with columns and rows, rather than in a graph. Though tables are visually less exciting, they are useful for communicating text-oriented data. Tables also are used when the disparity between series numbers is great or with particularly detailed data (see fig. 12.14).

Table charts can be tedious when they contain too much numerical data. In cases where you have more than five data groups or data series, consider a graph instead. Table 12.8 covers the available table chart templates.

Figure 12.14
Table charts are
great for text-
oriented data.

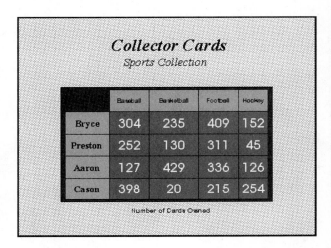

Table 12.8
Types of Table Charts

Chart Type	Description
Rows	This option enables you to alternate color by rows.
Columns	This option enables you to alternate color by columns
None	This option has no color division.

3D Riser Charts

CorelCHART! calls all bars that extend vertically from the category axis risers. As such, *3D riser charts* are really just another name for 3D bar charts. Essentially, all parameters pertaining to bar charts are relevant here. The main difference between 3D riser charts and the typical bar chart is the addition of the third axis that eliminates the need for a legend to identify each series of data. Three-dimensional risers enable you to add an illusion of depth to your charts (see fig. 12.15). Table 12.9 covers the available 3D Riser chart templates.

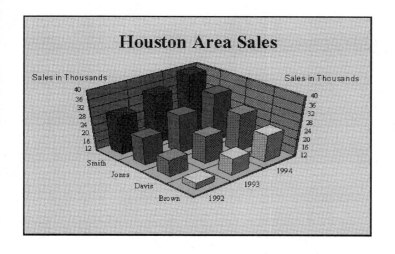

Figure 12.15
3D risers are similar to bar charts, but add an illusion of depth to your charts.

Table 12.9
Types of 3D Riser Charts

Chart Type	Description
3D Riser	This is a basic 3D bar chart. You can choose from four different riser shapes: Bars, Pyramid, Octagons, or Cut-Corner bars—rectangle bars with cut corners.
3D Connect Group	Points in a data group are connected to form floating lines or anchored 3D areas. The floating line types Ribbon and Step are suspended above the chart floor, enabling you to view the area beneath the data points. The Area option is essentially a 3D Area chart.
3D Floating Bars	3D riser chart with data depicted as floating objects, rather than bars that extend upward from the baseline. You can choose from Floating Cubes or the multi-sided Floating Spheres.

continues

Table 12.9, Continued
Types of 3D Riser Charts

Chart Type	Description
3D Connect Series	Points in a data series are connected to form 3D areas. The Area option displays as a 3D area chart. The floating line types, Ribbon and Step, are suspended above the chart floor allowing you to view the area beneath the data points.

3D Scatter Charts

Three-dimensional scatter charts basically are scatter charts with an added axis. As shown in figure 12.16, the third dimension allows you to show the correlation between three variables rather than two, like a traditional Scatter chart. Table 12.10 covers the available 3D scatter chart templates.

Figure 12.16
3D scatter charts show the correlation between three variables.

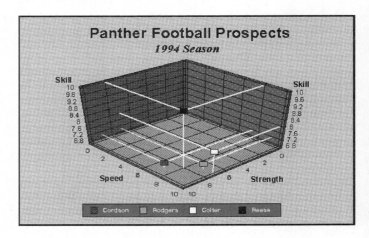

Table 12.10
Types of 3D Scatter Charts

Chart Type	Description
XYZ Scatter	Basic 3D scatter chart with three values per data point.
XYZ Scatter With Labels	3D scatter chart with labels for the data points.

Pictographs

You can use pictographs to replace the bars in bar charts and histograms with graphics images. Theses images might be from CorelDRAW!'s clip art library or any of your own CorelDRAW! files that are saved in CDR format. The bars in a bar chart showing sales per quarter, for example, could be replaced with images stacked upon each other (see fig. 12.17). This effect increases visual interest in your charts, but should be confined to charts with a limited number of data groups. Table 12.11 covers the available pictograph chart templates.

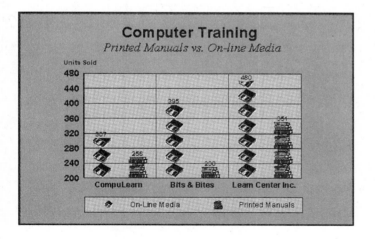

Figure 12.17
Pictographs use graphic images to plot the data values.

Table 12.11
Types of Pictograph Charts

Chart Type	Description
Horizontal Side-by-Side	Horizontal bar chart with the bars displayed as pictographs.
Vertical Side-by-Side	Vertical bar chart with the bars displayed as pictographs. The pictograph bars representing each data point are placed side-by-side along the Category axis.

Bubble Charts

Bubble charts are similar to scatter charts with a third data set added. The first two sets of data are represented on the horizontal and vertical axes, with the third data set represented by the size of the bubble (see fig. 12.18). The size of each bubble, or data marker, references the comparative cost of each of the properties. CorelCHART! includes bubble charts with labels and with dual axis. Table 12.12 covers the available bubble chart templates.

Figure 12.18
Bubble charts are effective for demonstrating three data values.

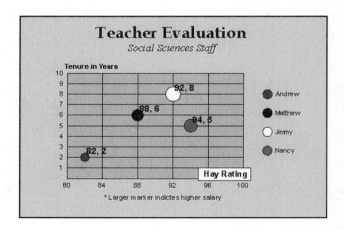

Table 12.12
Types of Bubble Charts

Chart Type	Description
Bubble	Basic bubble chart with three values per data point.
Dual-Axis Bubble	Bubble chart with a second value or Y axis is placed on the chart. Some areas are plotted against a second data axis to compare series that use different units of measure or that exhibit a large disparity in magnitude.
Bubble with Labels	Bubble chart with label identifiers next to each bubble marker.
Dual-Axis Bubble with Labels	Bubble chart with a second value or Y axis placed on the chart and with label identifiers for each bubble marker.

Radar Charts

Radar charts are used to display the variations of a series of data in relation to other data series. You can use radar charts to demonstrate the relationship between each series of data and the correlation between a specific series of data and the whole of the other series. For example, figure 12.19 illustrates how much time is spent on each phase of the production of three print projects. Table 12.13 outlines the available radar chart templates.

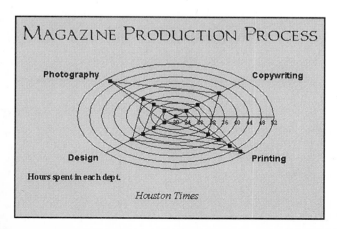

Figure 12.19
Radar charts demonstrate the relationship between series of data and their relation to the whole.

Table 12.13
Types of Radar Charts

Chart Type	Description
Radar	Basic radar chart.
Stacked Radar	The areas for each data group are stacked to represent the total value for a data group.
Dual-Axis Radar	Radar chart where some areas are plotted against a second data axis to compare series that use different units of measure or that exhibit a large disparity in magnitude.

Polar Charts

This chart type uses circular and radial axes to plot chart values (see fig. 12.20). The effect is to illustrate the distance and angle of how each data point sits from other data points and the chart's center. CorelCHART! offers a single and dual axis polar chart.

Figure 12.20
Polar charts use circular and radial axes to plot data.

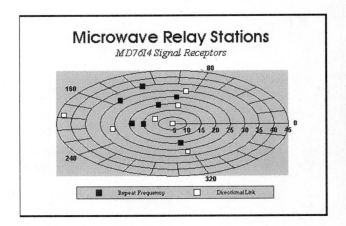

Gantt Charts

Gantt charts diagram a schedule of activities relating to a specific project. Figure 12.21, for example, diagrams two multi-media projects. The projects begin October 4 and are completed November 19. Each step in the production process is represented by a horizontal bar that shows the projected starting date and ending date. Thus, each bar illustrates the time required to perform a specific activity. The cumulative of all activity bars adds up to the total intended time span for the project.

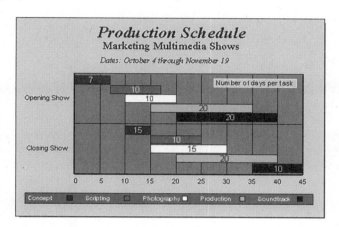

Figure 12.21
Gantt charts diagram project activities.

CorelCHART! provides a wide assortment of chart types giving you tremendous flexibility in creating and designing charts. Most sets of data can be expressed in many different chart formats, but usually one will stand out as being superior to others. The more you know about the various chart types available in CorelCHART!, the easier your job of producing effective, professional charts and graphs will become.

Basic File Mechanics—Opening and Saving Chart Files

CorelCHART! uses many of the same menu commands and dialog boxes as CorelDRAW! for performing basics functions such as opening and saving files. Familiarity with CorelDRAW! is advantageous when it comes to using CorelCHART!. This section covers the steps for opening and saving files, noting any features and options that specifically apply to CorelCHART!. If you're already familiar with the fundamentals of file mechanics, you might want to skip the following discussion.

Starting CorelCHART!

CorelCHART! is a separate program included with CorelDRAW!. It is installed along with Draw in the Windows Program Manager Corel 5.0 group. To start Chart, open the Corel 5.0 Group window and double-click on the CorelCHART! icon. The initial CorelCHART! screen appears with all of the menu selections unavailable except for the File and Help menus. All the operational functions become available when you open or begin a new file. As shown in figure 12.22, the CorelCHART! screen has many of the same tools found on the CorelDRAW! screen.

Figure 12.22
The CorelCHART! screen.

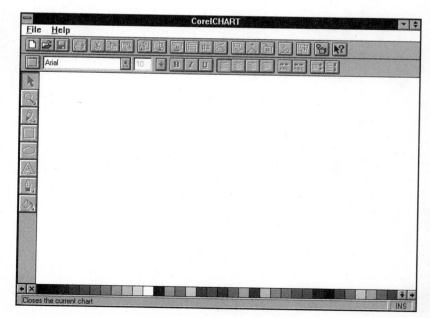

CorelCHART!'s screen includes a Toolbox for annotating charts with graphics shapes and text on the left. The Ribbon Bar under the menu bar provides quick access to several menu commands. For example, the first button creates a new chart file, while the eighth and ninth buttons import and export data. The Text Ribbon Bar located immediately above the chart area includes buttons and list boxes for formatting text objects. The status line at the bottom of the screen displays information about selected commands and tools.

Tip

To determine the function of a button, go over it with your mouse pointer; a description of the button appears in the status line. If you hover the pointer over the button for a few seconds, a little yellow fly-out menu appears, describing the button's function and the related keyboard shortcut.

Opening Chart Files

With CorelCHART!, you can have several files open at one time. This capability makes it easy to share data among charts and check for consistency when necessary. The actual number of files you can keep open at once is limited only by the size of the chart data and your computer's memory.

To open an existing CorelCHART! file, choose File, Open or click on the Open button in the Ribbon Bar. When the Open Chart dialog box appears as shown in figure 12.23, change over to the appropriate drive and directory to locate the CorelCHART! file you want to open. The CorelCHART! files located in the specified directory appear in the File Name box. CorelCHART! files have the file extension CCH. Click once on a file name to display a preview of the chart. Click on the Options button to display the file notes. The files size and date also are displayed. Choose OK or double-click on the file name to open the chart. If you previously opened other files, the last chart you opened is displayed and active in Chart View. As with other Windows applications, use the Window menu to switch to other open chart files.

Figure 12.23
The Open Chart
dialog box.

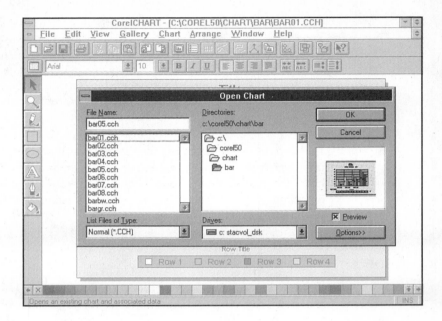

Saving Chart Files

Sometime during the creation of your chart file, you will need to save it. The first time you save a chart, select Save or Save As from the File menu or click on the Save button (the small computer disk) in the Ribbon Bar. The Save Chart dialog box appears (see fig. 12.24). Change to the drive and directory to which you want to save the file and then enter a file name in the File Name box.

To display a description of the chart in the Open Chart dialog box, enter it in the Notes box. You might use a description when you have several bar charts with the same background and basic layout and find it difficult to determine one from the other by looking at the preview. The description helps you identify the exact chart you want to open. You can use as many characters for the description as you need. After specifying the file name, directory, and description, choose OK to save the file. The new file name appears at the top of the screen in the title bar.

Whenever you make changes to a chart, you must save the file again before closing it. Select File, Save or click on the Save button, and the chart is updated with the latest changes. Select File, Save As if you need to change the directory, file name, or description of the chart you are updating.

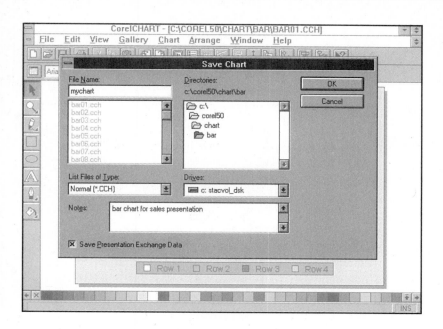

Figure 12.24
The Save Chart
dialog box.

Tip

It's wise to save often when working with any application, but it is particularly important in chart files with big blocks of numbers and text. Get into the habit of using the Save button or the keyboard shortcut Ctrl+S to save.

Adjusting Program Settings and Preferences

CorelCHART! gives you control over settings that affect how the program displays objects on the screen, and how it performs certain operations. You can change these settings at any time.

To adjust the program settings, select File, Preferences. The Preferences dialog box appears (see fig. 12.25). An X in the checkbox beside an option indicates that the feature is turned on. The Show Ribbon Bar option displays the button bar located immediately below the menu bar. The Show Text Ribbon Bar option displays the ribbon located right above the chart area. The Show Status Line displays the status line at the bottom of the screen. The Show Pop-Up Help command instructs CorelCHART! to display the function of a button when you position the mouse on it. The Interruptible Display option enables you to stop a screen redraw by clicking the mouse or pressing a key. This command is invaluable if you work on a slower computer.

Figure 12.25
The Preferences
dialog box.

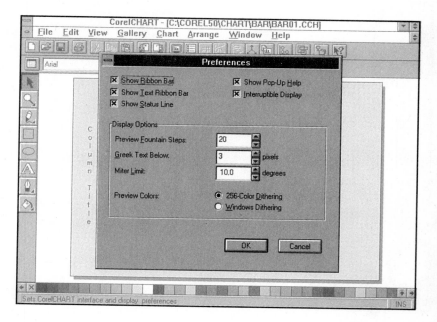

Other options include the Preview Fountain Steps, Greek Text Below, and Miter Limit. Because these commands work just as they do in CorelDRAW!, this section provides only a brief overview of these options.

✔ The Preview Fountain command determines the number of bands used to represent fountain fills on the screen. Selecting a low value (less than 20) speeds up screen redraws, but produces noticeable banding in your printed product.

✔ The Greek Text Below command simplifies the appearance of text below the size specified. Selecting a high value (maximum 500) causes the text to display as small blocks, resulting in faster screen redrawing. This option does not affect the appearance of text when printed.

✔ The Miter Limit command affects the appearance of corner joints. Any corner that is less than the Miter Limit will have a beveled point. Corners above the limit will come to a sharp point.

✔ The Preview Colors command controls how CorelCHART! displays colors on your screen and has no affect on the printed output. Selecting the 256-Color Dithering will result in smoother colors on-screen. However, unless you have a monitor or graphics adapter that can display 256 colors simultaneously, the Windows Dithering option is your only choice.

Chapter Snapshot

As an artist, you may be accustomed to drawing charts
mechanically by using rectangles to create bars and
wedges. CorelCHART! provides a powerful way to
create charts based on raw numerical data. In this
chapter, you learn to do the following:

✔ Create new chart files

✔ Move between the Data Manager and Chart View

✔ Use the Gallery menu to select additional chart
types

✔ Create and save CorelCHART! templates

✔ Enter and edit data in the Data Manager

✔ Calculate data with formulas and functions

✔ Autoscan and manually tag chart data

✔ Import and export chart data

✔ Format and print chart data

CHAPTER

Designing a Chart

Becoming proficient with CorelCHART! is easier if you understand how the program "thinks." Thus, this chapter introduces the two main components of CorelCHART!: the Data Manager and the Chart View. These two modules are used for entering data and designing charts. The chapter begins with the steps for creating charts, such as selecting a chart type and using sample data. There are also in-depth coverage for working with templates to streamline your charting efforts in CorelCHART! and the steps for selecting another chart type from the Gallery menu. The next section examines working with the Data Manager to enter, tag, and format your chart data.

Understanding the Data Manager and Chart View

When you work with CorelCHART!, you can switch back and forth between two windows that enable you to see the chart data in different ways. The *Data Manager* enables you to see the text and numbers entered into columns and rows like a spreadsheet ledger. The *Chart View* enables you to see the chart generated by the data in the Data Manager. The Chart View also is the place where you apply any finishing touches to complete the chart.

Understanding the Data Manager

The Data Manager is where you will begin producing charts. Here, you enter the text and numbers that comprise your chart. You enter data into an electronic ledger, or spreadsheet. This chart data generates the chart displayed in Chart View. For instance, text entered as titles in the Data Manager appears as the chart titles in Chart View. The Data Manager includes many of the powerful features found in spreadsheet applications such as Excel and Lotus.

Exploring the Chart View

After entering data in the Data Manager, switch to the Chart View to see your chart (see fig. 13.1). The Chart View is where you format the various chart elements. You can enlarge the title text, explode a pie slice, or change the color of the grid lines. The Text Ribbon at the top of the screen makes formatting text elements a breeze. The Chart View also contains a Toolbox, similar to the one used in CorelDRAW!. These tools can be used to enhance your charts with graphics shapes and text. Notice the Fill tool, which works the same as it does in CorelDRAW!, giving you access to many wonderful fill patterns and fountain fills.

The specific chart type—bar, line, or area, for example—depends on what you originally selected when you instructed CorelCHART! to create a new chart. However, you can easily change the chart type after creating and designing the chart without affecting the data in any way. For instance, imagine after designing and formatting a bar chart that you determine that a line chart will work better. Simply command CorelCHART! to switch to a line chart and let it do the work of composing the data in the new chart style. The whole idea is flexibility, giving you the power to create effective, informative charts.

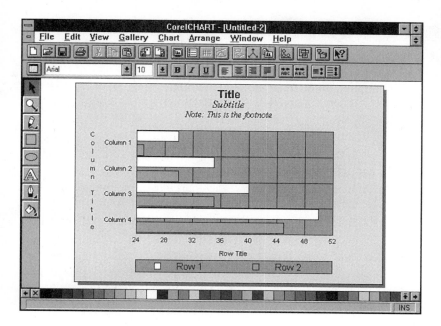

Figure 13.1
The Chart View
screen.

Moving Between Views

You will find yourself moving back and forth between the Data Manager and the Chart View frequently, especially when you first begin creating a chart. While some users might enter all the data at one time, others enter part of the chart data, switch to the Chart View to see how it looks, and then switch back to the Data Manager to enter more data. This way, you can watch as the chart is being built.

To switch from the Data Manager to the Chart View, click on the top button in the Toolbox (the rest of the tools are grayed out in the Data Manager). This button is called the Chart View button and looks like a tiny bar chart. Once in Chart View, the button changes to a tiny spreadsheet; clicking on this button takes you back to Data Manager.

You can see both the Data Manager and the Chart View at the same time by tiling the windows. The tiling options are in CorelCHART!'s **W**indow menu. You can choose to tile the windows vertically or horizontally.

Creating a New Chart

CorelCHART! requires that you select one of 16 main chart types when you create a chart file. If you are unsure what chart type works best with your data, refer to Chapter 12 for examples and discussion of available chart types. Keep in mind that after creating the file, it is possible to switch to another chart type if necessary. For instance, if you initially selected a bar chart and then decide to use a line chart, it's easy to change.

When you select a chart type, you are also selecting a template. Templates establish the chart type and formatting, such as colors and fonts. Actually, templates are just CorelCHART! files from which you "borrow" the chart type, style, and formatting codes for your new chart file. Think of the template as a starting point; after selecting a template, you can embellish and enhance the chart with your own personal design style.

To create a new chart, select **F**ile, **N**ew, or click on the New button in the Text Ribbon Bar. The New dialog box appears with the main chart types displayed in the Gallery list box on the left. Notice the bar is currently selected. On the right is the Chart Types list box where you see a visual display of the bar chart template. When you select a new chart type, the template changes to reflect the newly selected chart type. In figure 13.2, for instance, Area is the selected chart type, and the template shows an area chart. A description of the template and its file location also appear in the bottom of the dialog box.

Figure 13.2
The New
dialog box.

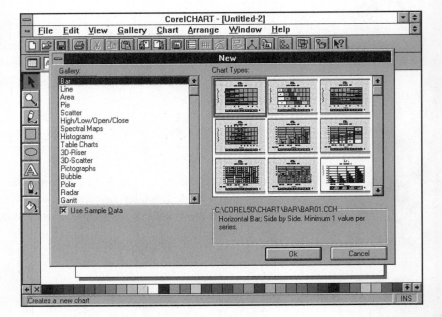

Tip   Press Ctrl+N to access the New dialog box.

Using the Sample Data Feature

Before choosing OK to create your chart, consider the Use Sample Data option under the list of chart types. The sample data option is turned on by default. If it is on when you choose OK, sample numbers and text are placed into the new chart. The sample data appears in the Data Manager and is used to generate the chart that you see in Chart View. As detailed later in this chapter, CorelCHART! requires that chart data be entered in a specific manner so that it can correctly identify all chart elements. Since the sample data is already properly entered, all you need to do is replace the sample data with your own. In addition, because the sample data is arranged in the required order, using the sample data can help teach you how chart data should be arranged in the Data Manager.

Turning off the sample data option gives you the ability to enter data in a blank spreadsheet. As you become more adept at using CorelCHART!, you might find turning off the sample data feature preferable, but take care to match the overall data layout structure used by the sample data. If you don't follow the structure, you could easily get some unexpected results. For instance, CorelCHART! expects titles to be entered in cells A1 and A2. If you enter a title in another cell it might be ignored or appear on the chart as another chart element such as a footnote or an axis title.

After selecting the desired chart type, choose OK to create a new chart. If the sample data option is left on, you are taken to the Chart View, where the sample data composes the chart. If the Sample Data option is turned off, you are taken to the Data Manager, which displays a blank spreadsheet.

The following steps illustrate creating a line chart using sample data:

1. Select File, New, or click on the New button. The New dialog box appears.

2. Select Line from the Gallery list box. The Line chart template appears on the right.

3. Make sure the Use Sample Data option is enabled and click on OK. As displayed in figure 13.3, a line chart created with the sample data appears in Chart View. If the sample data was turned off, the Data Manager appears displaying a blank spreadsheet.

Figure 13.3
A new line chart
with the sample
data option
turned on.

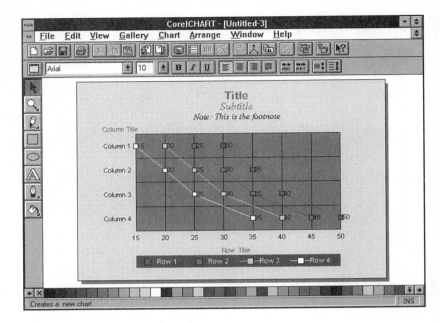

Working with CorelCHART! Templates

As previously discussed, when you select a chart type from the New dialog box, you also are selecting a template. Templates are simply regular CorelCHART! files from which you borrow the chart type and formatting. When you create a new chart file, you are using a copy of the template and any changes you make do not affect the original template. This section discusses how you can speed up your chart creation time by designing your own templates and applying new templates to chart files.

Creating Chart Templates

Although the templates help you get started, in many cases they will not fit your needs exactly. For example, you might need to add a company logo, change colors, or adjust font sizes. It is important to know that any chart you design can be used as a template for future charts. This means that after you design a chart that captures the "look" of your organization, you can use it as a template. Using your custom-designed chart file as a template is a tremendous time-saver. Because you arranged the chart style and formatting in advance, all you have to do when creating a new chart is enter the new data—the formatting will already be complete!

Creating a chart template is simply a matter of saving your chart file in one of the directories where CorelCHART! stores its template files. As mentioned earlier, when you select a chart type in the New dialog box, the template's file name and directory appear in the lower right corner. CorelCHART! stores the templates in the C:\COREL50\CHART directory path. For example, the bar chart templates are stored in C:\COREL50\CHART\BAR, and the area chart template is stored in C:\COREL50\CHART\AREA. When you save your custom chart files in one of these directories, you create a template that will be available for preview and selection when you create a new chart file.

In figure 13.4, for instance, several custom templates have been added to the bar chart category. Select the chart type and the desired template, then click on OK to create a chart file with the customized formatting.

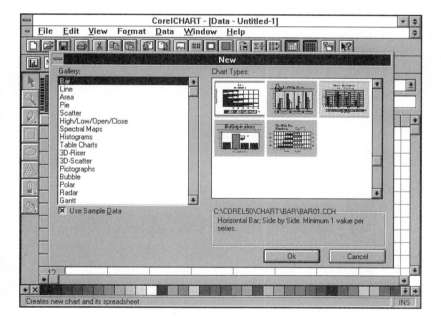

Figure 13.4
You can create your own templates and preview them in the New dialog box.

The path for storing template files is automatically created when you install CorelDRAW! 5.0. However, you do have the option to alter this path during installation.

Actually, a chart file can be used as a template regardless of what directory it is stored in, but you won't be able to preview it in the New dialog box unless you store it in one of the specific directories reserved for templates. The Apply Template command covered in the next section enables you to use any chart file like a template.

Applying Templates to Existing Files

The Apply Template command in the File menu enables you to apply a different template to a chart after it has been created. For instance, imagine you have to create a bar chart documenting each month's sales. After creating a bar chart and entering data for this month's sales, you could use the Apply Template command to apply the formatting from the chart you created last month. The chart type (which in this case already was a bar) and the formatting from the template are applied to the new chart. The Apply Template command, however, applies only the chart type and formatting, not the chart data. Therefore, the new chart looks just like last month's, but reflects this month's data.

The Apply Template command is an alternative to creating templates as discussed in the previous section. The main difference is that the templates you are applying do not have to be stored in the template directories. However, they must be stored in the template directories if you want to preview them in the New dialog box and thus use them as the initial template.

You can use one of your own chart files as a template or a CorelCHART! template file. The following steps illustrate applying the CorelCHART! line chart template to a bar chart:

1. Open the bar chart file. From the File menu, select Apply Template to display the Open dialog box.

2. Change to the drive and directory where the line chart is stored. The CorelCHART! line chart template is stored in C:\COREL50\CHART\LINE.

3. Select the file name of the file you want to use as a template. The Line chart template is called HLINE01.CCH. If the Preview box is checked, a preview and description of the template appear on the left. Choose OK to apply the template.

Using the Gallery Menu To Select Additional Chart Types

The Gallery menu provides access to all of the chart types available in CorelCHART!. You can use the Gallery menu to change a vertical bar chart to a horizontal bar chart, or a line chart to an area chart. The Gallery menu also is where you find the more complicated chart types, such as dual Y-axis, bipolar, and percent. The Gallery menu and the Apply Template command are similar because they both retain the previously entered chart data while changing the chart type. Changing the chart type through the Gallery menu applies a new chart type, but retains all formatting attributes you had previously made to the chart. However, when you apply a template, it changes the chart type and any formatting modifications you might have made such as new colors or fonts, and repositioning of text.

Using the Gallery menu lets you quickly experiment with different ways of presenting your data. After entering data into a line chart, you can use the Gallery menu to display your data in an area chart format. If an area chart isn't quite right either, you can easily take it right back to a line chart, or perhaps try a scatter chart. You can also use this technique to create several different examples of a chart, then let the end user of the chart, the presenter, decide which one best suits his or her needs.

When you select a main chart type from the Gallery menu, a fly-out menu appears listing the available formats for that type. Move to the first choice and press and hold the mouse button to see a preview of the chart format. Drag down to the other chart format choices to preview them. Releasing the mouse on a desired chart format applies it to your chart.

Chart Setup

CorelCHART! enables you to change the paper size and orientation at any time during the creation of your chart file. A chart file created in a 35mm slide format can be quickly changed to letter-sized paper. CorelCHART! examines the chart elements and places them in a similar location on the new page setup. This means you can take a chart designed for a 35mm slide and change its page setup to portrait-oriented, legal-sized paper with only minor adjustments in object placement. The ability to change the paper size and orientation after creating your chart makes it easy to transfer a chart originally used in a slide presentation to 4 × 5 film for publication in an annual report.

Generally, you will want to set up the correct paper size and orientation before you begin entering data and formatting the chart. Initially selecting the final paper size and orientation enables you to place objects exactly where you want them, as they will appear on the output. Remember that if you do change the page setup after composing your chart, you might have to reposition or readjust some chart elements. To control the paper size and orientation for a chart file, select File, Page Setup. The Page Setup dialog box appears as shown in figure 13.5.

III

Using Corel's Modules

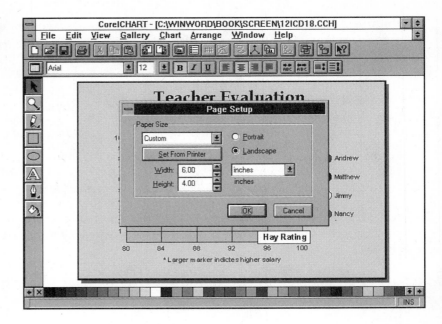

Figure 13.5
The Page Setup
dialog box.

Adjusting the Paper Size and Orientation

Click on the down arrow by Paper Size to reveal the available sizes; these are the same sizes available in CorelDRAW!. Select the desired size. The size of the paper appears in the Width and Height boxes. Because you cannot alter a specific paper size, the Width and Height boxes are grayed out. To set up a custom-sized page, select Custom from the list of Paper Sizes and enter the desired measurements in the Width and Height boxes.

With the exception of the envelope and slide paper sizes, most of the paper size options can be set up in Landscape or Portrait orientation. Click on the desired orientation.

Working in the Data Manager

Understanding how the Data Manager works is an important part of learning and using CorelCHART!. As discussed earlier, CorelCHART! uses the text and numerical data entered in the Data Manager to calculate the size and placement of the bars, slices, or other graphing elements that make up your chart. You can enter the chart data manually, or import it from another application, such as Lotus 1-2-3 or Excel. As you will see, the Data Manager is much more than a place for entering and labeling data. Indeed, the Data Manager can handle many of the functions you might perform in spreadsheet applications like Lotus and Excel.

Examining the Data Manager Screen Tools

When you begin a new chart using the sample data, CorelCHART! starts by displaying the chart in the Chart View. If you choose not to use the sample data when beginning your chart, Chart instead displays a blank spreadsheet in the Data Manager.

This section focuses on working with the Data Manager, so if you are in the Chart View, you should move to the Data Manager by clicking on the Data Manager button—the tiny spreadsheet at the top of the Toolbox. If the Sample Data Option was turned on when you began the new chart, the Data Manager displays the sample data. The Data Manager window, shown in figure 13.6, has many tools to help you enter the data that will generate your chart. At the top of the screen is the Text Ribbon Bar, which provides quick access to commands such as opening, saving, and printing files. The *Text Ribbon* provides buttons for formatting data, such as applying bold and italic. Below the Text Ribbon is the *Tag list*, which contains a list of the tags you'll use to identify the various types of chart data. The *Autoscan* button is used to search through the data and tag it automatically. To the left of the Autoscan button is the *Preview Box*, which displays a small picture of a chart. The *Contents* box displays the contents of the selected cell.

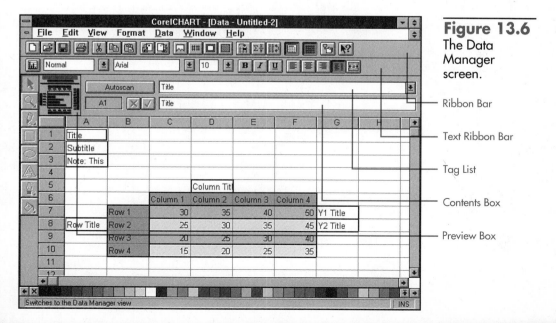

Figure 13.6
The Data Manager screen.

— Ribbon Bar

— Text Ribbon Bar

— Tag List

— Contents Box

— Preview Box

Examining the Data Manager Spreadsheet

A very important part of the Data Manager is the *spreadsheet window*. This is where you enter the text and numbers that will generate your chart. The spreadsheet consists of 240 vertical columns, denoted by column letters along the top, and 16,384 horizontal rows, marked by row numbers on the left. The small box at the intersection of each column and row is a *cell*. Each cell has a cell address that includes the column letter and row number. For instance, the first cell is addressed as A1. Text and numbers are entered into the cells of the spreadsheet.

Selecting Cells

Before you can enter data into a cell, you must first select it. When you initially open the Data Manager, the selected cell will be A1. The selected cell address appears at the top of the screen, and the selected cell is surrounded by a black border. To select another cell with the mouse, use it to position the cursor on the cell and click over it. To select with the keyboard, simply use the arrow keys to move to the cell you want. To select a group or *range* of cells, use the mouse to drag from the first cell to the last cell in the range. For example, as shown in figure 13.7, the cells from B2 to F10 are selected. The selected range in this case would be expressed as B2:F10. The colon between the cell references is interpreted as meaning *through*, as in cells B2 *through* F10. You can also select a range of cells with the keyboard. Click in the first cell and hold the Shift key as you use the arrow keys to move to other cells. All of the cells between are selected.

Figure 13.7
Selecting a range of cells in the Data Manager.

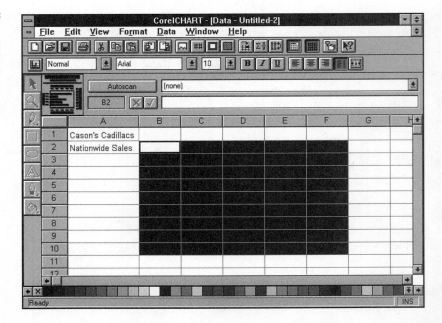

Tip

Click on the column letter to select an entire column of cells and on the row number to select an entire row of cells.

If there is data in the selected cell, the cell contents appear in the Contents box at the top of the screen. The sample data has also been tagged for placement in the chart. The tag name of the selected cell appears in the Tag list. For instance, in figure 13.8, A1 is the selected cell, the Contents box displays the title text, "Boomers Focus on Quality, not Quantity," and the Tag list displays "Title."

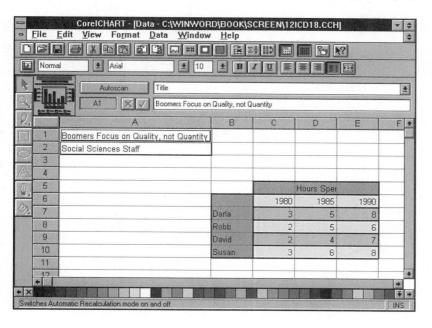

Figure 13.8
When a cell is selected, you can view the cell contents and tag name.

Moving in the Spreadsheet

You can move through the spreadsheet using the scroll bars. However, there are keyboard shortcuts for moving through the spreadsheet (see table 13.1).

Using Corel's Modules

Table 13.1
Keyboard Shortcuts for Moving
Through the Spreadsheet

Key	Spreadsheet Movement
arrow keys	Move one cell in the selected direction
Ctrl+Home	Move to cell A1
Ctrl+End	Move to the end of your data
PgDn	Move down one screen
PgUp	Move up one screen
Ctrl+PgDn	Move to the right one screen
Ctrl+PgUp	Move to the left one screen

Tip You can use the Go To button in the text ribbon to quickly move to a specific cell. Simply click on the Go To button, enter a cell address in the GoTo dialog box, and click on OK.

Entering Data in the Data Manager

To enter data in the spreadsheet, select the cell where you want the data to appear. Once the appropriate cell is selected, start typing. Your typed data appears in both the cell and the Contents box directly above the spreadsheet. When you have finished typing, press the Enter key to accept the data in the cell. Alternatively, you can use the arrow keys to accept the data by moving to another cell. If you decide not to accept the data after typing it, press the Escape key to cancel the entry.

Tip You can use the Enter Data button (the check mark) in place of the Enter key when entering data. Likewise, the Cancel Entry button (the X) can be used in place of the Escape key to clear data.

If you enter a long text string into a cell, the text may appear to be "cut off" in the cell. In such cases, the cell is not wide enough to display the text. This has no effect on how the data appears on your chart in Chart View. Widening columns is discussed later in this chapter.

Replacing Data

When you type data in a cell that already contains data, the old data is replaced by the new. Replacing data is the basic principle behind using sample data. Essentially, you are replacing the sample data with your own. Figure 13.9 shows the sample data CorelCHART! places when you create a new bar chart. The sample data is already tagged for placement in the chart. Therefore, all you need to do is select the cell containing the data you want to replace and type in the new data. For instance, when using sample data, cell A1 is tagged as the chart title, and A2 as the subtitle. You can replace the sample titles with your titles by typing on top of them.

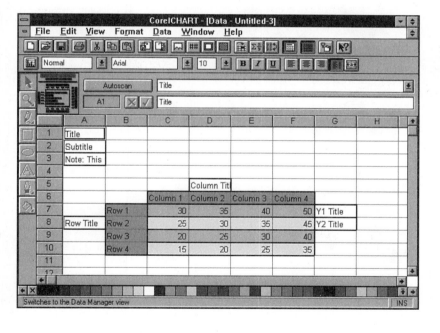

Figure 13.9

The Sample Data placed in the Data Manager screen.

Speeding Up Data Entry

The numbers used to generate your chart must be placed in a contiguous range of cells without any blank columns or rows. For instance, in figure 13.10, the numbers and headings appear in cells B6 through F9. The following steps can speed up your data entry time:

1. Select the range of cells in which you want to enter the data. The top left cell within the selected range is white. This is the active cell.

2. Type in the data for the active cell and press Enter. The active cell moves down to the next cell in the selected range. Type in the next set of data and press Enter again.

3. When you get to the bottom of a column within the selected range, pressing Enter takes you to the top of the next column. This shortcut prevents you from having to use the arrow keys to return to the top of each column.

Figure 13.10
Chart text and values are often placed in a contiguous range of cells in the Data Manager.

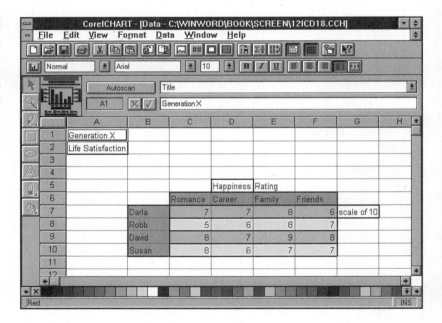

Editing Data

In many cases, the best way to edit cell contents is to retype the data in the cell and press Enter. For instance, if a cell currently shows a value of 100, and you want to change it to 525, just type in the new data over the old and press Enter to accept the new data. There may be times, however, when you want to keep what is already in the cell and amend it. For instance, if the chart title cell contains the name "ABC Company," and you need it to say "ABC Company Incorporated," rather than retyping the entire headline, select the cell you want to edit and click in the cell data in the Contents box. When an insertion point appears in the data, edit the data as necessary. When you are finished editing, press Enter and the updated data appears in the cell.

> You can also edit the cell contents by pressing the F2 key. This method enables you to edit the contents in the formula bar, or in the cell itself. After pressing F2, click in the cell or formula bar to place the insertion point and begin editing.

Calculating Data with Formulas and Functions

CorelCHART! provides tools to help you write formulas and functions for calculating chart data. For instance, you may need to determine an average of your company's entertainment expenses for the past five years or project the number of cars that will be sold in the coming year. If you have experience with spreadsheet applications such as Lotus 1-2-3 or Excel, you will find the formulas and functions in CorelCHART! quite familiar. If you are new to spreadsheet formulas and functions, the Formula Editor dialog box contains a calculator with which you can perform quick calculations. The next section discusses writing formulas and functions, including some pointers for novice spreadsheet users.

Entering Formulas

On the spreadsheet, formulas begin with an equal sign and are written using cell addresses instead of the actual number values. For instance, in figure 13.11, the formula =C7+C8 was entered into cell C9 to sum up the contents of cell C7 and C8. The formula appears in the Contents box, while the summed value appears in the cell. The formula adds up the contents of the specified cells. If the contents of either cell change, the formula recalculates to display the new value. For instance, if the number in cell C7 was changed to 100, the summed value in cell C9 would automatically recalculate to display 200.

When writing formulas to perform calculations, you employ basic math functions such as addition, subtraction, multiplication, and division. CorelCHART! requires that you place an *operator* between each of the cell addresses in your formula. The operators you use are, + for addition, – for subtraction, * for multiplication, and / for division. For example, the formula =C7+C8–C9 instructs CorelCHART! to add the contents of cells C7 and C8, then subtract the contents of C9. Keep in mind when you are writing formulas, that the operations will be performed in a specific sequence. The * and / operators take precedence over the + and – operators. That makes a big difference in the formula, =D7+D8/E8, where the division takes place before the addition. You can override this by inserting parentheses around the part of the formula you want to calculate first. For instance, =(D7+D8)/E8 instructs CorelCHART! to perform the addition first, and then the division.

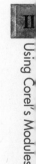

II

Using Corel's Modules

Figure 13.11
A formula using
cell addresses.

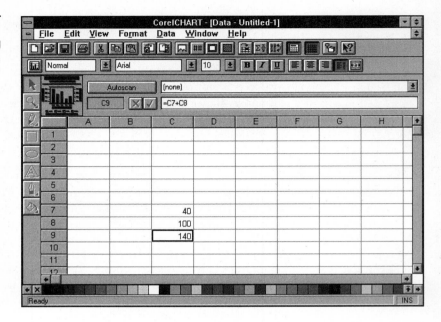

Figure 13.11
A formula using
cell addresses.

Formulas can be entered directly into the cell. After selecting a cell, type in the formula and press Enter. The formula is displayed in the Contents box, and the calculated value is displayed in the cell. The following steps illustrate how you might write a formula calculating the commission rate earned by each sales representative. In figure 13.12 the sales figures for two months are entered in cells C5 through D8, and the commission rate appears in D2.

1. Select the cell where you want the first commission rate to appear. Select E5 to start with the first salesperson, Tom.

2. Type =(C5+D5)*D2 to instruct CorelCHART! to add the two months' sales figures first, and then multiply that total by the commission rate in cell D2. Press Enter to compute the formula.

3. Move down to the next cell and repeat the above steps for the remaining sales representatives. Make sure you are using the correct cell references when entering the formulas.

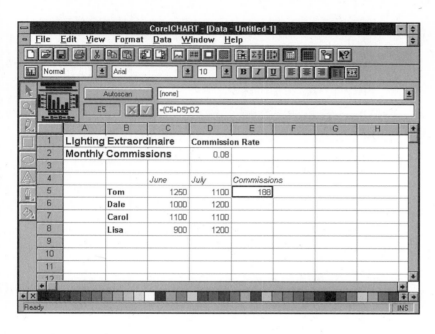

Figure 13.12
Entering formulas
to calculate sales
commissions.

Formulas can also be created in the Enter Formula dialog box and then placed in the spreadsheet. The Enter Formula dialog box works much like a standard calculator. As shown in figure 13.13, this dialog box contains a numeric keypad and buttons to calculate formulas. You can either click with the mouse on the desired numbers or operator buttons, or type the formula into the text box provided. Also contained within the dialog box are buttons to Cut, Copy, and Paste formulas from one cell into another cell or group of cells. The following steps use the Enter Formula dialog box to calculate the commission rate for each sales representative in figure 13.12.

1. Select the cell where you want the first commission rate to appear. Select E5 to start with the first salesperson, Tom.

2. From the **D**ata menu, choose Enter For**m**ula or click on the Enter Formula button in the Text Ribbon Bar. The Enter Formula dialog box appears. All formulas are entered in the Editor box.

3. Enter the formula (C5+D5)*D2 and click on the Enter button to place the formula into the cell. The result is displayed in cell E5. Notice that the formula is displayed in the Contents box.

4. Repeat the above steps for the remaining sales representatives. Make sure you are using the correct cell references when entering the formulas. If the Enter Formula dialog box blocks your view of the cells

you want to calculate, drag on the title bar of the Enter Formula dialog box to move it aside.

Figure 13.13
The Enter Formula
dialog box.

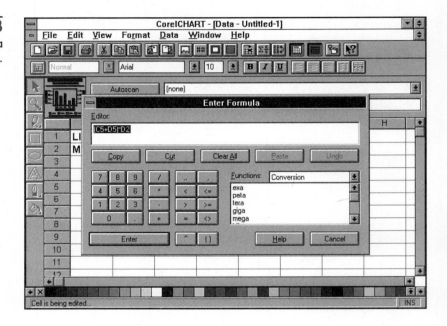

Entering Functions

The Enter Formula dialog box gives you access to prebuilt worksheet functions to perform mathematical calculations. Think of functions as shorthand formulas. For example, to add up eight cells of data, you *could* enter the rather lengthy formula, =B4+B5+B6+B7+B8+B9+B10+B11, or the shorter sum function, =SUM(B4:B11). The SUM function tells the Data Manager to total up the number values specified in the parentheses.

CorelCHART! includes over 300 functions to help you perform all sorts of number crunching. You can do everything from summing and averaging monthly sales, to finding the future and present values of annuities, to determining the monthly payment on your car loan. CorelCHART! includes functions for the following types of data manipulation:

- ✔ Conversion Functions
- ✔ Date and Time Functions
- ✔ DDE/External Functions

✔ Engineering Functions

✔ Financial Functions

✔ Information Functions

✔ Logical Functions

✔ Lookup and Reference Functions

✔ Math and Trig Functions

✔ Statistical Functions

✔ Text Functions

CorelCHART!'s functions work exactly like those found in the popular spreadsheet applications. For more information on using individual functions, refer to CorelCHART!'s online help topic, "Spreadsheet Functions."

All functions are utilized in the same basic way. First you select the function, then you enter the cell addresses of the numbers you want calculated. As an example, this section discusses using two frequently used functions, SUM and AVG (for averages). In figure 13.14, the goal is to total all company sales figures, then determine the average sales for all sales representatives. This can be accomplished quickly by using functions. The following steps illustrate the process for placing a sum function in cell D9 and an average function in D10.

1. Select cell D9 to create the formula to total the sales. From the **D**ata menu, select Enter Formula, or click on the Enter Formula button in the Text Ribbon Bar to display the Enter Formula dialog box.

2. Choose the type of function you need by clicking on the down arrow by Functions. The SUM is in the Math & Trig category. Scroll through the **F**unctions list to locate SUM(list). Double-click on the function to place it in the Editor box.

3. An insertion point is blinking between the parentheses in the function. Enter D3:D8 as the cells to be summed. Click on the Enter button to display the result in the spreadsheet. The formula appears in the Contents box.

4. Select cell D10 and press the F12 key—a shortcut for the Enter Formula command. Choose the Statistical function category and double-click on the AVG (list) function to place it in the Editor box.

I

Using Corel's Modules

5. Enter D3:D8 and click on the Enter button to place the sales average into the spreadsheet.

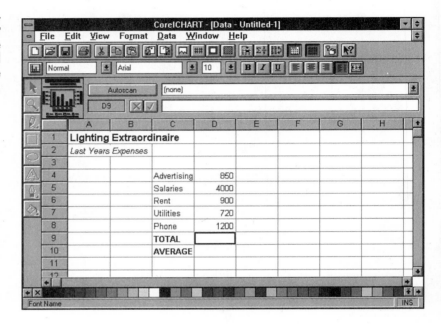

Recalculating Formulas and Functions

As mentioned earlier, formulas and functions are written using cell references so, if the number values change, the formula or function is automatically recalculated for the new data. The automatic recalculation feature can be turned on and off with the **A**uto Recalculate command in the **D**ata menu, or by clicking on the Auto Recalculate button in the Ribbon Bar. If automatic recalculation has been disabled, formulas and functions do not automatically recalculate until you select **R**ecalculate Now from the **D**ata menu.

Importing and Exporting Chart Data

The ability to transfer data between CorelCHART! and other applications can be a big time-saver. For instance, if the chart data has already been entered in another spreadsheet application such as Excel or Word for Windows, you can import the data into the Data Manager. Or, after entering the departmental sales figures in the Data Manager, you could be asked to place the figures in a Word for Windows table. CorelCHART! can export the data in a format Word for Windows can accept.

 If your chart data is entered in a Windows application, such as Word for Windows, you can also transfer it into the Data Manager by copying and pasting the data through the Windows Clipboard. For more information regarding transferring data from one Windows application to another, refer to your application reference manual. You will also find more about the copy and paste process in later sections of this chapter.

Importing Data

Imported data fills the cells of the spreadsheet in the Data Manager. Importing clears *all* existing data in the spreadsheet and replaces it with the new data. If the existing data is important, save it before importing any new data. It is important to consider this before importing, because the Undo command is not available to revoke the importing step. Table 13.2 lists the file types that can be imported into the Data Manager.

Table 13.2
File Formats That Can Be Imported into the Data Manager

Format	File Extension	Notes
Corel Sheet	CDS	The chart data in the Data Manager can be exported to this format.
Corel Sheet 4.0	TBL	Same as above, except for version 4.
Import from Text	TXT	Many applications, such as Word for Windows and WordPerfect, can export to this format.
Import from CSV	CSV	Many database programs, such as dBASE and Paradox, can export to this format.

continues

Using Corel's Modules

Table 13.2, Continued
File Formats That Can Be Imported into the Data Manager

Format	File Extension	Notes
Import from RTF	RTF	Many Windows applications, such as Ami Pro and Lotus for Windows, can export to this format.
Excel 3 & 4	XLS	Excel 3.0 and 4.0 spreadsheet files. (You can save version 5.0 files in the 4.0 format.)

After importing, you might need to rearrange the data to meet the requirements of the Data Manager for tagging and Autoscan. The data arrangement needed for CorelCHART! to correctly tag or *place* the data is covered later in this chapter. To import a data file into the Data Manager, follow these steps:

1. Select **F**ile, **I**mport or click on the Import button in the Text Ribbon Bar. The Import Data dialog box shown in figure 13.15 appears.

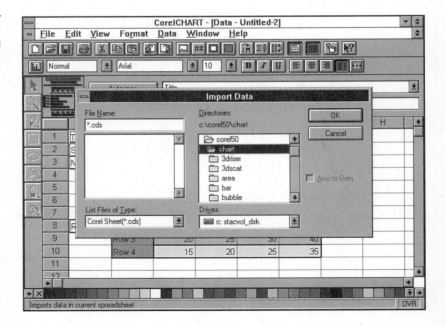

Figure 13.15
The Import Data dialog box.

2. Click on the down arrow by List Files of Type and select the file format to be imported, such as Excel 3 & 4.

3. Change to the drive and directory where the file to be imported is located. Double-click the desired file name to import the data. The data is imported into the Data Manager spreadsheet.

Exporting Data

Exporting saves the chart data in a format other applications can read. Table 13.3 lists the available formats for exporting the data in the Data Manager.

Table 13.3
Available Export File Formats

Format	File Extension	Applications That Accept Format
Corel Sheet	CDS	This data can be imported into another CorelCHART! file
Export to Text	TXT	Most word processing and spreadsheet applications can import text files
Export to CSV	CSV	Many spreadsheet and database applications can import the "Comma Separated Value" format
Export to RTF	RTF	Most Windows applications can import the "Rich Text Format "
Excel 3.0	XLS	Excel 3.0
Excel 4.0	XLS	Excel 4.0

To export a data file, follow these steps:

1. Select File, Export or click on the Export button on the Ribbon Bar. The Export Data dialog box shown in figure 13.16 appears.

Figure 13.16
The Export Data
dialog box.

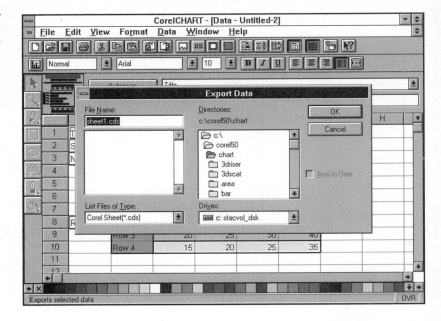

2. Click on the down arrow by List Files of **T**ype and select the file format to be exported, such as Excel 4.0.

3. Change to the drive and directory where you want to save the exported file. Enter a file name and click on OK. The file is saved in the new export format.

Tagging Data in the Data Manager

After entering the chart text and numbers, you are almost ready to switch to Chart View. Remember, Chart View is where you see the chart data transformed into a chart. But before switching to Chart View, you must tag the chart data. *Tagging* lets CorelCHART! know which cells contain the elements used to compose the chart in Chart View. For example, tagging tells CorelCHART! which cells contain the subtitle and data sets so that they can be placed correctly on the chart. You must tag every cell of data that you want to appear on the chart; however, not all data in the spreadsheet must be tagged. For instance, if you have included a note or comment on the spreadsheet, this data does not need to be tagged.

There are basically two ways to tag chart data, Autoscanning and manual tagging. The Autoscan method quickly scans your chart data and tags it automatically. With the manual method, you select the cell(s) for each individual chart element, and then apply a chart tag. This section will cover how to tag chart data with both the Autoscan and manual methods.

Identifying CorelCHART! Tag Names

Tagging requires that you assign *tag names* to the cells containing the data needed to compose the chart. Most of the tag names are relatively straightforward. For example, the Title tag is for the title data, and Subtitle tag for subtitles. Some tags, however, may require some clarification. Table 13.4 identifies the tag name for each chart element. Figure 13.17 shows how each tagged element is displayed on the chart.

Table 13.4
Tag Names and Corresponding Chart Elements

Tag Name	Chart Element
Title	Chart Title
Subtitle	Chart Subtitle
Footnote	Chart Footnote
Column Title	Category Axis Title
Column Headers	Category Axis Labels
Row Title	Series/Legend Title
Row Headers	Series Labels
Y1 Title	Data Axis Title
Y2 Title	Second Data Axis Title
Data Range	Number Values

Figure 13.17
Identifying chart
elements.

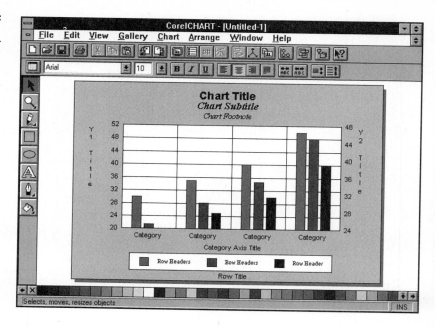

Examining the Effect of Sample Data on the Tagging Process

The sample data feature available when you first create a chart can make the entire tagging process easier. As discussed earlier in this chapter, the New dialog box includes an option for placing sample data in the chart. If the sample data feature is turned on when the chart is created, sample data is placed in the Data Manager which then generates the chart displayed in Chart View. If the sample data feature is turned off when you are creating a new chart, a blank spreadsheet appears ready for you to enter the chart data. If you switch to Chart View without entering and tagging data, a large, red null sign appears because there is no data to generate a chart. This section examines how sample data affects the tagging process.

Using Sample Data

Using the sample data option simplifies the chart creation process because the sample data is already tagged for placement in the chart. To see the tags, select the cell(s) and refer to the Tag List at the top of the screen. For instance, in figure 13.18, cells C6 through F6 are selected, and the Tag List identifies these cells as "Column Headers." Notice also that the Preview box signals how the cell has been tagged by highlighting that element in the chart picture.

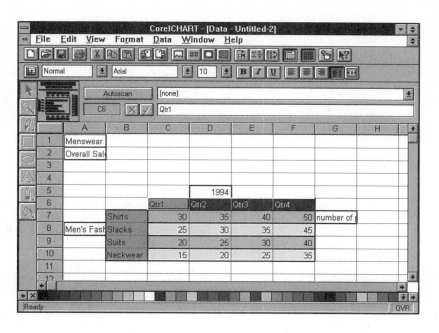

Figure 13.18
The Tag List displays the selected tag name.

The sample data for most chart types will look the same. Some chart types, such as spectral maps and tables, use slightly different sample data. The data itself is not particularly important; however, the way data is arranged and tagged is very important. Sample data is arranged in the order and orientation necessary for Autoscan to tag chart elements (Autoscanning is discussed in the next section). When Autoscan searches through the spreadsheet, it looks for a specific arrangement of the chart data. If the data is arranged according to the Autoscan requirements, your data is tagged correctly. If the data is not arranged according to the Autoscan requirements, your data may be missing or tagged incorrectly. For instance, the title text might appear as the footnote. Using sample data ensures that you are arranging the chart data in the manner specified by Autoscan. The sample data in figure 13.19 was replaced with chart data to illustrate the arrangement required by Autoscan.

Because the sample data is already tagged, when you replace it with your own data, your data will be automatically tagged. Then, when you switch to Chart View, your data composes the chart. It all works very smoothly until you need to add more categories of data than the sample data provides or to delete the categories you don't need. Whenever you deviate from the sample data, you will need to perform some re-tagging. Tagging with Autoscan and manual tagging are discussed in the next section.

Figure 13.19
Chart data using
Autoscan data
arrangement.

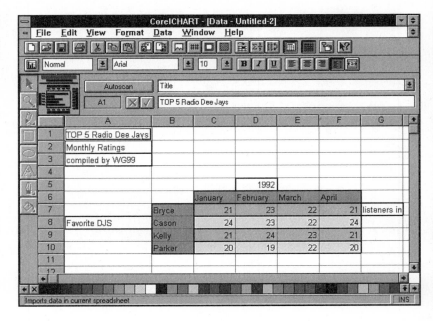

Creating a new chart without the sample data enables you to enter chart data into a blank spreadsheet. You can enter chart data to match the arrangement needed to Autoscan, or you can enter the data in whatever cells you choose and use the manual tagging method to identify the chart elements. However, even with manual tagging, you must still follow a few rules regarding where certain chart elements must be placed. For instance, all chart data must be entered with row headers (series labels) to the left of the number values and the column headers (category labels) above the data range. In general, it is recommended that you use the sample data to avoid any confusion about data arrangement and tagging.

Using Autoscan

Autoscanning searches through the data in the spreadsheet and tags it for placement in the chart. Whether you replaced the sample data or entered data into a blank spreadsheet, you can use Autoscan to quickly tag the data. In fact, it's a good idea to click on the Autoscan button whenever you are ready to switch to Chart View. This way, any changes to the data are automatically recognized. However, as previously discussed, the Autoscan feature only works if your data is arranged in a specific order. Figure 13.20 depicts a typical Autoscan data arrangement for most chart types. Matching your chart data to this layout lets you take advantage of the speed of Autoscan.

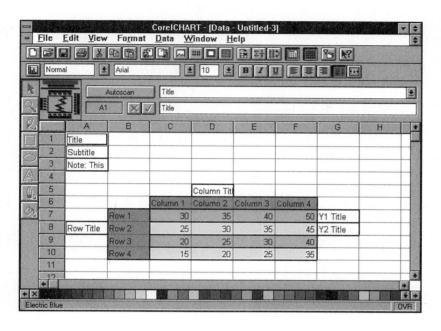

Figure 13.20
Autoscan chart
data arrange-
ment.

Autoscan searches the spreadsheet for a large block of cells comprised of numbers. It assumes that the top row of cells in that block are the column headers, and the left most column in the block are row headers. The rest of the block is scanned as the data range. You will encounter problems if you leave blank columns or rows in the data range. For example, the data in figure 13.21 would not compose an accurate chart because of the empty column. In addition, Autoscan requires that you have a column header for every column of numbers and a row header for every row of numbers. Again, problems would occur with this data because the last column of numbers has no header. The Row title must be to the left of the Row Headers, and the Column Title must be to the left of the Column Headers. The chart title, subtitle, and footnote should be placed in A1, A2, and A3 so that Autoscan can tag them correctly.

If you enter data into a blank spreadsheet or import it from another program, it might not match the arrangement required by Autoscan. In such cases, you can cut and paste the data to the proper location. In this way, the data matches the required arrangement so that you can take advantage of Autoscan.

To use Autoscan, select a single cell anywhere in the spreadsheet and click on the Autoscan button. If you select more than one cell, Autoscan will not scan properly. CorelCHART! scans through the data and tags it accordingly. After Autoscanning, the Data Range and Column and Row Headers are highlighted. To preview the tag names, click on a cell and refer to the Tag List at the top of the screen. After

Autoscanning, if your data is tagged incorrectly, it is probably arranged in the wrong order. To remedy this problem, try arranging it in the order specified in figure 13.20, and then click on the Autoscan button again. Once your data is properly tagged, switch to Chart View to preview your new chart.

Figure 13.21
Autoscan will not work if empty columns are placed between the chart data.

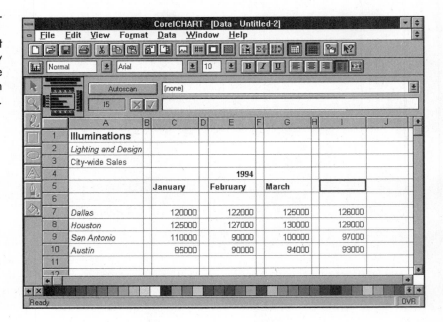

Manual Tagging

Though Autoscanning requires that your data be arranged in a specific order, you can vary from this order as long as you manually tag the data to identify each chart element. Figures 13.22 and 13.23 illustrate two ways you might enter data for manual tagging. As illustrated in both figures, manual tagging has a few requirements regarding how the data should be arranged. Manual tagging requires that column headers are placed above the data range, and row headers are placed to the left of the data range.

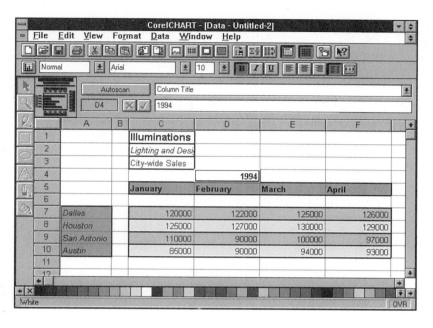

Figure 13.22
Arrangement of data for manual tagging.

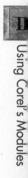

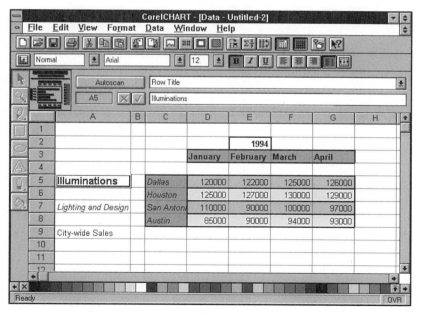

Figure 13.23
Another data arrangement for manual tagging.

Using Corel's Modules

To tag chart data manually, select the cell(s) that contain the data and then apply a tag from the Tag list. Though manual tagging is an easy process, you must tag every chart element. To help you select the appropriate tag, refer back to the previous section, "Identifying CorelCHART! Tag Names." The following steps illustrate how to tag the data range in figure 13.23.

1. Select the cell(s) containing the data you want to tag. For instance, select D5 to G8 to tag the data range in figure 13.23.

2. Click on the down arrow by the Tag List to reveal a listing of the tag names. You will have to scroll to see all the names.

3. Click on the desired tag name. Tag the cells D5 through G8 as the Data Range. The selected cell(s) are tagged; the Tag List displays the selected tag name.

Repeat this procedure until all chart elements have been tagged. When you finish tagging each element, switch to the Chart View to see if your data was placed correctly. If the chart elements do not appear correctly in the chart, you might have to return to the Data Manager to re-tag the data.

Rearranging and Manipulating Data

As you enter text and numbers to build a chart, you might need to rearrange and manipulate the data. For instance, you might need to delete data, move it to another row, or insert a column for new data. Rearranging data becomes especially important in the tagging process. As discussed in the previous section, tagging requires that the chart data be entered in a specific order. For instance, CorelCHART! expects you to place the category axis titles above the number values. To meet the arrangement of data required for tagging, you may occasionally have to rearrange your data so that it will be tagged appropriately. This section discusses deleting, moving, copying, pasting, and filling chart data in the Data Manager.

Many of the commands for rearranging data covered in the next sections are also available from CorelCHART!'s cell menu. To use the cell menu, position the mouse pointer in the cell(s) you want to edit and click the right mouse button. The cell menu pops up with choices for clearing, cutting, copying, and pasting data. Though these are the same commands found in the **E**dit and Fo**r**mat menus, the cell menu is designed to put these frequently used commands right at your fingertips.

Deleting Data and Formatting

The Clear command is used to delete or clear the contents of a cell or group of cells. Use this command when you want to eliminate any data from the spreadsheet. For instance, when you create a bar chart, CorelCHART! places four sets of sample series data. If your chart only requires three sets, just delete the fourth set of data. The Clear command also lets you delete cell formatting. This is useful when you want to keep the data, but delete the bold and italic formatting.

To clear all data or formatting, select the cell or cells containing the data you want to delete and select Edit, Clear, or press the Delete key. (You can also use the cell menu.) The Cut and Clear Options dialog box appears as shown in figure 13.24. The Xs by each item indicate what types of data and formatting will be deleted. By default, each of the options is marked to be deleted. You can customize what is deleted by clicking on the data type or features you do not want deleted. For instance, to delete all data except formulas, uncheck the Formulas option. To delete all formatting information except for the font, uncheck the Font option. After selecting the data and formatting you want deleted, click on OK to delete the specified data or formatting.

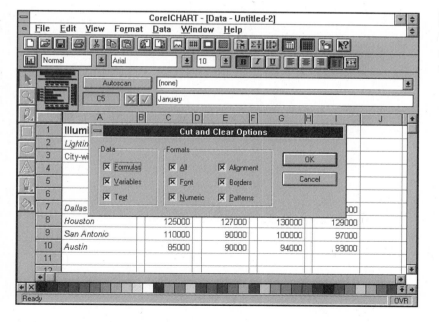

Figure 13.24
The Cut and Clear Options dialog box.

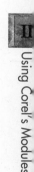

II

Using Corel's Modules

Cutting, Copying, and Pasting Data in the Data Manager

You can use the Cut and Paste commands to move data from one cell to another. The Cut command differs from the Clear command in that you can paste cut data elsewhere on the spreadsheet. Cleared data cannot be pasted elsewhere in the spreadsheet. The Copy and Paste commands enable you to copy data between cells.

Using Cut and Paste

The Cut command removes the selected cell data and sends the data to the Windows Clipboard. The Paste command is then used to place the data from the Windows Clipboard back into the spreadsheet at a new location. Use the following steps to cut and paste data in the Data Manager.

1. Select the cell(s) containing the data you want to move, and select Edit, Cut or click on the Cut button in the Ribbon Bar. (You can also use the cell menu.)

2. The Cut and Clear Options dialog box appears. This is the same dialog box used with the Clear command. In the dialog box, select the desired data and formatting options you want cut and click on OK. The data is removed from the spreadsheet.

3. Select the cell where you want to place the data and select Edit, Paste, or click on the Paste button in the Ribbon Bar. (You can also use the cell menu.) You only need to select the top left cell of the range you want the data pasted in—even if you are pasting multiple cells of data. The pasted data will use the selected cell as a starting point and then fill down and to the right with the rest of the data.

Using Copy and Paste

The Copy and Paste commands enable you to copy the contents of a cell to another. To copy and paste data, follow the same steps for cutting and pasting, except use the Copy command instead of Cut. Keep in mind that copying and pasting is a great way to copy data from one chart spreadsheet to another because it saves you the time of having to re-enter data such as titles, category axes, or headings.

Copying and Pasting Formulas and Functions

Building multiple formulas on a spreadsheet can be time-consuming. Imagine if you had to total the monthly sales of a hundred products. This would amount to one hundred formulas! Instead of writing all those formulas and functions individually, you can save a lot of time by copying and pasting them to other cells. Each time you copy and paste a formula, the pasted formula is essentially re-written for the new cell location. For instance, in figure 13.25, the formula in cell C8 reads =C4+C5+C6. When this formula is copied and pasted in cell D8, it is automatically adjusted to read as =D4+D5+D6. The change in the pasted formula occurs because of a process known as *relative cell referencing*.

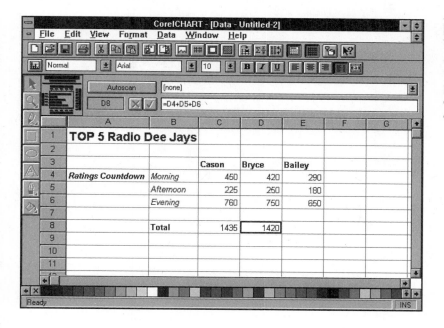

Figure 13.25
When you copy and paste a formula, the pasted formula adjusts for its new cell location.

Filling Data

The Fill commands provide you with another, often quicker way to copy data between cells. With the Fill commands, you can "fill" adjacent cells with data and formulas. You simply select a range of cells that includes the data you want to fill, and the cells you want the data to fill into. The Fill Down command lets you fill data from the top of the selected area down into the cells below. For instance, in figure 13.26 you could select cells G4 through G7 and fill the formula in G4 down into the other cells. Remember, the formulas adjust to calculate for the data relative to the new cell location. The Fill Right command lets you fill data from the left of the selected area to the right. In figure 13.26, you could select C8 through F8 and fill the formula in C8 to the other cells.

Figure 13.26
The Fill command
makes it easy to
copy data or
formulas to other
cells.

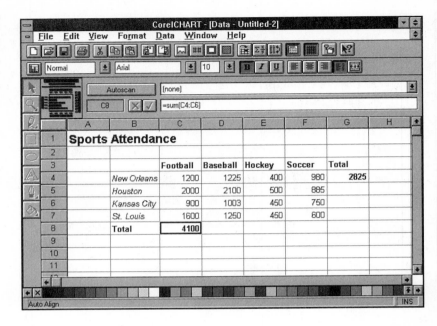

The Fill commands work only when you want to copy data to adjacent or "touching" cells. For instance, you cannot fill from cell B10 to D10, then skip to C10. If you want to copy data to nonadjacent cells, use the Copy and Paste commands. The following steps illustrate using the Fill Down command:

1. Select the cells containing the formula you want to repeat, and the cells where the formulas will be filled. In figure 13.26, the cells G4 through G7 are selected.

2. From the Edit menu, select Fill Down to fill the data from G4 to the other selected cells on the right.

Inserting Columns and Rows

In the charting business, it is not at all uncommon to update charts with new series of data. For instance, you may be asked to update a sales chart by inserting a row for a new sales representative. When you insert a column or row, any existing data moves over to make room for it. To insert a new column or row, use the following steps:

1. Select the column(s) or row(s) where you want the new columns or rows inserted. To select a column, click on the column letter. To select a row, click on the row number. To select more than one column or row, drag across several column letters or row numbers.

2. Select <u>E</u>dit, <u>I</u>nsert to add the new column(s) or row(s). When you insert a new column, any existing data is shifted to the right. When you insert a new row, any existing data is shifted down.

Your formulas and functions will adjust to the new location when you insert columns and rows. For instance, the formula C4*C5 in column C would change to D4*D5 when a new column C is inserted. However, even though formulas and functions adjust when you insert columns and rows, it's still a good idea to double-check them for accuracy.

Deleting Columns and Rows

You can remove data from a spreadsheet by deleting entire columns and rows. For instance, you could delete a row containing last year's sales figures. It's important to remember that deleting a column or row also deletes any data in the column or row. To delete a column or row, use the following steps:

1. Select the column(s) or row(s) you want to delete. To select a column, click on the column letter. To select a row, click on the row number. To select more than one column or row, drag across several column letters or row numbers.

2. Select <u>E</u>dit, <u>D</u>elete. The column(s) or row(s) and any data are deleted.

Adjusting Column Width and Row Height

When entering chart data, you find that longer text strings do not completely fit into a cell. By default, columns in the Data Manager spreadsheet are 50 points or about 3/4 inches wide, and rows in the spreadsheet are 15 points tall. If your text strings exceed these boundaries, the text appears cut off. Actually, all of the text is still there; it just appears cut off because the column is not wide enough. You can adjust the column width and row height to accommodate the text. For instance, the title "Working Safely" in figure 13.27 is cut off because the column is not wide enough to display all of the text. The top and bottom of the text are also clipped off because the row is not tall enough.

You can adjust the column width and row height to fit longer text strings. However, the column width and row height affect only what you see in the Data Manager, not in the Chart View. Even if your title is cut off in the Data Manager, the title still appears complete in the Chart View. You really only have to worry about column width and row height when formatting the spreadsheet to be printed.

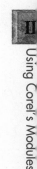

Figure 13.27
Examining data
that is too large
for the cell.

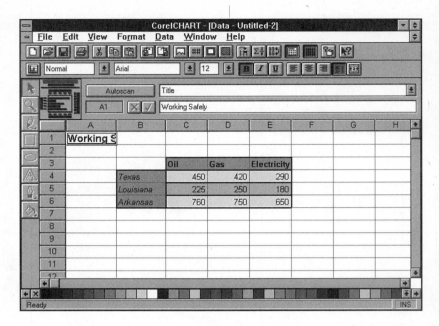

Adjusting Column Width and Row Height by Dragging

The easiest way to adjust the column width is to drag on the dividing line between the column letters. For instance, to widen column A, place the cursor on the dividing line between columns A and B. The cursor shape changes to a double-sided arrow. Drag the line to the left or right to adjust the width of the column. When the column is at the desired width, let go of the mouse button, and the column width is adjusted. To adjust the width of several columns at once, select all of them before dragging the width of one column.

The same process is used to adjust row height. Place the mouse on the dividing line between any two row numbers. Again, the mouse shape will change to a double-sided arrow. Drag up or down to increase or decrease the row height. Release at the desired height.

Adjusting the Width and Height with the Column Width and Row Height Commands

The Column Width command lets you enter a precise measurement for the column width. Select a cell in the column you want to adjust and choose Column Width from the Format menu. The Column Width dialog box shown in figure 13.28 appears. Type in a new width and click on OK.

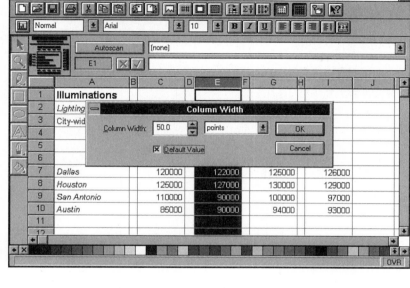

Figure 13.28
The Column Width dialog box.

The Row Height command functions similarly to the Column Width command. Select a cell in the row you want to adjust and choose Row **H**eight from the Fo**r**mat menu. The Row Height dialog box shown in figure 13.29 appears. Type in a new height and click on OK.

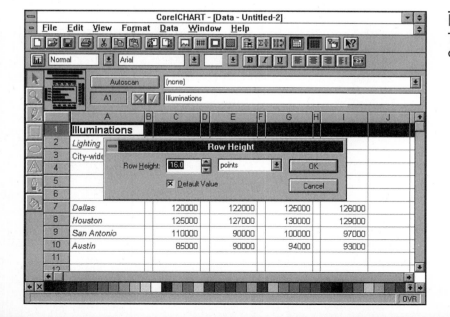

Figure 13.29
The Row Height dialog box.

> **Tip**
>
> A value of 0 (zero) in the Column Width or Row Height dialog box hides the row completely. This is a great way to hide sensitive data.

Using the Best Fit Command

The Best Fit command automatically adjusts the column width and row height to match the largest entry in the selected column or row. To use Best Fit, select the column containing the data you want fit and choose Best Fit from the Format menu. All cells in the column are adjusted to the width necessary to display the longest text string.

Sorting Data

CorelCHART!'s sorting feature helps you organize chart data in alphabetic or numeric order. For instance, you might need to sort a list of sales representatives alphabetically by last name. Information is sorted by a key. The *key* tells CorelCHART! which element of the data to use as a guide for the sort. For instance, to sort by city names, you would use column B as the sort key (see fig. 13.30). To sort by attendance totals, you would use column F as the sort key. The key is simply the category by which you want the data sorted.

Figure 13.30
Examining data
to be sorted.

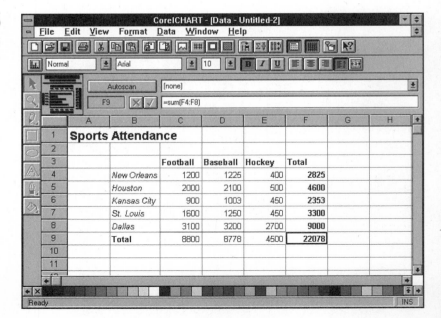

You can choose to sort the data by columns or rows. In figure 13.30, the cities and attendance figures are lined up in rows. To arrange the city names in alphabetical order, you would choose to sort by rows. However, the sports categories are lined up in columns. To arrange the sports categories in alphabetical order, you would choose to sort by columns. CorelCHART! assumes that you want to sort by rows unless you specify otherwise.

Before sorting, it is important to select all the data you want sorted. In figure 13.30, you would not want the cities sorted without the corresponding attendance figures, so both the city names and the attendance figures must be selected. The following steps illustrate sorting the data in figure 13.30 alphabetically by city name.

1. Select the cells you want to sort. In figure 13.30, cells B7 through F10 are selected. Notice this includes the city names and attendance numbers, but not the totals in row nine.

2. Select **D**ata, **S**ort or click on the Sort button in the Text Ribbon Bar to display the Sort dialog box shown in figure 13.31. Make sure **R**ow is selected for the orientation for sorting the data.

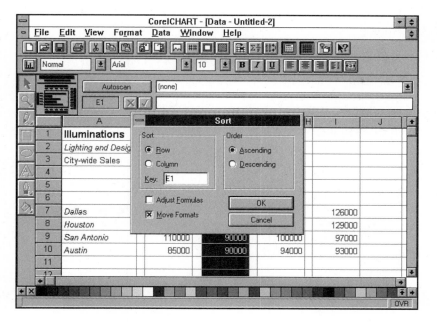

Figure 13.31
The Sort dialog box.

3. In the **K**ey box, enter B4 instructing CorelCHART! to use column B as the sorting key. You must type in a whole cell address, even though only the column letter will be used when sorting by rows, and only the row number will be used when sorting by columns.

4. The default sorting order is **A**scending, which sorts alphabetically from A to Z, and numerically from the lowest to the highest number. Descending sorts alphabetically Z to A, and numerically, highest to lowest.

5. Leave the **M**ove Formats option on so that all cell formatting is sorted along with the cell data. Click on OK, and the data is sorted alphabetically by city name.

Formatting in the Data Manager

Charts and graphs can instantly communicate a value-based concept. One glance at a bar chart and you can tell if sales are going up or down. One look at a pie chart and you can see which department has the highest expenditures. However, there is no disputing that real numbers provide more precise, concrete facts.

The chart data in the Data Manager can be formatted to create visually impressive documents that are easier to understand. The formatting options let you apply different fonts and type styles to titles, add currency symbols to number values, and embellish data with borders and shading. However, keep in mind that any formatting changes you make to the chart data in the Data Manager affect only the data in the spreadsheet; they have no effect on the chart itself.

Text Formatting

Formatting text in the Data Manager is similar to formatting text in other popular Windows applications such as Excel or Word for Windows. To change text attributes, simply select the cell or group of cells you want to change, then choose the appropriate menu command or click on the desired button on the Text Ribbon Bar. Figure 13.32 displays the Text Ribbon Bar.

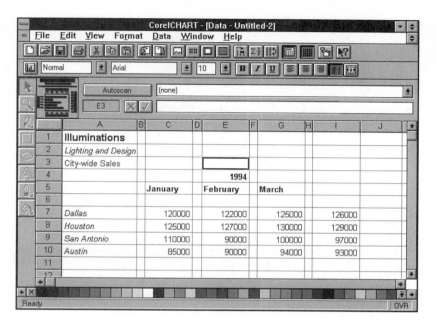

Figure 13.32
The Text Ribbon
Bar.

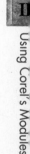

Changing Type Styles

To apply bold, italic, or underline to the chart data, select the cell(s) containing the data you wish to format and click on the (B) button for bold, the (I) button for italic, and the (U) button for underline. You can apply more than one type style to the selected cell(s). For instance, clicking on the bold and italic buttons creates bold-italic text.

Changing the Type Face and Type Size

To apply a new font, select the cells containing the data you want to change, and select Font from the Format menu. The Font dialog box displayed in figure 13.33 appears. In the Font list box, choose the desired font. In Font Style and Size list boxes, select the desired attributes. In the Effects section, click in the appropriate check boxes to apply Strikeout and Underline attributes. Click on the down arrow beside the Color option to select another color for the data. As you make changes, notice the text in the sample box. Click on OK to apply the selected font information.

Figure 13.33
The Font dialog
box.

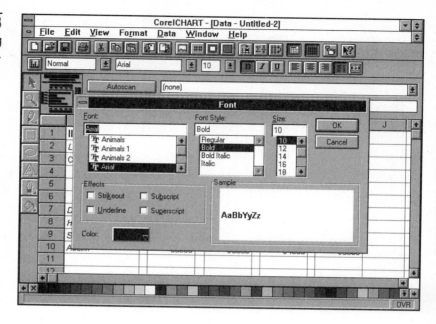

 Note   You can also access the Font dialog box by clicking the right mouse button on the selected cell(s). When the Cell menu appears, select the Font option.

Aligning Cell Data

You can adjust the alignment of the data within the cells with the Alignment buttons on the Text Ribbon Bar. There are four alignment buttons. From left to right, they are: Left align, Right align, Center align, and Auto align. To use the alignment buttons, select the cells containing the data you want to align and click on the desired button.

Numeric Formats

The numbers in the Data Manager spreadsheet can be formatted to display commas, currency, percentage signs, and decimal places. For example, the number 5,000 can be formatted to display as $5,000.00, 5,000 or 5000.00%.

CorelCHART! uses basic numeric formats and codes to apply numeric formatting. *General* is the default format, displaying up to 12 decimal places with no commas or currency. The Percentage format displays numbers with a percent sign (%). The Scientific format displays numbers in exponential (scientific) notation.

The numeric codes are similar to those found in Microsoft Excel. The codes are created with digit placeholders, such as number signs (#) and zeros (0), which represent your numbers. For instance, the format code #,##0 would format 3000 as 3,000. When choosing the desired format, look for the code that displays the attributes you need, such as currency, and the number of decimal places. If you select a format that does not display decimal places, CorelCHART! will round any decimal numbers. For instance, if you enter 3000.80 and apply the format #,##0, the number displays as 3,001. However, the actual number value is not changed. For example, even though the number 3000.80 is displayed 3,001, formulas calculating that value use 3000.80, not the displayed value of 3001. Table 13.5 lists the available numeric format codes in CorelCHART!.

Table 13.5
CorelCHART! Format Codes

Code	Data Entered	Data Displayed
###0	3000.80	3001
###0.0	3000.80	3000.8
###0.00	3000.80	3000.80
###0.000	3000.80	3000.800
###0.0000	3000.80	3000.8000
$###0.00	3000.80	$3000.80
#,##0.00	3000.80	3,000.80
#,##0.00DM	3000.80	3,000.80DM
$#,##0	3000.80	$3,001
#,##0	3000.80	3,001
#,##0DM	3000.80	3,001DM

As you can see, the zeros force the display of a specified number of decimal places. For instance, the code ###0.0000 forced the display of four decimal places even though only two were entered.

CorelCHART! also provides formats for displaying the time and date. The formatting symbols are: d for date, m for month, and y for year. For example, the code m-d-y displays the date September 1, 1993 as 9-1-93, while d-mmm-yy displays as 1-Sep-93.

Applying Numeric Formatting

To apply numeric formatting, select the cell or group of cells to be formatted, and then click on the Numbers button (##) in the Text Ribbon Bar or select Numeric from the Format menu. The Numeric Format dialog box displayed in figure 13.34 appears. Scroll through the list of formats to select the desired numeric format style. The Sample box at the bottom of the dialog box previews how the data will appear with the selected format style. When ready, click on OK.

Figure 13.34
The Numeric
Format dialog
box.

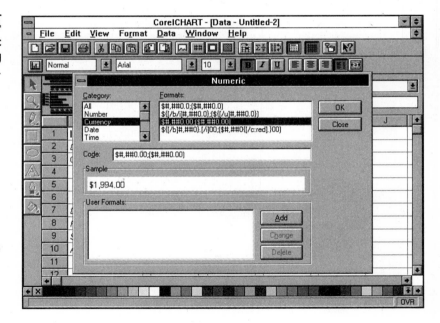

 You can also access the Numeric Format dialog box by clicking the right mouse button on the selected cell(s). When the cell menu appears, select the Numeric Format option.

Borders and Shading

You can embellish chart data with borders and lines to separate data and to mark totals and subtotals. For instance, it is common practice to add lines under subtotals and totals. Shading cells is another way to add emphasis and flair to your chart data. For example, column headings can be shaded to make them stand out on the page.

Applying Borders

Borders can be placed on all four sides of a cell or in combinations such as top and bottom, or left and bottom. Figure 13.35 shows a bottom border placed on cells B6 through E6, and an outline border around cells A10 through E11.

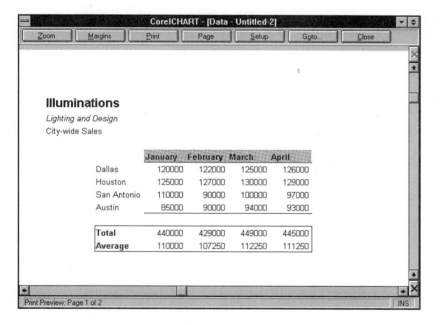

Figure 13.35
Print Preview of chart data illustrating the use of borders and shading.

To place borders, select the cells where you want the borders to appear, and click on the Border button or choose **B**orders from the **F**ormat menu. The Borders dialog box displayed in figure 13.36 appears. Choose **O**utline to place a border around the exterior of the selected cell(s). Choose **T**op, **B**ottom, **L**eft, or **R**ight to place borders on the different sides of the selected cell(s). To select a line style, click in the desired **S**tyle box. To choose a color, click on the down arrow by **C**olor and select a color. When you are finished making selections, click on OK to apply the border.

Figure 13.36
The Borders
dialog box.

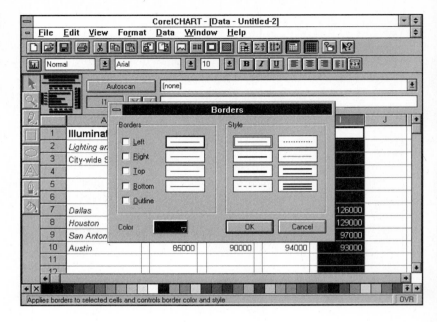

Applying Shading to Cells

Shading is often used to set off titles and column headings. You can select from several backgrounds and colors to shade cells. To apply shading, select the cells you want shaded and click on the Patterns button, or choose Patterns from the Format menu. The Patterns dialog box as displayed in figure 13.37 appears. Select the desired brush pattern, and click on the color buttons to create a colored pattern. Click on OK to apply the shading to the selected cell(s). The Data Manager always displays the sample data with some shading already applied. To view and print your own shading choices, you must turn off the default shading by selecting Chart Tags from the View menu.

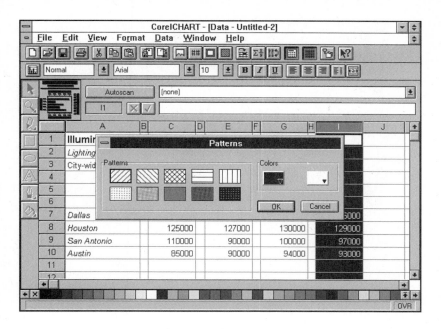

Figure 13.37
The Patterns
dialog box.

Printing in the Data Manager

After sprucing up the chart data with fonts, borders, and shading, you are ready to print. The printed copies of your data can be used to verify the figures for your resident number-crunchers or as audience hand outs supplementing the charts. Although printing in the Chart View is very similar to printing in CorelDRAW!, printing in the Data Manager is more like printing in a spreadsheet program such as Excel. For instance, you can print cell grid lines and create headers and footers. This section documents the special options of printing your chart data. Printing Chart View is covered in Chapter 14, "Formatting and Printing a Chart."

Previewing Your Document

CorelCHART! provides the Print Preview command to let you check the appearance of your printed chart data before sending it to the printer. To see how your chart data will look on the page, choose Print Preview from the File menu. The preview screen appears displaying a full page view of your document, as shown in figure 13.38. The buttons at the top of the screen control certain aspects of the Print Preview screen and the printed page. To exit Print Preview and return to the Data Manager, click on the Close button. Print Preview is introduced first so that you can view any changes made to the chart data, such as adjusting margins and building headers and footers.

Figure 13.38
The Print Preview
screen.

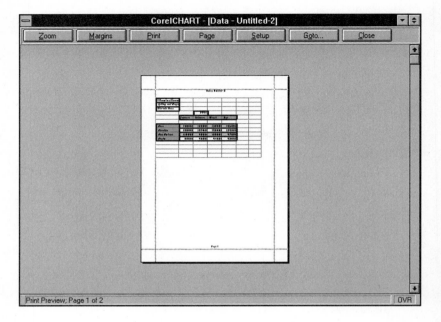

The Zoom button magnifies the page to the 100-percent view, or the approximate size your document will appear when printed. Click on the Zoom button to view the chart data at 100 percent; do it again to return to the full page view. Another way to zoom into the page is to use the mouse. Position the mouse cursor on the part of the page you want to zoom into. Notice the mouse shape changes to a magnifying glass. Click the mouse to zoom into that part of the page. Click again to zoom back out to the full page view.

The Margins button enables you to visually adjust the page margins in the preview window. Click on the Margins button to display dotted lines representing the margins. (These do not print.) Place the cursor on the margin you want to adjust, and it will change to a two-sided arrow. Drag the margin line to the desired position and release the mouse button. The chart data is redrawn on the screen showing your new margins.

Click on the Page button at the top of the preview window to open the Page Setup dialog box. This dialog box's options are covered in the next section, "Controlling Page Setup." If you have more than one page of chart data, click on the Go to button. Enter the page number you want to preview in the Go to Page dialog box, and click on OK. You can also use the Page Up or Page Down keys to move to the next or previous page in your document.

If you want to select a new printer or change printer parameters, click on the Setup button to display the Printer Setup dialog box. Setting up your printer is covered later in this section. When you are ready to print, click on the Print button to display options for printing the chart data. The Print dialog box is discussed in the next section. To exit Print Preview and return to the spreadsheet window, click on the Close button.

Controlling Page Setup

The Page Setup dialog box provides several options for creating professional-looking documents. If you are in the Print Preview window, click on the Page button. If you are in the Data Manager window, select Page Setup from the File menu. The Page Setup dialog box shown in figure 13.39 appears. By default, CorelCHART! uses 54 points as the top, bottom, left, and right margins for printed chart data. Enter the desired margin settings in the Left, Top, Right, and Bottom boxes. You can also click on the arrows to select a desired measurement. To use another measurement system such as inches, simply click on the down arrow by points and select the desired system.

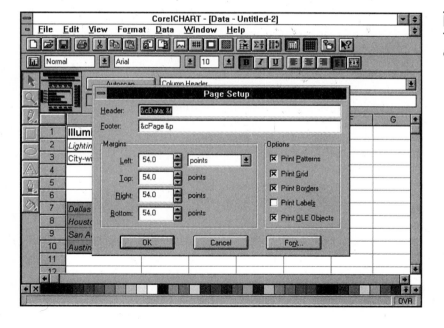

Figure 13.39
The Page Setup dialog box.

Creating Headers and Footers

Headers and footers are text, such as company names, dates, and page numbers, that can be placed at the top or bottom of each printed page. You can enter any text as header and footer text, but CorelCHART! provides codes for displaying the date, time, file name, and page number in the header or footer text. You can also enter codes to control the alignment of the header and footer text. Table 13.6 lists the header and footer codes available in the Data Manager.

Table 13.6
Header and Footer Codes

Code	Effect
&L	Aligns text against left margin
&C	Centers text between margins
&R	Aligns text against right margin
&D	Inserts the current date
&T	Inserts the current time
&F	Inserts the file name of the spreadsheet or chart
&P	Inserts the page number

Header and footer codes can be combined for specific results. For instance, the header code &C&T would center the time at the top of the page. The footer code &R&D would right-align the date on the bottom of the page. The alignment codes must appear before the data codes, otherwise the data will be left-aligned. You can also combine the codes with your own text to create custom headers and footers. For instance, the code &D&C John Smith &R &P would left-align the date, center the author name, and right-align the number.

To create headers and footers, enter the desired codes in the Header and Footer boxes in the Page Setup dialog box. Headers and footers can only be previewed in the Print Preview window; you cannot see header and footer text in the Data Manager.

Using Print Options

The Page Setup dialog box includes several other printing options unique to spreadsheet applications. For instance, you can print the cell grid lines, and row and column headings.

The Print Patterns and Print Borders are turned on, instructing CorelCHART! to print any shading or borders you have added to the data. To print data without any shading or borders, click on the Xs by the commands to turn these options off.

The Print <u>G</u>rid option prints the cell grid lines displayed in the Data Manager. Figure 13.43 shows chart data with the Print Grid option turned on. Turn off this option to print cell contents only.

To print the row numbers and column letters with your chart data, click on the Print Label<u>s</u> command. Turn on the Print OLE command to print embedded or linked objects created in another OLE server, such as a graphic from CorelDRAW!.

Printer Setup

After determining the margins and setting up any headers and footers, the next step is setting the parameters for your printer. From the <u>F</u>ile menu, choose P<u>r</u>int Setup. The Printer Setup dialog box appears. Here, you can choose a printing device and set up printing parameters such as paper size and orientation. Under Printers, click on the desired printing device, then click on the <u>S</u>etup button. A dialog box with information about the selected print device appears. Although the options available in the dialog box will differ based on the print device you have chosen, the basic output options—resolution, paper size, paper source, paper orientation, and number of copies—appear for every type of print device. For more information about setting up printers and the settings appropriate for your printer, refer to Chapter 11, "Basic Printing Techniques," Chapter 25, "Advanced Printing Techniques," and your printer manual. After selecting the desired options, click on OK to return to the spreadsheet.

Printing Your Chart Data

With the page and printer setup complete, you are ready to print. If you are in the Print Preview window, click on the Print button. If you are in the Data Manager window, select <u>P</u>rint from the <u>F</u>ile menu. The Print Data dialog box appears. Enter the number of copies you want printed in the <u>C</u>opies box. The First Page <u>N</u>umber option lets you specify the number to be assigned to the first page of your document. For instance, entering the number 10 would instruct CorelCHART! to start numbering the pages of your chart data at 10. This option is handy if you want the page numbers of your chart data to match up with documents created in another application.

The Print Cells section lets you print only specific columns and rows of your data. Printing only part of your chart data is great when you have added comments or notes on the spreadsheet that you don't want to appear on the printed document. By default, the <u>A</u>ll option is selected, indicating all columns and rows with cell data will print. To print only certain parts of the spreadsheet data, click in the <u>F</u>rom box. Enter the first column or row you want to print and then move to the <u>T</u>o box and enter the last column or row you want to print. For instance, you could print from column A to column F and from row 10 to row 30.

When chart data is more than a single page in size, you can use the Print Pages section of the dialog box to control which pages you want to print. The options in the Print Pages section are available only if the <u>A</u>ll option is selected for both columns and rows in the Print Cells section. Select the T<u>w</u>o-Sided Printing option to print the odd and even pages separately. By default, the All Pages option is selected, indicating that all the pages of the spreadsheet data will print. To print only specific pages, click in the <u>F</u>rom box and enter the first page you want printed. Then, click in the <u>T</u>o box and enter the last page you want printed. When finished selecting the desired print options, click on OK to print your document. A message box appears displaying the status of your print job as it is sent to the printer.

CorelCHART!'s extensive selection of chart types makes it one of the most powerful charting applications available. Regardless of the kind of data you want to present, CorelCHART!'s wide selection of chart types ensures that you will find the perfect way to express your information.

Now that you have a better understanding of some of CorelCHART!'s fundamentals, you are ready to begin creating a chart. The focus of the next chapter is entering text and numerical values used to compose your chart, and creating formulas to calculate your data.

Chapter Snapshot

This chapter explains how to design and print your charts. You will find that many of the formatting commands in CorelCHART! are very straightforward, especially if you are familiar with CorelDRAW!. You will learn to do the following:

✔ Select chart colors

✔ Use outlines and fills

✔ Annotate your charts with graphic objects and text

✔ Adjust bar thickness and spacing in bar charts

✔ Explode pie slices

✔ Display grid lines

✔ Display format legends

✔ Create pictographs

✔ Format chart text and graphic elements

✔ Print charts

✔ Transfer data between CorelCHART! and other applications

Well-designed charts not only communicate the data, they can impart an air of credibility and professionalism. CorelCHART! has the kind of tools and features you will need to design impressive, powerful charts that make your point crystal clear in a moment's glance.

14

CHAPTER

Formatting and Printing Charts

C harts and graphs create powerful first impressions that can make or break a sale, influence an investment, or win over a competitor. Whether you are plotting the number of television viewers during a ratings sweep or comparing the pitching speed of Hall of Fame baseball players, a well-designed chart grabs your attention as it leads your eye through an examination of the data. When designing charts, your goal is to enhance the chart's message and make it easy to understand.

After switching from the Data Manager to view your chart for the first time, don't be surprised if your mind races with all the changes and adjustments you want to make. Use the graphic elements at your disposal—typeface, size, style and alignment, design elements, such as rule lines and boxes, illustrations and color choices—to engage the viewer's eye and invite further examination of the chart.

Selecting Chart Objects

As with all graphics applications, you must select an object before moving, sizing, or formatting it. When you click on a chart object, such as a title, pie slice, legend, bar riser, or chart frame, the object becomes selected. Some objects display small buttons when selected; others display a gray outline. As displayed in figure 14.1, eight small buttons surround the chart title when selected, while an outline appears around the selected legend text. By default, only one object is selected at a time. To select more than one object, press and hold the Shift key as you click on the other objects.

Figure 14.1
Selected objects appear with a gray box or buttons surrounding the object.

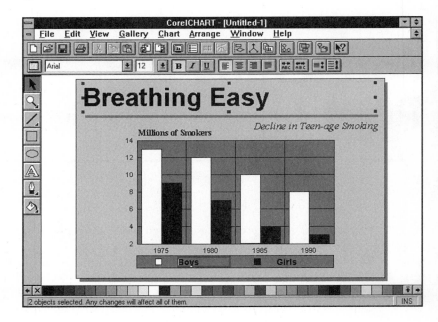

Changing Chart Colors and Outlines

As a designer, you know the impact of color cannot be overstated. Red can conjure up images of financial danger, blues often help keep the viewer calm, while rich metallic colors generally portray stability and strength. CorelCHART! gives you control over the fill and outline color of every chart element. In addition, all of the wonderful fountain and patterned fills found in CorelDRAW! also are available in CorelCHART!.

You can change the color of almost any chart object by following these basic steps. Select the object, then click on the desired color in the color palette or apply a fill using the Fill tool. To change the color of a bar riser, for example, select the bar, and then click on the desired color in the color palette. To apply a fountain fill to the chart background, select it and click on the Fountain Fill tool in the Fill tool fly-out.

Using the Color Palette To Apply Fill and Outline Colors

The color palette at the bottom of the CorelCHART! screen provides quick access to a wide range of colors. To display all of the colors in the palette, click on the up arrow button on the right side of the palette. Click on the button again to restore the palette to one row of colors.

 To display another color palette, choose **V**iew, Co**l**or Palette. Select the desired color model from the fly-out.

To apply a new fill color, select the object and click on the desired color in the color palette. Click on the button marked with an X in the palette to remove the fill of the selected object. To apply a new outline color, select the element and click with the right mouse button on the color in the color palette. Click with the right mouse button on the X button in the palette to remove the outline.

Using the Fill Tool To Apply Colors and Fills

CorelCHART!'s Fill tool is identical to the one found in CorelDRAW!. When you click on the Fill tool (the last tool in the Toolbox), the fly-out toolbar appears as shown in figure 14.2. The Fill tools in CorelCHART! work just as they do in CorelDRAW!, so this section provides a basic overview of using the tools. Refer to Chapter 7, "Understanding Outline and Fill," for more in-depth coverage.

If the color palette does not offer the specific color you need, you can use the Fill tool to access more color choices. CorelCHART! uses the same color models, such as PANTONE and Grayscale, found in CorelDRAW!. To apply a solid or uniform fill color, select the chart object you want to fill and click on the Fill tool. Select the Uniform Fill Color tool (the color wheel on the top row) to display the Uniform

Fill dialog box as shown in figure 14.2. Click on the down arrow by the Show list box and select the desired color model. Click on the desired color in the palette, and click on OK. The color is applied to the selected object. Use the tools on the bottom row of the Fill tool fly-out to apply no fill (X), white, black, 10% black, 30% black, and 70% black.

Figure 14.2
The Uniform Fill
dialog box.

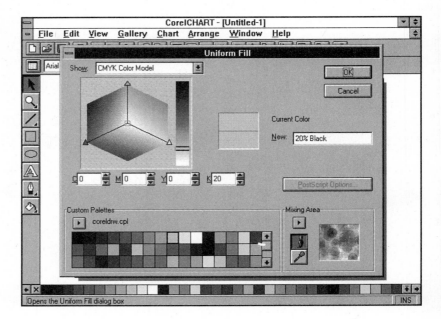

Applying Fountain Fills

Fountain fills are a great way to spruce up chart backgrounds (see fig. 14.3). You can apply fountain fills to almost every chart element including titles, legend text, chart frames, bars, and pie slices. To apply a fountain fill, select the object you wish to fill, and click on the Fill tool. From the fly-out, select the Fountain Fill tool (third on top row) to reveal the Fountain Fill dialog box. Select the fountain type, and choose the From and To colors for the fountain fill. Click on OK to apply the fill.

Applying Pattern Fills

Just as with CorelDRAW!, CorelCHART! offers two types of pattern fills: two-color and full color. Pattern fills can be applied to most chart elements, such as titles, frames, bars, and pie slices. To apply a pattern fill, select the object you want to fill, and click on the Fill tool. From the fly-out, click on the Two-Color Fill tool (fourth on top row), or the Full Color Fill tool (fifth on top row) to reveal the Pattern Fill dialog box. Click on the large button in the middle of the full-color pattern dialog box to display the available patterns. Select a pattern swatch and click on OK to apply the fill.

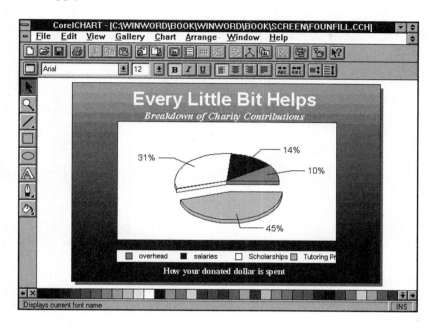

Figure 14.3
Fountain Fills can create interesting chart backgrounds.

Applying Texture Fills

Texture fills can add an interesting design touch in charts. Like pattern fills, texture fills can be applied to most chart elements, with the exception of chart text. To apply a texture fill, select the object you want to fill and click on the Fill tool. From the fly-out, click on the Bitmap Texture Fill button (sixth on top row) to reveal the Texture Fill dialog box as shown in figure 14.4. Select a texture from the Texture List and click on OK.

Formatting Outlines with the Outline Tool

CorelCHART! places black outlines around many chart elements, such as bars, frames, and legends. Unlike CorelDRAW!, however, in CorelCHART! outlines cannot be placed around chart titles and text. You can change the line color, thickness, or remove the line from objects with the Outline tool. Click on the Outline tool (the seventh tool in the Toolbox), to display the fly-out toolbar. Because many of the commands for formatting outlines are the same in CorelDRAW!, this section provides a basic overview of using the Outline tool. For more in-depth coverage, refer to Chapter 7.

Figure 14.4
The Texture Fill
dialog box.

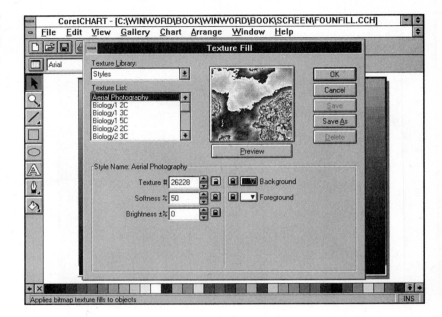

Changing Outline Color with the Outline Tool

Although you can apply outline colors with the color palette, the Outline tool offers many more color choices. After selecting the chart object you want to modify, click on the Outline Color tool (the color wheel on the bottom row) in the fly-out to display the Outline Color dialog box. Click on the down arrow by the Show list box, and select the desired color model. Select the color you want in the palette and click on OK to apply the outline color to the selected object. The tools in the bottom row of the Outline tool fly-out let you apply white, black, and percentages of black to the outlines.

Changing Outline Thickness

The tools on the top row of the Outline tool fly-out control line thickness. Click on one of the last six tools to apply a pre-set line thickness to the selected chart object. To set a custom line thickness, click on the Outline Pen tool (first tool on top row) in the fly-out. The Outline Pen dialog box as shown in figure 14.5 appears. Enter the desired line thickness in the Width box. Also available in this dialog box are options to change the line colors and dashed line styles. When finished making your line selections, click on OK to apply the outline formatting.

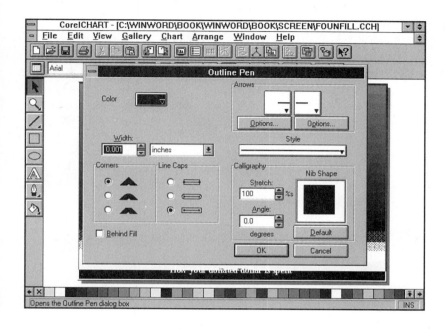

Figure 14.5
The Outline Pen
dialog box.

Working with the Chart Frame

The chart frame is the box that appears around your graph. You can enlarge the chart frame to give the graph greater dominance or reduce the frame to make room for another graph or additional graphic elements. To size the chart frame, select the frame and then drag one of the selection buttons. Just as in CorelDRAW!, drag one of the four corner buttons to scale the frame, thereby sizing it proportionally. Drag one of the inside buttons to stretch the frame, thus distorting the original shape. When sizing the frame, keep in mind that chart elements, such as bars, slices and axis text, also are reduced or enlarged. To move the chart frame, simply press and hold the mouse button in the middle of the frame and drag to the desired position. Release the mouse to redraw the frame in its new location.

You can't delete the chart frame; however, you can remove the fill and the outline with the button marked X in the color palette to create the same visual effect.

II

Using Corel's Modules

Selecting Chart Commands

CorelCHART! provides several ways to access the commands for designing and formatting charts. This chapter focuses on using menus to access commands. For instance, to adjust bar thickness, this chapter instructs you to select Bar Thickness from the Chart menu. However, CorelCHART! also provides pop-up menus to quickly access most commands. The pop-up menu can be displayed by clicking the right mouse button on the chart element you want to format. A context-sensitive pop-up menu appears displaying options for that particular chart element. For instance, clicking on a pie slice displays a pop-up menu that offers another way to adjust the pie thickness.

Displaying Titles, Data Values, and Other Text Elements

Chart titles, footnotes, axis titles, and legends can help make your charts quickly and easily comprehended. Chart titles inform the viewer of company names and dates. Axis titles and legends explain how data is organized and presented. CorelCHART! lets you control which titles and text elements are displayed in your charts. For example, you may decide to remove the subtitle and footnote in some charts, while in other charts you may want to display the data values on the bars, as illustrated in figure 14.6.

Figure 14.6
CorelCHART! enables you to display the actual data values on the chart.

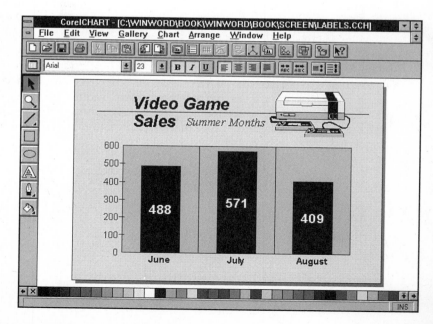

To control which text elements are displayed, choose Chart, Display Status or click on the Display Status button. The options in the Display Status dialog box vary according to the chart type. For instance, figure 14.7 shows the Display Status dialog box for bar charts. The check marks indicate which text elements are displayed. To display a text element, click in the appropriate check box. To remove a text element from the chart, click to clear the check mark. In a pie chart, for instance, turn on the Slice Labels and Slice Values options to display the labels around the pie.

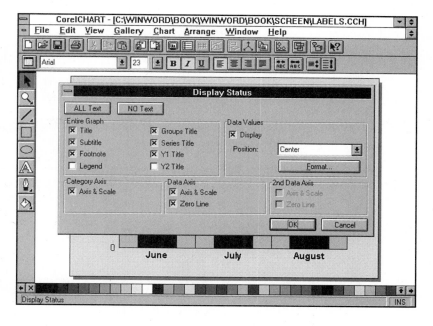

Figure 14.7
The Display Status dialog box.

You can display the data values on bar, line, and area charts by clicking on the Display checkbox under Data Values. Click on the down arrow by the Position list box to control where the data values are placed. For instance, in figure 14.6, the Center option was selected to display the data values in the center of each bar. After making the desired selections, click on OK, and the specified titles and text elements are displayed on your chart. Options for formatting chart text are covered in the following section.

Another way to turn off the display of titles and footnotes is to delete the data from the cell in the Data Manager.

Using Corel's Modules

Formatting Chart Text

The placement, size, and style attributes of chart text elements are some of your most important design considerations. Chart titles should catch the viewer's eye, axis titles should facilitate understanding, and legends should clarify chart data. In addition, there will probably be times when you want to annotate your chart with extra text to clarify and enhance the chart's message. The tools for formatting text are in the Text Ribbon Bar at the top of the screen (see fig. 14.8).

Figure 14.8
Use the Text Ribbon Bar at the top of the screen to control text attributes such as font and style.

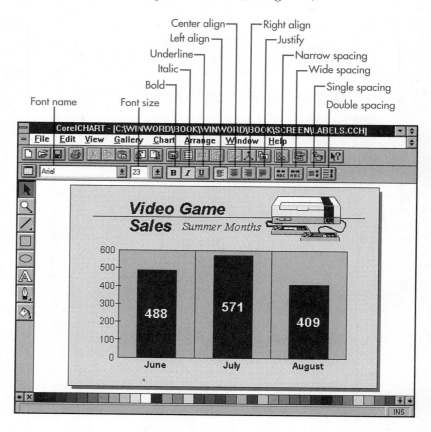

The text elements in CorelCHART! fall into two general categories. The main text type is chart text, which is entered in the Data Manager. Chart text includes chart titles, subtitles, footnotes, axis titles, and slice labels. The second type, annotated text, is entered directly on the chart with the Text tool. Both types can be sized and formatted; however, some chart text, such as the axis scales and titles, cannot be moved. This section details the options for formatting both types of text.

Applying color to text objects is covered in the previous section, "Selecting Chart Colors." Refer to the next section for information on creating annotated text.

Moving Text Elements

CorelCHART! enables you to move or reposition most chart text elements. You might want the footnote at the bottom of the chart, for example. Though you can move all annotated text, some chart text, such as axis text and slice labels, cannot be repositioned. To move a text element, select it and then drag the text to the desired location. An outline of the text appears as a reference point as you move text. Release the mouse when you have positioned the outline where you want the text to appear.

Applying Type Attributes

You can use all of your favorite fonts from CorelDRAW! in CorelCHART!. To apply a new typeface, select the text you want to change, and click on the down arrow by the Font list box in the Text Ribbon Bar. Click on the desired font, and the selected text is displayed in the new font. To change the type size, select the text, and choose a new size from the Font Size list box. Before changing the type size of axis and legend text, you must turn off the Autofit feature. Autofit is discussed in the following section, "Formatting Options for Axis and Legend Text."

The title, subtitle, and footnote also can be sized by dragging on the selection buttons. If you want a smaller type size, for instance, drag the selection handles in toward the center of the text. For a bigger type size, drag the handles away from the center.

The maximum font size is 72 points in CorelCHART!. If you need larger type, create it in CorelDRAW!, then copy and paste it into CorelCHART! by using the Clipboard.

You can add emphasis to text elements by applying bold, italics, and underline to text. In the Text Ribbon Bar, the B button creates bold text, the I button creates italic, and the U creates underlined text. To apply a type style, select the text and click on the appropriate button in the Text Ribbon Bar. If the button appears "pushed in," the style already has been applied. To remove the style, select the text and click to "pop out" the desired style button.

Using Corel's Modules

To maintain a uniform chart appearance, all axis text or legend text must be the same size. Therefore, when you change the typeface, size, or style of axis or legend text, all remaining axis and legend text will also be identically adjusted. In figure 14.9, for instance, enlarging the font for any value on the data axis enlarges the font for all numbers on the axis. The same is true for pie slice labels and values; changing the attributes of one affects all others.

Adjusting Text Alignment

You can adjust the text alignment of titles, subtitles, and other chart text to fit your particular chart design needs. In figure 14.8, for instance, the chart title is left-aligned, the subtitle is right-aligned, and the footnote is centered at the bottom of the chart. The Text Ribbon Bar includes four buttons for controlling text alignment (see fig. 14.11). Use the first button to set left-aligned text, the second for center-aligned, the third for right-aligned, and the last button for justified or "right & left aligned" text.

Figure 14.9
Any formatting changes made to axis data affects all data on that axis.

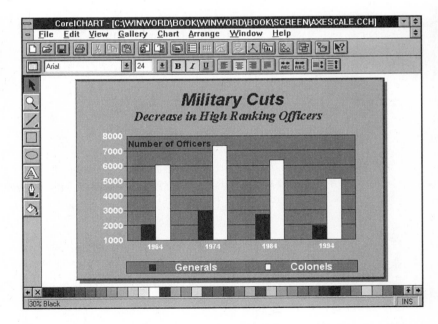

When you select a text element, the button representing the current alignment of the text is "pushed in." To change the text alignment, simply click on the desired alignment button. For instance, if a center-aligned chart title is selected, the Center Alignment button is pushed in. Click on the left-align button to align the text to the left side of the chart.

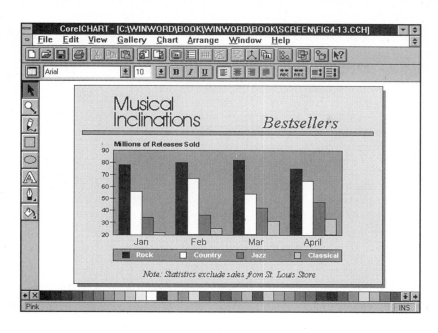

Figure 14.10
Chart text can be
left, right, or
center aligned.

 You also can move chart titles, subtitles, and footnotes to control positioning.

Adjusting Letter and Line Spacing

CorelCHART! provides a unique tool for adjusting the spacing between the letters in text elements. After selecting the text you want to adjust, click on the Decrease Spacing button in the Text Ribbon Bar (refer back to fig. 14.8) to reduce the amount of space between letters. Each time you click on the button, the space between the characters is decreased, bringing the characters closer together. To increase letter spacing, select the text element and click on the Increase Spacing button. Again, each click will increase the space between characters, spreading them out across the chart. You cannot adjust the letter spacing in axis text, pie labels, or legend text.

For text blocks that include more than one line of text, you can adjust the spacing between lines. After selecting the text you want to adjust, click on the Single Spacing or Double Spacing button (refer back to fig. 14.8). You may need to click several times on the buttons to achieve the desired effect.

Special Options for Formatting Axis Text

Most of the commands for formatting chart text also apply for the text and numbers along the X and Y axis. CorelCHART!, however, provides two features, Autofit and Stagger, that are unique to formatting axis text. The Autofit feature determines the best size, automatically sizing the axis text so that all the text can fit on the axis without overlapping. Of course, the more text you place on the axis, the smaller the type size will become. At times, you might find that the Autofit feature makes axis text too small. Before enlarging the text, you must turn off the Autofit feature.

To turn off Autofit, select the axis name from the Chart menu. In a bar chart, for example, if you want to size the data on the category axis, select Category Axis. From the submenu, select Autofitted Text or Autofitted Scale. Clicking on the Autofit command removes the check mark and turns off the feature. Click again to turn Autofit back on.

The Stagger feature also prevents any text overlap by alternating the placement of the labels on the axis. In figure 14.11, for example, Autofit was turned off so that the text on the category axis could be enlarged, then staggered to prevent overlapping. To stagger axis text, select the axis name from the Chart menu. From the submenu, click on Staggered Scale or Staggered Text.

Figure 14.11
CorelCHART!
enables you to
stagger axis text.

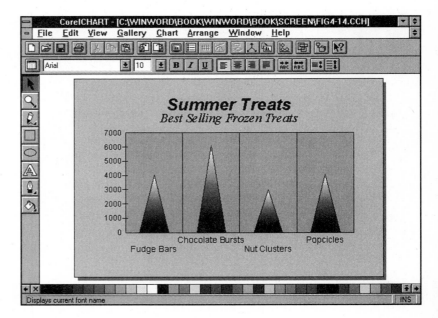

Tip By default, Y axis titles will display vertically. Press and hold the right mouse button on the title to reveal a pop-up menu. Turn off the Hotel Text feature to horizontally align the text.

Special Options for Formatting Legend Text

A descriptive, easy-to-read legend can assist in effectively communicating a chart's message. In figure 14.12, the legend is stacked vertically and used as a graphic element, adding some pizzazz to the chart. By default, legends are placed at the bottom of the chart, and the legend text is automatically sized to prevent any text overlap. You can move, size, and format the legend text to create the effect you need, although it may take several steps to get the legend exactly as you want it.

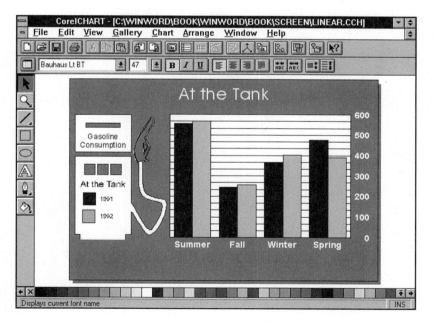

Figure 14.12
There are many options for formatting the legend in CorelCHART!.

Moving and Sizing the Legend

The legend box can be moved and sized just like any other graphic object. To move the legend, place your mouse inside the legend box and drag it to the desired location. Size the legend by dragging on one of the corner handles until you reach the desired size. Sizing the legend can change the orientation of the legend text and markers. Increasing the height and decreasing the width of the legend box, for instance, causes the markers to line up vertically instead of horizontally (see fig. 14.12).

Removing the Legend

Simple charts might not require a legend to explain the chart data. For a pie chart, instead of using a legend, you might opt to place the labels and values around the pie. To remove the legend from your chart, choose Chart, Legend or click on the Legend button in the Ribbon Bar. The Legend dialog box appears as displayed in figure 14.13. Click on the Display Legend option to remove the X. Click on OK, and the legend is removed from the chart display.

Tip

Click on the legend with the right mouse button to access the pop-out menu, then click on Legend to access the Legend dialog box.

Figure 14.13
The Legend
dialog box.

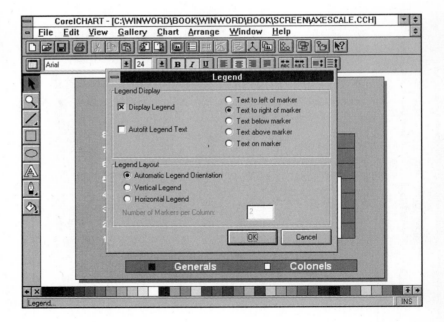

Working with Autofit

CorelCHART!'s Autofit feature automatically sizes legend text and prevents any overlap. If you want to enlarge or reduce the text size, you will first need to turn off Autofit. To turn off Autofit, select Legend from the <u>C</u>hart menu or click on the Legend button on the Ribbon Bar. In the Legend dialog box, click on the Autofit Legend Text option to remove the X in the text box. Click on OK, then adjust the size of the legend text with the Font Size list box on the Text Ribbon Bar.

Adjusting the Legend Layout

The legend text and markers can be vertically or horizontally oriented to create different effects. To change the legend orientation, select <u>C</u>hart, Legend or click on the Legend button on the Ribbon Bar. Under Legend Layout at the bottom of the dialog box, select Horizontal or Vertical Legend. You also can control where the legend text sits relative to the legend marker with the options on the right side of the dialog box. When you are finished modifying legend options, click on OK to observe the changes.

Annotating with Graphics and Text Objects

Adding graphics and additional text elements enables you to customize and enhance your charts. You might want to add a company logo, for instance, or a string of text that announces an increase in sales. Added text and graphics are called *annotations*. The tools in the Toolbox help you create annotated text and simple graphic objects, such as circles, squares, and arrows. Figure 14.14 identifies each tool in the CorelCHART! Toolbox. Because the tools for working with annotated objects work very much like those in CorelDRAW!, this section provides a basic overview. Refer to Chapter 2, "Creating and Drawing," for detailed information on drawing and manipulating graphics and text.

Note You also can import graphics from other applications. Transferring data into CorelCHART! is covered later in this chapter.

Figure 14.14
The CorelCHART!
Toolbox.

Pick tool
Zoom tool
Pencil tool
Rectangle tool
Ellipse tool
Text tool
Outline tool
Fill tool

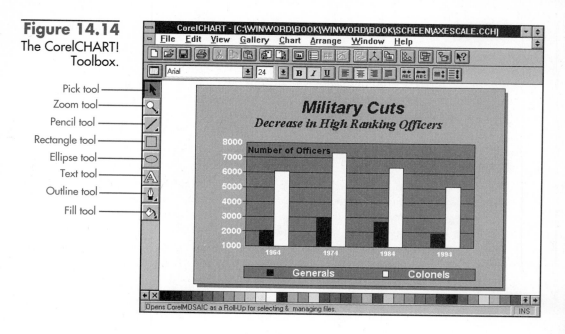

Adding Annotated Text

Annotated text is great when you want to add extra notes or comments on a chart. Unlike chart text, such as titles or axis text, annotated text is not linked to the Data Manager. Annotated text is added as an independent element on top of the chart, and can be manipulated separately from all other chart elements.

To create annotated text, select the Text tool, move to the chart area, and click. An insertion point appears indicating that you can begin typing. When you are finished typing, select the Pick tool to move the text string. Use the formatting commands described in the previous sections to change the typeface, size, and style.

For longer blocks of annotated text, you can draw a box with the Text tool to control the width of the text block. As you continue to type, the box depth will increase to accommodate all of your text.

Adding Annotated Graphics Objects

With CorelCHART!'s drawing tools, you can enhance your charts with lines, curves, rectangles, and ellipses. Any graphics object you draw automatically will be assigned the current default fill and outline attributes, such as color and line thickness. Refer to previous sections on selecting colors and outlines for more information on formatting graphic objects.

When you press and hold the mouse button on the Pencil tool, a fly-out toolbar appears displaying three drawing tools. The first tool, the Freehand tool, draws freehand curves. The second tool, the Straight Line tool, draws straight and diagonal lines. The third tool, the Polygon tool, draws closed polygon shapes. Use the Rectangle and Ellipse tools to add rectangles, squares, ellipses, and circles to your charts.

As in CorelDRAW!, holding the Ctrl key while drawing with the Ellipse or Rectangle tool creates perfect circles and squares. Hold down the Shift key while you draw with the Rectangle or Ellipse tool to draw the shape from the center rather than from one anchor point to another. Hold both the Ctrl and Shift key to draw perfect squares or circles from the center.

You can size, shape, and position all annotated objects the same way you would in CorelDRAW!. To move an object, position the mouse on the object and drag it to the desired position. To size an object, select the object and drag on one of the selection buttons. Use an object's corner selection buttons to scale the object proportionally. To change an object's proportions or "stretch" an object to a new shape, click on any of the four middle selection handles and drag.

Options for Formatting Category (X) and Data (Y) Axes

Many chart types work with a basic XY axis structure. In CorelCHART!, the bar, line, area, histogram, hi/lo, scatter, gantt, and bubble charts all have an axis running vertically up the side of the chart, and another running horizontally across the bottom of the chart. Regardless of the chart type, the commands for formatting the axes are basically the same. This section discusses the options for adjusting and formatting the axes in XY charts.

II

Using Corel's Modules

In polar charts, the two axes are placed on top of each other like a plus sign. In radar charts, one of the axes is circular, the other is displayed from the center of the chart to the outside edge. However, both chart types use the same formatting commands as basic XY charts.

If your chart is vertically oriented, the Y axis appears on the left and the X axis appears along the bottom. In a horizontally oriented chart, the axes are switched to display the Y axis running along the bottom, and the X axis on the left. Figure 14.15 illustrates how the axes are flipped when a bar chart changes from vertical to horizontal orientation.

Refer to Chapter 3, "Editing and Manipulating," for information about how to use the Gallery menu to change the chart orientation.

Most chart types refer to the X axis as the Category axis and the Y axis as the Data axis. However, these names can vary. A histogram, for example, uses the terms "Interval" and "Data" for the axis names, and a scatter chart identifies the axes as X-Axis and Y-Axis. In this section, all axes are referred to as either the Category axis or Data axis.

CorelCHART! also includes templates for creating dual Y axis and bipolar bar, line, and area charts. You will find that most commands for formatting the second data axis in dual Y axis and bipolar charts are identical to the commands for adjusting the primary data axis.

Placement of the Category and Data Axis

You can display the category and data axis text on different sides of the chart or on both sides. In figure 14.16, the category axis was placed at the top of the chart, and the data axis appears on both the left and right sides. Displaying the data axis on both sides of the chart provides the viewer with another axis against which data can be compared.

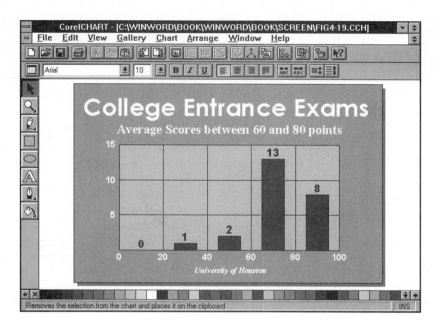

Figure 14.15
The axes are switched in vertically and horizontally oriented charts.

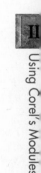

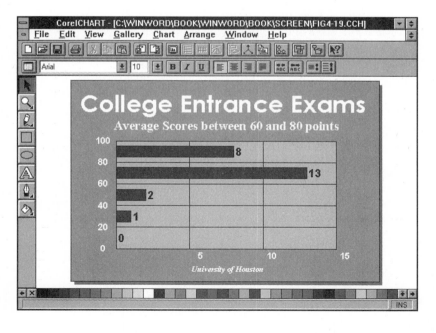

Figure 14.16
Chart with category axis placed at the top of the chart and data axes placed on both sides of the chart.

To adjust the display of the category axis, select Category Axis from the Chart menu. If the chart is vertically aligned, the submenu will offer the options Display on Top and Display on Bottom. If the chart is horizontally aligned, the submenu offers Display on Left and Display on Right. Clicking on the desired option places a check mark by the command, indicating it is turned on. Removing the check mark turns off the feature. To adjust the display of the data axis, select Data Axis from the Chart menu and click on the desired option.

Displaying Axis Grid Lines

Grid lines help lead the viewer's eye from a data set to the data axis. With CorelCHART!, you can display grid lines for both the category and data axis. You might find that too many grid lines clutter the chart. Tick marks, the small lines placed along the data axis (see fig. 14.17), provide an alternative to grid lines.

To display grid lines on the category axis, select Category Axis from the Chart menu. Click on the Show Grid Lines command in the submenu to place grid lines on the category axis of your chart. Click on the command again to remove the grid lines. CorelCHART! does not provide options for placing tick marks on the category axis.

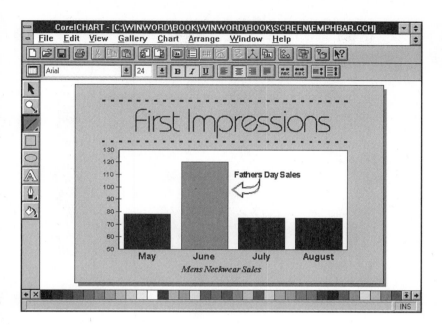

Figure 14.17
Tick marks are another way to format the Data Axis.

To display grid lines on the data axis, select Data Axis from the <u>C</u>hart menu. In the submenu, select Grid Lines. The Grid Lines dialog box, as shown in figure 14.18, appears. The dialog box controls the display of major and minor grid lines. Major divisions are the units between each numerical value along the data axis. Minor divisions are the units between the major divisions.

Click on the Show Major Grid Lines option to display grid lines along the major divisions. When Show Major Grid Lines is turned on, options for displaying the grid lines become available. Select Normal to display the grid line without tick marks, or Normal with Ticks to display the grid lines with tick marks outside the data axis. The three remaining options turn off the display of grid lines and place tick marks instead. The options for controlling minor divisions are the same as those for major divisions. After selecting the desired grid line options, click on OK. Refer to the previous section on selecting outline color and thickness to format the grid lines. All grid lines must use the same line width and color.

Using Corel's Modules

Figure 14.18
The Grid Lines
dialog box.

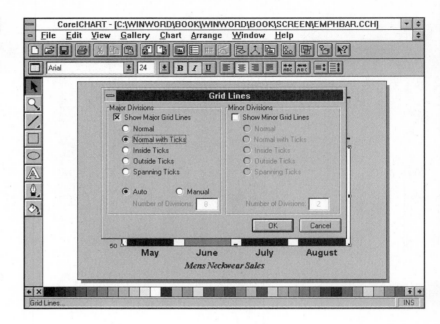

Scaling the Data Axis

The data axis scale provides a reference point to gauge the amount of a specific item. The scale is defined by a minimum and a maximum value with data points incrementally spaced between. CorelCHART! uses your chart data to determine the scale of numbers appearing on the data axis. For instance, if all of your chart values are under 50, the data axis might scale from a minimum of 0 to a maximum of 50. If your chart values range from 150,000 to 350,000, the data axis might scale from 120,000 to 360,000. You can adjust the scale on the data range to begin and end at the values you specify. In figure 14.19, for example, the data axis was scaled from 1,000 to 8,000.

To adjust the data axis scale, select Data Axis from the Chart menu. Select Scale Range from the submenu to display the Scale Range dialog box as shown in figure 14.24. By default, the Automatic Scale option is selected. Click on the Manual Scale option to enter customized starting and ending values. Enter the desired number values in the From and To boxes. In figure 14.20, for instance, 1,000 was entered in the From box and 8,000 was entered in the To box. Click on OK to return to the chart.

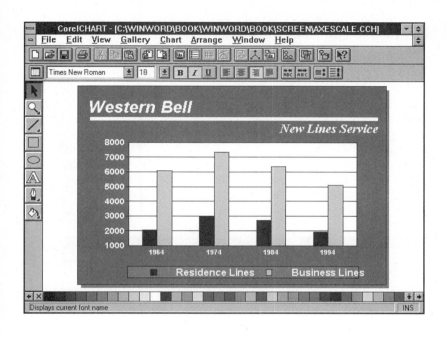

Figure 14.19
Chart with data axis scale adjusted.

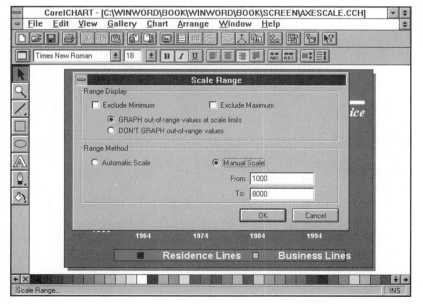

Figure 14.20
The Scale Range dialog box.

Selecting Linear or Logarithmic Scaling

CorelCHART! provides two types of scaling options: Linear and Logarithmic. The default option, Linear, is a standard scale representing an amount or quantity in evenly spaced increments. On a linear scale, for example, one division on the graph might represent $100, two divisions equates to $200, six divisions to $600, and so on. Logarithmic scales compress or expand the data values in powers of 10 as they ascend the Y axis so that the distance between each unit along the data axis decreases as you go up the scale. A logarithmic scale is generally used when there are large disparities in data values such that you must compare large and small quantities in the same chart. In figure 14.21, for example, some of the data values are as little as $20, while others are as much as $10,000. With a logarithmic scale, the numbers are more easily comprehended.

Figure 14.21
A chart with logarithmic scaling.

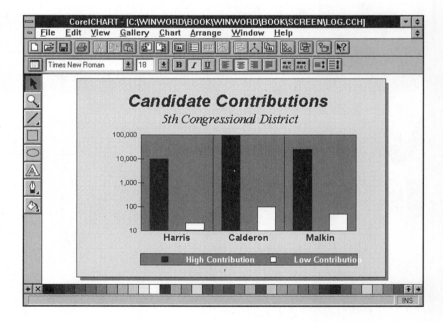

To change to a logarithmic scale, select Data Axis from the Chart menu. From the submenu, click on Log Scale. The Data Axis on the chart is redrawn to display as a logarithmic scale. It's important to note that on a logarithmic scale, you cannot display any minor grid attributes or manually adjust the scale range.

Formatting the Data Axis

You can apply numeric formatting, such as commas and decimal places, to the numbers along the data axis. In figure 14.22, for example, currency symbols are added to inform the viewer that the data axis is scaled in currency. To format the data axis, select Data Axis from the Chart menu. Select Number Format from the submenu to display the Numeric dialog box. The Numeric dialog box is the same one used to apply numeric formatting to data in the Data Manager. Select the desired formatting option from the list of choices and click on OK. Select $#,##0, for example, to add currency symbols to the data axis. Refer to Chapter 3 for a thorough examination of all the formatting codes and options.

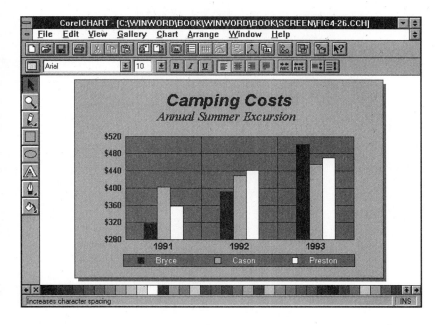

Figure 14.22
You can format the axes to display currency or other numeric formats.

Reversing Data Sets

There may be times when you need to reverse the order of the chart data. In the first chart in figure 14.23, for example, the data is displayed in the original order, while in the second chart, the data is reversed so the years appear chronologically backward and the order of the legend data is swapped. Rather than re-entering it in the Data Manager, CorelCHART! gives you an option to flip or reverse the data in Chart View. To reverse the chart data, select Data Reversal from the Chart menu. The submenu offers two options for reversing your data; Reverse Series and Reverse Groups. Choose Reverse Series to flip the order so that the first data series will be displayed last, and the last first. Choose Reverse Groups to swap the order of the categories on the X axis.

Figure 14.23
The Data Reversal
command
reverses the order
of data on the
category axis.

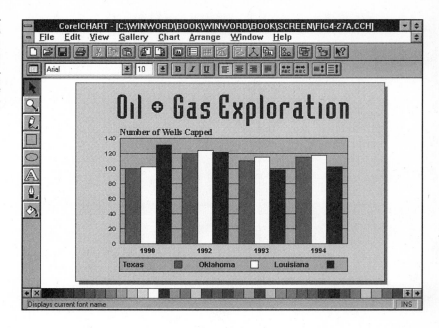

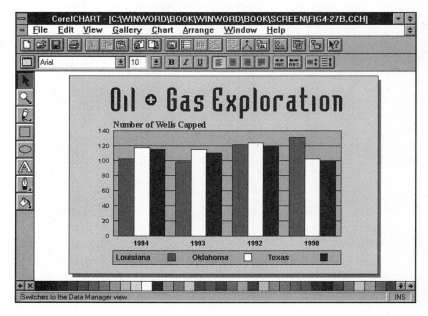

Note The Data Reversal and Data Analysis commands are not available for pie charts and some specialized chart types.

Using the Data Analysis Feature

CorelCHART! has tools to help you calculate and analyze statistical data in your chart. With the Data Analysis feature, you can quickly determine the mean, standard deviation, or averages for a set of data and then plot the figures as a line on your chart. The data analysis is done to one set of data at a time. In figure 14.24, the black line in the bar chart represents the mean sales for king-size beds. The white curved line represents the upward trend of queen-size bed sales throughout the year.

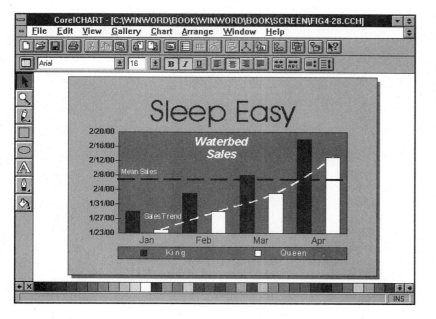

Figure 14.24
The Data Analysis command enables you to add (to your charts) lines representing means and trends.

To use the Analysis feature, select the bar, line, or area representing the series of data you want to calculate. Next, select Data Analysis from the **C**hart menu to display the Data Analysis dialog box as shown in figure 14.25. Select the desired type of data analysis and click on OK. For more information about CorelCHART!'s data analysis features, refer to online Help.

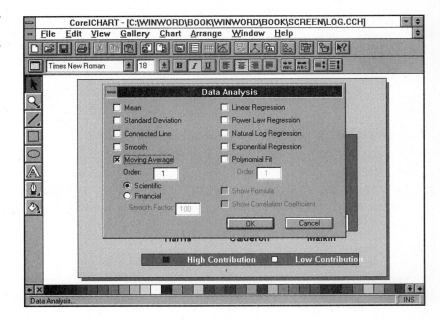

Figure 14.25
The Data Analysis
dialog box.

Formatting Charts

You will find that many of the previously discussed commands apply to most chart types. For instance, grid lines can be applied to all XY charts, including bar, line, and bubble charts. The Data Reversal and Data Analysis commands also are available in many chart types. However, there are a few commands that are specific to certain chart types. For example, you can only detach pie slices in a pie chart, and adjust the spacing between bars in a bar chart. The following sections discuss the special options and features for designing certain chart types. The chart types are alphabetized to make it easy for you to locate the options for each chart type.

Special Options for Bar Charts

Bar charts are ideal for examining and comparing data. In figure 14.26, for instance, the bar chart compares the voting habits of men and women. CorelCHART! provides many options for controlling the appearance of bar charts. CorelCHART! refers to the bars as "bar risers." The Chart menu offers a variety of options for designing bar charts, ranging from adjusting the bar thickness to selecting another riser shape.

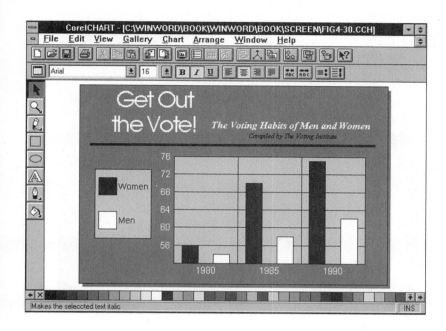

Figure 14.26
Example of a bar chart.

Emphasizing a Bar

You can change the color of one bar to focus special attention on that set of data. To change the color of one bar, select the bar and choose Emphasize Bar from the Chart menu. The emphasized bar is filled with gray. If desired, you can select a different color from the color palette.

Adjusting the Bar Thickness

Add extra flair to your bar charts by adjusting the thickness of the bars. Especially when working with two or three sets of data, widening the bars gives them more prominence on the chart. To control the bar thickness, select Bar Thickness from the Chart menu to reveal the submenu. You can preview each of the thickness options by pressing and holding the mouse button, and dragging down the list of choices. Release on the desired selection and your bars assume the specified thickness.

Adjusting the Bar to Bar Spacing

The Bar to Bar Spacing command enables you to control the amount of space between bars in the same category. Controlling the amount of space between bars can make charts much easier to read and interpret. As displayed in figure 14.27, "clustering" bars together helps the viewer distinguish between the skaters. To control the bar spacing, select Bar to Bar Spacing from the **C**hart menu to reveal the submenu. You can preview each of the spacing options by pressing and holding the mouse button, and dragging down the list of choices. Release the mouse button when you have reached the desired selection and your bars will assume the specified spacing.

Figure 14.27
Adjusting the spacing between bars helps the viewer separate and understand the chart data.

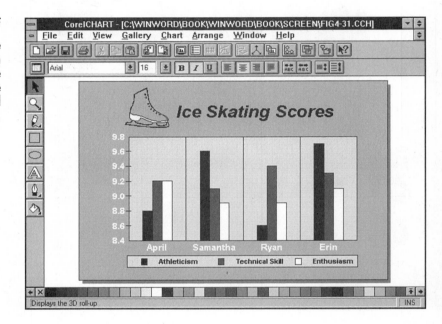

Changing the Marker Shape

By default, rectangular bars are used as the marker shapes. For special effects in your chart design, you can change the marker shape to circles, stars or some other graphic shape. For instance, in figure 14.28, a diamond shape is used to illustrate jewelry sales.

To choose another marker shape, select a bar riser from the data set you want to change. From the **C**hart menu, select Marker Shape. A submenu appears displaying the available graphic shapes. You can preview each of the shapes by pressing and holding the mouse button, and dragging down the choices. Release on the desired shape and the bars in the selected data set are changed.

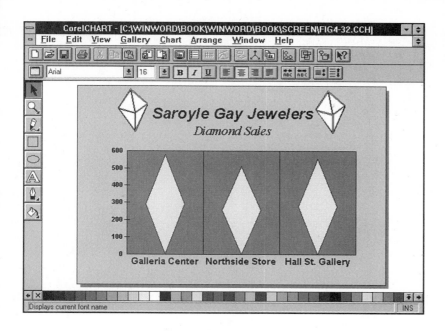

Figure 14.28
CorelCHART! enables you to change the marker shape in bar charts.

Creating Pictographs

The vertical height of the marker shapes represents the relative value of a specific set of data. Instead of stretching a single shape to illustrate the different data values, you can instruct CorelCHART! to stack the shapes as illustrated in figure 14.29. To stack the selected marker shapes, choose Show Pictograph from the Chart menu, or click on the Show Pictograph button.

In addition to stacking markers, you also can stack images from CorelDRAW! to create special effects. The CDR files or "pictographs" you select will replace the markers in a bar chart. For instance, in a chart documenting food sales at ball parks you could use hamburgers and hot dogs as pictographs. CorelCHART! includes templates for creating pictograph charts. They work basically the same as bar charts, except that the Show Pictograph command is already selected.

To change the markers in an existing chart to display with pictographs, turn on the Show As Pictograph command in the Chart menu. Next, click on the Fill tool to display the fly-out. Click again on the last button in the submenu to display the Pictograph Roll-Up as shown in figure 14.30. To import a CDR file as a pictograph, click on the Import button in the Pictograph Roll-Up. The Import Files dialog box appears. Change to the drive and directory where the file you want to import is located. Select the file name and click on OK. A preview of the file appears in the Pictograph Roll-Up. To display the image as a pictograph, select a bar riser from the data set you want changed and click on the Apply button. The bars are re-drawn with the selected CDR image.

Figure 14.29
Stacking Marker
Shapes with the
Show As
Pictograph
command.

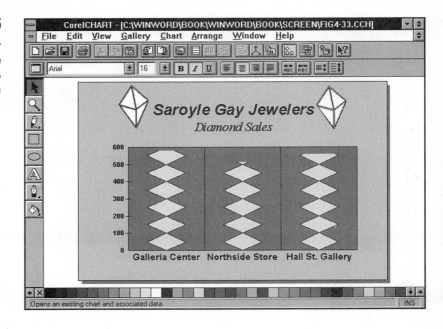

Figure 14.30
The Pictograph
Roll-Up menu.

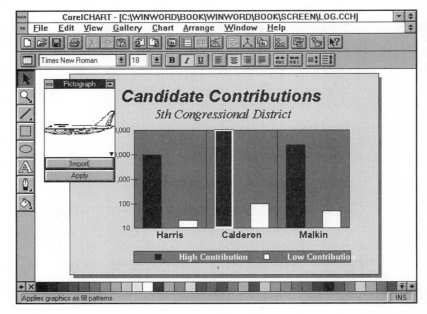

Using the Base of Bars Command

The Base of Bars command lets you adjust the data axis to begin scaling with the lowest number in the chart data, instead of zero. Select Base of Bars from the Chart menu, and select From Scale Minimum from the submenu. To reset the data axis to scale from zero, select From Zero Line from the Base of Bars submenu.

Note Area charts use the Base of Areas command to perform the same function as the Base of Bars command.

Displaying Data as a Line

In a bar chart, you can display one set of bars as a line to differentiate it from other chart data. For instance, in figure 14.31, the last set of data represents the average 200 meter sprint time. The average is displayed as a line to distinguish it from the other bars which represent individual sprint times. To display a series as a line, select a bar riser and choose Display as Line from the Chart menu.

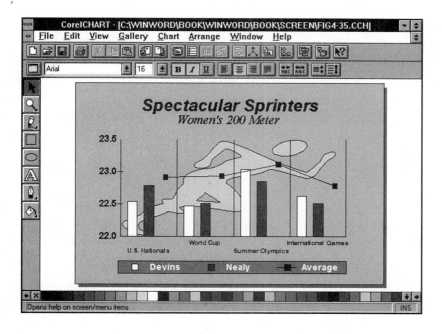

Figure 14.31
Displaying one series of data in a bar chart as a line.

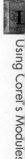

Special Options for High/Low/Open/Close Charts

High/low/open/close charts are typically associated with showing stock market buying trends. When building a high/low chart from CorelCHART!'s template, notice you can select a chart that displays just the high and low values, or one that displays the open and close values as well. As with bar charts, you can adjust the bar thickness in high/low charts. The steps for doing this are covered in the section "Special Options for Building Bar Charts." Unique to creating high/low/open/ close is the capability to adjust the width of the open and close markers.

To adjust the width of the open and close markers on a hi/lo chart, select Open and Close Width from the Chart menu. To preview the choices on the submenu, press and hold the left mouse button, then drag down the list of choices. Release on the desired selection and the markers assume the specified thickness.

Special Options for Histograms

A histogram plots the frequency of values within specified intervals. For instance, the histogram in figure 14.32 uses four intervals to demonstrate the frequency of cavities among 100 children. As with bar charts, you can change the bar/marker shape or stack graphic pictures in place of the bars to create a pictographic histogram. The steps for doing this are covered in the section "Special Options for Building Bar Charts." Unique to creating histograms is the capability to adjust the intervals against which the data is measured.

Figure 14.32
The interval axis can be adjusted to display the number of intervals you specify.

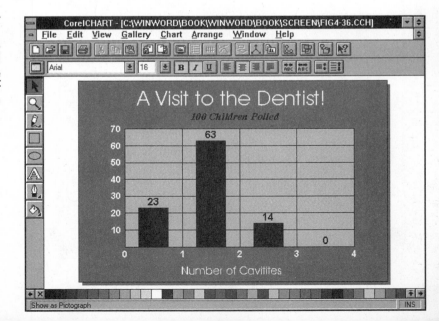

The interval axis in figure 14.32 is scaled in four intervals. You can customize the number of intervals to correspond with your chart data. Select Intervals from the <u>C</u>hart menu to display the Histogram Intervals dialog box shown in figure 14.33. Enter the desired amount of intervals in the text box. You can select the Automatic option to let CorelCHART! set the number of intervals. However, it might display more or fewer intervals than you need. You will find that setting your own number of intervals will produce the best results.

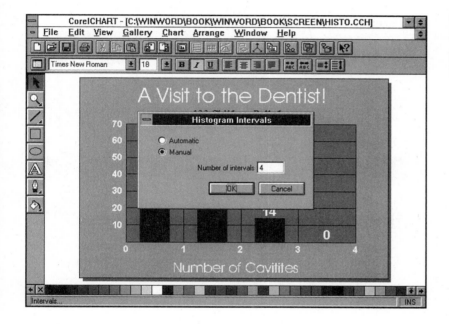

Figure 14.33
The Histogram Intervals dialog box.

Special Options for Line Charts

Line charts communicate relationships and trends. The line chart in figure 14.34 illustrates truck sales in Texas and Oklahoma. In line charts, small squares are placed on each data point in the line. These squares are called *markers*. In CorelCHART!, you can adjust the shape and size of the markers. In figure 14.34, the markers are displayed as triangular shapes.

Showing Markers

To turn off the display of the markers, select a line and choose Show Markers from the <u>C</u>hart menu. The markers for the selected line disappear.

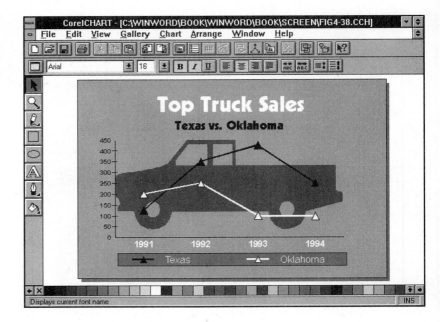

Changing the Marker Shape

By default, the marker shape is a small square. You can change the marker shape to circles, stars, or another graphic shape. To choose another marker shape, select a line and choose Marker Shape from the Chart menu. A submenu appears displaying the available graphic shapes. You can preview each of the shapes by pressing and holding the mouse button and dragging down the choices. Release the mouse button when you have reached the desired shape and the markers in the selected line are changed.

Controlling Marker Size

The size of the marker also can be adjusted. A larger marker shape can draw more attention to the lines in your chart. In a chart with many lines, however, you may want to reduce the marker size to eliminate clutter. To control the size of the markers, select a line and choose Marker Size from the Chart menu. A submenu appears displaying the available sizes. You can preview each of the sizes by pressing and holding the mouse button, and dragging down the choices. Release on the desired size and the markers in the selected line are changed.

Displaying Data as a Bar

In a line chart, you can display one set of data as a bar to differentiate it from other chart data. For instance, in a line chart illustrating cruise sales, the lines may represent the number of cruises sold, while the bars represent the revenue from the sales. To display a series as a bar, select a line, and choose <u>C</u>hart, Display as Bar.

Special Options for Building Pie Charts

Pie charts are simple, straightforward graphs that give you an immediate, intuitive sense of the proportions of the whole. As displayed in figure 14.35, pie charts can quickly show you which restaurant made the most milkshakes. Many designers enjoy working with the pie shape because the uncomplicated form makes it easy to adorn the chart with shadowing, tilting, and dimension.

Figure 14.35

Example of a pie chart.

Note This section discusses options for single pie charts. Most of the commands, however, also apply to ring and multiple pie charts.

Adjusting the Pie Tilt

Tilting the pie slightly backward adds an illusion of depth to your charts. To adjust the tilt of your pie chart, choose <u>C</u>hart, Pie Tilt. A submenu appears displaying the available tilt options. You can preview each of the options by pressing and holding the mouse button, and dragging down the choices. Release on the desired selection and your pie chart assumes the specified tilt. Keep in mind that while a slight tilt can add visual appeal, too much tilt can distort the shape of the slices and actually misrepresent your data. The slight tilt in figure 14.36 adds to the chart's overall appearance.

Figure 14.36
Pie tilt can be a subtle design element in pie charts.

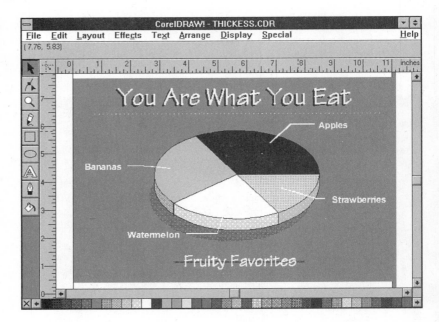

Adjusting the Pie Thickness

Controlling pie thickness is another way to add dimension and visual style to pie charts. As illustrated in figure 14.40, a thicker pie with just the right amount of tilt can make the chart appear as though you could almost reach out and grab it. To control the pie thickness, select Pie Thickness from the <u>C</u>hart menu to reveal the submenu. You can preview each of the thickness choices by pressing and holding the mouse button, and dragging down the list of choices. Release on the desired selection and your pie chart will assume the specified thickness.

Rotating the Pie

CorelCHART! places the slice for the first set of data at the top of the pie chart. If you think about the pie chart as a clock, the first set of data is placed at 3:00. The remaining sets of data wrap around the pie in a counter-clockwise fashion. With CorelCHART!, you can change the position of the pie slices by rotating the pie. To rotate the pie, select Pie Rotation from the **C**hart menu to reveal the submenu. A small preview of the pie chart appears at the top of the submenu, with the rotation choices listed beneath. As you drag through the rotation choices, watch the preview to indicate the amount of rotation. Release on the desired degree of rotation to rotate the slices of your pie chart.

Sizing the Pie

Depending on the length of the slice labels, you may want to reduce or enlarge the size of the pie. For instance, in figure 14.37, a smaller pie allows more room for the longer slice labels. On the other hand, with short slice labels, you may want to increase the size of the pie to add more impact to your chart. To size the pie, select Pie Size from the **C**hart menu to reveal the submenu. A small preview of the pie chart appears at the top of the submenu, with the size choices listed beneath. As you drag through the size choices, the preview will change representing the different pie sizes. Release on the desired pie size, and your pie chart assumes the specified size.

Figure 14.37
Consider the length of the slice labels when adjusting the pie size.

Using Corel's Modules

Note Another way to adjust the pie size is to size the chart frame. The size of the frame directly affects the size of the chart.

Controlling Slice Feeler Size

Slice feelers are the lines connecting the slice and the slice labels. CorelCHART! gives you control over the position, color, and line width of the feelers. As displayed in figure 14.38, the feelers are modified to begin deeper into the slice and end right outside of the slice to make more room for the slice labels.

Figure 14.38
CorelCHART!
gives you control
over the style and
location of the
slice feelers.

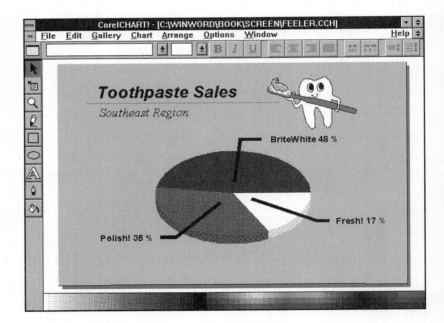

In a single pie chart you can adjust the position of all feelers at one time or each feeler individually. To adjust the position of one feeler it must be selected prior to selecting the Slice Feeler command, otherwise the changes will affect all slice feelers. In a multiple chart, your adjustments apply to all feelers in the same data series. To adjust the position of the slice feelers, select Slice Feeler Size from the Chart menu. The Slice Feeler Size dialog box appears (see fig. 14.39). The three black dots represent the points you can move to reposition the feeler. Drag the dots to change the length of each segment of the slice feelers. As you adjust the size of the feeler segments, the dialog box provides the horizontal orientation, feeler length and center distribution of the feeler.

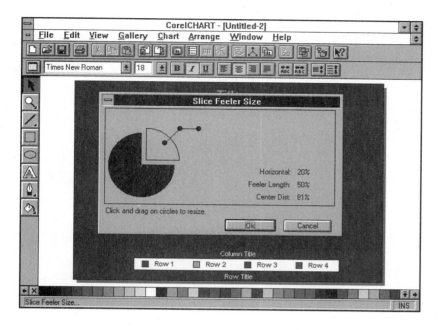

Figure 14.39
The Slice Feeler
Size dialog box.

You can change the color of the slice feelers by selecting one of the feelers and clicking with the right mouse button on the selected color in the color palette. To adjust the line width of the feelers, use the Outline tool. When you select this tool a fly-out menu appears with several preset line widths. To apply one of the preset widths, select a slice feeler and choose the desired thickness. All slice feelers must use the same line width and color. You can, however, draw a feeler with the Freehand tool and then format it to look at what you want. Refer to Chapter 7 for more information on using the Outline tool.

 Refer to the section "Displaying Chart Titles and Headings" for information on removing the slice feelers from the chart.

Detaching Pie Slices

Detaching or exploding a pie slice is a popular way to emphasize one set of data. As displayed in figure 14.40, the detached slice quickly becomes the dominant element as you examine and analyze the data. To detach a slice, select the slice you want detached (a selection outline will appear around the slice). Next, choose Detach Slice from the **C**hart menu to reveal the submenu. A small preview of the

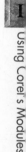

pie chart appears at the top of the submenu with a list of the detaching choices. As you drag through the choices, the preview will illustrate the different detaching options. Release on the desired detachment option and the selected slice will be detached. To rejoin the slice in the pie, select the detached slice and choose No Detachment from the Detach Slice submenu in the <u>C</u>hart menu.

Figure 14.40

Detached slices draw attention to certain sets of data

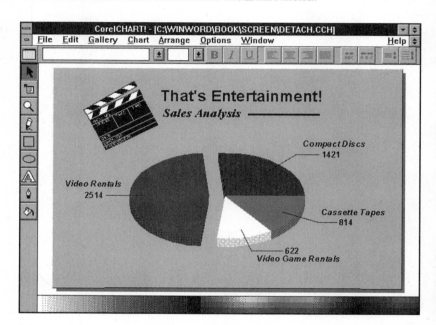

Deleting Pie Slices

To delete a pie slice, select the slice you want deleted and choose Delete Slice from the <u>C</u>hart menu. The slice is removed from the Chart View, but the data still appears in the Data Manager. To display the slice again, select Restore All Slices from the <u>C</u>hart menu.

You can delete slices to create build effects for presentations. For instance, the first chart could display a single slice, the next chart adds another slice and so on. Builds in CorelCHART! actually are created in reverse order of the way they are presented. First, create the chart as it will appear at the end of the build, with all slices displaying. Save the completed chart, delete a slice, and then save the chart file again under a different name. Next, delete another slice and save the file again. Repeat this procedure for each slice in the pie to create a build of pie slices for your presentation. Now when the charts are presented in the opposite order that you created them, the slices "build" to create the pie chart.

Adjusting the Pies Per Row in Multiple Pie Charts

Multiple pies are used to compare how a set of data changes over different periods of time. The chart in figure 14.41 provides a quick look at how advertising expenses have increased over the last four years. You can control the number of pies that display on each row. With six pies, for instance, you could place three on the top and three on the bottom. For charts with an uneven number of pies, you can't place more pies on the bottom row. That is, you can't place two pies on top and three on the bottom. Further, regardless of the number of pies on the bottom row, they always left align.

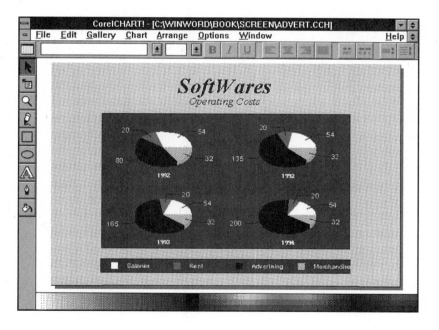

Figure 14.41
Multiple pie chart examining operating expenses over a four-year period.

To control the number of pies per row, select Pies Per Row from the <u>C</u>hart menu. The Pies Per Row dialog box appears. Enter the amount of pies you want displayed per row and click on OK.

Special Options for Spectral Maps

Spectral maps are specialized charts that indicate how a variable changes over a geographic area. Demographers, for example, might employ spectral maps to convey the increasing population growth in suburban areas. As with bar charts, you can adjust or reverse the data sets, and change the marker shape. The steps for doing this are covered in the section "Special Options for Building Bar Charts." Unique to creating spectral maps is the capability to change the range of colors used to generate the chart.

As illustrated in figure 14.42, the colors gradually change in a spectral map to illustrate the relationship between the values. The viewer understands that a great change in color denotes a great change in the chart values. To specify the colors used in the spectral map, select Spectrum from the Chart menu to display a submenu. Select Spectrum again to display the Color Range dialog box. This box lets you select the starting and ending colors for the blend in the spectrum. Click on the Start button and select a color, then repeat the same steps with the End button. The default number of divisions is 20, enter a different amount to create a rougher (fewer divisions) or smoother (more divisions) blend. When finished, click on OK to change the colors used in the spectral map.

Figure 14.42
The changes in color facilitate relationships and comparisons in spectral maps.

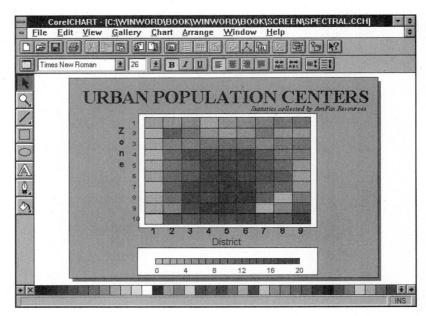

Special Options for Table Charts

Use a table chart when you have data that cannot be sufficiently expressed in a chart. In figure 14.43, the table details how many video games were sent to each city. This table chart provides the viewer with actual numerical values. Table charts consist of columns and rows. Every table chart has column headers in the top row, and row headers in the first column. Headers are generally used for table titles and headings. The intersection of a column and row is a cell. Data appears in the cells in the table, similar to how data appears in cells in the Data Manager.

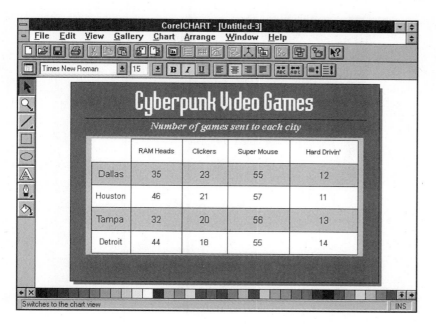

Figure 14.43
Table charts are
a great way to
present textual
data.

Adjusting the Table Divisions

Table charts can be designed with color divisions by row, column, or with no color divisions at all. Figure 14.46 shows a table chart with color division by rows. Notice how the alternating shades of gray on the rows assist the viewer in reading the table. To control the color divisions in a table chart, select Divisions from the Chart menu. The Table Chart Divisions dialog box as shown in figure 14.44 appears.

Click in the first check box, No Color Divisions, to use the same color in the whole table except the column and row headers. Click in the Color by Rows option to alternate colors from row to row. Click the Color by Columns option to alternate colors from column to column. By default, the header cells appear in a different color than the row or column data. To make the headers the same color as the columns or row, click on the Include Headers feature.

By default, the colors alternate every other row. You can enter a new number in the Number of rows per color text box to control the number of contiguous rows or columns you want to have the same color. For instance, if the number of rows per color option is set at 2, the color alternates between every two rows. When finished making selections, click on OK.

Figure 14.44
The Table Chart
Divisions dialog
box.

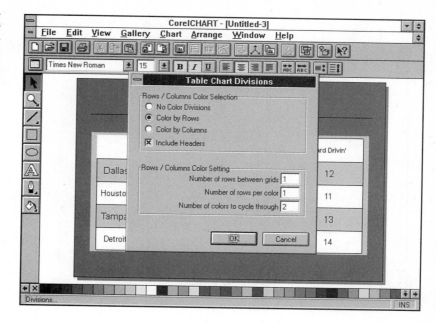

Changing Row or Column Colors

To change a row or column color, select a cell in the row or column you want to change. The cell displays a white border when selected. Click on the desired color in the color palette and the corresponding row or column colors are changed. Make sure you have the cell selected, not the text inside the cell. If you have the text selected, you will change the color of all the text, not the cell background.

Using the Grids and Borders Command

The Grids and Borders command enables you to adjust the display of the table grids and borders. Select Grids and Borders from the Chart menu to display the Grids and Borders dialog box as shown in figure 14.45. Use the grid matrix to control the display of various parts of the grid. Click with your mouse on whatever part of the grid you want to turn on or off. After making the desired selections, click on OK to view your choices. Even though the Grids and Borders dialog box enables you to turn off the display of grid lines between the columns and rows, they will still appear when you view the chart. To remove grid lines, select the line and choose the X in the Outline Tool fly-out.

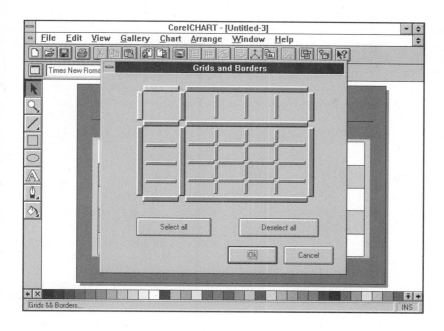

Figure 14.45
The Grids and
Borders dialog
box.

Formatting Table Text

CorelCHART!'s Autofit Table command automatically sizes the table text according to the data you enter. You will need to turn off the Autofit Table option before changing the size of table text. To turn off the Autofit Text feature, select Autofit Table from the <u>C</u>hart menu. The feature is turned off when there is no check mark by the command. Now, select a text string and choose a new type size from the type size list box at the top of the screen.

Adjusting Column Width and Row Height

The Autofit Table command discussed in the previous section also automatically adjusts the width of the columns in your table. When the Autofit Table feature is on, CorelCHART! examines the text entered in the Data Manager, and adjusts the column widths accordingly. For instance, a column containing the word "Computer" would be wider than a column containing the word "PC". The Autofit Text option also forces each row to be the same height, regardless of the amount of text entered in the Data Manager.

Turn off the Autofit Table command to make all of the columns the same width. The Uniform Cell Width and Uniform Cell Height commands become available when Autofit Text is turned off. If your table is set up with color division by columns, the width of the columns is controlled by the size of the text in the columns. The smaller the text, the narrower the columns. When the size of the text is changed, the column width will adjust to fit. The height of the rows is also based on the size of the text in the rows. The smaller the text, the shorter the row will need to be. As you enlarge the text, the row height will be increased to accommodate the text. Select Uniform Cell Height to instruct all rows to conform to the height of the tallest row.

Special Options for 3D Charts

3D charts essentially are bar charts with a third dimension, a Z axis, added to give the chart the illusion of depth. As shown in figure 14.46, X, Y and Z axes are used to plot the chart data. CorelCHART! provides extensive flexibility for modifying the dimensional aspect of 3D charts. Many of the options for formatting bar charts also apply to 3D riser charts, such as working with grid lines and changing the marker shape. Refer to the section "Special Options for Bar Charts" for more information.

Figure 14.46
3D charts use X, Y, and Z axes to plot the chart data.

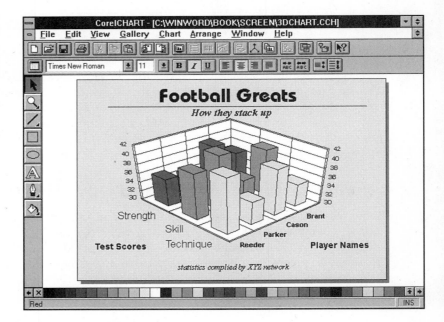

Adjusting the Viewing Angle

To adjust the viewing angle of your chart, choose Preset Viewing Angles from the Chart menu. From the submenu, you can choose from several different viewing aspects. To preview the choices, press and hold the left mouse button, then drag down the list of choices. Release on the desired selection, and your chart is redrawn accordingly.

Manipulating Riser Sizing

Select the Riser Sizing command from the **C**hart menu to adjust the size of the riser. The submenu offers several sizing options. To preview the choices, press and hold the left mouse button, then drag down the list of choices. Release on the desired selection, and your chart is redrawn accordingly.

Using the 3D Roll-Up

You can use the 3D Roll-Up to alter, adjust, and manipulate the dimensional aspect of 3D charts. Choose **3**D Roll-Up from the **V**iew menu to access the roll-up as shown in figure 14.47. The roll-up has four buttons for manipulating the chart dimension. Clicking on each button in the roll-up reveals different tools with red arrow tips for modifying the chart. Press and hold on the red arrow tips to manipulate the chart. Click on the first button to move the chart. Click on the second button to adjust the size and perspective of the chart. Click on the third button to change the axis length, and modify the thickness of chart floor or walls. Click on the fourth button to rotate the chart. As you adjust the chart's display, an outline of the chart displays as a reference point. Release the mouse button when you have positioned the chart outline where you want. After making changes in the roll-up, click on the Redraw button to display the changes or the Undo button to return the chart to its original shape and location.

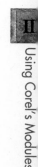

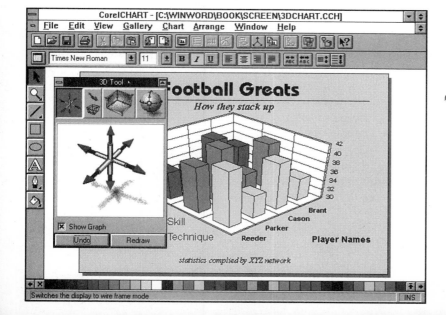

Figure 14.47
The 3D Roll-Up.

II

Using Corel's Modules

Applying Shading Effects

Much of the illusion of dimension with 3D charts can be attributed to shading effects. Think of shading as a light source hitting the chart, making some parts of the object appear lighter, and other parts darker. CorelCHART! gives you control over the shading on your chart. Choose AutoShade Cube from the <u>C</u>hart menu to make it look as though light is striking the chart floor and walls. Choose AutoShade Risers to create the effect of a light source illuminating the riser bars in the 3D chart. Click to remove the check marks and disable these features if you wish to apply fountain or patterned fills to the risers or walls on the chart.

Most of the commands covered in this chapter are only one mouse click away. By clicking the right mouse button you will reveal a pop-out menu that will show a list of commands pertaining to the type of chart that you are creating.

Transferring Data and Printing Charts

After you have designed all of these fabulous charts, there's no doubt you will want to use the charts in other applications. You might want to place a chart in a brochure created in CorelDRAW! or an annual report assembled in CorelVENTURA!. On the flip side, you might want to bring graphics created in CorelDRAW! or CorelPHOTO-PAINT! into CorelCHART!. Think of sharing or transferring data between applications as a two-way street. You can transfer data into CorelCHART! and you can transfer charts into other applications.

This section discusses the variety of methods for transferring data between CorelCHART! and other applications: drag and drop, copy and paste through the Windows Clipboard, and import and export files. The examples pertain to transferring data between Corel applications. However, you also can transfer data from other applications such as Word for Windows and Excel. Refer to the software documentation for more information. The section concludes with a look at the options and features for previewing and printing your chart files.

Copying Charts to Other Applications

To copy a chart into another Windows application, select Copy Chart from the Edit menu. This command copies all chart elements, including the background, to the Windows Clipboard so that you can paste the chart into another Windows application. After switching to the application where you want to display the chart, choose Edit, Paste.

 CorelCHART! supports Object Linking and Embedding, or OLE, which provides options for updating the chart after you have pasted it into another program. Object Linking and Embedding is a powerful way to share data between all Corel applications. For more information on OLE, refer to Chapter 26, "Understanding CorelDRAW! Filters."

Using Drag and Drop

Drag and drop is the quickest way to place a CorelCHART! file into another program. You can drag and drop a whole chart, but not its individual parts, into other applications. Drag and drop creates an embedded object in the receiving or client application. Not all Windows applications can receive charts in this manner. Check the applications documentation for information on Object Linking and Embedding. The following steps illustrate how to drag and drop a chart from CorelCHART! into CorelDRAW!

1. Size the CorelCHART! Chart View window and the CorelDRAW! window so that you can see both on your computer screen (see fig. 14.48).

2. Press and hold the mouse button anywhere in the Chart View.

3. Drag the pointer from the Chart View window to the CorelDRAW! window.

4. When the cursor becomes a blinking white arrow, release the mouse button to "drop" the data into the CorelDRAW! window.

Figure 14.48
Use the drag and
drop method to
quickly transfer a
chart into
CorelDRAW!.

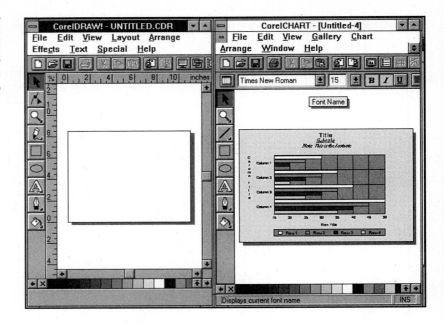

Using Cut, Copy, and Paste
To Transfer Data

The Cut, Copy, and Paste commands work just like they do in other Windows
applications. As displayed in figure 14.49, the CorelCHART! Ribbon Bar provides
buttons for cutting, copying, and pasting data. There is one difference with
CorelCHART!. Only annotated text and objects can be cut or copied to the
Clipboard. Individual chart elements such as titles, chart frames, or legends cannot
be cut or copied to the Clipboard.

The following steps illustrate transferring a graphic in CorelDRAW! to
CorelCHART!.

1. In CorelDRAW!, select the object(s) to be transferred, and choose
   Edit, Copy or click on the Copy button.

2. Switch to CorelCHART! and open the file where you want the graphic
   displayed.

3. Then choose **E**dit, **P**aste or click on the Paste button. The graphic is pasted on the chart. The pasted object can be moved and sized. However, you cannot change any object attributes, such as colors or fonts. If you want to alter the graphic, return to CorelDRAW!, make the changes and then repeat the steps for copying and pasting the object back into CorelCHART!.

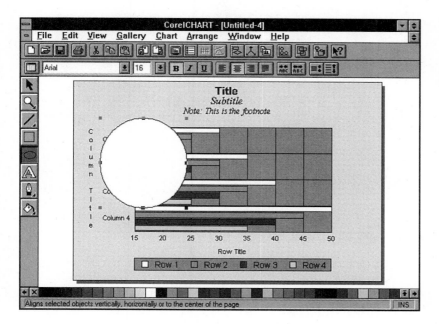

Figure 14.49
The Cut, Copy, and Paste buttons in the Ribbon Bar.

Data can be copied from the Data Manager in one chart file to the Data Manager in another. Refer to Chapter 3 for more information about Data Manager.

For special effects, you might try the Paste Inside command to paste graphics into the chart frame as shown in figure 14.50. After copying the desired graphic to the Clipboard, select the chart frame, and choose **E**dit, Paste **I**nside. The pasted graphic replaces the chart frame. It's important to note that the pasted graphic will be distorted to fit the frame size.

Figure 14.50
The Paste Inside command enables you to paste graphics inside the chart frame.

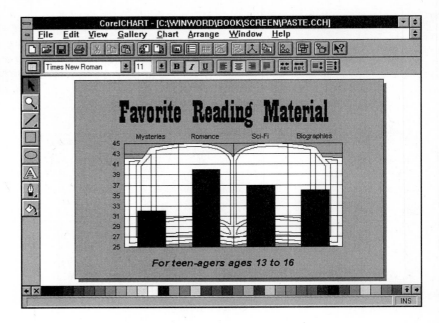

Importing Graphics

CorelCHART!'s import function gives you access to graphics created by other illustration and presentation programs, as well as clip art and scanned images. A scanned map, for instance, can be imported into a CorelCHART! file. The following steps illustrate importing a TIFF scanned image.

1. Select File, Import or click on the Import button. The Import dialog box as displayed in figure 14.51 appears.

2. Click on the down arrow by List Files of Type and choose TIFF Bitmap.

3. Change to the drive and directory and locate the file you want to import.

4. In the File Name box, select the file you want to import and click on OK. The imported TIFF file can be moved as desired.

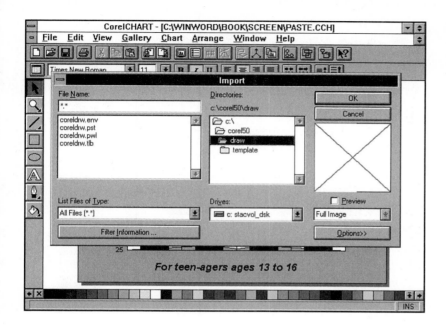

Figure 14.51
The Import
dialog box.

CorelCHART!'s Import and Export features work the same as CorelDRAW!'s. Refer to Chapter 26 for more information.

Exporting Charts

CorelCHART!'s Export feature saves the chart file in a file format that another application can read. For instance, you can export the chart to a Windows Metafile (WMF) file and then import the WMF into another application such as Aldus PageMaker or QuarkXpress. The following steps illustrate the steps for exporting a CorelCHART! file into the Windows Metafile format.

1. Choose File, Export or click on the Export Data button on the Ribbon Bar. The Export dialog box as displayed in figure 14.52 appears.

Figure 14.52

The Export dialog box.

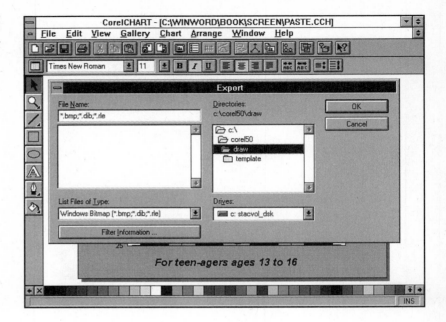

2. Click on the down arrow by List Files of **T**ype and choose Windows Metafile.

3. Change to the drive and directory where the file you want to save the exported file is.

4. In the File **N**ame box, enter a file name for the exported data. CorelCHART! automatically adds the correct file extension, such as WMF for Windows Metafiles. Click OK and the export file is created.

Printing Charts

All graphic designers know that the hard work put into designing graphics doesn't amount to much until it's printed and all the world can stand in awe of your talent. There are essentially two things that will direct the process of printing your charts. The first consideration is the type of media for your finished piece. Are you creating a 35mm slide, 4 × 5 film, or a black-and-white overhead transparency? Second, is the printing being done in-house, or are the chart files being sent to a service bureau for high-resolution output? The answers to these questions determine how you will proceed through the printing process. If your final output will be an overhead transparency printed on the Laserwriter at your desk, for example, you'll be managing the whole print job yourself. If the final output is a 35 mm slide, you can send the file to a service bureau where they will direct the printing.

This section covers basic printing features and options for printing charts in CorelCHART!. Because most of the printing features in CorelCHART! are identical to CorelDRAW!, they are discussed at length in Chapter 21, "Managing Color and System Calibration." The options for printing chart data in the Data Manager are detailed in Chapter 13, "Designing a Chart."

Designing in color when the output device is black and white can be frustrating because the conversion from color to black and white is unpredictable. You are better off to work with shades of gray when designing your charts to ensure that what you see is really what you get.

Setting Up the Printer

It's always smart to check the printer setup before printing to determine if the right printer, orientation, and paper size is selected. Like all Windows applications, CorelCHART! uses the printer drivers installed when you loaded Windows. To select a printer, choose File, Print Setup. The Print Setup dialog box appears displaying the current printer. If you want to print to another device, click on the down arrow by the printer's name. Select the desired printing device from the list of available printers. Click on the Setup button to display a dialog box with options for controlling page orientation and paper size. Click on OK in the Setup dialog box to return to the Print Setup dialog box. Click on OK again to setup the specified printer.

Printing Charts

To print a chart, open the file you want to print in the Chart View and select File, Print or click on the Print button. The Print dialog box appears. You can only print one chart file at a time in CorelCHART!, so the options, All and Current Page produce the same output—one printed chart. Unlike CorelDRAW!, you cannot print only selected objects in CorelCHART!.

Press Ctrl+P on your keyboard to access the Print dialog box.

Because you can only print one file at a time in CorelCHART!, you might find it easier to insert the charts into a CorelSHOW! presentation, and then print the presentation. Refer to Chapter 16, "Using CorelSHOW!," for more information on inserting charts into CorelSHOW!.

CorelCHART! can print up to 999 copies of your file. To change the number of copies, simply enter the desired number of copies in the Copies text box. If you are sending the chart file to be output at a service bureau, you may need to click on the Print to File option to create a "print" file. (Refer to Chapter 11, "Basic Printing Techniques," for more information on printing to file.)

To preview the chart before printing, click on the Options button. The Print Options dialog box appears (see fig 14.53). To preview your chart, click on the Preview Image option in the bottom left of the dialog box. The Print Options dialog box contains the options for adjusting the print image, such as Center and Fit to Page. At the top of the dialog box, click on the "tabs" marked Separations and Options to create color separations, and control fountain steps and curves. Refer to Chapter 11 for more of an in-depth discussion of these features. Click OK to return to the Print dialog box. After selecting the desired print options, click on OK to print the chart file. A status bar indicates the progress of the print job. Click on the Cancel button to terminate the print job.

Figure 14.53
The Print Options
dialog box.

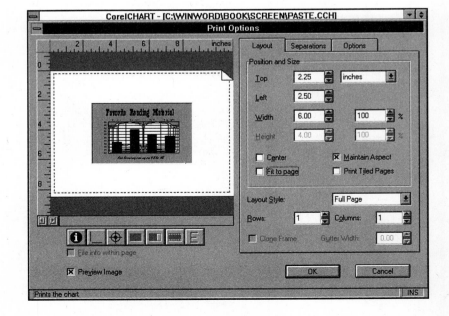

Chapter Snapshot

CorelTRACE! is a powerful utility in the CorelDRAW! suite of programs that enables you to convert bitmap images that include scanned clip art and photos into illustrations that you can can edit. In this chapter, you learn how to:

- ✔ Perform a basic trace
- ✔ Save your default TRACE settings
- ✔ Become familiar with the tracing options
- ✔ Use the OCR tracing method to scan text
- ✔ Tips for creating better traces

With CorelTRACE!, sketches, photographs, and even humble text become the raw materials for creating spectacular illustrations.

15

CHAPTER

Tracing Bitmap Images

CorelTRACE! is a powerful utility in the CorelDRAW! suite of programs that enables you to convert bitmaps that include scanned clip art and photos into CorelDRAW!-editable illustrations. With the click of a button, CorelTRACE! can save you hours of tedious work. This chapter describes what CorelTRACE! does, how to make easy "click and go" traces, and continues on to detail professional-level customizations to get just the look you are searching for.

CorelTRACE! does much more than simply trace bitmaps. You can easily turn photos and scanned clipart into very unusual looking pictures. For example, CorelTRACE!'s Woodcut feature makes clipart look like it was printed with an inked, wood-engravers block. CorelTRACE!'s Outline trace feature can quickly turn a scanned engineering drawing into an editable picture ready for further work. Tracing a photo and experimenting with CorelTRACE!'s various settings can make a strong, attention-getting graphic illustration. You can even use CorelTRACE!'s OCR (Optical Character Recognition) engine to convert scanned documents into text that is editable by your word processor.

Don't let CorelTRACE!'s simple interface fool you into thinking that it is a rudimentary little utility—it has features that most CorelDRAW! users never explore. This chapter takes you on a tour of these features, beginning with a description of how it works. You'll work through an example using CorelTRACE!'s easy-to-use default settings, and progress into advanced techniques for getting the most from CorelTRACE!. Most of the bitmap files used in this chapter are included on the *Inside CorelDRAW! 5, Fifth Edition CD-ROM* so that you can follow the examples using your own computer.

The Power of CorelTRACE!

CorelTRACE! is the bridge between the world of bitmapped pictures and CorelDRAW!. Bitmaps include scanned photographs, line art, and pictures from paint programs. While these bitmap images may be directly imported into Draw as components of a design, CorelDRAW! is primarily a vector illustration program. Therefore, you have limited control over how the imported images look.

Bitmaps are comprised of rows and columns of pixels (or picture elements) that make up an image. The pixels in a bitmap can be just black or white, different shades of gray, or different colors. The grid of rows and columns making up a bitmap is created at some fixed size; however, all bitmaps show the "jaggies" when enlarged enough.

By contrast, vector pictures are comprised of mathematical equations of lines and shapes that are infinitely scalable, always printing at the top resolution of the printing device. As a result, vector images provide smooth outlines and even fills in your illustrations. This is one advantage that illustration programs like CorelDRAW! have over bitmap (paint) programs.

CorelTRACE! converts bitmaps into fully editable vector shapes so that you can work with all of CorelDRAW!'s tools for creating unique designs. After conversion to vector art using CorelTRACE!, the artwork can be enlarged without worrying about the jaggies. See figure 15.1 for a comparison between an enlarged section of a bitmap and a traced line.

In a sense, CorelTRACE! imitates the familiar method of using tracing paper and a pencil over an existing picture to create a drawing. CorelTRACE! finds the shapes in a bitmap by searching for the boundary between light and dark pixels. Wherever a boundary is found, CorelTRACE! draws a vector line.

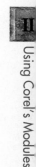

Figure 15.1
The bitmap
(shown in gray)
shows "jaggies"
when enlarged,
while the traced
lines remain
smooth.

Getting Acquainted with CorelTRACE!

CorelTRACE! has a split window interface that lets you see the bitmap to be traced in the left half, and a view of the resulting trace on the right. A Ribbon Bar at the top of the screen contains icons for quickly choosing different actions, while the Toolbox on the left side holds various selection and viewing tools. Figure 15.2 shows the CorelTRACE! screen open and ready for work and figure 15.3 depicts the buttons on the Ribbon Bar located near the top of the CorelTRACE! screen.

The buttons on the Ribbon Bar make choosing various tracing options a one-click task. Represented are buttons for tracing outlines, tracing centerlines, forms tracing, woodcut tracing, and more. Common file management tasks are included as buttons, too. Table 15.1 lists all file management and tracing options available from the Ribbon Bar.

Using Corel's Modules

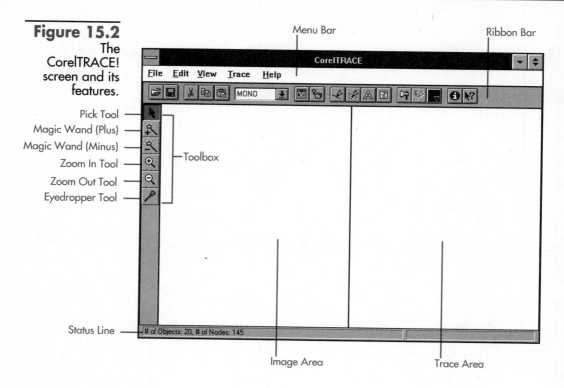

Figure 15.2
The CorelTRACE! screen and its features.

Menu Bar

Ribbon Bar

Pick Tool
Magic Wand (Plus)
Magic Wand (Minus)
Zoom In Tool
Zoom Out Tool
Eyedropper Tool

Toolbox

Status Line — # of Objects: 20, # of Nodes: 145

Image Area

Trace Area

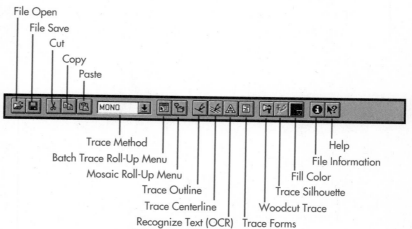

Figure 15.3
CorelTRACE!'s version 5 expanded Ribbon Bar.

File Open
File Save
Cut
Copy
Paste

Trace Method
Batch Trace Roll-Up Menu
Mosaic Roll-Up Menu
Trace Outline
Trace Centerline
Recognize Text (OCR)
Trace Forms
Woodcut Trace
Trace Silhouette
Fill Color
File Information
Help

Table 15.1
Buttons on CorelTRACE!'s Ribbon Bar

Button Name	Purpose
File Open	Displays the File Open dialog box.
File Save	Saves a tracing.
Cut	Cuts CorelTRACE! output to clipboard and clears the trace screen.
Copy	Copies CorelTRACE! output to clipboard, leaves traced image intact.
Paste	Pastes a previously copied bitmap in as a source image.
Trace Method	Selects the Trace Method from a drop-down list.
Batch Trace Roll-Up	Opens the Batch Trace Roll-Up to add files for unattended tracing of multiple files.
Mosaic Roll-Up	Opens CorelMosaic for file viewing.
Trace Outline	Traces the outlines of pixels in the source image, and fills closed shapes. The most common tracing mode.
Trace Centerline	Finds thin lines in source image and renders them as lines instead of thin closed shapes.
Recognize Text (OCR)	Finds and recognizes text in a scanned document.
Trace Forms	Traces lines in a scanned form and also recognizes any included text.
Woodcut Trace	Traces shapes using a woodcut engraving effect.
Trace Silhouette	Traces only the outside shape of an object and ignores interior detail.

Using Corel's Modules

continues

Table 15.1, Continued
Buttons on CorelTRACE!'s Ribbon Bar

Button Name	Purpose
Fill Color	Fills traced selection with a custom color. Works only with silhouette, woodcut, or with custom selections.
File Information	View source image information.
Help	View CorelTRACE! Help.

Table 15.2 describes the available tools from the Toolbox on the left side of the CorelTRACE! screen. They are listed in order from the top to the bottom of the CorelTRACE! Toolbox.

Table 15.2
The Tools in CorelTRACE!'s Toolbox

Tool	Purpose
Pick tool	Selects a rectangular area for tracing from the source image.
Magic Wand (Plus)	Selects an area for tracing based on color similarity in the source bitmap.
Magic Wand (Minus)	Deselects an area in the source image.
Zoom In tool	Magnifies an area of the source bitmap.
Zoom Out tool	Zooms back out.
Eyedropper tool	Samples a small area of the source image to set fill color. Useful with grayscale/color images.

Which File Formats Are Supported?

CorelTRACE! can read many different bitmap formats, including Windows bitmaps (BMP, DIB, RLE), CompuServe GIF files (GIF), JPEG compressed bitmaps (JPG, JFF, CMP), Kodak Photo CD files (PCD), Paintbrush format (PCX), Scitex

CT bitmaps (CT), Targa bitmaps (TGA, VDA, ICB, VST), and the popular Tagged Image File Format (TIF). If you have a scanner with a TWAIN driver, you can even scan directly into CorelTRACE! to save time.

CorelTRACE! saves traced files in only one format—EPS. These vector-format EPS files are imported into a CorelDRAW! file for further editing. Also, they can be placed directly into a word processor or page layout program for printing to a PostScript language printer. EPS files do not print to non-PostScript printers, however.

CorelTRACE! version 5 is an incremental improvement over version 4. Notably, the Tracing Options dialog box (choose **T**race, **E**dit Options...) now sports the "tabbed notebook" look to make changing trace settings easier.

CorelTRACE! still handles line art, grayscale, and color bitmaps with aplomb, and still offers a variety of tracing modes including Woodcut and OCR that were introduced with CorelTRACE! version 4. Before the major overhaul that distinguished CorelTRACE! 4 from older versions, Adobe's Streamline autotrace program was a part of every serious illustrator's arsenal. Now, Streamline's power is matched in nearly every area except speed, and surpassed in function by the many special features found in CorelTRACE!.

Quick Tracing with Defaults

CorelTRACE!'s default settings produce usable traces without much fuss or bother. The following steps can render most line-art bitmaps into EPS files that you can import into CorelDRAW! for editing. Be sure to save any open work in other programs that you might have running before trying to trace a bitmap. Bitmaps opened in Trace can be large enough to exceed your system's capabilities, potentially causing problems.

If you "get lost in the icons," CorelTRACE! has descriptions of the Ribbon Bar functions on the status line at the screen bottom. Place your cursor over a button for a couple of seconds and read the description that appears at the bottom. The expanded Ribbon Bar permits quick access to more options than before. **H**elp is now context sensitive—click once on the **H**elp button on the Ribbon Bar and then click again on the menu item or button that you would like explained.

Performing a Basic Trace

Double click on the Corel 5 *program group in Program Manager*

The Corel 5 program group window opens

continues

Using Corel's Modules

continued

Double click on the CorelTRACE! *icon*	Starts CorelTRACE!
Click on File	The File menu appears
Click on Open *(or press Ctrl+O)*	The Open dialog box appears

Navigate to the directory that contains the bitmap.

Click the down arrow of List Files of type	A list of file extension filters appears
Click on Paintbrush (*.PCX)	Available PCX format files show
Click on POSEYS.PCX	A thumbnail preview appears if the review box is checked (see fig. 15.4)
Click on OK	The file loads into the left window of Trace
Click the Trace Edges button	Tracing begins and displays in the right window (see fig. 15.5)
Click on File	The File menu appears
Click on Save Trace	The file is saved as C:/POSEYS.EPS

Figure 15.4
The Open dialog box displays thumbnails of selected files if **P**review is checked.

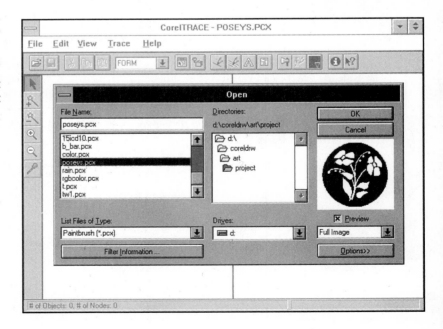

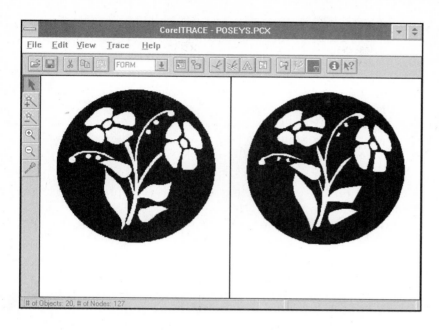

Figure 15.5
CorelTRACE!
displays the
original bitmap
on the left and
the resulting
traced image on
the right.

Now import the trace in CorelDRAW! for editing. Any missing lines or parts of the illustration that didn't get traced can be fixed. Best of all, you have the full power of CorelDRAW! available for creative coloring and shaping and all the other things Draw can do. If you want, add text and POSEYS becomes a new logo for the flower shop down the street.

Sometimes Trace turns short curved lines into straight lines, but a little node editing in Draw can fix that easily.

If you feel that your mouse hinders your creative freedom in CorelDRAW!, then draw your designs on paper the "old-fashioned" way and scan them for tracing. It is easy to embellish napkin sketches so that they result in finished illustrations using the powerful team of CorelDRAW! and CorelTRACE!. Remember too that using a TWAIN compatible scanner from within Trace makes scanning your hand-created art a snap.

The brief example above only hints at the versatility of CorelTRACE!. It can trace line art, color photos, engineering drawings, and produce a wide variety of differing effects. For example, a color photograph can be rendered in only black and white if you wish, or an engineering drawing can be rendered as true lines instead of filled shapes.

Tracing Outlines

Outline tracing is the default tracing method used by CorelTRACE!. Choosing Trace, Outline finds the outline of various shapes in the bitmap picture, or, as a shortcut, you can click on the Ribbon Bar showing a pencil and a single line. When finding outlines, Trace looks at the pixels that comprise the picture and follows the border between light and dark pixels. In color photos, it finds the border where different colors meet. You even control how accurately Trace follows the contours of the bitmap to achieve special graphics effects if desired.

Outline tracing produces a file having a series of closed and filled vector shapes that represent the picture. In most cases, this is the best way to reproduce your bitmap. The traced picture is actually a collage of overlapping, filled shapes that can be rearranged, resized, and recolored once the traced picture is imported into CorelDRAW!.

If you explore the Edit Options dialog box in the Trace menu, you will see CorelTRACE!'s new tabbed notebook metaphor that makes customizing options a snap. In the dialog box, you will see headings named Image, Color, Lines, Woodcut, and OCR, each of which contains several different options for customizing your trace. Each of these options is described in the following sections, and selected examples show what effect some of the more important choices have.

Protecting Your Default Settings

Before you begin to experiment with the default settings in the Tracing Options dialog box, make sure that you don't modify the original settings for the MONO, DITHERED, FORM, and COLOR trace configurations. These default files are configured to give optimum results for most work, but are too easy to accidentally change using the Edit Options dialog box. In particular, OCR is especially sensitive to changes made to the default settings.

Various trace configurations available in CorelTRACE! are saved in separate files named MONO.CTR, DITHERED.CTR, COLOR.CTR, and FORM.CTR in the Trace subdirectory. You can change the attributes of the files to read only using Windows File Manager as listed in the steps below.

Safeguard Your Defaults Using Read Only Attributes

Double-click on the File Manager *icon*   File Manager starts

Navigate to the CorelTRACE! subdirectory

Click on the file MONO.CTR	MONO.CTR is selected
Click on File, Properties	The Properties dialog box appears
Click on Read Only in Attributes	The box is checked
Click on OK	The file is now protected from accidental change

Repeat the steps above for DITHERED.CTR, COLOR.CTR, and FORM.CTR.

If you assigned the read-only attribute to the files, they can't be changed in CorelTRACE!. It will appear that you are making changes to the defaults, but they won't "stick" and then return to the default settings when you click on Save. If you want to use a custom trace setting, make the changes in the dialog box and save to a new file named "CUSTOM" or whatever you like.

Image Options

Figure 15.6 shows the Image options available in the Tracing Options dialog box. These options control how your trace is made. While the default options work for most situations, there are times when you have to adjust the default settings to obtain the results you desire. Because of CorelTRACE!'s split screen, you can see the results of a trace without having to leave the program. This makes experimentation with the various settings easy, and you can get just the right "look" to your trace in no time at all. Advanced users often tinker with the settings for artistic reasons. Read the following explanations to find out how each of the settings affects your trace.

Smooth Dithering

The first option check box, Smooth Dithering, gently blurs the halftone pattern of dithered images for better tracing. This is useful if you scan a printed image containing halftone color dots or if you are tracing a GIF format image that has dithered color. Because the GIF format is limited to 256 or fewer colors, many GIF images have dithered color to simulate other colors. In addition, many low-end scanners produce images that have few colors and dither the available hues to increase the number of apparent colors. Trace's Smooth Dithering option can be selected to improve the quality of the scan that results from these types of images. Smooth Dithering is turned on by default if you have the DITHERED configuration selected, but you can enable it for any custom trace configuration you want to create.

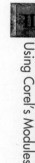

Using Corel's Modules

Figure 15.6
The Tracing
Options dialog
box showing the
Image settings.

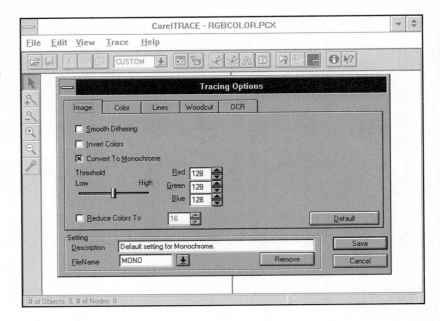

Invert Colors

Invert Colors changes black to white and vice versa. If you are using a color image, the colors invert too, appearing much like a negative for a color photograph. This is useful for some TWAIN interfaces (such as the Microtek TWAIN module for older 300Z scanners) that incorrectly transfer the image to CorelTRACE! as a negative. It can even be used after the scan is made so that you don't have to rescan the image. OCR work and centerline tracing in particular require black objects on a white background, so Invert Colors can be used if the colors are inverted in the scan or file.

Convert to Monochrome

The next setting, Convert To Monochrome, works in conjunction with the Threshold slider and controls the Red, Green, and Blue settings. It converts grayscale or color pictures to black-and-white images that have no intermediate tones. The default converts to black any tones darker than the medium shades. Any tones lighter than the medium shades get converted to white, resulting in a picture with no middle tones.

For example, figure 15.7 depicts a grayscale TIFF file having a wide range of gray tones. Figure 15.8 shows the photo loaded in CorelTRACE! with Convert To Monochrome selected using default values for Threshold. The default Threshold is 128 for all channels.

Figure 15.7
The original scanned photograph.

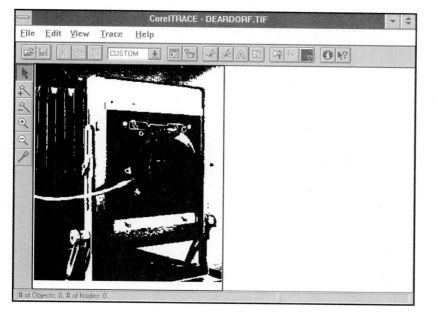

Figure 15.8
The scanned photo loaded using Convert To **M**onochrome default settings.

Figure 15.9 shows the same image loaded with Threshold adjusted to RGB (**R**ed, **G**reen, **B**lue) values of 73, and figure 15.10 shows the image with Threshold adjusted to 147 for all channels. Note that CorelTRACE!'s preview changes to reflect the different threshold values chosen, and that a higher threshold darkens the image.

Figure 15.9
The photo with
Threshold
adjusted to 73
for all channels.

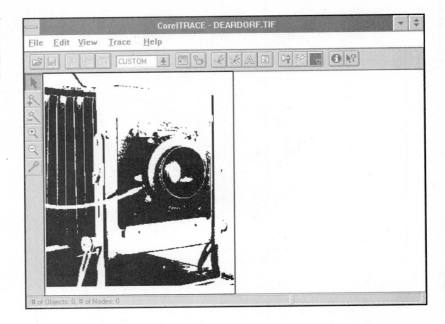

Figure 15.10
The photo with
Threshold
adjusted to 147
for all channels.

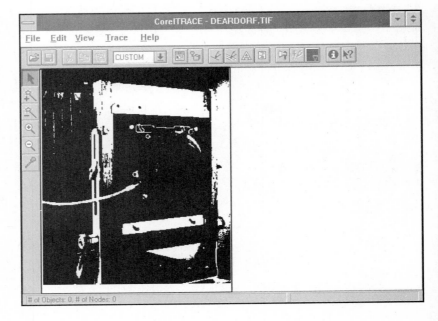

The previous example showed the effects of various Threshold settings on a gray-scale scan. If you have a color scan, you can individually adjust the Red, Green, and Blue channels to fine-tune the trace. For example, if you scanned a color logo, you can selectively adjust the color channels to drop out a color or other effects. Figure 15.11 is a color PCX file having the words RED and GREEN in red and green against a blue background. The default Convert To **M**onochrome setting makes all colors black in CorelTRACE!'s preview window.

After adjusting **R**ed to 255, and Green and Blue to 0, the word RED reverses out from the blue background as shown in figure 15.12. If the Red and Green are 0 and Blue is 255, the blue background becomes white, and the words RED and GREEN become black as shown in figure 15.13. Although this is a simple example, you can imagine many situations where you are given a color photograph or a color logo with which to work. If you experiment with these settings, you might find a better working combination than those the defaults produce.

Figure 15.11
A color bitmap file for tracing.

II

Using Corel's Modules

Figure 15.12
Threshold set to
Red=255,
Green=0,
Blue=0 in the
Tracing Options
dialog box.

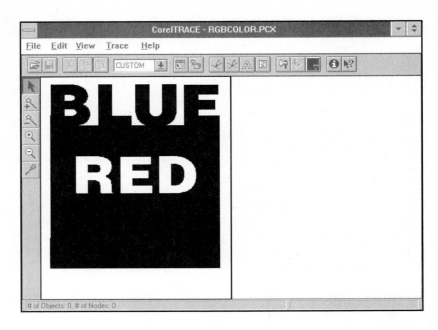

Figure 15.13
Threshold set to
Red=0,
Green=0,
Blue=255 in the
Tracing Options
dialog box.

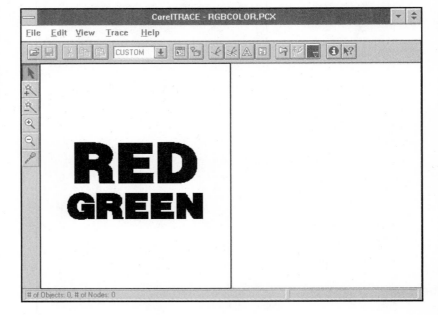

Reduce Colors

The last choice in the Image section of the Tracing Options dialog box is the Reduce Colors setting. You must deselect the Convert To Monochrome check box for this setting to appear as a valid choice. You can set this for any amount you desire from 2 to 256. As its description indicates, checking this setting reduces the colors in a trace.

There is one potential pitfall, however. If you load a grayscale bitmap into CorelTRACE! and then select a high number of colors (or shades of gray) to render the trace closer to the original, you only get up to four shades of gray no matter what you selected. The next section describes the options for color, and how these options interact with the Reduce Colors settings in this special case.

Color Options

To obtain more than four tones in a grayscale picture, you must click on the Color tab at the top of the Tracing Options dialog box and set the Selection Wand and Tracing Tolerance to a lower number using the slider bar. See figure 15.14 for a look at the Color options control in the Tracing Options dialog box. If you work through the math explained next, it is easy to see how the Color control limits the available colors (or shades of gray) in a trace.

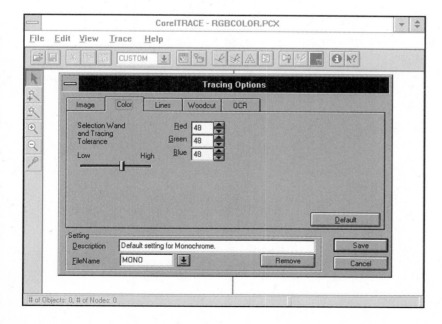

Figure 15.14
The Tracing Options dialog box showing the Color settings.

II
Using Corel's Modules

In a grayscale bitmap there can be as many as 256 different shades of gray. If the color option for Selection Wand and Tracing Tolerance is set to the default of 48, then the number of shades is reduced to 256/48 = 5.33, which would be rounded down to five available shades. If you change the Tracing Tolerance to the lowest value of 24 using the slider control, then the available shades of gray increase to 256/24 = 10.66 or 10 shades of gray. As you see, the Selection Wand and Tracing Tolerance setting limits the available colors regardless of the Reduce Colors setting. Figures 15.15 through 15.17 illustrate what these different settings do to the traced image.

Figure 15.15
A grayscale bitmap before tracing.

Figure 15.16
Bitmap traced
with **R**educe
Colors To 256,
Color Tracing
Tolerance set to
the maximum of
64.

Lines Options

Do you demand even more control over your trace? Additional options for custom tailoring your trace await you in the Lines section of the Tracing Options dialog box. These settings determine how accurately CorelTRACE! follows the original contours of the bitmap. You may elect to have a loose, freeform fit for graphic reasons, or a tighter, more accurate trace to better duplicate the original artwork.

The Lines section of the Tracing Options dialog box contains the following options: **C**urve Precision, **L**ine Precision, **T**arget Curve Length, **S**ample Rate, **M**inimum Object Size, and **O**utline filtering (see fig. 15.18). On the right side of the dialog box are settings that affect Centerline tracing; these will be covered later in this chapter.

II

Using Corel's Modules

Figure 15.17
Bitmap traced
with **R**educe
Colors To 256,
Color Tracing
Tolerance set to
the minimum
of 24.

Curve Precision

The **C**urve Precision setting determines how accurately the trace follows the original curves of the bitmap. The choices are Very Good, Good, Medium, Loose, and Very Loose. Very Good produces the most accurate trace, and Very Loose creates rounded approximations of the original shapes. This is useful for special graphics effects when a "free and loose" appearance is desired.

Line Precision

Line Precision governs whether the curves in the original render as straight lines or as curved lines. With a Very Loose setting, curves in the original are squared off using straight lines. Very few rounded curves will result. This creates an effect that resembles the angular shapes found in a "scratch board" rendering. Using a Very Good setting, curved lines are rendered as curves instead of being flattened into lines, and they are generally truer to the original.

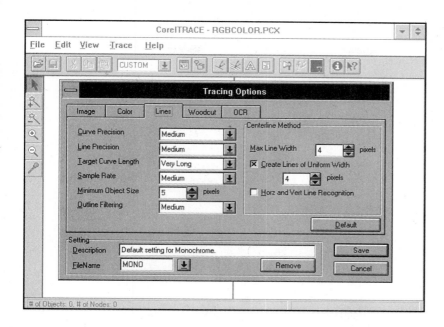

Figure 15.18
The Lines section of the Tracing Options dialog box.

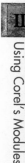

Target Curve Length

Target Curve Length is another setting that can affect the precision of the trace. If it is set to Very Short, the trace accuracy improves from the default of Very Long. The disadvantage is that node count and file size increase. Corel suggests that leaving the setting at Very Long results in satisfactory traces in most cases, although you should experiment if a trace is unsatisfactory.

Sample Rate

Sample Rate determines how CorelTRACE! looks at a row of pixels in an image. If it is set to Fine, CorelTRACE! "samples" the edge of a shape more frequently. This slows the trace, but the accuracy improves. If it is set to Coarse, CorelTRACE! averages consecutive pixel locations to position a trace line. If you have an image with jaggies, using Coarse helps smooth the curve. A setting of Medium is a good default.

By using various combinations of Curve Precision, Line Precision, Target Curve Length, and Sample Rate, it is possible to greatly affect the appearance of a trace. The following figures should be compared to the first example in this chapter and to the default trace that was described. Figure 15.19 shows a trace made with a combination of settings that rendered the picture as accurately as possible; compare this trace to the one at the beginning of the chapter that was made with CorelTRACE!'s default settings. Tables 15.3-15.5 list the line settings used to make various shapes.

Figure 15.19
An accurate trace very true to the original picture.

Table 15.3
Line Settings for Making an Accurate Trace

Line Setting	Value
Curve Precision	Very Good
Line Precision	Very Good
Target Curve Length	Medium
Sample Rate	Medium
Minimum Object Size	5 pixels
Outline Filtering	Medium

Figure 15.20 shows a trace made to have as many angular, straight lines as possible, and figure 15.21 shows a flowing, rounded trace.

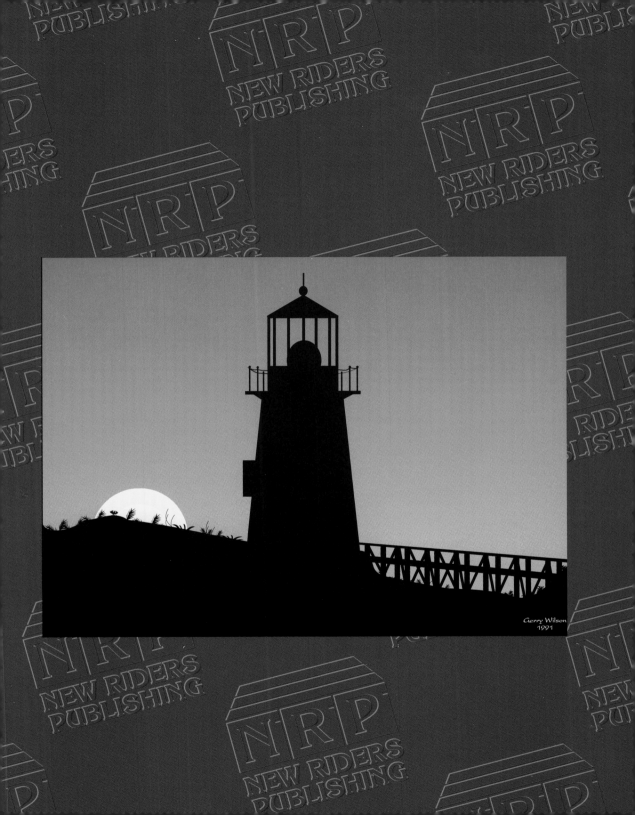

Gerry Wilson
1991

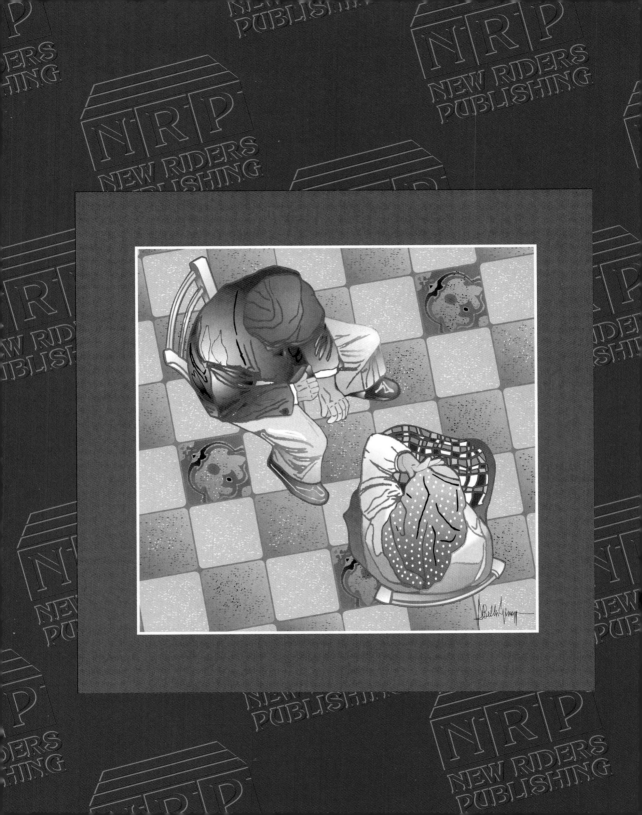

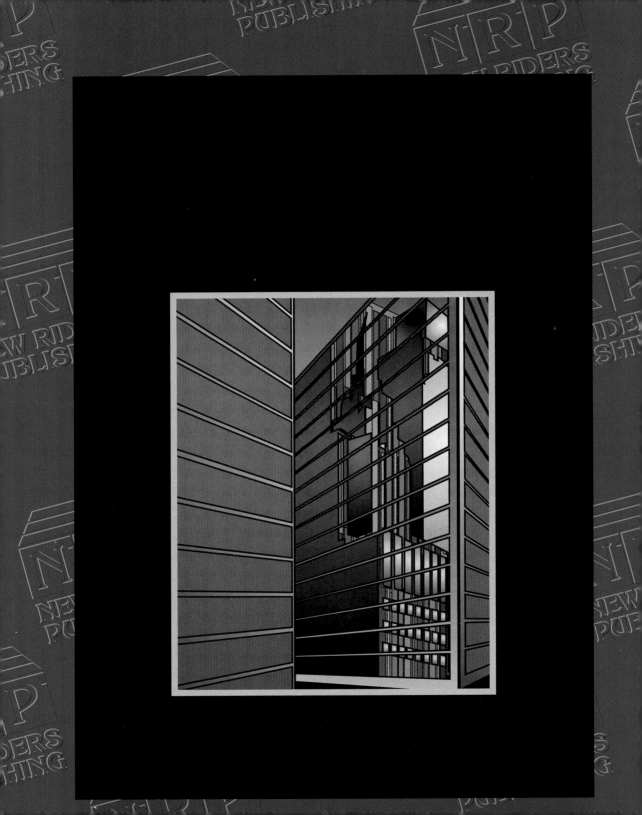

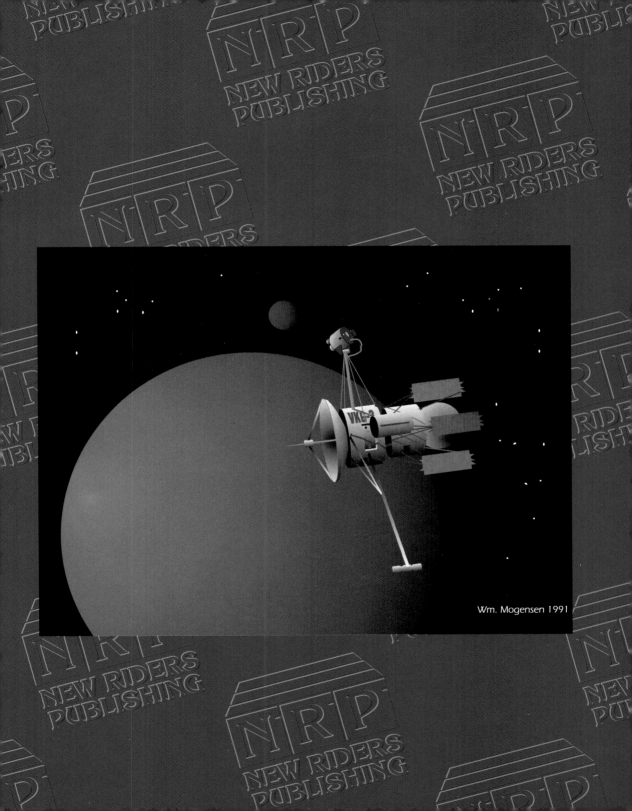

Wm. Mogensen 1991

"WOODROW"
3 Year Old, Cream colored Shar-Pei lost on July 11
Last seen in the historic area of Ghent.
If you have any information, please call:
555-7043

Grouper

LISA AGNES WINDHAM

Figure 15.20
A trace with
angular shapes.

Table 15.4
Line Settings for Producing Angular Shapes

Line Setting	Value
Curve Precision	Very Loose
Line Precision	Very Loose
Target Curve Length	Very Long
Sample Rate	Coarse
Minimum Object Size	5 pixels
Outline Filtering	Medium

II

Using Corel's Modules

Figure 15.21
A trace with rounded, flowing shapes.

Table 15.5
Line Settings for Producing Rounded Shapes

Line Setting	Value
Curve Precision	Very Loose
Line Precision	Very Good
Target Curve Length	Long
Sample Rate	Coarse
Minimum Object Size	5 pixels
Outline Filtering	Medium

Minimum Object Size

Minimum Object Size is a filter for specifying the minimum-sized object in the bitmap to be traced. The default Minimum Object Size setting is 5 pixels, which means that individual objects smaller than 5 pixels in area are not to be traced.

Instead, they are filtered out of the resulting traced picture. The default of 5 pixels should be sufficient for general purpose tracing because it removes unwanted scan artifacts and other small specks.

If you increase the Minimum Object Size number, larger items start to disappear from the trace. This has the added benefit of reducing the file size and complexity of the track, as well as other practical uses. Figure 15.22 shows a bitmap that has many small dots in the image. Figure 15.23 shows the resulting scan with a Minimum Object Size of 5 pixels, the CorelDRAW! default. It closely resembles the original and is comprised of 422 objects.

Figure 15.22
The original bitmap before tracing.

A bitmap that contains many small shapes is a good candidate for using a custom Minimum Object Size setting. Because of its complexity, it takes a while to import into CorelDRAW!. Figure 15.24 shows the same image traced with a Minimum Object Size of 30 pixels. Anything less than 30 pixels in size is not traced, which effectively filters out the smaller dots in the image. This trace contains 38 traced objects and is only 19 KB in file size. Figure 15.25 shows a trace with the Minimum Object Size set to 50 pixels, which eliminates all but the 21 largest shapes that comprise the image. This less complex file, only 14 KB in size, imports very rapidly into CorelDRAW! and displays much faster.

Figure 15.23
The bitmap after tracing with the default **M**inimum Object Size setting of 5 pixels.

Figure 15.24
The bitmap after tracing with **M**inimum Object Size set to 30 pixels.

Figure 15.25
With **M**inimum Object Size set to 50 pixels, only the very large shapes get traced.

As you see, the **M**inimum Object Size setting is very useful when you want to simplify a scanned image that has many small, isolated areas. Other times, you can set **M**inimum Object Size to a small number to capture as much detail as you can, with the trade-off of increased file size and slow editing.

Outline Filtering

Outline Filtering is the last setting that affects outline tracing in the Lines section of the Tracing Options dialog box. It has a greater effect on low resolution scans of 150 dpi or less. It smooths the trace lines of jagged edges in the original bitmap. The default setting of Medium should suffice for most scans, but you can use Smooth Points to help smooth the outline of a jagged original. If you use the Smooth Points setting on a drawing that has thin lines or shapes, they might disappear or appear broken along their length. If this occurs, reduce **O**utline Smoothing to either Medium or None.

Tracing Centerlines

Centerline tracing is used generally for technical, architectural, or other drawings comprised of mostly thin lines and, most importantly, only for black-and-white drawings. Figure 15.26 shows a drawing that is ideal for centerline tracing. This

Using Corel's Modules

image is a 600 dpi TIF file nearly ½ MB in size. You create a centerline trace by clicking on its button on the Ribbon Bar, or by selecting <u>T</u>race, <u>C</u>enterline. Figure 15.27 shows the resulting trace.

Figure 15.26
Technical drawings having thin lines are good candidates for using the Centerline feature.

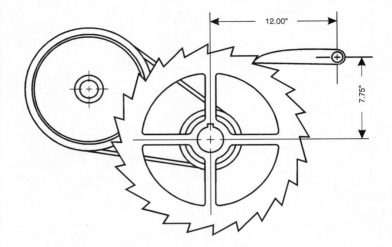

Figure 15.27
The drawing after tracing. CorelTRACE! creates the drawing using lines instead of filled shapes.

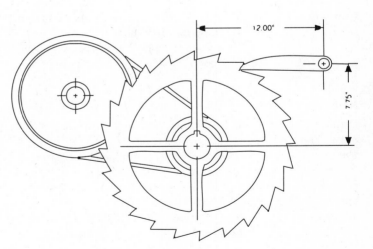

There are advantages and disadvantages to selecting a centerline trace. Because the lines are not closed shapes, they cannot be filled easily for shading effects in CorelDRAW!. However, the lines can be assigned any custom weight using the Pen tool. This makes it easy to bold some of the lines that make up one part in an illustration and to reduce the line weight for less important parts. You could use this technique to emphasize important components in a complex drawing.

Tip

Another potential problem is that Trace sometimes follows the "wrong" path where two lines intersect each other. After all, you know what the picture represents and understand where the lines are supposed to go at an intersection, but Trace doesn't have human intelligence. In Trace, a line sometimes takes a turn at an intersection instead of cutting across the intersecting line and continuing on. If this happens, you must break the lines during node editing in Draw and reconnect the line segments correctly. This doesn't affect much unless you are trying to give different parts of the picture different line weights.

Centerline Method Controls

When tracing centerline drawings, CorelTRACE! sometimes finds a filled area that can't be traced in centerline mode. When these are encountered among the lines, Trace reverts to its default mode and treats them like filled outlines. It follows the contour of the object and assigns it a fill instead of creating a line. An area where many lines come together in an all-centerline drawing is sometimes thick enough that Trace sees it as a filled shape.

Max Line Width in the Lines section of the Tracing Options dialog box controls the threshold between outline and centerline tracing methods. If you choose **T**race, **E**dit Options to open the Tracing Options dialog box, you see the settings for the Centerline Method section. The first setting, **M**ax Line Width, tells CorelTRACE! how to trace an object when the Centerline Method is used. If a line is greater than 4 pixels wide, it is treated as an outline shape. For example, if a simple circle made of a line thicker than 4 pixels wide is traced using the defaults, CorelTRACE! renders it as a combination of filled outline shapes instead of a line. A combination of a filled black circle and a smaller filled white circle results. The trace appears visually similar to the original, but you can't change the apparent "line thickness" easily in CorelDRAW! simply because it isn't a real line. You would have to change the relative sizes of the inside and the outside circles to change the apparent line thickness in this situation.

If CorelTRACE! insists on tracing your centerline drawing as a series of filled shapes, then change **M**ax Line Width to a higher number. As an example, the drawing shown in figure 15.25 was treated as an outline instead of a centerline when CorelTRACE!'s defaults were used. Because it was scanned at high resolution (600 dpi), each line is comprised of more pixels than a lower resolution scan would have caused. The one-point thick lines of the original produced a scan with lines approximately 8 pixels thick at 600 dpi, so CorelTRACE! made the initial trace in outline mode even though Centerline Trace was selected. CorelTRACE!'s **M**ax Line Width was then adjusted to 14 pixels (comfortably higher than the average line thickness), and the second trace progressed as expected in Centerline mode.

You can estimate the pixel width of lines scanned at 1:1 size using the following method:

1. Estimate the width of the original lines in points. In case you don't have a feel for line weights in points, type and line-thickness gauges are available in graphics arts stores. An average pencil mark is about one to two points thick. A freshly sharpened pencil line is about a half point thick.

2. Multiply the estimated line width by the resolution (in dots per inch) of your scan.

3. Divide the result by 72. The quotient is the thickness in pixels of the scanned lines.

Because CorelTRACE!'s <u>M</u>ax Line Width defaults to only 4 pixels, even a one-point line at 300 dpi is likely to be traced as an outline. As a result, only very fine lines would be traced as centerlines. Many believe that CorelTRACE!'s centerline defaults here are too limiting for most practical situations. Fortunately, it is easy to change. You might consider making a new trace setting having a higher <u>M</u>ax Line Width than 4 pixels if you do much centerline tracing. If you use a 300 dpi scanner for most work, choose a setting of 8 to 10 for better results. If you use a 600 dpi scanner, choose a setting in the 12 to 16 range. Save this setting to a different <u>F</u>ilename (such as NEWLINE) in the Tracing Options dialog box for later use.

<u>C</u>reate Lines of Uniform Width tells CorelTRACE! what thickness to assign to the lines after tracing. This is changed easily once the file is imported into CorelDRAW!, so it is of interest mainly to those who import the tracing directly into a page layout program for printing.

The final Centerline Method control is the <u>H</u>orz and Vert Line Recognition check box. When enabled, CorelTRACE! rotates the entire picture to straighten the horizontal or vertical lines it finds. Check this box if you have a drawing of mostly horizontal or vertical straight lines and desire to have them straightened. You should be aware that CorelTRACE! sometimes finds a strong diagonal line in the image and believes it to be a reference horizontal line. For example, figure 15.26 is made of many small lines, a few long, thin horizontal and vertical construction lines, and a prominent line representing the drive belt. When <u>H</u>orz and Vert Line Recognition was turned on for tracing this image, CorelTRACE! rotated the picture counterclockwise to make the drive belt horizontal. It didn't recognize the proper horizontal or vertical lines in that admittedly complex illustration. When used with appropriate subject matter, however, it can save much time.

Optical Character Recognition

Unique among tracing programs is CorelTRACE!'s capability to recognize text in a scanned image. It is especially useful if you happen to have a TWAIN scanner to scan printed text directly into CorelTRACE!. This eliminates the need for an intermediate scanning program and having to save large bitmap files on your hard drive.

If you choose the OCR Trace Method in CorelTRACE!, it searches for letterforms in the scanned image and converts them into editable text. Its recognition rate is remarkably high, especially if you can scan at 300 dpi or higher. Like any OCR program, Trace works best with clearly defined original material without broken letterforms or highly decorative typefaces. Also, avoid type that is printed over a background screen tint. Remember that OCR Trace Method works only with image resolutions of 200 dpi or higher and black-and-white images. A straight scan helps assure accurate recognition, too.

Image Source

While CorelTRACE! has OCR options for dot matrix print and fax fine format, the best results are obtained using the normal setting with higher quality type. If you have dot matrix or fax fine format documents, choose the appropriate option to maximize the recognition rate. To select these, choose Trace, Edit Options, and click on the OCR tab in the Tracing Options dialog box. A drop-down box contains the settings for dot matrix and fax fine formats.

Check Spelling

Also found in the OCR section of the dialog box is a check box to enable CorelTRACE!'s own spell checker. It may be faster to check for spelling errors in your word processor, but the feature is handy for quick jobs that don't merit a special trip through the word processor.

After using CorelTRACE! for OCR, you can save the text as an ASCII text file for importing into Draw, Publisher, or your word processor for editing. Any unrecognized text is represented by a tilde (~) character to make searching for errors easier.

If you need to keep a copy of the scan, save it as a Windows Bitmap (*.BMP) file by choosing File, Save, Image As, and typing a file name.

Do not change the default settings for the various tracing options found in the **T**race, **E**dit Options dialog box. If you overwrite the defaults with custom specifications, you could experience program errors and computer lockups during OCR operations. If you want to experiment with a custom Tracing Options setting, be sure to save it to a different **F**ilename (for instance, CUSTOM) to avoid overwriting the defaults.

Woodcut

Also unique to CorelTRACE! is the Woodcut tracing method. It simulates the appearance of a woodcut print by filling a traced shape with lines of varying thickness. To trace an image using the Woodcut setting, click on the Woodcut trace button on the Ribbon Bar or choose **T**race, **W**oodcut. There are several controls in the Tracing Options dialog box that affect the appearance of a Woodcut trace. Figure 15.28 shows the Woodcut section of the Tracing Options dialog box.

Figure 15.28
The Woodcut section of the Tracing Options dialog box enables customization of several settings.

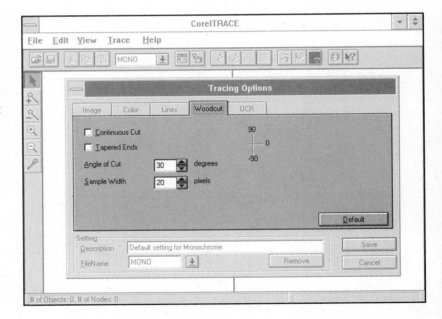

Continuous Cut

The <u>C</u>ontinuous Cut check box controls how the woodcut lines render in the lighter areas of a picture; if this box is checked, they don't just end where black meets white. Instead, the lines continue into the light areas, but become very narrow. This gives a background texture to mostly white pictures. Figure 15.29 shows the effect of a trace made with <u>C</u>ontinuous Cut enabled.

Figure 15.29
The <u>C</u>ontinuous Cut option in Woodcut tracing creates thin lines in the white areas of the original.

Tapered Ends

When the <u>T</u>apered Ends check box is enabled, the woodcut lines have pointed ends. This creates a "rougher" appearance in the trace than normal. Left unchecked, some woodcut lines have pointed ends, but many have squared ends. It is a subtle difference between the two, and it works well with some illustrations. You should load a file and experiment to see the difference for yourself.

II

Using Corel's Modules

Angle of Cut

The Angle of Cut option controls the angle that the woodcut lines take when rendering an illustration. The default angle of 30 degrees is a good setting for most illustrations, but you can change it to something else to create a different effect.

Sample Width

Sample Width controls the thickness of the Woodcut line. A smaller Sample Width creates thinner lines and shows more detail. If you have an illustration that has been scanned at low resolution or at a small size, then changing Sample Width to a lower number helps hold detail. Large, high-resolution scans would need a larger number to keep the file size reasonable and to reduce the number of woodcut strips across the picture. Figure 15.30 shows a Woodcut trace using the defaults and figure 15.31 shows the same traced image with Sample Width set to 10 pixels.

Figure 15.30
Image traced using Woodcut defaults.

Figure 15.31
Image traced using a Sample Width of 10 pixels.

Forms

The Forms tracing method is a combination of three different tracing methods. It finds horizontal and vertical lines and renders them in centerline mode; it finds and traces the outlines of larger graphics shapes; and it recognizes text in the form using OCR mode. You can trace a form by clicking on the Form icon on the Form button of the Ribbon Bar, or you can choose Form (B&W) from the Trace menu. You must have a scan that is comprised of just black and white and an image resolution of at least 200 dpi for this option to work. Don't confuse grayscale images that have middle tones with a true black-and-white (1-bit) bitmap.

After the trace is completed and saved, you can import the resulting EPS file into CorelDRAW! for editing, spell checking of the text, or even for changing the typeface. Be aware that the trace is not editable in a word processor because it is in the EPS format.

Other CorelTRACE! Tools

Even with all the options described previously, there are times when you demand even more control over your traced image. The selection tools along the left side of CorelTRACE!'s screen permit the sort of control you need.

II

Using Corel's Modules

The Pick Tool

The Pick tool is used to select a rectangular area for tracing. Simply click and drag your mouse to select the area that you wish to trace. Once selected, a moving dashed line (marquee) shows the area to be traced. This feature is often used to crop out unwanted areas from a scan but can be used for special effects. For example, if you select the lower half of a picture and trace it in Woodcut mode, you can then reselect another part of the picture for tracing in a different mode. In this way, you build your trace section by section, using different settings for different effects.

If you select an area to trace with the Pick tool and then change your mind, simply choose View, Clear Marquee. The selected area disappears, and you can either choose another area or go on to another tool. The Pick tool is limited to selecting rectangles, but the next tool, the Magic Wand, allows much more freedom to choose what to trace.

The Magic Wands

The Magic Wand (Plus) tool enables you to select irregular areas for tracing based on color similarity. If you click on an object using the Magic Wand (Plus) tool, it outlines the selected object with a moving marquee. You can hold down the shift key to select additional unconnected shapes for tracing.

If you selected too many objects, deselect some by using the next icon, the Magic Wand (Minus) tool. Simply click on any unwanted selection areas and they no longer show the "marching ants" marquee.

When using the Magic Wand tool with color or grayscale pictures, the area selected is based on color similarity settings in the Tracing Options dialog box in the Color section. Using a higher number permits a larger area to be selected because more colors or shades of gray are included. A smaller number limits the selection area to a very narrow color range, generally resulting in a smaller selection area. Because the numbers can be individually adjusted, you have considerable control over how the wand selects an area.

The Zoom Tools

You can zoom in to a small section of your bitmap to see small features by clicking in the Zoom In tool icon. This permits you to select small areas using the Magic Wand tool. This is not used often when tracing with defaults, but becomes indispensable for using the selection tools. If you want to return to the original view, click on the Zoom Out tool.

The Eyedropper Tool

The Eyedropper tool picks a color sample from the original bitmap for Silhouette or Woodcut tracing. The selected color displays on the Select Color button and is used to fill the traced areas.

The Silhouette Button

Using the Magic Wand enables the Silhouette button, which enables you to trace the outer profile of a selection area. A normal trace follows the outer profile of a selection area and continues on to trace details that lie inside the selection area. Trace Silhouette ignores anything inside the selection area and traces just the outside. This option is available when using the Pick tool also, but the result is always a trace of the rectangular selection area. Because that's not very useful, it is almost always used with the Magic Wand tools.

The Select Color Button

You can select from many different colors for Silhouette and Woodcut traces using the Select Color button. Clicking on it drops down a palette of different colored swatches. Other colors, including PANTONE and process colors, can be accessed using the More button. This opens the color selection dialog box that is familiar to CorelDRAW! users.

Some Tips and Hints

Experience is the best teacher for using CorelTRACE!. The program has a depth of features that is untouched by most CorelDRAW! users, and unless you explore the features yourself, you could miss something useful it has to offer. Following are tips based on hard-won experience to help you produce better traces in a shorter time. There is nothing wrong with learning from the efforts of others.

Lighting a Subject for a Better Trace

If you are responsible for creating a photograph to be traced, move the lights to one side of the subject to create interesting shadows. On-camera flashes tend to flatten the three-dimensionality of a subject and produce a less satisfactory trace. If the lights are on the side of the subject, the shadows create a three-dimensional form that traces better.

II

Using Corel's Modules

Touch-Up Scans in PhotoPaint

To save time later on, touch up scans in PhotoPaint before tracing. Cropping unnecessary detail and cleaning up the background can make a big difference when tracing.

If you have two different shapes that touch somewhere, Trace treats them as one large object. You can often "cut" a small connection between adjacent objects in PhotoPaint to force CorelTRACE! to see two different things. This saves time after the trace is imported into CorelDRAW! for editing.

Crop or Resample Bitmaps

The File, Open dialog box permits you to crop or to resample a bitmap to a smaller size before you open it in CorelTRACE!. Below the preview window is a drop-down box with Crop and Resample options. Use these to expedite work if you have large bitmaps to trace.

Export Text from CorelDRAW! for Tracing

If you export text from CorelDRAW! as a PCX or TIF bitmap file, you can use CorelTRACE!'s custom tools to change the appearance. For example, figure 15.32 shows exported text after tracing with the Woodcut setting. It began in CorelDRAW! as text surrounded by a white box and was exported as a PCX file. The white box behind the text provides a background that renders as thin lines when Continuous Cut is enabled in Woodcut Tracing Options.

If you are adventurous, you can even import the trace back into CorelDRAW! for export and tracing again. Use techniques like these to invent your own special type effects.

Figure 15.32
CorelDRAW!
text exported
as PCX and
traced with the
Continuous Cut
option checked,
and with Angle
of Cut set to
minus 60
degrees.

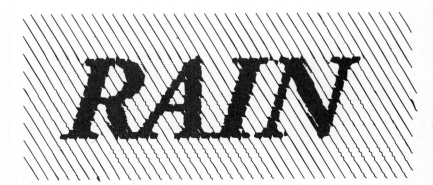

You have been given a quick tour of CorelTRACE!'s features, and now the rest is up to you. Using nothing more than time and your imagination, you can create any number of effects! Sketches, photographs, and even humble text become the raw materials for creating spectacular illustrations using Trace's powerful tools.

Chapter Snapshot

CorelSHOW! is the module that you will want to use to create a full-featured screen show. The module makes use of Microsoft's object linking and embedding (OLE) technology to build multimedia presentations. In this chapter, you learn to do the following:

✔ Follow the rules of OLE

✔ Use the Ribbon Bar and Toolbars

✔ Create a buildup screen show

✔ Use transitions and modify your presentations

✔ Add sound and animation to your work

✔ Move your presentations to other computers

Slide presentations that use the standard 35mm format are rapidly becoming a thing of the past. Multimedia presentations created in such programs as CorelSHOW! have become the rage in the corporate world. It's time to leave the static past behind and move into the interactive age!

16

CHAPTER

Using CorelSHOW!

CorelSHOW! is an application whose forte is creating and managing on-screen presentations. This module provides the tools to incorporate graphics, sound, and animation files.

Besides using Show to produce presentations, you can use it to automate printing jobs, such as overhead and 35mm slide presentations. Rather than using CorelDRAW! to open and print numerous overheads, you can put them together as a presentation in Show. Two advantages of bringing them into Show are that you can rearrange the order of the presentation materials and you only need to issue one print command. Now you can walk away and make yourself a peanut butter and jelly sandwich while Show and the printer do the rest.

CorelSHOW! has grown considerably since version 4. In its previous incarnation, CorelSHOW! was a simple workspace in which elements created in programs such as CorelDRAW!, CorelCHART!, CorelPHOTO-PAINT!, and CorelMOVE! were brought together. Today, Show's capability to display a wide variety of graphics is still deeply rooted in the OLE technology. Version 5, however, no longer relies on CorelDRAW! for its text functions. This improvement means that text slides are very quickly generated.

Another change to Show that greatly improves its performance is the addition of a Toolbar, which has buttons that provide access to file operations, copying and pasting functions, and text and paragraph formatting.

Getting To Know OLE

Show's capability is based on something that is built into Microsoft Windows. This underlying functionality is called OLE. Because OLE is such an integral part of Show, this discussion provides a good opportunity to get some rudimentary information on its operations.

OLE stands for Object Linking and Embedding. Its purpose in the Windows world is to keep track of mundane information, such as which files or programs you used to create objects in a document. Microsoft thinks this is intuitive computing. It is, but you must play by the rules and not move applications and files around on your computer. Also, applications must be designed to utilize the capabilities of OLE. Thankfully, Corel has designed its suite of program modules to be OLE-capable.

To successfully transfer information using OLE, the two programs must cooperate closely. In this process, one program is called the client and the other is termed the server. The *server* is the program that originates the information and "serves it up" to the *client*. The client then uses the transferred information as needed. Microsoft does not force any program to adopt all the functionality of OLE; therefore, an application can be OLE-capable and be only a server, only a client, or both.

You are probably thinking, "What's the big deal? I've been using the Windows Clipboard to transfer information to and from applications for years." True, but transferring items with the Clipboard often changes their construction—sometimes a lot. The item also becomes disconnected from the application that created it. If you need to revise something that went over the Clipboard, you might experience some problems.

Embedding

The power of OLE lies in its capability to create and maintain a connection between programs that share objects. If you need to make a change to your object, choose Edit, Edit Object. This process launches the server and loads your original file. Make your revisions, issue an Exit & Return command from the server and presto—your changes appear in Show. No fussing with exporting, importing, and intermediate files strewn all over the hard drive. This part is the embedding half of OLE. What could be quicker and easier?

Linking

Suppose that you want to change every place where you used your company logo on 150 different 35mm slides. No problem. The linking capability in OLE comes into play in this situation. If you used a link function when you added the company logo in the slide assembly process, Show can do the replacing with the Links command under the Edit menu. By updating the link of the master logo file, your Show presentation logo is updated on every slide. Now that's slick!

The Uh-Oh in OLE

As mentioned earlier, you must play by the rules in the OLE world. If you move the master file, the link is broken—keep that master logo file in the same spot. You also must plan which type of transfer to use for a new document: a static embedded transfer (that you maintain) or a dynamically linked transfer (that is automatically updated). Another point to remember: don't move those OLE server applications. Generally, their locations are added to the registration database at the time each program is installed so that Windows can keep track of where servers and clients can be found when their services are needed. (You didn't really think it was magic, did you?)

Finally, the last sticky wicket in the OLE scheme: OLE 2. Yes, Microsoft has upgraded OLE, and, as of this writing, it has proved to be more complicated than some developers counted on. Remember that CorelDRAW! modules that utilize OLE 2.0 functions might be less than reliable. Hopefully, you'll never experience OLE 2-related problems, like losing the link to the server application, but it does happen, so be prepared.

Starting CorelSHOW!

Enough talk of embedding, linking, and whatnot. The time has come to mouse your way over to Program Manager and double-click on the CorelSHOW! icon in the Corel Graphics program group. After the colorful title screen disappears, Show is displayed.

Like CorelMOVE!, the first thing you need to do is to use the File menu to open an existing presentation file or start a new presentation. Start a new presentation on which to practice the following exercises.

Starting a New Show Presentation

Choose File   The New Presentation dialog box appears

In the Start with Slides *text box, type* 4

If Page Settings are not 11 by 8.25 inches and Landscape, use the Page Setup button to change them.

Choose Page Setup   The Page Setup dialog box appears

continues

continued

At Page Size, select Screen

Click on OK   The Page Setup dialog box appears, then
                                                disappears

Click on OK   A new presentation window appears

You now are ready to create a five-page screen show. The next section helps you
become familiar with the tools that Show offers.

Touring the Presentation Window

The CorelSHOW! Presentation window supplies the blank pages and basic tools
needed to assemble and view your presentation elements. The following sections
describe the various components of the Presentation window (see fig. 16.1).

Figure 16.1
The
CorelSHOW!
screen.

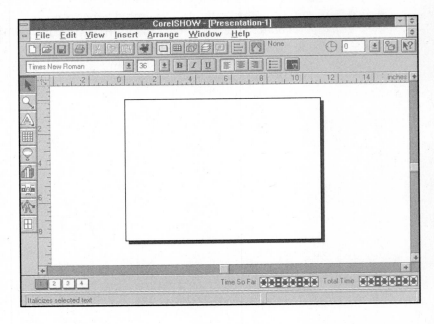

The menu bar provides selections for most of the functions used in Show. Select
each menu and examine the choices offered.

Below the menu bar is the first of two gray ribbon bars. The top one, known as the Button Bar, will be recognizable to older users of CorelSHOW! as a mixture of the new with the old. The newer buttons are shortcuts for some of the commands found under the <u>F</u>ile and <u>E</u>dit menus. The rest allow access to functions such as running a screen show, slide sorter, timelines window, and transition effects. Most of these functions also can be found under the <u>V</u>iew menu.

Below the top Button Bar is another. This is totally new and is called the Text Ribbon Bar. Notice a drop-down list of fonts available on your system, a handy drop-down list of font sizes, buttons to format the character, paragraphs, and color attributes of your text. Tables 14.1 and 14.2 show each item on these Toolbars and its purpose.

Table 16.1
The Button Bar Elements

Element	Name	Use
	New presentation button	Starts a new presentation file.
	Open presentation button	Opens an existing presentation file.
	Save presentation button	Saves the current presentation file to disk.
	Print button	Calls up the Print dialog box to print the current presentation.
	Cut button	Cuts the currently selected item from the presentation and places it onto the Clipboard.
	Copy button	Copies the currently selected item and places it onto the Clipboard.

continues

Table 16.1, Continued
The Button Bar Elements

Element	Name	Use
	Paste button	Pastes the current contents of the Clipboard onto the current slide.
	Screenshow button	For viewing your presentation on-screen.
	Slide Viewer button	For viewing and editing foreground objects on individual slides in the presentation (Show's default view).
	Background View button	For viewing and editing background objects.
	Speaker Notes View button	For viewing and editing speaker's notes associated with the presentation.
	Slide Sorter button	For viewing and arranging thumbnail versions of all the slides in your presentation. Simply drag slides into a new position to change their viewing or printing order.
	Slide Numbering button	Reorders slides by sequentially clicking on them with the mouse. This button is only available when in Slide Sorter mode.
	Timelines button	Calls up the Timelines window, which controls the duration of slides and elements on them.

Element	Name	Use
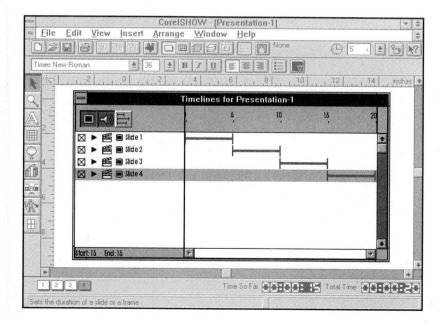	Transition button	For adding built-in effects that make the transition between pages more interesting.
0	Slide Duration Setting	For setting the amount of time a selected object or slide displays on-screen.

Press the Timelines button. The Timelines window is very similar to the Timelines Roll-Up in CorelMOVE!. Selecting this icon brings up a window that graphically displays all the elements in your presentation (see fig. 16.2). From this window, you can quickly see if a slide has elements on it or a cue assigned to it and for how long the slide is set to display. Any sound objects you insert in the presentation also are shown here.

Figure 16.2
The Timeline window.

You can limit the types of objects displayed in the window by selecting or deselecting the two icons at the top left. The third button enables the Zoom feature. You can magnify the scale of the timelines portion of the window. This is handy for grabbing the lines to manually adjust the time duration of each slide, element, or sound.

Each entry in the Timeline window represents a slide or an element on a slide. You can tell the difference by the little icon of a slide to the right of the slide number. The check box at the beginning of the timeline entry is a toggle switch that enables or disables display of the item. An X in the box denotes that it will be displayed.

The small triangle to the right of the enable box can be clicked on to reveal the separate elements that a slide contains. Click on one and you will see a Frame 0 entry. Each slide has a default Frame 0. As new elements are added, they too will appear as Frame items that are sequentially numbered. If an item is deleted from a slide, all Frame items are automatically renumbered. If a Frame item is selected, the corresponding Slide entry is also highlighted. This serves as a visual reminder of what slide you are editing.

The next icon to the right is used to set cues. Click on it to call up the Cue Information dialog box. Cues enable you to jump to other parts of your presentation or cause your show to pause and wait for user interaction. When a cue has been set for any condition other than Always and any action other than Continue, the icon will display closed. This is a visual clue that a cue is set for that element or slide.

Now it's time to continue with the rest of the tour.

Table 16.2
The Text Ribbon Elements

Element	Name	Use
Times New Roman ⬦	Font Name drop-down list	For selecting a font for the selected text
36 ⬦	Font Size drop-down list	For selecting a size for the selected text
B	Bold button	For applying the bold attribute to currently selected text
I	Italic button	For applying the italic attribute to currently selected text

Element	Name	Use
U	Underline button	For underlining the currently selected text
	Left Align button	For making the currently selected paragraph left aligned
	Center Align button	For making the currently selected paragraph center aligned
	Right Align button	For making the currently selected paragraph right aligned
	Bullet button	For applying the default bullet style to the currently selected paragraph
	Color selection button	For selecting and applying a color to the currently selected paragraph or highlighted text

Continuing down the left side of the CorelSHOW! screen, you see the Toolbar. Click on these icons to access the tools you need to create or modify the elements in your presentations. Table 16.3 lists these buttons and their uses.

Table 16.3
The Toolbar

Icon	Tool Name	Use
	Pick tool	For selecting, moving, and resizing objects.
	Zoom tool	For changing the viewing magnification of the page. Holding down the icon causes a fly-out to appear. The zoom choices are similar to those in CorelDRAW!.

continues

II
Using Corel's Modules

Table 16.3, Continued
The Toolbar

Icon	Tool Name	Use
A	Text tool	For adding text to your slide. Holding down the icon causes a fly-out to appear, offering access to the Paragraph Text tool or the Artistic Text tool.
	Background Library tool	For accessing libraries of backgrounds.
	CorelDRAW! tool	For accessing CorelDRAW! to create objects.
	CorelCHART! tool	For launching Chart to create objects.
	Corel PHOTO-PAINT! tool	For using PhotoPaint to create objects.
	Insert Animation tool	For inserting an animation file (the same function as selecting Animation from the Insert menu).
	OLE tool	For launching other OLE-capable applications on your system that can create valid objects.

Along the bottom of the Show window is another gray area that offers more tools to control your presentation.

On the left are icons that represent the pages in your presentation. Clicking on these icons moves you from page to page. Note that the page icons disappear and are replaced by the word Background when you select the Background button on the Button Bar. Because backgrounds apply to all the pages in your presentation, you do not need to switch from page to page. If you want to use a different background on a slide, select the slide, then choose View, Background, Independent. Next switch to Background View and assemble the new background.

The last two controls in the lower portion of the screen are time displays. The first control shows how much time the presentation takes up to the page you are currently viewing. The second display keeps track of the total time of your total presentation. Don't set your watch by these counters; they aren't very accurate. They do, however, provide a close estimate of your presentation length.

Now that you have experienced the who, what, and where of CorelSHOW!'s interface, it's time to move along and create a simple screen show.

Joe DeLook was going to a local business show, looking for new clients. He knew that a video presentation would be eye catching. This was the perfect job for CorelSHOW!. He made a simple five-slide screenshow that would play over and over. The show consists of an introduction slide and four others listing key advantages to using DeLook Designs. His project in CorelSHOW! is the basis for the following exercises.

The exercises call for certain fonts. They are Calligraph421 BT and DomDiagonal BD BT. If you do not have these fonts installed on your computer, take the time now to load them from the CD or substitute others of your choice.

Developing a Buildup Screen Show

A *buildup* is a series of slides displayed in succession. Each new slide adds more information to the previous slide. Bullet charts are ideal candidates for use of the buildup technique.

The following exercises work through making a four-bullet buildup screen show. The first slide displays the first bullet point. As the next slide is displayed, it appears as if the second point is simply added to the first. The third and fourth slides add the final bullet points to the previous two. The trick to making this technique work is to create the slide that displays the complete bullet list first.

Creating the Background

Screen shows need colorful backgrounds to make the displayed information look more interesting. The following exercise uses CorelDRAW!'s Texture Fill tool to produce a dark blue background. Feel free to experiment with other color schemes that suit your taste. The following steps use the five-page slide show that you started in the earlier exercise.

Creating a Background

Click on the Page 1 icon	Page 1 is displayed
Click on the Background tool on the Button Bar	The word Background replaces the page icons
Click on the CorelDRAW! tool	The CorelDRAW! window appears
Choose L̲ayout	The Layout menu appears
Choose P̲age Setup	The Page Setup dialog box appears
Click on the Page Size drop-down list	The drop-down list appears
Scroll down to the bottom of the list and select Custom	
In the W̲idth edit box, type **11.00**	
In the H̲eight edit box, type **8.25**	
Select the Landscape option	
Click on the Display tab	The bottom tab appears
Choose A̲dd Page Frame	
Click on OK	You are back in the Draw page window and the page border is highlighted
With the page border highlighted, click on the Outline tool	The Outline tool fly-out menu appears
Click on the Outline tool	The Outline fly-out appears
Click on None icon (top row, third from the left)	The outline disappears
Click on the Fill tool	The Fill fly-out menu appears
Click on the Texture Fill icon (top row, sixth from the left)	The Texture Fill dialog box appears
Select Samples in the Texture L̲ibrary *drop-down list*	
Select Clouds.Midday in the T̲exture	A preview of the texture is displayed
In the Brightness +-% edit box, type **20**	
Click on P̲review	Displays a preview of the texture
Click on OK	The Texture Fill dialog box disappears; the rectangle is filled with Clouds.Midday

Choose **F**ile	The File menu appears
Choose E**x**it & Return to CorelSHOW!	Your background appears in CorelSHOW!

Through OLE, the CorelDRAW! background object has been transferred and embedded into your presentation. If you need to change the background for any reason, simply double-click on it. CorelSHOW! launches CorelDRAW! and automatically loads the background object for you.

If for some reason the background doesn't fit perfectly, the remainder of the exercise will help.

Fitting the Background

Choose **A**rrange	The Arrange menu appears
Choose Fit Object to **P**age	Sizes the background to fill the entire page
Click on the Slide View tool in the Ribbon Bar	The page icons at the bottom reappear

Now that you have created a background, navigate through the page icons to confirm that each page displays the blue texture background. Most of the pages have a common header. You will now put this on the background layer.

Placing the Header on the Background Layer

Click on the Background tool on the Button Bar	
Click on the Text tool	The cursor turns to a cross hair
Click anyplace on the page	An insertion cursor flashes
Type **DeLook Designs**	
Click on the Pick tool	The text is selected
Click on the Font Name drop-down list	The list appears
Select Calligraph421 BT	The text turns to Calligraph421 BT
Click on the Bold button	The text becomes bold
In the Font Size edit box, type **73**	
Press Enter	The size of the text becomes 73

Joe DeLook wanted a drop-shadow effect for his type. This helps it to be more legible on the textured background. Next you will use the copy and paste commands to accomplish this.

Creating the Drop-Shadow Effect

Use the Pick tool to select the text

Choose <u>E</u>dit	The Edit menu appears
Choose <u>C</u>opy	The text is copied to the Clipboard
Choose <u>E</u>dit	The Edit menu appears
Choose <u>P</u>aste	The text is pasted directly on top of the original
Click on the Color Selector button	The drop-down palette appears
Select the Green square (third row, fourth from the left)	The text turns green
Click on the Zoom tool	The Zoom fly-out appears
Select the Magnify icon (first one)	The cursor turns to a magnifying lens with a + in it
Marquee-select the first several letters of DeLook	The view is zoomed in to the portion you designated

Use the Pick tool to select the green text and position it up and to the right as shown in figure 16.3.

Click on the Zoom tool	The Zoom fly-out appears
Click on the Page view icon (last one)	The view changes to display the entire slide

You can drag guidelines from the rulers, just the same as in CorelDRAW!. This will help you to line elements up. If the rulers are not visible, select <u>R</u>ulers from the <u>V</u>iew menu. Look under the <u>A</u>rrange menu for commands to access Setup and Snap To Guidelines.

You also might find it easier to work on the background slide elements with the texture-filled rectangle moved to the side. You can reposition it quickly by selecting it and pressing F4.

Use the Pick tool to marquee-select both pieces of text and position them at the top of the page. Joe Delook positioned the top of the letters at 1 inch down from the top and 1.25 inches from the left side.

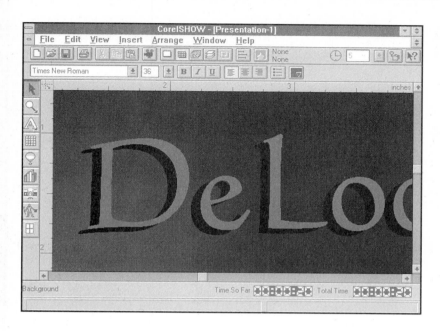

Figure 16.3
Proper position of text and drop shadow.

Joe used a yellow rule to set his slide header from the body of his slide. You will use CorelDRAW! again to make this rule.

Click on the CorelDRAW! tool

The CorelDRAW! window appears

Click on the Rectangle tool

The cursor becomes a cross hair

Draw a rectangle that is 9 inches wide by .22 inches high.

Click on the Outline tool

The Outline fly-out menu appears

Click on the Hairline icon (top row, fourth from the left)

The outline is changed to 1/4 point or .02 inches

Click on the Outline tool

The Outline fly-out menu appears

Click on the Black Color icon (second row, third from the left)

The Outline color is black

continues

continued

Click on the Fill tool	The Fill fly-out menu appears
Click on the Texture Fill icon (top row, sixth from the left)	The Texture Fill dialog box appears
Select Samples in the Texture **L**ibrary *drop-down list*	
Select Clouds.Midday in the **T**exture List *dialog box*	A preview of the texture is displayed
Click the Color Selector button	The color pallet appears
Select Yellow (third row, fifth from the left)	The color selector button turns yellow
Choose **P**review	A preview of the texture is displayed
Click on OK	The Texture Fill dialog disappears; the rectangle is filled with Clouds.Midday
Choose **E**dit	The Edit menu appears
Choose **C**opy	The rectangle is copied to the clipboard
Choose **E**dit	The Edit menu appears
Choose **P**aste	The rectangle is copied directly on top of the original

Use the Pick tool to position the top rectangle approximately .05 inches from the top and 0.5 inches to the right. Then use the Pick tool to select the bottom rectangle.

Click on the Fill tool	The Fill fly-out menu appears
Click on the Black Color icon (bottom row, third from the left)	The rectangle is filled with black
Choose **F**ile	The File menu appears
Choose E**x**it & Return to CorelSHOW!	Your drop-shadowed rule appears in CorelSHOW!

Use the Pick tool to position the yellow rule 1 inch from the left edge and approximately 1.89 inches from the top (see fig. 16.4). Use the To **B**ack command in the **A**rrange menu to place the yellow rule behind the text.

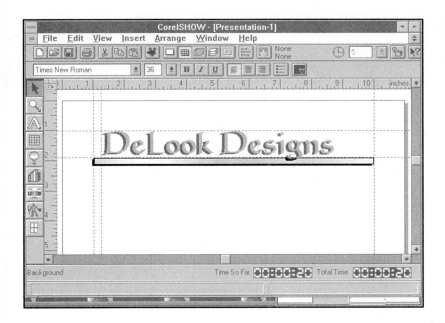

Figure 16.4
Proper position
of yellow bar
under heading.

Now that you have finished the common background for your slide show, click on the Slide View button on the Button Bar. The individual slides reappear along with the background. In Slide View mode, your background elements are inaccessible so you don't have to worry about moving them by accident.

Using Background Libraries

When you create a background that you want to use again, use the Save Background command under the File menu to store your background in a Background Library file (SHB). You can create new libraries or select the Insert in Library option to add a background to an existing SHB file. When you want to use a saved background again, click on the Background tool, and the Background Library window appears. You can use the Change button and browse the hard drive to locate the SHB file that contains the background you want. After you locate the file, you can access all the backgrounds stored in that library. Simply click on the background of your choice and it is placed into your presentation. Then click on the Done button to close the library window.

Using Corel's Modules

Be careful when looking through Background libraries. If you click on one, it replaces the existing background for the currently selected slide. If the background you deleted was not previously saved in a library, you will have to redo all your work.

Creating a Bullet Chart

As mentioned earlier, the bullet chart you create has four bullet points. You will now use CorelSHOW!'s text functions, automatic bullet making, and color functions to make the slide.

Making Your Bullet Points

Click on the Page 4 icon	The Page 4 icon turns gray
Select the Text tool	The cursor becomes a cross hair
Click on the cursor anywhere on the page	An insertion cursor blinks

You are ready to type the four sentences that make up the bullets. Remember to start each sentence with a space and press Enter only at the end of the sentence.

Type **Innovative Designs**

Award Winning Creative Team

State-of-the-Art Facilities

Quick Turnaround

Click the cursor anyplace on the slide	The insertion point is no longer active in the text block; the text block is selected
Click on the Text tool	The cursor turns to a cross hair
Click anyplace on the page	An insertion cursor flashes
Click on the Font Name drop-down list	The list appears
Select DomDiagonal BD BT	The text turns to DomDiagonal BD BT
Click on the Bold button	The text becomes bold
In the Font Size edit box, type **49**	
Press Enter	The size of the text becomes 49

Click on the Bullet button on the Text Ribbon Bar	The default bullet style is applied

Once again, you will create a drop-shadow effect for this type.

Use the Pick tool to select the text

Choose **E**dit	The Edit menu appears
Choose **C**opy	The text is copied to the Clipboard
Choose **E**dit	The Edit menu appears
Choose **P**aste	The text is pasted directly on top of the original
Click on the Color Selector button	The drop-down palette appears
Select the Yellow square (third row, fifth from the left)	The text turns yellow
Click on the Zoom tool	The Zoom fly-out menu appears
Select the Magnify icon (first one)	The cursor turns to a magnifying lens with a + in it
Marquee-select the first several letters of text	The view is zoomed in to the portion you designated

Use the Pick tool to select the yellow text and position it up and to the right as shown in figure 16.5. Try to make it look consistent with the drop shadow you made for DeLook Designs.

Click on the Zoom tool	The Zoom fly-out menu appears
Click on the Page view icon (last one)	The view changes to display the entire slide

Use the Pick tool to marquee-select the two text blocks and center them on the page.

Working with Bullet Styles

CorelSHOW!'s new text-handling features make short order of bulleted items. You have tremendous flexibility to use any character in a symbol font that the program recognizes for bullets. You also can change the size and color of the bullet used. These options do not affect the text settings you use for the text itself.

The following exercise uses the **B**ullet Style command under the **E**dit menu to change the bullet color of the yellow text to green.

Figure 16.5
Correct position
of bullet points
and drop
shadow.

Changing the Bullet Color

Choose **E**dit	The Edit menu appears
Choose **B**ullet Style	The Bullets dialog box appears
From the Font drop-down list, select CommonBullets	The characters in the CommonBullets font appear
Select the first solid bullet (top row, second column)	
In the Size edit box, type **100**	
Click on the **C**olor *selector button*	The color palette appears
Select Green (third row, fourth from the left)	The Color selector button turns green

Make sure that the **E**nable Bullet option in the lower left of the dialog box is selected.

Click on OK	The Bullets dialog box disappears

The color of the four bullets is now green.

You now should have a screen that looks similar to figure 16.6. This slide is the final one in the four-part series. You will use the Copy, Paste, and Delete functions to create the first three slides in the buildup series.

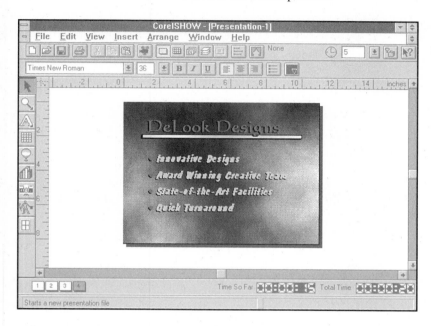

Figure 16.6
The completed bullet points slide.

Completing the Bullet Buildup

Use the Pick tool to select the yellow text block and the drop shadow text block

Choose **E**dit	The Edit menu appears
Choose **C**opy	The two elements are copied to the Clipboard
Click on Page 3 icon	Page 3 appears
Choose **E**dit	The Edit menu appears
Choose **P**aste	The two elements are pasted onto slide 3
Click on the Text tool	The cursor turns into a cross hair
Click the cursor at the end of the last bullet	The insertion point is after the word Turnaround
Drag the cursor to highlight all the text after the last bullet	Quick Turnaround is highlighted

continues

continued

Press the Delete key	The text disappears
Press the Backspace key until the bullet disappears	
Click the text cursor anywhere to deselect the yellow text	

Use the same procedure to remove the last bullet point from the drop shadow text block.

Marquee-select the two text blocks of three bullets

*Choose **E**dit*	The Edit menu appears
*Choose **C**opy*	The two elements are copied to the Clipboard
Click on Page 2 *icon*	Page 2 appears
*Choose **E**dit*	The Edit menu appears
*Choose **P**aste*	The two elements are pasted onto slide 2
Click on the Text tool	The cursor turns into a cross hair
Click the cursor at the end of the last bullet	The insertion point is after the word Facilities
Drag the cursor to highlight all the text after the last bullet	State-of-the-Art Facilities is highlighted
Press the Delete key	The text disappears
Press the Backspace key until the bullet disappears	
Click the text cursor anywhere to deselect the yellow text	

Use the same procedure to remove the last bullet point from the drop shadow text block.

Marquee-select the two text blocks of two bullets

*Choose **E**dit*	The Edit menu appears
*Choose **C**opy*	The two elements are copied to the Clipboard
Click on the Page 1 icon	Page 1 appears
*Choose **E**dit*	The Edit menu appears
*Choose **P**aste*	The two elements are pasted onto slide 1

Click on the Text tool	The cursor turns into a cross hair
Click the cursor at the end of the last bullet	The insertion point is after the word Team
Drag the cursor to highlight all the text after the last bullet	Award Winning Creative Team is highlighted
Press the Delete key	The text disappears
Press the Backspace key until the bullet disappears	
Click the text cursor anywhere to deselect the yellow text	

Use the same procedure to remove the last bullet point from the drop shadow text block.

You have finished assembling your bullet buildup. Now is a good time to save the work that you have accomplished so far.

Saving the Bullet Presentation

Choose **F***ile*	The File menu appears
Choose **S***ave*	The Save Presentation dialog box appears
Use the **D***irectories and Dri***v***es lists to move to the directory in which you want to save your file.*	
In the File **N***ame text box, type* **DELOOK1**	
Click on OK	The Save Presentation dialog box disappears and your file is saved to disk

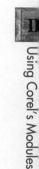

Displaying Your Screen Show

Now that you have four slides in your show, take a look at what you have created. There are several options that affect the way your presentation displays on the screen.

Choose **F**ile, Pre**f**erences and the Preferences dialog box appears (see fig. 16.7). On the Presentation tab, you can select one of two options that control the timing of your screen show: **A**utomatic Advance to next slide or **M**anual Advance to next slide.

Figure 16.7
The Preferences
dialog box.

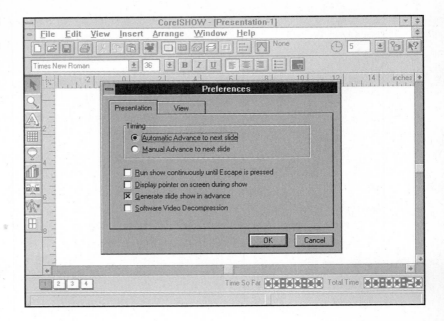

Automatic Advance uses the time shown in the Slide Duration text box to display the current slide for the set time period. It then automatically displays the next slide for its set duration. This procedure continues until the end of your show. If you want to lengthen or shorten the duration of a slide's screen time, simply click in the Slide Duration text box and type the value you want. Alternatively, you can choose from one of the preset values in the drop-down list next to the text box. The default setting for slide duration is 5.

Tip

If you set a slide and all objects on it to a duration setting of 0, the display of that slide is suppressed during the screen show.

The Slide Duration text box has two functions. If you select the slide background or workspace background (not an object on the slide), it controls the time of display for that slide. If you have selected an object on the slide, you are controlling how long the highlighted element displays. Using this feature, you can have two elements on a slide and set the total length of the slide display to 10, with the first element set to display for 5 and the second element for a duration of 8. This staggering of display times is a way of adding more appeal to your screen presentations.

Choose the <u>M</u>anual Advance option button for hands-on control of how long each page in your show displays. To move to the next page, double-click on the left mouse button or press any of the following keys: PgDown, down or right arrow, F6, Enter, or the spacebar. To move backward in a presentation, double-click on the right mouse button or use any of the following keys: PgUp, up or left arrow, or F5. Move to the first slide in the presentation using the Home or F9 keys. Jump to the last slide using the End or F10 keys. Press Esc in Automatic or Manual mode to end the screen show.

The next three option settings in the Presentation Options dialog box control other aspects of the show.

"<u>R</u>un show continuously until Escape is pressed" is pretty self-explanatory. "<u>D</u>isplay pointer on-screen during show" enables you to use the arrow cursor to point to objects during the screen display. This feature is essential when interactive shows are being played. Finally, "<u>G</u>enerate slide show in advance" enables Show to compose the screen show before you run it. This option eliminates any gaps in moving from one slide to the next. Sometimes you might need to deselect this option; for most shows, however, it should be used.

It's time to start your screen show. Make sure <u>A</u>utomatic Advance and <u>G</u>enerate screen show in advance are selected before proceeding.

Running the Screen Show

Click on the Screen Show icon on the Button Bar	The cursor turns into an hourglass and the status bar at the bottom shows the progress in generating the screen show
When the Start Screen Show dialog box appears, click on OK	The CorelSHOW! window disappears and the screen show starts

Your presentation takes up the full screen of the monitor and should advance from the first bullet-point slide to the last. If your show starts over because you have selected the continue option, press Esc to stop it. After the screen show ends, you are returned to CorelSHOW!

If you noticed that any of the bullet points seemed to move or jump when the next point was displayed, the text object probably was moved slightly. This problem is easy to fix: just follow the steps you used to make the slides to duplicate the one that doesn't align properly.

Modifying Your Presentations

You have gotten to see most of the creation features of CorelSHOW!. Now you learn to do some fine-tuning and to modify your shows. What if you need to add or delete slides or pages from your presentation? The following exercises demonstrate how easy these tasks are to perform.

Adding Pages

Click on Page 4 icon	The Page 4 icon turns gray
Choose Insert	The Insert menu appears
Choose Slide	The Insert New Slide dialog box appears
In the Insert pages *text box, type* **1**	
Select After current	
Click on OK	The page icons on the bottom bar have increased to five

That's all there is to adding pages in a presentation.

How about deleting, you ask? No menu command exists for deleting pages. This task must be taken care of from the Slide Sorter mode. Simply click on the page you want to remove from the presentation and press the Delete key. Presto, it's gone! You also can rearrange the order of your slides from the Slide Sorter view.

First you need to finish the presentation the way Joe designed it. A key slide, the introduction, is missing. In the next few exercises, you assemble the introduction slide and use the Slide Sorter mode to move it to the first position.

The introduction slide doesn't have the common title, but it does share the same blue background, so you can use the Independent background feature to make this slide's background different.

Assembling the Intro Slide

Click on Page 5 icon	Page 5 is displayed
Choose View	The View menu appears
Choose Background	The background options menu appears
Choose Independent	The background disappears

Click on Page 4 icon	Page 4 is displayed
Click on the Background View button on the Button Bar	The background for slide 4 is displayed
Click on the blue texture-filled rectangle	The rectangle is selected
*Choose **E**dit*	The Edit menu appears
*Choose **C**opy*	The background is copied to the Clipboard
Click on the Slide View button on the Button Bar	Slide 4 appears
Click on Page 5 icon	Page 5 appears
Click on the Background View button on the Button Bar	Page 5's blank background appears
*Choose **E**dit*	The Edit menu appears
*Choose **P**aste*	The blue background is pasted onto Page 5's background layer

Now that you have the independent background in place for the introduction slide, it is time to move it to the first position in the presentation.

Moving Pages Around

Click on the Slide Sorter view icon on the Button Bar	Thumbnail views of the five slide are displayed (see fig. 16.8)
Click on and hold the Page 5 icon	The page is highlighted
Drag the icon past the first slide	A bar appears before slide 1
Release the mouse button	Slide 5 is placed at the beginning and all slides move down one position

An alternative way to rearrange slides is to use the numbering tool.

Click on the Numbering tool in the middle of the Button Bar	Activates the numbering tool
Click on the slides in the order that you want them	The slides are highlighted

The slides are automatically rearranged when you click on the last slide in your series.

Figure 16.8
The Slide Sorter
view.

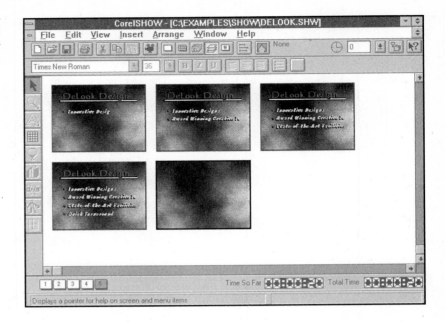

As you have seen, modifying and fine-tuning your presentations is easy using the built-in tools that CorelSHOW! supplies. Using another technique for importing items into Show finishes this presentation.

Inserting Existing Files

You have used CorelSHOW!'s OLE capabilities to add CorelDRAW! elements to your presentation; next, you use the Insert command to bring in a Draw file that has already been prepared. This file is the finishing element on the introduction slide.

Inserting a CorelDRAW! Object

Click on Page 1 icon	Page 1 is displayed
Choose **I**nsert	The Insert menu appears
Choose **O**bject	The Insert Object dialog box appears
Choose Create from **F**ile	The Browse button appears
Choose **B**rowse	

Use the Dri<u>v</u>es and <u>D</u>irectories lists to move to the EXAMPLES\SHOW subdirectory on the *Inside CorelDRAW! 5, Fifth Edition CD-ROM.*

Click on INTROSLD.CDR

Click on OK

All the type for the intro slide was added in one fell swoop. This feature enables you to incorporate your previously developed CorelDRAW! artwork. It also can come in handy to bring things in grouped so that you have less work keeping them lined up.

Adding Transitions

Now that you have the basic show together, you need to add a little pizzazz. A transition will do nicely. A *transition* is a special effect that controls the way a slide or the objects on it enter or exit the screen display. Finish off the presentation by adding a transition to the type object you just inserted on the first slide.

Adding a Transition to the Introduction Slide

Click on Page 1 icon	Page 1 appears
Click on the text object	The object is selected
Click on the Transition Effects button on the Button Bar	The Transition Effects dialog box appears (see fig. 16.9)
In the Opening list, select CurtainOpen	
In the Closing list, select WipeUp	
Click on Pre<u>v</u>iew	The Preview display shows a small preview of both effects
Click on OK	The Transition Effects caption now reads CurtainOpen, WipeUp

You cannot see the effects of your transition until you run the screen show. Run it and watch as the text on the first slide "opens" from the center out to the edges and then "rolls up and away" at the end of the slide duration time.

Transitions can be applied to the slide or to the separate elements on the slide. This concept is the same as the time duration feature. However, transition effects cannot be set for slides that use the <u>C</u>ommon background. You can only set slide transitions for slides that have <u>I</u>ndependent backgrounds.

Figure 16.9
The Transition
Effects dialog
box.

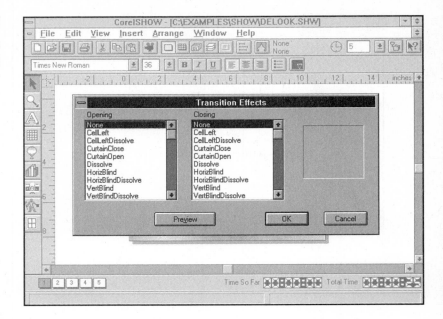

Transitions are much more noticeable on objects such as graphics and text. Objects can have opening and closing transitions. If you are trying for a specific look using several transitions on more than one object contained on the same page, it is important to know how Show paints the objects on your screen. It paints the bottom (back) layers first and the top (front) layer last. If you want an object to appear last when the page is displayed, select the object and use the commands under the **A**rrange menu to bring it to the front. This idea of layers is not hard to grasp because other Corel modules use it as well.

Adding Other Objects

The principles and techniques shown earlier to embed graphics objects apply to all the different objects with which Show can work—whether they are backgrounds created in PhotoPaint or animations created in Move. Some points to keep in mind regarding sound and animation are outlined in the following sections.

Sounds

You can use the **S**ound command in the **I**nsert menu to embed sound files in your Show presentations. You can only incorporate Microsoft-compatible WAV files. If you have WAV files that do not play in Show it's because they don't meet

Microsoft's specifications completely. You won't be able to hear sounds unless you have a sound board installed in your system or have installed Microsoft's poor man's solution: the PC speaker driver.

The PC speaker driver is a software solution that enables you to play WAV files through the small speaker in your computer. You can find this driver on many bulletin boards or get it directly from Microsoft. It is by no means a quality sound solution, but it does work. You might be surprised at how many people are impressed by even the simplest bells and whistles.

Animations

Mixing the movements of animation with charts, graphs, and word slides makes for a very memorable and impressive presentation. Show can accept files saved in the following formats: CorelMOVE! (CMV), Autodesk Animator (FLI, FLC), Video for Windows (AVI), and Quicktime (MOV). You can use the Animation tool in the Toolbar or the <u>A</u>nimation command in the <u>I</u>nsert menu to call up the Insert Animation dialog box. This dialog box gives you access to any animation file on your system. Click on the <u>O</u>ptions button to reveal settings that you can use to get the most out of your animation files. Some types of files cannot make use of all the options shown. Such is the case with CorelMOVE! files, which cannot be set to display F<u>u</u>ll Screen—they simply do not resize. Some Autodesk Animator files can take advantage of this option, but the result might not look very good on your monitor. You have to experiment to find optimal settings for your presentations.

 You cannot make changes to a presentation after it is saved as a screen show file. Save a new presentation as an editable file first, then as a screen show file. For existing presentations, save the screen show file under a different name or in another directory.

Taking Your Shows on the Road

CorelSHOW! enables you to save a presentation so that it can only be run as a screen show and cannot be edited or changed by the viewer. This is the best way to distribute your presentations to others. In addition to running on your computer, the screen show also can be shown on another computer.

To save a file as a screen show, choose <u>F</u>ile, Save <u>A</u>s and select the <u>S</u>creen Show option box. Give it a unique file name.

For CorelSHOW! PLAYER to operate, your system must have Microsoft Windows version 3.1 or higher installed.

If you are going to display your presentations on computers that do not have CorelSHOW! installed, you need to distribute the portable screen show player program, SHOWPLR.EXE, and the presentation that has been saved as a screen show file (SHR). Copy these files to the remote machine's hard disk for best performance.

On the remote machine, load SHOWPLR.EXE by either double-clicking on it in the File Manager or by using the <u>R</u>un command in Program Manager. When the CorelSHOW! PLAYER dialog box appears (see fig. 16.10), use the Dri<u>v</u>es and <u>D</u>irectory lists to move to the location of the screen show file you want to display. In the lower portion of the dialog box, there are some options that you can set, if you want, then press Play. Your screen show will play back as if the remote machine had CorelSHOW! installed on it.

Figure 16.10
The CorelSHOW!
PLAYER dialog
box.

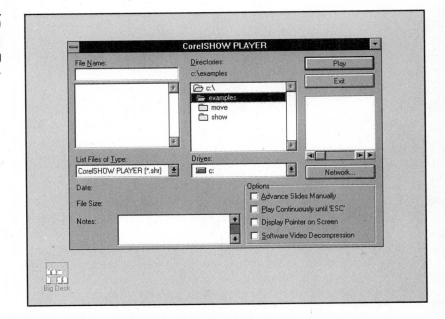

CorelSHOW! offers you the tools to create presentations and screen shows that use state-of-the-art features. Using OLE-capable server applications opens up great possibilities. As programs upgrade to take advantage of OLE's functionality, the capability to combine objects that previously were incompatible becomes a major attraction.

Chapter Snapshot

Will the next Chuck Jones spring from your basement (even if it's not Pismo Beach)? If you have ever had the fantasy of creating your own Saturday-morning cartoons, then CorelMOVE! is for you. In this chapter, you learn to do the following:

✔ Explore the process of animation with actors, props, backgrounds, layers, sound, and storyboarding

✔ Use CorelMOVE!'s menus, Toolbox, and Control Panel

✔ Build and tweak actors and props

✔ Add motion and work with cels

✔ Use Object Linking and Embedding (OLE) to create and place your actors

✔ Give your actors direction by path-editing

✔ Add sound to your animations

✔ Use libraries to save your animation elements

The animation for Chameleon Racing Boats you create in this chapter does a great job of introducing the capabilities of CorelMOVE!. And the exercises you complete help to hone your newfound animation skills. After creating the walking lizard, you will be ready to build more complex animations.

17

CHAPTER

The Basics of CorelMOVE!

orel Corporation's quest is to provide a package that produces every type of graphics image you might need. CorelMOVE! is the newest module to be integrated into the CorelDRAW! suite of applications and is designed to fill the need for a multimedia authoring tool. CorelMOVE! enables you to create animation sequences that can include sounds and special effects.

This chapter teaches you the basics of CorelMOVE!. It introduces the fundamentals of animation and explains how these relate to CorelMOVE!. You see how simple creating animation can be and get an idea of the powerful features CorelMOVE! has to offer to the budding animator.

Thanks to CorelMOVE!, the exciting world of sound and motion falls within the grasp of anyone with the desire to learn and experiment.

What is CorelMOVE!?

Like the screen shows produced by CorelSHOW!, the animations you create with CorelMOVE! are transportable to other computers running Windows. Besides using CorelMOVE! to play back your Move files, with the proper drivers installed, you can play back your animations by using the Microsoft Media Player. You are given the choice in the installation of CorelDRAW! to install the animation drivers for Video for Windows (with extension AVI) and Quicktime for Windows (MOV). The Media Player application was automatically installed by Windows in the Program Manager's Accessories Group.

CorelMOVE! has grown to meet the need to integrate other animation file formats that have become popular. You now have the ability to export your animations to the MPEG Movie (MPG) and PICS Animation (PCS) formats, as well as produce Mac PICT images for viewing on Macintosh systems.

Tip CorelMOVE! files have a CMV extension. Autodesk Animator files have FLI or FLC extensions. Quicktime movies have a MOV extension.

When you couple CorelSHOW!'s capability to import CorelMOVE! and Quicktime files and sequences created in Autodesk's Animator program, adding animation sequences to all your screen shows makes creating true multimedia presentations a reality.

CorelMOVE! animations are developed by rendering graphical elements, actors, and props as separate components. These components are assembled and edited into finished sequences. Added sound effects and cues complete a multimedia production. This modular concept offers you the flexibility to "mix and match" the elements you create. Elements can be organized into libraries for easy retrieval and use in other animated productions.

Exploring Animation

Animation is the process of bringing to life that which is inanimate. Common animation techniques are based on the way live-action motion is photographed for movies. In a movie, scores of photos are snapped every second to capture motion in progress. Each separate picture is called a *frame*. When played back, the projected image appears to be moving.

In animation, artists create the individual frames. Artists must study and draw in sequence every progressive part of a movement (see fig. 17.1). Sound like a lot of work? It is! Computers and programs like CorelMOVE!, however, make it much less difficult.

Figure 17.1
Renderings needed to animate walking motion.

Walt Disney, perhaps the most famous animator of all time, elevated the process of animation to an art form. He perfected techniques used to make animated characters seem more lifelike. He combined his characters with perfectly coordinated sound tracks, placed them on stunning background paintings, and painstakingly recorded his masterpieces on film.

For many of us, the most familiar form of animation is the common cartoon. You can carve away many hours on a Saturday morning digesting the surreal antics of talking dogs, muscle-bound superheroes, and zany aliens. The techniques used to produce these "not-quite-Disneylike" features are closely related to CorelMOVE!'s style of animation.

With CorelMOVE!, you create and coordinate the same three basic animation elements that all traditional animators work with: actors, props, and sounds. Sound is not really a necessity; in fact, only those who have sound boards installed in their computers can use sound in CorelMOVE!. (This gives you a great excuse to buy that sound board you have been drooling over.)

Actors

Actors are the most important elements in your animated creations, but they also are the most complex items to develop. Actors usually are made up of several cels depicting each phase of a movement. There are instances, however, when an actor can be just one cel in length.

Cel is short for cellulose acetate—the clear material on which traditional animators paint their characters. The material must be transparent so that the background painting shows through as each frame of the progressive motion is photographed in sequence.

You must know what your actors are going to do so that you can map out and dissect their movements. Then you are ready to render your individual cels. This important planning stage, called *storyboarding*, is discussed later in the chapter.

Props

Props are rendered just like actors. However, because they don't need to show different stages of motion, they are rendered on a single cel only. Props are still very versatile. They can be completely stationary or manipulated with Move's built-in transitions during the course of your movie. *Transitions* are special effects that enhance the way props enter and exit your animation. Good use of props adds depth to your animations.

Backgrounds

Backgrounds are the scenery against which the actors and props move. Background paintings often are major productions in big-budget animations. You need backgrounds in CorelMOVE! animations because you don't want your actors and props cavorting around a stark white screen. As far as CorelMOVE! is concerned, backgrounds are considered props. Usually, you render them at a size that covers the entire animation window and place them on the bottom layer.

Layers

CorelMOVE! uses the same concept as CorelDRAW! when it comes to layering items. You can move an element to the front of everything else, to the back, or anywhere in between. CorelMOVE! makes it exceedingly easy to rearrange the layering of animation elements.

An actor can never be placed behind a prop. Props always appear on a layer behind actors.

Sound

If you have a sound board installed in your system, background sounds can be incorporated into the show to make it much more exciting and professional. Move's capabilities in the sound department have grown over the last year. Not only does Move offer a built-in WAVE file-recording and editing tool, it also has expanded its importing capabilities to allow incorporation of several different sound types from several different computer systems. In the Import Sound dialog box, you now can select from the following choices: Video for Windows (AVI), CorelMOVE! (CMV), Promotion Animation (MWF), WAVE files (WAV), AIFF Audio (AIF), MacSND (SND), Sound Blaster Audio (VOC), and Amiga SVX (SVX).

As you become more experienced, you might even synchronize recorded voices with a character's movements to make it appear that the character is talking. Unfortunately, CorelMOVE!'s fundamental design does not make this a very practical idea if you are expecting to take your animation to another system. Proper synchronization of sound and video is lost very rapidly when exporting to a movie format or playing your Move file on a computer that has a different processor or video card.

Storyboarding

The first step in producing your animation is planning. Answer the questions who, what, when, and where before you start the actual animation process; this saves a tremendous amount of time redoing work later. The traditional term for this step is *storyboarding*. You plan your animation by sketching single frames and placing them in the order they appear in the animation. Only key frames need to be rendered: those that show a different view of an actor, a new prop entering or exiting the scene, or the beginning of a new scene.

How much work should you put into storyboarding? If your animation is simple and you are working alone, your storyboard can be simple and sketchy. If you are working with many others on an elaborate project, the storyboard must be detailed enough to give everybody sufficient information to "see" the movie and be able to complete their specific tasks.

So then, talking dogs, muscle-bound superheroes, and zany aliens parading around your computer screen are only a few steps away, right? Yes and no. Some factors that affect the overall quality of your productions must be considered.

For the best possible animations, you need better-than-average computer power. CorelMOVE! is carrying out many instructions and is pushing tons of pixels around on your screen. The number of cels in your actor, the speed at which you want your animations to move (frames per second), the number of actors and props used in your show, and the incorporation of sound are all factors that have a dramatic effect on your computer's performance. Even a simple animation can bring a weak CPU with a small, slow hard disk and minimal RAM to a crawl. Do not dismiss the importance of a fast video system. Accelerator cards and systems that incorporate local bus, EISA, or PCI architecture keep your animations zipping along. Of equal concern is the amount of hard disk space you have free on your computer. Animations can grow extremely large, very quickly. Keep plenty of empty space around, or you might find yourself unable to save the masterpiece you just spent hours perfecting.

If you are serious about animation, buy the biggest, fastest hardware you can afford. You won't regret it. If you are simply getting your feet wet, experiment with CorelMOVE!. See what you can do with the resources you have. You will undoubtedly be surprised by what you accomplish.

Another factor is experience. Animation is an art. Walt Disney honed his skills over time; it paid off. Your practice will too. Reading imparts to you the experience of others, so go to the library and check out some books on animation. Subscribe to magazines that specialize in multimedia.

Study the work of other animators. To this end, the samples supplied by Corel on the CD are an invaluable source of information. Open them up. Examine them closely. Look at all the actors and the cels that make them move.

Finally, have patience. Consider that one minute's worth of animation in a typical high-quality animated film is composed of 1,440 cels. In CorelMOVE!, you won't make anywhere near that number of cels, but the basic principles still apply. The work can be tedious. If you take your time, you can produce professional-looking animations.

Joe DeLook Goes Multimedia

Last year, Joe's old pal, Rip Raster, had a project for DeLook Design that allowed Joe to use CorelMOVE! to create a multimedia show to attract potential buyers' attention. This project was a huge success and helped Joe to continue his use of animation and multimedia presentations.

Now Joe uses CorelMOVE! to make presentations to potential clients of his own. He's seen the way sound and motion can really affect people. Joe has a very important presentation to make to the Chameleon Racing Boat Company. Chameleon is known worldwide for their fast boats and flashy paint jobs. DeLook Designs has a chance to design all the graphics used on Chameleon's entire line of racing boats.

Joe wants to customize his presentation to the Chameleon executives, so he's going to develop a short, animated introduction which later he will incorporate into a presentation he has developed in CorelSHOW!. Joe's project in CorelMOVE! is the basis for the exercises you follow here.

If you are ready, pull up your director's chair, put on your favorite beret, and grab your megaphone. Next stop—Movieland!

Starting CorelMOVE!—Lights, Camera, Action!

First you must start CorelMOVE! and become familiar with its tools. Then you can work through a simple example to see the way an animation, with actors and props, is created.

Upon installation, CorelDRAW! 5.0 creates a Program Group in Program Manager called Corel 5. In it, you find the CorelMOVE! icon. Double-click on the icon to start the program. After a few seconds, CorelMOVE!'s window stares you in the face.

Understanding the CorelMOVE! Workspace

CorelMOVE! has two work areas: the Animation Window and the Editor. Unfortunately, when you start CorelMOVE! you are in neither. You see only a bleak-looking, gray backdrop and an anemic menu bar. All the menus except File and Help are inaccessible. You do not have much choice here; you need to start a new file (see fig. 17.2).

Starting a New Move File

Click on File

Click on New   The Select Name For New File dialog box
                                                 appears (see fig. 17.2)

In the File Name *text box, type* **Test1**   The CMV extension is automatically added to
                                                 the end of the file name when you choose OK

Use Drives and Directories to store the file where you will remember it. Do yourself a favor and don't choose a floppy disk.

Click on OK   You now are in the Animation window, and
                                                 the name of your file is displayed in
                                                 CorelMOVE!'s title bar

---

Figure 17.2
Starting a
new file.

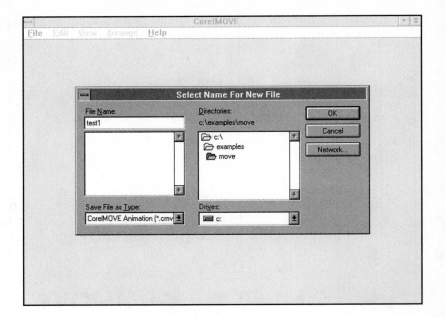

Touring the Animation Window

The Animation window is the workspace where you assemble and arrange the elements of your animation. You assign to actors movements (paths) across the image area and specify the entering and exiting transitions for your props. This is not where you create the actors and props; that is done in the Editor. The global parameters of your animation are set or modified from this workspace. These parameters include how big (in pixels) your animation window is, how many frames long it runs, and how fast it plays back.

Now is the best time to become familiar with the Animation window. At the top, notice that the menu bar has come to life. All but one of the menu titles are now accessible. Right in the middle of the screen is the Animation Screen area. The Toolbox is positioned along the left side, and the Control Panel rests along the bottom (see fig. 17.3).

Menus

You can now scan each menu and get a look at the available options. This is your chance to play detective and investigate. It doesn't do any harm to click on Cancel to get out of any dialog boxes. Take note of Import in the File menu and Insert Object in the Edit menu. Although they look the same, they serve slightly different purposes. If you select the <u>T</u>imelines, <u>C</u>el Sequencer, or <u>L</u>ibrary Roll-Up menus under <u>D</u>isplay, more toys appear. You get to use these options later.

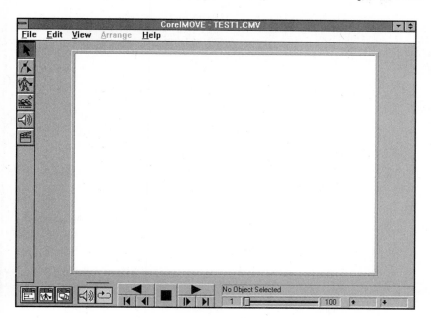

Figure 17.3
CorelMOVE!'s Animation window.

Frame Window

All of the elements of your movie are assembled and played back inside the frame window area. You can change the height and width of the frame from the <u>A</u>nimation Information dialog box under the <u>D</u>isplay menu. Keep in mind that your animations are played on other computers that might not run the same video resolution as yours. If yours produces an animation with a frame size of 800 × 600, and you attempt to play it back on a system with 640 × 480 (VGA), 120 pixels on the right side and 140 pixels on the bottom of your creation get lopped off.

Toolbox

Six tools are available in CorelMOVE!: Pick tool, Path tool, Actor tool, Prop tool, Sound tool, and Cue tool. Table 17.1 shows each tool and its purpose.

Table 17.1
The Toolbox Tools

Icon	Tool Name	Use
![Pick tool icon]	Pick tool	For selecting or moving actors and props; works just like the Pick tool in CorelDRAW!.
![Path tool icon]	Path tool	For selecting actors and applying paths to them; also for selecting and editing existing paths. Similar to the Shape tool in CorelDRAW!.
![Actor tool icon]	Actor tool	For creating new actors. It opens a dialog box that enables you to choose the editor of your choice: Move's paint editor, Paint, or Draw 5.0.
![Prop tool icon]	Prop tool	For creating new props. It opens a dialog box that enables you to choose the editor of your choice: Move's paint editor, Paint, or Draw 5.0.
![Sound tool icon]	Sound tool	For placing sounds into a CMV file. It opens a dialog box that enables you to use CorelMOVE!'s Wave Editor to record and modify WAV files.
![Cue tool icon]	Cue tool	For creating cues. The Cue Information dialog box appears. Cues enable you to automatically start, stop, pause, or jump to other frames in your animations. Cues can also be "chained" together to add a great deal of user interaction and playback flexibility.

Control Panel

Starting on the far left of the Control Panel are icons that display the <u>T</u>imelines, <u>L</u>ibrary, and <u>C</u>el Sequencer Roll-Up menus. These are tools you use to fine-tune your animations; they activate the same roll-ups you saw under the <u>D</u>isplay menu.

In the middle is a cluster of seven VCR-style push-button controls. These are used to play your animation in a variety of ways. To the left of these playback controls are two more controls. The top one shows a speaker, and the bottom one has an oval shape with an arrowhead on it. Table 17.2 shows these controls and their functions.

Table 17.2
Control Panel Controls

Icon	Control Name	Function
	Stop	Stops playback of your animation
	Forward	Plays back your animation (with sound, if enabled)
	Forward One Frame	Plays back one frame each time you click on it
	Reverse	Reverses playback of your animation (without sound, even if enabled)
	Reverse One Frame	Reverses playback one frame each time you click on it
	First Frame	Moves to frame one
	Last Frame	Moves to last frame
	Loop	Provides continuous playback of your animation until the Stop button is clicked

II

Using Corel's Modules

continues

Table 17.2 Continued
Control Panel Controls

Icon	Control Name	Function
	Enable Sound	Enables sound during normal forward playback (has no effect if you do not have a sound board installed)

Rounding out the Control Panel is a slider control that enables you to move through the frames comprising your animated production. The numbers on either side of the slider inform you which frame you are viewing and the total number of frames in your animation. Other status fields on the Control Panel display important information about the currently selected actor or prop. You are kept aware of the selection's type, name, number of cels, and in which frames it enters and exits the animation.

Creating and Modifying Actors and Props

The other workspace you use to create animations is the Editor. CorelMOVE! is unique among animation packages because it offers a choice of four different editors for creating or modifying actors and props: the built-in Move bitmap editor, the Paint 5.0 module, CorelCHART! 5.0, and CorelDRAW! 5.0. Which one you use depends on an array of factors.

The Move editor and Paint are bitmap-based paint programs. If you are comfortable with this type of program and their tools suit your needs, use them.

If charts play a part in your animation, CorelCHART! is a natural to work with, and when you use CorelDRAW! 5.0 as your editor, you get the power of a vector-based drawing package. All the tools available in Draw are at your disposal. The combined power of the different applications pushes CorelMOVE! ahead of the pack.

As you examine each editor's tools and functions, you realize that each has strengths and weaknesses. The beauty of CorelMOVE! is that you are not locked into using just one editor. Use them all; what works for you is the right tool for the job!

To examine the editors, you need to have something to edit. Tell CorelMOVE! that you want to create or modify an actor or prop with the following steps:

Creating a New Actor

Select the Actor tool	The New Actor dialog box appears

In the Object **N**ame *text box, type*
TestActor

Although CorelMOVE! assigns arbitrary names for your animation elements, it's a good idea to supply unique names that make them easy to identify. These are not file names, only labels.

Click on the **C**reate New *option*

Click on CorelDRAW! 5.0 Graphic in the Object **T**ype *list*

Click on OK	CorelDRAW! starts

Through the magic of OLE, CorelDRAW! starts and a link is established between it and CorelMOVE!. *OLE* stands for object linking and embedding, a Windows feature that enables you to create files that share and transfer information between OLE-capable applications, such as Move, Draw, Chart, and Paint. OLE makes it possible to dynamically edit animation elements created in Draw or Paint directly from Move. If you look closely, you see that this is not a common circumstance in CorelDRAW! (see fig. 17.4).

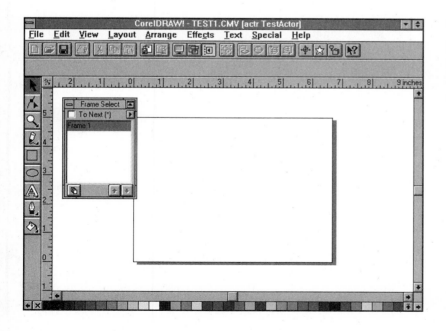

Figure 17.4
Using CorelDRAW! 5.0 as the editor.

Using Corel's Modules

The text in the title bar at the top indicates that the file it is linked to is Test1.CMV. It also reveals that this element is an actor and displays its name.

A new roll-up menu called Frame Select is conspicuously positioned in the upper left corner. Think of it as a modified version of the normal Layers Roll-Up menu. This roll-up provides everything you need to use CorelDRAW! to create multiple-cel actors.

There are other changes in the File menu. Update initiates the "rendering" function and uses OLE to transfer all your work from Draw to Move. Exit & Return does the same thing; however, it closes this instance of Draw. If you're sure that you won't do any more editing to this actor, or you're running low on Windows resources, use Exit & Return. Save Copy As enables you to save the current drawing as a native CDR file.

Take more time to look around, then choose Exit & Return. When you are presented with the Import Imaging Options dialog box, click on Cancel.

Now create a new actor using CorelPHOTO-PAINT!. The same types of changes have been made to Paint's File menu and title bar. The biggest difference between this editor and Draw or the Move editor is the lack of support for making the individual frames that comprise an actor. What Paint excels at is making elaborate scenery that moves because it's really a one-cel actor moving along a path.

Creating Your First Actor

You are ready to create your first actor. Cancel everything you have been doing to get back to the Animation window. Take a deep breath; in a few seconds, you will push the Actor tool icon on the Toolbar yet another time.

Following Joe DeLook's lead, you will create the animation that he designed as the intro to his Chameleon Racing Boat presentation. He was familiar with the company's logo (see fig. 17.5) and wanted this graphic to be an integral part of his animation sequence.

Joe's ideas started to come together as he went through his storyboarding process. The concept he ended up with was a lizard walking on screen from the left and stopping in the middle of the screen. The lizard would merge into the company logo and dissolve, through special effects, into nothing.

Joe felt he was ready to render his lizard drawings. He already had the ending lizard drawing—it would be the same as the company logo. Now he needed to create the beginning drawing and all the other key renderings, which, when played back, would make the lizard look like it was walking. Joe quickly realized that he did not have enough knowledge of how a lizard walked, so he went to do research

at the local pet store. On returning to the studio, he produced the sketches shown
in figure 17.6.

Figure 17.5
The Chameleon
Racing Boat
logo.

You don't have to do all the work for this exercise because Joe's work
has been provided on the *Inside CorelDRAW! 5, Fifth Edition CD-ROM*
that accompanies this book; you can find all the necessary files in the
EXAMPLES\MOVE subdirectory. Someday, however, you will have a
project that will cause you to retrace many of the key planning steps Joe
followed.

Before you start the next exercise, you need to set certain options.

Changing the Animation Window Size

Click on **E**dit	The Edit menu appears
Click on Animation Info	The Animation Information dialog box appears
In the **W**idth *text box, type* **600**	
In the **H**eight *text box, type* **380**	
Click on OK	

Figure 17.6
Sketches of key
positions during
a lizard's walk.

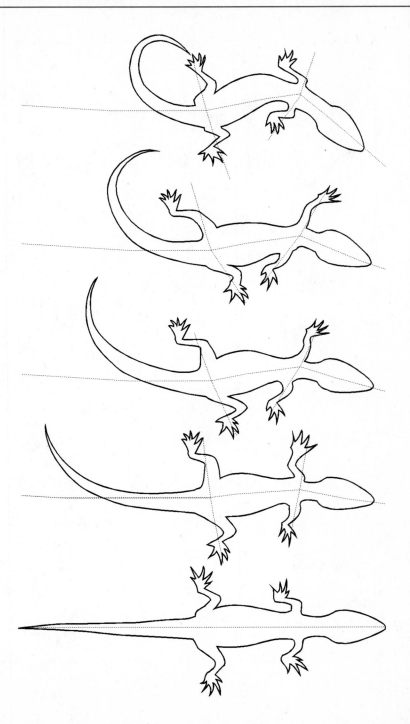

Now it's time to push that Actor button. When the New Actor dialog box appears, name your actor **Lizard1**. Choose CorelDRAW! 5.0 Graphic as your Object Type. Make sure that Create New is still selected and click on OK.

When CorelDRAW! is ready, follow the directions in the next exercise to render your walking lizard.

Joe took his initial drawings, then refined and scanned them. Next, he ran them through CorelTRACE! to get vector graphics, which are easily manipulated in CorelDRAW!. He rendered five drawings that showed one complete lizard stride—from a completely straight position to the curled position found in the logo. Finally, he stored each of them in separate CDR files.

The following steps show how to use CorelDRAW!'s Import feature to bring Joe's drawings together to make the multiple-cel lizard actor.

Creating a Lizard

Click on File

Click on Import   The Import dialog box appears

Click on the List Files of Type   The List of file types drop-down list appears

Click on CorelDRAW! *(*.CDR)*   The List of file names shows only CDR files in the current subdirectory

Use the Drive and Directories to move to the CD-ROM drive and the EXAMPLES\MOVE subdirectory.

Click on LIZARD1.CDR

Click on OK

Using Corel's Modules

Tip   When working in an editor, the terms frame and cel are interchangeable. They cannot be used interchangeably when working in the Animation window, however.

What you see is the first position for your lizard. It is, by default, placed on Frame 1. Notice that Frame 1 is highlighted in the Frame Select Roll-Up. To import the rest of the lizard drawings, it is necessary to add more frames to your actor.

Using the Frame Select Roll-Up Menu

Most motion is highly repetitive. Regularly shaped objects, such as balls or boxes, have very few distinctive views. Sometimes, merely variations in shadowing or coloring distinguish one key frame from another. Irregularly shaped objects, such as lizards and people, are not as simple to animate, but there still is a lot of repetitive motion that makes having cut and paste functions a real pleasure. This is where the Frame Select Roll-Up menu shines.

To start the lizard walking, you need to insert more cels into your actor's sequence. You only need enough cels to show one complete stride of the lizard—four frames—so three more renderings besides the original are sufficient. Eventually, you will use the Frame Select Roll-Up menu and its pop-up menu to add more frames, fill them with renderings, and then copy and modify these renderings to animate complete striding motion.

The Frame Select Roll-Up menu has, just below the title bar, a small button with a black triangle (see fig. 17.7). The fly-out menu is accessed by clicking on it. From this menu, you can easily insert cels, delete cels, copy items from one cel to another, and set options that help in viewing your cels.

Figure 17.7
The Frame Select fly-out menu.

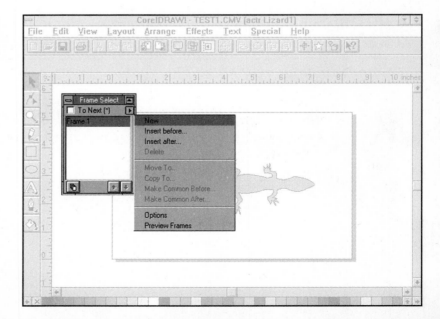

Making the Lizard Walk

On the Frame Select Roll-Up menu, click on the fly-out menu button (a triangle)	The fly-out menu appears
Click on Insert after	The Insert New Frames dialog box appears
Type **3**	
Click on OK	The Frame Select Roll-Up menu shows a frame count of 4
Select Frame 1 *from the Frame Select Roll-Up menu*	The lizard appears
Select Frame 2 *from the Frame Select Roll-Up menu*	The lizard disappears

If you see the outline of the lizard on a frame on which it should not be, it's because it's still selected somewhere else. This can be beneficial, but if it's annoying, simply click anywhere on the frame to deselect the rendering.

You are ready to import the next rendering of the lizard.

Click on File	
Click on Import	The Import dialog box appears

You can use the Import icon on the Toolbar instead of clicking on File, Import.

Click on the List Files of Type *drop-down list*	The List of file types appears
Click on CorelDRAW! (.CDR)*	The list of file names shows only CDR files in the current subdirectory

Use the drive and directory areas to move to the CD-ROM drive and the EXAMPLES\MOVE subdirectory.

Click on LIZARD2.CDR	
Click on OK	

Use the same procedure to select the next frame in the Frame Select Roll-Up and use Import to bring Lizard3.CDR into frame 3 and Lizard4.CDR into frame 4. In case you're wondering, Lizard5.CDR won't be used until the creation of the merger with the Chameleon Racing Boat logo; the last frame of the third stride.

The Frame Select Roll-Up provides you several ways to see how the animation is progressing. You could click on each frame in the Frame select window very quickly—crude, but it works. Another method is to use the up and down arrow keys at the bottom of the roll-up to cycle through the cels. This is a better method, but not the best.

Another is to press the Preview button on the bottom left of the roll-up. This presents a box with a small thumbnail view of the separate cels. First, they are rendered one at a time; then you can select Preview to automatically view all the cels one after another. Up and down arrows are provided so that you can step through each frame at your own pace. When you're finished previewing your work, choose OK.

As you preview the cels, notice that the lizard's legs appear to be moving properly, but his body is shifting around when it should be fairly stationary. This bouncy, jumpy motion is not the desired effect. The individual lizard renderings need to be shifted to align the body positions better. Another item on the fly-out roll-up helps with this.

Using the Onion Skin

Click on the Frame Select fly-out menu

Click on Options   The Frame Options dialog box appears

Click on **N**ext Frame   The Next Frame option is activated

Click on **P**revious Frame   The Previous Frame option is activated

Click on In **F**ront   The In Front option is activated

Click on OK

The colors that you select for the wireframe are also used to display the names of the frames in the Frame Select Roll-Up. This makes it easier to distinguish which wireframe belongs to which frame.

Now you will be able to see the rendering on the current cel, and wireframe views of the renderings on the frame before and after it. The wireframe colors correspond to the colors on the color selector buttons in the Frame Options dialog box. If you want to change these colors, go back into the Frames Option dialog box and click on the color icons. The color selectors act like those found in CorelDRAW!.

The In <u>F</u>ront option determines if the before and after wireframes are placed in front of or behind the current rendering. Note that CorelDRAW!'s "edit in wireframe" toggle switch operates as usual; this also aids in viewing your animation cels. Highlight each frame in the Frame Select Roll-Up and see the benefits to using the Onion Skin option.

The next task is to align the individual lizards to create a smooth walking motion. To achieve this, you will position the renderings so that the shoulders of the upper legs and the base of the neck are in the same approximate position. Don't worry about precise placement. You will use the position of the lizard on Frame 1 as your starting point.

Positioning the Lizard

Click on Frame 2	The lizard on Frame 2 appears
Click on the Lizard rendering	The rendering is selected

Use Draw's Zoom tool to get in closer and position the lizard so that the upper shoulders and neck area look as they do in figure 17.8. Following the same procedures, continue to Frames 3 and 4, making the same types of adjustments.

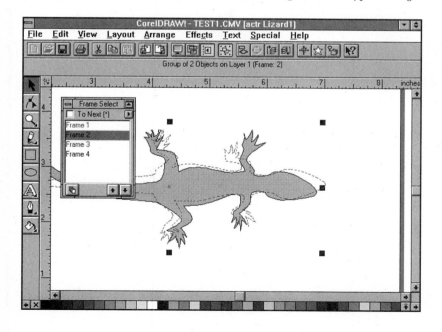

Figure 17.8
Positioning lizard renderings using the Onion Skin option.

II

Using Corel's Modules

You will need to preview your stride sequence again using any of the methods previously mentioned. When you are satisfied that what you are previewing is a lizard taking one stride forward, it's time to return to Move and see what it looks like there.

Returning to Move

Click on <u>F</u>ile	The File menu appears
Click on E<u>x</u>it & Return	The Rendering Frames dialog box appears and shows the progress of its exporting functions

Next, the Import imaging options dialog box appears, enabling you to control how the renderings are converted for Move's use. You can experiment with the Perform high quality dithering, but it is best to leave it checked for this exercise.

The options grouped in the transparent color area are very important. When you return from CorelDRAW!, your vector images are transformed into bitmap images—just like TIFF or PCX files. This transparency feature means that any image you set on a layer lower than the actor will show through. This often is not what you want, so these settings control which colors it should or should not make transparent when images are converted. Choosing <u>N</u>one makes your actor display within a gray rectangle. If you don't want your actor to have any transparency, pick the color that does not appear in your renderings. The Color <u>t</u>olerance setting enables a range of colors, starting at the color you choose, to be made transparent.

Click on <u>W</u>hite

In the Color <u>t</u>olerance *text box, type* **0**

Click on OK

The bounding box that surrounds an actor or prop denotes the entire space that it will occupy in the animation. For an actor, this means the complete range of motion depicted in the sequence of cels. This causes the bounding box to be much larger than some of the renderings in some cels.

OLE takes care of shutting down CorelDRAW! and placing the actor in the Animation window. If all goes well, Lizard1 is ready to strut his stuff. Your actors initially will display with a bounding box composed of moving dashed lines. This box indicates that the actor is selected. If you need to, reposition the lizard to the center of the Animation window by moving the cursor anywhere within the selection area and clicking and dragging the actor to its new position.

Now let's see some action. Click on the forward VCR button on the Control Panel and watch the lizard dance. Pretty wild, huh? If the Loop push-button is depressed, the animation plays continuously until you click on the Stop button. Let it run, and observe that the slider control moves and the Frame Counter status fields change. After you are sufficiently dizzy, click on the Stop button.

When you need to make changes to your actor, double-click on it. This brings up the Actor Information dialog box (see fig. 17.9). You can modify almost every aspect of the actor by changing the values in the text boxes. This dialog box also is the gateway back to CorelDRAW!. Click on the Edit Actor button at the lower left to launch back to Draw. The actor is loaded and ready to edit. The same procedure is used for props.

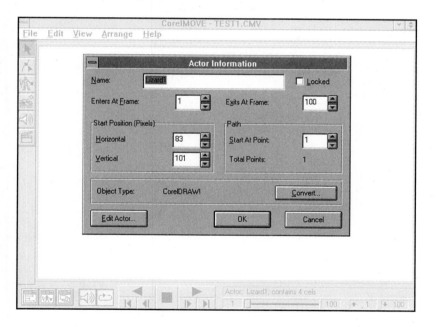

Figure 17.9
The Actor Information dialog box.

Using Corel's Modules

Because the rest of his strides are not rendered, the lizard's movement appears spastic. This is overcome by editing Lizard1 in CorelDRAW! to complete the walking motion. Double-click Lizard1 and click on the Edit Actor button. When CorelDRAW! is up and running, use the Frame Select Roll-Up menu to add more cels and to finish two more strides.

Finishing the Lizard's Cels

Click on Frame 4	The lizard on Frame 4 appears
On the Frame Select Roll-Up menu, click on the fly-out menu button	The fly-out menu appears
Click on Insert after	The Insert new frames dialog box appears
Type **3**	
Click on OK	The Frame Select Roll-Up shows a frame count of 7

Here, the copy and paste functions of CorelDRAW! make short order of finishing the repeating parts of the lizard's strides. First get the lizard back to his starting position, then start on the second stride.

Click on Frame 3	The lizard on Frame 3 appears
Click on the lizard rendering	The lizard is highlighted
On the Frame Select Roll-Up menu, click on the fly-out menu button	The fly-out menu appears
Click on Copy To	The To? arrow appears
Click on Frame 5	You are now on Frame 5, and the lizard from Frame 3 is copied to Frame 5
Click on Frame 2	The lizard on Frame 2 appears
Click on the lizard rendering	The lizard is highlighted
Click on the fly-out menu button	The fly-out menu appears
Click on Copy To	The To? arrow appears
Click on Frame 6	You are now on Frame 6, and the lizard from Frame 2 is copied to Frame 6
Click on Frame 1	The lizard on Frame 1 appears
Click on the lizard rendering	The lizard is highlighted
Click on the fly-out menu button	The fly-out menu appears
Click on Copy To	The To? arrow appears
Click on Frame 7	You are now on Frame 7, and the lizard from Frame 1 is copied to Frame 7

Check that the position of the last lizard matches up well with the previous cel. If not, reposition it now. You have finished the complete striding motion on the top side. Preview your work. When you are ready, you will add more cels and use Draw's mirror function to render the second stride that moves the lizard's legs and tail in the opposite direction.

Click on Frame 7	The lizard on Frame 7 appears
Click on the fly-out menu button	The fly-out menu appears
Click on Insert after	The Insert new frames dialog box appears
Type **5**	
Click on OK	The Frame Select roll-up shows a frame count of 12
Click on Frame 6	The lizard on Frame 6 appears
Click on the lizard rendering	The lizard is highlighted
Click on the fly-out menu button	The fly-out menu appears
Click on Copy To	The To? arrow appears
Click on Frame 8	The lizard from Frame 6 is copied to Frame 8
Click on Effects	The Effects menu appears
Click on the Transform Roll-Up menu	The Transform Roll-Up appears
Click on the Scale/Mirror icon	The roll-up changes to display the Scale and Mirror options
Click on the Vertical Mirror button (see fig. 17.10)	
Click on Apply	The lizard is mirrored

Although the lizard will be moving his legs and tail to the opposite side, these motions are the same as the first, only mirrored; that is why you can use the Mirror function. Position the Transform Roll-Up menu so that it's out of your way.

Once again, you will use the Onion Skin option to position this rendering. Unfortunately, the Onion Skin options are not saved when you exit CorelDRAW! and return to Move, so you will need to reset them for this editing session. Remember that the upper shoulders and neck are what you are trying to keep in the same general area. When you are finished, you should have something that looks like figure 17.11. Let's complete this portion of the sequence.

Figure 17.10
Using the
Transform
Roll-Up menu.

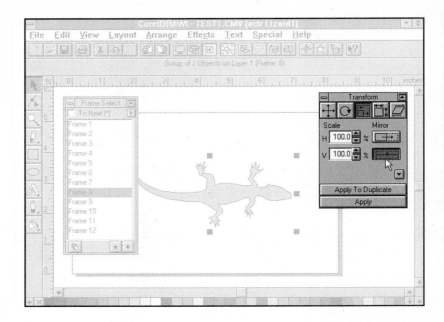

Figure 17.10
Using the
Transform
Roll-Up menu.

Figure 17.11
Positioning the
mirrored lizard
rendering.

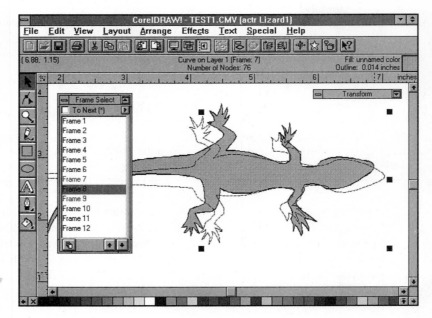

Continuing the Lizard's Cels

Click on Frame 5	The lizard on Frame 5 appears
Click on the lizard rendering	The lizard is highlighted
Click on the fly-out menu button	The fly-out menu appears
Click on Copy To	The To? arrow appears
Click on Frame 9	The lizard from Frame 5 is copied to Frame 9
Click on the Transform Roll-Up	
Click on the Vertical Mirror button	
Click on Apply	The lizard is mirrored

Reposition this lizard and using the above techniques to copy Frame 4 through Frame 10, mirror and position this lizard. Creating the return motion will be simple copying. You won't need the Transform Roll-Up any longer, so you can go ahead and minimize it.

Click on Frame 9	The lizard on Frame 9 appears
Click on the lizard rendering	The lizard is highlighted
Click on the fly-out menu button	The fly-out menu appears
Click on Copy To	The To? arrow appears
Click on Frame 11	The lizard from Frame 9 is copied to Frame 11
Click on Frame 8	The lizard on Frame 8 appears
Click on the lizard rendering	The lizard is highlighted
Click on the fly-out menu button	The fly-out menu appears
Click on Copy To	The To? arrow appears
Click on Frame 12	The lizard from Frame 8 is copied to Frame 12

When you preview your work, you see that the lizard takes two strides, one to each side. The last stride ends just before the starting position, which is appropriate. As the walking sequence is played in a continual loop, the last cel and the first cel will match up perfectly.

To get back to Move, choose File, Exit & Return to and set the Transparency options to White with 0 Color tolerance.

Now that you are back in Move, you can see the fruits of your labor. Push the forward VCR control and watch the lizard continually stride. After a while, this will become boring for both you and the lizard. That's because he's getting (and going) nowhere.

Now it's time to give the lizard a little push in the right direction. First, you'll move Lizard1 to a good starting point. You can do this by selecting and moving it with the mouse or by changing the Start Position coordinates in the Actor Information dialog box; the latter method makes it easier to work through the example.

Moving the Starting Position

Double-click on Lizard1   The Actor Information dialog box appears

In the **H**orizontal *text box, type* **-377**

In the **V**ertical *text box, type* **126**

Click on OK

Lizard1 is now positioned in the far left of the Animation window. To get it to move across the screen, it needs a path to follow. A simple path needs only two points: a beginning and an end. The coordinate pair your actor starts from is the *beginning node*; the coordinate pair your actor finishes at is the *end node*. A very active actor has a complicated path with many intermediate nodes.

To assign a path to an actor, select the actor with the Path tool. Path nodes can be set anywhere in Move's Animation window or gray backdrop.

Using the Path Edit Roll-Up Menu

Select the Path tool from the Toolbox and click on Lizard1. The Path Edit Roll-Up menu appears, and the actor is surrounded by a bounding box. Move your mouse to the middle of the Animation window and click once about halfway down the side as shown in figure 17.12. If a new node is not made, make sure that the Allow Adding Points option at the bottom of the Edit Path roll-up menu is checked, then try it again.

A line is drawn between the starting node (which you can't see because it's off the screen) and a black circle, which designates the end node. A two-node path is not very exciting. Lizard1 needs more motivation for you to get the most from him; more nodes get things popping. First, get your ending node in the right spot. The next two exercises demonstrate these procedures.

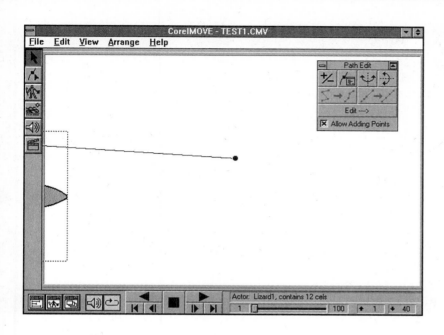

Figure 17.12
Using the
Path tool.

Changing a Node's Position

Click on Lizard1 *with the Path tool*	Lizard1 is selected and the beginning and end nodes are connected by a line
Double-click on the end node	The Point Information dialog box appears

The Point Information dialog box can be accessed for every node on a path.

In the Horizontal *text box, type* **87**

In the Vertical *text box, type* **130**

If not already checked, select the
Loop To Here *option*

Click on OK	Lizard1 repositions

As you run your animation, you will see the lizard jump from the left edge of the screen to the middle and then get nowhere for the duration of the animation. This is because there are no intermediate points on the path.

Paths are used to make your actors move about the screen. Think of the cels as someone jogging in place; all the right motions are there, just no direction.

How do paths relate to cels and frames during playback in the Animation window? For every frame in the animation, in this case 100, the actor displays a cel. If there is a path, the actor displays the next cel at the next path point. If there are more path points or frames than there are cels in an actor's sequence, then the actor will play over continuously at the end of the path until the frames run out.

Let's add some more points to Lizard1's path to achieve smooth forward motion.

Adding More Nodes to a Path

Click on the +/- button on the Path Edit Roll-Up *menu*	The Scale Path dialog box appears
In the **D**esired *text box, type* **40**	
Click on OK	

You now have 40 nodes on the path. Push the Forward button on the Control Panel and watch the fun. The Scale Path dialog box is used to delete, as well as add, nodes to a path.

Why is the lizard running to the middle of the screen, remaining there and gyrating away? Because the last node is set as the Loop To Here node. The Loop To Here (LTH) node performs a special function. See what happens when you change its location to another node on the path.

Changing the Loop To Here Node

Click on Lizard1 with the Path tool	
Double-click on any node on the path	The Point Information dialog box appears
Click on the Loop To Here option	
Click on OK	

Now play back your animation. As you see, changing the LTH node makes a big difference in the way your animation works. Experiment by changing the LTH node setting to different nodes on the path.

You should understand the logic behind this behavior. After an actor runs through its sequence of cels (in this case 12), it immediately moves to the LTH node and plays its sequence over and over until the allotted number of frames in the animation expire. So, when the LTH node is set at the end of the path, the lizard stops there and runs through its entire sequence; it has no place left to go. If set to the first node, the lizard moves to the end of the path, jumps to the first node, then runs the whole path again. This repetition continues until all the frames of the animation run out.

If the LTH node is set to a node other than the end, a connection line is drawn between it and the end node. This line is now part of the actor's path. If you add nodes to the path, nodes are added to this line segment. If this is not what you want, set the LTH node to the end of the path, add your new nodes, and then reset the LTH node.

You are making progress. Now you know how to make your actors move continuously along a path throughout the length of your animation.

There are a host of other functions on the Path Edit Roll-Up menu that help immensely when working with paths and nodes. Here are a few:

✔ You can move a series of consecutive nodes by selecting them using the Shift+Click technique.

✔ You can delete nodes on a path by selecting them and pressing the delete key.

✔ You can make a path smoother by selecting a range of nodes and pressing the Smooth Path icon (first icon, second row). This function takes the path points and makes more of a straight line between them. This is a progressive function; the more times you press it, the closer the selected nodes get to being a straight line.

✔ The next icon over from Smooth Path is the Distribute Path tool. This function takes a selected range of points and makes all the spaces between them even. You only need to use this function once.

As you develop your animation, you might need to add or delete frames from your animation. Use the Animation Info dialog box to accomplish this.

Changing the Number of Frames

Click on **E**dit	The Edit menu appears
Click on Animation In**f**o	The Animation Information dialog box appears
In the **N**umber of Frames *text box,* type **120**	
Click on OK	

You used the Animation Information dialog box earlier to set the size of the Animation window, and now you have used it to change the number of frames in your animation. You can always tell how many frames your animation has by looking at the status box to the left of the slider control. There are other settings in this dialog box that affect your animations.

One important setting is Speed. The lower the number in this box, the slower your animation runs. The maximum is 18, and that's a good setting unless you have specific reasons to change it. The caption indicates that this is a frames-per-second setting. In reality, it's not. It is a relative number and there are many factors that determine the real playback timing of the animation—the biggest is how fast your video card is.

Backing It Up

Lizard1 looks rather lonely on a blank screen. A background does wonders at this point. Because this element does not move, it can be a prop. Creating props is a snap with CorelDRAW!.

Any element you place or import is positioned in the animation at the current frame. Always move to the frame in which you want the element to appear before selecting the Place or Import command.

Making the Background

Use the Frame slider control to go to Frame 1	
Click on the Prop tool in the Toolbox	The New Prop dialog box appears
In the Object <u>N</u>ame *text box,* type **Background**	
In the Object <u>T</u>ype *list, click on* CorelDRAW! 5.0 Graphic	
Select the <u>C</u>reate New *option*	
Click on OK	CorelDRAW! starts
Select the Rectangle tool	

Drag out a rectangle approximately 8.50" × 5.50" and position it in the middle of your page.

Click on the Fill tool	The Fill fly-out menu appears
Click on the Texture Fill tool *(top row, sixth from the left)*	The Texture Fill dialog box appears
Select Samples *in the* Texture <u>L</u>ibrary *drop-down list*	
Select Gouache wash *from the* <u>T</u>exture List	
In the Brightness *edit box, type* **40**	
Click on the Preview button to see *what your texture looks like*	
Click on OK	
Click on the Outline tool	The Outline fly-out menu appears
Click on the X *icon* *(top row, third from the left)*	Any Outline disappears
Click on <u>F</u>ile	
Click on E<u>x</u>it & Return to	

When the Import imaging options dialog box appears, choose None; set the Color tolerance to 0. This will ensure that no transparent holes appear in the background.

Back in Move, position your background to cover the entire Animation window. If your background doesn't fill the Animation window, CorelDRAW! is a simple double-click away and you can edit it. View your animation and see how it looks.

Now use the <u>T</u>imelines Roll-Up menu to control when your elements enter and exit the animation.

Using the Timelines Roll-Up Menu

Select the Timelines icon from the Control Panel or choose <u>T</u>imelines Roll-Up from the <u>V</u>iew menu to bring the roll-up on-screen. The Timelines Roll-Up menu is crucial to getting that "top-down" view of your animation. It lists all the elements of your animation by category: first come actors, next props, third sounds, and finally cues. Each section is separated by a line. As you can see, Lizard1 is on top with Background underneath. If you do not see them in the listing, check to see if the Actor and Prop buttons at the top of the Timelines Roll-Up menu are depressed.

III

Using Corel's Modules

Click on the fly-out button at the top, to the right of the icons. The roll-up expands and displays multicolored timelines (see fig. 17.13). Each timeline indicates the frame at which an element enters the animation, the amount of frames the element displays, and at what frame it exits.

Figure 17.13
The Timeline
Roll-Up.

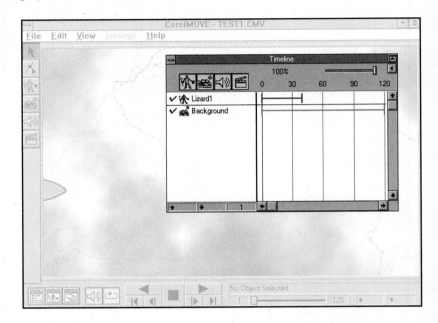

 Tip

When you place an element into your animation, its starting position is set at the frame you are working on. By default, the duration extends for the duration of frames in the animation. Sounds are an exception because their timelines are set to the approximate amount of frames it will take to play the sound file.

The Timelines Roll-Up is very intuitive. You can modify the timing aspects of all components from this roll-up. This is more efficient than jumping to many different dialog boxes to accomplish the same results. You can turn an item off by clicking on the check mark at the beginning of its entry. You can even double-click on the element to bring up the Edit dialog box.

As your cursor passes over a timeline, it changes shape. Your cursor can take three different appearances, indicating what part of the timeline you would be affecting. Use the following exercise to arrange Lizard1's duration on-screen.

Moving Timelines

Click and hold on the left end of the Lizard1 timeline	The cursor turns to an arrow pointing left
Drag the end of the timeline to Frame 40	The status bar at the bottom reads 40

If you have problems grabbing the end of a timeline, use the slider at the top of the Timeline Roll-Up to zoom in on the line you need to modify (see fig. 17.14).

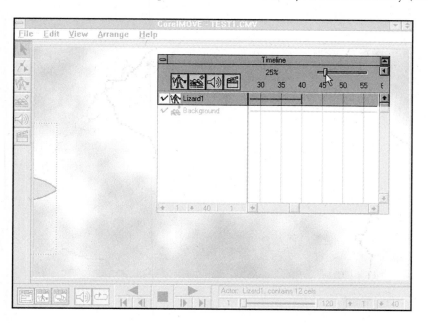

Figure 17.14
Using the slider control to zoom in on timelines.

Play with each element's timelines, then play back your animation to see the results. Become familiar with the versatility and control built into this very useful roll-up menu.

Connecting Actors and Props

You can connect small, individual sections of animations, with one section beginning as another is ending, to help reduce the number of cels that you must render. An animation having a figure walk on screen, turn and face the audience, stand still, and then start to talk, for example, could be done with four actors rather than one actor in one long sequence. The walking sequence would be the first actor.

The actor turning would be the second. Standing still could be an actor or even a prop. The actor talking would be a fourth cel sequence. When strung together, the individual parts would form one fluid animation.

The advantage of this approach is twofold: most motions are repetitive and these components could be used over again elsewhere. And your computer's resources are not taxed by loading large actor sequences. The downside to this technique is that you must carefully plan out the starting and ending renderings for each sequence so that the transition from one actor or prop is not noticeable.

You are going to use the preceding techniques to connect Lizard1 to the Chameleon Racing Boat logo. You will use one actor and two props for this exercise. The actor will be three cels. It will consist of the last rendering of the striding sequence, an intermediate drawing of the lizard, and then the lizard in the logo position. This actor will make the transition to the logo smooth. The first prop is the lizard portion of the logo. The second prop will be the text portion of the Chameleon Boat logo.

Why use props for this part of the animation? Joe wanted to use some of the special transition effects built into Move, and transitions can only be applied to props.

Bringing It All Together

Use the Frame slider control to go to Frame 40	
Click on the Actor tool	The New Actor dialog box appears
In the Object **N**ame *text box, type* **Lizard2**	
Click on **C**reate New	
Select CorelDRAW! 5.0 Graphic *as your* Object **T**ype	
Click on OK	CorelDRAW! starts
On the Frame Select Roll-Up menu, click on the fly-out menu button	The fly-out menu appears
Click on Insert after	The Insert new frames dialog box appears
Type **2**	
Click on OK	The Frame Select Roll-Up shows a frame count of 3
Select Frame 1 *from the Frame Select Roll-Up*	

Click on <u>F</u>ile

Click on <u>I</u>mport   The Import dialog box appears

Click on the <u>L</u>ist Files of Type   The list of file types appears
drop-down list

Click on CorelDRAW! (*.CDR)   The list of file names shows only CDR files in
                                                        the current subdirectory

Use the drive and directory areas to move to the CD-ROM drive and the EXAMPLES\MOVE
subdirectory.

Click on LIZARD4.CDR

Click on OK

Select Frame 2 *on the*
Frame Select Roll-Up

Click on <u>F</u>ile

Click on <u>I</u>mport   The Import dialog box appears

Click on the <u>L</u>ist Files of Type   The list of file types appears
drop-down list

Click on CorelDRAW! (*.CDR)   The list of file names shows only CDR files in
                                                        the current subdirectory

Use the drive and directory areas to move to the CD-ROM drive and the EXAMPLES\MOVE
subdirectory.

Click on LIZARD5.CDR

Click on OK   Lizard5.CDR appears

Select Frame 3 *on the Frame Select*
Roll-Up

Click on <u>F</u>ile

Click on <u>I</u>mport   The Import dialog box appears

Click on the <u>L</u>ist Files of Type   The list of file types appears
drop-down list

Click on CorelDRAW! (*.CDR)   The list of file names shows only CDR files in
                                                        the current subdirectory

Use the drive and directory areas to move to the CD-ROM drive and the EXAMPLES\MOVE
subdirectory.

Click on LIZARD6.CDR

Click on OK   Lizard6.CDR appears

Now that you have the three renderings, position them as shown in figure 17.15. The shoulders and neck are the areas to focus on. Preview your work; when you are satisfied, use Exit & Return to to get back to Move. Don't forget to select White as your transparent color in the Import imaging dialog box.

Figure 17.15
Proper position for Lizard2 renderings.

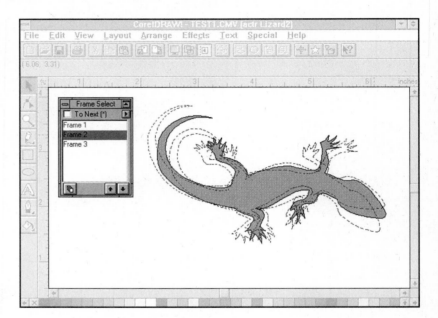

Once you are back in Move, position Lizard2 so that it is in exactly the same position as Lizard1. Use the arrow keys to move the actor one pixel at a time. When this step has been completed, use the Timeline Roll-Up menu to make Lizard2 enter the animation at Frame 41 and exit at Frame 43. You also can accomplish this by double-clicking on the actor and entering these numbers in the Enters At Frame and Exits At Frame text boxes in the Actor Information dialog box.

To set the lizard logo prop, use the steps in the following exercise:

Setting the Lizard Logo Prop

Move to Frame 43	The last cel of Lizard2 is visible
Click on the Prop tool in the Toolbox	The New Prop dialog box appears
In the Object Name *text box,* *type* **Lizlogo**	
Select the Create from File *option*	

Click on **B**rowse	The Browse dialog box appears

Use the drive and directory areas to move to the CD-ROM drive and the EXAMPLES\MOVE subdirectory.

Click on LIZARD6.CDR

Click on OK	The New Prop dialog box appears again
Click on OK	The Import imaging options dialog box appears
Click on White	
Click on OK	The new lizard rendering appears

If you already have files that can be read by Move, using the above technique is faster than OLEing to CorelDRAW!. Position Lizlogo to display in the same position as the last cel of Lizard2. Use the Timeline Roll-Up to make Lizlogo enter at Frame 44 and exit at Frame 100.

Move to Frame 45	Lizlogo is visible
Click on the Prop tool in the Toolbox	The New Prop dialog box appears

In the Object **N**ame *text box,*
type **Chamlogo**

Select the Create from **F**ile *option*

Click on **B**rowse	The Browse dialog box appears

Use the drive and directory areas to move to the CD-ROM drive and the EXAMPLES\MOVE subdirectory.

Click on CHAMLOGO.CDR

Click on OK	The New Prop dialog box appears again
Click on OK	The Import imaging options dialog box appears
Click on White	
Click on OK	The Chameleon Boating Racing logo appears

Position Chamlogo as shown in figure 17.16. Use the Timelines Roll-Up to make it exit at Frame 101. Now you must add those transitions.

Double-click on the Lizlogo prop	The Prop Information dialog box appears
Click on E**d**it *in the Transitions section*	The Transitions for Prop dialog box appears
Under E**x**it Transition, *select* Checkerboard	The Steps edit box appears

In the S**t**eps *edit box, type* **5**

continues

continued

*Click **P**review to see how the effect will look*	
Click on OK	The Transitions for Prop dialog box reappears
Click on OK	
Double-click on the Chamlogo prop	The Prop Information dialog box appears
*Click on **Ed**it in the Transitions section*	The Transitions for Prop dialog box appears
*Under **E**ntry Transition, select* Iris	The Steps edit box appears
*In the **S**teps edit box, type* **5**	
*Under **Ex**it Transition, select* Circular Wipe	The Steps edit box appears
*In the **S**teps edit box, type* **5**	
*Click **P**review to see how the effect will look*	
Click OK	The Transitions for Prop dialog box reappears
Click OK	

Figure 17.16
Positioning the Chameleon Racing Boats logo.

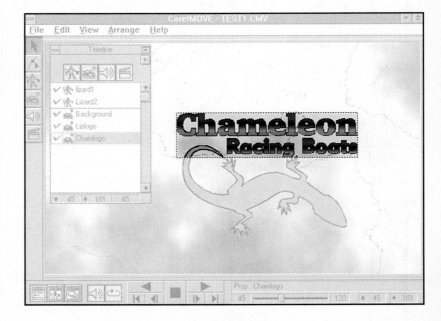

That's it! You've completed the animation. It's time to preview your work. Does it seem like a lot of work? I think Walt Disney felt the same way. But there is satisfaction in hard work.

What About the Rest?

You've produced a few seconds of animation and have used only a handful of the tools that CorelMOVE! has to offer the budding animator. The following sections briefly describe some of the other CorelMOVE! tools.

The Cel Sequencer Roll-Up Menu

CorelMOVE! provides special functions that enable you to make your actors more dramatic without redrawing them. Included in these special functions is the ability to change the display order of your actor's cels. Learning to use these options, found on the Cel Sequencer Roll-Up, saves time and helps you to produce more advanced animations. You can apply these built-in special effects to your actors with a few mouse clicks.

Tip The Cel Sequencer effects can be applied only to actors. If a special effect is needed for a prop, use a transition.

You access the Cel Sequencer Roll-Up in either of two ways: click on its icon at the bottom (third from the left) or select Cel Sequencer Roll-Up from the View menu. When the roll-up appears, it might have no values because it's dynamic—it only displays information about the currently selected actor. Click on Lizard1 and numbers will appear (see figure 17.17).

Tip The number of frames in which an actor is displayed can be determined and adjusted using the Timeline Roll-Up.

The top row displays the number of the frame that is affected by the settings in the Cel and Size settings below. The second row tells you the number of the cel that is be displayed at the frame. Under normal circumstances, this is the same order that they were created in the editor. You see as you scroll through the frames that they repeat in the same sequence. The last row is the Size row. Unless it has been changed for some reason, the size of all frames is set to 100 percent.

Figure 17.17
Clicking on Lizard1 causes numbers to appear.

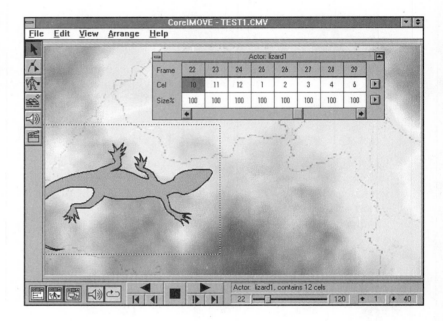

Double-click to highlight any of the numbers in the Cel and Size rows to make a change. You also can use the two fly-out menu buttons on the right side of the roll-up. These offer several means to select frames and apply preset size and cel order changes.

Now you are ready to use the Cel Sequencer to customize the display of your actor's cels to finish off the striding motion of Lizard1.

Changing an Actor's Cel Order

Click on Lizard1	The Cel Sequencer Roll-Up displays Lizard1's sequence info
Click on the Size fly-out button	The Size menu appears
Click on Select All	The Size row for all frames is highlighted
Click on the Size fly-out button again	The Size menu appears
Click on Random	

Review your work. That's pretty wild, eh? The best way to become familiar with these options is to experiment with them. They can have some side effects for which you need to compensate, but they do save lots of time if used properly.

The Library Roll-Up

The key to CorelMOVE!'s flexible nature is its capability to save and organize animation elements. You collect your actors, props, and sounds and save them in libraries. When you need a previously created element, simply load the library that contains it, and place it into your new production.

The Library Roll-Up provides the functions needed to manage your libraries and their members (see fig. 17.18).

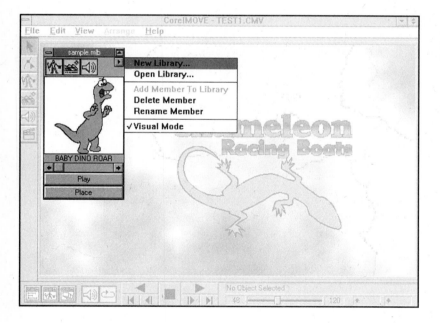

Figure 17.18
The Library Roll-Up.

Making Use of a Library

Click on the Library icon in the Control Panel or click on <u>L</u>ibrary Roll-Up *under* <u>V</u>iew	The Open Library dialog box appears

Use the drive and directory areas to move to the drive and directory on which you installed Corel5. Navigate to the MOVE\SAMPLES subdirectory.

Click on SAMPLE.MLB	
Click on OK	The Library Roll-Up appears

Use the scroll bar and arrow buttons to move through the library and view all the elements. Press the Play button to view an actor's cel sequence. Use Place to insert the currently displayed element into your animation.

Continue with the exercise to create a new library for the Chameleon elements.

Click on the fly-out button	The Library Roll-Up menu appears
Click on New Library	The New Library dialog box appears
In the File <u>N</u>ame *text box,* *type* **Chameleon**	

Use the directories and drives areas to choose where you want to store your library.

Click on OK	The Library Roll-Up title bar displays: CHAMLEON.MLB
With the Pick tool, click on Lizard1	A bounding box appears around Lizard1
Click on the fly-out button	The Library Roll-Up menu appears
Click on Add Member To Library	Lizard1 is placed in the Chameleon library; Lizard1 is displayed in the status line under its picture

If a picture of Lizard1 is not displayed, choose Visual Mode from the fly-out menu. Click on the Play button to watch Lizard1 run through its cels, and click on Stop when you are finished. Repeat the preceding steps for each member you want to add to the library.

Adding Sound

With a sound board installed in your computer, you can elevate your animations to the level of multimedia extravaganza. Well, almost.

WAV files come in several different "flavors." If your WAV file does not play, it might not be 100-percent compatible with Microsoft's specification for WAV files.

By using the Sound icon in the Toolbox, you can use Move's internal Wave Editor to record, manipulate, and place files into your animation. If you have access to other sources for WAV files, you can use the File, Import command.

The Timelines Roll-Up comes in handy to start and end the sound at the appropriate frames. Make sure that you allow enough frames in between the start and stop positions to accommodate the length of your file. Placing simple sounds in your animation is not very complicated; however, it takes a good deal of experimentation to synchronize your sounds with the visual elements of the animation.

Chapter Snapshot

Corel's suite of applications provides you with the tools you need to produce multimedia presentations. By using CorelMOVE! and CorelSHOW!, you can create professional-quality presentations. In this chapter you learn to:

✔ Use the Cel Sequencer to repeat cels

✔ Use the Morph function

✔ Save morph control points

✔ Create an interactive presentation

✔ Add sound to the presentation

CorelDRAW! enables you to build presentations that combine animation, morphing, special effects, and sound. As you continue to learn these techniques, you will recognize that it's easy and profitable to become a multimedia bug.

Advanced CorelMOVE! and CorelSHOW!

Multimedia is the buzz word in the graphics world these days. You now must contend with multimedia-ready computers and multimedia authoring programs. Some presentation programs offer users the ability to make their own multimedia presentations. Where did this come from?

Less than a decade ago, presentations were big deals. Making 35mm slides was a specialty that took many days and involved artists and photography specialists. Each person in the production chain had to be skilled and experienced, and special equipment was needed.

Presentations had evolved far beyond a simple slide show with someone talking over it. Adding music, film, and video clips was fairly commonplace if you could afford it. These presentations became productions in their own right. It took many projectors, monitors, video recorders, synchronizers, mixers, and skilled operators to bring everything together and make things work.

These productions were saved for special occasions. The majority of business presentations were still using black-and-white overheads and 35mm slides.

Computers had a hand in both of these scenarios. Today, though, the personal computer and software such as CorelMOVE! and CorelSHOW! have changed things drastically. Very impressive presentations can be developed by just about anyone. The price of the software and hardware needed is no longer prohibitive.

The affordability of portable computers with large hard drives, color screens, and sound boards enables exciting presentations with animations and sound to be carried anywhere. No more crews of people dragging in tons of equipment and searching for wall outlets and extension cords.

Corel and Multimedia

The Corel suite of applications can be used to put together multimedia presentations. Images you use to present your ideas are rendered in CorelDRAW! or CorelPHOTO-PAINT!. Animations are produced in CorelMOVE!, and CorelSHOW! is used to wrap the whole thing up in a nice, neat package.

The multimedia experience does have its price—it costs you in effort, time, and sometimes frustration. Eventually, if you catch the multimedia bug and continue your journey down the technological highway, you should learn more about sound files, video cards, monitor resolutions, color depths, and perhaps even CD-ROM recording technology.

The exercises you complete in this chapter are designed as extensions of those completed in the CorelMOVE! and CorelSHOW! chapters. If you have not completed these chapters, do so before proceeding.

In addition, you need to load specific fonts so that you can follow the exercises exactly and to enable the example files on the accompanying CD to display properly. Check to make sure you have the following fonts installed:

- ✔ Calligraph421 BT
- ✔ DomDiagonal BD BT
- ✔ Geometr706 Md BT

If these fonts are not installed, take the time to do so now.

Note It is not absolutely necessary to load these fonts. If you don't, however, CorelSHOW! substitutes fonts that might not look as attractive.

All files used in this chapter are found on the *Inside CorelDRAW! 5, fifth edition CD-ROM* in the EXERCISE\CH18 subdirectory.

Joe DeLook's Multimedia Extravaganza

Joe has a big presentation to make to the Chameleon Racing Boat company. They're looking for someone to handle all graphics design and production work for their team of racing boats. This is a great opportunity for DeLook Designs, and Joe wants to impress the decision makers at the presentation. He's going to pull out all the stops and make a flexible, interactive screen presentation.

Joe is planning to include the animation (with some production refinements) that was produced in Chapter 17, "The Basics of CorelMOVE." He will incorporate the animation into a personalized version of the bullet presentation that was developed in Chapter 16, "Using CorelSHOW!."

Advanced CorelMOVE! Tools

Joe's Chameleon animation has undergone a few modifications. The starting position of the lizard has been changed, and the lizard acts more like a Chameleon by changing colors. Also, the boat connection is emphasized graphically, by adding a racing boat image to the animation. Some special production challenges presented themselves. These challenges are easily overcome with the help of CorelMOVES!'s advanced tools.

Using the Cel Sequencer

A new lizard actor that changes colors has been rendered. This new actor consists of nine frames. The first three are the transition from the "straight" position to the "curled" position found in the Chameleon Racing Boat logo. The next six frames contain the "curled" position rendering with different colors applied.

Although the color changes look fine when previewed in CorelDRAW!, when played in Move, they go by too quickly and don't have the best visual impact. An initial reaction is to double-click on the actor, OLE back to CorelDRAW!, and add more cels. At this point, examine some considerations that would cause you to think a little more before you double-click on the actor.

After working on an animation for many hours you'll soon get tired of the time it takes to use the OLE route of importing elements into your creation. There also is the uncertainty of whether adding just one more frame for each color change would be enough of a change. The dread that you might spend many more hours modifying this lizard to get it right makes you long for a better way. The better way is the Cel Sequencer Roll-Up menu, which can be used to change the order in which an actor's cels are displayed.

In the following exercise, you get a hands-on lesson in how to use the Cel Sequencer to repeat the cels you want displayed in a particular frame.

First, load the LIZARD-1.CMV file from the EXERCISE\CH18 subdirectory on the accompanying CD. You can play this back several times to get an idea of some of the improvements that have been made to the animation you created in Chapter 17. Lizard2 is the actor you want to modify. Lizard2 enters the animation at Frame 41 and exits at Frame 49. That's enough frames to display its nine cels.

Before you can customize Lizard2's cel sequence, you have to increase the amount of frames it is set to display. To do this you can use the Timelines Roll-Up menu (see fig. 18.1), which is very handy to have open. You also can double-click on the actor to get to the Actor Information dialog box and enter a new frame number in the Exits At Frame edit box.

Figure 18.1
The Timelines
Roll-Up menu.

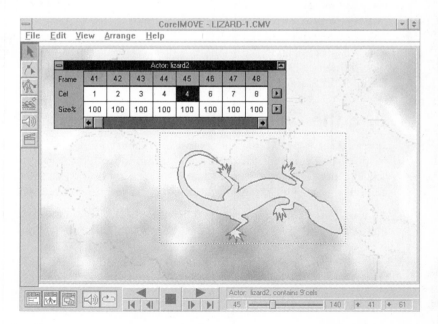

What should the new exit frame number be? Six frames of color changes exist, and you want to set each to display three times. This makes 18. Add the first three cels and you get a total of 21. Therefore, the new exit frame would be 61. When you have made the exit frame change to Lizard2, continue with the exercise.

Using the Cel Sequencer to Modify an Actor's Playback

Move to frame 41

Use the Pick tool to select Lizard1	Lizard2 information is displayed in the status line next to the Frame Slider control
Click on **E**dit	The Edit menu appears
Click on **V**iew	The View menu appears
Click on **C**el Sequencer Roll-Up	The Cel Sequencer Roll-Up appears with Actor: Lizard2 in the title bar
In the Cel row, under Frame 45, double-click on the 5	The 5 is highlighted and moved up and to the left
Type **4**	The Cel number is changed to 4
In the Cel row, under Frame 46, double-click on the 6	The 6 is highlighted and moved up and to the left
Type **4**	The Cel number is changed to 4
In the Cel row, under Frame 47, double-click on the 7	The 7 is highlighted and moved up and to the left
Type **5**	The Cel number is changed to 5
In the Cel row, under Frame 48, double-click on the 8	The 8 is highlighted and moved up and to the left
Type **5**	The Cel number is changed to 5
In the Cel row, under Frame 49, double-click on the 9	The 9 is highlighted and moved up and to the left
Type **5**	The Cel number is changed to 5

Using Corel's Modules

Now you have three frames that display Lizard2 cel 4, and three frames that display cel 5. Continue using the Cel Sequencer to change frames 50, 51, and 52 to display cel 6; frames 53, 54, and 55 to display cel 7; frames 56, 57, and 58 to show cel 8; and finally, frames 59, 60, and 61 to show cel 9.

Now use the Timelines Roll-Up or the Prop Information dialog box (double-click on the prop) to change Lizlogo1 to enter at frame 61.

Take a look at your animation. Now the changing colors of the Chameleon have much more importance, and the transition to the final logo is very smooth. When you are finished scrutinizing the work you have accomplished on the lizard, watch the transition effect on the final lizard and the entering of the boat.

Joe wanted to have more of a message here. DeLook Design's job was to transform plain boats into colorful showpieces worthy of the Chameleon name. The Transition effect just was not sending the right message. He needed something more spectacular and eye-catching—morphing.

Using CorelMOVE!'s Morph Function

Joe had played with this feature before, and he knew it could create really cool effects but had to be used with care. Move's Morph tool is not as sophisticated as some he had seen demonstrations of, but he knew he could get something that would impress the Chameleon executives. Joe wanted to use the Morph function to transform a plain racing boat into a fully decorated Chameleon racer.

What are some of the limitations that Move users need to keep in mind? First, the Morphing function is available only through CorelMOVE!'s internal editor; it cannot be used on PhotoPaint- or Draw-created actors. This is not a drastic problem, however, because any editor or prop can be converted to a CorelMOVE! object so it can be edited on the Move paint editor.

The bigger problem with this conversion strategy is that it is a one-way street. Once you convert to a Move object, you cannot go back. If you are not sure of what you can expect, copy your element first and then paste it back in. Convert the copy and experiment with it until you have the effect that you want.

The second problem you might find is that the morphing process adds stray "garbage" to the intermediate cels it creates. Again, this is not an insurmountable problem. Use the editor's paint tools to touch up the imperfections. Be aware that the Move paint editor is somewhat primitive when compared with PhotoPaint or one of the other high-end bitmap editing programs. Try to have your actor or prop in ready condition before converting to a Move object. (This includes proper sizing.)

How Morphing Works

The reason you can only morph actors is that you need two objects to start the process. If you have a one-celed actor, the <u>M</u>orph Cel command under the Effects menu is unavailable until you insert another cel. On the first frame you place the

From image and the next frame the To image. You must be on the cel with the From image when you select the **M**orph Cel command.

When the Morph dialog box appears (see fig. 18.2), you see two picture boxes. These are labeled From and To. On these images you plot control points that give plenty of flexibility over the morphing process. These control points are matched sets. When you use the Pick tool to click in one image, a corresponding point is placed in the same position on the other image. If you leave all the matching control points in the default positions, a very gradual change from one image to the other occurs.

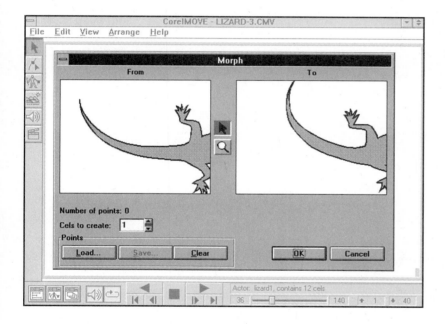

Figure 18.2
The Morph dialog box.

For really wild morphings, click on one of the control points in a set and drag it to a very different spot in the image. Experimentation is the name of the game with setting these control points, and depending on the From and To images, you might get very spectacular results or very ugly.

One of the easiest ways to get complicated drawings, like the Chameleon racing boat, into a position to use the Morph command is to start in CorelDRAW!.

Joe figured out that he needed two drawings of the same racing boat; one very plain and the other in full Chameleon regalia. He created the finished drawing of the decorated version as BOAT1.CDR and then removed the custom touches and used the Save As command to save

continues

the drawing as BOAT2.CDR. From these two drawings (located in the EXERCISE\CH18 subdirectory on the *Inside CorelDRAW! 5, Fifth Edition CD-ROM*), you are able to create the three elements that make up the complete boat action sequence.

The first element is a prop of the plain boat. A prop is used because we can add a Transition to it as it enters the animation and because it stays in one position for quite a few frames. The second element is a two-celed actor used to make the morphing sequence. The From cel (number one) is the plain boat, and the To cel (number two) is the customized boat drawing. After the morphing process is complete, however, a total of 12 cels are in the boat actor. The final participant in this sequence is a one-celed actor of the customized boat. This needs to be an actor so that a path can be added to it. This makes it move off to the left in the animation window.

If you run the Lizard-1.CMV file and examine the frames from 119 on, you see there are only two elements in the current boat sequence. By following the next exercises, you create three new ones to replace these.

Making the Plain Boat Prop

Use the Frame slider control to move to Frame 90	
Double-click on the boat	The Prop Information dialog box appears
In the Position (Pixels) section, make a note of the numbers in the Horizontal *and* Vertical *edit boxes. The Horizontal number should be 184 and the Vertical number should be 204*	
Click on the Prop tool	The New Prop dialog box appears
In the Object Name *edit box, type* **Plain Boat**	
Click on Create from File	The Browse button appears
Click on Browse	The Browse dialog box appears
Use the Drives and Directories lists to move to the EXERCISE\CH18 *subdirectory on the accompanying CD*	
In the File Name *list, double-click on* BOAT2.CDR	The Browse dialog box disappears
Click on OK	The cursor changes to an hourglass, after the rendering process Plain Boat prop appears

Select the original Boat prop	A bounding box appears around it
Press the Del key on the keyboard	A Delete "Boat" dialog box appears
Click on OK	The original boat disappears
Double-click on Plain Boat	The Prop Information dialog box appears
In the <u>H</u>orizontal *edit box, type* **184**	
In the <u>V</u>ertical *edit box, type* **204**	
Click on OK	Plain Boat moves to the correct position (see fig. 18.3)

While you are here, you should set the opening Transition effect for this prop.

In the Transitions *section, click on* E<u>d</u>it	The Transitions for "Boat Prop" dialog box appears
In the <u>E</u>ntry Transition *list, click on* Checker Board	The Steps edit box appears
In the <u>S</u>teps *edit box type* **7**	
Click on <u>P</u>review	A sample of the effect is shown
Click on OK	The Prop Information dialog box appears
Click on OK	You are back in the animation window

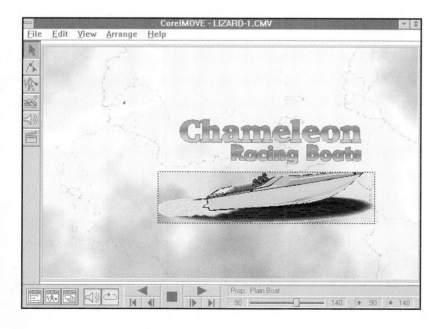

Figure 18.3
Plain Boat prop
after correct
positioning.

Using Corel's Modules

If you run the animation now, you see the plain boat appears and is then replaced by the customized boat. When the customized boat moves off, however, Plain Boat is still on-screen. This is because the default for any new element is to enter the animation at the frame you were on when you created it and to display until the end of the animation. Use the Timeline Roll-Up or the Prop Information dialog box to adjust Plain Boat's exit frame to 97.

Creating the Morphed Actor

Use the Frame Selector slider to move to Frame 97	
Select the Actor tool	The New Actor dialog box appears
In the Object Name edit box, *type* Morph Boat	
In the Object Type, *click on* CoreDRAW! 5.0 Graphic	
Click on OK	CorelDRAW! appears
Click on File	The File menu appears
Click on Import	The Import dialog appears
From the List Files of Type *drop-down list, select* CorelDRAW! (*.CDR)	Only CDR files are shown
Use the Drives and Directories *controls to move to the* EXERCISE\CH18 *subdirectory on the accompanying CD*	
Double-click on BOAT2.CDR	The plain boat appears on Frame 1
On the Frame Select *Roll-Up menu, click on the fly-out menu button*	The fly-out menu appears
Click on Insert after	The Insert New Frames dialog box appears, with a 1 in the edit box
Click on OK	Frame 2 appears in the Frame Select Roll-Up
Click on Frame 2	Frame 1 is replaced by a blank Frame 2
Click on File	The File menu appears
Click on Import	The Import dialog appears
From the List Files of Type *drop-down list, select* CorelDRAW! (*.CDR)	Only CDR files are shown

Use the Drives and Directories *controls to move to the* EXERCISE\CH18 *subdirectory on the accompanying CD*	
Double-click on BOAT1.CDR	The plain boat appears on Frame 2
Click on File	The File menu appears
Click on Exit & Return to actor appears	After the image is rendered, the Morph Boat
Double-click on Morph Boat	The Actor Information dialog appears
In the Horizontal *edit box, type* **184**	
In the Vertical *edit box, type* **204**	
Click on OK	Morph Boat moves to the correct position directly over the Plain Boat prop

Now for the fun part—morphing. First, convert the actor to a CorelMOVE! object and edit it. All of these functions are carried out through the Actor Information dialog box. When you are ready, double-click on Morph Boat.

Morphing the Actor

In the Actor Information *dialog box, click on* Convert	A dialog box asking if you are sure you want to convert your actor to a CorelMOVE! object appears
Click on OK	The Object type caption in now reads CorelMOVE! 5.0
Click on Edit Actor	The Move paint editor appears with cel 1 of Morph Boat displayed
Click on Effects	The Effects menu appears
Click on Morph Cels	The Morph dialog box appears

The procedure to make the morph effect is to use the Pick tool (found in the center between the two image windows). It is used to plot control points in the From and To image windows, select the number of cels you want the effect to occur over (this number of cels is inserted in between the start and end cel), and then click on OK.

It is best to place your first control point in the From image window. When you click the mouse button to set a control point, you see an X and Y coordinate. Also, a running total of points currently set is displayed. These status messages help you keep track of what you are doing as you set points.

Another important visual cue that helps as you set control points is that the points are matching pairs. The active set is shown in red, all others are green. When you reselect any point by clicking on it with the Pick tool, it turns red; its matching point in the other image also turns red. When you initially set a point, both points are set at the same X and Y position. You can drag a control point to a new position in either window; however, the corresponding control point does not move unless you drag it.

Should you need to zoom in closer for finer control over control point placement, click on the Zoom tool underneath the Pick tool. Click the left mouse button in either image to zoom in, and click the right mouse button to zoom out. If you hold down the left mouse button, you can drag the image in the window to view areas not currently visible. To remove all the control points, click on the Clear button.

It would take considerable space to describe the exact position X and Y coordinates of each control point used to make the morph effect in the example. It also would not teach much about what actually is happening as you set and move control points. The best way is for you to experiment to see how things work. You can always choose Exit from the File menu and choose not to apply the morphing modifications you have made.

When you are done experimenting, you can use another feature found in the Morph dialog box to reconstruct the exact control point layout. This feature enables you to save a layout of control points and then load them again to achieve the same morphing effect.

Applying Previously Set Control Points

In the Points section, click on Load	The Load Control Points dialog appears
Use the Drives and Directories *controls to move to the* EXERCISE\CH18 *subdirectory on the accompanying CD*	
In the File Name *list, double-click on* BOAT2.MPH	The points are loaded and applied to both images (see fig. 18.4)

In the Cels to create *edit box,*
type **10**

Click on OK   The Morphing cels message appears

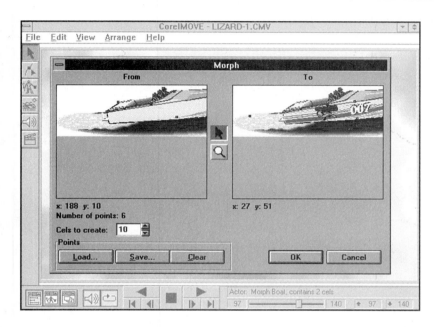

Figure 18.4
The Morph
dialog box with
loaded control
points.

Morph rendering can take some time and the amount of time varies. Some factors that cause the process to take longer are: size of renderings, how many cels you are creating during the process, and how fast your computer is.

After the morphing is complete, you can use the scroll arrows under the Paint toolbox to move through each cel that has been created and inserted into your actor. You probably note some black and gray areas in the upper left area, as well as stray pixels along the top of the cels. This "garbage" is a by-product of the morphing function. Figure 18.5 shows the use of the selection tools to marquee-select these areas on each cel. After you have selected them, press the Delete key to remove them. Make sure to set the background color to white before doing this. This is accomplished by selecting the Eyedropper tool and right-clicking any white area of the cel.

When you are satisfied with the effect, choose **F**ile, E**x**it and answer Yes to the Close Paint Window and Apply changes dialog box.

Once again, it is necessary to adjust the timeline of this element. Use the techniques you have learned previously to have Morph Boat exit the animation at frame 120. Morph Boat is only 12 cels long, but its on-screen duration is set for many more frames. Use the Cel Sequencer as you have before to set frames 109 through 120 of Morph Boat to display cel number 12.

When you have completed this last step and play back the animation, you see the effect Joe had in mind. The plain boat dramatically transforms into a customized racing boat and then speeds off screen.

You now have completed the advanced exercises for the Move portion of this project. If you want to use the animation you just completed in the Show portion of this chapter, save it to a subdirectory on your hard drive. If you would rather not take up the 1.2 MB of space required, that's OK. The complete animation is included on the CD as LIZARD-2.CMV

Figure 18.5
Selecting morph "garbage" to be removed.

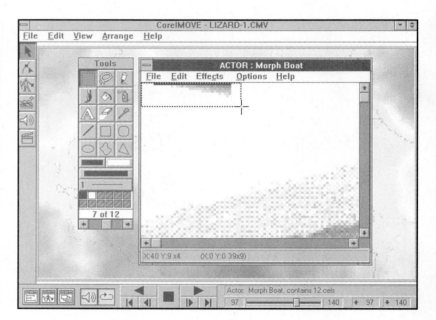

Using CorelSHOW! To Make an Interactive Presentation

An interactive presentation is one that can change according to input from a user or another program. The ability to simply end a presentation rather than view it to its completion is an example of interactivity. The flexibility to jump to a completely different area of a presentation, to back up or go forward, and to repeat specific information are examples of much more complicated interactivity.

CorelSHOW! enables a good measure of control to make your presentations interactive and flexible. In the following exercises, you incorporate the animation completed with the morphing sequence into a presentation. You add navigational buttons to the slides in your show to enable the user to end the show, to move to the next slide, and to start the presentation over again.

The key to this interactive capability is the Cue function. In traditional terms, a cue is the signal to start something. In Show, a cue is a setting to do something. It can start an action such as playing a sound file or an animation. It also can signal a pause for a specified amount of time. It can even wait until a certain action has occurred, such as clicking on an object, and then go to a specified location in the presentation. It is this last behavior we implement in the completion of this project.

 First, you need to copy the initial presentation file from the accompanying CD to a subdirectory on your hard drive. The file is called DELOOK1.SHW and is in the EXERCISE\CH18 subdirectory. It is approximately 1.2 MB in size.

Some Precautions

CorelSHOW! uses a lot of disk space to save your presentation file. The presentation you are going to make will balloon to nearly 5 MB. An even greater concern for many users is that Show uses tremendous amounts of disk drive space as you are developing your presentation. Depending on what you have on your slides, your file might need .25 to 1.5 MB per slide.

You must have a SET TEMP=drive\subdirectory setting in your AUTOEXEC.BAT file that points to a subdirectory with enough space to hold your presentation. It is entirely possible to run out of space and not be able to save the work you have done. This TEMP space is NOT the same as your SWAP file. Your SWAP file space is not used by CorelSHOW!.

It is recommended that you have at least 20 MB free on the hard drive that is pointed to by the SET TEMP variable before you start this portion of the example project.

Planning the Presentation

Joe DeLook's multimedia extravaganza is based on the screen show he put together. Some changes have been made: a new slide with background has been placed at the start, and the introduction slide has been simplified. The remainder of the presentation remains the same, except the position of the contents has been moved up to accommodate the added navigational buttons and their captions.

Joe used CorelDRAW! to make some marble-like, 3D buttons. They have the same type of VCR icons on them as the playback controls in Move. A marble button designates forward, backward, and end. Each of the drawings is found on the accompanying CD.

In the following exercises you will insert two of these three buttons on each slide and then align them on the bottom corners. Next, add captions to explain what each button does. Finally, add cues to the buttons to cause the presentation to react to the users interaction.

Guidelines have already been positioned to help in correctly placing the buttons and text. Make sure that S__n__ap to Guidelines under the __A__rrange menu is on before positioning your elements.

When you have loaded the DELOOK1.SHW file into CorelSHOW! and have moved to page one of the presentation, you are ready to start the next exercise.

Adding the Animation

Click on __I__nsert   The Insert menu appears

Click on __A__nimation   The Insert Animation dialog box appears

In the List Files of __T__ype *list,*
select CorelMOVE! Animation
(*.CMV, *.MWF)

Use the Dri__v__es and __D__irectories controls to move to the EXERCISE\CH18 subdirectory or the subdirectory in which you saved your version of the LIZARD.CMV file. On the CD, the file you need is LIZARD-2.CMV. When you locate the file you are going to use, double-click on it.

Center the animation toward the top as shown in figure 18.6. If you are having difficulty centering the animation horizontally because it is snapping to the left or right guidelines, use the Zoom tool to get in closer. The Snap to feature is more flexible and enables finer movement adjustments at higher magnification levels.

With the animation positioned correctly, you can use the F5 button to play your presentation. The presentation plays the animation and then each of the five slides automatically. If it does not, check the P__r__eferences options under the __F__ile menu to see that __A__utomatic Advance to next slide is set on, under the Timing section.

Next, you will add the buttons to the individual slides. Make sure you are on slide number 1 before continuing.

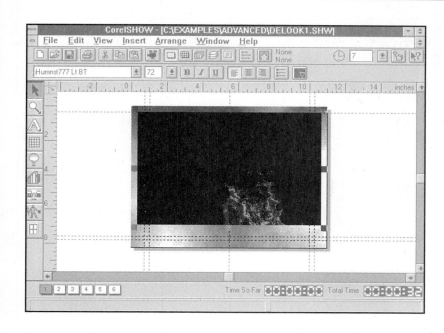

Figure 18.6
Animation positioned properly on slide 1.

Inserting the Marble Buttons

Click on **I**nsert	The Insert menu appears
Click on **O**bject	The Insert Object dialog box appears
Click on Create from **F**ile	The Browse button appears
Click on **B**rowse	The Browse dialog box appears
Use the **Dri**ves *and* **D**irectories *controls to move to the* EXERCISE\CH18 *subdirectory on the accompanying CD*	
Double-click on MARBLE1.CDR	The Insert Object dialog box appears again
Click on OK	The marble button appears in the middle of the slide

Using the Pick tool, position the button in the lower right corner. Next, use the same method to insert MARBLE2.CDR and position it in the lower left corner. You should now have a slide that looks like figure 18.7.

The left button is the "end presentation" button, and the right button is the "advance to next slide" button. Many people do not instinctively understand this, so it is best to give them a hand by placing captions next to the buttons.

Figure 18.7
The first two
marble buttons
in position.

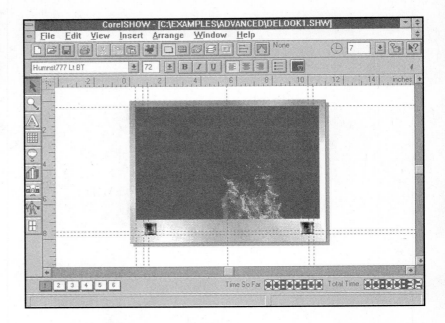

Making Button Captions

Click on the Text tool	The cursor becomes a crosshair
Click to the right of the End *button*	An insertion marker is placed next to the button
Type **Press to end show**	
Highlight the text by dragging the text cursor over it	
Select Geometr706 MD BT *from the Font Name drop-down list*	The text is changed to the correct font
Select 20 from the Font Size drop-down list	The font size changes
Click on the Pick tool and position the text to the right of the button (see fig. 18.8)	
Select the Text tool	The cursor becomes a crosshair
Click to the left of the Advance button	An insertion marker is placed next to the button
Type **Press to advance**	

Highlight the text by dragging the text cursor over it	
Select Geometr706 MD BT *from the Font Name drop-down list*	The text is changed to the correct font
Select 20 *from the Font Size drop-down list*	The font size changes
Click on the Pick tool and position the text to the left of the button (see fig. 18.9)	

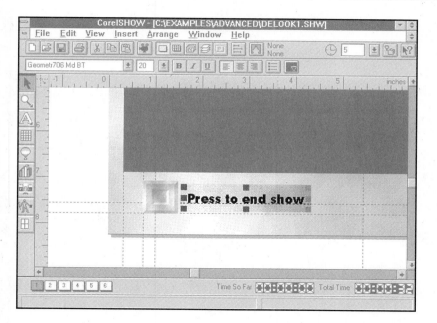

Figure 18.8
Proper position of the End button caption.

The interactive controls are taking shape. They also need to function, however, so next add the cues that cause the show to operate under the user's control.

Adding Cues

Click on the End button	The button is selected
Click on View	The View menu appears
Click on Timelines	The Timelines window appears and Slide 1 is highlighted

continues

II

Using Corel's Modules

continued

Click on the small triangle next to the check box	The arrow points downward and all the elements on Slide 1 are displayed; Frame 2 is highlighted, this is the End button
Click on Frame 2's Cue *control*	The Cue Information dialog box appears
In the Conditions *drop-down list, select* Wait for	Two more drop-down lists appear to the right
In the next drop-down list to the right, select Mouse Click on	The next list box changes to reflect the frames available to click on for this slide
From the Frames *drop-down list, select* Frame 2	
In the Actions *drop-down list, select* End Presentation	
Select Update	The word Continue is replaced by End Presentation (see fig. 18.10)
Click on OK	The Cue Information dialog box disappears

Figure 18.9
Proper position
of the Advance
button caption.

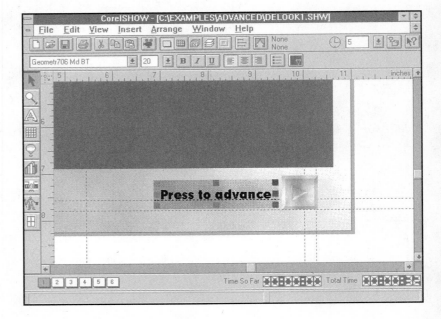

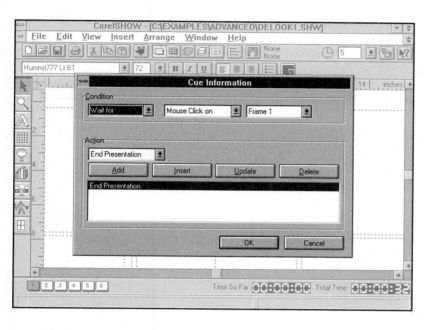

Figure 18.10
The Cue
Information
dialog box
settings for the
End button.

You have programmed the End button to end the presentation any time it is clicked on with the mouse. Next, program the Advance button to move to the next frame when clicked.

Programming the Advance Button

With the Pick tool, select the Advance *button in the right corner*	Frame 1 is highlighted in the Timelines window
Click on Frame 1's Cue *control*	The Cue Information dialog box appears
In the Conditions *drop-down list, select* Wait for	Two more drop-down lists appear to the right
In the next drop-down list to the right, select Mouse Click on	The next list box changes to reflect the frames available to click on for this slide
From the Frames *drop-down list, select* Frame 1	
In the Actions *drop-down list, select* Goto Slide	A number edit box appears
In the Slide *number edit box, type* **2**	

continues

II

continued

Select Update	The word Continue is replaced by Goto Slide 2
Click on OK	The Cue Information dialog box disappears

That is how you set cues to respond to mouse clicks. Explore the Cue Information box for a while, and you start to see the potential for setting up all types of interaction with the user.

Because all but the last slide share the End and Advance buttons, it is a simple matter of copying these four elements and pasting them onto slides 2, 3, 4, and 5.

You have to adjust the "Goto Slide number" to reflect the next slide, and the "Mouse Click on...Frame number" setting to the frame number assigned to the End and Advanced buttons. The frame number for each button is not necessarily the same for each slide. These numbers are assigned in numerical order according to when the element was placed on the page.

The Timelines window is the only place to get information about what Frame number is assigned to the End and Advanced buttons. This is a real inconvenience. Hopefully, Corel will change this feature as well as make the Timelines window into a real roll-up like those found in CorelMOVE!.

After you have copied the navigational buttons and captions to the next four slides and have reset the End and Advance cues, you should copy another set of buttons to slide 6. The button layout is different, but you can still use the End button and captions as templates for the new elements. The next exercise walks you through bringing in the final button, setting its cue, and revising its caption. When you are ready, make sure that you are on slide 6.

The Final Buttons

With the Pick tool, select the Advance button

Press the Delete key on the keyboard	The button disappears

Select the End button on the left side of the screen and position it in the right corner, where the Advance button was

Select the Text tool	The cursor turns to a crosshair
Highlight the Press to advance *caption and type* **Press to end show**	
Highlight the old End *caption on the left side of the page, and type* **Press to start again**	
Click on **I**nsert	The Insert menu appears
Click on **O**bject	The Insert Object dialog box appears
Click on Create from **F**ile	The Browse button appears
Click on **B**rowse	The Browse dialog box appears
Use the Dri**v**es *and* **D**irectories *controls to move to the* EXERCISE\CH18 *subdirectory on the accompanying CD*	
Double-click on MARBLE3.CDR	The Insert Object dialog box appears again
Click on OK	The marble button appears in the middle of the slide

Using the Pick tool, move this button to the bottom left corner (see fig. 18.11). Use the Timelines window to identify its frame number, and use the Cue Information dialog to set the **C**ondition to "Wait for...Mouse Click on...Frame 11" and the **A**ction to "Goto Slide 2." Don't forget to choose **U**pdate before clicking on OK.

Now you are ready to run your slide show. When it plays, you are in control. The presentation does not proceed until you click on one of the buttons. Play with all the buttons for a while and make sure everything works as intended. If it doesn't, check the settings in the Cue Information dialog box for any button that does not respond properly.

Let's Have a Little Noise

Sound really makes your presentation come alive. As described in Chapter 16, "Using CorelSHOW!," Show is capable of playing back WAV files. Show doesn't have any outrageous sound features, just straightforward playback of WAV files. The sound is played back at the time designated in the Timelines window.

Keep in mind that sounds are not added to individual slides; they are played back according to the start time you set for them. Also, when the WAV file is imported into the presentation, its playback duration is figured automatically, and the timeline is set for enough time to play it back one time. If you modify the length of a WAV's timeline, it's possible to make the sound repeat. If this is what you want, it takes some experimenting to get things just right.

Using Corel's Modules

Figure 18.11
The Start Again
button and
caption.

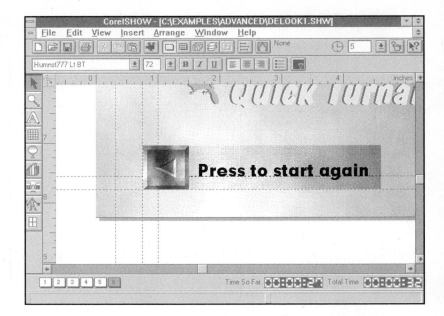

To add emphasis to the start of each slide, add a file called CHIMES1.WAV. To make the beginning animation stand out, use one called TADA1.WAV. Both of these files are found on the *Inside CorelDRAW! 5, Fifth Edition CD-ROM* in the EXERCISE\CH18 subdirectory.

Adding WAV Files

Move to Slide 1	
Click on **I**nsert	The Insert menu appears
Click on **S**ound	The Insert Sound dialog box appears
Use the Dri**v** es and **D** irectories *controls to move to your Windows directory or the* EXERCISE\CH18 *subdirectory on the CD*	
Double-click on TADA1.WAV	The WAV file is added to the bottom of the Timelines window; the starting time is automatically set for the beginning of the slide and the duration is set long enough to enable one playback

Move to Slide 2

Click on **I**nsert	The Insert menu appears
Click on **S**ound	The Insert Sound dialog box appears
Use the **Dri**v**es** *and* **D**irectories *controls to move to your Windows directory or the* EXERCISE\CH18 *subdirectory on the CD*	
Double-click on CHIMES1.WAV	The WAV file is added to the bottom of the Timelines window; the starting time is automatically set for the beginning of Slide 2 and the duration is set long enough to enable one playback

Follow the preceding instructions to add CHIMES1.WAV to Slides 3, 4, 5, and 6. When you are finished, press F5 to view your interactive multimedia presentation. The addition of the WAV files was simple, yet it really makes a difference.

The amount of free disk space you have is what limits the amount of sound you can add. WAV files can get very big, but strategies exist to keep them as small as possible: making the sample rate 8 bits instead 16, and recording files at 11 or 22 KHz rather than the maximum of 44 KHz. Each time you reduce one of these specifications, you are cutting the file size by half. You are, however, degrading the quality of your sound file at the same time. It is a trade-off you have to experiment with. Remember that most PC sound systems do not give you excellent sound quality anyway, so a happy medium can be reached without too much worry.

A Finishing Touch

Now make one more modification to the presentation to give it that professional touch. When the animation starts, the buttons also display rather abruptly. This detracts slightly from the animation. If we set the buttons and captions to display after the animation is finished and give them a transition effect, then the proper attention is given to each element.

To accomplish this task, lengthen the time duration of Slide 1 to 11 seconds and move the timelines for the buttons and captions to start at 7. Then add an Entering Transition to all the items except the animation. When you are ready, move to page one.

II

Using Corel's Modules

The Final Touches

Click on the background of Slide 1

In the Slide Duration *edit box,*
type **11**

Click on the Timelines button on   The Timelines window appears
the Button Bar

Move to the top of the Timelines window and enlarge it enough to zoom in on the timelines of
the End and Advance buttons. The timelines for the buttons and their associated captions are
shorter than the animation. Grab each of the four timelines in the middle and move them so
that the beginning point is at 6 and the end point is at 11 (see fig. 18.12). You are able to
monitor this by watching the status bar at the bottom of the Timelines window.

Move the Timeline window out of your way

Marquee-select both buttons   All four items are selected
and their captions

Click on the Transition Effects button   The Transition Effects dialog box appears
on the Button Bar

In the Opening list, select
HorizBlindDissolve

Click on OK   The Transition Effects dialog box disappears

Figure 18.12
Adjusting a
button's timeline.

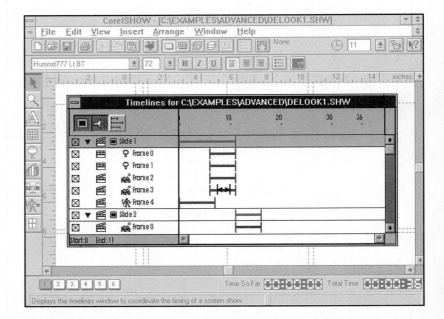

When you play back the presentation, the timing of the button and caption appearance is much more appealing. The effort put toward small refinements and fine-tuning the timing pays off in making your presentation stand out. The name of the game is impressing the audience. Sound, animation, transitions, and timing all contribute to making that lasting impression.

Chapter Snapshot

CorelPHOTO-PAINT! 5.0 has become a clear contender among the Windows image retouching programs. In this chapter, you learn the following:

✔ Set up PhotoPaint preferences

✔ How to place images in PhotoPaint

✔ Work with Photo CD images

✔ Use various filter types to retouch or add special effects to an image

✔ Work with canvases and fills

✔ Techniques for preparing print files

Clearly, CorelPHOTO-PAINT! has become a product that is up to doing the job as you need it done.

19

CHAPTER

Using CorelPHOTO-PAINT!

With the release of CorelDRAW! 5.0, CorelPHOTO-PAINT! is becoming a major player in the scanning and manipulation environment. Built into the overall product, you will find calibration tools that allow accurate monitor and printer setup. Additionally, there are built in functions for selecting a scanner set up or defining your own. Support for Kodak's PhotoCD format makes available a whole world of images on CD-ROM that enhance the potential for productive creativity. Capabilities have been added to the program to make it a much more flexible creator's product. By using a combination of tools, almost any effect or task can be performed on a project.

This chapter gives you an overview of the general features of PhotoPaint, old and new, and demonstrates how to use them. Some of the most important feature improvements are in the interface and how the program is used. By making these changes, Corel has made PhotoPaint an easier program to interact with.

System Requirements

Although PhotoPaint contains some great new changes, the program takes up about 30 MB of hard disk space. When you consider that PhotoPaint subdirectories alone take up 3 MB, this is not exactly a code light program. Add to it the other modules used, and PhotoPaint is without a doubt a heavy-weight program.

Also consider the size of some images. A 16-color RGB PCX is going to be much larger than a black-and-white image. Likewise, a 24-bit Truecolor CMYK TIFF is going to be geometrically larger still. Opening and editing these images requires real muscle to get the job done right. The more RAM memory and hard drive storage space you have, the better chance you have of producing high-quality results.

Setting PhotoPaint Preferences

The first time you open PhotoPaint, you should set your system preferences. The preferences, as in version 4.0, are centralized. These commands make using version 5.0 easier. They have been greatly expanded from the simple At Startup (now called On Startup) and Units choices in 4.0.

From the Special menu, select Preferences. The Preferences dialog box contains a number of check boxes and also requires that you make some configuration decisions (see fig. 19.1).

Across the top of the box are two card file tabs, General and Advanced. When you open Preferences, it defaults to the General card file. By clicking your mouse on Advanced, you are shown the preferences for the colors of the various marquees that you might use at different times, and where your plugins are stored (see fig. 19.2). You can Insert or Delete a number of plugin files in which PhotoPaint can look.

Each marquee type is a different color by default, but you can choose to make any number of them the same.

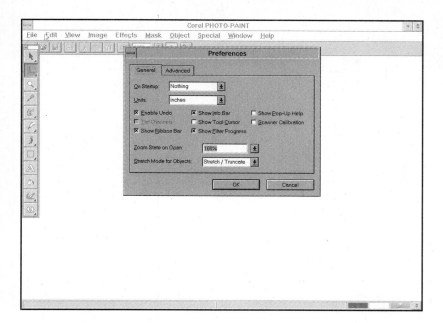

Figure 19.1
The Preferences
dialog box.

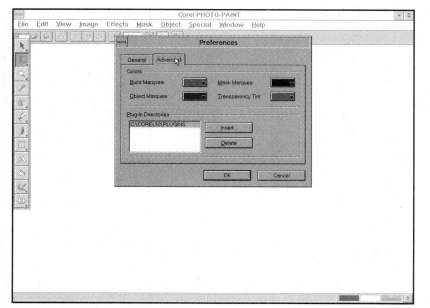

Figure 19.2
The Preferences
Advanced
dialog box.

II

Using Corel's Modules

The <u>O</u>n Startup option enables you to choose what you want PhotoPaint to do at launch. The choices are: Nothing, Open File, or New File. If you select Nothing, then CorelPHOTO-PAINT! launches and waits for you to tell it what to do. The other two choices are self-explanatory.

<u>U</u>nits defines the universal measurement default on launch. You always can change the measurement where needed, as it just gives the default setting. As for the check boxes, play with them until you find the launch combination that most appeals to you.

How the <u>Z</u>oom State On Open and <u>S</u>tretch Mode for Objects options are set in Preferences is very important to the starting state of the files you work with. The default choices in the roll-downs are Best Fit and Stretch/Truncate. In most cases, these will be the best choice to start with until you are comfortable changing to other file opening states. Best Fit opens the image in its entirety in full view. If necessary, it reduces the image size while maintaining the aspect ratio, thereby avoiding any distortion of the image and allowing you to see the whole image.

<u>S</u>tretch Mode for Objects refers to altering the aspect ratio of an object. If you stretch or shorten its aspect ratio, you want to retain the edge definition of the original file to avoid distorting the original file's integrity. The Anti-Alias option provides a computational technique used to maintain the smoothness of angles and curves, particularly on the monitor or with course printing screens. This technique adds or detracts pixel information to maintain a regularity seen in edges. With fonts or line art, this is fine. With images, this could mean that edge data becomes fuzzy or oversharpened and it might not appear natural.

If you are familiar with 4.0 and its calibration methodology, SURPRISE!, the Calibration menu and Display menu are no longer available. They really didn't go away; what took place was more like the disbandment of a military unit. The menu item was renamed <u>V</u>iew and its table of organization was restructured. Some things stayed, some were transferred elsewhere, while others, such as Calibrate, were mustered out of the corps. Be assured that in this case the early retirement was needed and well deserved. It was a cumbersome process at best.

Monitor calibration is discussed in detail in Chapter 21, "Managing Color and System Calibration." You are encouraged to read this and to perform a monitor calibration.

Before an image is brought into PhotoPaint for manipulation, there are two changes to the program that you should view. The first of these is the <u>O</u>pen command in the <u>F</u>ile menu and the second is the C<u>o</u>lor Roll-Up in the <u>V</u>iew menu.

A number of options have been changed in the Open dialog box. A scroll-down window under the preview has been added. This scroll-down window gives you the option of opening the full image, cropping the image before it opens, resampling it, or selecting a partial area of the image. The Filter Information button opens a dialog box that tells you the type and version of the selected filter. In the lower right corner, there is another button called Options. This button, when clicked, extends the Open dialog box and shows information on the selected file. This enables you to decide if you have opened the correct image.

After an image has been opened in PhotoPaint, almost every interaction with it requires the selection of color from the Color Roll-Up. As such, it is important to understand a structural change in how the Color Palette works. When an image is opened, it is in a default color mode, for example, CMYK, RGB, or grayscale. Each of the color models has its own color conventions. When a color is selected from the Color Roll-Up palette, it is constrained. The palette is completely interactive with the image color model that is selected. If the image selected is an RGB image, then all selectable colors in the palette will be RGB color only. Likewise, if the image is grayscale, than the color palette will only allow shades of gray to be supplied. This type of interactivity is prevalent throughout the program. Recognition of it helps you to learn how to use this program successfully.

Getting Images into PhotoPaint

There are a number of ways in which images can be brought into PhotoPaint. Thanks to the Twain technology, they can be scanned directly into PhotoPaint, read off any removable media, or accessed from a CD-ROM. Different considerations must be taken into acccount with each of them.

Twain technology is a set of standards developed by the desktop scanner manufacturers in conjunction with the major software developers as a standard set of conventions used in creating a scanner driver interface. While every manufacturer builds in differences pertinent to its own products, by maintaining the conventions laid out in the Twain technology standards, any scanner can scan directly into any software that supports and is fully compliant with Twain.

The first method is through CorelPHOTO-PAINT!'s File pull-down menu. In the menu, click on Acquire Image. You will then have two selections, Select Source or Acquire. Unless you use more than one scanner, it is not necessary to access the Select Source menu. To scan, click on Acquire. The scan will be completed when you follow the setup and scan procedure required for the scanner you are using.

The sophistication of the scanner's use and setup is determined solely by the manufacturer and the operating software that comes with the scanner.

Figure 19.3
Acquire/Select Source pull-down menu.

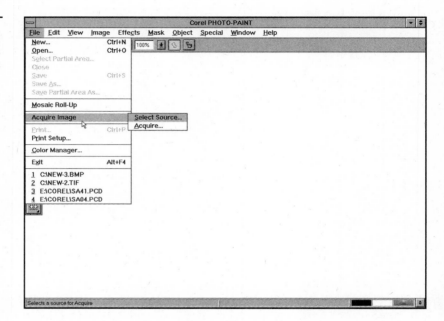

To scan accurately, it is imperative that you go through the entire calibration process that is laid out in Chapter 21. This is essential to assure the most efficient and productive way to scan images directly into PhotoPaint. As an extra, Corel has included an industry standard Color Target to be used for calibration.

If your images are from a traditional drum scanner or you are outputting to a PostScript imagesetter, you should work with your imaging service bureau to ensure that the information you are using for your calibration is accurate and appropriate.

Another method that can be used is off-line scanning. Off-line scanning can be done either at the workstation that is used for PhotoPaint, or at a separate workstation. The ultimate effect is essentially the same. In most cases, off-line scanning is more productive in getting images scanned. There are several reasons for this.

PhotoPaint is not a front-end scanning engine. It is an image retouching program that enables you to scan directly into the program. Generally this is done with utilities that are supplied by scanner manufacturers for that purpose. Some scanners' front ends are sturdier than others, while some are easier to use. In almost all cases, images scanned with these scanning utilities will need to be retouched in an image processing program. As such, many features that should not be left out often are.

A front end is the interface that is used for communication between the scanner and a computer. It's a combination of hardware and software, or in the simplest form, it's a scanner driver and a SCSI connection. For a more sophisticated scanner, it could be a special interface card and a full-blown application to control the scanner. Because scanners are "dumb" devices, a front end is necessary.

The alternative is to use a scanning utility that is compatible with a number of scanners and printers, and addresses as many scanning issues as possible before sending the image to the retouching program. The most well-known of these utility programs is Ofoto 2.0 for Windows from Light Source. With Ofoto, the scanner and printer are defined. The pair then is characterized to work together. This is done by outputting an Ofoto Scanning target on the printer and scanning it back. Ofoto reads the data from the target, compares it to the information that is stored on the original document and the two drives, and adjusts the scanning curves accordingly. When in use, the program batch processes scanning, pre-scanning, cropping, sharpening, basic color adjustments, and straightening. This way, you reduce the time spent scanning a number of images.

The second method of acquiring data is from removable media, such as when you obtain images from a digital imaging center to include in your documents. The removable media can take any number of forms and should be treated no differently than any other image stored on the local hard drive or network. Keep in mind, however, that removable media is more subject to failure from impact than the hard drive in your machine, which gets backed up. Treat removable media with care. Remember, a floppy disk and CD-ROM are both removable media. The difference is that CD-ROM is solid state data, while a floppy disk (along with all magnetic media) is affected by environmental issues. That is, the recorded data can be easily lost by impact, exposure to heat, extreme cold or moisture, rapid temperature change, dirt and grime, or mechanical failure of the disk itself.

II

Using Corel's Modules

The third method to get images into PhotoPaint is by using Photo CD. Photo CD was developed by Kodak as a method of scanning, globally correcting, adjusting, and storing images to ensure baseline image continuity and useability. What is unique about Photo CD is how the file is written to the Photo CD.

Photo CD is written to the disk in such a way that it incorporates five different resolutions and four color depths. This information resides within the image format and is selected at the time of acquire.

The Resolutions and Color Depths are as follows:

Resolution	Colors
*Wallet (128 × 192)	*256 Grayscale
*Snapshot (256 × 384)	*16 Color 4 Bit
*Standard (512 × 768)	*256 Color 8 Bit
*Large (1,024 × 1,536)	*16.7 million Color 24 Bit
*Poster (2,084 × 3,072)	

To acquire a Photo CD Image directly into PhotoPaint, select File, Open. Before opening the image file, a dialog box called Photo CD Options opens (see fig. 19.4). In this dialog box, you can select Resolution, Colors, and Preview. Text at the bottom of the box indicates what the image size will be with the combination that is selected. The Apply Image Enhancements check box can be disregarded because all image enhancements can be made within PhotoPaint.

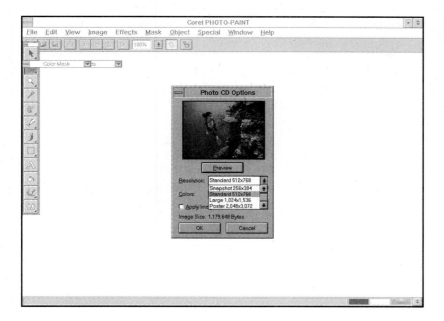

Figure 19.4
The Photo CD
Options dialog
box.

CorelPHOTO-PAINT! Filters

After the image is opened in PhotoPaint, you have an unlimited number of choices. The one area where the most options have changed is in the Effects menu. The number of filters that now are available has increased. Additionally, many of the filters that were scattered about the various menus now are centralized in the Effects menu. As these are the heart of the retouching capabilities, it is vital that you become familiar with what they do.

As mentioned, a lot has changed with PhotoPaint 5.0 in relation to filters. Filters now are grouped together as subsets of the Effects menu. A few of the filters still can be accessed by using hot keys but for the most part, applying a filter requires using the mouse or movement keys to navigate through the menus.

A couple of the filters have been eliminated, but many more have been added. Overall, the filters still can clearly be grouped as two distinct sets, even though the program no longer separates them accordingly.

To see how the various filters' looks apply, refer to the PhotoPaint manual. Note in some cases, however, that the range for each filter is not done justice. Many of the filters can give some very striking and powerful effects, but the examples shown are not extreme uses of the filters. So while the application example shown in the manual might be very sedate in appearance, it could also give drastic and highly artistic results.

The first group of effects is special effects or creative filters and the second group is retouching filters. It is pretty safe to say that the following list is one of the most comprehensive filtering lists available from any desktop image retouching application available today. Understanding what these different filters do, in particular the Special Effects filters, is highly subjective and is best understood through playing. Table 19.1 is meant to give you a feel for each filter before you start playing with it. Remember that the effects are cumulative with the combined use of multiple filters, and in some cases negative, but the filters will clearly give you effects you have not even considered. As you play with filters, take notes on what you do. You might stumble upon a combination of filters that produce a really cool result that you'll want to reproduce some day.

Table 19.1
Special Effect Filters

Filter Name	Description
Artistic/Pointillism	Creates the effect attained by painting with the tip of a paintbrush and spotting the canvas instead of brushing it. Similar to the works of Georges Seurat.
Artistic/Impressionism	Adds a light stroking pattern on a defined curve path to the overall image appearance. Depending on the transparency, edge, and number of strokes selected, the degree of "disrupted reality" varies. Similar to the works of Claude Monet.
Fancy/Edge Detect	By setting a color and sensitivity, this filter isolates all the edges and changes all other color information, creating a charcoal-like texture.

Filter Name	Description
Special/Contour	Finds the edges, isolates them, colors them, and obliterates all other color information, leaving a skeletal representation of the original image.
Fancy/Outline	Finds the outline information and creates a highlight pattern with it, leaving all other color information intact, giving an electrical appearance.
Fancy/Emboss	According to image density, Emboss "rates the depth" of image and replaces the color with a designated gray in a selected direction. The result is very similar in appearance to hammered sheet metal.
Fancy/Invert	Reads all the highlight and shadow details and reverses them, creating a "positive negative" image.
Fancy/Jaggy Despeckle	The image's sharpness is distorted, creating an overall soft image. The degree of "unsharpness" is adjusted by a maximum width and height of 5 pixels.
Fancy/Motion Blur	This is a common effect most often used with athletes and cars to generate a feeling of motion. On a directional basis, the image is blurred by a speed factor to create an effect similar to a slow-motion camera shot of something moving.
Noise/Add Noise	Destabilizes the smoothness of the image, similar to using a coarse filter when developing a picture.

continues

Table 19.1, Continued
Special Effect Filters

Filter Name	Description
Noise/Remove Noise	This filter is just the opposite of Add Noise. This makes a coarse, grainy image appear more focused and sharp.
Noise/Maximum	This filter induces a greater clarity and detail in a dark image by reducing the amount of color in all areas.
Noise/Median	Overall smoothing of file.
Noise/Minimum	This filter brightens and smoothes highlight areas.
Mapping/Pixelation	This filter restructures the image with either round or square magnified pixels according to a selected width and height.
Special/Posterize	This filter flattens the dynamic structure of the color to give a very flat, surrealistic effect.
Special/Psychedelic	This filter is very strange and colorful. You must see it to understand it. Play with it.
Special/Solarize	This filter shifts the color value of all pixels below a preset threshold to a portion of the red color gamut according to its color value.

The following chart lists the Artistic filters that have been added with version 5.0. Add More Noise and Edge Emphasis have been eliminated.

Table 19.2
New Special Effects Filters

Filter Name	Description
Mapping/Vignette	Vignette creates an oval cameo window of the image. The sharpness of the vignette and color of the background are selected. The color of the background is limited to black, white, or pen selected
Mapping/Tile	Tiles the image into a given area. You select the number of tiles horizontally and vertically and the program repeats the image accordingly.
Mapping/Swirl	The effect that this filter creates is best described as water down the drain. The higher the angular selection the more pronounced the draining effect. The effect is only centered on the image. To do a partial offset, select an area of the image, cut it out, and put it back in place as a new image. Then re-insert the image into the original image with the desired offset from center. This creates an interesting effect.
Mapping/Punch-Pull	Imagine grabbing the center of an image and pulling it forward or backward. That is what punch-pull does.
Mapping/Map to Sphere	This filter wraps/distorts the image around a cylinder or a sphere.
Mapping/Glass Block	This filter is similar in application to tile, except the image remains intact behind the image. Portions of the image are mirrored from block to block.
Mapping/Impressionist	This filters out a portion of the details to give a speckled effect.

continues

Table 19.2, Continued
New Special Effects Filters

Filter Name	Description
Mapping/Ripple	This filter applies a sine wave to an image. The pattern is adjusted just like in math class; period (duplication of pattern), amplitude (height of hills and valleys), and Ripple type (the direction of application).
Mapping/Smoked Glass	This effect basically reduces the dynamic range of an image and adjusts the transparency.
Mapping/Wet Paint	This filter looks like wet paint running down a canvas, reminiscent of elementary school art class.
Mapping/Wind	This is a variation on the motion blur filter.

The following is a list of filter effects that are used for image retouching and not artistic manipulation. That is not to say that they can't be used for that purpose, but their primary use is to "fix" images.

Table 19.3
Retouching Filters

Filter Name	Description
Color/Brightness and Contrast	This filter alters the differences between highlight and shadow areas and increases or decreases the detail accordingly. It is especially useful in opening up detail in dark areas.
Special/Threshold	This filter sets a color value to 0 for all colors. Any colors below the threshold become 0 and all colors above are unaltered.

Filter Name	Description
Color/Gamma	This filter adjusts the midtone grayscale independent of highlights and shadows, increases the detail.
Color/Hue & Saturation	This filter affects the value of the colors. Hue shifts the colors through a color wheel orientation based upon RGB, while Saturation alters the amount of color present in relation to the original balance
Sharpen/Sharpen	Sharpen is used to enhance the edge details. Because all colors have edge areas, this filter makes very drastic changes, so, to avoid distortion, apply only small percentages of sharpen.
Sharpen/Enhance	Called Enhance Detail in version 4.0, this filter has been modified to allow for discrete adjustment of smooth-ness or sharpness of image.
Sharpen/Unsharp Masking	A combination of both the Sharpen and Enhance filter, the Unsharp Masking effectively executes a simultaneous application of the two filters with an averaging of the combined filter effect. It sharpens edge detail and smoothes the detail of smooth areas.
Sharpen/Adaptive Unsharp Mask	This filter is similar to the Sharpen filter in that it sharpens the edge detail. It recognizes and "ignores" non-edge details more effectively.

continues

Using Corel's Modules

Table 19.3, Continued
Retouching Filters

Filter Name	Description
Soften/Smooth	This filter pixel blends color areas to reduce transition of color, giving a less harsh image appearance.
Soften/Soften	This filter is similar to Smooth, but a greater amount of image detail is retained. It is less likely to plug up shadows or blow out highlight areas.
Soften/Diffuse	Generally a destructive filter, Diffuse shifts the pattern of pixel colors to unfocus images.
Color/Tone Map	Tone map has been expanded in a number of ways. It still serves to correct inaccuracies in the color balance, and is color model intuitive. If you are working in CMYK, RGB, or Grayscale, it enables you to adjust the curve according to the appropriate color components. The overall use of the tool is much more apparent than in prior versions. An interesting aside with this filter is that, in the past, PhotoPaint viewed this as a calibration tool and not as a filter for retouching.

Filter Name	Description
Tone/Equalize	This filter enables you to view the Highlight-Midtone-Shadow detail as a histogram and enables you to reset the midtone point and truncate/expand the highlight shadow tone end-points, effectively reducing or expanding the dynamic range of the image.

The filters in table 19.4 are new filters that have been added to version 5.0. The Filter Smooth/Blend has been removed as its functionality has been incorporated into a number of other filters.

Table 19.4
New Retouching Filters

Filter Name	Description
Soften/Directional Smooth	This filter smoothes the differences in adjacent pixel colors in a single angular vector. Some detail is lost to this filter process.
Sharpen/Directional Sharpen	This filter analyzes the different values of colors and applies the sharpening in a specific direction.
Sharpen/Edge Enhance	This filter sharpens specifically those edge colors that have different values.

Because the following three filters effect the geometry of image and not the colorimetry, they don't really fall into either of the prior classes and should be treated as a separate category. They are, however, in some ways similar to the artistic filters.

II

Using Corel's Modules

Table 19.5
Transformation Filters

Filter Name	Description
Transformation/3-D rotate	This filter changes the position of the image on a flat cube face to another face at a different angle. Although the orientations are height and width, the alteration is actually on the X-, Y-, and Z- axes.
Transformation/Perspective	This filter alters the orientation of an image so that it looks like you are viewing it from an angle. The image does not necessarily require a trapezoidal shape, just as long as it maintains a 4-point rhomboid wire frame.
Transformation/Mesh warp	This filter contours the image over a landscape setup using a wireframe grid.

Fills and Canvases

With the new version of PhotoPaint, canvases have remained effectively the same, while fills have changed. These capabilities are important for you to understand if you want to use them correctly.

A canvas is a bitmap image, as well as a background. Essentially, a canvas would be used to build a project in lieu of working on a flat tint or white paper. If all your work is done in the CPT format (Corel's native format for PhotoPaint), then canvases remain separate objects, removable and editable until the image is merged to be saved in another format. As soon as the images are merged or converted into another format, they are no longer separate objects, but rather a single image file. If canvases are used with other formats, such as TIFF (the standard image format for the prepress industry), then every time the image is saved, the canvas is saved as part of it. It is never separable.

Note An interesting use of canvases is to make a background, such as wallpaper in Windows.

Fills come in two flavors, tile and texture. While the types of files have remained the same, the way they are accessed and edited, if applicable, has been vastly improved (see fig. 19.5). All fills can now be edited from the Fill Roll-Up menu. There are 5 distinct types of Fill:

> Color Fill
>
> Fountain Fill (also known as Color Gradient Fill)
>
> Bitmap Fill
>
> Texture Fill
>
> No Fill Fill

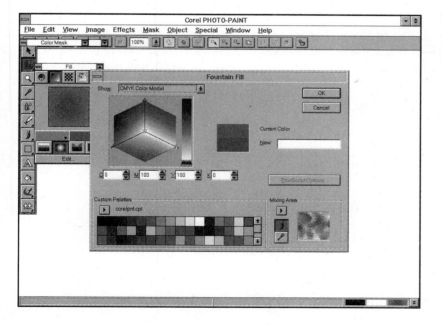

Figure 19.5
The Fountain Fill
dialog box.

Using Corel's Modules

The Color and Fountain fills are created from flat tint colors and can be adjusted for any color you desire. They are fully editable from the Roll-Up/Edit button. When this button is selected, the Color Palette dialog box opens up. While editable color information varies interactively, the basics are the same. The Show dialog box enables you to select the color model in which you want to work. This could be one of the myriad of color models that Photo-Paint now supports:

CMYK

RGB

HSB

Grayscale

Uniform Colors

PANTONE Spot

PANTONE Process

FOCALTONE

TRUEMATCH

Each of these color models has different uses and approaches to how it is applied. Use the model that best fits your working environment, that makes the most sense for you and the way you work, and that fits into your production flow.

Bitmap fills are just what the name implies—fills that use a bitmap as the underlying, composing element. Any bitmap can be used as a fill, however, it must be imported as bitmap fill to be used as such. At that point, any image area filled with a bitmap fill will have a repetition of that image. Importing files is done using the Import dialog box as shown in figure 19.6.

Texture fills are made up of patterns of flat tints that have been used to create patterns. PhotoPaint comes with an extensive library of texture patterns that can be used as texture fills or can be edited to create new ones. By its very nature, a texture fill's potential to be either attractive or ugly is limited only by imagination.

The final type of fill present on the roll-up menu is the No Fill fill. This does not appear to be a fill at first glance. When you consider its uses, however, that assumption needs to be re-evaluated. This fill is handy when an image area needs to be filled with absolutely no color. Using this fill ensures that no color sneaks in by accident.

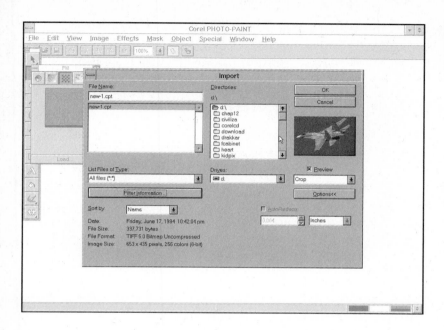

Figure 19.6

The Import
dialog box.

Tools

The tools that are available in version 5 are not much different than those that were available in version 4. The biggest difference comes in their organization and interactivity.

The tool buttons can still be arranged in either a grid or as a toolbar. In the grid format, all the tool buttons are always visible. In the toolbar format, only one button, representing a number of tools that have been grouped together according to function, is available. When you need to perform a function with a button related to a button on the toolbar, click on that button, and a fly-out menu appears with the related buttons. When a tool is selected from the fly-out menu, it becomes the primary button on the toolbar for the time being. A nice feature of the tool buttons is their interactivity.

Some of the tool buttons are task specific. If one affects masking but not Object/ Layer editing, when a task is being performed in which one of these task specific buttons cannot be used, it disappears from the tool ribbon. So at various times, different buttons might not be present on the tool ribbon.

The settings for the application of a tool are important when using the tools. The Tool Settings Roll-Up menu proves to be a vital asset for this task. It enables you to set all parameters that are appropriate to each tool, making it as effective as possible. Because the method in which each tool is used determines its successful or unsuccessful application, you should use the Tool Setting Roll-Up regularly.

Preparation for Printing

Hopefully, before you finish editing, a decision is made regarding the image's final use. Preferably, that decision is made before you start doing any work, otherwise, accurate calibration of the process goes out the window. Because of the flexibility of working in the CPT mode, all image editing should be done in that mode.

If the image is going out to a PostScript imagesetter for four-color separation and then to a 35mm slide, two conversions need to be made. To make conversions, choose Image, Convert To. The color models that you can convert to are as follows:

Color Type of Image	Color Depth of Image/Output Type
Black/White	Line Art Printer Halftone Screen Halftone
16 Colors	(4 bit)
Grayscale	(8 bit)
256 colors	(8 Bit)
RGB Colors	(24 bit)
CMYK Colors	(32 bit)

For output purposes, any images that start as Photo CD or are edited as CPT must be converted to CMYK or RGB. CMYK is used for imagesetter output and RGB for slide output. After the images are converted to their respective color model, they should be saved to the appropriate format by choosing File, Save As. If you use the CMYK color separation, save the file in TIFF 6.0 format. RGB should be saved as a bitmap file.

Photo CD format and CPT format are not industry-accepted output formats. As such at this time, no one makes an output device that specifically outputs hard copy in the native format of each. As such, for color hard copy the generally accepted formats are CMYK for ink printing processes and RGB composite final images.

When printing in the RGB color setting the Options function in the <u>F</u>ile, <u>P</u>rint dialog box should be on. The first file card visible in the dialog box is Layout. If the image is going out for 35mm slide output, there is no reason to add any marks around the image area or to adjust any of the other options. Click on the Separation file tab to open that card. Then make sure that the Separations button is clicked off. The file is now ready to print. If the image is going to an online film recorder, select the device. If it is going out-of-house, print it to file.

If the image is going out to an online PostScript imagesetter, the printing process needs to be handled a little differently. Again, go into the <u>F</u>iles, <u>P</u>rint Options dialog box. In the Separations file card, Separations must be on, and all four color plates should be highlighted. On the Layout file card, all the scroll downs can be left alone. On the right side of the page, Preview image should be selected. In addition, the printer options should be selected as appropriate. From left to right under the image box they are: Right-Wrong reading, Positive Negative film, Density strip, color bars, registration marks, crop marks, and id slug. These options are selected dependent upon what your printer needs; you should discuss this with him. Printers hate fixing bad film, and they hate putting it on their presses even more.

Chapter Snapshot

With version 5, CorelMOSAIC! is thoroughly integrated into Corel's applications to become an extremely valuable file management tool. In this chapter, you learn how to:

✔ Run Mosaic as a separate utility

✔ Run Mosaic from a roll-up menu

✔ View your graphics files in thumbnail fashion

✔ Use Mosaic directories, catalogs, and libraries to organize your files

✔ Use drag and drop to copy, move, or delete files

CorelDRAW! files can eat up much of your hard disk space and be difficult to manage. CorelMOSAIC! is perfect to use to view, compress, and manage files.

CHAPTER

Using CorelMOSAIC!

With release 5, Mosaic has been thoroughly integrated into Corel's suite of applications and provides many useful features for graphic file management. In previous versions, CorelMOSAIC! was a separate utility program packaged with CorelDRAW!. With release 5, a roll-up subset of the Mosaic program is available in all the major Corel applications. The Mosaic program can be used to view files, compress files, and manage files.

File Viewer

In addition to displaying the file name, CorelMOSAIC! can show a *thumbnail,* or miniature picture of the file. This is a visual clue that enhances the meaning of an eight character file name. Thumbnails are added, or embedded, into a file when it is created. CorelDRAW!, for example, enables you to choose to include one (when you save) and to specify the thumbnail's resolution. It's easy to create lots of files in little time, but it's sometimes difficult to remember their file names. Now you can display files graphically, along with their file names.

File Compressor

Most graphics files can be made substantially smaller through compression. With CorelMOSAIC!, you can create libraries of your files and automatically compress and decompress them by dragging and dropping them. Thumbnails, if available, are included in the libraries to assist in searching for a file without decompressing and opening it.

File Manager

Files can be moved or copied from one directory (or drive) to another, or can be deleted. Mosaic provides a visual confirmation that you are dealing with the right file. Optional description fields are available in Mosaic collections that expand the descriptions of the files. Additionally, you can search for files with keywords.

In this chapter, you learn the ways in which Mosaic organizes *collections,* Corel's name for all Mosaic files, of images in directories, catalogs, and libraries.

Mosaic as Application versus Mosaic as Roll-Up

As a separate, stand-alone utility, CorelMOSAIC! is capable of heavy duty file management and runs much like any Windows program. Batch operations—in which you can convert many files at a time to a different format—are available only in this mode. This program enables you to open more than one collection at a time, and drag and drop between them.

The Roll-Up mode is available in all of Corel's suite of programs —Draw, Photo-Paint, Trace!, Ventura Publishing, Show, Chart, and Move. In Roll-Up mode, you can have only one collection open. Roll-Up mode is where you look for a file, confirm it visually, and either import it by dragging it off the roll-up and dropping it in your main window, or start the underlying Corel application by double-clicking on the image.

 See table 20.1 for a complete list of file types and the application with which they are associated.

Additional differences between Mosaic as a stand-alone utility and Mosaic as a roll-up include the following:

✔ When you open the Mosaic Roll-Up, it defaults to the Windows directory and builds a collection of files. The Mosaic application "remembers" the last collection you had open, and reloads it.

✔ The roll-up does not have a menu bar.

✔ The stand-alone program includes a File, Preferences section to change the size and look of the thumbnails. Selections here do not affect the roll-ups, however.

✔ The stand-alone program can have multiple collections open at once; roll-up Mosaic can have only one.

File Types Supported

Throughout all of the Corel applications, there is a common set of *filters,* translators to convert files, used to import and export files. In the roll-up version, all valid file types will be selected. In the Open dialog box of the Mosaic application, you have many choices of types of files to include in a collection.

The following table describes the valid file extensions, and the import filters each uses. The column labeled *DDE Application* shows the Corel program that is launched if you double-click on the thumbnail or select Edit.

Table 20.1
Valid Mosaic File Types

File Extensions	Import Filter	DDE Application
CLC	Corel Catalog	CorelMOSAIC! application only
CLB	Corel Library	CorelMOSAIC! application only
FLI, FLC	Autodesk FLIC Thumbnail	
GIF	CompuServe Bitmap	CorelPHOTO-PAINT!
CCH	CorelCHART! Thumbnail	CorelCHART!
CDR, PAT, CDT	CorelDRAW! Thumbnail	CorelDRAW!
SHW, SHB	CorelSHOW! Thumbnail	CorelSHOW!
EPS, PS, AI	EPS (Placeable)	CorelDRAW!
JPG, JIFF, JTF, CMP	JPEG Bitmap	CorelPHOTO-PAINT!
PCD	Kodak Photo CD Image	CorelPHOTO-PAINT!
CMX, WAV, AVI, CMV	RIFF Thumbnail	
TGA, VDA, ICB, VST	Targa Bitmap	CorelPHOTO-PAINT!
TIF, SEP	TIFF Bitmap	CorelPHOTO-PAINT!
BMP, DIB, RLE	Windows Bitmap	CorelPHOTO-PAINT!
PCX	Windows Paintbrush	CorelPHOTO-PAINT!
CMX	Corel Presentation Exchange	
CPT	CorelPHOTO-PAINT! Image	CorelPHOTO-PAINT!

File Extensions	Import Filter	DDE Application
EPS	CorelTRACE!	CorelDRAW!
CT, SCT	Scitex CT Bitmap	

Starting Mosaic Roll-Up

Roll-Up Mosaic can be started in every Corel application three different ways:

- ✔ **By the menu.** Choose File, Mosaic Roll-Up and the roll-up opens.

- ✔ **With a keyboard shortcut.** Alt+F1 selects the Mosaic Roll-Up in every application.

- ✔ **With the button bar.** Each of the new Ribbon Bars contains a button to activate Mosaic.

In CorelDRAW! 5 only, you can access Mosaic by automatic startup. If you would like the Mosaic Roll-Up available on the screen every time you open Draw, you can set this option. The following exercise shows you how to have one Mosaic Roll-Up appear on your screen whenever you start CorelDRAW!:

Setting Up Automatic Load of Mosaic Roll-Up

Choose View   The View menu appears

Choose Roll Ups   Opens the Roll-Ups dialog box
                                (see fig. 20.1)

Click on Mosaic-1 in the list box   Highlights Mosaic-1 and activates the three
                                        check boxes to the right

There are two entries for Mosaic in the list box, Mosaic-1 and Mosaic-2. Both can be chosen if you want to have two Mosaic roll-ups available when you open CorelDRAW!. Here, just choose one.

Click on Visible and Arranged   Places an "X" in the boxes

The other option, Rolled Down, enables you to specify that the Mosaic Roll-Up will be in the fully opened, rolled-down form, when CorelDRAW! starts. If you select either the Arranged option or the Rolled Down option, you will automatically get the Visible option.

At the bottom left of the dialog box is a section called Start Up Setting with a drop-down list box.

Click on the down arrow   Opens a short list of choices

II

Using Corel's Modules

Click on the Custom *option and choose* Save Custom	Saves your custom settings (or resaves them if you have saved them before)
Click on OK	Closes the dialog box and you are finished

To verify that it works, exit from CorelDRAW! and restart it.

Figure 20.1
New Collection
dialog box.

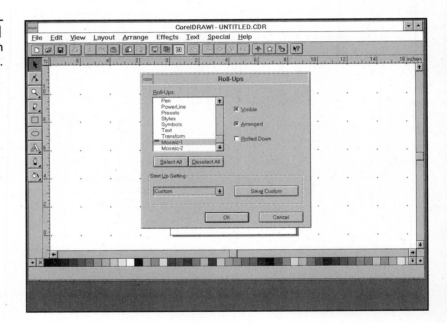

Placing Mosaic Roll-Up

If you plan to keep the Mosaic Roll-Up on your screen, find some convenient, out of the way spot to move it (click on the title bar and drag it). You need only allow for the title bar part of the roll-up—that's all that will be visible when rolled up.

Placing the rolled-up title bar at the bottom of your window causes the roll-up to open upward. When you roll it up again, the title bar remains in this new position, not where you left it.

Roll-ups are notorious for using a lot of your Windows system resources. Using too many roll-ups will degrade your system's performance to the point where Windows may become unstable.

Never select the option to load all the roll-ups on start up. It's good practice to completely close any roll-up that you will not be using for a while.

Using the Mosaic Stand-Alone Application

The first difference you might notice when you start the stand-alone version of Mosaic is that it's exactly the way you left it. The stand-alone version of Mosaic "remembers" what collections, and in what order, you had open when you last used the program. This is a major advantage of the stand-alone version over the roll-up version.

If you normally use the same directories for your work, just open them and leave them open when you exit from the program.

With the roll-up version, you must change your directory every time, assuming you do not want the Windows directory. This procedure takes a little time, but it is easy.

Viewing a Directory

Any time CorelMOSAIC! is on your screen, you can look at the graphics files in any directory. You also can easily change the directory. This exercise will show you how to quickly create a view of any directory, showing the thumbnails of the files it contains.

Looking in a Directory—in Stand-alone Mosaic

Choose File	Opens the File menu
Click on Open Collection	The Open Collection dialog box appears
Using the drive and directory list boxes, choose a directory	Highlights a directory
Click on OK	Closes the Open dialog box and displays the images from this directory in a new window in Mosaic

Note that double-clicking on the directory is the same as clicking once and then clicking on OK.

In the upper right hand corner of the Mosaic Roll-Up is a small icon of a file folder (see fig. 20.2).

Click on File folder icon	Drops down the directories box
Using the drive and directory list boxes, choose a directory	Highlights the directory and the drop-down box closes
Click on OK	Images from this directory in a new window in Mosaic

Figure 20.2
Title bar of
Mosaic Roll-Up.

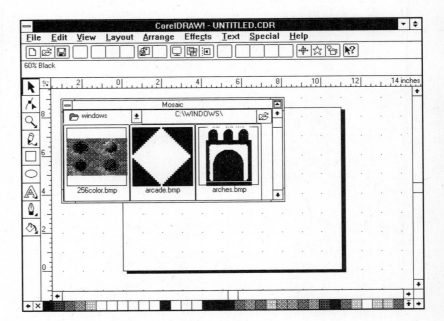

Corel has sped up the loading and drawing of Mosaic collections in version 5. If you have multiple collections open, Mosaic draws the one you can see first and does not draw any thumbnails that are hidden.

Tip
You can stop, or interrupt, the loading and drawing of thumbnails by clicking the mouse button anywhere in the window. To resume the loading and drawing of thumbnails, press Esc.

Opening a Catalog or Library

All three types of collections, directories, catalogs, and libraries, look very similar on the screen.

Directory collections are produced when you point to a directory with Open Collection. They do not store the thumbnails in a file and re-create them each time you open a directory collection.

Catalogs do have a file saved in the directory you choose that contains all the thumbnails. A good example of a catalog is the one included with the clip art.

Libraries have two files. One file contains the thumbnails, and the other file contains the compressed files of the library.

Creating a Catalog or Library in the Stand-alone version of Mosaic

Choose **F**ile	Opens File menu
Click on **N**ew Collection	Opens New Collection dialog box
Enter your new file name	File name appears in File **N**ame box

If you type your file name first, you don't need to select the file name box because it's ready to accept typing when the dialog box first opens. You also do not need to type a file extension—Mosaic adds it in the following step:

Under List Files of **T**ype you have two choices: Corel Library (*.CLB), and Corel Catalog (*.CLC).

Click on type of collection	Highlights collection
Choose a directory for your new collection	Changes target directory
Click on OK	Closes dialog box and displays empty collection in Mosaic

At this point, you have created either a new catalog or a new library, but it is empty. The next step is to move files into it.

It's helpful to understand the difference between **F**ile, **N**ew Collection and **F**ile, **O**pen Collection. Use **F**ile, **N**ew Collection only to create a catalog or library that does not exist. Use **F**ile, **O**pen Collection to open any directory, catalog, or library that you have previously created.

Dragging and Dropping a Selection

Dragging and dropping is probably one of the handiest features of CorelMOSAIC!. With two or more collections open in either the roll-up or the stand-alone version of Mosaic, here's how you move, copy, and delete a file:

Copying a File

Click on a thumbnail and hold down the mouse button	Selects thumbnail
Holding down the mouse button, move the mouse cursor to another collection	Changes mouse cursor shape
Release the mouse button	The Confirm File Copy dialog box appears
Click on Yes	The file is copied into the new collection

Moving a File

Click on a thumbnail and hold down mouse button	Selects thumbnail
Holding down mouse and the Shift key, move the mouse cursor to another collection	Changes mouse cursor shape
Release the mouse button and the Shift key	The Confirm File Move dialog box appears
Click on Yes	The file is moved into the new collection

Deleting a File

In the stand-alone version of Mosaic only, you can delete files from any collection.

Click on a thumbnail	Selects a thumbnail
Choose **E**dit	Opens **E**dit menu
Click on **D**elete	The Confirm File Delete dialog box appears
Click on OK	Deletes file and closes dialog box
Click on Yes	

Using the Delete key on your keyboard does the same thing as **E**dit, **D**elete in the menu, but is quicker.

Launching a Selection

Table 20.1 lists the file types Mosaic will read. Notice the column labeled *DDE Application*, which lists the Corel programs associated with certain file types. With Mosaic open—either as the stand-alone or roll-up version—you can double-click on a thumbnail and start the Corel application for this file, with this file automatically loaded at startup.

After the program is running, and the file is loaded, you can edit this file and save it. Exiting from the program returns you to the point from which you left.

Understanding Libraries

Libraries, sometimes called archives, contain one to several compressed files. Most graphics files, and CorelDRAW! files in particular, can be substantially reduced in size with compression techniques. Many archiving programs are available. PKZIP from PK Ware, for example, makes files smaller by removing and encoding redundant information.

In one test, PKZIP reduced 20 CorelDRAW! files, originally containing 3,991,794 bytes, to 1,354,125 bytes, or approximately one-third of the size. CorelMOSAIC! can accomplish similar results. The same files, when moved to a Mosaic library, took up only 1,461,189 bytes.

Because hard disk space is always scarce, compressing files into libraries is well worth the effort.

Tip

After your files are compressed into libraries, they can be moved to floppies for storage. You may need to add and delete files to get your libraries to fit. If a library is too big, drag files out of it until the library is small enough to fit.

Understanding Thumbnails

Thumbnails are low-resolution bitmap representations of graphics files that are embedded in the files themselves. These small figures enable you to see approximately what the file will look like when it's loaded. Without thumbnails, the entire file would have to be read and loaded before you knew whether you had the right file. Most modern graphics programs, including CorelDRAW, use thumbnails to give you a preview of the file in the Open Drawing dialog box. Figure 20.3 shows CorelDRAW!'s Open Drawing dialog box with a thumbnail of one of the MS Windows wallpaper bitmaps.

Figure 20.3
The Open Drawing dialog box from CorelDRAW!.

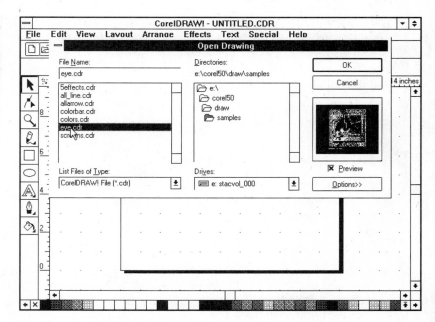

Tip

Use the lowest resolution of a thumbnail that displays enough detail of the file. Thumbnails increase the size of your file and file loading time.

Files with Thumbnails

Most graphics files have thumbnails embedded; most text documents do not. Wherever possible, CorelMOSAIC! displays a thumbnail or attempts to create one. If, however, you specify to omit a thumbnail when you create the file, Mosaic does not display one.

Earlier in this chapter, table 20.1 listed the import filters available to Mosaic. Most of them have "Thumbnail" in their description, meaning that they can either find the thumbnail in the file or create one. See figure 20.4 for some examples of thumbnails.

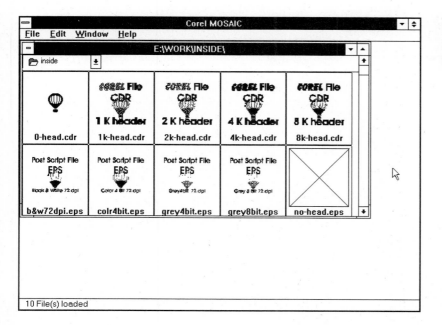

Figure 20.4
Examples of thumbnails.

Using Corel's Modules

Sizing Thumbnails at Creation

Corel applications give you control over thumbnails. In Draw, when you first save a file, you have the option of deciding the size of its embedded thumbnail. In the Save <u>A</u>s dialog box, you can choose from None to 8 KB. None excludes it and 8 KB is the highest resolution. Each size in between adds the stated amount to the file size—an 8 KB thumbnail adds 8 KB to the size of the Draw file. You can always change the size later by performing a different Save <u>A</u>s command.

EPS files have embedded TIFF pictures to show thumbnails. When creating an EPS file, you can specify its resolution (amount of detail), and whether it is grayscale or color. Although CorelDRAW! thumbnails are fixed in size, EPS thumbnails are not. The resolution and the number of colors change the size of the thumbnail, and, therefore, the size of the whole file. Be aware that even with some small TIFF bitmaps, an 8-bit color thumbnail can easily double the size of the file.

Managing Your Graphics Files

As you begin to use CorelDRAW! and other graphics applications more and more, you'll notice that the files you create are gobbling up your hard drive. Most graphics files are considerably larger than text files, so disk space will quickly become scarce. (Of course, the very large hard disk requirements of modern applications are certainly taking their toll. The Corel suite alone can take over 50 MB.)

The following are some practical suggestions to help you better manage your precious space:

✔ Create a separate subdirectory for the exclusive use of graphics files. Create this directly off the root directory so that it is easy to find and quick to point to when saving your files. You might call this directory something like "Images" or "Graphics."

✔ Create subdirectories, under this "Images" directory, that contain only EPS files or CDR files from Draw. After you start saving files to this subdirectory, you will find that most programs will begin to use this as their default. This saves you time in choosing a place to put the file you are saving. Finding files later is simple: they are in only one place.

With your graphics files all in one place, Mosaic can easily create a collection whenever you start the stand-alone version of Mosaic, or when you point to the directory with the roll-up version. You also can delete unwanted files in the stand-alone version of Mosaic with <u>E</u>dit, <u>D</u>elete.

Finally, if you decide to use Mosaic's library function to compress your files, you need only drag them from one Mosaic window to another.

Backing Up Your Files

There are many methods, media, and programs available to back up your files. Regardless of how you do it, Mosaic offers you a very nice alternative. By using Mosaic's library functions, you can first compress your files, and then copy the whole library to your backup media. Thus, not only do you conserve disk space, but you can easily and visually browse the library to select a file you want to restore to your system.

Part Four

Advanced Topics

Chapter Snapshot

Until the release of CorelDRAW! 5, color calibration
was left to the ultra-advanced CorelDRAW! user. Now,
however, even beginners can control color consistency.
In this chapter, you do the following:

✔ Learn why calibration is important

✔ Calibrate by using CorelDRAW!

✔ Calibrate your scanner and color printer

✔ Verify color accuracy

✔ Use version 5's new color tools

✔ Create a system profile

Learning to calibrate your system gives you a competitive advantage, which you need to succeed in today's
graphics environment.

CHAPTER

Managing Color and System Calibration

Color calibration within the PC environment is not new, even though lately it seems we hear more and more about it. Competition between platforms has taken its toll on the computer industry. Environments, such as the Apple Macintosh System, that have had much more success with the science of desktop publishing have made it frustrating for PC users. Only recently has the capability to produce full and accurate color documents come easily to our world.

Years ago, conventional color systems operated by large prepress film houses already had calibration in place. It was something that experts or specialists had to be contracted to set up, and it was time-consuming and expensive. Color calibration through the computer is not new, it's just relatively new to the PC.

Now that color is readily available and widely used on desktop systems, things have changed a bit. Color is not as costly or as time-consuming to set up and maintain as it used to be. The color control and flexibility you envied in big systems of the past is not only within your reach, it's staring you right in the face!

Until the release of CorelDRAW! 5, color calibration was something only the ultra-advanced CorelDRAW! user attempted. Now, with the release of version 5, new hope exists for even the most basic user who wants to control color consistency and quality.

This chapter not only gives you a basic understanding of the principles of calibrating a system, it also gives you insight into the new color management tools available. First, you see how color calibration was achieved without any software automation and how CorelDRAW! version 4 enabled basic system controls. Then, you are taken though the basic step-by-step system profile creation now available in version 5.

Why Should You Calibrate?

Why should you bother with color calibration? Here is a fundamental example of how knowing about and implementing color calibration directly benefits you and your work.

Your boss or favorite client picks you to design their next series of full-color brochures. It's a lot of work, but you've been waiting for a chance like this to come along. You have years of training and a bundle of original ideas. Besides, you can do everything by computer and be finished in no time flat!

After skipping a week of lunches and coffee breaks, and working through your weekend, you're finished. The proofs look out of this world, and the boss and client both love them. Now all you have to do is print them. Unfortunately, when the film and color overlays come back, the colors are awful. The blues are no longer blue, they're more purple. Your reds are more like orange. Your browns have all turned yellowish. What began as a work of beauty has turned into something quite hideous. Was it your colors? Read on.

In the world of color production, there are almost as many variables in the process as there are reproducible colors. The key to achieving proper color is controlling these variables and knowing your equipment. With color technology changing almost weekly, however, it is a real challenge to keep up. This chapter is an attempt to teach you the basics of producing color documents on your desktop computer—ones you can hold in your hand that look reasonably similar to what you had in mind.

The desktop color production world, for the most part, consists of color scanning, a desktop color proofing device, a color monitor, your eyes (and the eyes of others), and anyone connected in one way or another to your computer. Presume that you eventually need to reproduce your ideas in mass quantity, by way of an imagesetter and printing press or equivalent. For the first part, you need to have a color monitor and a quality video card capable of at least 256 colors.

Setting the Scene

Some of the more sophisticated monitors sold these days come with their own calibration software utilities, as do some software packages such as CorelDRAW! and PhotoPaint. A few independent software calibration packages also are on the market, and they promise to do the job. Regardless of how you calibrate your monitor, you must do a few very basic things before you begin. Following these steps ensures a controlled environment for viewing your colors, whether on your monitor or on your hard-copy original.

✔ **Warming up.** First, turn on your monitor and let it warm up for at least half an hour to make sure the color display has stabilized. Next, obtain a color swatch of some sort to match a color model to your software program. A spot color model is probably the best one to use, and make sure your swatch is recent. Some swatches can fade over time if left in bright sunlight or even bright office lighting.

✔ **Lighting.** Set the lighting in your work area close (if not exactly) to your usual working light level. Controlled lighting is ideal; pull the shades to keep natural light from entering the room. As the lighting levels change during the day, so do the spectrum of light your eyes let in and the look of colors on your monitors.

✔ **Power protection.** Make sure that your system is protected from power surges (if you haven't already). Power levels can fluctuate during various times of the day and can affect the color generation of your monitor. It's a wise choice to do this anyway if you value your motherboard or the data stored on your hard drive.

✔ **Comfort levels.** Set the brightness and contrast controls on your monitor to comfortable levels. After you have set these controls, get some tape to hold them in place. You don't want these settings to move after you have calibrated.

✔ **Background color.** Set the background color of your monitor to a neutral gray. The background color can affect the way you view other colors on your screen. A red background, for instance, makes all other colors look less red in comparison.

✔ **Choose your weapon.** You can select either an independent calibration software package that you trust, or use the features built into the software package you are using.

IV

Advanced Topics

Calibrating Using CorelDRAW!

The print engine of CorelDRAW! features a section for color correction that enables the color button to be active. Inside this section are the tools used to create your own color circuit and to preview the image you are about to print using that particular color circuit. By selecting the prepress button in this section, you can make adjustments to the six colors that appear on your monitor (red, green, and blue [RGB], and cyan, magenta, and yellow [CMY]. As each of the six color boxes is selected, the color selection dialog box is presented, enabling the monitor color to be mixed to closely match the printed version. By matching each of these six colors to the six print equivalents from your color swatches, you can inform the color circuit generation process of the capabilities and properties of the destination device.

This calibration method is meant only to give you accurate screen color representation in CorelDRAW! and does not in any way affect the output device behavior. This data is then used to bring the Preview in the Color dialog box closer to actual true color (based on SWOP standard). It is more of a "normalization" than a calibration. Also in this section are the tools used to compensate for other printing processes, such as press type, dot gain, under color removal, and black point (these are referenced in more detail later in this chapter). After you make adjustments to these colors under the calibrate selection, you have to name your creation (smt file). Even on a 486, 66 MHz machine, it takes about 10 minutes to write the file.

Calibrating your monitor in PhotoPaint is a little different than in CorelDRAW!. Go to your Display menu and select Calibrate. CorelDRAW! actually describes this method in detail in technical support fax document #4006. It describes the following procedure: "Adjust the gamma value until the desired look is obtained on the monitor. A gamma range of 1.3 to 2.1 has proven to be suitable for a wide range of monitors. The desired result is that the colored bars look like they are moving smoothly from one section to the next. You should feel free to experiment as the results are highly subjective; no correct setting exists. Increasing the gamma value is similar to turning up the brightness control on the monitor. This does not affect the image, only the monitor it is being viewed on."

Knowing Your Monitor

After you have set the colors on your monitor, consider taping samples of the colors you use most often around the perimeter of the screen. This is so that you can monitor lighting changes. Daily power fluctuations can affect the way your monitor renders color. Also, this gives you a quick reference as to exactly how the colors with which you are working should really look. Remember, your monitor is no replacement for your own eyes, which are capable of seeing many more colors.

Gamma

Gamma is a measure of contrast that affects the midtones of an image. Gamma is commonly used to describe the relationship of the output density to the original density (changes in brightness) across the midtones when you are performing color correction on an image. Adjusting the gamma enhances detail to the middle grayscale values or midtones. It does not affect the shadow (darkest) areas or the highlight (lightest) areas of the scanned image. When gamma correction is applied, the image looks much closer to the original.

Calibrating Your Scanner

If you have the good fortune to purchase (or perhaps you already own) a scanner, you are well on your way to reducing or eliminating your color separation and halftones costs. Having a scanner at your disposal also gives you access to a world of unlimited creative opportunities. Besides, for the few thousand dollars a scanner costs (depending on which one you choose), it will pay for itself in due course.

With a few cables to hook up and some software to load, installing a scanner is fairly simple. When you first install it, you might find that the first image you scan won't be quite perfect. Keep in mind that the scanner is just a recording device. Just like a stereo amplifier, you might have to adjust the base and treble a bit to hear all the sounds (or in this case, see all the colors).

Considerations Before Scanning

When you scan an image, you need to make a number of decisions concerning resolution, compression type (if any), and format (including TIFF, BMP, TGA, EPS, or PCX). These decisions are determined by the intended use of the image. For most, a desktop flatbed scanner—especially with color—is used as a proofing place-holder for a high-quality image to be inserted manually or electronically later (if you're planning to go to laser imagesetting for offset printing). It also is used as a design element or artistic image in layout, graphics, or multimedia software. For simplicity, try the TIFF or tagged image file format unless you need a specialized format. The TIFF file format is widely accepted and usually importable into most graphics, layout, or even word processing programs.

During scanning, all RGB (red, green, blue) color information is recorded for each bit of resolution. Most scanners record in this format—the same format in which the image is rendered from your monitor. Before you go any further, be absolutely sure you have calibrated your monitor for variables, such as room lighting, and monitor settings, such as brightness and contrast. Also be sure to set and adjust the red, green, blue (RGB), and cyan, magenta, and yellow (CMY)

IV

Advanced Topics

monitor colors in your software package. Doing this ensures a controlled medium from which to measure the scanned image results.

Scanner Proofing

Use the following basic steps to proof what your scanner has recorded:

1. Scan the image in your favorite scanner-acquire utility.

2. After scanning, open the image in a photo-editing package such as CorelPHOTO-PAINT!. Then compare the original continuous tone photo to the image appearing on screen. More often than not, the image appears darker than the original.

3. From the Image menu, select Color, Gamma. Correct the screen image to match the original as closely as possible. Use the Preview feature to view before accepting the changes.

After going through a series of trial and error exercises, you probably find that your monitor works best at a Gamma setting range of between 1.6 to 2.0 (from a range option of 0.10 to 10.0). After determining which setting works best, you should be able to rely on the image you see on your monitor to be as close in color, brightness, and contrast to the original as possible.

After going through the comparison process, you can be fairly sure that any color scan from that particular scanner using these monitor settings gives a fairly accurate screen representation. Your own monitor-to-scanner relationship varies depending upon which monitor and scanner you use. By trial and error, though, you eventually discover the best value.

Calibrating Your Color Printer

Desktop color printers are relatively new to the consumer market when compared to the software capability of color on the desktop. Prices on new-technology printers presently are on a continuous downward spiral, and quality is on its way up. You might be using a black-only laser printer to proof all of your color documents, and you aren't alone. Many artists and designers get by with only the color they see from their monitors and the experience they have acquired from using the same color schemes over and over again.

Various Printer Technologies

A multitude of color printer manufacturers in the industry use various printing technology such as laserjet, bubble-jet, laser, color sublimation, or thermal wax transfer. These technologies vary widely in the way they interpret and then re-produce color. In addition, two completely different breeds of printers exist: PostScript and Non-PostScript. (Slightly biased sounding isn't it? It's sort of like saying the sky is either blue or it's non-blue.)

Keep two concepts in mind even before you begin calibrating your printer: PostScript versus Non-PostScript, and resolution. PostScript-based color printers have color PostScript algorithms written into their drivers that cannot be altered. The accuracy of these PostScript printers is dependent upon how their drivers read the color information from the print engine of your software (for instance CorelDRAW!). Because they cannot be adjusted, you either have accurate color or you don't.

Non-PostScript printers have drivers that interpret the color from your print engine, but usually have some type of utility to control red, green, blue (RGB), intensity, and gamma setting. Then, consider another determining factor: the resolution of your printer. If your printer is a PostScript-based QMS Colorscript 100, for instance, your resolution is 300 dots per inch (dpi). Then, the screen frequency—the line of screen that the printer reproduces—is only about 42 lines. This means your color output is so coarse you probably won't be concerned about critical color accuracy. To achieve accurate color comparisons, you need to select a color printer that produces at least 400 dpi.

Proofing the Color Results

Before beginning this process, you must first make sure that your monitor has been calibrated. The next step is to obtain a recently printed (preferably in the last six months) color swatch that gives you an accurate comparison to your color printer's output. The most common is probably a PANTONE Spot Color Selector, but you also can use a PANTONE Process Color Selector.

Create a document consisting of colors you use most often. The easiest way to do this is to create a square with a label such as "PANTONE XXX" centered under it. Move a copy of it beside the first square by holding down the command key (to constrain it) and clicking on the right mouse button. For subsequent copies choose Edit, Repeat until you have the first row.

Then, select the entire first row and create a row below the first (command+click the right mouse button), and then select repeat until you have enough colors to suit your needs. Create a file with 15 spot colors and 15 process colors. Try to include things like company logos, favorite colors, or simple colors that are on the brighter side of the color wheel. Avoid dark colors, such as dark brown, violet, or dark blue, that look almost black. Don't bother with graduated or radial fills. They look neat on the screen, but you can't find a comparison if you are using a

IV

Advanced Topics

traditional color swatch. Make sure to include samples of 100 percent for cyan, magenta, yellow, and black. Be sure to position a neutral 20-percent screen tint of black in the background. This reduces the amount of contrast between the colors you are viewing and the white of the paper onto which you are printing. Next, print the file to your color printer.

Compare the results of the color output to the colors on your swatch. Here is where those who can adjust the color on their printers depart from those who cannot (generally, PostScript printer owners from Non-PostScript owners). The saving grace is that if you are unable to adjust your color printer's output, at least you know whether your output is too dark or light, or too red, green, or blue. From here, you just have to imagine the correct color. If you can adjust the color on your printer, base your decision on the comparison to the swatch. It might seem like a hit-or-miss approach, but achieving accurate color is worth all the work. How many attempts you make is determined by how close you want your color to be.

Back to the Monitor Again

Now you have all of your CorelDRAW! documents in true color. Think back for a moment to when you calibrated your scanned images for viewing on your monitor. You made adjustments to the gamma setting of the images so that you could see accurate color on the screen. Now that you are going to calibrate your images for output, you must use basically the same principles. The biggest difference is that the color printers generate a detailed image that contains much more information than what you see on your monitor. Monitors only tell you part of the story. They show only the midtone values of the image controlled by the gamma value. When you adjust the gamma value of a scanned image, you are controlling the midtones (the only tones) you can see on the monitor. The printer, however, can reproduce much more by reproducing a wider range of highlights and shadows.

Using an image from the color scanner that you plan to use most often (preferably tagged image file format, TIFF), import this into the CorelDRAW! document you have just used to calibrate your printer. Print the file to the color printer and examine the results. Most likely, you are looking at something quite different from what you see on your monitor. When calibrating your monitor, you discovered you had to make adjustments to the gamma to get accurate screen representation. You have to surpass what the screen shows and compensate for the printer. Your screen image might not look accurate when compared to the original, but it prints correctly.

To adjust the scanned image to print correctly on your color proofing device, use a program capable of editing brightness and contrast, such as CorelPHOTO-PAINT!. PhotoPaint can make these changes quite accurately.

Open the scanned color image in PhotoPaint and, under Image, Color, go to brightness and contrast. Here you must perform careful and controlled changes to the image, storing each change to the original image as a separate TIFF file. Make a note of the file name and the changes made to the file as you go. Start with brightness increasing by percentages of 10. Then move to contrast and intensity and do the same. Then make a separate CorelDRAW! file to import the sample TIFF images to for printout and comparison. Be sure to label each image. Crop the samples to a specific area using the crop tool (select the bitmap image, select the node editor, and move the middle handles on the bitmap) to save time and costly print materials. After you have the right combination of commands to match your original, you can make those same changes to any image from that particular scanner and be sure that your color proofing device provides you with accurate color.

Experts warn that if you plan to have your film color separated for reproduction on a traditional printing press, you should remove the image before sending your file to the service bureau. Replace it either with a professionally scanned image from an ultra-high resolution drum scanner from a service bureau, or mechanical film separations produced in the traditional way.

Do not rely on flatbed scanners to produce proper scanned color images.

After you have gone to the trouble of calibrating your monitor, scanner, and color-proofing device to ensure accurate color, go the rest of the way to the film and printing stages. After you have a properly imaged set of film, the next step is to make a laminate proof or *match print*. This match print is made through a specialized process in which each film separation is exposed to a micro-thin color carrier sheet. Then all the carrier sheets are bonded together onto a white backing. The aim is to simulate printing the job on a press. Just having a color overlay proof, or color key, does not suffice, especially if this is one of the last stages in your system calibration.

Once you have something you can rely on to accurately represent the results of the film output, you must return to your monitor with your laminate proof. Look closely at the even screen tints, the graduated fills, and the scanned images. Check your colors carefully. By matching your proof to what actually prints on the press, you now can trust your monitor's colors. Because you have a fully calibrated system, every stage reflects the proper colors.

IV

Advanced Topics

Verifying Color Accuracy

Return to your monitor with the color print and compare the reflective colors you see to the colors rendered from your monitor. Do not worry if they don't match exactly. Remember, your eyes can see a much wider range of colors than your monitor can render. Your press match might be printed at 150 lpi and in process color with fountain fills, and even the highest resolution monitor is not able to render the colors exactly. What you should be looking for is colors that are way off like mauves that should be purple, oranges that should be red, light greens instead of dark greens, and sky blues instead of navy blues. At this point, if you notice that colors are not exactly as they should be, it might be time to readjust your monitor calibration. Use the method described at the beginning of this chapter, only add your color press match to the equation for better accuracy.

Checking Your Final Film

If you find that your press match colors do not match your monitor's colors, and they aren't even close to the colors you originally asked for from the file, it might be necessary to inspect the film from the digital imagesetter.

Sometimes, as the file is digitally imaged, human error creeps in and you might not be holding exactly what you asked for. Digital imagesetting involves many different processes—some informational and some physical—and it is not uncommon for errors to occur in outputting film. You need to check to make sure your film is the correct resolution (dpi), line screen (lpi), and density. The easiest way to check the density of your film is by examining the densitometer scale printed by CorelDRAW!. This scale usually is divided up into increments of 10 percent. Accuracy should be off by two percentage points at the most. In other words, if you ask for a 20-percent screen, you should have something in between an 18 and 22-percent screen tint.

If you have never checked film before, you might want to consult someone who is experienced. Try your printer first. If he has a stripping department, his film strippers likely are qualified. Make sure you go over everything with them. That way, you can pick up some pointers. A couple of useful items for checking over the film yourself are a screen finder and a screen percentage guide. The *screen finder* tells you the angle of the screens and the line resolution on your film. The *percentage guide* enables you to compare screen tints on your film in negative form.

You need to get a hard copy of your printout and verify what the screen percentages on the film should be. Write them down on the hard copy printout for easy reference. A light table helps, but you can use a window or a bright light to enable you to see what's on the film.

Color Overlay Proofing

Producing a color overlay is something that might not be necessary if you are printing a two-color job where one of the colors is black. But, if you are printing two or three spot colors together, or your job is based on process color (CMYK), you are wise to have a color overlay produced.

Color overlays, sometimes referred to as color keys, are composed of four layers of film representing each of the colors you have set up in your file. They are produced by contacting the output film to a colored carrier film, and then assembled onto a white backing sheet. In the case of process color film, the overlays are assembled (from the bottom up) yellow, magenta, cyan, and then black. This gives you a fairly accurate representation of what the final printed product should look like. The only drawback to color overlays is the small amount of color distortion created by looking at colors through four layers of polyester carrier film. The thickness of carrier film can cause the colors to appear darker than normal (by up to 5 percent in some cases).

Color Press Match

In cases where highly accurate process color is required, it might be necessary to have a press match made of the film. A press match is made much the same way a color overlay proof is made, except the overlay film is micro-thin. The final layers are bonded together for a comprehensive composite that almost exactly matches the colors on the final press-printed piece. A press match is deemed a closer match than color overlays due to the color distortion sometimes found in color overlay film. In addition, press matches cost more to produce than color overlays.

CorelDRAW!'s New Color Management Tools

Among other exciting new features, CorelDRAW! version 5.0 contains features that help smooth out some of the rough spots of calibration. Color management features enable you to develop a profile of your entire system by integrating the specific characteristics of your monitor, scanner, and printer into a saved CCS file. According to the documentation for this version, a color management system is meant to ensure that colors are accurate and consistent between the various devices involved in the publishing process so that the final result is predictable. This new feature examines the relationships between the color models of the RGB (phosphors) of monitors and scanners, and the CMYK (pigments) of printers, and builds up a configuration file to smooth out the rough spots involved in jumping between them.

If you operate a system that uses more than one scanner or printer, you can load the saved configuration that stores the characteristics of the file. Most users need go no further than the first dialog box; specify their monitor, printer, and scanner combination; indicate whether they are working with images or line art; and save their configuration as a system profile.

In addition, advanced user tools enable editing of the characteristics of those particular devices or customizing of devices not found in the listings provided. It is recommended, however, that the gamma and white point of your particular monitor be adjusted because these differ even within identical monitor brands. The white point is the temperature (usually measured in degrees Kelvin) your monitor must reach to achieve an accurate representation of white. This can be done interactively using the advanced user feature.

After building your own system profile, version 5.0 enables color correction by offering a selection of different screen-rendering modes. By selecting either none (no color correction), fast, accurate, or simulate printer, the user can view work being created using all the information about the devices built into their profile.

CorelDRAW!'s Color Manager

The theory of color management is to have a system of checks and controls in place to ensure that color is rendered consistently from device to device. To better understand CorelDRAW!'s color management system theology, you must first consider the concept of how color is perceived, rendered, and compared.

Color matching is basically the physical selecting and matching of one color to another in an effort to communicate ideas. In other words, when you thumb through a color swatch, you are selecting and matching a color for identification purposes. These colors are contained in a color model (usually the manufacturer of the basic recipes used to create those ink colors), and each color is assigned a catalog number. If you were to use PANTONE 246, for instance, someone on the other side of the globe could pick up her PANTONE color selector and not only see the same color but know exactly how to achieve it.

Note   These color matching systems have not been around all that long. PANTONE only introduced the first color model in the early 1960s.

In today's desktop color industry, many different types of devices render color, some of which use their own weird and wonderful methods to produce results.

Monitors render in something called *phosphor color* (RGB), while some desktop printers render color in *pigment color* (CMYK, also known as process). Each of these various devices has its own set of capabilities and variations. To complicate matters, other desktop printers use the RGB color model instead of CMYK to render their output. To make matters even worse, consider that CMYK is based on a four-dimensional color model, and RGB is a three-dimensional model.

Corel's Color Manager has incorporated the three evils that make up an effective color management system: characterization (which describes the properties of the particular unit); calibration (which compensates for device color variances); and transformation (which is the accurate conversion of information from one color model to another). The color management system also must take into account the range of colors (color gamut) possible on that particular device, and the range of difference between the darkest black and the whitest white (dynamic range).

Using CorelDRAW!'s color handling features has been made quite easy. All color information is shared between CorelDRAW!'s sister applications, and pretested device profiles for a wide range of monitors, desktop printers, imagesetters, and scanners are included in the package.

Select **F**ile, **C**olor Manager in CorelDRAW! 5.0 to select the particular monitor, scanner, and printer (fig. 21.1). Once selected, that particular combination can be saved and named as a system profile for later reference. Gray component replacement, dot gain, and under-color removal rates can all be incorporated into these profiles. Custom configurations can be created for particular printing press types, paper, ink models, and virtually any variable.

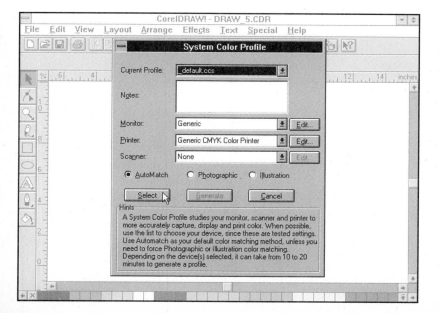

Figure 21.1
Selecting a monitor, printer, and scanner in the System Color Profile dialog box.

To create a basic system profile, follow these steps:

1. Choose File, Color Manager to bring up the System Color Profile dialog box.

2. Choose a monitor.

3. Choose a printer.

4. Choose a scanner. (This step is optional, not everyone has this type of equipment.) This function can only be done from an application that supports the use of that type of device (such as PhotoPaint or Ventura).

5. Use the space provided in the Notes box to catalog exactly which monitor, desktop printer, imagesetter, printing press, and paper type you are using.

6. Click on Generate to bring up the Generate Profile dialog box and give your new profile a name.

7. Click on OK to save the profile.

Another feature available to the user is choosing how the monitor renders your images on screen. Three modes of color rendering are available: Automatch, Photographic, or Illustration.

Select the Photographic matching method to optimize how your monitor renders scanned images to the screen. What CorelDRAW! does at this point is ignore all other color object information on your page to focus on accurate scanned-image color information. For this, the system profile uses the information available for the monitor and scanner you have built into your profile.

Select the Illustration matching method to tell CorelDRAW! you want it to concentrate on rendering color information for vector-based objects only (objects created within CorelDRAW!). The information on your monitor and printer is used to render a color image as accurately as possible to the screen.

If your file uses both vector-based illustration-type color objects as well as scanned images, CorelDRAW! interpolates a compromise between the two rendering methods that use information built into all three device capabilities and limitations.

Advanced User Practices

Accessing and using advanced user features might be necessary in cases where the particular device you are building into your system profile is not listed in the pre-tested hardware list that came with CorelDRAW! 5.0. Similarly, your device might be listed, but you need to adjust or customize the settings. By selecting <u>E</u>dit in the System Color Profile dialog box, a number of dialog boxes can be accessed.

Advanced Monitor Calibration

You can calibrate your monitor one of two ways: numerically or interactively. The first way is quite simple. Find out from your monitor's documentation (or contact the manufacturer) how to obtain the RGB gamma and chromaticity values, and the white point temperature for the particular monitor you are using. Calibrating your monitor numerically is as easy as entering these numbers (fig. 21.2). Once entered, save your particular profile under a different name.

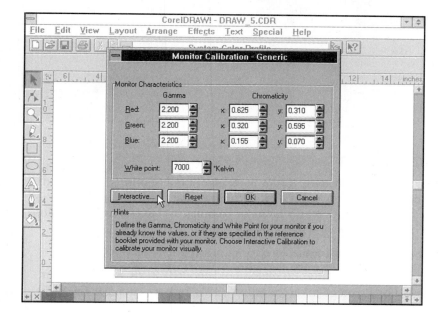

Figure 21.2
Calibrating a monitor numerically.

The second way to calibrate your monitor is interactively (fig. 21.3). It is not recommended that you do this unless you are professionally trained. This involves using specialized devices such as a colorimeter and a spectrophotometer. If you do not know whether you have one of these in your office, you probably don't. The latter sells for about $20,000 and is a highly sophisticated and specialized unit. You should almost never have to calibrate your monitor interactively. Monitors' numeric values for gamma and chromaticity are virtually identical from monitor to monitor for a particular model.

Figure 21.7
Calibrating the
RGB color model
printer.

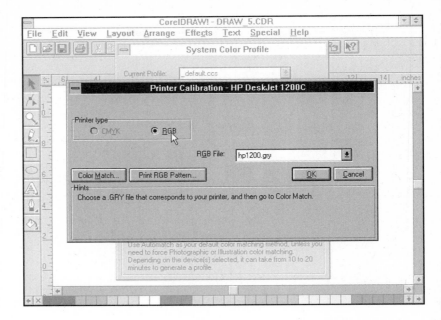

2. Click on Print **R**GB Patterns. When the Print dialog box appears, choose a printer. Once again a test pattern file called RGB80 is printed to your printer, and 80 little squares are printed.

3. Use the spectrophotometer or colorimeter again to measure the color values of the grayscale squares only in numerical sequence (from 65 to 80) and enter the values in an ASCII file in three columns: X, Y, and Z separated by a space. Once complete, name the file with a GRY extension and copy it into your COREL50\COLOR subdirectory.

4. Return to the Printer Calibration dialog box and choose the GRY file you have created.

5. Click on Color **M**atch. The Printer Characterization dialog box appears. Establish printer characterization according to one of the two methods described previously. Upon returning to the Printer Calibration dialog box after characterizing the printer, click on OK.

Calibrating Your Scanner

If a pretested file exists for your particular scanner, then you need only select that scanner type in the main System Color Profile dialog box, save the profile, and you're done. But if none exists, you have to create your own. For this, you need to have a properly scanned image to work from. Corel supplies a calibration target. Follow these steps:

1. Scan the target image or one you have already determined is sufficient.

2. In the scanner calibration dialog box located under edit in the System Color Profile dialog box, choose image.

3. Choose the scanned target (.TIF) file you have created. If necessary, click Browse and locate the file.

4. Choose a reference file. If necessary, click Browse to find the file. The reference file must have the extension REF.

5. Click on Scanned Target. The Scanned Target dialog box appears (see fig. 21.8).

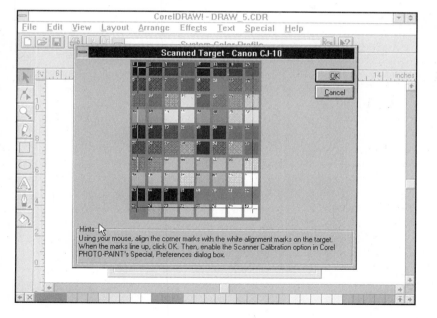

Figure 21.8
The Scanned Target dialog box.

IV

Advanced Topics

6. Frame your selection by dragging each of the four corner markers so that they frame the entire grid. The Color Manager compares the values of the colors framed to the values in the reference file and performs the calibration for you.

7. Click on OK, and the Save Scanner File dialog box appears.

8. Name the file and save it to your COREL50\COLOR subdirectory.

The color calibration process of your system can take weeks to complete and might not always be accurate the first time around. It also is prone to many variables, so don't forget any of the steps you took to achieve your success. The adjustments made to your color system toward perfect results are well worth the effort. Everyone involved—from your clients to your printer—will thank you for it, and it might give you the competitive advantage you need to succeed in this increasingly competitive industry.

Chapter Snapshot

When CorelDRAW! opens it relies on a special group of files to tell it some critical information about things like where it was last and what it was doing. These special configuration files have become critical to the operation of the program and how it can better serve users.

This chapter shows you how to get your hands dirty when it comes to manually editing and customizing the special powers of Draw 5's configuration files. You'll learn how to:

✔ Understand CorelDRAW!'s "secret" language

✔ Take proper precautions before editing files

✔ Identify and edit Corel's five basic configuration files:

✔ CORELAPP.INI (applications)

✔ CORELDRW.INI (CorelDRAW)

✔ CORELFLT.INI (import/export filters)

✔ CORELFNT.INI (fonts and symbols)

✔ CORELPRN.INI (printing)

Understanding how the controls are set and how they work will give you more control over Draw by using the Windows controls to set up and maintain your program settings.

CHAPTER

Customizing Window Controls for Better System Performance

S lowly, but surely, the Corel engineers have been making it easier for users to change the settings within CorelDRAW!'s modules, but there are still some key controls that have remained accessible only by braving the secrets of the INI files that control the program modules themselves. With the information in this chapter, you will find out how to navigate your way through the mysterious codes found in these special files.

Knowing the Secret Language

The configuration files are first written during the initial install of CorelDRAW!.
The settings for some options are dependent on which options you select during
the install. Before exploring these INI files, be aware that it is extremely easy to get
screwed up if you're not quite sure of what you're doing. Take precautions to
protect the setting already existing just in case your changes don't work out.
Opening the files and editing their contents can be very tricky. You have to watch
out for hazards such as case-sensitive characters, extra carriage returns, and spaces
where there should or shouldn't be any.

Certain characters perform special functions when used alone or sometimes in
combination with other characters. For instance, a line preceded by a semicolon is
ignored by Draw when it reads the INI file, allowing the engineers of the program
to write cryptic little notes to the person reading the file. You will usually see these
at the beginning of each file.

These comments or remarks can give insight into some of the codes that control
various settings for the program to follow when starting up. A title surrounded by
square parentheses as in "[Config]" identifies a certain section or group of settings
clustered together, in this case a title identifying some configuration settings. An
equal sign usually points to a path name or setting identifier as in:
`ProgramsDir=C:\COREL50\PROGRAMS` telling Draw where to look for certain files,
and `FountainPresets=coreldrw.ffp` telling Draw which fountain fill settings file to
load when booting up. In many cases, an equal sign followed by a "0" (as in
`ThisSetting=0`) indicates that that particular setting has been turned off by the
user, and an equal sign followed by a "1" (as in `ThisSetting=1`) has been activated
or turned on by the user. Watch out for this one because it isn't always the case!
You will see as you read further that in the fonts setting area a 1 means something
entirely different!

Backing Up First

Do yourself a huge favor and back up your files. Even if you aren't planning to
open the files, it is a good idea to make backups of them. Follow these steps to
ensure that nothing goes wrong:

1. Open your Windows File Manager and create a new and separate
    directory on your hard drive. Call it something like MYCONFIG and
    store it in a safe spot. Do not create this directory anywhere within
    your COREL50 directory. Draw might find these files before it finds
    the files it's supposed to and *really* screw you up.

2. Select the drive where your COREL50\CONFIG files are stored and select all the files ending in INI.

3. While holding down the Control key, drag the files into that directory. This makes copies of the files instead of moving them.

4. To be even safer, also put these files onto a backup disk and label it "CorelDRAW! 5 backup INI files" and date it.

Doing this before going any further in this exploration of the config files ensures that you can recover should something awful happen like spilling a cup of coffee on your keyboard or an earthquake or power failure while you're editing one of these files.

Opening INI Files

To open any of the INI files you can use your Windows Notepad utility. Simply open Notepad in Program Manager (usually found in the Accessories group window) and select open. Change the file name extension to INI instead of TXT and open the COREL50\CONFIG directory. The various INI files will appear in the file name window. Double-click on the file you want to open.

Editing the Settings

After editing the file, to save any changes you have made to the settings, resave the file under the same name with the same extension INI. You should use the INI extension instead of TXT because Notepad might default back to the TXT file format when you're not looking.

Looking at Config Files

All the settings you have selected in CorelDRAW! are stored in various places in five configuration files: CORELAPP.INI, CORELDRW.INI, CORELFLT.INI, CORELFNT.INI, and CORELPRN.INI. To pick up where it left off, Draw uses these as sort of memory files. They can tell Draw which fonts to load, which import and export filters it has available to it, and which preferences its last user set up. The more features built into a program, the larger and more complicated these configuration files become. The many settings these files remember include defaults, paths to other modules, roll-up settings, Clipboard handling, color settings, and the list goes on.

IV

Advanced Topics

CorelDRAW!'s General Application Initialization File: CORELAPP.INI

This configuration file is one that almost every program looks at to know where to look for various other files and modules that are located on your hard drive. This configuration was written after performing a custom install of CorelDRAW! 5 and might not be exactly identical line by line to the CORELAPP.INI file for your own program; the basic features are covered, however.

Contents of the CORELAPP.INI file in C:\COREL50\CONFIG:

```
Line 1; Descriptions for the [Config] section options below
     ;
Line 2; ProgramsDir=? Directory for program files
Line 3; DataDir=? Directory for data files
Line 4; CustomDir=? Directory for custom files
Line 5; ColorDir=? Directory for color files
     ;
Line 6; DrawDir=? Directory for CorelDRAW! files
Line 7; ChartDir=? Directory for CorelCHART! files
Line 8; ShowDir=? Directory for CorelSHOW! files
Line 9; PhotoPaintDir=? Directory for CorelPHOTO-PAINT! files
Line 10; MoveDir=? Directory for CorelMOVE! files
Line 11; TraceDir=? Directory for CorelTRACE! files
Line 12; MosaicDir=? Directory for CorelMOSAIC! files
Line 13; VenturaDir=? Directory for CorelVentura! files
Line 14; TagWriteDir=? Directory for TagWrite! files
     ;
Line 15; FontsDir=? Directory for wfn fonts
Line 16; FiltersDir=? Directory for filters
Line 17;
Line 18; BigPalette=? 0 = NO, 1 = YES default=0
Line 19; BigToolbox=? 0 = NO, 1 = YES default=0
Line 20; FontRasterizer=? 0 = NO, 1 = YES default=1
Line 21; TTFOptimization=? 0 = NO, 1 = YES default=1
     ;
Line 22; TextureMaxSize=? max texture bitmap 257
Line 23; height & width in pixels
     ;
Line 24; SpellLanguage=? English, French, German, default=English
Line 25; Swedish, Spanish, Italian,
Line 26; Danish, Dutch, Finnish
     ;
```

```
Line 27; SpellDict=? Spelling dictionary file default=IENC9231.DAT
Line 28; HyphenateDict=? Hyphenation dictionary file
        default=HENDP148.DAT
Line 29; ThesaurusDict=? Thesaurus dictionary file
        default=RENTI301.DAT
      ;
Line 30; See the "REFERENCE" section in CorelDRAW's On-Line Help
Line 31; for more information.
      ;
Line 32; SystemColorProfile=? System Color Profile
default=_default.css

[Config]
Line 33 ProgramsDir=C:\COREL50\PROGRAMS
Line 34 DataDir=C:\COREL50\PROGRAMS\DATA
Line 35 CustomDir=C:\COREL50\CUSTOM
Line 36 ColorDir=C:\COREL50\COLOR
Line 37 DrawDir=C:\COREL50\DRAW
Line 38 ChartDir=C:\COREL50\CHART
Line 39 ShowDir=C:\COREL50\SHOW
Line 40 PhotoPaintDir=C:\COREL50\PHOTOPNT
Line 41 MoveDir=C:\COREL50\MOVE
Line 42 TraceDir=C:\COREL50\TRACE
Line 43 MosaicDir=C:\COREL50\MOSAIC
Line 44 VenturaDir=c:\corel50\ventura
Line 45 TagWriteDir=c:\corel50\config
Line 46 FontsDir=C:\COREL50\SYMBOLS
Line 47 FiltersDir=C:\COREL50\PROGRAMS
Line 48 FountainPresets=coreldrw.ffp
Line 49 SpellLanguage=English
Line 50 SpellDict=ienc9231.dat
Line 51 HyphenateDict=hendp148.dat
Line 52 ThesaurusDict=renti301.dat
Line 53 BigPalette=0
Line 54 BigToolbox=0
Line 55 FontRasterizer=1
Line 56 TTFOptimization=1
Line 57 TextureMaxSize=257
Line 58 UseClippingForFills=3
Line 59 [Color Calibration]
Line 60 SystemColorProfile=PROFILE1.ccs
Line 61 ProfileMatchMode=0
```

```
Line 62 [TempPaths]
Line 63 Cleanup=1

Line 64; The following section specifies the contents of the
CorelMetafile
Line 65; which will placed on the clipboard by CorelChart! and
CorelDraw!
Line 66 0=C:\TEMP
Line 67 [ClipboardCorelMetafile]
Line 68 CalligraphicPen=0
Line 69 1BitBitmaps=1
Line 70 8BitBitmaps=1
Line 71 24BitBitmaps=1
Line 72 CompressedBitmaps=1
Line 73 MonoBitmapFills=1
Line 74 FountainFills=1
Line 75 FountainSteps=20
Line 76 VectorFills=1
Line 77 BezierCurves=1
Line 78 HoleSubpaths=1
Line 79 RectsAndEllipses=1
Line 80 RotatedRectangles=1
Line 81 RoundedRectangles=1
Line 82 RotatedEllipses=1
Line 83 EllipticalArc=1
Line 84 PenStyle=1
Line 85 TextCharacter=1
Line 86 Text=1
Line 87 RotatedText=1
Line 88 TextInRectangle=1
Line 89 TextInParallelogram=0
Line 90 TextInPerspective=0
Line 91 ExactText=0
Line 92 OutlineSeperate=0
Line 93 BinaryBitmaps=1
Line 94 WireFrameOnly=0
Line 95 VectorMaxPolygonSize=4096
Line 96 CurveFlatness=0
Line 97 MiterLimit=0
Line 98 [Registration]
Line 99 UserName=Firstname Lastname
Line 100 SerialNumber=CD5-XXX-XXXXXX
```

Key Features Controlled by CORELAPP.INI

The following sections explain just what the preceding code means and how it affects CorelDRAW!.

Lines 1-32

Note that all of these entries are preceded by a semicolon indicating to the program to ignore all information contained on these lines. This material is basically a listing of instructions to the person viewing this configuration file.

Lines 2-5

These describe how the program booting up will find its program, data, custom, and color files.

Lines 6-14

These tell you how the program will find its partner programs such as CorelDRAW!, CorelCHART!, CorelSHOW!, CorelPHOTO-PAINT!, CorelMOVE!, CorelTRACE!, CorelMOSAIC!, and TagWrite! directories.

Lines 15-16

These describe how the program will find its symbol and font data files, and how to look for its filters.

Lines 18-21

These show what the zeros and ones after the palette, toolbox, font rasterizer, and true type font optimizer mean on (NO) and off (YES) and what the default setting is.

Lines 22-23

These tell how the maximum texture bitmap size is determined.

Lines 24-26

These describe how the program finds its available language and which language is the default, in this case English.

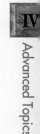

IV

Advanced Topics

Lines 27-29

These tell where the spelling, hyphenation, and thesaurus dictionaries are located.

Lines 30-31

This is a message to the viewer of the file to refer to CorelDRAW!'s online Help reference section to gain more insight into these utilities.

Line 32 System Color Profile Default

This tells the program how to look for its System Color Profile default file.

The next section contains actual instructions to the program reading this file. If changes are made here they will affect the program settings. Be very careful and thorough from here on.

Lines 33-58 Config Paths

These describe Config paths, files, and settings. As described above, lines 33-45 tell where to look for all of the files relevant to the other program modules. Lines 46-47 are the font and filter paths.

Lines 53 and 54 Palette and Toolbox Controls

These indicate that the big palette and big toolbox features (also available in previous versions 3 and 4) are turned off. If you are visually handicapped, you might want to turn these on by changing the 0s to 1s.

Line 55 Font Rasterizer

This setting controls Draw's font rasterizer, which has the capability of improving the look of fonts printed at smaller sizes. Disabling this feature drastically slows down screen redraw and printing times. It might be necessary to disable the font rasterizer in cases where certain printer drivers have trouble printing; this is usually indicated by small type printing incorrectly. The default setting is on (FontRasterizer=1).

Line 56 TrueType Font Optimization

This is Draw's hotline into the Windows TrueType font engine. Again, some printer types or screen drivers may not work properly with this feature and it might be necessary to disable it. The default setting is on (TTFOptimization=1).

Line 57 Maximum Texture Bitmap Size

This setting controls how wide and tall (in device pixels) the bitmap texture may be before the resolution of the bitmap is reduced. The default resolution of the bitmap is 120 dots per inch. The texture generator is optimized for thresholds that are a power of two plus one. A value set below 129 causes the screen preview to slow down. Default setting is 257.

Line 60 System Color Profile

This tells Draw which color profile was last selected. When Draw starts up again it will resume using this same color profile. System Color Profiles are created using the new Color Manager feature, which enables you to maintain consistent color representation between your color monitor, color printer, and color scanner.

Line 63 Temp File Purging

As Draw operates, it creates various temp files on your hard drive that store information Draw might need to perform a specific function (such as an undo, or a change made between saves and auto backups). When activated, this handy feature tells Draw to automatically delete these files when you exit the program. The default setting is on (Cleanup=1).

Line 66 Clipboard Temp File Location

This tells Draw in which directory to store the temporary Clipboard information. As mentioned in the notes contained within the file, this applies to CorelDRAW! metafiles placed on the Clipboard by CorelCHART! and CorelDRAW!.

Lines 67-97 Clipboard Options

This is one of those sections Draw warns not to play around with unless you know exactly what you are doing. These features control how certain items are handled when they are copied onto the Clipboard; a good rule of thumb here is "if it ain't broke, don't fix it."

Lines 98-100 Registration Information

This is the information each module displays during start-up. If you spelled your name wrong, got married, or just wanted a change, you can enter it here. This is also where the programs get their information when you select the Special/About menu at the far right of the screen.

IV

Advanced Topics

Draw's Main Initialization File: CORELDRW.INI

Contents of the CORELDRW.INI file in C:\COREL50\CONFIG:

```
Line 1; The Preferences sections may be changed by the user.
Line 2; All other sections should not be altered by the user.
      :
Line 3; See the "REFERENCE" section in CorelDRAW's On-Line Help
Line 4; for more information.
      [Config]
Line 5 Window=0,0,1020,690,1
Line 6 PaintArea=C:\COREL50\CUSTOM\PNTAREA.BMP
Line 7 [Settings]
Line 8 MaxCharsToDrawDuringKern=25
Line 9 LastImportIndex=0
Line 10 LastExportIndex=0
Line 11 LastSavedCDRImageHeaderSize=8
Line 12 DimensUnitsStyleIdx=0
Line 13 DimensPrecisionIdx=2
Line 14 DimensPlacementIdx=1
Line 15 DimensAbbrevIdx=0
Line 16 DimensLabelHorizontal=0
Line 17 DimensLabelCentered=0
Line 18 DimensShowUnits=1
Line 19 EditPreview=1
Line 20 GridFlags=0x2A
Line 21
Line 22 ShowBitmaps=1
Line 23 HighResBitmaps=1
Line 24 ShowOnScreenPalette=1
Line 25 DefPaletteMethod=0x5
Line 26 ColorCorrection=0
Line 27 LoadRollupsOnStartup=0
Line 28 ArrangeRollupsOnStartup=0
Line 29 SaveRollupsOnShutdown=0
Line 30 SaveExchangeData=1
Line 31 ToolBoxVisible=1
Line 32 ToolBoxFloating=0
Line 33 ToolBoxGrouped=1
Line 34 ToolBoxFloatPos=0,0
Line 35 ToolBoxNumTools=1,9
```

```
        [Preferences-1]
Line 36 DupOffset=250,250
Line 37 NudgeOffset=100
Line 38 MiterLimit=450
Line 39 ConstrainAngle=150
Line 40 UndoLevels=4
Line 41 AutoCenterPowerClip=1
Line 42 RightMouseButton=3
        [Preferences-2]
Line 43 AutoPan=1
Line 44 InterruptableRefresh=1
Line 45 ManualRefresh=0
Line 46 FullScreenCrossHairs=0
Line 47 ShowObjectsWhenMoving=1
Line 48 DelayToDrawWhileMoving=500
Line 49 Fountain=20
Line 50 ShowStatusLine=1
Line 51 StatusLineOnTop=1
Line 52 SmallStatusLine=0
Line 53 StatusLineMenuHelp=1
Line 54 ShowRibbonBar=1
Line 55 ShowPopUpHelp=1
        [Preferences-3]
Line 56 CurveTightness=5
Line 57 SnapTightness=5
Line 58 AutoReduceTightness=4
Line 59 AutoTraceTightness=5
Line 60 StraightTightness=5
Line 61 CornerThreshold=5
Line 62 MinExtrudeFacetSize=125
        [Preferences-4]
Line 63 EditTextOnScreen=1
Line 64 ShowRollupFontSample=1
Line 65 MinCharsToBreak=3
Line 66 SmallCharsThresholdPxl=9
Line 67 CalligraphicClipboard=1
Line 68 TextOnClpMetafile=0
        [Preferences-5]
Line 69 MakeBackupWhenSave=1
Line 70 AutoBackupMins=10
Line 71 OptimizedPalette=0
Line 72 HighResRotatedBitmaps=1
```

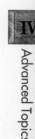

IV

Advanced Topics

```
Line 73 WindowsDithering=0
        [ConfigUnits]
Line 74 PenSize=0x1
Line 75 PageSizeUnits=1,1
Line 76 DupOffsetUnits=1,1
Line 77 GridOrgUnits=1,1
Line 78 TranslateUnits=1,1
Line 79 TileUnits=1,1
Line 80 BitmapScrollIndex=0
Line 81 TextSize=0x4
Line 82 GutterWidth=0x1
Line 83 NudgeOffsetUnit=0x1
Line 84 ColorModel=0x2
Line 85 OnScreenPaletteIndex=0
Line 86 LineStyleScrollIndex=0
Line 87 ArrowScrollIndex=0
Line 88 SymbolSize=1
Line 89 SymbolScrollIndex=0
Line 90 SymbolLibrary=0
Line 91 AutoReduceUnits=0x1
Line 92 MinExtrudeFacetSizeUnits=0x1
        [SaveConfig]
Line 93 PaperSize=11000,8500
Line 94 PaperSizeType=0x1
Line 95 PaperOrientation=0x1
Line 96 PaperColor=CMYK100,0,0,0,0,USER
Line 97 ShowPageBorder=1
Line 98 PageLayout=0x1
Line 99 FacingPages=0
Line 100
Line 101 LeftPageFirst=0
Line 102 GridOrg=-5500,-4250
Line 103 GridFreqX=4.000500
Line 104 GridFreqY=4.000500
Line 105 Units=1,1
Line 106 WorldUnits=0x1
Line 107 WorldScale=1.000000
Line 108 WorldPageUnits=0x1
Line 109 WorldScaleInUse=0
        [DispInfo]
Line 110 ScreenSize=1024,768
```

```
Line 111 DlgFontHeight=16
         [Directories]
Line 112 ImportVector=C:\COREL50\CUSTOM
Line 113 Print=C:\COREL50\DRAW\
Line 114 Template=C:\COREL50\DRAW\TEMPLATE
Line 115 TextImport=C:\COREL50\DRAW
Line 116 WaldoDocs=C:\WINDOWS\SUBDIRECTORY\SUBDIRECTORY
Line 117 Paint=C:\COREL50\DRAW
         [DimensLabelFormat]
Line 118 Suffix=""
Line 119 Prefix=""
Line 120 Linear=0.00""
         [LastUsed]
Line 121 1=C:\WINDOWS\SUBDIRECTORY\SUBDIRECTORY\FILENAM1.CDR
Line 122 2=C:\WINDOWS\SUBDIRECTORY\SUBDIRECTORY\FILENAM2.CDR
Line 123 3=C:\WINDOWS\SUBDIRECTORY\SUBDIRECTORY\FILENAM3.CDR
Line 124 4=C:\WINDOWS\SUBDIRECTORY\SUBDIRECTORY\FILENAM4.CDR
         [RollupSettings]
Line 125 LastFillRollupPageUsed=0
Line 126 [ObjectDataFieldNames]
Line 127 Name=1,0,0,1,0,1,0^General
Line 128 Cost=1,1,1,0,1,4,0^$"$"#,##0.00
Line 129 Comments=1,0,0,0,2,1,0^General
Line 130 CDRStaticID=1,0,0,0,3,1,0^General
```

Explanation of Key Features of the CORELDRW.INI File

For the most part, this area sets up Draw's settings and preferences. The first four lines of this text file also offer a warning and some instructions for the user. The warning is a reminder that fooling around with the Settings area might not be such a good idea—and they're right. Entering an incorrect value could really foul things up here.

Lines 7-35 Draw Control Settings

These settings control how Draw handles things such as kerning, importing and exporting indexes, the new dimensioning and labeling features, palettes, roll-ups, color correction, and toolbox settings.

Lines 12-18 Dimensioning and Labeling Settings

These next seven lines control the options found in the new Dimensions Roll-Up, which can only be accessed by selecting View\Roll Ups\Dimensions, or by using the Dimensions Roll-Up shortcut of Alt+F2 (see figs. 22.1 and 22.2).

Figure 22.1
Dimension Roll-Up options (left button selected).

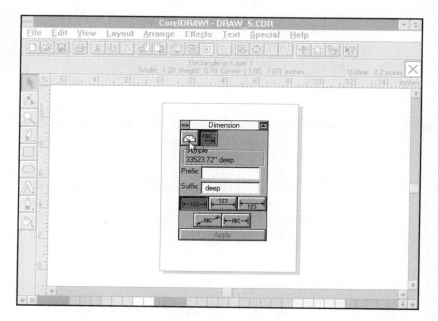

Lines 24-25 On-Screen Palette Controls

This setting tells Draw whether to show the bottom of the screen palette (0 for off and 1 for on). The codes following `DefPaletteMethod=?` tell Draw which palette to use: `0x0=none`, `0x1=uniform colors`, `0x2=custom colors`, `0x3=FOCOLTONE colors`, `0x4=Pantone Spot colors`, `0x5=Pantone Process colors`, and `0x6=Trumatch colors`.

Line 26 Color Correction Control

This controls which color correction method is in use. Here 0=none, 1=fast, 2=accurate, 5=fast with printer simulation, and 6=accurate with printer simulation.

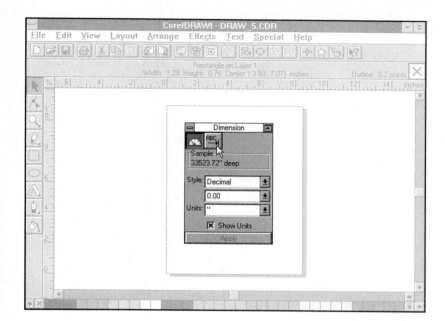

Figure 22.2
Dimension Roll-
Up options (right
button selected).

Lines 27-29 Roll-Up Controls on Start Up

These settings tell Draw what to do with the roll-ups and which ones to load (see fig. 22.3). There are 19 in total, so watch out for this one. If you choose to load all roll-ups on start up, be sure you have lots of free RAM. Roll-ups take up quite a bit of memory and can substantially limit the use of other programs depending on how much RAM your system is equipped with. To load all 19 roll-ups it is recommended that you have at least 32 MB of RAM on your system. Another hazard to look out for here is that only one of these features can be selected at a time (1 meaning on and 0 meaning off) although they can all be selected off.

Lines 31-35 Toolbox Controls

These settings indicate the toolbox settings. ToolBoxVisible=1 means the toolbox is selected to appear, ToolBoxFloating=0 toolbox is not floating, ToolBoxGrouped=1 toolbox is grouped, ToolBoxFloatPos=X,X lets Draw know the last known position of the toolbox origin mark, and ToolBoxNumTools=X,X means how many tools are showing.

IV

Advanced Topics

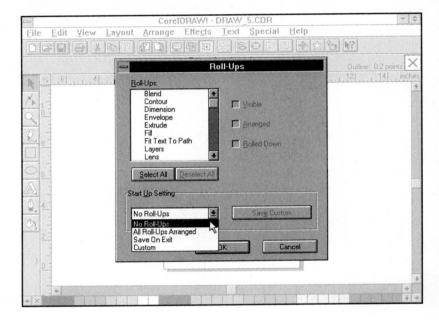

Figure 22.3
The Roll-Ups dialog box with selection options.

Lines 36-42 General Preferences

These are the first group of settings the Draw engineers have set out as safe to tinker with. They control everything found in the Special\Preferences\General dialog box, shown in figure 22.4. Note that like many of the settings previously mentioned, they can all easily be controlled from within Draw.

If you examine the settings here (in the preceding list of code), you will see that they match those found in the Preferences\General dialog box and are even set up in the same order. The last entry here controls the uses of the right mouse button as follows: 0=object menu, 1=2x zoom, 2=character, 3=edit text (shown here), 4=full-screen preview, and 5=node edit. This is one of the more valuable things to set up to relieve some of the time spent accessing the pull-down menu bars or hitting Ctrl+Alt keyboard combinations.

Lines 43-55 View Preferences

Likewise, these are the same controls you will see set out in the Special\Preferences\View dialog box (see fig. 22.5). They control all of the features Draw has that relate to how the program reproduces your images on screen, including refresh, display of moving objects, draw delays, fountain stripe rendering, the status bar, and the sometimes distracting pop-up help control.

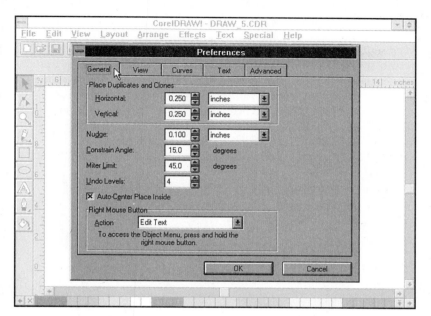

Figure 22.4
The Preferences/ General dialog box.

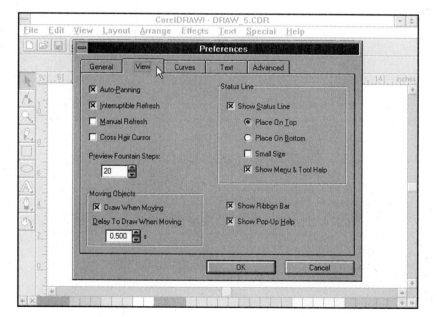

Figure 22.5
The Preferences/ View dialog box.

IV

Advanced Topics

Lines 56-62 Curve Preferences

In Special\Preferences\Curves you will see all of these options displayed (see fig. 22.6). They control how the auto-trace function of the Bézier tool traces scanned objects such as TIFF files imported into Draw. They include critical controls to the function of this important tool such as tracking, threshold, auto-join, and auto-reduce. The values indicated all refer to pixel size except for the minimum extrude facet size, which is user-adjustable and in this case measures 0.125 inches.

Figure 22.6
The Preferences/
Curves dialog
box.

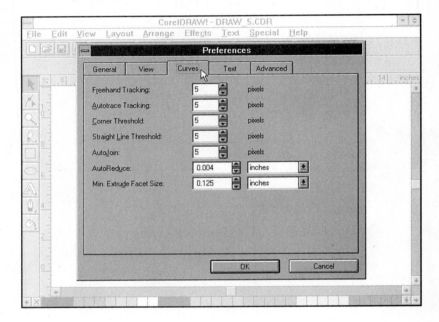

Lines 63-68 Text Preferences

These controls can be found in the Special\Preferences\Text dialog box and control, and include the finer details of text handling such as the on-screen text editing option, Text Roll-Up font sampling, and text greeking at a user-selected limit (see fig. 22.7). Line 65 controls something quite unique, though. The Minimum Line Width setting refers to the least number of characters that Draw will allow to fall on the last line of text wrapped inside an envelope; this is a great feature to become familiar with if you use this effect frequently. In the INI it is referred to as MinCharsToBreak=3 or, in this case, Draw is set to enable a mini-mum of three characters on the last line of a text envelope wrap.

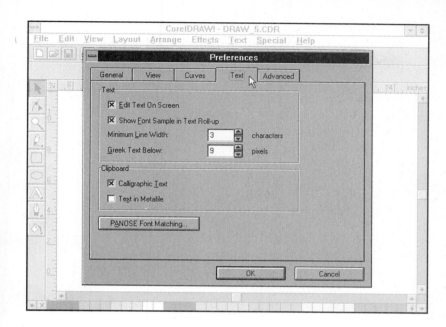

Figure 22.7
The Preferences/
Text dialog box.

Lines 69-73 Advanced Preferences

Access these controls by selecting Special\Preferences\Advanced (see fig. 22.8). They set up Draw to do things such as make a backup every time you save your file, length of time between autobackups (10 minutes, as it is setup for here, may be a little short if you find yourself working on very large files), high resolution rotated bitmap control, and Windows dithering.

Lines 74-92 Miscellaneous Settings

This area is a bit of a potpourri of options ranging from Draw's favorite pen sizes, color and measuring controls, scrolling options, symbol libraries, and various user-selected unit measuring increments. They are linked into the other controls found in this INI file and Corel recommends (with good reason) that you leave these alone and let Draw make any adjustments to these settings as it sees fit.

Lines 93-109 Saved Settings

Draw looks at these settings to let it know which paper size, page setup, and grid and scale setup was last in use and uses them for its next file. Lines 93-100 relate directly to the Page Setup dialog box, including paper size, orientation, paper color, page border, layout style, facing pages, and left or right page first (see figs. 22.9, 22.10, and 22.11).

IV

Advanced Topics

Figure 22.8
The Preferences/
Advanced
dialog box.

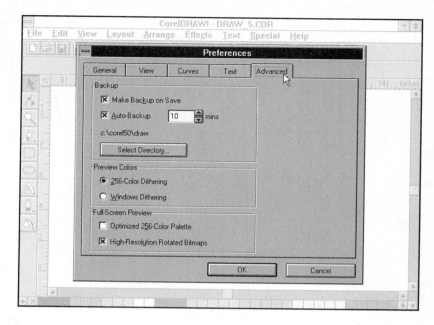

Figure 22.9
The Page Setup/
Size dialog box.

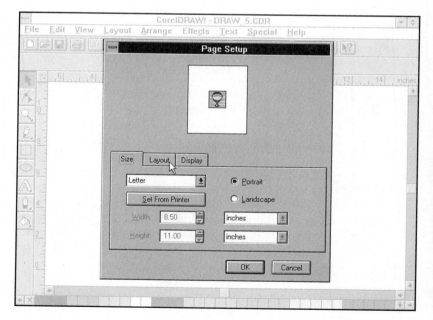

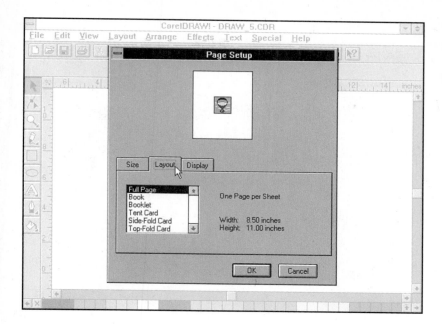

Figure 22.10
The Page Setup/
Layout dialog
box.

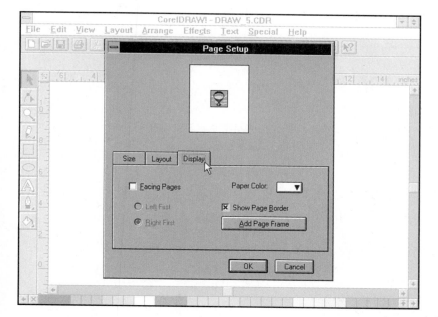

Figure 22.11
The Page Setup/
Display dialog
box.

IV

Advanced Topics

Lines 101-109 list all of the options presently selected from the Grid & Scale Setup dialog box, including grid origins, grid frequency, unit measure used, and world units presently selected (see fig. 22.12).

Figure 22.12
The Grid & Scale
Setup dialog box.

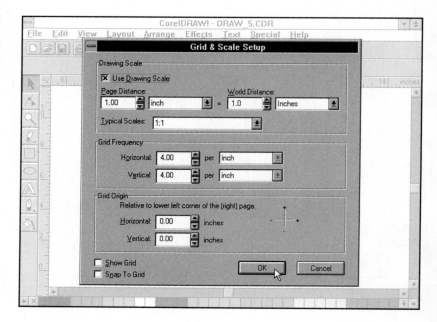

Lines 112-130 Miscellaneous

The rest of these settings relate to miscellaneous directories containing files Draw needs to keep track of for importing and exporting functions and should not be tampered with.

Draw's Import and Export Filter Arsenal

CorelDRAW! 5 comes with even more import and export filters than ever before, opening all sorts of avenues for the average user to work with other applications. What follows is the list of import and export filters available with the full install. The list is lengthy and that's definitely a good thing if you are regularly preparing files for use with other programs or platforms. They range in use from internal filters for use with Corel's other modules to other file formats such as page layout, word-processing, CAD programs, video compression, and static image file formats. There's something for every one!

Contents of CORELFLT.INI in C:\COREL50\CONFIG:

```
        [ImportFilters]
Line 1  CDR=IMPCDR,"CorelDRAW!",*.cdr,11
Line 2  CMX=IMPCMX,"Corel Presentation Exchange",*.cmx,21
Line 3  CDRCCH=IMPCDRTH,"CorelDRAW!",*.cdr,10
Line 4  CDRCMX=IMPCDR.DLL,"CorelDRAW! Graphic",*.cdr;*.pat,19
Line 5  CDRTH=IMPCDRTH.DLL,"CorelDRAW! Thumbnail",*.cdr;*.pat;*.cdt,8
Line 6  CMXTH=IMPCDRTH.DLL,"Corel Presentation Thumbnail",*.cmx,8
Line 7  CMVTH=IMPCDRTH.DLL,"CorelMOVE Thumbnail",*.cmv,8
Line 8  CCHCMX=IMPCCH.DLL,"CorelCHART Chart",*.cch,20
Line 9  CCHTH=IMPTIFF.DLL,"CorelCHART Thumbnail",*.cch,8
Line 10 SHWTH=IMPSHWTH.DLL,"CorelSHOW Thumbnail",*.shw;*.shb,8
Line 11 TRACE=IMPAI.DLL,"CorelTRACE",*.eps,2
Line 12 CPT=IMPCPT,"CorelPHOTO-PAINT Image",*.cpt,16
Line 13 BMP=IMPBMP.DLL,"Windows Bitmap",*.bmp;*.dib;*.rle,1
Line 14 GIF=IMPGIF.DLL,"CompuServe Bitmap",*.gif,1
Line 15 CGM=IMPCGM.DLL,"Computer Graphics Metafile",*.cgm,2
Line 16 JPEG=IMPJPEG.DLL,"JPEG Bitmap",*.jpg;*.jff;*.jtf;*.cmp,1
Line 17 PCD=IMPPCD.DLL,"Kodak Photo CD Image",*.pcd,1
Line 18 PCX2=IMPPCX.DLL,"Paintbrush",*.pcx,1
Line 19 CT=IMPCT.DLL,"Scitex CT Bitmap",*.sct;*.ct,1
Line 20 TGA=IMPTGA.DLL,"Targa Bitmap",*.tga;*.vda;*.icb;*.vst,1
Line 21 TIFF=IMPTIFF.DLL,"TIFF Bitmap",*.tif;*.sep;*.cpt,1
Line 22 WMF=IMPWMF,"Windows Metafile",*.wmf,12
Line 23 WMF2=IMPWMF,"Windows Metafile",*.wmf,23
Line 24 AI=IMPAI.DLL,"Adobe Illustrator 1.1, 88, 3.0",*.ai;*.eps,2
Line 25 DXF=IMPDXF.DLL,"AutoCAD DXF",*.dxf,2
Line 26 GEM=IMPGEM.DLL,"GEM File",*.gem,2
Line 27 IMG=IMPIMG,"GEM Paint File",*.img,22
Line 28 HPGL=IMPHPGL.DLL,"HPGL Plotter File",*.plt,2
Line 29 PIF=IMPPIF.DLL,"IBM PIF",*.pif,2
Line 30 PIC=IMPPIC.DLL,"Lotus PIC",*.pic,2
Line 31 PICT=IMPPICT.DLL,"Macintosh PICT",*.pct,2
Line 32 DRW=IMPDRW.DLL,"Micrografx 2.x, 3.x",*.drw,2
Line 33 EPS=IMPEPS,"PostScript (Interpreted)",*.eps;*.ps,18
Line 34 EPS2=IMPEPS.DLL,"EPS (Placeable)",*.eps;*.ps;*.ai,7
Line 35 RIFFTH=IMPCDRTH.DLL,"RIFF Thumbnail",*.wav;*.avi,8
Line 36 FLITH=IMPFLITH.DLL,"Autodesk FLIC Thumbnail",*.fli;*.flc,8
Line 37 GEN=IMPGEN,"Ventura Generated File",*.gen,24
Line 38 AMI=W4W33F.DLL,"Ami Professional 2.0, 3.0",*.sam,9,1
Line 39 TXT=IMPTXT,"ASCII Text",*.txt,14
Line 40 TXT2=IMPTXT8,"ASCII Text (8-bit)",*.txt,25
```

IV

Advanced Topics

```
Line 41 EXL=W4W21F.DLL,"Excel for Windows 3.0, 4.0",*.xls,9,1
Line 42 L123=W4W20F.DLL,"Lotus 123 1A, 2.0",*.wk?,9,0
Line 43 L1233=W4W20F.DLL,"Lotus 123 3.0",*.wk?,9,2
Line 44 PRNTAB=IMPPRN,"Lotus/Excel Print Table",*.prn,27
Line 45 MSWW6=W4W49F.DLL,"MS Word for Windows 6.0",*.doc,9,0
Line 46 MSWW2=W4W44F.DLL,"MS Word for Windows 2.x",*.doc,9,1
Line 47 MSWW1=W4W44F.DLL,"MS Word for Windows 1.x",*.*,9,0
Line 48 MSW=W4W05F.DLL,"MS Word 5.0, 5.5",*.*,9,2
Line 49 MSWM2=W4W54F.DLL,"MS Word for Macintosh 5.0",*.*,9,2
Line 50 MSWM=W4W54F.DLL,"MS Word for Macintosh 4.0",*.*,9,1
Line 51 RTF=IMPRTF,"Rich Text Format",*.rtf,13
Line 52 TWRTF=IMPTWRTF,"Tagwrite - Style Match RTF",*.rtf,28
Line 53 TWWP5=IMPTWWP5,"Tagwrite - Style Match WP 5.x",*.*,29
Line 54 TWSGML=IMPSGML,"Tagwrite - SGML / Custom Template",*.*,30
Line 55 WP60=W4W48F.DLL,"WordPerfect 6.0",*.*,9,1
Line 56 WP51=W4W07F.DLL,"WordPerfect 5.1",*.*,9,1
Line 57 WP50=W4W07F.DLL,"WordPerfect 5.0",*.*,9,0
Line 58 WPG=IMPWPG.DLL,"WordPerfect Graphic",*.wpg,2
        [ExportFilters]
Line 59 CPT=EXPCPT,"CorelPHOTO-PAINT Image",*.cpt,16
Line 60 BMP=EXPBMP.DLL,"Windows Bitmap",*.bmp;*.dib;*.rle,1
Line 61 GIF=EXPGIF.DLL,"CompuServe Bitmap",*.gif,1
Line 62 CGM=EXPCGM.DLL,"Computer Graphics Metafile",*.cgm,2
Line 63 JPEG=EXPJPEG.DLL,"JPEG Bitmap",*.jpg;*.jff;*.jtf;*.cmp,1
Line 64 OS2=EXPOS2B.DLL,"OS/2 Bitmap",*.bmp,1
Line 65 PCX=EXPPCX.DLL,"Paintbrush",*.pcx,1
Line 66 CT=EXPCT.DLL,"Scitex CT Bitmap",*.sct;*.ct,1
Line 67 TGA=EXPTGA.DLL,"Targa Bitmap",*.tga;*.vda;*.icb;*.vst,1
Line 68 TIFF=EXPTIFF.DLL,"TIFF Bitmap",*.tif,1
Line 69 WMF=EXPWMF,"Windows Metafile",*.wmf,12
Line 70 WMF2=EXPWMF,"Windows Metafile",*.wmf,23
Line 71 AI=EXPAI.DLL,"Adobe Illustrator",*.ai;*.eps,2
Line 72 AT1=EXPAT1.DLL,"Adobe Type 1 Font",*.pfb,5
Line 73 DXF=EXPDXF.DLL,"AutoCAD DXF",*.dxf,2
Line 74 EPS=EXPEPS.DLL,"EPS (Placeable)",*.eps,7
Line 75 EPS2=EXPEPS,"EPS (Placeable)",*.eps,17
Line 76 GEM=EXPGEM.DLL,"GEM File",*.gem,2
Line 77 HPGL=EXPHPGL.DLL,"HPGL Plotter File",*.plt,2
Line 78 PIF=EXPPIF.DLL,"IBM PIF",*.pif,2
Line 79 PICT=EXPPICT.DLL,"Macintosh PICT",*.pct,2
Line 80 SCODL=EXPSCODL.DLL,"Matrix/Imapro SCODL",*.scd,2
Line 81 RTF=W4W19T.DLL,"Rich Text Format",*.rtf,9,0
Line 82 RTF=IMPRTF,"Rich Text Format",*.rtf,13
```

```
Line 83 TTF=EXPTTF.DLL,"TrueType Font",*.ttf,5
Line 84 AMI=W4W33T.DLL,"Ami Professional 2.0, 3.0",*.sam,9,1
Line 85 TXT=IMPTXT,"ASCII Text",*.txt,14
Line 86 EXL=W4W21T.DLL,"MS Excel for Windows 3.0, 4.0",*.xls,9,1
Line 87 L123=W4W20T.DLL,"Lotus 123 1A, 2.0",*.wk?,9,0
Line 88 L1233=W4W20T.DLL,"Lotus 123 3.0",*.wk?,9,2
Line 89 MSWW2=W4W44T.DLL,"MS Word for Windows 2.x",*.doc;*.*,9,1
Line 90 MSWW1=W4W44T.DLL,"MS Word for Windows 1.x",*.*,9,0
Line 91 MSW=W4W05T.DLL,"MS Word 5.0, 5.5",*.*,9,2
Line 92 MSWM2=W4W54T.DLL,"MS Word for Macintosh 5.0",*.*,9,2
Line 93 MSWM=W4W54T.DLL,"MS Word for Macintosh 4.0",*.*,9,1
Line 94 WP51=W4W07T.DLL,"WordPerfect 5.1",*.wp;*.*,9,1
Line 95 WP50=W4W07T.DLL,"WordPerfect 5.0",*.*,9,0
Line 96 WPG=EXPWPG.DLL,"WordPerfect Graphic",*.wpg,2
         [CorelAIExport]
Line 97 V88Header=aihead.dat
Line 98 V88Header2=aihead2.dat
Line 99 V3Header=ai3head.dat
Line 100 V3Footer=ai3foot.dat
         [CorelBMPImport]
Line 101 ImportCorel30RLE=0
         [CorelDXFExport]
Line 102 InchHeader=dxfhead.dat
Line 103 MMHeader=dxfhead2.dat
         [CorelHPGLExport]
         Plotter Units Per Inch=1016
Line 104 [CorelEPSImport]
Line 105 Dlg Text Format=1
Line 106 VMSize=2
         [CorelFilterDirectories]
Line 107 LastImport=-1
Line 108 -1=C:\WINDOWS\SUBDIRECTORY\SUBDIRECTOR
         [Common Dialog]
Line 109 Dlg Preview=0
Line 110 Dlg Selected Only=0
Line 111 Dlg Backup=0
Line 112 Dlg Bitmap Load=0
Line 113 Dlg AutoReduce=0
Line 114 Dlg Reduce Low Value=0
Line 115 Dlg Reduce High Value=40
Line 116 Dlg Reduce Units=0
Line 117 Dlg By Reference=0
Line 118 Dlg Add to File List=0
```

IV

Advanced Topics

Draw's Endless Font and Symbol Supply

You need fonts you say? Look no further than CorelDRAW!'s CD disc two. The list includes fonts from a variety of collections divided into categories as follows: Basic, Casual, Design, Education, Formal, Fun, Presentation, Printer, Publisher, Signs, Technical, Template, Theatre, and General. Corel has so many included on the CD that they warn users not to install them all (they number 825 at last count) for fear that even the most sophisticated user will quickly run out of hard disk space.

Historically, Draw has not been the greatest program when it comes to font handling. Oh sure, the image on the screen looks good and so might the basic desktop laser print. But experts will often moan when asked to judge how Draw fonts print on high-resolution digital imagesetters. The Corel engineers have gone to great pains this time around in an effort to quell the screams of those who rely on accurate font rendering when it comes to output time.

During the initial installation of the Corel collection of programs, the font selection information is stored in a file called CORELFNT.INI, which Draw examines on startup, during screendraw, and when it comes time to print the font. The following is a list of a simple variety of fonts, huge as it may be.

Contents of the CORELFNT.INI file in C:\COREL50\CONFIG:

```
        [Fonts]
Line 1; To use WFN fonts provided in CorelDRAW! 2.x. and earlier,
Line 2; add the appropriate lines from your old CORELDRW.INI (2.x)
Line 3; or WIN.INI (1.x) AS IS (WFN filename is case sensitive).
Line 4; for example:
Line 5;Avalon=15 avalon.wfn
Line 6;DawnCastle=3 castle.wfn
Line 7;Lincoln=1 lincoln.wfn
Line 8;Toronto=15 toronto.wfn
Line 9;GeographicSymbols=1 geograph.wfn
Line 10;MusicalSymbols=1 musical.wfn
        [Symbols]
Line 11 Arrows1=arrows1.wfn
Line 12 Arrows2=arrows2.wfn
Line 13 Awards=awards.wfn
Line 14 Balloons=balloons.wfn
Line 15 Borders1=borders1.wfn
Line 16 Borders2=borders2.wfn
Line 17 Boxes=boxes.wfn
Line 18 Buildings=buildngs.wfn
```

```
Line 19 Bullets1=bullets1.wfn
Line 20 Bullets2=bullets2.wfn
Line 21 Bullets3=bullets3.wfn
Line 22 Business&Government=business.wfn
Line 23 Computers=computer.wfn
Line 24 Electronics=electrnc.wfn
Line 25 Festive=festive.wfn
Line 26 Food=food.wfn
Line 27 Furniture=furnitur.wfn
Line 28 GeographicSymbols=geograph.wfn
Line 29 Household=househld.wfn
Line 30 Hygiene=hygiene.wfn
Line 31 Landmarks=landmark.wfn
Line 32 Medicine=medical.wfn
Line 33 Military=military.wfn
Line 34 MilitaryID=militid.wfn
Line 35 MusicalSymbols=musical.wfn
Line 36 NauticalFlags=flags.wfn
Line 37 People=people.wfn
Line 38 Plants=plants.wfn
Line 39 Science=science.wfn
Line 40 Shapes1=shapes1.wfn
Line 41 Shapes2=shapes2.wfn
Line 42 Space=space.wfn
Line 43 SportsFigures=figures.wfn
Line 44 Sports&Hobbies=hobbies.wfn
Line 45 Stars1=stars1.wfn
Line 46 Stars2=stars2.wfn
Line 47 Technology=tech.wfn
Line 48 Tools=tools.wfn
Line 49 Tracks=tracks.wfn
Line 50 Transportation=transpo.wfn
Line 51 Weather=weather.wfn
        [FontMapV20]
Line 52 aardvark.wfn=Aardvark 0,606,0,0
Line 53 adelaide.wfn=Adelaide 241,0,0,0
Line 54 alto.wfn=Alto 238,0,0,0
Line 55 amy.wfn=Amy 314,0,0,0
Line 56 ARABIA.WFN=Arabia 291,0,0,0
Line 57 architec.wfn=Architecture 237,0,0,0
Line 58 avalon.wfn=Avalon 567,543,551,543
Line 59 BAHAMAS.WFN=Bahamas 276,276,0,0
Line 60 BAHAMAHY.WFN=BahamasHeavy 299,0,0,0
```

IV

Advanced Topics

```
Line 61 BAHAMALT.WFN=BahamasLight 276,0,0,0
Line 62 ballroom.wfn=BallroomTango 255,0,0,0
Line 63 banff.wfn=Banff 528,0,0,0
Line 64 bangkok.wfn=Bangkok 559,606,0,0
Line 65 bard.wfn=Bard 275,0,0,0
Line 66 bassoon.wfn=Bassoon 225,251,0,0
Line 67 bedrock.wfn=Bedrock 123,0,0,0
Line 68 beehive.wfn=Beehive 584,0,0,0
Line 69 bodnoff.wfn=Bodnoff 638,0,0,0
Line 70 briquet.wfn=Briquet 255,0,0,0
Line 71 brisk.wfn=Brisk 200,0,0,0
Line 72 brochure.wfn=Brochure 279,0,0,0
Line 73 brooklyn.wfn=Brooklyn 583,606,575,606
Line 74 campaign.wfn=Campaign 216,0,0,0
Line 75 cancun.wfn=Cancun 322,0,0,0
Line 76 carino.wfn=Carino 263,0,0,0
Line 77 carleton.wfn=Carleton 344,0,0,0
Line 78 casablca.wfn=Casablanca 528,591,496,543
Line 79 cas_antq.wfn=CasablancaAntique 220,0,251,0
Line 80 casperof.wfn=CasperOpenFace 269,0,0,0
Line 81 centold.wfn=CenturionOld 528,575,520,0
Line 82 copprpot.wfn=CopperPot 346,410,0,0
Line 83 cosmic.wfn=Cosmic 206,0,0,0
Line 84 cosmic2.wfn=CosmicTwo 409,0,0,0
Line 85 cottage.wfn=Cottage 268,0,0,0
Line 86 cuprtino.wfn=Cupertino 646,0,622,0
Line 87 dauphin.wfn=Dauphin 237,0,0,0
Line 88 CASTLE.WFN=DawnCastle 276,315,0,0
Line 89 dixiland.wfn=Dixieland 795,0,0,0
Line 90 eklektic.wfn=Eklektic 321,0,0,0
Line 91 ERIE.WFN=Erie 283,339,0,0
Line 92 ERIEBLAK.WFN=ErieBlack 315,339,0,0
Line 93 erie_ctr.wfn=ErieContour 387,0,0,0
Line 94 ERIELITE.WFN=ErieLight 276,291,0,0
Line 95 expo.wfn=Expo 360,0,0,0
Line 96 florence.wfn=Florence 222,0,0,0
Line 97 france.wfn=France 512,543,0,0
Line 98 Frankstn.WFN=Frankenstein 323,0,0,0
Line 99 frankgo.wfn=FrankfurtGothic 520,543,528,543
Line 100 frankgoh.wfn=FrankfurtGothicHeavy 559,0,567,0
Line 101 freeport.wfn=Freeport 370,0,0,0
Line 102 fuji.wfn=Fujiyama 378,441,378,449
Line 103 fuji2.wfn=Fujiyama2 291,0,291,0
```

```
Line 104 fujibold.wfn=FujiyamaExtraBold 528,0,535,0
Line 105 fujilite.wfn=FujiyamaLight 370,0,362,0
Line 106 galleria.wfn=Galleria 474,0,0,0
Line 107 gatineau.wfn=Gatineau 496,528,488,535
Line 108 geograph.wfn=GeographicSymbols 740,0,0,0
Line 109 gil_ubld.wfn=GilbertUltraBold 333,0,0,0
Line 110 glacier.wfn=Glacier 236,0,236,0
Line 111 goldmine.wfn=GoldMine 344,0,0,0
Line 112 symbols.wfn=GreekMathSymbols 606,0,0,0
Line 113 griffon.wfn=Griffon 264,0,0,0
Line 114 griffn_s.wfn=GriffonShadow 264,0,0,0
Line 115 harpoon.wfn=Harpoon 227,0,0,0
Line 116 heidlbrg.wfn=Heidelberg 250,0,0,0
Line 117 homeward.wfn=HomewardBound 551,0,0,0
Line 118 ireland.wfn=Ireland 173,0,0,0
Line 119 jupiter.wfn=Jupiter 252,0,0,0
Line 120 kabana.wfn=KabanaBook 315,0,0,0
Line 121 kabana_b.wfn=KabanaBold 326,0,0,0
Line 122 keypunch.wfn=Keypunch 295,0,0,0
Line 123 koala.wfn=Koala 223,240,0,0
Line 124 kornthia.wfn=Korinthia 345,0,251,0
Line 125 Lincoln.WFN=Lincoln 244,0,0,0
Line 126 LINUS.WFN=Linus 165,0,0,0
Line 127 memorand.wfn=Memorandum 591,614,0,0
Line 128 monspace.wfn=Monospaced 598,598,598,598
Line 129 motor.wfn=Motor 465,0,0,0
Line 130 musical.wfn=MusicalSymbols 386,0,0,0
Line 131 mystical.wfn=Mystical 232,0,0,0
Line 132 nebraska.wfn=Nebraska 535,543,512,520
Line 133 brunswik.wfn=NewBrunswick 559,606,559,598
Line 134 nwfdland.wfn=Newfoundland 348,0,0,0
Line 135 neworder.wfn=NewOrder 377,0,0,0
Line 136 newordre.wfn=NewOrderEngraved 415,0,0,0
Line 137 ottawa.wfn=Ottawa 535,535,543,543
Line 138 palette.wfn=Palette 337,0,0,0
Line 139 palmsprn.wfn=PalmSprings 559,575,528,543
Line 140 paradise.wfn=Paradise 425,0,0,0
Line 141 paragon.wfn=Paragon 205,0,0,0
Line 142 penguin.wfn=Penguin 276,307,0,0
Line 143 PENGLT.WFN=PenguinLight 276,0,0,0
Line 144 pipeline.wfn=Pipeline 237,0,0,0
Line 145 posse.wfn=Posse 71,0,0,0
Line 146 PRESDENT.WFN=President 276,0,0,0
```

```
Line 147 ANTIQUE.WFN=ProseAntique 260,252,0,0
Line 148 renfrew.wfn=Renfrew 567,0,0,0
Line 149 southern.wfn=Southern 543,598,559,630
Line 150 stamp.wfn=Stamp 575,0,0,0
Line 151 surreal.wfn=Surreal 357,357,0,0
Line 152 swz.wfn=Switzerland 535,559,543,567
Line 153 swzblack.wfn=SwitzerlandBlack 622,0,606,0
Line 154 SWZCOND.WFN=SwitzerlandCondensed 252,252,252,252
Line 155 SWZCONBK.WFN=SwitzerlandCondBlack 244,0,244,0
Line 156 SWZCONLT.WFN=SwitzerlandCondLight 220,0,220,0
Line 157 SWZINSRT.WFN=SwitzerlandInserat 244,0,0,0
Line 158 swzlight.wfn=SwitzerlandLight 535,0,543,0
Line 159 swznarrw.wfn=SwitzerlandNarrow 441,465,449,465
Line 160 techncal.wfn=Technical 252,0,252,0
Line 161 thunder.wfn=ThunderBay 533,0,0,0
Line 162 timpani.wfn=Timpani 591,598,614,606
Line 163 timpanih.wfn=TimpaniHeavy 669,0,701,0
Line 164 toronto.wfn=Toronto 520,535,512,528
Line 165 umbrella.wfn=Umbrella 299,0,0,0
Line 166 unicorn.wfn=Unicorn 417,0,0,0
Line 167 uptown.wfn=Uptown 338,0,0,0
Line 168 usablack.wfn=USABlack 622,0,622,0
Line 169 usalight.wfn=USALight 535,0,543,0
Line 170 viking.wfn=Viking 491,0,0,0
Line 171 vogue.wfn=Vogue 236,276,0,0
Line 172 zurich.wfn=ZurichCalligraphic 0,0,472,0
         [PSResidentFonts]
Line 173 Arial-Normal=Helvetica 1
Line 174 Arial-Bold=Helvetica-Bold 1
Line 175 Arial-Italic=Helvetica-Oblique 1
Line 176 Arial-BoldItalic=Helvetica-BoldOblique 1
Line 177 Courier New-Normal=Courier 1
Line 178 Courier New-Bold=Courier-Bold 1
Line 179 Courier New-Italic=Courier-Oblique 1
Line 180 Courier New-BoldItalic=Courier-BoldOblique 1
Line 181 Symbol-Normal=Symbol 1
Line 182 Times New Roman-Normal=Times-Roman 1
Line 183 Times New Roman-Bold=Times-Bold 1
Line 184 Times New Roman-Italic=Times-Italic 1
Line 185 Times New Roman-BoldItalic=Times-BoldItalic 1
Line 186 Avalon-Normal=AvantGarde-Book 3
Line 187 Avalon-Bold=AvantGarde-Demi 3
Line 188 Avalon-Italic=AvantGarde-BookOblique 3
```

```
Line 189 Avalon-BoldItalic=AvantGarde-DemiOblique 3
Line 190 Brooklyn-Normal=Bookman-Light 3
Line 191 Brooklyn-Bold=Bookman-Demi 3
Line 192 Brooklyn-Italic=Bookman-LightItalic 3
Line 193 Brooklyn-BoldItalic=Bookman-DemiItalic 3
Line 194 Dixieland-Normal=ZapfDingbats 3
Line 195 GreekMathSymbols-Normal=Symbol 1
Line 196 NewBrunswick-Normal=NewCenturySchlbk-Roman 3
Line 197 NewBrunswick-Bold=NewCenturySchlbk-Bold 3
Line 198 NewBrunswick-Italic=NewCenturySchlbk-Italic 3
Line 199 NewBrunswick-BoldItalic=NewCenturySchlbk-BoldItalic 3
Line 200 PalmSprings-Normal=Palatino-Roman 3
Line 201 PalmSprings-Bold=Palatino-Bold 3
Line 202 PalmSprings-Italic=Palatino-Italic 3
Line 203 PalmSprings-BoldItalic=Palatino-BoldItalic 3
Line 204 Switzerland-Normal=Helvetica 1
Line 205 Switzerland-Bold=Helvetica-Bold 1
Line 206 Switzerland-Italic=Helvetica-Oblique 1
Line 207 Switzerland-BoldItalic=Helvetica-BoldOblique 1
Line 208 SwitzerlandNarrow-Normal=Helvetica-Narrow 3
Line 209 SwitzerlandNarrow-Bold=Helvetica-Narrow-Bold 3
Line 210 SwitzerlandNarrow-Italic=Helvetica-Narrow-Oblique 3
Line 211 SwitzerlandNarrow-BoldItalic=Helvetica-Narrow-BoldOblique 3
Line 212 Toronto-Normal=Times-Roman 1
Line 213 Toronto-Bold=Times-Bold 1
Line 214 Toronto-Italic=Times-Italic 1
Line 215 Toronto-BoldItalic=Times-BoldItalic 1
Line 216 ZurichCalligraphic-Italic=ZapfChancery-MediumItalic 3
```

Key Items in the CORELFNT.INI File

First a bit of background on what you are seeing in the list. Lines 1-10 contain information on using fonts provided with earlier versions of CorelDRAW! back to before version 2.x. These instructions are followed by lines 11-51, which refer to the WFN symbol collection that comes with Draw 5. Earlier in the Config section of CORELAPP.INI, you saw on line 46 the instruction FontsDir=C:\COREL50\SYMBOLS telling Draw where to look for the WFN files it needs to load symbols into the symbols library you see in the Symbols Roll-Up. Here is where the reference to these WFN files is made. To the left of the equal sign you see the actual name Draw lists in the Symbols Roll-Up selection, and,

IV

Advanced Topics

to the right of the equal sign, you see the file name containing the data needed to build those particular symbols. If the file isn't there, Draw won't list it; conversely, if the reference isn't made here, then Draw also won't list it. Knowing how this works may come in handy if you are in the habit of making up your own symbols libraries.

Further down, on lines 52-172, you see the section called FontMapV20. Here you have the WFN fonts produced by and for earlier versions of CorelDRAW!. On the left of the equal sign, notice the abbreviated name of the WFN file, and, on the right, see the name as it appears in the fonts listing in Draw. Following that are a series of numbers that refer to the actual font identification number, each of which is separated by a comma. The first number represents the identification of the "normal" style, the second refers to the "bold" style, the third refers to the "italic," and the fourth refers to the "bold italic." The numeral 0 means no font exists for that particular style.

Next on lines 173-216, in the PSResidentFonts section, notice that there are two font names on each line. On the left of the equal sign you see the name that Draw refers to the font as, and on the right of the equal sign you see the actual name of the font as the industry knows it as. Each is followed by a number. These numbers are what Draw looks at when it goes to send your file to the printer. A 0 means that the font will not be resident on the printer and Draw is to download the font to the printer before sending the file information. A 1 means that the font is resident only on older printer types, such as the early laser printers of 9 or 10 years ago. A 3 means that the font is resident on the printer for sure and Draw won't bother taking the time to download the font information.

Draw's Printing Controls

The initial install of CorelDRAW! 5 creates a file to control various printer functions and settings. Here you will see the printer settings that Draw looks at when you select File\Print or Ctrl+P to find out what to do in certain instances depending on which type of printer you are using. This file is short and sweet, but settings listed here are critical to printing and will determine whether you will have success in printing.

Contents of the CORELPRN.INI file in C:\COREL50\CONFIG:

```
        [Config]
Line 1  TextAsClip=0
Line 2  PreviewImage=0
Line 3  UseColorProfile=1
Line 4  DumpEntireBitmap=0
Line 5  WarnBadOrientation=1
```

```
Line 6  PSBitmapFontLimit=8
Line 7  PSBitmapFontSizeThreshold=75
Line 8  PSComplexityThreshold=1500
Line 9  PSOverprintBlackLimit=95
Line 10 PSRegistrationMarkType=1
Line 11 PSDownloadType1Fonts=1
Line 12 PSConvertTrueTypeToType1=1
Line 13 PSSpotFountainsAsProcess=1
Line 14 PSColorBitmapsAsGrayscale=1
        [PSDrivers]
Line 15 MGXPS=1
Line 16 PSCRIPT=1
Line 17 AGFAPS=1
        [PSScreenSets]
Line 18 RT230.INI=RT Screening - Lino 230/200
Line 19 RT260.INI=RT Screening - Lino 260
Line 20 RT300.INI=RT Screening - Lino 300
Line 21 RT330.INI=RT Screening - Lino 330
Line 22 RT500.INI=RT Screening - Lino 500
Line 23 RT530.INI=RT Screening - Lino 530
Line 24 RT630.INI=RT Screening - Lino 630
Line 25 HQS230.INI=HQS Screening - Lino 230
Line 26 HQS260.INI=HQS Screening - Lino 260
Line 27 HQS300.INI=HQS Screening - Lino 300
Line 28 HQS330.INI=HQS Screening - Lino 330
Line 29 HQS500.INI=HQS Screening - Lino 500
Line 30 HQS530.INI=HQS Screening - Lino 530
Line 31 HQS630.INI=HQS Screening - Lino 630
        [PSScreenFreqDefaults]
Line 32 300=60
Line 33 600=80
Line 34 1000=100
Line 35 1200=133
Line 36 1270=133
Line 37 1693=133
Line 38 2540=150
Line 39 3386=200
```

Lines 1-14 Basic Printing Settings

This first Config section sets out the most important settings involving the printing process.

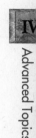

Line 1, `TextAsClip`, (turned off here) describes whether to convert text to curves.

Line 2, `PreviewImage=0`, leaves the print preview window in File\Print\Options\Print Options blank until selected on within Draw.

Line 3, `UseColorProfile=1`, indicates the setting controlled from the File\Print dialog box found in the bottom left area of the screen. In this case, it is selected as enabled.

Line 4, `DumpEntireBitmap=0`, determines how bitmaps are sent to the Hewlett-Packard series IV printers. If you happen to be using this printer and its printer driver's graphics mode is set to raster bitmaps, it will print as transparent. To prevent this from happening, leave this control at the default of off and all bitmap images will be sent to the printer one raster line at a time. In instances where this method overloads the printer when printing files containing many fountain fills, try setting the printers graphics mode to HPGL/2.

Line 5, `WarnBadOrientation=1`, is a great feature and guarantees to save you wasted printouts. Leave it in the on position to warn you when your page orientation doesn't match what is presently selected on your printer. Even if you switch printers while still in the File\Print dialog box, it will jump up and tell you that something's amiss. It might also be worth remembering that this feature cannot be controlled from within Draw and can only be set by editing this INI file or by using a third-party vendor program such as SetDraw or Corel's INI Editor.

Line 6, `PSBitmapFontLimit=8`, limit tells Draw the maximum number of fonts it can rasterize at a time when sending information to the printer. The range is 0 to 250 and the default is 8 fonts.

Line 7, `PSBitmapFontThreshold=75`, is the height of a bitmap font character measured in pixels according to the resolution of the PostScript printer. The higher the value, the longer the font will take to print. Draw uses this value to decide if the font can be rendered by a PostScript printer (if the font is not resident). Before Draw will convert characters to bitmap printing, though, they have to meet certain conditions. The font must not be listed in your CORELFNT.INI file, it may not have any scale, skew, envelope, outline, or fountain fill applied, and scale and fit to page can not be enabled in the Print menu. The range for this setting is 0 to 32,767 and the default value is 75.

Line 8, `PSComplexityThreshold`, is a nasty-looking instruction to give Draw, but fairly simple to comprehend. This setting helps Draw decide whether a fill path is too complex to print on a PostScript device, or if it should be chopped up into sections. The value entered here is the number of segments in an individual path. If the fill path to be printed has more segments than the setting entered here, it will be chopped up into smaller parts without changing its appearance. The default setting is 1500; however, if you are having trouble printing a file containing a ton of fountain fills across complex paths, try lowering this to 200 or 300. This will let Draw know to go ahead and break it into smaller, more digestible chunks for the printer to handle. The smaller type sizes might not look that great, but at least the file will print and your fountain fills will come out right. The range for this setting is from 20 to 20,000.

Line 9, `PSOverprintBlackLimit=95`, means that when Draw's auto-trapping feature "always overprint black" is enabled (during separations printing on a PostScript device), all black objects with a screen percentage value between 95 and 100 (solid black) will overprint all objects beneath them. The allowable range for this setting is between 0 and 100, but it is highly recommended that you leave it right where it is. Setting this value to less than 95 percent will cause white space to appear on separation layers. Not a great idea.

Line 10, `PSRegistrationMarkType=1`, simply means that the registration reference marks set for color separations in the **F**ile**P**rint\\Options\\Print Options dialog box are selected.

Line 11, `PSDownloadType1Fonts=1`, is the function that indicates fonts are not resident on the printer and tells Draw to go ahead and download the font before sending the file information. This option is found in the **F**ile**P**rint\\Print Options\\Options dialog box.

Line 12, `PSConvertTrueTypeToType1`, can also be found in the **F**ile**P**rint\\Print Options\\Options dialog box. As the instruction implies, it tells Draw to go ahead and convert TrueType fonts to type 1 fonts.

Line 13, `PSSpotFountainsAsProcess=1`, controls the colors in the file and commands Draw to print any spot colors it finds as process colors using the program's process color conversion tables.

Line 14, `PSColorBitmapsAsGrayscale=1`, converts all color information to shades of gray so that you can print on devices that do not support color.

Lines 18-31 RT and HQS Screening

Draw has built-in screening technology settings found in the **F**ile**P**rint\\Options\\Separations menu when Print Separations and Edit Custom Halftone are selected. This particular device screening was initially released with version 5 and more device screening scripts are to follow.

Lines 32-39 Default LPI and DPI Settings

These settings tell the printer that Draw is printing to a particular film resolution, as well as which screen frequency to use if none is selected within the Advanced Screening Technology dialog box.

IV

Advanced Topics

Chapter Snapshot

Besides all the wonderful graphics tools you'll find in the CorelDRAW! 5 box, you've also acquired the equivalent of a small type foundry collection consisting of Type 1 and TrueType fonts. With 830 high-quality typefaces at your disposal, your designer's loft can be a garden, or it can be a jungle if you don't understand a few things about how digital fonts should be managed. This chapter covers the following:

✔ How TrueType and Type 1 fonts are created

✔ How to manually install and remove fonts

✔ The differences between Type 1 and TrueType fonts, and how their construction can affect your work

✔ The best ways to manage your font collection

Fonts play a heavy role in the design business and learning to manage them pays off.

CHAPTER

Font Management Techniques

The following are three really good ways to bring a fast PC to its knees:

✔ Apply a CorelDRAW! texture fill to an 8 1/2-by-11 page frame

✔ Stick a peanut butter sandwich in the 5 1/4 drive, then type the DISKCOPY command

✔ Install more than 20 percent of CorelDRAW! 5's font collection

While the first two are sort of common sense "don'ts," the last point is not so obvious. At first glance, having a comprehensive typeface collection installed is an invaluable benefit. But this benefit can become a deficit if you don't understand the ins and outs of managing typefaces, how they're created, their impact on your Windows environment, and the best way to use them in a CorelDRAW! design or layout.

Too Much Type

It should come as no surprise to Windows 3.1x users that the horsepower required to rasterize scalable fonts on-the-fly within applications has to come from somewhere. It's not magic; every installed TrueType or Type 1 font takes up system resources. When your system resources are low, all types of flaky things can happen, including system hangs and crashes. If you have too many typefaces installed, you are allowing resources ordinarily allocated to your applications to be stolen. In round numbers, when you have more than 250 typefaces (TrueType, Type 1, or both in combination) installed, you will notice a significant decrease in speed in all of your Windows programs and Windows itself.

There are 830 typefaces in two different type formats on the CorelDRAW! CD-ROM that you can install. You might already have a category or two installed if you picked them during CorelDRAW!'s Setup. In this chapter, though, you'll learn how to install and remove fonts manually to arrive at a custom typeface collection on your hard drive that suits your individual needs.

The first choice you need to make is which typeface format you want to use—TrueType or Type 1. Even though equivalent fonts (such as Times New Roman and Times New Roman PS) might appear the same on-screen, some subtle differences exist in their construction. Understanding font architecture and font origins makes it easier to decide which type of font to use in your work.

Type 1s and TrueType

TrueType (originally developed by Apple Computer Systems and Microsoft) and PostScript Type 1 (originally developed by Adobe Systems) are *scalable* font technologies. They both define the outline of each character in a typeface as a mathematical description. While each type of font format uses different math to describe the outline, the basic font rasterizing (displaying) process is the same. When you choose a typeface and point size, the vector math that describes each character is accessed to build and display the characters at the size (scale) you've specified.

Although CorelDRAW! can use both types of typefaces in a single document, it's not wise to follow this practice. The technologies of the typefaces are similar, but most printers and other output devices are geared more toward either Type 1 or TrueType, but not both. Service bureaus are terrific places to get your design work put on a page or film at high resolutions; you should familiarize yourself with which font technology they use, and perhaps use the same font format to keep things synchronous.

When you run CorelDRAW! Setup, you are asked to select one or more collections of TrueType typefaces for installation or to make selections from the assorted list of fonts, also in the TrueType format. CorelDRAW! *does not* automatically install Type 1 PostScript typefaces for you, even though Type 1s are on the CD.

You can work faster and smarter in CorelDRAW! if you choose a single format of typeface and stick to it, regardless of which typeface format suits your needs best. To decide which format is right for you, you need to understand how digital fonts work, and why they sometimes don't work.

The Advantages of PostScript

Adobe Systems invented the Type 1 font format and based it on their PostScript descriptor language. PostScript is a remarkable programming language that is used to describe how a page should look and print. Type 1 fonts use the PostScript language to describe how a letter is shaped, how large it should be, and its position relative to the page. PostScript isn't used just to build and print fonts, and that is where it differs from TrueType technology, which is only used for font building.

PostScript does different things when applied to different publishing needs. It can create digital halftone cells necessary for accurately printing a grayscale or color image from a printing press. Encapsulated PostScript images (which CorelDRAW! can create) are *device independent*. Device independence means a document created as an EPS file can be read by IBM-PCs, Macintoshes, and many variants of the UNIX operating systems.

Both of these capabilities are important points for CorelDRAW! designers who create designs for high-quality printed output. If you send your work to a service bureau or imaging center (most of which currently are Macintosh and PostScript based), and if your work contains fountain fills, blends, or images from Photo-Paint, you'd be wise to export CorelDRAW! graphics as EPS images and use Type 1 typefaces in your designs.

Type 1 PostScript fonts produce the best results when printed to a PostScript-based printer, imagesetter, or film recorder. But they also produce clean, sharp type when printed to a PCL-based printer(such as an HP LaserJet).

If your intention is to install a luxurious amount of fonts for your design work, having enough hard drive storage space can become a concern. Simply put, Type 1 typefaces take up less room on your hard drive. On an average, they take up 10,500 fewer bytes than the same typeface in the TrueType format—10,500 bytes alone isn't going to flood your hard disk, but if you were to copy all of the Type 1 typefaces from the CorelDRAW! CD onto your hard disk (hint: don't), they would take up 8.8 MB less space than if you had copied all of the TrueType to your drive.

The Disadvantages of PostScript

PostScript Type 1 typefaces are not inherently supported by Windows, as is TrueType. To use Type 1 typefaces, you must use a PostScript type management program to allow Windows and Windows applications to use Type 1 typefaces. This means that you have to devote some of your system's resources to running the type manager. The most commonly used type management program is Adobe Type Manager (ATM).

Adobe Type Manager comes bundled with many applications, including CorelVENTURA.

PostScript printers usually are more expensive than PCL-based printers. This is partially due to the PostScript interpreter licensing fees printer manufacturers pay to Adobe, but also because PostScript printers rely less on your computer's computational power for processing than PCL printers. That is, they require more memory and must contain more data processing circuitry.

PostScript printing is slow compared to PCL-based printing. You pay for the accuracy, precision, and fidelity of the final printed image in time.

TrueType Advantages

TrueType is the font format that is built into Windows. Like Adobe's Type 1, TrueType is a scalable font technology that produces different font sizes on-the-fly. The most positive aspect about TrueType is that anyone who has Windows can use it without running a third-party type manager.

TrueType also is inexpensive. Microsoft single-handedly brought average typeface prices down, from $30 to $50 a font to $1 or less (in some cases), through its commercial offerings in TrueType collections. Type 1 prices now have dropped due to TrueType's pricing structure, but still are typically more expensive. As a CorelDRAW! user with 830 fonts available on the CorelDRAW! CD, it might be a while before you feel the urge to purchase additional typefaces, but if you share documents, the TrueType format is a good choice because buying matching font sets costs less.

TrueType fonts print faster to both PCL and PostScript printers because only the characters used in a document are sent to be processed for printing, not the entire typeface. If you've typed the headline "WOW" in Arial TrueType, for example, the print driver only processes and sends the uppercase W and the uppercase O. If you used a Type 1 typeface for the same headline, all 256 characters in the typeface are sent for processing, even though only the uppercase W and O are used.

TrueType Disadvantages

The mathematics that are used to describe each character in a TrueType font are less efficient than the mathematics used to describe the same character in a Type 1 format. Because the PC is performing the calculations, users frequently ignore this reality; but if you want to optimize your system and get better font handling performance from your applications, you should consider the math behind your typeface format choice.

Using the less efficient TrueType system of mathematical equations increases the file size of the font and its complexity because more nodes are required to describe accurately the arcs that make up the outline of the typeface. The more complex (more nodes) something is, whether it's a graphical object or a typeface, the harder it is to print it successfully. In this chapter, you'll take apart a character using CorelDRAW! to see how many nodes are needed to define the same character in TrueType and Type 1 format.

Service bureaus and imaging centers in general give you untold grief if you bring files to them that use TrueType fonts. Most imaging centers have standardized on Type 1 typefaces and might not own any TrueType. If this is the case with your local imaging place, your file can't be processed without the substitution of an equivalent Type 1 font. If the service bureau can (and will) substitute an equivalent font, you still might not get the results you expect. The TrueType font width, kerning, letter, and word spacing of the same typeface, from the same font vendor, is slightly different than in Type 1 format.

Another reason why your service bureau or imaging center might show you their exit sign instead of a print is that nearly all imagesetters (high-resolution printers used to produce film for print presses), color print proofing devices, and film recorders are PostScript devices in 1994. PostScript drivers must convert the information in a TrueType outline font to a Type 1 format that can be sent to the device. Adobe refers to converted TrueType as *synthetic Type 1*, but cautions against using this synthetic font. PostScript devices have been known to successfully

IV

Advanced Topics

process and print TrueType, but you never know when this process will be successful. Often, a file will not print completely if it contains TrueType, especially if you've used a mixture of TrueType and Type 1 in your file.

How Scalable Fonts Work with PCL Printers

If your CorelDRAW! artwork is going to be output from a PCL printer, there's a nominal difference in quality between TrueType and Type 1 formats. Printer Command Language doesn't care about a font's native descriptor language; both TrueType and Type 1 fonts are rendered to a bitmap format by the printer driver (a file on your hard drive supplied by Microsoft or an OEM printer manufacturer) and then sent to the printer.

A document in CorelDRAW! contains information about the size, type, and format of the fonts used. When you print the piece to a PCL printer, this information is sent to the print driver for processing into a format that the printer can understand. The print driver takes the information about each character's outline, then determines where the printer puts dots of toner on the paper to fill the outline and create a readable character. Figure 23.1 is an oversimplified illustration of how the bits of font information are mapped to a grid. This processing takes place within your computer. When it finishes its calculations, it sends the instructions to the printer.

Figure 23.1
PCL printers follow print driver instructions on how an outline of a character is filled with dots.

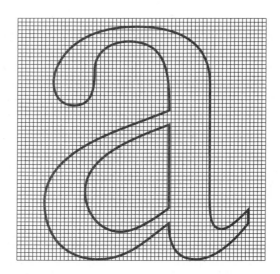

Both TrueType and Type 1 fonts are sent and printed to a PCL printer as bitmaps made up of the same size dots. They print just fine, but there is *no* native language support to make them cleaner than the print driver makes them.

Resolution Enhancement is a patented method of bringing more pleasing prints to PCL-based Hewlett-Packard printers by varying the size of the dots of toner. This produces smoother, less jagged curves than toner dots that use the same size. Other, non-PostScript manufacturers have similar methods of enhancing print quality.

Resolution Enhancement technology, however, does not add refinement to either TrueType or Type 1 typefaces; it only works with the typeface format that is native to the printer. HP uses a type format called Intellifont that can take advantage of Resolution Enhancement. This is not a widely supported type format, and CorelDRAW! does not provide you with type in the Intellifont format.

How Scaleable Fonts Work with a PostScript Printer

The PostScript print driver, like the PCL driver, plays an important part in preparing your file for printing to a PostScript device. The PostScript print driver takes all the information CorelDRAW! provides about the page (both the graphics and the type) and creates a PostScript file that the printer's PostScript interpreter can process. Like a PCL driver, the PostScript print driver does its work within your computer. When it's finished, the driver passes the file to the printer's PostScript Interpreter. The PostScript Interpreter then processes the information (within the printer) into a set of instructions that tells the printer what to do to reproduce the page.

The print driver doesn't perform anything extraordinary with Type 1 typeface because type information is already in the vector PostScript format that the PostScript interpreter can read and use. But when you use a TrueType font in a document, the printer driver must either convert the TrueType's vector format to a bitmap (like the PCL printer does) or convert it to the type of vector format that a Type 1 typeface uses. Whether it converts to bitmap or to Type 1, vector math depends on what settings you've made in <u>S</u>end to Printer As: section of the print driver's Advanced Options section. These options can be set in CorelDRAW! by choosing <u>F</u>ile, P<u>r</u>int Setup, then choosing <u>S</u>etup, <u>O</u>ptions, and Ad<u>v</u>anced when you have a PostScript printer chosen as your output device.

Adobe recommends that you send TrueType to PostScript devices as bitmaps. This doesn't produce as clean and smooth a result as converting to Type 1 math, but it's more of a foolproof method of printing. The conversion of TrueType to Type 1 math doesn't always work, and your finished print might be missing text areas.

IV

Advanced Topics

No hard-and-fast rule exists for printing TrueTypes as a bitmap or allowing their conversion to Type 1s. If you're printing to your own PostScript printer and you have time to experiment, choose <u>S</u>end to Printer As: Adobe Type 1. If you want to be safe and can afford to sacrifice a little quality, choose <u>S</u>end to Printer As: Bitmap (Type 3).

Choosing Your Fonts

As mentioned earlier, too many fonts residing on your hard disk can cause general problems with Windows performance, regardless of whether they're written to the Type 1 or TrueType format. Basically, there are three reasons for "font congestion" on a system.

Fonts take up space where they are stored. A typical font can weigh in at 55,000 bytes. This amount alone is a negligible sum, but if you've loaded 200 fonts, you might have 11 MB less hard disk space. Many people never remove a font after it's installed and outlived its novelty, so I wasn't surprised when I visited a friend who's a "font addict" and discovered he had over 50 MB of fonts choking his available hard disk space.

TrueType fonts have to be registered in the WIN.INI file that comes with Windows 3.x. This is a text file that tells programs specific details about how they should operate. Microsoft has set an upper limit of 64 KB for WIN.INI's size. Type 1 fonts, by default, are installed as auto-downloaded to your printer when you add them to ATM, and these, too, need to be registered in WIN.INI under the [PostScript,LPT] section. With long path names entered (for example, **Avant Garde Book Oblique BT (TrueType)=TT0155M_.FOT**), WINI.INI approaches the limit for its file size, and strange, unpleasant things happen to Windows and your applications.

Both Adobe Type Manager and the TrueType engine in Windows operate as Terminate-and-Stay Resident programs (TSRs). That is, they're always running as programs in the background while you work in CorelDRAW! and other applications, ready to hop in and display Aardvark Bold in a blink of an eye if this is your command. This hop turns into a limp when the scalable font TSRs have to keep track of an excess of different fonts.

You can take preventative measures to avoid font overkill on your system. You need to decide which typeface format is for you, then make an honest evaluation of which fonts you really need in your business and which ones are superfluous and fanciful. Appendix E, "CorelDRAW! Fonts," shows a graphical chart of CorelDRAW! 5 fonts as arranged in groups. In the next section, you'll get a first-hand look at how the two type technologies build their characters. By looking at the structure of a font, you'll get a pretty clear idea of why "font stress" can occur on your system.

Choosing a Compact Font Format

As mentioned earlier, TrueType files typically are larger than their Type 1 equivalents. Most of the reason for this is that outline fonts are made up of nodes that arcs pass through, and the equations that describe how an arc arcs is different between the two formats.

If you've ever converted text to curves in CorelDRAW! to create a custom logo, you know that converted text is made up of nodes along the text's outline. Type 1 fonts are easier to modify with the Shape tool when converted to curves because the math (Bézier) used to describe them is a little more elegant than TrueType's. Bézier curves are a pain in the neck to design with, but they provide the most efficient way to express a curved line within a font outline. Nodes and segments are a graphical interpretation of math that CorelDRAW! uses when you make a design. The more shapes and nodes you have, the larger the resulting file will be.

The next set of exercises is provided as an example of how CorelDRAW! and other applications handle TrueType and Type 1 fonts. You need Swiss 721BT in the Type 1 format from CorelDRAW!'s CD and Adobe Type Manager v 2.5 or later installed and running to participate. You don't have to follow along, but if you at least read the exercise, you might draw some conclusions of your own about the font format you use in CorelDRAW!.

Adding a Type 1 Font from CorelDRAW!'s CD

Place the CorelDRAW! CD containing the CorelDRAW! fonts in the CD-ROM drive	Makes the entire collection of fonts available for copying to hard disk
Double-click on the Adobe Type Manager *icon in Program Manager*	Launches Adobe Type Manager
Click on **A**dd	Displays the Add ATM Fonts menu
Double-click on the drive letter of the CD-ROM drive in the **D**irectories *list*	Displays and selects the directory structure of the CorelDRAW! CD in the **D**irectories list

continues

continued

Double-click on the Fonts *subdirectory, then double-click on the* type1 *subdirectory*	Displays and selects the CorelDRAW! Type 1 fonts, arranged in categories alphabetically
Double-click on the **S** *subdirectory in the* **D**irectories *list*	Displays the fonts contained in the S subdirectory in the Available **F**onts window
Scroll down to Swis721 BT *and click on it*	Selects Swis721 to add to Adobe Type Manager, as shown in figure 23.2
Make sure that the **I**nstall as autodownload fonts for the PostScript Driver *box is not checked*	Prevents ATM from adding a line to WIN.INI about this font's hard disk location if you have a PostScript driver installed

You might not ever want to use this typeface again. If this option is dimmed, don't worry; ATM will not add this font to WIN.INI if you don't have a PostScript driver defined in Windows.

Bump your Font **C**ache *up to 256 KB*

By default, ATM's Font Cache of 96 KB is conservative for users with more than 50 fonts installed. This improves screen redraw in Windows applications, and you'll scroll in windows faster.

Click on **A**dd, *then click on* E**x**it

ATM displays a dialog box that prompts you to restart Windows to affect the change. This refers to the change to the size of the font cache, not the addition of the typeface, which doesn't require restarting Windows. Don't let it restart; you can continue with the exercise, and the font cache will increase the next time you start Windows.

Choose R**e**turn to Current Windows Session to dismiss the dialog box and continue. Swis721 is available to use in Windows programs, especially CorelDRAW!, the proving grounds for our font experiment.

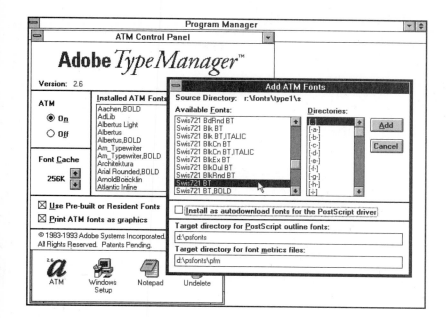

Figure 23.2
Select the SWIS721 BT Type 1 font to add through Adobe Type Manager.

Comparing Font Technologies

The reason you should have Swis721 loaded in Adobe Type Manager at this point is that it bears a remarkable similarity to Windows Arial, a TrueType font that came with Windows 3.1x. Both Arial and Swis721 BT are variations on the classic Helvetica typeface owned by Linotype AG. If you check the total size of the files that make up Arial and Swis721 BT in File Manager, you'll find that ARIAL.TTF and ARIAL.FOT equal 66,998 bytes, while 0003a___.PFM and 0003a___.PFB come in at 53,958 bytes.

In theory, a lowercase "a" from both Arial and Swis721 BT fonts should have the same curves and an equivalent number of nodes connecting the curves to look the same. But because the fonts use different font technologies to describe the outline of an "a", they don't. Type 1 fonts use Bézier curves as a model for the mathematical expression of a character's shape, while TrueType outlines are made of splines.

Having two typefaces on your system with the exact same name is a problem maker. Applications don't know which font is which, become confused, and cease to work. Windows, when faced with this font identity crisis, ignores the Type 1 and only deals with the TrueType. Never load identically named fonts that are in two different font formats.

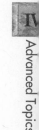

continues

This is why we didn't ask you to load both SWIS721s in the TrueType and Type 1 format for the experiment to follow.

In the next exercise, you'll type a character from Arial and one from Swis721 BT, then convert them both to curves to see their construction from a view in CorelDRAW!.

Double-click on the CorelDRAW! icon. Choose the Text tool, then click an insertion point on the Printable Page.

Type a lowercase **a**, then press Ctrl+ spacebar to switch to the Pick tool and select the "a". Press Ctrl+T. The dialog box for setting font type, size, and other parameters displays in the drawing window.

Converting Fonts to Curves

Choose Arial *from the* Fonts *list, then type* **250** *in the* Size *field and click on OK*	Provides you with a good view of the Arial font
Left mouse click and drag the selected character to the right, then right mouse click before releasing both buttons	Creates a duplicate of the Arial character, which is presently selected
Press Ctrl+T, then choose Swis721 BT *from the* Fonts *list, and click on OK*	

You now have two nearly identical lowercase "a"s in the drawing window; the left is a TrueType font, the right is a Type 1 font, as shown in figure 23.3.

Click on the Zoom *tool, then choose the* Fit in Window *tool from the fly-out menu*	Zooms you into the closest maximum view of the objects in the drawing window
Choose Edit, *then* Select All *(or double-click on the* Pick tool)	Selects both characters
Choose Arrange, Combine *(Ctrl+L)*	

This is the quickest way to change multiple Artistic Text objects to curves at once. You also can select one Artistic Text object at a time and use the Convert to Curves (Ctrl+Q) command, but it's more fun to watch all the nodes appear this way.

Choose the Shape tool	Displays the nodes in an active selection

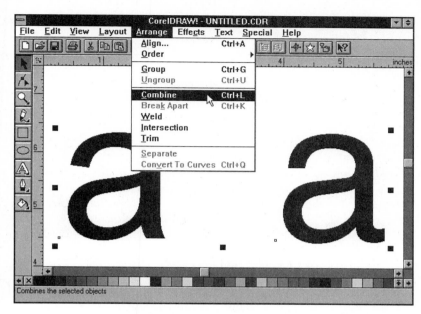

Figure 23.3
The geometry of
the fonts might
be similar, but
their construction
is not.

As you can see in figure 23.4, there are more nodes in the left object than the right.
Thirty-seven points of inflection make up a lowercase "a" in Arial TrueType, while
only 23 are required for the Type 1 equivalent.

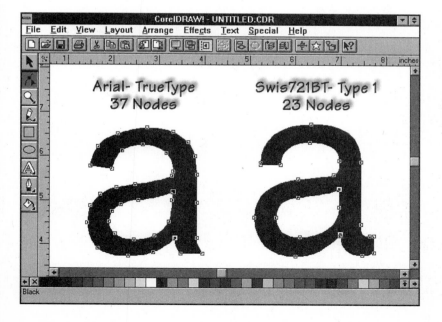

Figure 23.4
Spline-based
TrueType fonts
require more
nodes to express
an arc than
Bézier curve
Type 1 fonts.

IV

Advanced Topics

While the combined object is still selected, press Del, then Alt+F4 (File, Exit) to exit CorelDRAW!. The point's been made about the relationship between font file sizes and the nodes used to create the outline of a character. You don't need to save this masterpiece.

Splines and Bézier curves are mathematical expressions used to define arcs. Although a character composed of only straight lines is represented by a similar number of nodes, most typefaces contain an abundance of rounded serifs and characters.

You'll get to design a custom font in Chapter 24, "Building Your Own Font," but regardless of how carefully you draw the path to economize on nodes, a character exported as a TrueType contains more nodes than you originally define. As sort of a post-exercise experiment, the lowercase Swis721 BT "a" was exported as both a Type 1 and a TrueType. The result is shown in figure 23.5. On the left is a Swis721 BT lowercase "a". In the middle is the same "a" exported as a Type 1, and on the right is the same "a" exported as a TrueType font. All three were then typed in CorelDRAW!'s drawing window and converted to curves.

Figure 23.5
All three characters began as a Type 1. The right "a" is a TrueType converted to curves.

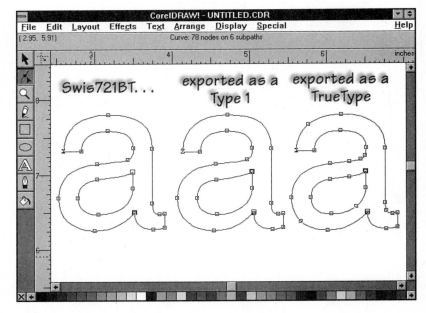

Splines require a node about every 45° of an arc to describe a curve. If you don't have one there, the export process adds one.

Because you have the option to use TrueType or Type 1 from CorelDRAW!'s CD, you have the following good reasons to choose Type 1 as your typeface format:

✔ The font file typically takes up less hard drive space

✔ When you convert Type 1 to curves in CorelDRAW!, you have fewer nodes to tangle with when you want to modify the text as a graphical element

✔ Service bureaus prefer computer graphics created with Type 1 because they're written in PostScript, the same native language as most high-resolution imagesetters

Managing Your Font Collection

CorelDRAW!'s Setup program warns users that choosing a total of more than 100 fonts from the various groups will result in poor Windows and CorelDRAW! performance. A few tricks, tips, and software programs are designed to cope with an oversized collection of typefaces, and the following sections address a designer's need.

Installing a Special Occasion Font

There will be times when you'll want to use a seasonal, decorative, or incredibly splashy display font. After that, there's no reason for it to be installed. If, for instance, you're designing a logotype that cries out for Pump Triline, you're presented with an "either/or" situation: manually uninstall a font to make way for Pump Triline, or choose a font other than Pump Triline for your design. This compromise is unacceptable for a designer. It's like receiving a crayon box with the blue crayon missing.

If you presently have all the fonts you need for everyday work, but still need one more to use in a single assignment, here's how to perform a little one-on-one font management.

(Briefly) Adding a TrueType Font

From Program Manager, double-click on the Control Panel *icon in the* Main *group, then double-click on the* Fonts *icon*

Opens the Fonts box, where you can install and uninstall TrueType fonts

Click on the **A**dd *button, then choose the* CorelDRAW! CD *from the* D**ri**v**es** *and* **D**irectories *listings*

continues

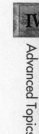

continued

Double-click on the Fonts *subdirectory, then the* TTF *subdirectory, then* P	The TrueType fonts appear in the List of Fonts window

Make sure that the Copy Fonts to Windows Directory box is checked. You'll slow your system down otherwise. Windows will attempt to fetch PumpTriD from the CD every time you want to use it, unless the file is copied to your hard disk.

Click on PumpTriD *in the fonts listings* window, *then click on* OK, *as shown if figure 23.6*	Adds PumpTriD to the fonts that CorelDRAW! and other applications can use

Figure 23.6

TrueType is added through the Windows Control Panel Fonts utility, not Adobe Type Manager.

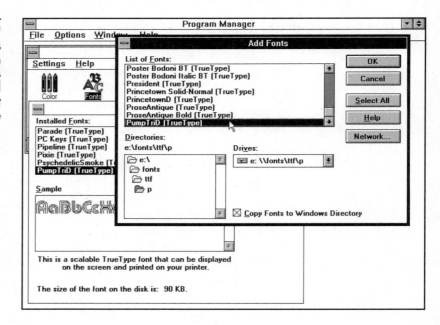

After you've done the exercise, you might want to remove PumpTriD from your collection of fonts, as well as your hard drive. Although you will see how to remove the font at the end of the exercise, if you installed a category of fonts during CorelDRAW! Setup, removing the font is a little different.

The CorelDRAW! Setup does not add the *.TTF TrueType file to WINDOWS\SYSTEM, but instead places the TTF file in the Fonts subdirectory beneath the Corel50 subdirectory. When a TrueType is added to available fonts, a *.FOT locator file is created and placed in the Window's SYSTEM subdirectory to point Windows to the sub-directory where the font file actually is stored. In this case, it would point to the drive where you installed CorelDRAW! and then to the Fonts subdirectory in the Corel50 directory tree.

With the **C**opy Fonts to Windows Directory box checked, PumpTriD is placed in the Windows Directory, which makes it easy for Windows to uninstall the font when the time comes. CorelDRAW! Setup and other third-party TrueType install programs provide an automatic way to add fonts, but sometimes complicate matters with their elegant workarounds.

Text As a Graphical Design Element

We have a logo in this section for a fictitious pizza parlor that needs the sort of pizzazz PumpTriD has. The ELMER.CDR file is on the *Inside CorelDRAW! Fifth Edition CD-ROM*, and now's a good time to swap CDs in preparation for the assignment. Bauhaus Heavy BT was used for part of the logo. PumpTriD is a stylized variation of Bauhaus, so the two fonts will work together and add the sort of visual resonance that attracts people to ads.

Your charge is to add a text element to the Famous Elmer's Country-Fried Pizza logo, then remove the PumpTriD TrueType font from your hard drive without ruining the finished logo for future use!

If this sounds like a magician's trick, it's not. It's simply using some of the power of CorelDRAW! to assist you in managing fonts you have only occasional use for.

Applying the New Font to a Graphic

From File Manager, copy the ELMER.CDR *file from the* CHAP23 *subdirectory on the* Inside CorelDRAW! Fifth Edition CD-ROM *to a working directory on your hard disk*

Double-click on the CorelDRAW! icon

Launches CorelDRAW! in the Corel group in Program Manager

continues

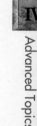

IV

Advanced Topics

continued

Choose File, Open (Ctrl+O, or click
on the Open button on the Ribbon Bar)

Choose the drive and directories location where you copied the ELMER.CDR *file from the drop-down lists, click on* ELMER.CDR *in the* File Names *window, then press OK*	Loads the ELMER.TIF file into Corel's Drawing Window
Click on the Zoom tool, choose the Zoom In tool from the menu fly-out, then marquee-zoom (click+diagonal drag) around the logo design, so you have about one screen inch of empty space around the logo	Zooms you into a comfortable viewing resolution for this assignment
Double-click on the Text tool	Displays the Text Roll-Up

Alternatively, you can choose Text, Text Roll-Up (Ctrl+F2), but this is CorelDRAW! 5, so why not take advantage of it?

Click and insertion point to the
right of the word "Famous"

This is the starting point of where you can start entering text directly.

Type **ELMER'S**

You can choose someone else's name if you feel they look like this cartoon.

Press Ctrl+spacebar	Switches to the Pick tool and selects your present Artistic Text entry
Click and drag on a corner selection handle in a direction away from the selection, stop when the status line displays that the text is 55 points	Scales the selection up so it's more the size of the rest of the text in the logo
Click on the font selection box toward the top of the Text Roll-Up, then type **P**	Makes the font list active, and scrolls you to the "P" section of available system fonts on your system
Scroll until you find PumpTriD, *then click and hold on the font name*	Displays a preview fly-out of the font, as seen in figure 23.7
Click on the Apply *button on the* Text Roll-Up	Applies PumpTriD to the selected Artistic Text

Figure 23.7
Click on the font name on the list (not the font name window) to display a preview of the selected font.

Applying Finishing Touches and Converting the Text

In the next example, you'll see how the dotted boundary box around moving selections can help you "eyeball" the angle of rotation for this new text piece. Frequently, designers have to match the angle of type that's already set in a piece. By watching the boundary box as you manually rotate selected text, you can get a fairly accurate idea of how much spin should be put on the selection. Make this text a permanent part of the ELMER.CDR logo now.

Customizing a Logo

Click a second time on the selected text	Puts the selection into the Rotate/Skew mode, and the selection handles turn into Rotate/Skew handles
Click and drag (slowly!) upward on the lower right rotate handle, then stop when the horizontal lines of the box are at the same angle as the FAMOUS part of the graphic	Causes the dotted boundary box representing extremities of the selected text to change angle, as shown in figure 23.8

continues

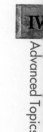

IV

Advanced Topics

continued

Figure 23.8

Selections
remain in place
until you release
the mouse
button.

 Unlike the example in this book, when you're working with different colored objects, you can place the one you want to rotate directly on top of the one you're trying to match for rotation angle.

Click again on the selection when it's been rotated to the right degree	Rotates the selection and puts the text back in selection mode
Click and drag the selected text into place beneath the FAMOUS lettering	

Use the arrow keys to nudge it into precise placement if your Nudge settings (set in **S**pecial, **P**references, General) are less than 1/100th of an inch.

Click on the Convert to Curves *button on the Ribbon Bar (or choose* **A**rrange, Con**v**ert to Curves; Ctrl+Q), *as shown in figure 23.9*	Converts the text to curves

You're free now to delete PumpTriD from your TrueType collection because the curves can no longer be edited as text.

Figure 23.9
Only
CorelDRAW!'s
Artistic Text can
be converted to
curves, unlike
Paragraph Text.

Save your work under a new name, then exit CorelDRAW!. Use the Fonts utility in Control Panel to remove PumpTriD from your active TrueType fonts. In Control Panel's Fonts dialog box, choose **R**emove, then check the **D**elete Font File from Disk box, and choose **Y**es. You have a safe copy of it for future use on the read-only Corel CD and have discovered a new method for managing fonts while you work.

Using PANOSE for Font Management

If you change your mind in the future about the spelling of Elmer, or any other Artistic Text you've converted to curves, you can forget about changing it if you deleted the font used and forgot which one of the 800+ fonts this one was. A "failsafe" method for converting text to curves in a document, yet retaining some editability, is to set up a new layer (Ctrl+F3). Use the Copy to command from the Layers Roll-Up's fly-out menu to copy the text to the new layer. Then double-click on the new layer title on the roll-up to display the New Layer options menu. Give the layer invisible, nonprintable, and locked attributes. Save your file.

The next time you open the file, the PANOSE matching system will pop up and tell you exactly what typeface is missing. This is the information you need to locate the missing typeface on the Corel CD. Write down the typeface name, choose Cancel, and exit CorelDRAW!. Reinstall the typeface, and you're back in business.

IV

Advanced Topics

When you reopen the file after having installed the typeface, unlock the layer it's on, and you're ready to edit.

CorelDRAW! has several beautiful display faces, and the experimentalist in you should definitely set aside some time to consider their usefulness within specific design assignments. But in terms of managing the overwhelming bounty you've purchased, knowing how to move them in, converting a text string to curves, then moving the font off your hard disk is an approach well worth considering.

Making Your Own Collection of CorelDRAW! Fonts

I am convinced that some people have Aaachen (or Aardvark) as an installed font because it's at the top of the alphabetical list of fonts. This same rationale has kept AAAA Plumbing and Ace Transportation Services in business by people who don't browse their telephone books.

But as contrary as it might seem, the more fonts you own, the more selective you should be. As previously discussed, too many fonts can slow your programs and flood your hard disk. The font categories CorelDRAW! Setup offered should be considered suggestions for the intermediate to advanced user. You should assemble a collection of your own fonts because only you know your specific assignments. And where to begin is easy.

Setting a Limit to Your Font Appetite

Set a maximum number of fonts that you want permanently installed on your system from the CorelDRAW! CD. If you've been collecting fonts since last year, you probably have a healthy collection already, so set your max at 100 fonts. If you've only begun your collection, you might want to set a limit of 200 or so. If you've been using CorelDRAW! 4 this past year, decide your own limit, but you probably have too many installed before you begin.

You might also upgrade your working set of fonts by replacing existing ones from the CD. URW Software (part of the URW type foundry), one of the oldest and most respected European font firms has contributed to the CorelDRAW! CD this year, and their renderings of Plaza, Enviro, and several other fonts are far superior to many identical commercial fonts, and even past CorelDRAW! versions. Remove the font equivalent you're now using from ATM or Windows, and load a better rendered face from the CD.

Give yourself a healthy balance of display (headline) and body text (paragraph) fonts. CorelDRAW! handles long documents 100 percent better than previous versions, giving you a new reason to load more body text fonts. And because fonts are accessible to all Windows applications, your new font collection can be used in word processing programs, Aldus PageMaker, CorelVENTURA, and similar desktop publishing applications.

The down side to body text fonts is that they don't travel singularly, and you'll want to include several versions of the same font family in your collection. Font families often carry different weights and italic and bold-italic versions. Don't cheat yourself by only installing, Goudy Old Style normal, for example, to keep your total number of fonts down. Sooner or later you'll need to italicize or bold a phrase and you'll be stuck.

The following is a list of "The Author's 100"; these are the fonts you never want to get caught without in an 11th hour crunch. Take a look at Appendix E for a quick visual reference of the fonts listed here. The legend here segments the recommended fonts into different categories; you might see some overlapping because the best fonts typically are the ones you can get the most mileage from in a variety of design situations.

Key	Font Type
D	Headline/Display Text. Not useful for more than 50 characters at a time.
P	Paragraph (body copy) Text. Highly readable at small point sizes (for example, 12 point); ideal for setting articles and this book.
WH	Work Horses. Multifunctional fonts, ideal for everyday use in a variety of business and design situations.
F	Fortune 500 Fonts. Upper-crust, conservative typefaces. Safe; you won't get chided or fired for using them in business reports and collateral material.
T	Tuxedo Fonts. Too formal for everyday use, yet perfect for invitations, initial caps, and social announcements.
I	Inspired Fonts. Revival and contemporary typefaces; not perfect for every assignment; go in and out of fashion, but can add a fresh touch to a page.

With the exception of some of the more exotic display fonts, most of these recommendations have at least one alternative weight so that body copy can be set in a similar style font for use in an assignment. With a little imagination (and by looking at some of the examples in this book!), these hundred fonts can be used to create thousands of different looks for scores of different graphical assignments:

Font	Keys
American Typewriter (Normal, Bold)	D/P/WH
Architektura	D/I
Avant Garde (Normal, Italic, Bold, Bold-Italic)	P/WH/F
Balloon (Normal, Bold)	D/WH
Bauer Bodoni (Normal, Italic, Bold, Bold-Italic)	P/WH/I
Benguiat (Normal, Bold)	D/P/I/WH
Bernard Fashion	D/I/ T
Bernard Modern (Normal, Italic, Bold, Bold-Italic)	D/P/I/ T
Bodoni Poster (Normal, Italic)	D/I
Bookman (Normal, Italic, Bold, Bold-Italic)	D/P/F
Bremen	D/I
Bremen Black	D/I
Broadway Engraved	D/I
Brush Script (or Brody)	D/I/WH
Carta (Symbol font)	D/WH
Caslon (Normal, Italic, Bold, Bold-Italic)	D/P/I/F
Caslon Open Face (or Atlantic Inline)	D/I/T
Century Schoolbook (Normal, Italic, Bold, Bold-Italic)	D/P/F
Engraver's Gothic	D/T/F
Engraver's Old English	D/T

Eras Black	D/I/F
Eras Book	D/P/I/F
Franklin Gothic (Normal, Italic, Bold, Bold-Italic)	D/P/WH/F
Franklin Gothic Heavy (Normal, Italic)	D/WH/F
Futura Book (Normal, Italic)	
Futura Medium (Normal, Italic)	D/WH/F/I
Futura Extra Black (Normal, Italic)	D/WH/F/I
Futura Black Condensed (Normal, Italic)	D/WH/F/I
Futura Condensed (Normal, Italic)	D/WH/F/I
Futura Bold Condensed (Normal, Italic	D/WH/F/I
GaramondNo4CyrTCYLig (Normal, Italic, Bold-Italic)	D/P/WH
GaramondNo4CyrTCYMed	D/P/WH
Goudy Old Style (Normal, Italic, Bold, Bold-Italic)	P/WH/I/F
Handel Gothic	D/ I/F
Swiss 721 (Normal, Italic, Bold, Bold-Italic)	D/P/WH/F
Swiss 721 Black (Normal, Italic)	D/WH/F
Swiss 721 Black Condensed (Bold, Italic)	D/WH/F
Swiss 721 Condensed (Normal, Italic, Bold, Bold-Italic)	D/WH/F
Swiss 721 Extended	D/WH/F
Kabel Book	D/P/WH/I/F
Kabel Ultra	D/WH/I/F
Kunstler Script (Normal, Bold)	D/T
Lithos (Normal, Bold) (or Neuland)	D/I

IV

Advanced Topics

continues

Font	Keys
Mona Lisa & Mona Lisa Recut	D/I
Mr. Earl (or Oz Handcraft)	D/I
Zapf Humanist 601 (Optima) (Normal, Italic, Bold, Bold-Italic)	D/P/WH
Serpentine Book	D/P/I
Serpentine Black	D/I
Snell Black	D/T
Stencil	D/WH/I/F
Tekton (Normal, Italic, Bold, Bold-Italic)	P/WH/I/F
Zapf Dingbats (Symbol font)	D/WH

CorelDRAW!'s CD also offers a collection of fonts known as the Dutch family. This collection is not included in the preceding list because Dutch is a variation of Times Roman, which is probably installed on your system. A variation of Times Roman ships as TrueType with Windows 3.1x and is commonly found on most versions of Adobe Type Manager as a Type 1 family.

Fonts manufactured by different companies sometimes bear synonymous names to industry standard names for both TrueType and Type 1. Bitstream's Humanist series, for instance, is otherwise known as Optima; the Swiss family is better known as Helvetica and a more widely accepted name for Brisk is Bisque.

Due to a strange court decision many years ago, manufacturers are allowed to copyright the name of a font, but not the actual design. At their best, some versions of popular classic typefaces, such as Peignot (Exotic 350), are faithful and might actually reproduce better than the version from the foundry that holds the copyright on the name. Other times you might find a shareware font that looks suspiciously similar to a popular font that simply won't work right on your system. In this case, the font was designed amateurishly by someone who ripped off an existing typeface, and you're better off not using it.

In either event, the CorelDRAW! catalog lists some of the alternative names for their offerings, and you should familiarize yourself with industry standard names.

Sooner or later you'll need to engage a service bureau for imagesetting your deign work, and it might not have the foggiest idea what Harpoon (Hairpin) is.

Industrial Strength Font Management

The preceding sections have covered the hands-on approach to managing a large number of typefaces. But if you have several different clients with entirely different preferences of design, you might want to check out a font management utility. Programs, such as Font Minder by Ares Software, enable the designer to hand pick different fonts and arrange them in a group. This group then can be activated or deactivated before starting CorelDRAW!. So if you have a special set of fonts for Fred's flyers and a different one for Larry's layouts, you can quickly swap the necessary group of fonts in and out of your system while keeping your permanent, everyday collection to a minimum. FontMinder Introductory version 2.0 located on the CorelDRAW! 1 CD can give you a taste of automated font management capabilities. Run SETUP.EXE in the FONTMNDR subdirectory of Corel's CD to install the program.

More advanced font management utilities also can delete fonts from your hard disk. This is *not* the same as deactivating a font. You should carefully read the documentation that accompanies a font management program. Different companies use different terminology for deactivating groups of typefaces.

In addition to font management, some font utilities offer renaming and kerning pair capability. Font Monster version 3.5x, by Leapin' Lizards (Steve Fox) of Taiwan is a wonderful shareware utility that renames a font anything you choose, in addition to grouping and moving fonts. This renaming capability enables you to standardize your font collection. The GaramondNo4CyrCYLig, for example, is a ponderously long name for Garamond. Simply use a program such as Font Monster to rename the font.

Final Thoughts on Adopting Font Families

Since most of us are introduced to the English alphabet at an early age, the reality that a typeface, the garb a written word is dressed up in, is mostly taken for granted. Those of us who realize a font's importance as a design element can add a layer of art to written communication, giving the content of a phrase some form. Never forget though, that a digital font is more than a vehicle for creating splendid graphical design; it's a technology and a tool. And as with any collection of tools, the craftsperson would be well served by deciding on a "toolbox" before the collection becomes unwieldy in number!

Use some of techniques described in this chapter to develop good font management practices, use the font management software you're comfortable with, and based on your personal needs, create a toolbox of your own.

Chapter Snapshot

Creating your own typeface will enhance your worth as a designer. Although CorelDRAW! doesn't have a special utility for creating fonts, it does have the innate power residing in the Drawing Window. If you want to create an original font, all you need is the knowledge of some basic typographic conventions, and the steps covered in this chapter. In this chapter, you learn to do the following:

✔ Set up a page layout specifically for creating fonts

✔ Create a gothic, serif typeface

✔ Discover some of the secrets of professional font-making

✔ See how to create and access extend characters

24

CHAPTER

Building Your Own Font

You've seen in this book how CorelDRAW! bridges the artistic gap between text and graphics objects. That's because typefaces are simply designs that have special codes assigned to them that are mapped to a keyboard.

Creating a Typeface Template

Windows programs that use TrueType and Type 1 typefaces must have a lot of font information available to them as they rasterize text to your monitor (and eventually to a printer). In addition to the outline of the font (the actual typeface character you see), "white space" is also part of a font's data. When a character is typed, some of the space you see surrounding a character is actually part of the font data, and shouldn't be confused with kerning and leading.

The first step to creating a custom typeface is to design a template in which each character in the typeface is drawn, white space and all. This helps you to achieve consistency between each character in the set. When creating a typeface template, you must pay attention to, and plan for, what the dimensions of the components of a typeface character will be and the amount of room that will go in between the characters.

Here's how to set up a template for a font in Corel's Drawing window:

Building a Template for a Character

Double-click on the Printable page border (or select <u>L</u>ayout, <u>P</u>age Setup)	Displays the Page Setup dialog box
Choose Custom *from the drop-down list of page sizes, and choose points from both the* <u>W</u>idth *and* H<u>e</u>ight *drop-downs list boxes*	

Typefaces are usually measured in points, not inches. Because the page will be a square, it doesn't matter whether you choose <u>L</u>andscape or <u>P</u>ortrait.

Type **750** *in both the* <u>W</u>idth *and* H<u>e</u>ight *entry fields, as shown in figure 24.1, and then click on OK*	This is a little larger than the typefaces you'll design on the template; the "master" characters will be 720 points, but you'll need a little "play" when designing and positioning them

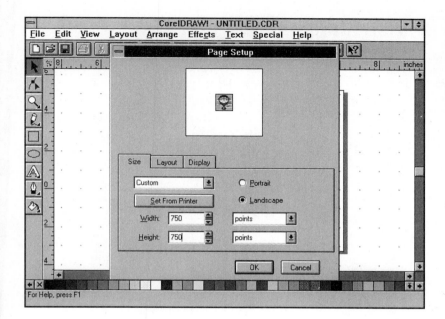

Figure 24.1
The Page Setup menu contains standard printing page sizes in addition to the custom option.

Type Measurement Conventions

From the earliest days of printing, type foundries and commercial presses developed the need for a standard unit of measurement. They settled on the *point*. Traditional typesetters used 72.27 points to equal an inch. When Adobe Systems defined the size of the point for their PostScript language and Type 1 fonts, they cut that down slightly to 72 points per inch. This measurement has become the standard for electronic type.

In the last set of steps, you established a working page size of 750 points by 750 points. In this space, the character you design will be 720 points. Although people generally don't type letters at 720 points (10 inches tall), professional type designers draw the characters at this size or larger. Designing at large scale and then shrinking the work down, minimizes any small inconsistencies in the design and sharpens up the edgework, just as with traditionally generated, physical artwork.

In the next exercise, you reset CorelDRAW!'s rulers and zero origin to settings more appropriate to the task at hand.

IV

Advanced Topics

Making a Point about Typography

Double-click on the intersecting box between two rulers, on the upper left corner of the drawing screen, to get 0" starting at the lower left corner of the Printable Page	Resets the zero origin of the rulers, in case you moved them prior to reading the chapter
Double-click on the middle of either ruler (or select Layout, *then* Grid & Scale Setup)	Displays the Grid and Scale Setup dialog box
Click on the drop-down list boxes for the Horizontal *and* Vertical Grid Frequency, *as shown in figure 24.2, set them to points, & give a 0.50 value to both*	Changes your ruler increments

This is an important trick to remember, because it's not the most obvious of CorelDRAW! options. You should make sure that the Show Grid box is checked.

Click on OK	Closes the Grid and Scale dialog box and returns you to the Drawing window
Choose the Zoom tool, click on the Zoom In+ tool, and click and drag a fairly tight area over the lower left corner of the Printable page outline	Displays a close-up of the area where you'll reset the zero origin and establish guidelines for creating fonts
Click and drag horizontal and vertical guidelines out from the rulers, to 30 points on both sides	Sets the location where the zero origin will begin relative to the template
Click and drag the zero origin (the little square that intersects the rulers) so that it's located exactly on the intersection of these two guidelines	Sets the new zero origin; your screen should look like figure 24.3 (except, of course, without the note and the "motion lines")

Ctrl+Y enables Snap to Grid mode. It makes it easier to bring the origin over the intersection of the guidelines. Press Crtl + Y to toggle this function off when you're done repositioning the zero origin.

Click on the Zoom tool, and select the Zoom to Page tool (the far right button on the fly-out menu)

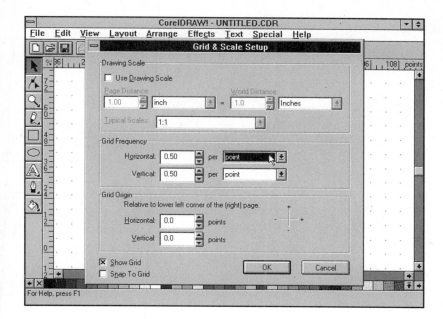

Figure 24.2
Use the Grid
and Scale Setup
command to
display different
ruler increments.

The Grid and Scale Setup dialog box is also useful on occasions when you have to design something far larger than a Printable page (maximum dimensions 30" by 30"). If you have a floor plan layout or something that you need to design to scale, in the Grid and Scale Setup dialog box, set the World Distance in the Drawing Scale area to the increments you are comfortable working with, and leave the Page distance at 1 inch, for example.

Corel's Rulers, Contour, and Transform Roll-Ups will then show you these translated measurements in place of the real distances on your page.

The Architecture of a Font

As mentioned earlier, each character in a typeface is surrounded by a white space, the area that separates one character from another. This means that the height of a 720-point capital letter doesn't occupy all 720 points of the *point size*. There's a difference between the height of a capital font letter, or cap height, and point size. The difference between the *cap height* and the *point size* is used by *descenders,* the bottoms of letters, such as "g" and "y," that descend below a font's baseline to a point above the following line of type.

IV

Advanced Topics

You'll add guidelines to the typeface master template next to help you consistently define where each character sits within the 720 point square design area. The easiest way to "spec" these characteristics is to get them from a few characters in a typeface that already exists.

Figure 24.3
The new origin point is now set on the intersecting guidelines.

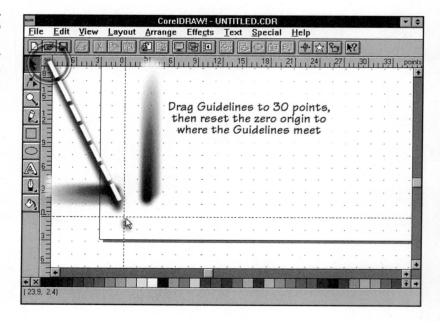

Drag Guidelines to 30 points, then reset the zero origin to where the Guidelines meet

Here's how to add to your type foundry glossary and make a font with precision:

Using a Reference Guide for Creating a Font

Choose the Text tool, and then click an insertion point with the cursor anywhere on the Printable page

By default, you'll be typing in Artistic Text

*Type **N**, and then press Ctrl+spacebar*	Toggles to the Pick tool with the "N" selected
Press Ctrl+T	Displays the Character Attributes options menu

"N" is the character you'll use to measure cap height for your font.

Choose Arial *in the* **F**onts drop-down box *and set the point* Si**z**e *to 720, and then click on* OK	Returns you to the font template with an uppercase "N" as your guide for the cap height within your template

If you can't find Arial, there's something wrong with your Windows configuration, because this TrueType font automatically installs when you install Microsoft Windows 3.1.

Whether it was an MIS Director's wish or your own deletion of Arial, you can substitute Avant Garde BT, Swis721 BT (normal), or any other fairly unexotic-looking font for this part of the exercise.

Click and drag the capital "N" so that its outline touches the left and bottom guidelines

This may take more than one move; the selection box around fonts does not exactly describe the letter's boundaries, but instead may fall outside of the character. Use the arrow keys to nudge the "N" into position, if necessary.

With the "N" selected, press the spacebar to go back to the Text tool. Type lowercase **a**, *and* **g**	This gives you the raw material for establishing an x-height and a descender for any font you might create in the future
Click and drag guidelines to the top of the "N," the top of the "a," and to the bottom of the "g"	Respectively, these are a font's Cap Height, X-Height, and Descender line, as illustrated in figure 24.4
Click and drag a vertical guideline to the right of the "N," to about 48 points on the horizontal ruler	This is a guide for the width of a typical character, although you'll want to use your own artistic judgement when creating a "W" and an "I"

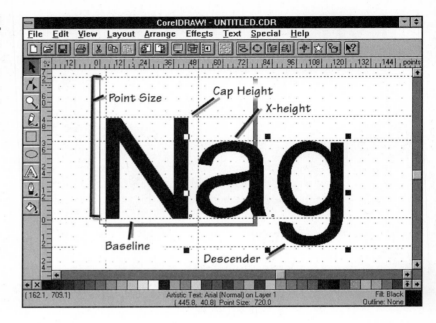

Creating Your Own Font

As you saw in the last steps, a 720-point capital letter only comes up to around 500 points or so. By setting a Guideline at this point, and by keeping all the characters you design sitting on the baseline, the resulting typeface looks aligned when you use it to type sentences and paragraphs.

The typeface you'll begin in this section won't have lowercase letters, but instead you'll reuse the 26 alphabetical letters to create a small-cap lowercase set. This is primarily to conserve space in this chapter; you have a lot of ground to cover.

Describing a Typeface

Generally, there are two kinds of non-decorative/non-symbol typefaces: *display* (or headline) and *body text*. Body text typefaces, such as Garamond, Baskerville, Palatino, and Times Roman, are very hard to imitate because their components are expertly measured and optimized to "read" at small point sizes. For this reason, you'll be creating a display typeface in this chapter where precision is important, but not as critical.

For both kinds of typefaces, there are Roman and Gothic varieties. *Roman* fonts are made of thick and thin strokes. *Gothic* fonts are made with single, even strokes. You'll create a gothic font, because CorelDRAW!'s Contour effect makes even-stroke characters easy to produce.

The doodads you often see at the ends of Roman font strokes are called *serifs*. When a character line ends in a serif, it's a little easier to read because the eye follows the slope. Historically, serifs were also added to fonts so that printing ink would give the character a clean edge where a character ended. Your typeface will be a serif, gothic typeface because the Contour effect "flutes" the end of the paths it creates from your original designs. And frankly, it looks sort of nice on a type-face.

When is a Font a Typeface?

Traditionally, the term "typeface" referred to the design of a family of lettering. This group typically consisted of a Normal, **Bold**, ***Bold-Italic***, and *Italic* member. Type only came in fixed point sizes because each letter was set from individual metal slugs aligned in rows to create words and lines of type. A 12-point metal slug of Times Roman Italic was a *font*, belonging to the Times Roman typeface. A 12-point piece of Times Roman Bold was a different font that also belonged to the Times Roman typeface.

But scaleable, digital typography like Adobe Type 1 and Microsoft/Apple TrueType has no fixed point size, so there are no real "fonts" in your PC. Conversely, some display faces, such as Plaza and Beehive, have no alternate family members (only Normal), so these aren't strictly considered "typefaces."

It's okay, therefore, to refer to a particular set of characters, such as Times Roman, as either a font or a typeface.

The Beginning of Your Alphabet

Let's begin with the letter "A." Now that the guidelines have been set up, you can add pages to your document; the guidelines will be displayed on all subsequent pages.

The primary rule to follow in creating Type 1 and TrueType fonts is that a character must consist of a closed path. It can have several subpaths, however. This is where the Contour Roll-Up, the Weld, and Combine commands make the task a lot simpler.

IV

Advanced Topics

Here's how to create the first character in your hand-crafted font:

Creating a Frame for a Font Character

Press PgDn, and then click on OK	Displays the Insert Pages dialog box and adds one page to the template
Press Ctrl+F3, and then double-click on the Guides title	Displays the Layers Roll-Up and the options menu for the Guides Layer
Check the Locked box, *make sure the* Set Options for All Pages *box is checked, and then click on OK*	Prevents your carefully plotted guidelines from getting bumped as you design
Click on the Layer 1 *title on the* Layers Roll-Up	Moves you to the Layer on which you'll be working
Double-click on a ruler, and set the Grid Frequency *to inches again*	The Contour Roll-Up, which you use throughout this assignment, is hard to use when set to points
Choose the Freehand tool and draw a teepee shape within the guidelines you've set up; it should be made up of three nodes and two line segments; the node where the segments meet should touch the Cap Height Guideline	This is one of the two components used to build the capital letter "A"
Draw a crossbar for the teepee	Completes the wireframe shape of the "A," as shown in figure 24.5

Tip   You might want to unlock the Guidelines Layer from time to time to add more guidelines for the crossbar, the midpoint of the character width, and so on. Consistency between different characters is important for easy readability.

Choose Edit, Select All, *and then choose* Arrange, Combine (Ctrl+L)	Combines the two open paths into one open path; remember the phrase "open path," as it plays a major part in the font creation

Select Effects, Contour Roll-Up
(*or press* Ctrl+F9)

The Contour effect
"thickens" the wireframe
of the "A," creating a
closed path around it

With the "A" wireframe selected,
set the Contour Roll-Up Offset *to*
.5 inches, Steps to **1**, *and then*
press Apply

The Contour effect has
created a nice, even path
around the "A," as shown
in figure 24.6

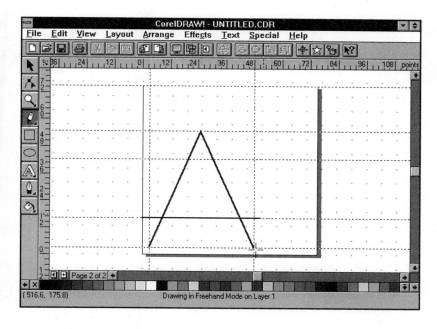

Figure 24.5
Create a
skeleton shape
of your custom
font first.

Tip

Contours are dynamically linked to the shape you've created them
from. You can use the Shape tool to click and drag on a node of your
wireframe "A" letter to change the Contour outline, if you think it needs
tweaking.

Finalizing a Font Outline

The Contour effect is a very useful tool for creating a closed path around an open
one, giving the capital "A" a nice even stroke almost automatically.

IV

Advanced Topics

Figure 24.6
The Contour effect cannot be created inside of an open path; the effect must be created to the outside of the "A".

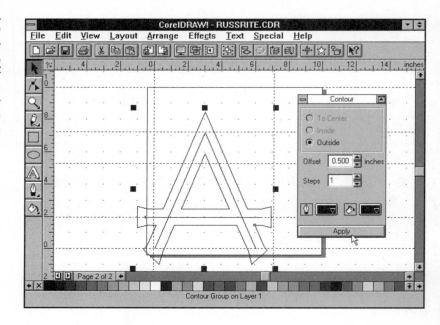

Because the Contour effect surrounds the original wireframe, the cap "A" now exceeds the Cap Height you defined. This will be corrected, and a little refining will be performed on the letterform in the next exercise. Before you can edit the Contour outline, it must be separated from the wireframe "A." Contours are dynamically linked to their Control Objects, and you cannot directly edit them as such.

Here's how to break the link between the effect shape and the Control Object:

Making the Contour Editable

Click on the Contour that surrounds the teepee shape, and then choose **A**rrange, **S**eparate

The bond between the wireframe you drew and its corresponding Contour is gone, and you can't indirectly change the Contour by altering the wireframe anymore

Click on an empty area of the Printable page, and then click on the Contour again

Separated Contours are grouped objects of one, and you need to select only the separated Contour group now

Click on the Group/Ungroup button on the Ribbon Bar	Ungroups the group of one Contour; it is now editable

As you can see in figure 24.7, after you separate and ungroup the contour paths, you are free to delete the wireframe you drew by selecting it and pressing Del (you no longer need it).

With the Contour outline selected, left mouse click over the black swatch on the color palette, and then right mouse click over the "x"	Gives the "A" a black fill and removes the outline; contour shapes based on open paths aren't filled, and filling them now makes them easier to edit in the future

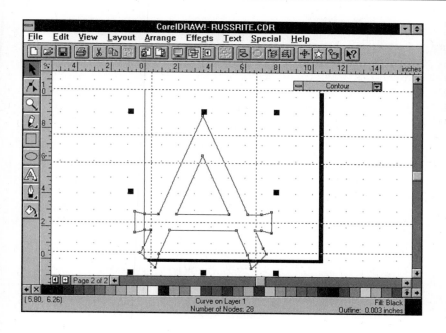

Figure 24.7
Separate and ungroup the Contour shapes, then delete the original wireframes.

Tip Neither Adobe Type Manager nor Microsoft Windows acknowledges the use of a fill or an outline attribute within font information. When you get to the section where you export individual characters, you'll see that the preview window only shows you a black filled shape of the paths you've created.

Thus, you can color a font purple, and give it a three-yard wide outline. Although this might be amusing, the information is discarded when the font is exported.

Now is a good time to save your work. From the File menu, click on Save (or simply press Ctrl+S). This display face will take on a look used earlier in this century for advertisements; I'm calling my font RUSSRITE.CDR after Russel Wright, the famous ceramics designer whose Atomic Age dinnerware has similar lines and flow.

Refining Your Character

Your new letter "A" is a bonafide character now, and you should do a little tweaking and resizing to get it ready for exporting.

It is vital that the characters be positioned right next to the vertical and horizontal guidelines you set at zero earlier, and that you maintain a consistent cap height throughout your alphabet. You can let the descenders in the letters "Q" and "J" go beneath the baseline, as you normally see with commercial fonts, and it's okay to let a serif stick out a little to the left of the vertical guideline. The guidelines are for consistency throughout the lettering, and also for the positioning CorelDRAW! uses for font data when it exports your letters. The "white" around a character is data, too.

Here's how to get the letter "A" to sit within the cap height and the baseline:

Refining a Font Outline

Click on the Shape tool, marquee-select the nodes at the bottom of your "A" beneath the baseline, and then drag them up so they meet the baseline (see fig. 24.8)	Places the letterform above the baseline, insuring your set of characters lines up properly when a text string is typed using your font
Repeat the preceding step to the nodes descending below the baseline on the other side of the "A"	Makes the "A" less lopsided
Choose the Pick tool	
Click the upper right corner selection handle and drag it in to meet the cap height guideline	Resizes the letter

Click and drag inside the letter shape Repositions the letter,
if necessary

Press PgDn to open a fresh page three. In the next section, you learn about some problems and solutions that concern letters with a curved outline.

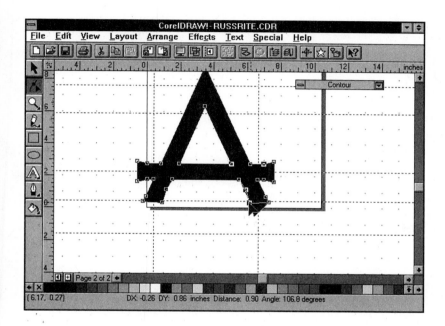

Figure 24.8
Unless you're going for an effect, the bottoms of letterforms should meet the baseline you've set.

Using Open Paths To Create Your Alphabet

You've learned one technique for creating a character using only straight lines. Unless you want a typeface (or font) to look like a wood carving, you need to address how curved lettering can be built. Using the Contour effect offers an advantage: if you set the Contour to the same value each time you apply the effect, each character in the alphabet will have a consistently sized stroke.

The reason why you want to work with open paths when creating a typeface is because the Contour effect treats closed paths differently than open ones. An open path forces the Contour to draw a closed shape all the away around the path's periphery, whereas a closed path only produces a Contour around the outside of it. This spells the difference between typeface characters approximately 1" in stroke width and .5".

IV

Advanced Topics

In the next exercise, you create the second letter of this font. Here are the first steps in creating a master character that contains curves:

Adding a Second Letter to The Font

*Use the Freehand tool to create a
figure similar to that shown
in figure 24.9. Start with straight
segments, and do not close the shape*

Select the Shape tool

Double-click on a node to display the Node Edit Roll-Up, *and then convert as many segments to curves as you like, and fuss with the shape until it becomes an eye-catching capital "B"*	Creates the wireframe for the second letter in your typeface

 If you've accidentally closed the shape, use the Break Apart button on the Node edit Roll-Up to open the path. The path does not need to be individual line segments like the **A**rrange, Brea**k** Apart command performs; paths simply need to be open, not closed.

On the Contour Roll-Up, click on the Apply button	A Contour surrounds the wireframe letter

Sometimes when a node with Cusp properties connects two segments at a severe angle, you get a "spike" sticking through another part of the Contour. To correct this problem, click and drag to reposition the node using the Shape tool, as shown in figure 24.10.

Eliminating Unnecessary Nodes

There is a disadvantage to applying a Contour to a curved line segment that you won't see until you separate and ungroup the Contour. The Contour effect places oodles of nodes along the path of a curve, far more than are necessary to describe the arc. If a closed path has too many nodes, the geometry is too complex to be exported as a typeface character.

In the following exercise, you learn how to separate the wireframe from the new Contour letterform, and get rid of superfluous nodes on its periphery:

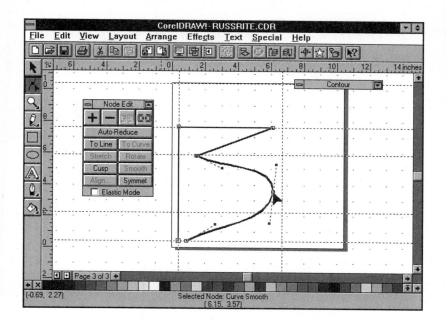

Figure 24.9
An open path still creates a Contour consisting of closed subpaths.

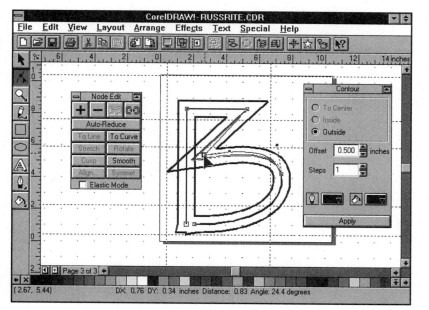

Figure 24.10
A Contour linked to its originating shape can be modified by changing the location of the nodes.

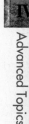

IV

Advanced Topics

Finishing the Second Font Character

When you're happy with the shape of your letter, select the Contour with the Pick tool, choose **A***rrange,* **S***eparate, and then ungroup the "B" the same way as you did to the "A"*	This makes the uppercase letter "B" editable; you can delete the wireframe now
Choose the Shape tool, and select the Contour letter	You'll see about a billion nodes defining the curved bottom
Marquee-select all of the nodes in the letter, and then press the Auto-Reduce button on the Node Edit Roll-Up, as seen in figure 24.11	CorelDRAW! reduces the number of nodes that support the shape of the arc (about 1 every 120° except for abrupt changes in the path)
If the Auto-Reduce feature doesn't reduce this shape back to a total of 30 or 40 nodes, click on a few nodes with the Shape tool, and then press Del	Manually deletes the superfluous nodes

If the curve changes radically, press Ctrl+Z to Undo, and select a different node that seems less vital to the outline of the letterform.

Resize and reposition the letter so that it meets the Baseline, Cap Height, and far left guidelines. Delete the wireframe "B" inside the Contour With the Contour selected, right mouse click on the "X" on the color palette, and then left mouse click over the black swatch.

Press Ctrl+S	Saves your work

An "Outline" for the Rest of the Alphabet

You now know how to create subpaths using an open path, and how to refine the Contour you apply around a letterform. There is not really much left to review in terms of creating these letters. You'll want to use the **C**ombine command, and not Weld, if you want to create two shapes (but one path) that don't overlap within the typeface character.

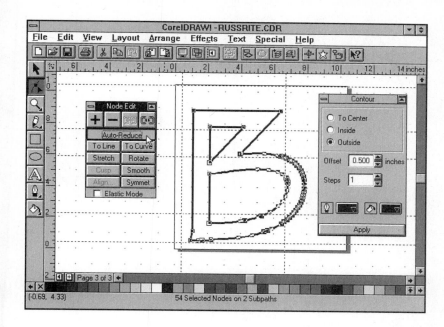

Figure 24.11
Auto-Reduce reduces the manual labor of editing out superfluous nodes along a path.

In figure 24.12, you have the complete wireframe guide for *RusselWrite*. It would be well worth your time to complete this alphabet before moving to the section on exporting, simply because it's fun to be able to use your custom-crafted font.

Even if you don't pursue creating RusselWrite (normal), you should try creating a collection of letterforms or shapes. There is a mock assignment at the end of this chapter that shows you how to manipulate your font in CorelDRAW!.

If you're simply browsing this section, RUSSRITE.TTF, the finished version, can be found on the *Inside CorelDRAW!, 5 Fifth Edition CD-ROM* for use in the exercise at the end of the chapter.

The Finer Points of Typography

Before learning about exporting fonts, take a small step back from this grand campaign to get a little perspective on how a font pulls together visually. Notice in figure 24.12 that the crossbars of characters like "H," "F," and "G" have the same relative heights. This improves readability. A good way to test how well your font works is to copy various letters to make a short sentence, reduce them all to the same height (14–18 points for a display font is good), and print a copy.

Figure 24.12
Draw these
paths, and then
apply Contours
to them to create
the letterforms
and punctuation
you'll need later.

There is no hard and fast rule for character widths, except those that common
sense dictates. An "M" should usually be wider than an "I," for example. You might
want to use a guideline from an established font that you like. Click and drag a
guideline at the width of the "M" from Arial, drop it on your design space, and
work with your own "M" (and other letters).

Numbers, punctuation marks, and extended characters (such as cent signs and trademark symbols) are also necessary letterforms to include in a font export. You can always go back to any typeface, original or not, and add a character. It's a real drag, however, to get cooking with your own font and be short the punctuation you need.

Extended characters are so named because they fall outside the range of a conventional typewriter keyboard. Because a 101 keyboard is not a typewriter, and because 8-bit code creates 256 registers for characters in a font, designers have added foreign characters, ligature characters (such as a custom "ff" and "oe"), and bullets to font creations. You learn how to assign one of your letterforms an extended character, and how to use one later in this chapter.

In the next exercise, you learn how to create an accented "E" to be included in your font set. Extended characters are very useful sometimes, particularly if the business you work for has an overseas office.

Here's how to re-use the letterform "E", and borrow a standard typeface character to align the relative position of the accent mark.

Creating An Extended Character

Click on the page control on the bottom left of the Drawing Window	Displays the Go To Page dialog box
Type 1, *and then click on OK*	Sends you to page one of the document
With the Pick tool, click on the Arial capital "N" you left here earlier, and then press Ctrl+C (**E**dit, **C**opy, *or use the Copy button on the Ribbon Bar*)	Copies the "N" to the Clipboard
Press Ctrl *and click on the right arrow on the Page Controls*	Takes you to the last page in the document
Press PgDn, *and then click on OK*	Adds a new page
Press Ctrl+V (**E**dit, **P**aste, *or use the* Paste button *on the Ribbon Bar*)	Pastes the letter "N" the same relative position as where you copied it
Click the left arrow *on the page controls*	Moves you to the page with your "E" letterform on it

continues

continued

Right-mouse clicking forward or backward page control keys moves you by five pages at a time.

Select the "E", and then left-click and drag it off the Printable page; don't release the mouse button yet	Moves the "E" onto the Desktop layer of the document, a layer all pages have in common
Right-mouse click, and then release both buttons	Places a duplicate of the "E" on the Desktop layer
Ctrl+click the right arrow page control key	Sends you to the last page of the document. The duplicate "E" is visible to the side of the Printable page
Align the "E" to the baseline on your new page	This gets the "E" in the same relative position as the "N"
Click on the "N", *and then choose the Text tool*	An insertion point appears behind the "N"
Press backspace, hold the Alt *key while typing* **0201** *on the keypad (not the row of numbers), and then release the* Alt *key*	The acute "E" extended character displays for the Arial font
With the Freehand tool, draw a line similar in angle and size to the accent mark above the Arial "E"	This is the wireframe for the accent for your own character
Use the Contour Roll-Up to apply an outline around your accent mark wireframe, separate the wireframe from the contour, ungroup it, and then position the mark above your "E"	You are creating your own extended character
Select the "E" and the accent mark, and then choose **A**rrange, **C**ombine *(Ctrl+L)*	You get a character that looks very similar to that shown on the left side in figure 24.13. You can delete the accented Arial character anytime

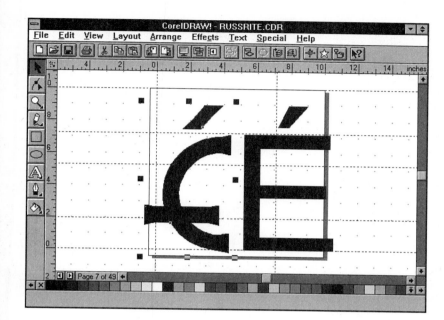

Figure 24.13
A valid character for export must be one closed path (a combination of subpaths is okay too).

Creating a "Blank" Character

Before exporting a character, here's an exercise that's also a really excellent TIP that my editors wouldn't let me put in a box off to the side...

If you don't fill all 256 registers of a typeface when you export, CorelDRAW! assigns the first character you export to all the blank registers. Which means with RusselWrite here (which has less than 75 characters), theoretically, every time a user of this font types an asterisk, for example, he produces an "A." Which is a pain in the word processor, you know?

In the next exercise, you create a bullet that fills all the vacant registers in a font you export.

Here's how to commence the font export with a bullet:

Exporting a Font/Filling the Registers

Using the page controls, go to the page before the letterform "A." It should be page 2, but perhaps you've arranged your document differently.

When you're at the page with the   The Insert Page dialog
"A" on it, press PgDn   box appears

continues

continued

Click on the **B***efore radio button, and then click on OK*	This adds a page between the Arial Nag page and the capital letter "A" you'll export
With the Ellipse tool, Ctrl+click+diagonal drag a circle about 2" in diameter	This is the bullet you'll use to fill the blank registers in the RusselWrite font
Press Ctrl+spacebar, and then reposition the bullet so that it is aligned between the Cap Height guideline *and the baseline, and flush against the left margin*	This makes the bullet "float" in a text string you type with your new font, as shown in figure 24.14

Again, it is not necessary to fill the shape to be exported as a font, but it improves visibility as you work.

Figure 24.14
Create a shape that fills character registers for which you have no character designed.

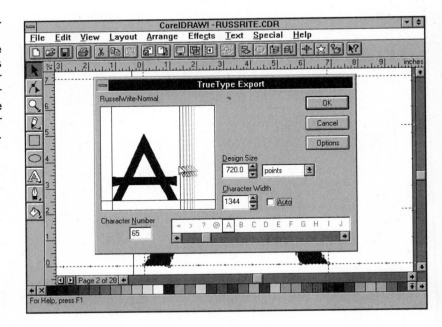

Exporting the Font

Here's the exciting part: after you have all your characters neatly guidelined on their own pages, CorelDRAW! does the rest for you.

You have some options when you export your typeface design, the first of which is what format you want your typeface to be read as. Even though there weren't a lot of positive things to say about the TrueType format in the last chapter, in this section you learn how to export your font as a TrueType font for a not-so-obvious reason.

Original fonts have commercial possibilities. CompuServe and local bulletin boards are chock full of fonts, and most of them seem to be:

1. Created by David Radowski, and

2. In the TTF TrueType format.

If you ever meet Mr. Radowski (I believe that he frequents Columbia University School of Music in Manhattan), I'll let him explain why he's possibly the most prolific designer of shareware fonts, but the reason for the TrueType format is a very simple one: your customer doesn't need Adobe type Manager. TrueType has native support in Windows, pure and simple. People who might buy your fonts don't need to buy anything else if they only own Windows 3.1*x*.

The export procedure is almost identical for either the Type 1 or TrueType format.

Here's how you export RusselWrite (Normal) as a TrueType font:

Making a TrueType Font

Select the bullet with the Pick tool.

It's critical that nothing except the bullet is selected. If you still have a wireframe or anything else on this page, make certain you don't accidentally select anything except the bullet.

Choose File, Export, *(or click on the Export button on the Ribbon Bar) and scroll in the* List Files of Type *drop-down list box until you find* TrueType Font (*.TTF), *and then click on it*

Selects the format for the font you are going to export

Name the TTF font file in the File Name *field, and check the* Selected Only *check box*

IV

Advanced Topics

continues

continued

You can easily identify your font creations and uninstall them if you have a special subdirectory containing the originals with original file names, as seen in figure 24.15.

Click on OK	You are transported to the Options dialog box
Type up to 34 characters for a typeface name (both upper- and lowercase letters work)	
Type **750** *in the* Space Width *field*	This is the spacing between words when you type with the typeface. It's an arbitrary value, and for fonts with narrow widths, 500 is a frequently used value

Tip

By default, Corel assigns an equal value of 2,048 to both **G**rid Size and Space Width, which can often yield wider inter-word spacing than you'd like. The Grid and Space are not point sizes; they are mathematical values that take into account some automatic proportioning.

You also have the opportunity to reset the Space Width field, after you define the first character in a font, by clicking the Options box after you've exported your first character.

Check the Symbol Font *box*	This will be covered a little later
Click on OK, and then click on **Y**es *in the TrueType Export dialog box*	This confirms saves to the RUSSRITE.TTF file

Exporting, Part II

In the TrueType Export dialog box, there's a scrolling window of available characters to which you assign your bullet character, with the corresponding code or Character **N**umber to the left of it. These are the Windows ANSI code numbers that correspond to a character in a font.

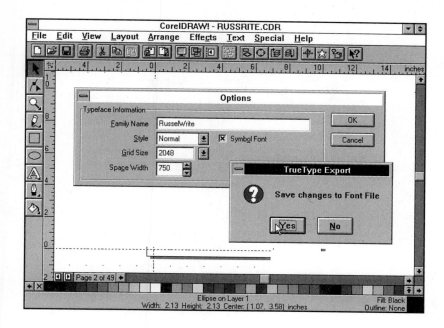

Figure 24.15
You name the TTF
file for your font
before exporting.

You need a place to put the bullet where it won't be overwritten when an actual character needs to occupy a register.

In the next exercise, you see where a character's white space is located within the font format, and which character is a good one to fill with the bullet.

Here's how to continue exporting the RusselWrite font:

Assigning a Character an ANSI Code

Type **255** *in the Character Number field, as shown in figure 24.16*

This takes you to the position of the character in the scrolling preview window. It's a lowercase "y" with an umlaut over it (which won't be used for this display face). All the letters are dimmed, because you haven't made an entry yet.

Click on OK

Figure 24.16
Set word spacing options and your font's name in the Options box.

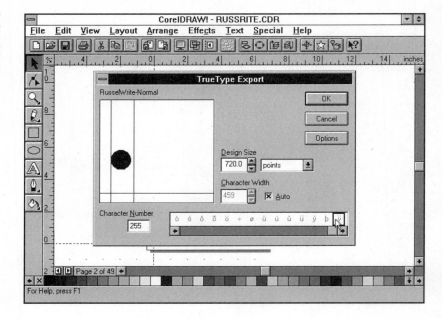

At this point, every character in RusselWrite is now a bullet. Let's change this now.

Press PgDn, *select the "A" with the Pick tool, and then press the* Export button *on the Ribbon Bar*	Selects the uppercase "A" for export
Click on RUSSRITE.TTF *in the* File Names box of the TrueType Export *options box, and then click on OK*	Selects the font you've created. You can now add a character to it
Scroll in the preview window until you see the capital "A" (character number 65); click on it	Assigns the letterform you've selected to RusselWrite's character number

 CorelDRAW! automatically advances the default character number. You must pay attention to which number you're assigning letterforms to, or you'll wind up typing **ZdGHmM#*?"I** in the future with your font.

If you like, uncheck the Auto *box, and click and drag on the right line near the "A"*	This is how you can manually fine-tune Character Width

Adjusting it, as shown
in figure 24.17, can
improve kerning when
you use the typeface

Tip

Character Width has nothing to do with the design of your character;
you do not squash it if you move the width line closer to the character.
Character Width is actually the "air" to the right of your design that
precedes the next letter in a word.

Click on OK

You have your first
genuine character
exported for RusselWrite

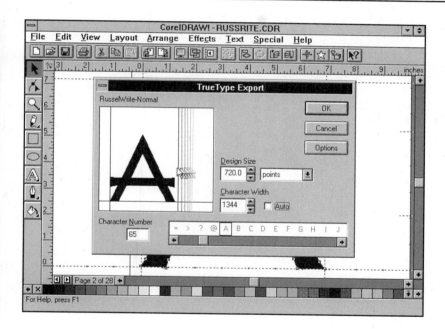

Figure 24.17
Set the character
width and the key
to which you
want to assign
your letter in the
TrueType Export
dialog box.

Stop

If you've deselected the Auto Character Width to more tightly kern a
character, be sure to check the Auto box for the next export. If you
don't, you wind up with more space after a character than you need.

You need to repeat the preceding steps for each character. Press PgDn to advance to the letter "B," select it with the Pick tool, click on the Export button, and then click on RUSSRITE.TTF in the File Name box.

When you hit a descending character, "J" or "Q," for example, notice that the preview window clips off the descender part of the character, as shown in figure 24.18.

All is well; do not panic. Descenders are supposed to go below the font's baseline, and although the preview window shows you only part of the character, the entire character will export, display, and print correctly.

Figure 24.18
Characters with descenders might appear to be clipped, but they export for use just fine.

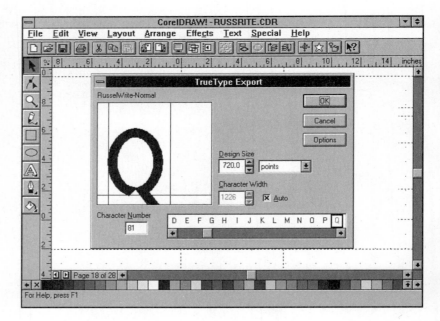

Tackling the Lowercase Letters

Lowercase letters are important to a typeface, even if they're a rehash of the uppercase designs. You can get away with this when designing a display font, because they are generally considered one-of-a-kind "designatures," and exhibit more character than consistency. Unless you type all day with the Caps Lock key engaged, the RusselWrite font will be a frustrating typing adventure without lowercase letters.

Here's how to add lowercase letters, made from the same letterforms you've already created:

Creating a Lowercase Alphabet

Press the page control to get the
Go To box, and type the number of
the page where "A" is

You'll start at the top
of the alphabet again to
export "small caps" for
RusselWrite

Select the "A," choose File, Export,
and then double click on RUSSRITE.TTF

This is the first
character for export as
lowercase

Scroll over to character 97, the
lowercase "a," and set the Design
Size to 1,000 points

This is roughly 3/4 of
the capital height in
this font, a good height
for "small caps" (see
fig. 24.19)

Click on OK

The "A" is exported to
the lowercase font
register

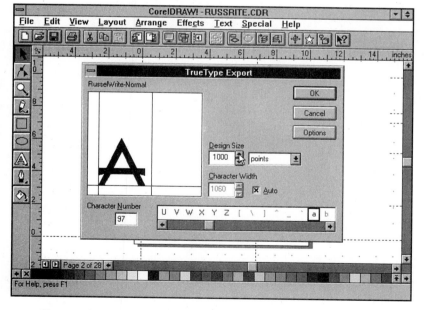

Figure 24.19
Small caps
generally work
well at about
3/4 the size of
regular
uppercase
characters.

Repeat the same steps you performed for exporting the capital letters. When
you're done, export the "odds and ends" characters using the same steps, except
set the character size back to 720. In figure 24.20, you can see the accented "E"

character as character number 201. Use the preview window as a visual guide for exporting extended characters; match the preview selection up with the character in the window at the left.

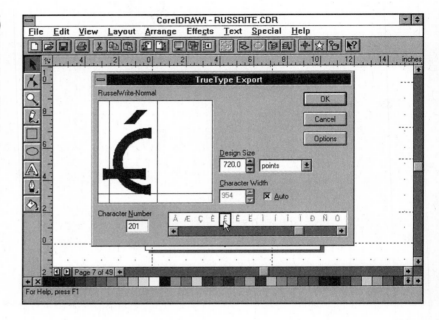

Figure 24.20
The extended character codes enable users to access foreign language characters and symbols within a font.

When you're finished, exit CorelDRAW!. In the following section, you install a hand-crafted TrueType font.

Installing Your Custom Font

CorelDRAW! does not automatically install a typeface you've created, so here's the brief installation procedure:

1. In Windows Program Manager (or another Windows shell like Norton Desktop for Windows), double-click on the Control Panel icon.

2. Double-click on the Fonts icon within the Control Panel group, and click on the Add button.

3. In the Drives and Directories windows, select the location you exported RusselWrite to. In figure 24.21, you saw a MY_STUFF subdirectory set up on drive D for the TrueType creations.

4. Click on RusselWrite in the List of **F**onts window, and then click on OK.

CHARMAP.EXE is a utility shipped with Windows that helps you find a regular, or extended character. As the proud parent of a new font, opening and selecting RusselWrite from Character Map can be a very gratifying experience. Even if you don't feel like a proud parent now, check out figure 24.21 anyhow.

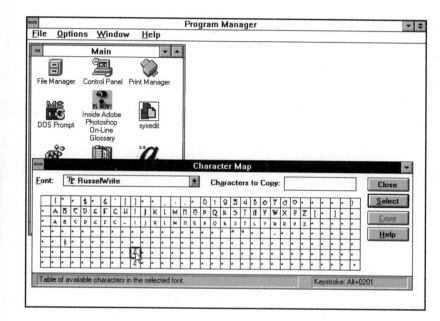

Figure 24.21
CHARMAP.EXE can display TrueType and Type 1 character assignments in a font.

Putting Your Font To Work

What good is a custom font if you don't use it? You might have asked yourself this question throughout this chapter, and here's the acid test: can you, the CorelDRAW! designer, work with a font you made yourself?

Read on, and see some of the wonderful possibilities that are in store for you and your font creations in CorelDRAW!.

In the next exercise, you use a template that was made for a place setting to be featured at every overcrowded, undersized table at the Cafe Brusque, a mock-European spot that brushes customers away with its waiters' attitude and pricing structure. RusselWrite can be used for many different assignments, but this one works particularly well, because it's a display face with a hint of art deco.

IV

Advanced Topics

Here's how to add a classy heading to the place setting of Cafe Brusque:

Adding Custom Text to a Design

If you don't have a custom font yet, load RusselWrite using the Windows Font utility before beginning. It's RUSSRITE.TTF, and it's in the CHAP24 subdirectory of the *Inside CorelDRAW! 5, Fifth Edition CD-ROM.*

Open CorelDRAW!, and then open BRUSQUE.CDR *from the CHAP24 subdirectory on the* Inside CorelDRAW! 5, Fifth Edition CD	This is the file you add text to; Layer 1 (containing the design) is locked, so by default, you work on Layer 2
Double-click on the Artistic Text tool, *make an insertion point above the coffee pot in the design, type* **CAF** *(hold* Alt+press 0201 *on the keypad), press* Enter, *and then type* **BRUSQUE**, *as shown in figure 24.22*	

You'll use the Text Roll-Up in a moment, so you can sort of multitask by double-clicking on the Text tool as you begin entering Artistic Text. This brings up the Text Roll-Up.

With the Text tool's I-Beam cursor, highlight what you've typed, and then click on the down-arrow key on the fonts window of the Text Roll-Up	Displays a drop-down list of available fonts, both TrueType and Type 1
Choose RusselWrite, *as shown in figure 24.23, click on the Center align button, and then click on* Apply	Displays a preview fly-out menu of the font chosen

Fine-Tuning a Custom Font

Although you have Café Brusque in the RusselWrite face within the design at the moment, notice that the letter and line spacing isn't perfect. This is because CorelDRAW! doesn't offer kerning pair or other adjustment when you export a font. The solution is to use the Pick and Shape tools to refine the short string of text.

Figure 24.22
Use the Alt key and the zero+3-character code to access the accented "E" (an extended character).

Figure 24.23
You can make almost any adjustment to text with the Text Roll-Up; no menuing necessary.

IV

Advanced Topics

Most serious designers like to manually kern headline text. Here's how to manually adjust Artistic Text:

Fitting the Text into the Design

Choose the Pick tool, select the Artistic Text, and then click+drag the bottom right corner selection handle in a four o'clock direction

This scales the text so that it fits better within the design space

Choose the Shape tool, *and click+drag up on the text arrow handle to the bottom left of the Artistic Text. Stop when the two text lines appear to have tighter leading, as shown in figure 24.24*

This adjusts Inter-Line spacing, which most commercial fonts actually require

Note

You also can press Ctrl and use the Shape tool on the left text arrow handle to adjust inter-paragraph spacing.

When the Shape tool is applied to the right text handle, it's a whole 'nother ball game. Click+dragging on the right handle increases/decreases character spacing, and Ctrl+click+dragging affects inter-word spacing.

Notice the "F" and the "É" have poor spacing between them. To fix this...

Click on the node that precedes the letter "É"

Selects only the "É"

Press Ctrl+drag to the left, as shown in figure 24.25

Moves the character closer to the "F"

The Ctrl key constrains movement of the character to a straight line, so your line should be perfect now.

Figure 24.24
Use the Shape tool to adjust Inter-Line spacing.

Figure 24.25
Hand-kern characters by click+dragging on a text node with the Shape tool.

IV

Advanced Topics

Copying a Text Style

The owner of Café Brusque would like to believe his beverages are priceless, but not literally. The price list on this table setting is blank, but not for long.

Here's how to use Artistic Text and the handcrafted font to display small caps within the font (without having to use the Text Roll-Up):

Using Small Caps for An "Effect"

Choose the Artistic Text tool, and on a vacant area of the Printable page, type **Small $4.95** *using both upper- and lowercase letters, and then press Enter;* on *the second line, type* **Medium $6.95**, *and then press Enter;* on *the third line type* **Large $11.95**	This is the text to be added to the table setting design
Press Ctrl+spacebar	Toggles you to the Pick tool and selects the text
Choose <u>E</u>dit, Copy Attributes <u>f</u>rom	A dialog box appears, asking you what attributes you want copied to the selected text
Click on the <u>T</u>ext Attributes check box, *and then click on OK*	Your cursor becomes a huge arrow
Click on some text to "adopt" its size, alignment, and choice of font.	
Click on the CAFÉ BRUSQUE text, as shown in figure 24.26	The prices you typed become set in RusselWrite, centered, and a little too large for the space in the design

Click+drag on a corner selection handle, toward the center of the Artistic Text selection.	Scales the text down so that it fits in the design area.

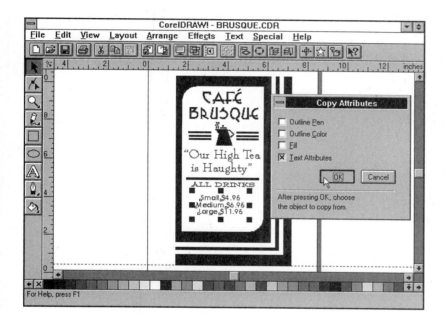

Figure 24.26
The Copy Attributes command can be used with text or graphical properties, or a combination of both.

Figure 24.27 shows the finished design. RusselWrite serves the design well.

Symbol Font Attributes

If you've bought Pi fonts (symbol sets) from Bitstream or other manufacturers in the past, you might have been a little startled when you rolled down the Symbols Roll-Up in CorelDRAW! 5. Regardless of whether Corel installed it or not, any font containing a Symbol or Decorative attribute is read by Corel upon startup and appears on the Symbols Roll-Up.

In figure 24.28, you can see that RusselWrite is displayed on the Symbols Roll-Up as a category. Certainly, you can use <u>S</u>pecial, Create <u>S</u>ymbol to add symbols to a

IV

Advanced Topics

category, but this is a very special quality about the Roll-Up and CorelDRAW!, because any font you create with this program can then be used as a makeshift drop cap in your page layout work.

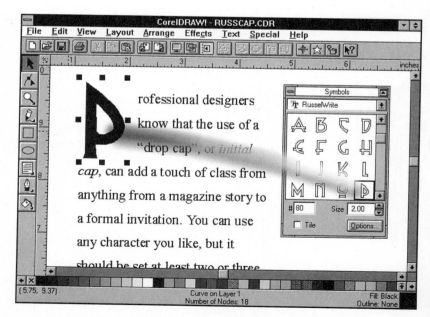

It's strange to think that for a chapter on fonts, we've now run out of words! In a nutshell, if you use the steps shown in this chapter to create your own typefaces, you'll enhance your worth to the business community as a designer. If you own a scanner and learn the ins and outs of CorelTRACE!, it won't be very long before you perfect a technique for creating a "signature" font— a typeface made from your own handwriting (or someone else's, but let's keep it legal here!).

CorelDRAW! brings the artist in everyone a little closer to the surface, because whether you're a wordsmith, or a dyed-in-the-wool graphics-type, the two worlds of self expression unite in a workspace that treats digital objects all the same way.

Chapter Snapshot

The professional illustrations you create mean nothing if you cannot output them. Output problems can cause you serious problems. This chapter provides the answers to most of the printing problems that can crop up. In this chapter, you learn:

✔ To construct your files so that they don't overload your printer

✔ The main causes of printing failure

✔ To test printer integrity

✔ To print to imagesetters

✔ To prepare a PRN file

✔ Print in color

✔ Work with spot and process color

✔ Troubleshooting tips

Knowing how to get printing results is what separates the amateur from the professional. This chapter arms you with the tools you need to print high-quality finished work.

25 CHAPTER

Advanced Printing Techniques

By now, you have a good idea how CorelDRAW! tools work and have seen the type and drawing power you have at your fingertips. CorelDRAW! is no slouch when it comes to flexibility and versatility—you can create just about anything you need.

It is great to create masterpieces you can view on your monitor and even proof at your desktop printer, but what happens if your file takes all day to print, or worse, doesn't print at all? What about when it gets to the final targeted printer? What if you run up against problems not mentioned in the CorelDRAW! manual? Where do you look first when trying to solve specific printing problems?

This chapter answers all of these questions—and many you haven't thought of yet—and starts you on your way to hassle-free printing. It helps you discover that there's more to printing than pressing a few buttons and sipping coffee while the machine does all the work.

Street-Proofing Your Files

If you're having problems printing, before you take apart your desktop printer, take a close look at the file you're printing. Some printers cannot digest some of the features offered in CorelDRAW!. The following is a list of file characteristics that, more than likely, choke the printer:

✔ Too many different fonts. CorelDRAW! users often are overwhelmed by the massive number of fonts available with the program, leading them to use as many different type styles as possible. All that font information being sent to the printer's (usually) tiny memory causes an overload.

✔ Too many nodes on one of the objects on your page. As incredible as it might seem, there is a limit to how many nodes can be on a single object. This doesn't have to be a single separate object if you are in the habit of using the Link command. Linking several objects together has its advantages, but when it comes to printing, remember not to link too many objects! CorelDRAW! doesn't tell you whether you have exceeded the limit either.

✔ File size is too large. Too much information can cause the printer to time out.

✔ Blending from a spot color to a process color. Yes, it is possible and does happen. When trying to print a document with this kind of blend on an object, you might get everything except that particular part to print. At least the printer has isolated the problem for you. You are likely using the PANTONE Spot Color palette and blending from one of the PMS colors to one of the process colors. CorelDRAW! enables you to complete this blend, but it never prints.

✔ Printing to your color printer while your file contains fractal fills that have been enlarged by more than 400 percent. Once again, too much information is contained in the bitmap images that make up that fractal fill.

✔ Altering the screen frequency to a higher setting than the default of the printer. The default is usually around 42-line for the average everyday 300 dpi laser printer. Setting this value higher increases the number of bits of information per inch that the printer has to interpret.

✔ Fountain fill exceeds 7.25 inches. This might not cause headaches if your desktop printer is equipped with generous amounts of RAM. When taking your file further down the road to higher resolution imagesetters, however, the PostScript information needed to create a blend might exceed the memory of the RIP and cause it to choke.

✔ Flatness setting is set too low. This is one of those more complex issues where your file contains a curve that is used as a clipping path for a complex fill like a bitmap image or a PostScript fill, or it could be a curved object containing a complex fill. The flatness setting selection button can be found in Print/Options/Options of version 5.

General Printing Tips

The rule to follow when planning your job for successful printing is easy to remember—keep it simple. You can give the same project to three different people and find that they use three completely different strategies to achieve the same result. One prints beautifully, the next takes a long time to print, and the last one doesn't print at all.

Those who take their files to the final stages of printing and have high-resolution film generated should be wary of some important limitations and restrictions. Follow these general rules when creating files to prevent surprises when heading for the imagesetter.

Don't use too many type fonts. For the average newsletter, poster, publication, illustrative diagram, and so on, try to limit your use to a maximum of five different fonts. Your designs print much faster and might even look a bit more coherent.

Don't link multiple objects together unless the total number of linked nodes does not exceed 200. While it's true that CorelDRAW! version 5 enables the user to set the maximum number of nodes in an object, this doesn't necessarily mean the tiny memory on your printer is capable of handling excessive amounts of data. Keep your objects simple.

Avoid creating multiple-color graduated fills. Blending from one color to another isn't taboo of course, but it is possible to create custom blends. These types of fills print fine on the desktop printer, but the amount of information needed to separate this type of blend at high resolution can cause an imagesetter to crash. Try using the Blend option and blending from one colored object to another. It might seem like a lot of work at first, but you might end up doing it anyway when your job doesn't print.

If you intend to image film separations, check your file for use of multiple palettes. The quickest way to do this is to use the tab selection feature. Tab from object to object while watching the upper right-hand corner of your screen for the color specifications display. It might get tricky when you have to start checking the outline color of your objects, but it also can save you money by not requiring you to print costly and unwanted film separations at the service bureau stage of your production.

IV

Advanced Topics

A quick shortcut exists if you are going to print to process color separations only, and you find a lot of spot colors mistakenly used in your file. You can use the Convert Spot Colors to CMYK option in the Separations dialog box. If your file is set to print to process color and just one additional spot color, however, you must use the first method.

Do not attempt to use fractal fills if your document is targeted for a digital imagesetter. Fractal fills, as attractive as they are, contain so much color information that attempts to image these digitally usually fail. This is recommended only when the images are being exported from CorelDRAW! to a dedicated proprietary imaging system (Scitex, for example).

Before you send files to any printer, clean them up. Delete any of the paste-board scraps you might have left over from creating the file. This reduces the file size and reduces the amount of data sent to the printer. When your file is imaged, CorelDRAW! sends information about all pages to the printer—not just the objects within the page parameters. Do not just cover them up with white boxes—delete and simplify.

When importing scanned images into CorelDRAW!, try not to over scan your images. Users often try to scan to the maximum resolution, but in most cases it isn't necessary. Only scan one to two times the line screen (lpi) of your final output. For a final film resolution of 150 lpi, for example, don't scan beyond 300 dpi. Higher resolution scanned images take up more disk space and take much longer to image.

Crop scanned images in an image-editing program. If you do this in CorelDRAW!, it causes time-consuming calculations to be performed even for the part of the image you don't need.

Rotate scanned images in an image-editing program such as CorelPHOTO-PAINT!. Rotating in CorelDRAW! causes unnecessary calculations to be performed at the imaging stage.

Avoid nested EPS files. This is when you import an EPS file into another file, save it, and export it again as an EPS file, and then import *that* file into *your* file.

Avoid nested fonts. Nested fonts refer to a typeface used in an EPS file, which is imported for use into another file. Problems can occur if the file was created on a different computer with a different set of fonts installed. On your computer, the file might print an incorrect font or not print at all.

To print faster and reduce the chances of your file not printing at all, install additional RAM on your desktop printer's memory (provided the printer's memory is expandable—check the operators manual to be sure). Most printers operating at a minimal RAM capacity of 2 MB regularly bite the dust when fed complex documents. Five megabytes is a good RAM size.

Testing Printing Integrity

If your file is complicated, you might consider disguising your desktop printer as a high-resolution imagesetter and printing the file to it. This is much better than finding out at the last possible moment that you might not get the results you expected from the imagesetter at the local service bureau.

Experts recommend a program called LaserCheck from Systems of Merritt, (205)660-1240, which disguises your desktop printer as a digital imagesetter. The program works by residing on your printer's internal memory much the same way as downloaded fonts do. When a file comes through for printing, the program is capable of reducing the image to fit onto a letter-size page, printing crop and registration marks, and listing all fonts used in the file in the margin of the page. This is great for CorelDRAW! users who regularly send out for digital output. LaserCheck is reasonably priced at $150.

Printing to Imagesetters

When you finish all work in your file and clean up the messes made on the paste board, you will likely head to the nearest imagesetter to get the final printout onto high-resolution film. Whether it's paper or film you require, and no matter which resolution you request—1270, 2540, or 3600 dpi—this is the test of whether your file prints.

If your desktop printer hiccuped once or twice during previous printouts, the file took more than an hour to print, mysterious blank pages came out of the printer, or you thought you smelled smoke once or twice, it gets much worse at this stage. If the printer cut through your file like a hot knife through low-cal margarine, you shouldn't have any troubles at all.

At a service bureau, it is highly recommended to print to the imagesetter directly from the original CorelDRAW! source file. This way, you don't have to prepare a large and cumbersome print (PRN) file.

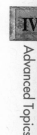

Preparing a Print File

Suppose that you are forced to prepare a print (PRN) file so that you can output your file to film. Don't panic, it's possible (just terribly inconvenient). Historically, Microsoft Windows drivers (previous to version 3.54) have been riddled with errors, and have given PRN file preparation a bad rap. If you have PSCRIPT.DRV version 3.58 or higher, you're safe. Follow these steps to check which driver version you have:

1. In Program Manager, open Control Panel, usually found in the Main group window (see fig. 25.1).

Figure 25.1
Control Panel in the Main group window.

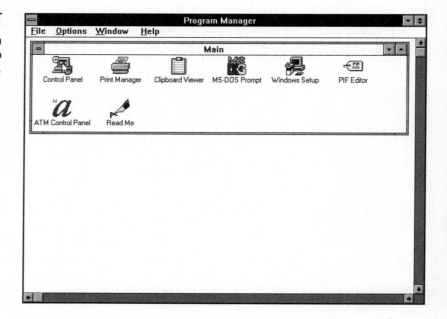

2. Double-click on the Printers icon (see fig. 25.2) to open the Printers dialog box (see fig. 25.3).

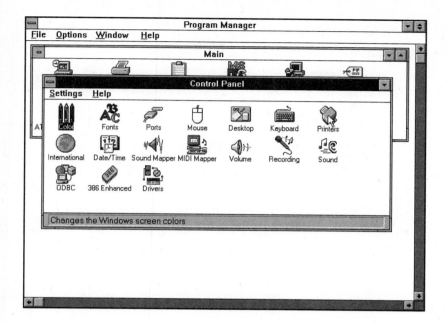

Figure 25.2
The Printers icon in Control Panel.

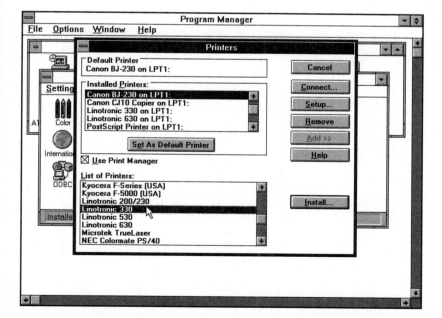

Figure 25.3
The Printers dialog box.

IV

Advanced Topics

3. Click on Setup.

4. Click on About and note the version number (see fig. 25.4).

Figure 25.4
The About
dialog box with
the current
printer driver
information.

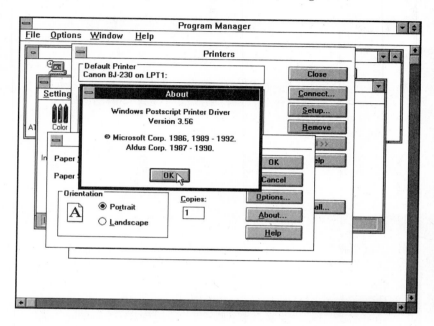

If you don't have a recent version, contact your nearest Microsoft office or your service bureau, or obtain the most recent driver from the Microsoft Windows Forum on CompuServe (if you have access).

The following procedure shows you how to prepare a print (PRN) file. Before printing though, you need to set up the proper System Color Profile. Using Color Manager under the File menu, select the System Profile. If you have not yet set up a corresponding system profile for you monitor, printer, and if necessary, scanner, then do so now. You might only need this particular system profile for making your print files. If this is your first attempt to make a system profile, refer to Chapter 21, "Managing Color and System Calibration."

1. With the file you need to print opened in CorelDRAW!, first choose File, Print. While in this dialog box, select the Pages to print, Printer, Print Quality, and Print to File options. If you know for sure that your print file is being printed from a Macintosh-based service bureau platform, then select the For Mac option also. This leaves out the two control characters (^ ^) that Windows places at the very beginning of the PostScript file that might confuse the printer.

2. Continue to set the rest of your print options as needed. How you do this depends on the particular setup of your file, the type of output you require, and the device you are printing to. If this is your first time preparing a Print File and you are sending your file to a service bureau, it is strongly recommended that you skip ahead to Chapter 27, "Working with Service Bureaus."

3. After this is complete, click on OK in the main Print dialog box. Another Print to File box appears and enables you to name the file and save it to a particular directory on your hard disk.

When creating a print file, don't save it to a floppy disk drive. First, save it to your hard disk. If you need to copy it to a floppy, do that later.

User-Defined Page Sizes

If the page setup you have selected for your file doesn't match any of the standard page sizes supplied with your driver, you might want to select the User Defined page size when choosing the setup of your printer.

The User Defined option is found in the main Print dialog box under the File menu in CorelDRAW! by selecting Setup and at the bottom of the list of paper sizes. Remember, this is not the page setup size of your file. It is the size of the space your printed file must fit into. Therefore, if you need to print any information outside of your page perimeter, such as crop marks, registration marks, or any file information, you need to select at least 0.5 inches extra around the edges of your file image. If you don't select a larger page, this information definitely is not imaged with your file.

Note also that the units of measurement are in 0.01 inch increments. If you want to print a tabloid size file (11 inches by 17 inches) with crop marks, you need to select a page size an extra inch wider and longer than your file size. In the width box, enter the inches in hundredths, in this case 0.12 of an inch. Do the same for the length. Better yet, enter the inch measurement of the paper size you require and add two zeros to it. The resulting page description then corresponds to this measure.

IV

Advanced Topics

Banding

Banding was once a much-talked-about subject around the service bureau, which generated differing opinions on how to eliminate the appearance of stripes in the graduated fills produced by programs such as CorelDRAW!

Banding is the result of mathematical calculations that the imagesetter's RIP performs. When the gradation from one shade or color to another is calculated, the imagesetter renders a series of parallel screen tint stripes at various thicknesses and increments to fake a smooth progression of ink percentages. The width and frequency of these stripes is dependent on the resolution and screen frequency the imagesetter is recording, and the number of gray steps per gradation that the software has instructed the imagesetter's processor to calculate. Studies have shown the human eye is sensitive to banding steps larger than one thirty-second of an inch.

 Although CorelDRAW! enables the user to blend from one spot color to another, avoid doing this. The screen can render this blend, but your printer most likely cannot.

When asked to produce a certain number of gray steps in a fountain fill for a certain resolution and screen frequency, the RIP simply calculates the square of dpi divided by lpi and multiplies that figure by the percentage of gray change in the fountain fill over a given measure. Gray change is the change in the percentage of ink required between one point and another. The calculations are as follows:

$$(\text{dpi}/\text{lpi})^2 \times (\% \text{ gray change}) = \text{Number of stripes}$$

or, the number of stripes is equal to:

$$(\text{Printer resolution divided by screen frequency requested})^2 \times \text{ink percentage change}$$

The banding you see printed from your average desktop laser printer can be fairly harsh. Using this formula, you can calculate the number of stripes this type of laser printer is giving you. Assuming it is a 300 dpi laser printer and that you have asked for a gray change from 0 percent (white or transparent) to 100 percent (black or solid ink), the calculations look like this:

$$(300 \text{ dpi} \times 60 \text{ lpi}) \text{ multiplied by } 100\% \text{ equals } 25 \text{ stripes}$$

Therefore, if you have an object 5 inches long that requires a 0-percent to 100-percent fountain fill from one end to the other, your laser printer renders 5 stripes for every inch of fill for that object (25 stripes divided by 5 inches).

The following table shows how the number of stripes changes as the resolution and screen frequency of the output changes. If you are outputting your files to 1270 dpi, Corel recommends that you set your fountain stripes to 128. For 2400 dpi, set them to 220 fountain stripes. Setting these values lower results in banding, but faster print times. Raising them does not lessen banding, but definitely increases the printing time.

Percentage	dpi:	300	1270	2540	1270	2540	2540	2540
Gray change	lpi:	60	90	120	133	120	133	150
10	2	19	11	9	44	36	28	
20	5	39	22	18	89	72	57	
30	7	59	33	27	134	109	86	
40	10	79	44	36	179	145	114	
50	12	99	56	45	224	182	143	
60	15	119	67	54	256	218	172	
70	17	139	78	63	256	256	256	
80	20	159	89	72	256	256	256	
90	22	179	100	82	256	256	256	
100	25	199	112	91	256	256	256	

Note The maximum number of steps for any object is limited to 256 stripes by the PostScript interpreter.

To avoid banding, it also can be advantageous to lower the screen frequency of your output. What this does is reduce the amount of detail the imagesetter can render. Most of the time, however, the visibility of banding can be significantly reduced by increasing the amount of resolution. Increasing the film resolution of your output from 1270 dpi to 2450 dpi, while maintaining the maximum number of fountain steps and the same screen frequency, should do the trick.

IV
Advanced Topics

To reduce the amount of visible banding, the service bureau output operator should be instructed to set the fountain strips to the maximum possible in the CorelDRAW! options when output is being sent to an imagesetter.

Printing in Color

In most cases, basic desktop color production in CorelDRAW! isn't as critical as some of the experts of the industry might lead you to believe. If you stick to the same color palette, none of your different-colored objects touch each other, and your page size is standard, you usually have very little to worry about. But what if you didn't or can't keep it simple and are forced to advance past the basic uses of palettes?

The spot color palettes in CorelDRAW! can be recognized by the way in which they are displayed in the palette window. Whenever you select a spot color, you are selecting a new and different color of ink represented by a number. This type of numbering system ensures that when you select a specific ink number you and your printer are working with the exact same color no matter what. Each time you select a new color, it means the person printing your job has to mix another new batch of ink just for that color.

When you use process colors, you are using a combination of the four basic colors found in nature: cyan, magenta, yellow, and black, commonly referred to as C, M, Y, and K. No matter how many colors you specify from the process color palette, you never have to print more than these four basic ink colors. The process color palette uses different amounts of these four basic colors to reproduce virtually any color the eye can see.

It is possible to take things a bit further and use both the spot and process color palettes together. In these cases, you need to consider that the minimum number of inks you are using is five: four process and one spot. Each time you add another spot color you increase the total number of inks used—and the printing bill. Five, six, seven, or more colors of ink can be quite effective if used properly.

When proofing to a black-and-white desktop printer, preparing complex color documents using process color, spot color, or a combination of both can become a problem. (Not everyone can afford brand new shiny color printers!) What happens if you get stuck having to proof a color illustration on-screen and, even worse, from a black-and-white printer? Much can be lost in the translation when proofing files containing color objects to a black-and-white desktop printer. Fine details, such as 0.2-point color outlines, that you can't quite make out on-screen can be completely forgotten about when proofing in black and white.

Creating color images on-screen is a function for which you must draw on your talent and skill. For many, creating is the easy part. Ensuring that the colors on-screen and those printed are indeed the colors you had in mind is a completely different matter. If you are creating a document and color is a concern to you, see Chapter 21, "Managing Color and System Calibration" to get a better understanding of all of the factors involved.

Working with Spot and Process Color

Whether you are preparing your file for reproduction in spot color, process color, spot and process colors, or just black, how you proof your color documents is critical. As outlined in Chapter 21, when you view your color objects on your monitor, you basically see RGB, meant to represent the specific reflective colors you have asked for. Process colors are reproduced on the monitor in the same way, but what goes on behind the scenes is entirely different.

An easy way to think of this is to imagine where the colors are being created. With spot colors, the printing press operator is physically mixing the ink. Therefore, you need only specify a color number when it comes time to separate the film. All objects specified in that color number are represented on the same overlay. For process color, the four printing inks already are mixed and waiting. It is your computer program, in this case CorelDRAW!, that does the mixing. For each color you specify, CorelDRAW! produces different percentages of those inks onto the C, M, Y, and K film overlays which, when combined on the printing press, should match the colors you see on your screen.

Spot Tints and Process Screens

When is a tint a screen, and when is a screen a tint? For those who are new to the world of film, there's probably no difference. To a printer, however, it makes a big difference. When people talk about screen tints of spot colors, they are talking about lighter shades of mixed inks. When they say process magenta screens, they know exactly to which angle the dots are supposed to line up, in what sequence that particular color should be laid down on the printed page, and maybe even the screen frequency of the film.

With spot colors, the concept is easier. Someone says "I'd like a 20-percent screen tint of purple," and it's pretty easy to imagine purple, just a lot lighter. Experience tells you when certain ink colors do or do not work well in certain screen tint percentages. Spot color screen tints usually are rounded off to 10-percent increments, or for the really picky person 5 percent. CorelDRAW! enables the user to select any screen, whether process or spot color, to be specified in 1-percent increments.

IV

Advanced Topics

Note

Spot color screen tints do not have to be imaged at any particular angle because they seldom overlap. CorelDRAW! sets these screen tint angles at a default of 45 degrees.

Process screens are a bit more complex than spot screens because there are four of them, and in most cases, these ink colors are laid down on the printed page overtop of each other. It is a little more difficult to imagine someone getting excited about a color such as C100, M20, Y34, and K12 (this is how printers usually specify process colors) by simply describing it in those terms. It would probably take you a while to decipher that it's a greenish color. If someone said aqua or algae, however, you'd be much closer to the mark in your mind. It's only human nature to associate colors with things, not numbers. This in itself makes working with process colors a bit scary. In addition, these inks have to be imaged onto film at specific angles. In most cases these angles are preset so that distracting patterns, known as *moirees*, don't occur when the screens are placed overtop of each other. The angles for process color screens are as follows:

Process color	Screen angle
Cyan	15 degrees
Magenta	75 degrees
Yellow	0 degrees
Black	45 degrees

Halftoning

Halftone is a term given to an image made up entirely of different sized dots set down in a consistent pattern. This is a name that has carried over from the traditional days of photographically recording a continuous tone photograph or image onto film through something called a halftone screen. This halftone screen looked something like a film negative with rows and rows of little clear spots on it where light could shine through. These halftone screen holes were sort of foggy around their perimeters, and the longer a light was shone through these little holes, the larger the exposed dot became. Now, technology has changed considerably, but the term has remained. The key is that where film could reproduce dots perfectly, the digital imagesetter has to build each dot from information (resolution) provided by the original scanned image.

Each halftone dot must be digitally made up of a group of smaller dots joined together. This is where scanning resolution comes in. Usually, the higher the resolution of the scan, the more detailed information is available to the imagesetter rendering the film. This also is where the screen frequency (lpi) of the film comes into play. The lpi of the film that the digital image is rendered to must be at least half the resolution of the scan. Or conversely, the scanning resolution should be twice the lpi of the final output film. So, if you are producing 150 lpi film negatives, you need to scan to at least 300 dpi.

Color Correction

Before heading into the area of color correction, you should browse through Chapter 21. It exposes you to the niceties of color correcting your monitor, scanner, printer, or color proofing device through to the final color proof or pressmatch stages. If you are new to color correcting, Chapter 21 will give you a much better understanding of the way CorelDRAW! (and your computer) handle it from a software point of view.

Consider some physical limitations and variations. First and foremost is the accuracy of the film you are sending to the printer. Most service bureaus pride themselves on producing film within two to three percentage points of the screen values you have specified in your file.

Dot gain refers to the dots making up the screens on your film becoming larger or spreading. This spreading is small, if not microscopic, and is not visible to the naked eye. It still affects your printed images. After you have handed over your film to the printer, it then has to be made into plates. These are installed on the rollers of the press. From film to plate and from plate to paper, dot gain occurs. It is sometimes more and sometimes less, depending on factors such as whether the plates are paper or metal, and the absorbency of the paper to which you're printing.

Individually, these inaccuracies might sound trivial considering all the digital and physical transformations the information goes through to end up as a printed product. When you take a closer look, however, you might find that, when all of the inaccuracies are compounded, they can significantly affect the color of the final printed product.

In CorelDRAW! version 5 no specific feature controls dot gain. Instead, in Color Manager under the File menu, an area exists where specific custom-made system profiles can be developed to suit the exact characteristics of your printer. In the case of printing presses, the user has all the necessary tools to build a profile reflecting not only the characteristics of the printing press but the monitor and scanner printer being used. To do this, it's necessary to compare the file you have created to the film and final printed product to determine the percentage of dot gain for that specific press. Using this same process, you might need to make specific profiles that describe the dot gain caused by absorption with certain paper types.

Trapping Techniques

Trapping is the practice of overlapping film (representing different colors) to ensure that the printed product has precise-looking registration and is easier to print. If you have ever come across someone who strips film for a living, he talks about things such as light colors biting into darker colors, and black things trapping colored things. The more you find out about trapping, the more you understand how frustrating it is to print a job on a printing press that hasn't been trapped. Being a CorelDRAW! user, trapping is totally under your control.

Untrapped work can be quite hideous-looking, and it's pretty easy to tell when a job hasn't been trapped properly. If the registration of the press is off by a hair, what you see is little slivers of the paper background showing through between one side or the other of the printed image. This is caused when paper going through the printing press shifts a little, and the ink falls in a slightly different spot than it's supposed to. The faster the press operates, the less control the operator has to prevent that shift from happening. Registration is a lot more controllable on sheet-fed presses than on a faster, more high-volume press like a web-offset.

Common Approaches to Trapping

Whether you are using spot color or process colors in your file determines how you trap them. Before you actually get into the trapping differences between the two, here is a real-life example:

Imagine you are trying to spray paint a sign with stencil-lettering sheets. You need one of the more important words on your sign in red for more emphasis. The only paint you have is black, yellow, and magenta, and the hardware store down the street is closed.

You decide to use black for most of the lettering, and you know that if you spray yellow and magenta on top of each other you'll end up with a nice red color to make that particular word stand out. The first color, yellow, goes down pretty easy. When you spray the magenta overtop of the first, though, something goes terribly wrong, and all of the lettering becomes messy looking.

What do you do? Start over? No way, there must be a way to fix it so that it looks okay. In the end, you decide to use black magic marker, draw a black outline around the letters, and hide all that mess.

Compare what you did here to what a printing press would do. In process color printing, yellow ink would go down on the paper first because it is the lightest color and least affects the final printed image. Magenta, the next darkest color, would follow. (The next would normally be cyan, but in this example you didn't use it.) Finally, black would go down last. In this example, the black ink was used to hide the poor registration of the stenciling sheets. In real life on a printing press, this also would be the case. The key point here is that the black magic marker you outlined the type with actually went overtop of the ink already on the sign. This is known as *overprinting*. What you did—in a very simple way—was trap the yellow and the magenta ink into the black ink. In process color printing, that is usually all you can do. Anything more would begin to alter the colors of your images. You wouldn't use yellow to trap into a cyan, for example, because where the overlap occurred would turn an awful green color, and that would be just as bad, if not worse, than not trapping.

In spot color trapping things are a bit different because you aren't mixing colors of ink together on the press to create new ones. In most cases, you are just trying to prevent colored objects that touch each other from overlapping a little. The trick is knowing which colored ink overprints another.

Trap Planning

First, you need to make trapping the last consideration. Trapping isn't something meant to stop you from using your creative juices to produce the best work you possibly can. It's merely one of those technical things necessary to ensure what you have already created makes it through the printing press stage intact.

Plan traps for spot-color jobs differently from process color traps. The best thing you could do before attempting to apply traps for the first time is to talk to your printer (not the one on your desktop). The printer might have suggestions that could greatly add to the final outcome of your printed images, or he might suggest having the file run through a professional electronic trapping system like a Scitec. If the second is suggested, don't try trapping any of your files. The first thing these systems do is strip out all trapping or overprinting information in the files and replace it with their own.

Desktop Trapping Basics

The chapter in the CorelDRAW! manual about creating color separations goes into detail regarding how to perform proper trapping using CorelDRAW!. Read this section thoroughly if you have not had experience in this area. All trapping problems have solutions. You have created a work of art, for example, that is made up of process colors and (to keep it simple here) one spot color object.

Here of course you are getting a bit fancier with your layout and actually are incorporating a photograph you happen to have taken illustrating the subject.

1. Set up a rectangle in your process color file representing the exact finished size of the photograph.

2. Use a uniform fill of any spot color.

3. Apply a 1-point outline to the object using the same spot color.

4. Select the outline to overprint. This causes the surrounding background colors to creep into the outline by half of its thickness.

When the final film negative separations are printed out, you have a separate negative that acts as a mask for the halftone, and it is trapped by all four background process colors.

If you actually have just a spot color object, this technique works exactly the same way. Making the outline a bit thinner makes the trap a little less effective, but is better than no trap at all. A trap applied to a 0.5-point outline, for instance, only allows for a 0.25 overlap into the background which might not be enough to ensure that the printing press registration be able to have any play at all.

Automated Trapping

As a user of CorelDRAW! you can do some general types of trapping with the click of a button. If you look in the Separations dialog box, you see an option whereby all items that are specified as printing between 95-percent to 100-percent black overprint all other colors of ink in the film separations generated. After this option is selected, Auto-Spreading also becomes available. Selecting this option enables you to select a trap to be created for each object that overprints by the point measure selection indicated below the Auto-Spreading selection.

The overprinting option can save hours of time spent selecting overprinting options for each of the black objects in your file. It is meant to be primarily used for process color film separations, however, and might not be all that useful if you have set your file up with spot colors, especially if none of those colors happens to be black. The Auto-Spreading feature should not be used, however, if the file being output contains black type less than 20-point in size. The Auto-Spreading feature is set up only to add a thin outline to the outside of an object (in this case each character), and would not only significantly slow down imaging time, but might cause undesirable results to the appearance of your typeface.

Other types of trapping involve sending your file to a specially designed trapping system capable of correctly trapping not only the black in your file but all colors including spot and process. These programs usually work by the user creating a composite color print file (or in some cases an EPS file) containing all the color information, and then downloading that file through the system. Many programs do this type of specialized work and your particular printer or specialized prepress prep business equipped with a system such as this has specific requirements. You need to check with them for their exact needs.

Specific Reproduction Methods

Most of the instructions dealing with advanced printing techniques in this chapter have been slanted toward preparing film separations for the purposes of offset printing. But once again, as a CorelDRAW! user you also have the capabilities of doing much more than just this. Besides the traditional service bureau operation of imaging film negatives, they also are capable of imaging film for use in producing silkscreen and also might be equipped with image recorders to make color transparencies.

Silkscreening

Film used in producing traditionally silkscreened products, such as print-making, T-shirts, and special signage, is produced to different specifications than your run-of-the-mill offset-printing film negatives. Silkscreeners don't use negatives. All film used must be produced in positive or black image on clear background. Except in very special cases, this film does not need to be high resolution. Because of the way their screens are produced, the resolution of the film doesn't need to be any higher than the resolution of the screen.

Silkscreener's screens aren't actually made of silk anymore. Today the screens are made of woven polyester strands similar to the screens that keep the bugs from infiltrating your home. The stretched screen has a light-sensitive solution spread over it, which seals all of the openings. The film positive is laid on top of the dried solution and the entire setup is then exposed to a high-intensity light source similar to burning a plate for a printing press. Where the light film is clear, the solution hardens and seals the openings. The solution remains soft where the black image of the film is. The unexposed part is then rinsed away and the screen is left to dry.

Note Because the image is exposed to the underside of the screen, it must be in a positive. To ensure a proper contact to the screen for maximum image transfer, it must be imaged emulsion side up.

IV

Advanced Topics

The screens containing the image are stretched onto a frame and laid on top of the product to be imprinted. Wherever there is an opening in the screen, ink can pass through from one side to the other. Ink representing your image is spread over openings in the screen and an imprint is produced by the ink soaking through to the other side. The resolution of the screen is determined by how many available openings the screen contains per inch. This resolution is much more coarse than any high-resolution film available from an imagesetter and this is the reason that a normal or 1270 dpi resolution film is more than adequate for silkscreening work.

When ordering film from a service bureau for use in silkscreening be sure to ask for film positive, emulsion up, and no more than 1270 dpi resolution. As for the line of screen, check with the individual supplier to find out what the capabilities of their equipment and screeners are.

Slide Image Recorders

If you have produced slides for presentations over the last dozen years or so you have noticed significant technological changes in the way they're produced. Programs such as CorelDRAW! now make it simple to produce visuals for presentations. The advances and availability of image recorders for slide generation have made watching homemade slide presentations a thing of the past.

Service bureaus or specialized slide imaging centers enable slide producers to image their visuals onto 35 millimeter, medium format (2.25-inch), or large format (4-inch by 5-inch, or 8-inch by 10-inch) color transparency film. These images are usually available in various resolutions. Because the images are enlarged by huge proportions, by the time they make it from the slide projector to the screen, the higher the resolution the better. In most cases, the average image center offering 35 millimeter slide imaging has two basic resolutions: 2,000-line or 4,000-line. These measures indicate the number of dots per inch.

A higher-quality, less common resolution you might have available from your imaging center is 8,000-line. This is more expensive, but infinitely more desirable if your images are going to be presented to a large audience where the enlargement factor reveals the lower resolutions and distracts from the subject matter.

When selecting an image center, ask which file types they accept. Several methods are available and your particular supplier might be quite fussy about which format you can send to them. They might ask you to prepare a special export file format, or if you're lucky they'll accept your CorelDRAW! source file—you won't have to waste time exporting files for them and them transferring those onto a disk.

In CorelDRAW! 5.0, the three most popular formats the imaging center might ask for are Computer Graphics Metafile (CGM), Scan Conversion Optical Description

Language (SCD), pronounced "Skodle," or Encapsulated PostScript (EPS). The latter being the most expensive and most desirable. You should consider a number of issues when first setting up for slides and just as in preparing your files for digital output, you must dodge certain software hazards. CorelDRAW! provides some time-saving features, but also enables you to create something the image recorder won't like very much.

Tip To select Page Setup double-click on the page border on your screen with the left mouse button.

When selecting a page format, select the Slide size under Layout/Page Setup. This sets your page to exactly 11 inches by 7.33 inches landscape (only) orientation. There is a good reason for this: you must follow a 2 by 3 proportion necessary for slide imaging; and you cannot image slides portrait style. Choose Add Page Frame to add a rectangle to your page exactly the size of your paper size. Use this rectangle to add a background color to your file if necessary.

If you are allowed to send source files to the slide imaging center be sure to use the Multiple-page feature in CorelDRAW! 5. This makes it much simpler for you, and the person imaging your files doesn't have to open different files every time he images a page. This is a good habit to get into, no matter how your file is reproduced.

If you are forced into providing files other than source files, you likely are providing CGM, EPS, or SCD files. If you have had even the most basic exporting experience, preparing these files is a relatively simple task. If it is your first time doing so, be sure to consult CorelDRAW!'s Technical Reference Manual, which outlines each of the various export file types or how to install the various export filters if you did not install them during your original CorelDRAW! 5 installation.

Before sending source files or exporting files be sure that you have done a bit of file clean up work. Failure to do so might result in some disappointing results. Be sure to provide your slide imaging center with color proofs of what your slide should look like, or at least a black-and-white proof with some basic colors indicated. Here are some guidelines to remember:

✔ Delete all information outside the page perimeter. As opposed to digital imagesetting machines, if any objects are laying on the paste board of your file they corrupt the slide recorders output. This usually can be recognized as horizontal stripes across the slide.

✔ CGM and SCD export formats do not support the use of imported bitmaps (BMP).

✔ CGM and SCD do not support PostScript textures or fountain fills other than straight horizontals or verticals.

✔ If you use SCD format, select the option Include All Artistic Attributes, which allows support for special pen shapes, corners, and pen effects. Patterned lines, however, are not supported.

✔ Try to use blends instead of fountain fills in your files. Blends take less calculations to image than fountain or radial fills.

Specialized Sign-Making

Truck lettering, real estate signage, park signs and the like are perfect candidates for the next special use of CorelDRAW!. Computerized vinyl letter-cutting systems for sign making such as CADLinkPlus from ThermaZone Engineering, Inc. of Ottawa, Canada, is one of the definitive leaders in this field. Programs such as this accept different file formats, including DXF, where the fill patterns are completely ignored and only the outlines of the objects in the files are used. The information contained in a DXF file is used for its object information. That data then can be manipulated by the operator of the CADLinkPlus system and then sent on to a plotting device equipped with an extremely sharp razor knife, which cuts out the self-adhesive vinyl shapes.

Maximizing Printing Power

Don't be satisfied with slow printing if you know that your equipment should be capable of producing much faster results. You can do a number of things to make sure that you are getting your money's worth. The computer and printer you have are supposed to be time savers, not time wasters!

First check the setup of your printer to make sure that your Transmission Retry Time is set to 600. Follow these steps:

1. Go to Program Manager and open the Main Windows group. Now open Control Panel, then Printers.

2. Select the printer you are printing to and choose <u>C</u>onnect. There you see the Transmission Retry Time selection. Set it to 600.

3. While you are there set the Device Not Selected to 0, and (if you are very low on hard disk space) turn off Print Manager by deselecting the Use Print Manager option.

Print Manager temporarily writes the printing information to your hard drive while you are printing so that you can continue working. If you're extremely low on hard disk space you might consider turning this off temporarily while your file prints. If you do have very little hard disk space left, start backing up your data. You should not use the last 5 percent of your hard disk space for any reliable data integrity.

Why Won't It Print?

Why won't it print. Unfortunately, with many variables to contend with, even making an educated guestimate is sometimes impossible.

First check to see if your printer has paper in it. Yes, it might sound silly, but these things happen to even the most experienced of users. Especially if you are printing to a networked printer used by many different people.

Next, tab through your document to check for objects that contain too many nodes. Try simplifying the ones you suspect might be causing the problem. Check for too many objects combined or welded together. Break these apart if you suspect them and try printing again.

Are you working off a network? Is the CorelDRAW! program running off of a file server or through a network? Networks are notorious for slowing down printing, saving, and opening. The solution, unfortunately, is to purchase an individual program for your particular machine.

Do you have any fountain or radial fills that graduate from one spot color to another? Even though this is a great feature, it might not work properly. Again, experienced users say that graduated fills between spot colors is something to avoid at all costs.

Does your computer have enough RAM to support all the programs you have open, including Windows, CorelDRAW!, Print Manager, and all the data that is needed to calculate and print your file? It is recommended that you operate your system with at least 4 MB of RAM. The more the better, however.

Have you tried using a higher Flatness setting (Print/Options/Options) or Auto-Increase Flatness? If your file has any quirks in it this is a good way to iron them out to at least get a reasonable printout.

Have you used any of the multiple-color fountain fills? These slow down printing considerably and in some cases might not print at all depending on how many colors you have used.

IV

Advanced Topics

PostScript Error Information

The makers of PostScript page description language have provided a very basic way of shedding light on the errors that can trip up a desktop printer or digital imagesetter. It provides vague and generic messages about the error that has taken place in printing your file and usually appears on a blank page (or might be printed on its own page after some of your file prints). These messages are very cryptic and can range in anything from font downloading messages to actual printing errors.

The three most common that apply to printing are LIMITCHECK, RANGECHECK, and TIMEOUT. LIMITCHECK relates to too many nodes on an object or combination of objects. TIMEOUT is an indication of the setting of your printer's Transmission Retry time set as mentioned earlier in the Control Panel, Printers, Connect dialog selection in Windows Program Manager.

The PostScript error handler is a little utility that is built into the Windows printer driver and is available only if you are printing to a PostScript printer. It can be activated in one two ways.

1. Go to Program Manager and double-click on the Main, Control Panel, and Printers icons to access the Printers dialog box.

2. Then select one of the PostScript printers you have set up in this listing.

3. Choose Setup, Options, Advanced and look at the bottom left corner. To activate the PostScript Error Handler, click in the box beside Print PostScript Error Information (see fig. 25.5).

The second way to activate the PostScript error handler is directly from the print menu in CorelDRAW!:

1. Choose File, Print.

2. In the first dialog box, select the printer you are printing to and choose Setup, Options, Advanced and the Advanced Options dialog box will appear.

3. To activate, check the Print PostScript Error Information box.

CorelDRAW! version 5.0 provides the user plenty of advantageous tools with which to produce a wide variety of projects. The best-kept secret to date seems to be how to obtain proper printing results. Whether you are a novice or a seasoned professional, this chapter has taken you through some of the more hazardous areas of working with not only CorelDRAW! but any program.

Program	For version(s)	File extension(s)
Lotus 1-2-3	1A, 2.0	PIC
Lotus 1-2-3 for Windows 3.0		WK?
Macintosh PICT		PCT
Micrographx	2.x, 3.x	DRW
Microsoft Rich Text Format		RTF
Microsoft Word for Windows	1.x	*
Microsoft Word for Windows	2.x	DOC
Microsoft Word for Macintosh	4.0	*
Microsoft Word for Macintosh	5.0	*
PostScript (interpreted)		EPS, PS
SCITEX		CT, SCT
Targa Bitmap		TGA, VDA, ICB, VST
Text		TXT
Tagged image file format (TIFF) 5.0		CPT, SEP, TIF
Windows Bitmap		BMP, DIB, RLE
Windows Metafile		WMF
WordPerfect Graphic		WPG
WordPerfect 5.0	5.0	*
WordPerfect 5.1 for Windows	5.1	*
WordPerfect 6.0 for Windows	6.0	*

Advanced Topics

General Import Filter Categories

Quite a few application filters are newly built into Draw's import collection, including a few improved filters worth noting: Corel's internal Presentation Exchange (CMX), SCITEX (CT, SCI), Ventura generated (GEN), and Tagwrite (RTF).

AutoCAD Filters

AutoCAD programs are favorites of architects and engineers from a wide cross section of industries. If you want to export a drawing from AutoCAD into a DXF format that Draw's filters understand, use the utility called DXFOUT that comes with the AutoCAD application. Draw can import a file exported from these applications as long as they are compatible with one of these two common formats: DXF or PLT. Once again, though, you have to be wary of importing files produced by AutoCAD versions 11 or 12, because some of the features available in these versions are not fully supported in Draw.

If you can influence the options selected when the file is actually exported from the AutoCAD application, you might want to consider these tips:

✔ The first thing you might notice upon importing a DXF file is that Draw enlarges the objects substantially when importing them, even though they are centered on the page. Objects can be scaled after importing.

✔ If the file you are exporting is created from a three-dimensional image, be sure the image is being viewed at the desired angle before exporting.

✔ Avoid using text justification. Multiple variations are not supported. Non-standard characters import as a "?" character. Panose font-matching takes place on import. Text size and skewing is adjusted to conform to the limitations of Draw.

✔ Avoid overly complex files. Draw's filter (or the available memory on your system) might not be capable of handling excessive import file sizes. If you find your file size is too large, try exporting it from AutoCAD using an HP7475 Plotter. Perform a Plot-to-file of your drawing, then import the file into Draw using the HPGL .PLT import filter.

✔ If you have problems with the dimension entities changing, try going back to AutoCAD and exploding the dimension entity before exporting.

✔ The variable line width available in AutoCAD is not supported in Draw, and therefore, the minimum line width applied to lines applies as the default.

✔ Raising curve resolution increases file size substantially. Lowering curve resolution makes the file size more manageable.

✔ Solid and trace entities are filled as long as the view is not set as three-dimensional.

✔ Points transfer into Draw as ellipses at the smallest size possible. Extruded points come in as line segments with two nodes. PDMODE is not supported.

✔ Files exported as "entities only" might import incorrectly because they contain little or no header information.

You should keep these tips in mind when exporting to DXF format. In addition, Draw does not support the following special features of the AutoCAD program:

✔ Draw cannot read shape entities such as SHX files.

✔ Polygons with variable-width polylines are not supported, including elevation (group 38), mesh M and N vertex counts (groups 71 and 72), smooth surface M and N densities (groups 73 and 74), and smooth surface type (group 75).

✔ Three-dimensional shapes, such as cones, spheres, and tori, and three-dimensional extrusions of circles, arcs, text, and polyline extrusions are not supported.

✔ The following features also are not supported: invisible lines in three-dimensional face entities, automatic wireframes, hidden lines removal, binary DXF format, and paper space entities with a Model Space. In addition, AutoCAD layers cannot be mapped to CorelDRAW! layers.

EPS File Formats (Placeable & EPS, PS, and AI)

Several different types of EPS filters now ship with Draw 5: Placeable EPS; PostScript (interpreted) EPS and PS; Adobe Illustrator created EPS; and CorelTRACE! EPS. Knowing which one to use can be tricky, especially if you don't know where the file came from in the first place. To find this information, select the All Files (*.*) selection at the top of the import filter list, click on Options at the bottom right of the dialog box to expand it, and click on the file for which you would like information. At the bottom left corner, you see all the pertinent information you need to choose the correct filter. You are not able to use the All Files selection for importing EPS files because more than one EPS filter type exists. Draw requires you to specify manually exactly which filter type to use when importing any EPS file. When importing, Draw asks which method to use when handling text (see fig. 26.7). If you are not sure whether you have all the fonts needed for the EPS file, you might want to import the EPS file using text as curves first to check. Otherwise, Draw uses the Panose font-matching utility to match any fonts not found installed on your system.

Figure 26.7
The Import EPS dialog box.

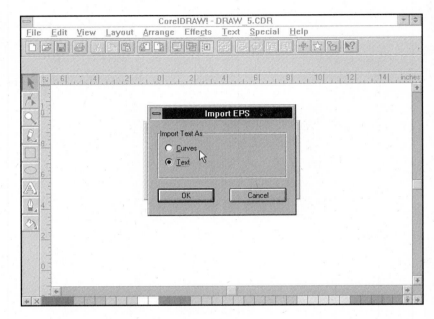

Placeable Encapsulated PostScript files contain a small bitmap image, called a header, that represents the imported information and displays in Draw. Neither objects nor text contained in the placeable EPS files are editable.

PostScript (interpreted) formats are mostly used for importing PRN or print files. This filter uses the PostScript information describing the page for a digital imagesetter or other PostScript printer to represent the image in Draw. If any fountain fills are described in the file, you might quickly run out of memory because of the complex way these fills are described to the PostScript printer. If it is imperative that you import a file containing fountain fills and you do run into memory problems, you might need to open up your CORELFLT.INI file and change the VMSize=n to a larger number.

Draw supports all Adobe Illustrator formats including versions 3.0, 88, and 1.1 created on either Macintosh or PC platforms. Imported AI or EPS files from Adobe Illustrator using this filter will come into Draw as fully editable groups of objects which can be ungrouped.

The CorelTRACE! EPS filter is specifically designed to work with files generated solely by CorelTRACE! and does not work on any other EPS file type. Objects entering Draw through this filter are grouped objects and fully editable when ungrouped.

Bitmap Filters

Draw suppports 12 bitmap types including BMP, CPT, CT, GIF, PCX, TGA, TIF, JPG, JFF, JFT, and PCD. These types each support black-and-white, color, and grayscale bitmaps and enable setting resolution of the imported image before importing. Each bitmap import enables you to crop the image or resample by changing the resolution of the image.

Windows and OS/2 bitmaps are fully supported, as well as CorelPHOTO-PAINT!, GIF, PCX, Targa (TGA), TIFF, and SCITEX formats. TIFF 6.0 supports the JPEG compression and CMYK data, and SCITEX format supports only full 32-bit color images.

Hewlett-Packard plotter formats are supported as HPGL and HPGL/2 PLT format. The PLT filter enables scaling and resizing of images. Curve resolution can be set, although the higher the curve resolution the bigger the file size. Corel recommends a curve resolution of 0.004 inches. HPGL does not support color; however, upon importing the file, you have the option to assign a color to each pen number. If you do not, Draw assigns the colors for you. You also are able to set pen width, velocity, fills, line types, and text.

Photo CD

The much-hyped Kodak Photo CD is fully supported and available for import into Draw (see fig. 26.8). You have the option of importing from a selection of five sample resolutions including Wallet, Snapshot, Standard, Large, and Poster. These range in file sizes from 24,500 bytes for Wallet to over 6 MB for Poster. The Photo CD filter imports color images into Draw only as RGB, however, and should probably be imported into an image-editing package such as CorelPHOTO-PAINT! where the color model can be converted to CMYK for print reproduction.

You also have the option of importing in a variety of color ranges including 256 grayscale, 16 (4-bit), 256 (8-bit), or 16.7 million (24-bit) colors (see fig. 26.9). A Kodak Image Enhancement also has been added to ensure that colors are correct (even if they are RGB).

IV

Advanced Topics

Figure 26.8
Importing Photo
CD images into
CorelDRAW!.

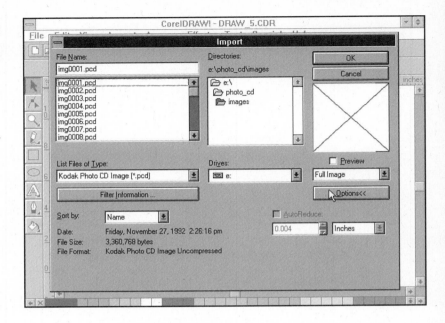

Figure 26.9
The Photo CD
Options dialog
box.

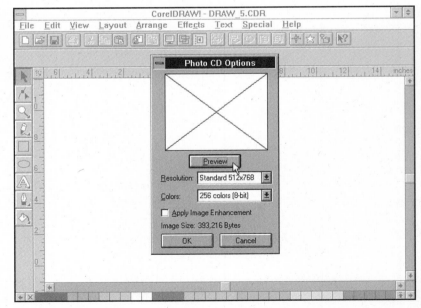

Mastering Draw's Export Filters

According to some experts, the export function is one of the most critical functions of a graphics program. If it does not work, many feel the program is worthless. Corel engineers must have had expert advice on this subject because they seem to have covered all bases.

Similar to importing, exporting to various file formats enables you to prepare your Draw files for use in other programs and platforms. Exporting is critical for preparing graphics files for use in programs such as page-layout and word-processing packages.

One of the best ways to succeed in preparing files for export is to know the limitations of your target program. If you are preparing a multi-color graphic file for use in a program that does not support color trapping, you should not bother going to the trouble of setting up complex and time-consuming overprinting and color-object editing. Or, if you have used patterned lines in your Draw file and your target program does not support patterned lines, you should come up with an alternative before exporting your file. You quickly find out that not all features supported in Draw are supported in other page-layout or word-processing programs.

Corel's Export Arsenal

Below you see (in no particular order, and taken straight from Draw's CORELFLT.INI file) what you would be equipped with if you selected a full install of all exporting filters during your initial install of CorelDRAW! version 5.

```
CPT=EXPCPT,"CorelPHOTO-PAINT Image",*.cpt,16
BMP=EXPBMP.DLL,"Windows Bitmap",*.bmp;*.dib;*.rle,1
GIF=EXPGIF.DLL,"CompuServe Bitmap",*.gif,1
CGM=EXPCGM.DLL,"Computer Graphics Metafile",*.cgm,2
JPEG=EXPJPEG.DLL,"JPEG Bitmap",*.jpg;*.jff;*.jtf;*.cmp,1
OS2=EXPOS2B.DLL,"OS/2 Bitmap",*.bmp,1
PCX=EXPPCX.DLL,"Paintbrush",*.pcx,1
CT=EXPCT.DLL,"Scitex CT Bitmap",*.sct;*.ct,1
TGA=EXPTGA.DLL,"Targa Bitmap",*.tga;*.vda;*.icb;*.vst,1
TIFF=EXPTIFF.DLL,"TIFF Bitmap",*.tif,1
WMF=EXPWMF,"Windows Metafile",*.wmf,12
WMF2=EXPWMF,"Windows Metafile",*.wmf,23
AI=EXPAI.DLL,"Adobe Illustrator",*.ai;*.eps,2
AT1=EXPAT1.DLL,"Adobe Type 1 Font",*.pfb,5
DXF=EXPDXF.DLL,"AutoCAD DXF",*.dxf,2
EPS=EXPEPS.DLL,"EPS (Placeable)",*.eps,7
```

```
EPS2=EXPEPS,"EPS (Placeable)",*.eps,17
GEM=EXPGEM.DLL,"GEM File",*.gem,2
HPGL=EXPHPGL.DLL,"HPGL Plotter File",*.plt,2
PIF=EXPPIF.DLL,"IBM PIF",*.pif,2
PICT=EXPPICT.DLL,"Macintosh PICT",*.pct,2
SCODL=EXPSCODL.DLL,"Matrix/Imapro SCODL",*.scd,2
RTF=W4W19T.DLL,"Rich Text Format",*.rtf,9,0
RTF=IMPRTF,"Rich Text Format",*.rtf,13
TTF=EXPTTF.DLL,"TrueType Font",*.ttf,5
AMI=W4W33T.DLL,"Ami Professional 2.0, 3.0",*.sam,9,1
TXT=IMPTXT,"ASCII Text",*.txt,14
EXL=W4W21T.DLL,"MS Excel for Windows 3.0, 4.0",*.xls,9,1
L123=W4W20T.DLL,"Lotus 123 1A, 2.0",*.wk?,9,0
L1233=W4W20T.DLL,"Lotus 123 3.0",*.wk?,9,2
MSWW2=W4W44T.DLL,"MS Word for Windows 2.x",*.doc;*.*,9,1
MSWW1=W4W44T.DLL,"MS Word for Windows 1.x",*.*,9,0
MSW=W4W05T.DLL,"MS Word 5.0, 5.5",*.*,9,2
MSWM2=W4W54T.DLL,"MS Word for Macintosh 5.0",*.*,9,2
MSWM=W4W54T.DLL,"MS Word for Macintosh 4.0",*.*,9,1
WP51=W4W07T.DLL,"WordPerfect 5.1",*.wp;*.*,9,1
WP50=W4W07T.DLL,"WordPerfect 5.0",*.*,9,0
WPG=EXPWPG.DLL,"WordPerfect Graphic",*.wpg,2
```

Again, a more simplified way to look at it follows:

Program	File extension(s)
Adobe Illustrator 88, 3.0	AI, EPS
Adobe Type 1 font	PFB
AutoCAD DXF	DXF
CompuServe Bitmaps	GIF
CorelCHART!	CCH
CorelDRAW!	CDR
CorelPHOTO-PAINT!	PCX
GEM files	GEM

Program	File extension(s)
Computer Graphics Metafile	CGM
HP Plotter HPGL	PLT
IBM PIF	PIF
JPEG Bitmap	CMP, JPG, JFF, JTF
Macintosh PICT	PCT
OS2 Bitmaps	BMP
Matrix/Imapro SCODL	SCD
Encapsulated Postscript	EPS
SCITEX	CT, SCT
Targa Bitmap	TGA, VDA, ICB, VST
Tagged image file format	BMP (TIFF) 5.0
True Type Fonts	TTF
Windows Bitmaps	BMP, DIB, RLE
Windows Metafile	WMF
WordPerfect Graphic	WPG

Popular Exporting Formats

The following is a list of the export formats you might use for a specific target program such as a page layout or word processing program. Because of the variety of printer types on the market, the list is divided into two basic printer types: PostScript and Non-PostScript (unless the format being exported to uses a proprietary printer type).

IV

Advanced Topics

Application	Filter PostScript	Non-PostScript
Ami Professional	EPS	WMF
Delrina Perform	GEM	GEM
PageMaker	EPS	WMF
CorelVENTURA!	EPS	CMX
WordPerfect	EPS	WPG

For page layout and other programs with graphics-editing capabilities:

Application	Filter type
Adobe Illustrator	AI
Arts & Letters	WMF, EPS (using decipher)
AutoCAD	DXF
GEM Artline	GEM
Macintosh-based vector	Macintosh, PICT, AI
Micrografx Designer	CGM
PC Paintbrush	PCX

For specific devices, use the following export filter format:

Device type	Filter
Matrix, Genegraphic, Solataire film recorder	SCODL
Computer-driven cutters, machines, or plotters	HPGL or DXF outlines

Bitmap Formats

The exporting to bitmap filters include Windows BMP, CompuServe GIF, Paint-brush, Targa TGA, and TIFF formats. On importing bitmaps, you have the option of scaling up or down the image (see fig. 26.10). Be careful when enlarging any bitmap images. Resolution of the bitmap decreases when it is scaled up or enlarged at all. If you reduce the size or scale down the bitmap, the result is satisfactory.

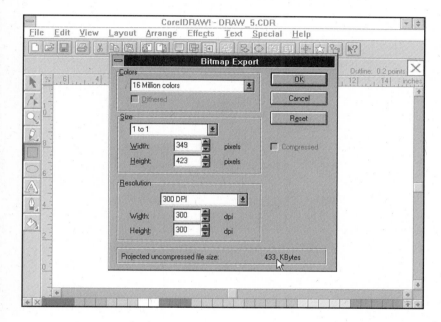

Figure 26.10
The Bitmap export dialog box.

Make a note of how much you scaled the bitmap down. If it was more than 50 percent, you might consider sampling it at a lower resolution initially. This is because reducing the size of the bitmap image compresses the resolution and might result in wasted information and wasted disk space. A good rule to follow is to always maintain an image resolution twice that of the final line screen resolution of the final output. If you are going to be making digital output from your file at a line screen of 150 lines per inch, you need only maintain an image resolution of 300 dots per inch.

IV

Advanced Topics

Draw bitmap formats also support some compression types:

Format type	Compression available
Windows Bitmap	RLE (run-length encoding) for 4- or 8-bit BMP files.
Compuserve GIF	LZW (GIF version 89A).
Paintbrush	RLE (PCX version 3.0).
Targa TGA	Both RLE-compressed color-mapped and RLE RGB are supported. 24-bit color TGA files are automatically exported as RLE-compressed RGB bitmaps.
TIFF	Draw 5 supports TIFF 4.2, 5.0, and 6.0 filter formats. If your objects are CMYK the filter automatically uses version 6.0. For 24-bit color you get the 5.0 filter, and for 8-bit or 256-color or less you get the 4.2 version filter.

Bitmap filters also support a number of additional options including colors options, a dithered colors option, compression, resolution, and size. Draw also indicates the projected file size of the exported file. JPEG or Joint Photographers Experts Group compression also is supported.

Encapsulated PostScript Formats

EPS filters support several formats and come equipped with options for setting text controls, converting color bitmaps to grayscale, setting fountain stripes, and setting the resolution of the image header (see fig. 26.11).

You can set the header resolution from 1 to 300. Although a very low resolution header reduces file size, it also lessens the user's ability to recognize details of the image on the screen and might sometimes make it difficult to position the image in the target program. The color of the header also reduces the file size, and if you don't mind a black-and-white representation of your color image, this also can greatly reduce the export file size.

In EPS formats, texture fills are not supported and are replaced with solid gray fills. Text should be exported to include fonts so that CorelDRAW! can download the font information into the EPS file. Text also should be exported as text, not curves, unless the number of characters is minimal and does not excessively enlarge the file size. In that case, just choose As <u>C</u>urves and Draw omits the font downloading information.

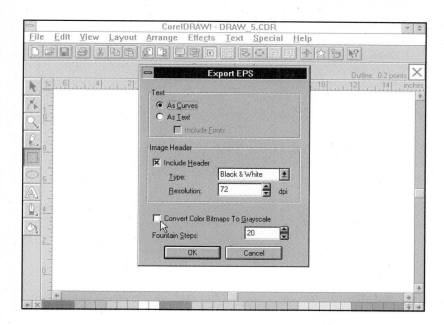

Figure 26.11
The Export EPS
dialog box.

The Adobe Illustrator export format, popular on the Macintosh platform, enables you to select which version of Illustrator to use to format your file (see fig. 26.12). Version 1.1, 88, or 3.0 selections are available. You also have the option again of exporting text as curves or as text. A Use Macintosh Characters option also becomes available after the As Text option is selected. This might come in handy if you had used an extended character set such as a foreign language character or other special characters.

Exporting to SCODL Format

SCODL format is primarily used for generating slide files on film recorder hardware. After you select this export filter, you will see that very few user options are available. If you have placed a colored rectangle for a background color in your file, whichever option you select here (black or white) is overridden (see fig. 26.13).

IV

Advanced Topics

Figure 26.12
The Export
Adobe Illustrator
dialog box.

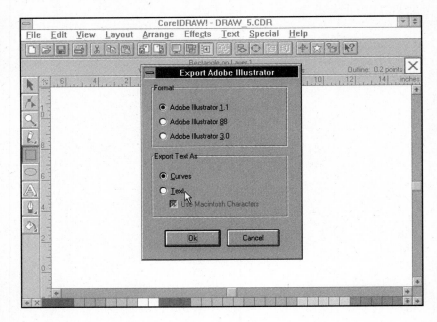

Figure 26.13
The Export
SCODL dialog
box.

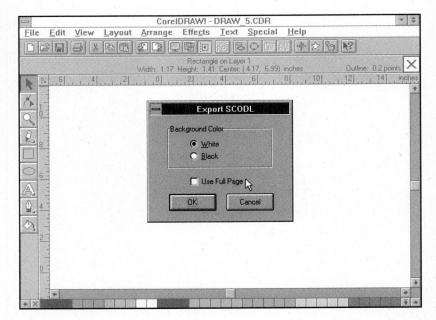

If you are preparing slides from Draw, select the Slide page size in Page Setup to be sure your page is set to the proper aspect ratio for slide formatting. Slide proportions follow a two-to-three ratio, which does not match a regular letter-sized page proportion.

When using this format, be sure not to allow your text or drawn objects to come too close to the frame of your page, or you might get an overflow error when imaging the file. The overflow error can usually be recognized by a series of horizontal colored lines across the slide. If you have used calligraphic text and would like to retain that effect, click in the Calligraphic Text box in Clipboard under Text options in Preferences. Unfortunately, PostScript textures, bitmaps, and two- and four-color patterns are not supported through this filter.

Using AutoCAD Formats

Although Draw has many features that AutoCAD misses, this works as a disadvantage when it comes to exporting into DXF format (see fig. 26.14). A number of necessary changes are made to the attributes of objects moving through this filter and into AutoCAD. One of the most critical changes is the fact that objects that do not have an outline assigned to them in Draw are automatically assigned an outline in the DXF format, so all text is converted to noneditable curves.

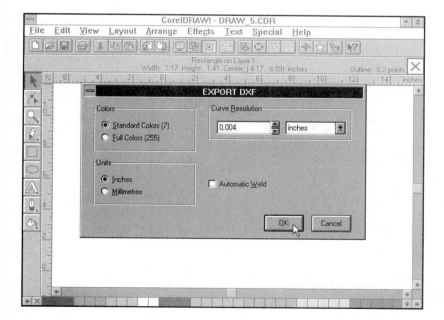

Figure 26.14
The Export DXF dialog box.

Other features not compatible between the two programs include calligraphic pen effects, patterned lines, arrowheads, varying line weights. Bitmaps are not supported, and layer information is not matched. Texture fills are not supported and result in solid gray fills. Color formats, when selected as Full Colors, might not match exactly the color scheme you have selected in your Draw file. If you used any of these features expecting them to all filter through to DXF, you were probably disappointed.

Using JPEG Compression

JPEG and MPEG are said to provide superior compression for various image formats. JPEG or Joint Photographer Experts Group compression is compatible with a wide variety of programs and platforms. Draw supports a number of JPEG formats including JPEG Interchange format (JFIF), TIFF JPEG (JTIF), and LEAD format (CMP).

The JFIF format is not actually true JPEG but is definitely used more widely than pure JPEG. This format is useful for creating compressed files to be used on PC, Macintosh, or UNIX platforms (see fig. 26.15).

Figure 26.15
The Export JPEG
dialog box.

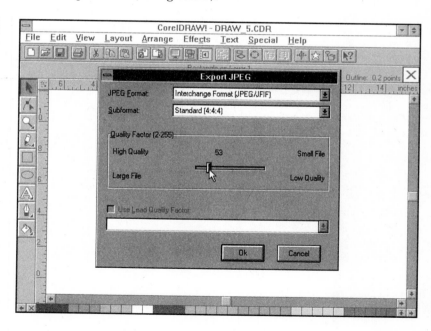

TIFF JPEG, or JTIF, uses TIFF 6.0 for JPEG compression supporting the full CMYK color model. These JTIF files cannot be created by a usual TIFF export filter, nor can they be imported using an ordinary TIFF filter. The JPEG filter must be used to ensure proper data compression.

LEAD format is the best JPEG compression but tends to be more non-standard than even true JPEG or JTIF. Draw supports the LEAD compression standard.

Using HPGL and Plotter Formats

The HPGL (Hewlett-Packard Graphical Language) and Plotter (PLT) export filter is by far the most complex-looking of Draw's collection of export filters. It is designed primarily for adapting files to be used on flatbed plotters, vinyl sign cutters, and automated industrial cutting machines. The HPGL dialog box is sub-divided into three tabbed Options areas: Pen, Page, and Advanced. Before beginning preparation for exporting, you should be aware that some features are not supported beyond Draw into the HPGL or PLT file formats. These machines do not operate on the same principles as the average desktop bubble-jet or laser printer, and require a different type of instruction from the application.

Because these types of printers reproduce the images using colored pens instead of bubble-jet or laser, you see an abundance of pen controls available in this filter. The Pen Options tab of the filter enables you to first choose the pen and then its color assignment, as well as its width and velocity (see fig 26.16). The color selection list contains 256 colors and a custom color pen setting. You also are able to save any of these Pen settings to a pen Library file in order to create a custom library of your own.

The Page Options tab enables you to scale your exported file to exact enlargement or reduction and include other controls such as Fit to Page, preformatted or custom page sizes, orientation, and plotter origin settings (see fig. 26.17). Be careful, the origin you set must match the origin setting on the plotter you are using. If your plotter normally starts plotting at the bottom left of the plotter page then set it there. If your origin is incorrectly set, the image being plotted will most likely go out of bounds.

The Plotter units setting enables you to adjust the number of plotter units on which your particular plotter operates. The norm and default is 1,016 units per inch, but check your plotter to make sure. Otherwise, your images might become distorted.

Figure 26.16
The Pen Options
tab of the HPGL
Export dialog
box.

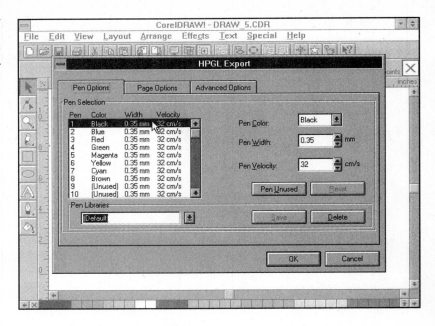

Figure 26.17
The Page
Options tab of
the HPGL Export
dialog box.

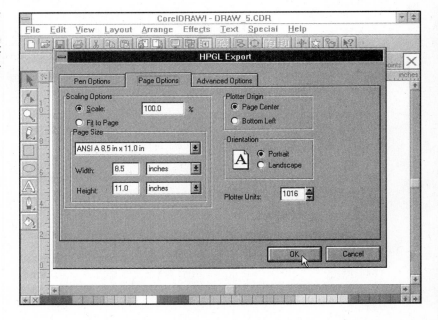

The Advanced Options tab of the HPGL export dialog box includes settings for simulating a fill pattern using pen hatching and cross-hatching, the frequency and angle of which are adjustable here (see fig. 26.18). An option also exists to remove hidden lines. It basically tells the plotter to ignore any lines describing objects hidden by other objects. Automatic Weld is a useful function for sign-cutters. The objects that overlap each other are allowed to become one outlined object. This feature only works on single or combined objects, or text objects when Text to Curves is selected. If you are unsure whether this feature works on the objects you have created for export, use the Draw Weld tool before attempting to export the file.

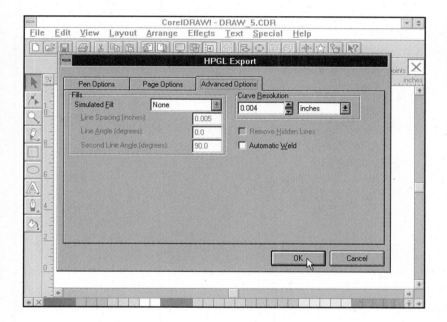

Figure 26.18

The Advanced Options tab of the HPGL dialog box.

Curve resolution also is controlled in Advanced Options. Again, as in other filters, the range is between 0.0 and 1.0 inches. The higher the value set here, the smaller the file size is. The default setting for curve resolution is 0.004 inches.

Exporting Fonts

The Adobe Type 1 and TrueType fonts filter enables the user to make objects into Type 1 fonts or TrueType compatible characters or symbols. When this export filter is selected, the last font name used or exported to is displayed in the Family Name field. Options include assigning a style such as normal, bold, normal italic, or bold italic, and selecting whether it is a symbol font (see fig. 26.19).

Advanced Topics IV

Figure 26.19
Assigning a style
in the Options
dialog box.

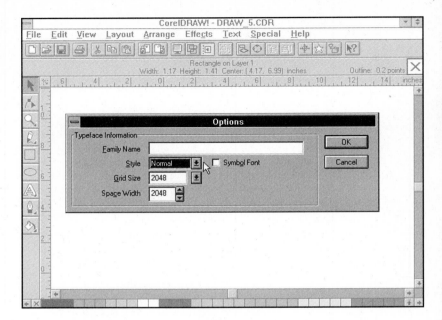

After you have selected the font name and style and clicked on OK, the filter takes you to another dialog box where you can set the size of the character you have created and build a spacing width setting into the font using Space Width. Leave the **D**esign Size setting at the default of 720 points unless you know this does not work for your font. Setting the **C**haracter Width at Auto enables Draw's filter to automatically calculate the amount of space required between the characters of your font collection. Below that, you see the Character **N**umber assignment that enables you to assign a keyboard button to the character you are exporting, which follows the Windows 3.1 character map settings (see fig. 26.20). The Options button takes you back again to the first Options dialog box.

Exporting to Macintosh PICT

Last, but certainly not least, is the popular Macintosh PICT (PCT) export format. Not many options are available to the user in this filter except the critical Export text as Curves or Text option, and the Macintosh character set option. This is slightly different when it comes to special extended character sets such as foreign language or symbol characters (see fig. 26.21).

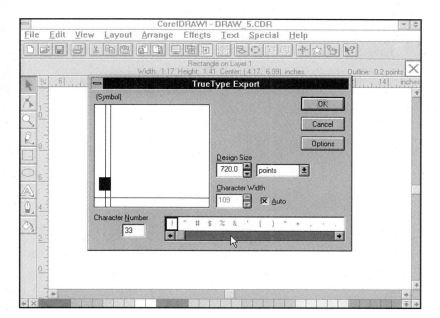

Figure 26.20
The Character Number assignment in the TrueType Export dialog box.

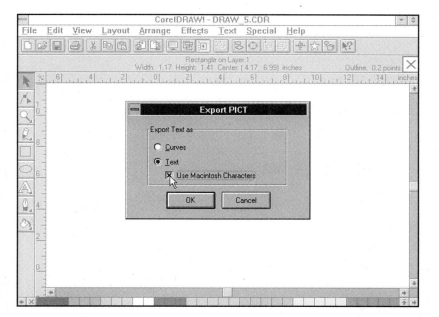

Figure 26.21
The Export PICT dialog box.

IV

Advanced Topics

As most filters do, this one also comes with its set of limitations including unsupported bitmaps, PostScript texture fills, and two- and four-color pattern fills. This filter also converts all objects with both outlines and fills to two separate objects: one for the outline and one for the fill.

Fountain fill steps are determined by the setting of your Preferences\View dialog box. Color-matching is made as closely as possible, however the best color model to use is 24-bit, which translates through the filter virtually identical to Draw's colors.

Chapter Snapshot

CorelDRAW! 5 provides the necessary tools to create expert layouts and illustrations. All of your hard work will not matter, however, if you cannot get high-quality output. This chapter discusses the following topics:

- ✔ The reproduction process
- ✔ The role the service bureau plays
- ✔ Understanding the terminology
- ✔ How to choose a service bureau
- ✔ Understanding the printing technology
- ✔ What you should expect to pay
- ✔ Supplying third-party fonts
- ✔ Troubleshooting problems

Many different production processes are involved in creating digital output. This chapter explains the process so that you can concentrate on creating the best art you can.

CHAPTER

Working with Service Bureaus

B
ack in the old days, traditional businesses such as word-processing, typesetting, and prepress stripping houses carried most of the technical know-how. If you prepared text, artwork, or photographs for any of these technical processes, you more than likely went through accredited or formal training to do a highly specialized job. The industry has changed substantially, however. Those highly specialized jobs that slowed down production schedules (and stretched budgets) now are replaced by the miracles of modern technology. Faster, cheaper, and usually better work is produced as a result.

By purchasing software programs such as CorelDRAW!, anyone can have the tools necessary to create expert layouts and illustrations. With version 5.0, the tool arsenal has been expanded to a point at which even the most demanding professionals can achieve their objectives. Artists who may not be familiar with the final stages of reproduction, however, might find themselves forced into unfamiliar territory. If you are one of these people, read on.

Understanding the Reproduction Process

Traditional businesses that used to handle just type, art, or camera work for the most part no longer exist in their old format. Many of these processes have been replaced by you, the desktop publisher. Whether you are keyboarding the text, drawing the illustrations, or taking the photographs, you are now the crux of it all. But now that you have completed the creative process of assembling all the elements in a manner that delights your authors, editors, and clients, you still have a few final hoops to jump through: The reproduction process.

Offset printing remains a standard in the industry. Budgeting your electronic artwork from your computer to a printing press now requires film. Film is used to produce printing plates that eventually are fastened to the rollers on the printing press. Each basic color specified in your file requires a separate layer of film to produce a separate printing plate for the press.

The Role of the Service Bureau

If you are using process color (four-color) to reproduce your work, for instance, you will need to generate four separate pieces of film. In the case of process color, you will need one sheet of film each to represent cyan, magenta, yellow, and black (commonly known as C, M, Y, and K). More complex projects might require additional spot colors printed together with the process colors. This usually is done to achieve accurate color for a company logo or a metallic ink that cannot be reproduced accurately, even by mixing process colors. For each additional color, a new, separate piece of film is required.

The term *service bureau* describes the relatively new business that has filled the need for film from electronically created artwork. They are businesses that are quite proud of the services they provide and, as the name implies, rely on customer service for their future success. They are usually operated by someone who has seen how desktop publishing and computers are changing business needs and environments.

Working at a service bureau usually requires a high level of computer literacy. It might even require the need to be familiar with publishing software on the market for several different computer platforms. The highly trained output operator's most challenging job is troubleshooting client files. Problems caused by improperly created files from inexperienced electronic artists can create lots of grief for everyone involved.

But problems are less likely to occur if you're fully prepared for the experience of buying digital output. Usually, there is a solution to a problem. Whether you're a first time purchaser of output, or a seasoned professional, this chapter shows you some of the weird, wonderful world of service bureaus.

Preparing Your Files for Digital Output

Having your files converted, or *imaged,* to film can be an emotional experience. As an electronic artist in the final stage of the production process of a project, you might feel as if you're being squeezed from both ends. From behind, you have performed all the processes up to the desktop publishing stage, and a few of those stages likely dragged beyond their due dates. Subsequently, all of the other stages were pushed back. Then, as you look ahead, you see the printing press waiting. Throughout your entire production process, that original delivery date has always remained constant. Everyone looks to you to make up for the lost time.

If you're new in the business, this can be a time of great stress and anxiety, but it doesn't always have to be that way. Prepare yourself and allow enough time in your schedule for imaging mistakes. Any seasoned professional will tell you planning is the key. The following questions should be considered:

- ✔ What will your creation be made up of?
- ✔ How many colors will there be?
- ✔ Will it be made of electronically scanned images or original art and photographs?
- ✔ Have you trapped your color images or do you even need to?
- ✔ What type of paper will your job be printed onto?
- ✔ What about the printer? Do you have one lined up yet?
- ✔ Has this service bureau ever worked with you before?
- ✔ Have they ever worked with electronically created film before?

It's wise to ask yourself as many questions as possible before heading out the door to the service bureau. Start thinking about answers to all of the questions that will be asked of you. As the artist, it is your responsibility to know the answers.

Consulting with Your Printer

The printer you select should be one with whom you are comfortable and who you trust. If you need referrals for a good printer, ask around. Look for a printer that has some experience in dealing with digitally created art or film. It would be advisable for them to have basic camera resources. They should be capable of basic film-stripping and plate-making or at least have a dedicated prepress service to do this work for them. Make sure that the service you hire can coordinate film stripping—unless you don't mind handling this complex, highly skilled process yourself.

After you have a printer selected, and the bureau has assigned someone to look after your account, ask for a tour of the facilities. This is not only educational, but serves as an investment in networking. You are likely to meet a press operator, camera person, and production manager. These are the professionals who are responsible for your job. Learn their names in case you need their assistance (and, if you are a beginner at this, you will).

A key part of meeting and touring around the print shop you settle upon will be to get a behind-the-scenes look into how advanced their operation is. Are they experts and up-to-date on technology or are they accustomed to getting napkin-style art and laser-printed type? This will make a huge difference in the amount of time you will have to dedicate to helping them out if there are problems with the film.

Before you order your film, ask the printer if they have any special requirements. For instance, if they are going to print your project "two-up" (the placement of two identical images on each side of the press sheet), will they require two complete sets of film, or can they duplicate it themselves? Do they need a certain line screen? Are they able to provide halftones if you need them? Will they handle the color separations if required? Do they require a color proof or match print of the film? Can they provide this themselves? Will you get to see a blueline or blueprint of the job before it goes to press? Will you be required to carry out a press proof? It may seem like too many questions at first, but think of it as an investment. You only have to learn this information once and much of it is given in Table 27.1.

Understanding the Terminology

Entering into discussions with either the printer or the service bureau can be pretty intimidating if you're unfamiliar with their language. Communication is critical, and you discover that service bureaus have a unique language all their own. If you are unsure of just what they are trying to tell you, ask questions.

Table 27.1 lists the most confusing terms you might encounter at a service bureau. Some may be obvious to you, but take a look just to avoid any surprises.

Table 27.1
Common Service Bureau Terminology

Term	Definition
All fonts resident	Describes the situation where all the fonts you have used to create your document are already loaded into the memory of the printer you are using, and no additional font code is required.
BBS	Acronym for bulletin board service; software that controls the traffic of files being transmitted from a remote location through a modem. Service bureaus use this as a convenience for their customers to send in their files.
Bleed	Describes when images in your file have overlapped the page boundaries set in your page setup.
Composite	A hard copy printout of all colors and overlays used in a file.
Compression package	A program that shrinks a file to a size that fits onto a disk; or to shorten the time it takes to transmit a file by modem.
Crop marks	The horizontal and vertical marks that indicate the outside corners of a page.
Crosshairs	In CorelDRAW!, the traditional target dots (also known as registration marks) used for matching up multiple layers of film on top of each other.
CT scan	Continuous tone scan.
Default	A preset factor in a software program or hardware configuration.
Density	Service bureau reference to the value measurement given to the relative opaqueness of a developed film negative.

continues

Table 27.1, Continued
Common Service Bureau Terminology

Term	Definition
Dot gain	This term refers to what happens on a press when ink dots hit the paper. When larger dots of ink soak into paper, the printed image becomes slightly larger and more distorted than is intended. This can be compensated for at the film imaging stage by adjusting the size of the dots.
Download	The action of transmitting a file from a central computer system to a remote computer system, or from a file server to a workstation.
DPI	Stands for dots per inch and refers to film, scanning, or printing resolution, which is the maximum number of dots (or more accurately "bits") that can be counted in one linear inch of a scanned image or film. Do not confuse dots per inch with the term "lines per inch," which refers to the number of rows of dots counted in one linear inch of a screen tint.
Driver	A program routine that contains the instructions necessary to control communication between software and peripherals; also called a device driver.
Drum scanner	A scanner whereby the original is loaded onto a drum-shaped holder that spins at high speeds while the data is recorded by a laser.
DTP	In the world of service bureaus, this stands for desktop publishing. However, if seen in the career ads in the newspaper, it often stands for data processing.
Emulsion	The silver-based coating on one side of the imaging film that is sensitive to light.

Term	Definition
	The emulsion side of the film is identified as the dull, non-reflective side. Unfortunately, it can be easily scratched off.
Extension	The three letters, preceded by a period, found at the end of a filename. It usually indicates the originating program of the file. For instance, all CorelDRAW! drawings have the same extension of CDR, and versions 3, 4, and 5 all share the same extension (unlike versions of other software by other companies).
Flatbed scanner	A scanner whereby the original is placed face down on a stationary document glass (much like a photocopier) and a reflection-sensitive light bar passes below it and records the data based on the reflected image.
Flatness	Describes the detail to which curves in your drawing are drawn. Setting the flatness level may affect how smooth your curved lines will be after being imaged—how many straight-line segments are used to make the curve. Flatness affects the printed image, not the screen image.
Font conflict	Virtually non-existent now, this problem plagued service bureaus in the early days before font identification standards were set. The resulting error was usually having fonts you had asked for replaced by completely different fonts.
Fonts	This is now known as the digital description of a typeface. The name has been carried over from the early days when typesetting systems used large metal or nylon discs with images of letters cut out of them to represent typefaces.

continues

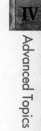

IV

Advanced Topics

Table 27.1, Continued
Common Service Bureau Terminology

Term	Definition
GCR	Gray component replacement during a separation is a technique for reducing the amount of cyan, magenta, and yellow in an image and replacing it with appropriate amounts of black.
Grayscale	Describes an optional "densitometer scale" image available in Print Options when separations are selected. From the days of manual camera work, it was a small strip of continuous-tone paper, graduated in steps from dark to light gray, which was placed along with the originals being shot on a graphic arts camera to ensure the proper film exposure and developing.
HQS	High-quality screening. A software feature much boasted about by Linotype, makers of the linotronic imagesetter line, which is built into their raster image processor (RIP). The purpose of HQS software is to give optimum screen angle when imaging process color separations with the aim of avoiding moires. The RIP adjusts the angle of the screen just slightly depending on the frequency of dot requested. See *RIP, moires.*
Imaging	The mechanical process of transforming digital information into machine instruction language with the purpose of exposing light-sensitive film by way of a laser. This is a term that printers use, so expect to hear it.
Imagesetter	Describes basically any printer that generates a hard copy image. It is synonymous with any machine that produces high-resolution film output.

Term	Definition
Laminate	Pronounced "'la-mi-nit" and also known as laminate proof, it is the name given to multiple layers of microthin, clear, and colored carrier film bonded together to a paper backing, and produced from film generated by the file you want to print. Once produced, is a close representation of the colors the press will print.
Landscape	Describes the orientation of your page. In CorelDRAW!, landscape describes a page that has greater width than height. (See *Portrait.*)
Line art	1) Any artwork that is not made up of color or screen tints and is only composed of solid black or solid white. 2) An image made of simple, drawn lines.
Linen tester	A small magnifying glass that is used to closely examine film or originals.
Linotronic	A line of imagesetters manufactured by Linotype.
Loop	Same as a linen tester, a small magnifier used to closely examine film or originals.
LPI	Stands for lines per inch, refers to the number of rows of dots counted in one linear inch of a screen tint or halftone screen. Not to be confused with resolution.
Moires	The effect when two or more film screens are aligned at incorrect angles and look like a blurry checkerboard or tartan pattern. This is one of the hazards to watch for in film production and can detract from the quality of photograph reproduction.

continues

IV

Advanced Topics

Table 27.1, Continued
Common Service Bureau Terminology

Term	Definition
Nested fonts	This is caused by selecting All Fonts Resident when exporting from a drawing program such as CorelDRAW!, and subsequently importing into another program. If the imagesetter cannot find the font in memory because its data is buried within other data, it substitutes a default font (usually courier) into the imported file.
Nesting files	This is caused by exporting a file that already contains a file imported from another source such as an EPS file. For more information, read about *filters* in Chapters 3 and 10.
PKZip	The most common compression program used in service bureaus.
Plate	For service bureaus: a color separation or film overlay that represents a color of ink. When printing: the paper or metal sheet that is installed onto the press and is produced directly from your film.
Portrait	Refers to the page orientation that has a page height larger than the width. (See *Landscape*.)
Print file	A PostScript text file created by selecting Print to File in the Main Print selection box. Can be recognized by the extension .PRN and contains all informational code necessary to describe the document you are printing.
Processing	1) In film processing, exposed film is taken to a film processing machine for developing, fixing, washing, and drying. 2) In image (data) processing, it refers to the data file that has been sent to the raster image processor of the imagesetter.

Term	Definition
Processor	The machine that physically develops, stops, fixes, washes, and dries the actual imagesetter film.
Raster graphic	Term given to any type of file that contains bitmapped images, such as BMP, TIFF, and PCX.
Registration	The accuracy in matching one film overlay to another according to the alignment markings imaged onto the film and the images on the film itself.
Resident scans	Scanned images that are stored at the service bureau to be inserted or used as link files when imaging client files.
Resolution	The measure of detail that is recorded onto the film by the imagesetter.
RIP	Raster image processor; basically a computer solely dedicated to calculating data and sending it directly to the imagesetter.
RRED	Right reading emulsion down; describes how the film is imaged. When RRED film is held with the emulsion side facing away from you, the images and type read from left to right.
RREU	Stands for right reading emulsion up, and describes how the film is imaged.
Screen frequency	Term used to describe the LPI or number of rows of dots countable in one linear inch.
SelectSet	Name of a line of imagesetters developed by AGFA, Inc.

continues

IV

Advanced Topics

Table 27.1, Continued
Common Service Bureau Terminology

Term	Definition
Separations	Term given to a set of film overlays that, when combined, make up a composite image.
Source file	The original file created by a program like CorelDRAW!, as opposed to a print file.
Spooler	A type of software program service bureaus use to regulate the jobs going to the imagesetters. Basically a traffic manager for all data sent to film. Files can be held in the spooler until it is necessary to image them in a timely manner.
System profile	A file generated by the CorelDRAW! version 5.0 color management system. It describes the hardware your system uses, compensates the screen image, and can also affect the output results.
Transparency	1) A color print generated onto a clear carrier for the purpose of producing an overhead cell for an overhead projector. 2) A term often used to describe a diapositive continuous-tone slide. If your service bureau deals in slides and overheads, you might need to clarify this term.
Upload	The action of transferring a data file from a computer system to a remote computer.
Vector graphic	What you create when you use the drawing tools in CorelDRAW!. Lines, objects, and curves representing fonts are all vector-based. Bitmaps, PCX files, TIFF files, and so on are not.

Familiarizing Yourself with the Technology

Before charging into your service bureau with disks in hand, it is good to know a little about what is behind the bureau's magic. Whether your project is just a simple one-pager or a huge manual filled with scans and color separations, the bureau operators pay more attention to customers who are well-informed about their business and the technology that runs it.

The Different Types of Imagesetters

There are two main types of imagesetter film processes in use. The first is a *roll-fed* or *capstan* system whereby a 200-foot roll of film is loaded at one end much the same way film loads into a 35 mm camera. This film is then exposed by a laser before it ends up in a take-up cassette. Tiny rollers coax the film through the machine and tug it so that it is perfectly taut. Theoretically, you could create a document the width of the roll (usually 12 or 18 inches) that extends the entire length of the roll (200 to 250 feet)—although you would want to keep a fire extinguisher handy for when the RIP explodes. The operator determines when the cassette is full and removes it for film processing, just as you would when your 35 mm camera finishes its film.

In the second type, the drum model, a 22-inch by 26-inch sheet of film is vacuum-sealed to the inside of a half-barrel-shaped drum. The laser mechanism mounted above moves back and forth across the film to expose it. Once the film imaging is complete, the exposed sheet is moved into a take-up cassette, and an unexposed sheet takes its place.

The most significant difference in the way these two types of imagesetters operate is that the film moves and the laser does not in the capstan, and the laser moves and the film is stationary in the drum.

Processing Film and Paper

The terms paper and film are a bit deceiving. Paper is really film that just looks like paper because it has a white polyethylene-based carrier with a layer of light-sensitive emulsion on it. Film, however, is exactly that—film. Specifically, it is highly sensitive orthographic (or line) film just like that used in the traditional prepress houses.

After being exposed by the laser of the imagesetter, both types of film must run through a film processor for the image to appear. These processors can be quite high-tech and incorporate all sorts of bells and whistles to keep them operating smoothly and efficiently.

IV

Advanced Topics

Film processors automatically process, fix, wash, and dry the film by pulling it through a series of rubber and steel rollers. During this process, variables such as film processor speed, water temperature and filtration, chemical replenishment rate, and how often the processor is cleaned are all important factors that affect the quality of the output.

A well-set-up processing system has a fresh and constant supply of filtered water controlled by a temperature regulator. Apparently, even the quality of the city water supply can be a factor. In areas where the water is more acidic than normal, adjustment to the chemistry dilution might be required. In areas where excessive rain floods the water supply, water may become muddier than usual, affecting purity levels.

These processors must be periodically tested by way of a control strip that tells the operator what the chemistry's condition is, and whether the equipment needs to be serviced or not.

Looking for a Good Service Bureau

A responsibility that has fallen on the electronic artist seems to be ensuring that the film outputs correctly and that operations at the service bureau run smoothly. The artist inevitably is dragged into any problems that crop up, which is the best motivator for selecting a reliable bureau from the outset. As the artist, you want to make the bureau workers your best friends. You want them to recognize your voice when you call and monitor your files as they journey through the imaging stages. You should also consult with them about planning your production schedules.

Your best bet for finding a good service bureau is through word of mouth, but beware of the opinions you hear. Some companies are judged solely on their prices. You might even witness price wars between competitors. Five dollars versus five-fifty per page sounds like a big spread—and it is, if you deal in volume the way the bureaus do—but good service is not based on just low prices! There are many other factors to consider; rush charges, processing surcharges, punctual service, clean output, common courtesy, and assistance during emergencies are all critical factors to weigh.

Where To Find a Reliable Service Bureau

Begin your search by asking colleagues who work in the same field as you. Next, call your printer—he may have already worked with a service bureau in the past. If you subscribe to a commercial e-mail network such as Internet, America Online, or

CompuServe, look for listings there. CompuServe's Corel forum has a downloadable file called SERVBU.EXE that uncompresses into a Windows help file called SERVBURO.HLP. This file has names, addresses, phone and fax numbers, and BBS numbers of Corel-approved service bureaus throughout the U.S. and Canada. Some even have toll-free numbers. Just remember, you could always consult the phone book as a last resort.

To install the file after uncompressing, follow these steps:

1. Place the file into your COREL50\DRAW directory and, using Program Manager, set up a new item icon in your Corel50 window group.

2. Browse until you locate the file.

3. Set the command to:
   WINHELP C:\COREL50\DRAW\SERVBURO.HLP
   assuming that your Corel50 directory is in the root of your C drive. If not, add the correct path.

4. A new Windows help icon appears in the window. Double-click on it to open.

Be absolutely sure to ask whoever answers the phone about whether they accept CorelDRAW! files and which versions they use. Service bureaus that do not allow source files to be sent should fall down to the bottom of your list.

The reason for this is quite simple: It is a major inconvenience when they aren't capable or refuse to accept original files. It means that you must supply them with print (or PRN) files—this is not good news. Print files are tricky and time-consuming to prepare, and are usually large and unwieldy to transport. Continue your search until you either find a source-file-compatible supplier or run out of choices.

Visiting the Service Bureau

Once you have picked out a service bureau, pay them a visit and tour their facilities. An early weekday morning is a good time. Let them know whether you are an experienced electronic artist or just a beginner. Ask to see how they calibrate their imagesetters. If they are a well-run shop, their machines are calibrated at least once a day. Do they have their imagesetters controlled by a print spooling system? Are they set up with a bulletin board so that you can transmit your files by modem if you so need?

Ask to see their film processors. This gives you the chance to see if their processors are run out of a pail of water (an extremely bad practice), or if they have a properly installed, temperature-controlled water filtration system. If you hold environmental issues high, ask how they dispose of their chemical waste. Find out how they store their film. It should not be piled high in a corner somewhere, but instead should be kept in a dry, dark area with some sort of stock rotation system so that they use only the oldest film.

How do they package up their film output? Do they use staples that could scratch your film while it is in transit? Do they include a nice cardboard reinforcement to prevent damage? Do they cut your pages apart for you, or just roll up the film in a tube and let you do the rest? Take a close look around. If you choose to have your work output there, this is probably the only time you get to see the facility and talk in person to the operators or owners before the real work begins. Do your best to make a good impression of yourself; sometimes, you will need these folks to bend over backward for you.

After the tour, you will have a better understanding of how efficiently their business runs. This is no small reflection on how efficient and conscientious they will be with your files. Before you go out the door, grab a handful of order forms and a price list for future reference.

The Mom-and-Pop Shop

Unless you have no choice in the matter, steer clear of service bureaus that remind you of a home business or a two-person shop that doesn't look like a professional establishment. They might still be in the learning processes of imaging and have a long way to go. Remember that this is a relatively new technology. Set-up costs are high, the learning curve is long, and inexperience is deadly. You don't want anyone using your files to learn the business.

The Specialized Service Bureau

Taken to the other extreme, some businesses specialize in only slide or transparency imaging. All they usually have are image recorders that produce slides from desktop publishing applications. Their market is very focused, and it can be quite difficult to find one that offers good service at a moment's notice. If you stumble onto one of these places, write down their number. You might need their special service one day.

The Professional Service Bureau

The one to find. The professional service bureau has competitive prices, puts value on customer service, is accustomed to high volumes of film, and is prepared for the complex problems. Once you find a truly professional service, stick with it. They will take care of you.

The Printer's Internal Imagesetting Service

Some print shops serve the client's need to have one-stop shopping, so they set up their own internal, electronic prepress service. The staff are sometimes moved in from other areas slumping in work load due to the advent of desktop technology. If your printing supplier has one of these departments, they might be worth considering as an output source. The staff is probably quite experienced, with a good understanding of the printing process. Unfortunately, these shops do not price competitively. In fact, it is not unusual to expect prices 300 percent higher than output from a typical service bureau.

What Should You Expect To Pay?

Buying output is like buying anything else these days. If you don't know what your film is worth, you might find out later that you paid too much. You should always expect a discount for quantity. In fact, most service bureaus actually advertise discounts when more than 5, 10, 25, 50, 100, or 200 pages are imaged. Also, if you have an extremely simple file without any spot colors or scanned or imported graphic files, and you need a large quantity of pages, talk to the manager or owner of the business. She just might want your business badly enough that she will give you an additional discount.

The following is an example of typical prices for 1270 resolution paper and film output. Take into account price fluctuations for inflation, area, supply, silver prices, and local price competitiveness.

Size	Paper/film	over 5	over 10	over 25	over 50
Letter	9-13	8.50-13	8-7.50	11.50-6.50	9.50-8
Legal	11-16	10.50-15.50	10-9.50	14-7.50	11.50-10
Tabloid	16-24	15-23	14.50-13.50	20.50-11	16.50-14.50
16×20	24-36	23-34	21.50-20.50	30.50-17	25-21.50
22×26	32-48	30-45.50	29-27	40.50-22.50	33.50-29

These prices are based on output delivered in one business day (24 hours).

What Quality Service Should You Expect?

When you receive your output, it should be perfect (barring any of your errors). The fact that the RIP could process through the PostScript imaging data describing your page, means the imaging part of the process had to have gone smoothly. If there was a problem and your output does not look as you expected, it is due to the fact that your instructions were inaccurate or the service bureau is not giving you the service you have paid for. This might sound like misplaced blame, but there is a reason for it—lack of proofing.

Before your output is ever packaged and the courier is called, someone should have given it that one critical eye to make sure that you would be satisfied (and that you would avoid a wasted courier charge and a time delay). If they had found a problem, you could have been contacted to help find the cause.

You can expect that your output will be sent to you properly and on time. Expect the convenience of having it sent to you by courier, and expect the courier's charge on your invoice. You have enough to do without wasting time arranging for couriers.

If you are in a hurry for your output and order a bureau's quick service, expect to pay surcharges. These range anywhere from a three-hour service with a 50-percent surcharge, to a one-hour service with a 100-percent surcharge.

If your files are extremely complex, you might be charged an extra processing surcharge. Most service bureaus follow a rule of thumb that each letter-sized page should generally take about fifteen minutes to image, after which you might be charged up to one dollar per every extra minute. This is not an uncommon practice, but keep in mind that good customers are rarely charged.

Although equipped with PC-compatible computers and the ability to output from CorelDRAW!, there are service bureaus who would penalize you for insisting on sending in source files. These businesses would charge you a 50-percent markup for outputting directly from the source files. Stay away from these places; they obviously don't need you as a customer!

What the Service Bureau Expects from You

As the client requesting output, you are expected to complete their order form correctly the first time around; one wrong box marked on an order form could mean improper output, and you would be left paying for useless material—and not just monetarily either. The service might remember you the next time you call or bring in a job and perceive you to be a problem customer. You might lose the status of being a good customer and get inappropriate service.

Finding a Common Platform

If source files are acceptable to the service bureau, you will save a lot of extra work. There are advantages to this, the best being that if there is a problem, you can save time by allowing one of their operators to correct the error in the original file. You avoid having to solve the problem yourself, resending the file by courier or modem, and wasting time.

But if you are unable to find a PC-equipped bureau, then the next most common platform you will find is a Macintosh-based platform. Macintosh-platform-based service bureaus began as the most common type due to the popularity burst of Macintosh computers over the last 10 years, but this is quickly changing. In the not-so-distant past, service bureau operators would shiver at the thought of having to output a print file, because they were nearly always created incorrectly. Ask them if they recommend any special instructions to prepare a print file. They may have their own way of doing things. The hazards you must first consider are things like whether to include any large scanned images if you have them built into your file, any special printer drivers you will need to obtain from the service bureau, and how will you get your file to the service bureau. You will not need to pull out your hair just yet, though; there are solutions for every situation. Further on in this chapter you will find all the information you need.

If your service bureau requires a print file, ask them how they would like the file prepared before you create it. They might have preferences you aren't aware of, such as presetting your emulsion up or down, or setting the line screen defaults and/or screen angle defaults.

IV

Advanced Topics

Supplying Third-Party Fonts

Although CorelDRAW! comes with 825 fonts of all styles, weights, and characters, you might use a font from a third-party supplier, or even a font you created yourself. This is a common case if your client has a special corporate font or one that must match other materials they have already produced. If such is the case, tell the service bureau on their order form. Do not rely on them to check over your file for you. Most order forms clearly state that the client must specify and supply all fonts used in the document.

Corel ships a basic font package that installs with the program. If you only use fonts from this collection, you have nothing to worry about. However, if you use a font from the CD-ROM disc supplied with versions 4 and 5, indicate which ones on the output order form. The bureau will need to install them onto the computer that will send output to the imagesetter.

As for third-party fonts, there are two options. If a special font is used for simple headlines, use the Convert to Curves feature. If you use a special font for something such as body type or paragraph type, send the font file along with your file. You will need to supply them with both the TIFF and FOT files for each special font you use.

Supplying Special Files

If you work solely in CorelDRAW! and have happily imported various types of files into your file, do not worry about sending the originals of those files. CorelDRAW! builds in all the data necessary to describe them for the imagesetter. However, if you use a layout program such as Aldus PageMaker or Quark XPress, and you have imported your CorelDRAW!-created graphic files into one of these programs, you might have to include them with the job.

Layout programs sometimes incorporate linking features whereby only the screen image is available while viewing the laid-out pages on your monitor. When printed, a layout program checks to see if the files placed into it are nearby, or if they are still in the same directory from which they were imported. When the main layout program file is sent to the service bureau for output, they might not print properly if those files are missing from the same directory as the program file. The safest route is always to include these imported files along with your job.

Maintaining Your Credibility

In your haste to make up time on an upcoming deadline, it is easy to forget to send special files or fonts needed to output your job. Make yourself a checklist and follow it religiously. If the service bureau sees you as reckless or absent-minded, they will no doubt consider problems with your output to always be your fault.

Output operators are only human, and you should not expect them to second-guess you or your type of work.

If you send your files by modem, fax in your order and promptly call them to let them know you have done so—they appreciate this level of diligence. If you bring in a disk, make sure everything needed is there. If you consistently have problems, your output may be quietly placed in the bottom of the cue, and hence there goes your good service.

Answering the Nitty-Gritty Questions

If this is your first time ordering output, you are in for a treat. This is nothing like playing 20 questions, the information they need is very specific: software, version numbers, screen frequency, negative, positive, film, paper—the variables seem endless. You must be absolutely sure that you have given the service bureau the correct instructions. Failure to do so wastes your time and money. Output can be quite expensive. If you need your 50-page, four-color book output to film and you mistakenly check off "paper" on the order form, guess who pays? If you wanted a 150-line screen, did you select 100-line because you were not familiar with the terminology? Same story—you pay. Complete their form carefully, including every scrap of information you can think of. Fax them a sample order to see if they understand what you are asking for. Never assume they will second guess you.

Preparing Your Files for Output

Before sending in your file, clean it up. Whether it is a CorelDRAW! or another file, be sure that you delete any extra artwork or imported files that might be on the pasteboard outside of the page area. Not only does this make your file size smaller, but it also images faster, saving time you might otherwise have to pay for if it were to take more than the allotted 15 minutes. If the output operator sees a big mess outside your page area, he or she will not clean it up for you!

Preparing a Print File

Ignore any horror stories you have heard about print files. They are relatively easy to create, but be alert. One wrong click of the mouse and your output is a wasted effort. Follow these procedures:

1. Open your file and select <u>F</u>ile, <u>P</u>rint.

2. Select your imagesetter as your printer (see Chapter 25, "Advanced Printing Techniques," for more information on choosing a printer).

IV

Advanced Topics

Make sure that you are using the Windows printer driver version 3.56 or later. Previous driver versions contain errors. If you are working with an older driver, you can obtain a newer version from the service bureau, CompuServe, Microsoft, or the Aldus forum.

3. After setting the print requirements to match the parameters of your printer (or following any special instructions as requested by the service bureau), select Print to file in the lower left area of the main Print menu box. If you know that the print file will be downloaded directly from a Macintosh computer, select For Mac (see fig. 27.1). Doing this deletes the two control characters that your Windows printer driver automatically inserts.

Figure 27.1
The Print to File
dialog box.

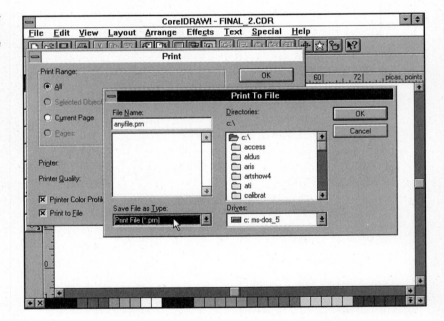

If you have selected to print any of the reference information such as crop marks, registration marks, calibration bar, densitometer bar, or file information, remember to allow a larger page size, such as those sizes that end in "extra."

4. When you select OK in the Print dialog box, you see a new Print to File option box appear that allows you to name the file and save it to a specific directory.

When preparing a print file, never choose the All Fonts Resident selection in the Print Options dialog box. This should only be selected in cases where the person preparing to send the file to the printer has memorized all of the fonts in their printer's memory and is absolutely positive that all the font information the file needs is available.

After your computer has finished writing the file to disk, make a note of the file's size. Could it fit onto a 3.5-inch floppy disk? Probably not—this file contains every bit of information necessary to output your file: Windows information, font, page size, screen frequency positive or negative, crop marks, and everything you selected. The service bureau will set the proper resolution and set up for paper or film as you requested; simply take this file and download it directly to the imagesetter. They do not even have to run Windows in order to print this file.

Checking Your Print File

Making a print file has been a risky business because there was never any way of verifying that what printed to file was really what you wanted. You had only your memory and concentration skill to rely on. An excellent program available to CorelDRAW! users is PRN View (version 2.1) written by Corel engineer Rus Miller (see fig. 27.2). This utility is available for downloading from the Compuserve Corel Forum. To use this utility follow these steps:

1. Download the self-extracting ZIP file called PRNVW.EXE and set it up in its own directory.

2. Double-click on the file in File Manager to extract the four files contained inside.

3. Set up the application as you would any application in Program Manager/New for a new item.

4. Once installed, locate or create a print file you want to check out.

IV

Advanced Topics

Figure 27.2
The PRN Viewer interface.

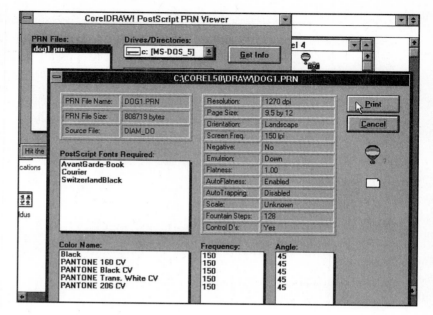

5. The print file is described in full detail, including all fonts used, paper size, orientation, resolution, etc. There's no guessing whether or not you pressed all of the right buttons. If you want, you can print all of this onto hard copy for later reference. You also can refer to this information when completing your output order form.

Best Time To Send Your Job

Service bureaus earn their living in two ways: by imaging as much as they can in as short a time as possible with as little hassle as possible; and by maximizing profits through rush charges. If you plan your time properly and religiously stick to your production schedule, you will not fall into the latter category.

How they maximize their machine time is simple. By day, they keep the imagesetters as busy as possible, interrupting the flow at any time for high-paying rush imaging. They keep busy by using powerful print spoolers to regulate the flow of data to their machines. If a frantic customer, blood-thirsty for a page of output, runs in the door, willing to pay anything for a piece of film—no problem. They can save his hide by holding all of their other work in the print spooler queue and giving his file the highest priority. Non-urgent and regular work is mostly imaged at night, when their most complex files are also processed. Files are sent to the spooler and the data is stored until the imagesetter is ready for it. The machines can merrily crunch away virtually uninterrupted.

The best time to send in your work is late afternoon when you have the best chance to have your job spooled up to image overnight and ready first thing in the morning. This might not work 100 percent of the time, but it is definitely the best time to try.

The average output order form can be a menacing-looking piece of work. Software, platform, fonts, resolution, screens, color separations, scans, and on and on. You might not even know what half of it means at first. Bureau managers are definitely not forms designers, but you can be sure that everything they need to know to do their job is on that hideous-looking form. Figure 27.3 is an actual order form from a service bureau. Actual names and addresses have been changed to protect the innocent.

Client information and shipping instructions are straightforward.

You might want to find your own courier if the service bureau charges a premium on top of their service.

Platform is not so critical because the software package you are using probably gives that away pretty quickly—but fill it out anyway. Program and version number are critical because the service bureau might not be as technologically current as you.

Tip

When completing an order form for imaging source files, request that the File/Print/Options Fountain Steps be set to the maximum of 250 for the smoothest blends possible.

Complete the Fonts used section carefully. If you cannot remember all of the fonts you used, there is a utility program called Font Checker available from the Corel Forum library in CompuServe. The downloadable file name is CDRCHECK.EXE, and it uncompresses to give you a nifty program capable of checking all the fonts used in your file. It might occasionally indicate that you have fonts that you are sure you did not use (see fig. 27.4). Keep in mind that this is freeware.

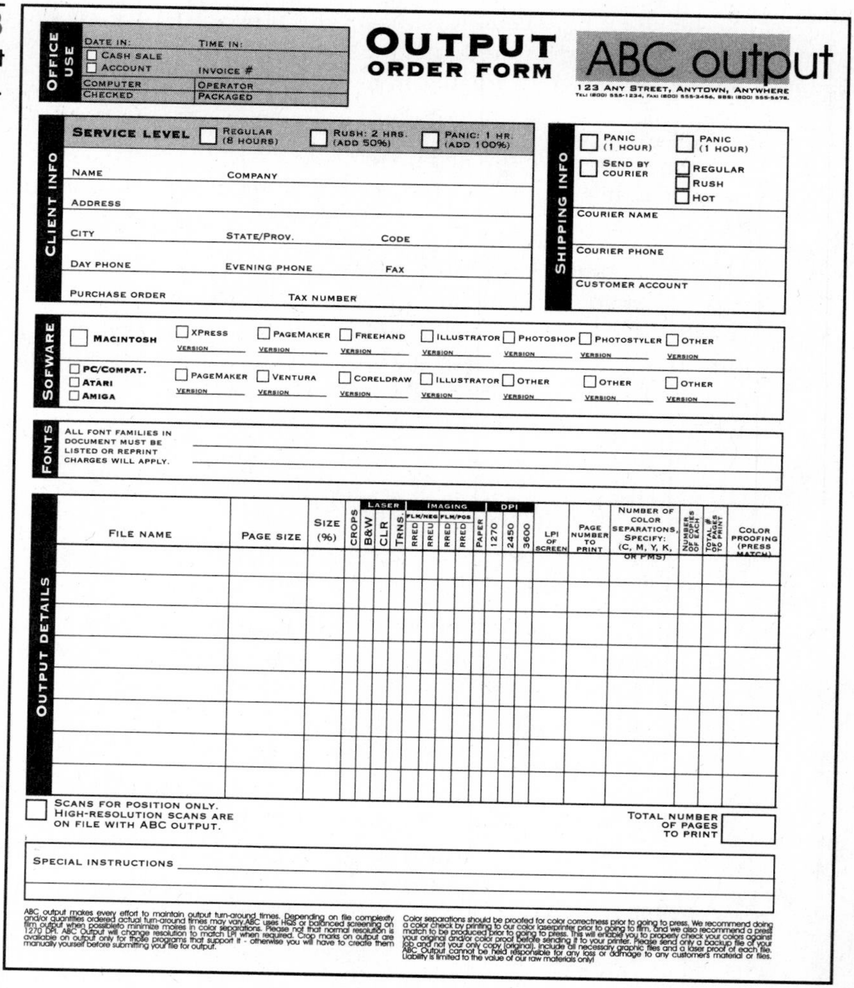

Figure 27.3
A sample output
order form.

This program is courtesy of Corel engineer Rus Miller. It will also tell you the file
size, the number of objects, the page size, and the page orientation. Service
bureaus have also been known to use this program when outputting from
CorelDRAW!.

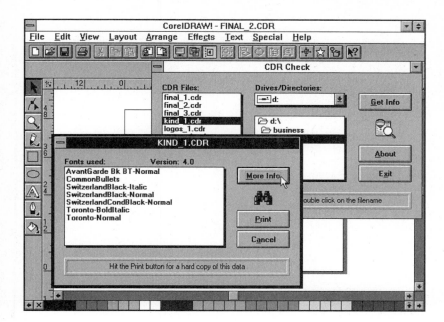

Figure 27.4
Freeware from
Corel enables
you to see what
fonts you used in
a file.

Send the bureau laser proofs of your pages. This might at least get them to take a second look at your file before they send it to the imagesetter. If there are going to be problems, the operators might be able to catch it just by glancing over the proof. They may even notice something you missed and give you a call to let you know.

Include a repeat of your instructions in a TXT file and save it to the same disk that your output files are on. Use Windows Notepad to create a repeat of the instructions you have asked for on the order form. Include your name, company, phone, date, and all pertinent information like file names, program and version used, and output requirements for each file. Service bureaus are busy places with literally thousands of files per week going through their hands. In case your files somehow get separated from your order you will have a backup—and the service bureau will have no excuses!

Getting Your Files to the Service Bureau

No matter what type your files are—print files, source files, scanned images, or font files—you might find it difficult to get them to the service bureau (or anywhere else for that matter). If the files are too big to fit onto a floppy disk, you are stuck finding another of the many methods available; file compression, file transmission through a modem, bulletin boards, removable hard disks, removable media, or e-mail uploading to name a few of the most common. Each has its own advantages and disadvantages, and choosing the best method depends on you and your service bureau. It is worth asking them how they want a file sent when you are calling around. To some, it may be an insurmountable obstacle they may not want to deal with. To others, it is only routine.

Compression Programs

The best and most common method is to compress your files using a data compression program. The most widely used in the industry is a shareware program called PKZIP, mentioned earlier in this book. It is available from PKWare, Inc., (414) 352-3670. The latest version released is 2.04g.

PKZIP lets you shrink a file or multiple files (and types) by as much as 95 percent depending on the file type. CorelDRAW! files usually compress to about 65 percent of the original size—more than half. Features in this newest release also enable for spanning multiple disks after compression of the file exceeds your available disk space. The beauty of this program, apart from being freeware, is that the people to whom you are sending a file do not need to have PKZIP installed on their system. PKZIP allows you to make a self-extracting file that explodes (usually in a fraction of a second) to its original size when the files icon is double-clicked in File Manager. The program comes with its own set of simple instructions and can be run under Windows MS-DOS prompt.

When creating print files for downloading from the Macintosh platform, another advantage to using PKZIP is that a ZIP file can be uncompressed onto a Macintosh computer using a program called Stuffit, available from Aladdin Systems, (408) 761-6200.

Doing this on the Macintosh end is fairly easy once you have Stuffit loaded. Take your PC-formatted disk containing the print file and put it into the Macintosh drive, which can read PC disks. With a Macintosh system utility called Apple File Exchange, convert the file using the default conversion. Once the file has been converted, open Stuffit, find the file, and, by using the Full Menus feature of the program (this one usually trips up everybody) under the Options menu, select Unzip and presto, you are ready to download.

If you do adopt PKZIP as part of your arsenal of tools, you quickly discover that it comes in handy for all sorts of things. Use it for archiving files onto backup disks and compressing large files for modem transmission to the service bureau.

Remote File Transmission

A bulletin board service (BBS) is something the professional service bureau likely has available for its customers. This setup enables you to transmit your files to them through a phone line without ever having to leave the comfort of your own computer. The only catch is that you need a modem to do it, but the necessary software is already loaded onto your computer!

For computer users, modems are the convenience device of the nineties. It is hardware capable of converting data into sound or vice versa much the same way a fax machine works. If you decide to go out and purchase one, it is worth spending a few extra dollars for a fast one with multiple uses. A modem capable of doubling as a fax or other tool is very useful, but speed and reliability are the most important features to look for. If your modem is slow at transmitting data, you could end up wasting time *and money* rather than saving it.

Select a modem that is either 2400 or 9600 baud (baud is the rate or speed at which data is transmitted). If the sole purpose of this modem is to transmit files to the service bureau, be sure that they at least have an equivalent or faster modem than you. If yours is faster than theirs, you're wasting your money; the speed of the exchange of information between modems is determined by the rate of the slowest of the two. You likely will select the 9600 baud model. If your service bureau has gone to the expense of setting up a bulletin board system, they probably want to be compatible with as many clients as possible and have the system controlled by a fast modem. *Today's models can go up to 57,000 baud.*

After installing a modem to your computer, the easiest way to hook into a BBS is to use a Windows-supplied software utility called Terminal. This is a pretty primitive program, but it has everything needed to transmit your files. If you do get lost while using it, consult the help menu; otherwise, go ahead and open it up with the following procedures:

1. Open the program (usually found in the Accessories Group) in Program Manager by double-clicking on the icon.

2. Go directly to the Settings/Communications menu and set the correct COM port, baud rate, data bits, stop bit, and the parity and flow control settings. The most common setup for this is 8 data bits, 1 stop bit, no parity, and Xon/Xoff flow control. (Don't be too concerned with these terms' meanings yet.) If the service bureau has any special settings that must be set, you might need to contact them to find out what they are.

3. Under the Settings menu again, select Phone Number and enter the correct number of the BBS. If you are dialing from within a large office environment where you need to dial a special prefix to get an outside line, enter this number first, followed by a comma and the BBS number. The comma inserts a pause, allowing time for the phone line to open.

IV

Advanced Topics

Figure 27.5
The Communications dialog box used to set connection information.

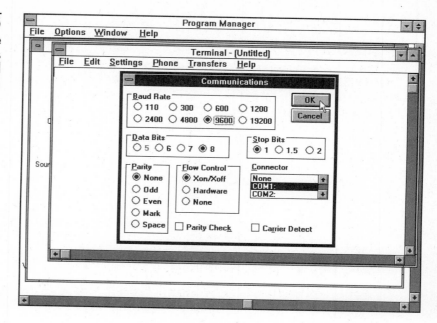

4. If you have a pulse-dial telephone, under Settings, select Modem Commands. Enter ATDP (for attention, dial pulse) where it says Dial Prefix. If you have a tone-dial telephone, select Modem Commands and enter ATDT, if it isn't already there.

5. After you have done this, you are ready. Select Phone/Dial to connect to the BBS. If it truly is a BBS system, the program at the other end will give all the instructions you need to send your file. Once you enter the area where you actually send your file, select Transfers/Send Binary File and choose the file you want to send. Once transmission has begun, you may go back to working in other programs under Windows, but watch out—any heavy demand put on your computer's processor slows the rate at which data leaves your computer's hard disk. Also, keep an eye on it from time to time to be sure that you know when your file transfer is complete. If you aren't watching carefully when it finishes, you might not be able to tell if the transfer was successful or not.

6. A thermometer-style progress bar at the bottom of the screen lets you know how much data has been sent. After completion, log off the system and select Phone/Hangup, and you are done.

Removable Media

If you choose not to use the modem route, or your files are too big to transmit over a modem, consider acquiring some type of large-format, removable media method. There is an abundance of products on the market, but again, consult your service bureau. They might be able to help you choose hardware that is best suitable for you both.

The most common medium type in the industry is removable magnetic disks that commonly hold 40 or 80 MB of data. They can be removed from the drives and used for data storage or data transport. Early models were plagued with problems with faulty and fragile disks, but those problems have been ironed out. Models on the market today boast a high reliability rate, and expert users routinely use this hardware for moving large files around for things such as imagesetter output.

An older, less popular format is the Bernoulli drive, which also is a magnetic drive capable of storing large amounts of data. It is quite antiquated though, and not recommended for data integrity and reliability. At best, it should only be used as a last resort, as this technology is becoming out-of-date.

E-Mail

Another transfer method is the e-mail route. If your service bureau is wise and has provided for files to be sent in by multiple methods, they might allow you to send by e-mail. Large commercial networks such as CompuServe, America Online, and Internet have provisions for sending data from one place to another more quickly and effectively than conventional modems. In situations where you are sending files a long distance, this method also helps you to avoid long-distance phone charges.

Paper versus Film: Not too Little, Not too Much

There are many different methods of reproduction that imagesetter output can take once it leaves the service bureau. As the artist and originator of the file, you probably know what is needed; you know one thing at least—you want the highest quality possible. But, in some cases, it might not be necessary to pay for the highest quality possible. With imagesetting, there are many different quality levels from which to choose. This section gives insight as to how not to order a Cadillac when all you need is a Chevette.

IV

Advanced Topics

Choosing Paper or Film

Film negatives are usually the norm in the printing industry, as well as a few others, but do you always need it? Maybe not. For instance, a community newspaper has the type of production methods that involve a lot of little pieces of art like company logos, faxed artwork, laser-printed ads, and halftones produced onto photomechanical transfer material (PMT), which is eventually going to be joined up somehow with a layout, usually text and editorial. In a case like this you wouldn't go to the expense of making film negatives of your output as well as all those little pieces of art; better just to manually paste-up all of those logos and artwork onto one layer and shoot it onto film with a stat camera. After all, many of those materials come to the newspaper in a quick-and-dirty format. Also, newspapers run at such a high speed that they wouldn't be able to maintain the detail of a very fine line screen. Most newspapers are printed with a 65- or 85-line screen, perfect for paper output.

On the other hand, some artists prefer paper output over film. Unfortunately, this sometimes ends up being a waste if the targeted method of reproduction is a sheet-fed press. Paper output must eventually be shot onto film as a final step in the production process. The unfortunate aspect is that sheet-fed presses run at a relatively slow rate and, therefore, can hold a much finer dot of screen. The cameras that are used to photograph the reflective properties of the paper output in order to get the images onto film aren't capable of focusing on excessively fine detail, so getting paper output is sometimes the wrong way to go.

Choosing High Resolution versus Low Resolution

There are three basic selections from which to choose when getting paper or film output: 1270, 2540, or 3600 dpi. These values measure the amount of bits or dots per inch that the imagesetter's laser will have to work with to construct the detail of your output onto the film.

If you require paper output, don't select any resolution greater than 1270 dpi or a line screen greater than 100 lpi. In the case of output for a newspaper, the paper images will need to be shot onto a film negative later anyway. Again, unfortunately, many cameras are not capable of focusing on detail exceeding 1270 dpi, and the same story goes for when the line screen is too fine—too much detail for the camera to pick up. A rare case where you might want to exceed 1270 dpi for paper output is if the images contained on that paper output were targeted for enlargement of more than 400 percent. In this case, it would probably be wise to ask for the highest resolution. The lpi would need to be determined mathematically by calculating the final size of the enlargement and then working back to the output size.

For film, use the 2540 dpi because the film comes in direct contact with the printing plate when it is burned; you need every possible detail to show up on the plate for the press. The higher quality the press you want, the higher quality resolution you need. For the most part, though, 2540 dpi is fine.

If you were creating artwork for such high-quality printing as used in bank notes, stock certificates, stamps, certain types of legal tender (nice work if you can get it), then you likely would select the 3600 dpi resolution and a much higher lpi of 200 to 300. Presses that print this type of work operate much slower than regular sheet-fed presses and can hold a much finer dot pattern. If you need to get an idea how much detail can be reproduced with this high of a screen and film resolution, just look at a stamp. The high degree of detail you will see reproduced on the stamp is a direct result of using an extremely high screen frequency.

RRED, RREU, Negatives and Positives

These first two short forms referring to the emulsion side of the film are enough to make any first-time film order a nightmare. They are unknown terms for those who haven't a clue about film, and worse, they don't even spell a word, so it's easy to forget what they mean. It can be pretty confusing for those who have spent their entire careers in front of a computer screen but have never actually had the chance to work with film.

RRED and RREU mean Right Reading Emulsion Down and Right Reading Emulsion Up. Right reading refers to film orientation relative to the reader when the film is not upside down and is readable from left to right. To determine if film is RRED or RREU, place the film on a table. Which way is the emulsion (or dull side) facing while you are reading it, down or up? If it's facing down, then the film is RRED and vice versa. Simple.

Choosing Emulsion Up or Down

Choosing either RRED or RREU depends on the production method you use. For offset printers, you will require film negative and RRED 99 percent of the time. Without droning on about the dynamics of printing press operation, suffice it to say that the emulsion side of the film must directly contact the printing press plate when exposed, and the resulting image must be backward-reading.

Making Sure that You Get What You Paid For

Service bureaus are operated by human beings who, in turn, operate machines—the critical term being human beings. Imagesetting is a far-from-perfect science that combines the precision of computers, the properties of physics and science, and the unpredictable (and occasionally rushed) imagesetter operators. When you receive your output, look it over before you send it to the print shop. It is not recommended that you courier your output directly from the service bureau to the printer. How do you know when you are getting value for your output dollar? Read on.

Casting a Critical Eye

When examining your actual output (apart from proofing the copy and checking the scanned images), check for things such as scratches, dirt, poor film density (or show-through), banding, screen frequency, and anything that verifies or demerits that you got what you paid for. Taking the time to look over your film is just as important as completing the output order form correctly. If the service bureau got what it needed, so should you.

There are a few simple tools that can help to verify your order's quality. Get a loop (or magnifying glass) of magnification of at least ten to check the resolution of the film. The best type to get is a free-standing model that holds steady while you look through it. Examine the edges of the smallest lettering to determine the smoothness of curves, dots, and holes. Through experience, you will be able to recognize 1270 from 2540 dpi easily, but it will definitely take a few examinations. Ask the service bureau for some samples of each when you first visit them to give you some reference material. They usually have pails of scrap film that they save for silver recovery and likely will be happy to hand over a few scraps.

Another useful tool is a simple-looking plastic overlay called a screen finder. The screen finder can be purchased at your local art and drafting supply shop for under 10 dollars and can enable you the determine the lpi or screen frequency of your output. The screen finder comes with instructions, but the short version is as follows:

1. Place your film on a light table or white piece of paper. A light table is a glass-top table with a built-in light source used to do film work. A window would work, also.

2. Find an area on your film that contains a screen and place the screen finder flat on top of it. The screen finder has a series of curved lines in the center of it that all seem to converge at the same point and a series of symmetrical measurements beside them.

3. Notice that the lines on the screen finder seem to develop a pattern when placed over the screen. Rotate the finder clockwise until the pattern that you see in the center points to the measurements along the side.

4. Determine which measurement most closely aligns with the pattern you see and that will tell you the screen frequency or lpi of your film.

If you receive paper, look for smudges of dirt or what looks like little black dust spots over the images on the output. If any are found, they are likely silver deposits caused by a dirty processor. If they are dark enough or excessively large, they could show up on the film when it is shot by the camera. The camera person must then spend extra time (you do pay for this) to clean up the image to get a good, clean image onto the plate for the press.

The screen finder also has examples of screen tints including 5, 10, 20, 30, 40, 50, 60, 70, 80, 90, and 95 percent. By closely comparing these samples to how your film is supposed to appear, you are able to determine whether the imagesetter was calibrated properly for correct density and whether your ink colors are accurate or not. At this point, sending it back to the service bureau for rework might be necessary. They may rerun the page(s) or do a rewash of the paper.

Scratches on your film are definitely cause for alarm. They are the result of a dirty processor. The silver deposits do not stick to film, but they do cause tiny hairline scratches and these might show up on the printing press plate. Send the output back for rework.

If your film looks bluish or greenish, this is no cause for alarm. This is the result of the film being packaged too soon after processing and is harmless to your images. If the color makes you nervous, leave the film out in the open light for an hour or so and the color will disappear.

IV

Advanced Topics

Problems that Affect Printing

Moires or checker-board patterns in your process color separations are caused by incorrect screen angles generated by either incorrect settings in your CorelDRAW! Print/Options/Separations (Ctrl+P/Options/Separations) selection or by over-riding software built into the RIP of the imagesetter. These usually show up either on the color key produced from your film before printing, or (unfortunately) while it's on the press. Again, you may have to check the screen angles of your film before sending it to the printer. If you are unsure about checking screen angles, ask your print shop to verify the angles for you. It's a tricky job and this is something only the most advanced users are able to do. If you find that the angles are incorrect, send them back. Process color screen angles should be as follows:

Cyan	15 degrees
Magenta	75 degrees
Yellow	0 degrees
Black	45 degrees

Banding is the last and final item you should check for, and this is something you might find only in the screen dots of a graduated fill. Banding appears like a series of steps in what is supposed to be a nice, smooth conversion from one dot size to another. You notice banding more in higher lpi and dpi film than in lower because this film reveals much more detail. The most common cause of this is an exceedingly low Fountain Steps setting in the Print/Options selection. The default changes with the device requested, but the maximum available from the software is 250 steps. Ask for this specifically on your output order form.

Banding stripes can appear quite noticeably in color-separated film even with the Fountain Strips set to the maximum. This occurs when the RIP has calculated for four colors to increase or decrease simultaneously, but alters the steps for each color to alternate with each other. The band usually is more noticeable in colors such as yellow and magenta. Don't be alarmed when you see this; it's usually just a characteristic of digital output and might not show up in your final printed product. Again, if you are unsure or unsettled by it—consult your printer.

Taking Your Output to the Press

When you have all you need as far as digital output goes, and you arrive at the printer's door, rest assured that, because you have made it this far through the process, you will be considered not only an expert in computers but also prepress. You are bringing the printer film that they can put right onto the press. They will consider you something of a nineties person, "hip," and "with it."

There is a downside, though. The printer might not be so happy to see your digital output. This situation can arise because many before you have tried and failed at producing successful film. Not to mention that you are now swaggering through a field where some printers once made a killing in profits: Film assembly used to be expensive, costs were high, printers who offered film services—and most do—made money from it. They might be a bit sheepish about trusting your work, and some might try prematurely to blame your output if there are problems. Walk cautiously amid their offices.

What the Printer Needs

Bring your film, your unscanned continuous-tone photographs, hard-copy artwork, color proofs, and anything else you can think of to make life easier for your printer. If your printing requires reproducing photographs, you will need to provide a complete composite of your job indicating reductions or enlargements of the photographs and cropping instructions. You will have indications on your film for exact positions for each photograph. If your photographs are color and will be printed in color, you may even have had them digitally scanned and incorporated into your film. If not, supply your photographs to the printer so that they can do this for you. When reproducing color photographs in full process color, one money-saving shortcut is to have all of your photographic prints made to the exact reproduction size. Printers will recognize this type of planning as the makings of a good final printed product.

Stripping Up Your Film Output

Stripping is a job done by someone who has had years of experience working with film and printing presses. When your job reaches the film negative stage, it is stripped into a format determined by the type of press it is to be run on. This is a fairly mysterious process that takes painstaking accuracy on the part of the manual stripper because they align film registration by hand and eye. However, some print shops have computerized cameras that place the images automatically into what is called signature format. A *signature format* is basically a collection of pages arranged as if you took a piece of paper, folded it several times into a small book, numbered the pages, and unfolded it. You see that some pages are upside down and some are rightside up according to their position in the book and on the page. The printer's signature is then printed and heads for a folding machine and subsequently a huge cutting machine, or "knife" as they call it. Then, if it's a book you've created, from there it likely goes to a stitcher, bindery machine, and/or collator. And, you thought you had done all the work?

Checking for Correct Color

If your project is multi-color, you will need to have some sort of color proof made before it goes onto the press. Again, there are several different ways to make a color proof, the most common and cheapest being a color key. A *color key* is made by exposing each represented layer of film onto a matching clear color overlay and is assembled by attaching each layer of that overlay film to a white paper backing. When all overlays are registered to each other and viewed at the same time, the result is a fairly accurate composite color proof of the entire printed job.

A color proof of your color choices helps accurately reproduce output, and provides the press a progressive guide to ink quantities and disbursement. Most printers insist that some form of color proof be included with the film. Either you provide it or they make it for you, but you must have one.

Part Five

Hardware Concerns

Chapter Snapshot

By far one of the most aggravating problems that can crop up in a PC is a memory error. When it occurs, the problem often is sporadic, coming and going without rhyme or reason. Fortunately, memory problems don't crop up very often. When they occur on your PC, however, you can use the procedures provided in this chapter to find the problem and cure it.

This chapter covers the following topics:

✔ Memory problems

✔ Memory banks and memory arrangement

✔ Memory-testing procedures

Although problems caused by memory failure are not common, this chapter will help you pinpoint problems.

CHAPTER 28

Memory Considerations

When you do experience a memory-error or problem with your PC, the cause might not even be a bad chip or memory module. It could just be that a chip or module is loose in its socket. Because such simple-to-fix problems are the most common, they are the ones this chapter covers.

When a memory-error occurs, you might receive an error message. Sometimes the memory error can help you find the memory chip or module that's experiencing the problem. Often, though, the memory-error does not reference the correct memory and does not help you identify the problem. So I am foregoing a discussion of memory-error messages and concentrating on the procedures that you follow with or without an error message. If your system manual includes a list of memory-error messages and solutions, however, you still might want to try the manual's suggested solution first.

Before you begin, you need to understand the way memory is organized on the motherboard or memory adapter.

Understanding Memory Banks

Memory is arranged on a motherboard in banks. The banks are identified on the board by a painted rectangle surrounding each bank. A typical 386 or 486 motherboard includes 2 banks, Bank 0 and Bank 1, and each consists of 4 system sockets, for a total of 8 sockets. Some 386 and 486 systems include 16 SIMM sockets—4 sockets per bank for a total of 4 banks. Typical 286 and prior systems use 4 rows of DRAM sockets (2 rows per bank, and still a total of 2 banks). Some 286 systems use SIMMs or SIPs rather than DRAM chips, and their memory is organized like typical 386 and 486 systems. Figure 28.1 shows the memory banks on a typical 486 motherboard.

Figure 28.1
The memory banks on a typical 486 motherboard.

Why am I telling you about memory banks? I'm describing them because there are a few important points to remember when installing memory. If you just installed new memory and are having a problem, the cause might be the way the memory in each bank is installed. Following are some points to check:

✔ Do memory speeds match in each bank? All the memory in a bank must be of equal speed. You can install memory of different speeds in a PC, but all the SIMMs, SIPs, or DRAMs in a bank must have the same speed.

✔ Are the banks filled properly? When you install memory, the banks must be filled in specific ways according to the amount of RAM you're installing and the design of the motherboard. Check your system manual to determine whether you filled the banks properly.

✔ Did you set the proper switches? When you change the amount of memory in the system, you usually have to change jumper or switch settings on the motherboard according to the amount of memory that is installed on the motherboard.

Whether you just installed new memory or your memory problem seems to have cropped up from nowhere, you can follow several procedures to try to eliminate the problem. First, however, a few words of caution:

Memory chips are very vulnerable to damage by static electricity. To avoid any more damage to your system's memory than it has suffered already, be extra cautious about discharging the static from your body before touching any chips or memory modules. Avoid touching the chips themselves if you can help it, and try to touch only the chip's casing and not any conductive pins, on the chip or on a SIMM or SIP. Keep a hand on the chassis whenever you can to provide an easy path to ground for any nasty static in your body.

Check Memory Seating

Memory errors or problems often are caused by poor contact between the memory chip or module and its socket. DRAMs and other types of chips have a tendency to wiggle out of their sockets over time due to vibration and changes in temperature. You also could have installed a chip improperly. To check memory seating, follow these steps:

1. Turn off, unplug, and open the system.

2. Discharge yourself (do this often throughout the procedure).

3. Find your system's memory.

4. For DRAMs: After you discharge again, examine each of the DRAMs to verify that the pins on each of the chips are inserted into their sockets properly. Look for pins that are bent under the chip or are outside the socket. If you find any pins out of their sockets, remove the chip, straighten the pins, and reinstall the chip, and make sure you get all the pins in their sockets.

5. For DRAMs: After you verify that all the pins are properly installed, press down firmly on the top of each chip to ensure that each one is seated in its socket (see fig. 28.2).

Figure 28.2
Seating a
memory chip in
its socket.

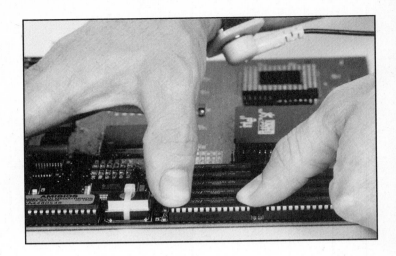

6. For SIMMs and SIPs: Verify that each memory module is seated in its socket securely. For SIPs, verify that no pins are bent and that all pins are inserted in their sockets correctly. For SIMMs, verify that the tabs for each socket are holding the SIMM securely in the socket (see fig. 28.3).

7. Plug in the system and turn it on to test it. If the problem disappears, close the system—the problem is solved. If the problem persists, continue with the next troubleshooting procedure.

Rearrange Memory

You might be able to eliminate the problem by rearranging the memory in the system. Just the act of removing the memory and reinstalling it sometimes fixes the problem (due to a loose or dirty contact). To rearrange memory, follow these steps:

1. Turn off and unplug the system. Remember to discharge your static often throughout this procedure.

2. In systems with DRAMs on the motherboard, you may need to remove the motherboard in order to remove the DRAMs. If the memory with which you are working is installed on an adapter, remove the adapter. In systems with SIMMs or SIPs, you should be able to remove the memory without removing the motherboard. For SIMMs/SIPs on an adapter, remove the adapter before trying to remove the memory modules.

3. If all the memory in your PC is the same capacity, swap the memory from one bank with the memory in the other. If you have different-

capacity memory in each bank, check your system manual to determine whether you can swap capacities between banks. If you can, you probably should reset some jumpers or DIP switches on the motherboard. (The system manual explains these settings.)

If you can't swap memory, skip the rest of this procedure and go to the next procedure.

4. After you reinstall the system's memory, plug in and turn on the system to test it.

Figure 28.3
Checking socket seating of a SIMM.

Minimize and Substitute Memory

This procedure essentially is a trial-and-error process of elimination to determine which chips or modules are causing the problem. You begin by removing all the system's memory, then reinstalling it in minimal amounts, and testing the installation.

If the installed memory functions properly, install more and test it again. If you have a bad memory chip or module, you eventually will narrow down the possibilities regarding which chip or module is causing the problem.

Follow these steps:

1. Turn off and unplug the system. Discharge your static often.

2. Refer to your system manual for the minimum RAM you can install in the system.

3. Install the minimum RAM, filling up the first bank. Remember to configure the motherboard's jumpers or DIP switches to specify the amount of memory installed.

4. Turn on the system and access its system setup configuration program (CMOS setup). In the CMOS setup, specify the amount of memory installed in the system, save the changes, and then reboot the system.

5. After the system reboots, test it to see if it functions properly. If you receive a memory size mismatch or memory-related CMOS error, you probably have not configured the system properly for the amount of memory you have. Check your settings and try again.

6. If you do not receive a CMOS or mismatch error but still experience the problem, remove the memory from the system and set it aside. You already might have found the bad memory. Replace it with an equal amount of other memory, such as another set of SIMMs, and turn on the system to see if it works.

7. If, after swapping memory, you still experience the problem, you may have a problem with the motherboard or memory card. Stop now and call the technical support department where you purchased the PC, explain the troubleshooting process you have used, and ask for assistance in locating the problem.

8. If the system functions normally after you install the first set of memory chips, SIMMs, or SIPs in Bank 0, turn off and unplug the system, and then install another set of memory in Bank 1. Reconfigure the board's jumpers/DIP switches, reconfigure CMOS setup, and then

reboot and test the system. If the system malfunctions, you have narrowed down the potential cause of the problem.

At this point, you can begin extensive swapping of the memory in and out of the system to identify the chip or module causing the problem; however, this will take a lot of time. Instead, I recommend that you remove the memory from the bank causing the problem and take it to your favorite PC fix-it shop. Have the memory tested there, and then replace the faulty chip or module.

Clean Pins

The pins that connect the DRAMs or SIMMs/SIPs in their sockets can become oxidized or just dirty from crud floating around in the air in your office. A dirty contact causes problems, often intermittently. If your system uses DRAMs, I feel sorry for you. You probably will need to remove the motherboard to remove the DRAMs. If you work with a memory adapter, you're lucky—the adapter is easy to remove. Removing SIMMs or SIPs from a system seldom requires removing the motherboard. If you're working with SIMMs/SIPs on an adapter, however, you need to remove the adapter. To clean your pins, follow these steps:

1. Turn off and unplug the system.

2. Discharge your static, and if necessary, remove the motherboard or adapter that contains the memory.

3. For DRAMs: Carefully remove one row of DRAM chips. Apply some isopropyl alcohol to a soft cotton cloth, and then wipe the pins on each DRAM. Reinstall the chips, and then repeat the procedure for the other rows of chips. Use a dry cotton cloth to wipe away any excess alcohol from the chips.

4. For SIMMs: Carefully remove the SIMMs from one bank. Clean the pins on the SIMM module's edge connector with a clean rubber eraser (see fig. 28.4). Rub the eraser over the pins to remove any oxidation or residue. Perform this cleaning procedure away from the PC so you don't get any eraser crumbs inside the PC or on the adapter.

Figure 28.4
Cleaning the
edge-connector
pins on a SIMM.

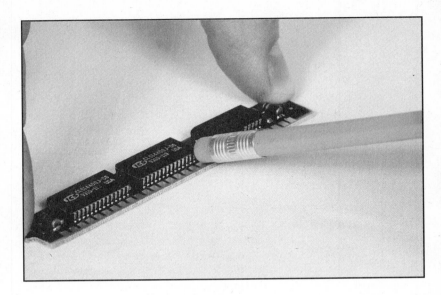

5. For SIPs: Carefully remove the SIPs from one bank. Clean the pins on the SIPs with a soft cotton cloth dipped in isopropyl alcohol. Remove any excess alcohol with a dry cotton cloth.

6. Replace the memory in the bank and repeat the process for the other bank(s).

7. Let the system sit for a few minutes to allow any remaining alcohol to evaporate.

8. Plug in the system and turn it on to test the system.

Seek Help

This procedure doesn't require a set of steps—just an explanation. If you have followed the procedures to this point and still experience memory problems, I suggest you call the technical support department at the place in which you purchased the PC and ask for help troubleshooting your memory problem. Let them figure out what the memory error messages, if any, are trying to tell you.

If you can't resolve the problem through technical support, I suggest you take your PC to your favorite computer technician/fix-it shop so that they can check the PC's memory. You could spend days trying to troubleshoot the problem and never find it. If you haven't solved the problem by now, turn it over to a professional to solve.

If you just can't stand the idea of taking your PC to someone else to fix, and if you have the money to spend on some additional memory, try the following procedure. (If you haven't located the problem yet, you probably need some new memory anyway—the memory you purchase for the next procedure will not go to waste.)

Replace Memory

If you're willing to spend some time coaxing your PC back to health, you can begin swapping out your PC's memory with new memory that you know is good (at least, you have to assume that new memory you just purchased is good). In this procedure, you selectively replace memory until you eliminate the bad chip or module. Follow these steps:

1. Read through your system manual to determine which type of memory to buy for your system. If your system contains DRAMs, buy enough DRAMs to replace one row of chips. If your system uses SIMMs or SIPs, buy one SIMM or SIP (whichever is used by your system).

2. After buying the new memory, leave it in the packaging until you're ready to install it. (Remember to discharge your static often during this procedure.)

3. For DRAMs: After discharging your static, remove one row of DRAMs from their sockets and set them aside where they will not get mixed up with your new DRAMs.

   Install the new DRAMs in place of the one(s) you removed.

   Plug in and turn on the system to test it.

   If the problem goes away, package the old DRAMs and a) throw them away; b) stick them on a shelf for testing at a later date; or c) take them to a PC fix-it shop to be tested.

   If the problem persists, remove the new DRAMs and set them aside. Reinstall the old DRAMs in the first row, then remove the DRAMs from the second row and set them aside. Install the new DRAMs in the second row and retest the system. If the problem persists, repeat this step until you have replaced each row with the new DRAMs and tested the system each time. If the problem still persists, the problem is probably in the motherboard or memory card. Call for help or have the PC serviced by a technician.

4. For SIMMs: Remove the first SIMM from Bank 0 and set it aside. Install the new SIMM in its place, and then turn on and test the system. Continue swapping the new SIMM for an old one in each bank until you have swapped and tested each SIMM. When you do not experience the problem, you have located the bad SIMM. Make a tie clasp out of it. If the problem persists, the trouble must be in the motherboard or memory card. Call for help or have the system serviced.

5. For SIPs: Follow the process described in step 4.

The type of trial-and-error testing described in this procedure can take quite a bit of time, but is worthwhile if you're trying to avoid paying for a service call.

Chapter Snapshot

Generally, installing a new video adapter doesn't involve much work, and connecting a new monitor to your PC doesn't take much effort. You should have little trouble with either task. This short chapter covers the following topics:

✔ Issues to consider when you buy a video adapter

✔ Video resolution

✔ Issues to consider when you buy a monitor

✔ Procedures for configuring a video adapter

✔ Procedures for adding RAM to a video adapter

✔ Windows video tips

If you are a professional graphics artist, this chapter provides valuable information for achieving high-quality images.

CHAPTER 29

Video Adapters and Monitors

The *video adapter* is the PC device that actually generates the image you see on the monitor. The video adapter converts the data coming from the CPU into something the monitor can display. The three most important issues related to video adapters are resolution, color, and speed. To understand resolution, you need to understand how an image is displayed on the monitor. CorelDRAW! will perform much better if you install a high-speed video card. In fact, of all add-ins you can install, a video card improves CorelDRAW!'s performance more than any other item.

Understanding Video Adapters

An image on the monitor consists of numerous small dots called *pixels*, which stand for "picture elements." (Actually, pixels are more like short horizontal lines, but dots are a good analogy.) Think of the image as a sand painting—each grain of sand that makes up the painting represents a pixel of a certain color.

Because your monitor is a fixed size, only a fixed amount of space in which to paint the sand painting is available. If your grains of sand are large, the image looks blocky. If the grains are small, the image is more refined.

The smaller the grains, the more grains that can fit in the same amount of space, thus improving the image quality. That's what image resolution is all about—the more pixels, the higher the resolution and the better the image quality.

Higher resolution also means you can display more information on the screen. In Windows, for example, you can display more cells of a spreadsheet, more of a word processing document, or simply more program windows on-screen. Figures 29.1 and 29.2 illustrate the same spreadsheet using two different video resolutions.

Figure 29.1
An Excel
spreadsheet at
640×480
resolution.

Microsoft Excel - SHAFT.XLS

			Stepped Shaft Designer							
	All lengths in inches, weights in pounds						Polar	Radius of	Twisting	Maximum
Segment	Length	Inside Dia.	Outside Dia.		Volume	Weight	Moment	Gyration	Moment	Horsepower
1	2	0	0.5		0.79	0.22	0.006	0.177	0.025	45.56
2	5.3	0	3		12.49	3.54	7.952	1.061	5.301	9841.12
3	2.8	0.1	0.5		0.88	0.25	0.006	0.173	0.025	45.49
4	4.5	0.1	0.75		2.30	0.65	0.031	0.263	0.083	153.72
5										
6										
7										
8										
9										
10										
Total:	14.6				16.45	4.67				45.49
Segments	4									
Material:	Steel		Density:	0.2836	lb/in^2		RPM	3600		
			Ult strength:	65000	lb/in^2		Safety			
			Shear mod:	12000000	lb/in^2		factor		2	

Ready   NUM

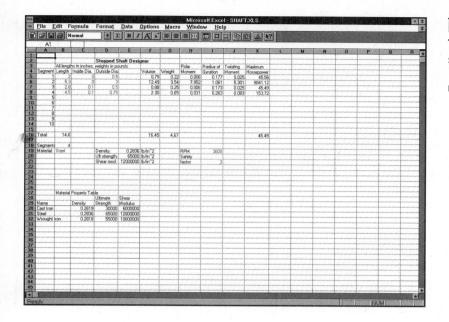

Figure 29.2
The same spreadsheet at 1024×768 resolution.

V

Hardware Concerns

Standard Resolutions

The PC industry supports a number of standard video resolutions, each described by the number of horizontal and vertical pixels that make up the display. The following list defines today's most popular video resolutions and includes some recommendations for each:

✔ **720×350.** This resolution is offered by a Monochrome Graphics Adapter (MGA). MGA adapters are inexpensive and offer a good solution if you don't need color.

✔ **640×480.** This standard VGA resolution is the minimum I recommend for either DOS or Windows. VGA resolution is acceptable on 14-inch and 15-inch screens.

✔ **800×600.** An 800×600 resolution is great for Windows because you can display much more data on-screen at one time than you can with a VGA adapter. This resolution works well on all monitor sizes.

✔ **1024×768.** This resolution is great if you work with drawing programs or want to cram as much data onto the screen at one time as possible. At this resolution, you might find text hard to read on a 14-inch monitor. You should use a 15-inch or larger monitor for this resolution.

✔ **1280×1024.** This resolution is great for image-processing applications (working with photos, for example), drawing applications, and other applications that require a fine image quality. You should use a 17-inch or larger monitor for this resolution.

Adapters that provide even higher resolutions than those described in the preceding list also are available. These adapters are for special-purpose applications and often are too expensive for the average user (and not particularly useful, either).

Most video adapters support a number of different display modes. An adapter that can display in 1280×1024 also can display using the lower resolution modes described in the list.

When you're evaluating a new video adapter, determine whether the adapter uses interlaced display mode or noninterlaced display mode. In *interlaced* mode, the adapter paints every other scan line of the image in the first pass and then paints the other scan lines "in between." A *noninterlaced* adapter paints all scan lines in one pass. A noninterlaced display generates less image flicker and is better for extended use of the PC.

Noninterlaced adapters are more expensive than interlaced adapters. Also, some adapters generate a noninterlaced display in some modes but generate an interlaced display in other modes.

About Color

The number of colors that a video adapter can display also is an important point to consider when you're buying a new adapter. I don't recommend monochrome displays because color enables you to organize your data better. I recommend a 16-color display as a minimum. Also available are adapters that can display 256 colors, 32,000 colors, or even more. The more colors the adapter can display, the better the image quality for images that make extensive use of color. Usually, these images include digitized photos and computer-generated art or photorealistic images (photo-like images generated by the computer).

If you work only with spreadsheets and word processing documents, you don't need the capability to display a million colors, so pick an adapter that suits the type of work you do (typically, a 16-color or 256-color adapter). Keep in mind that as with resolution, the adapter can use different color modes. An adapter that can display 32,000 colors also offers modes for 256-color and 16-color display.

If you increase the number of colors the adapter can display, you will need more memory on the adapter. To display 256 colors, for example, the adapter generally requires at least 512 KB of video RAM. Increasing the resolution also increases the video RAM requirement.

To display 256 colors at a resolution of 1024×768, the adapter generally requires at least 1 MB of video RAM. Most adapters sold today provide at least 1 MB of RAM on the adapter. You should check the standard amount of RAM supplied on the adapter and whether you can add more RAM to increase the capabilities of the adapter.

Getting the Scoop about Monitors

A video adapter basically is useless without a monitor, so it's a sure bet that your PC includes a monitor. If you're shopping for a new monitor, keep the following points in mind:

✔ **Scan rate/refresh rate.** The monitor must match the capabilities of the video adapter. You can match the scan rate and refresh rates of the monitor to the video adapter, but you might find matching the display resolution easier. Make sure that the monitor you're buying supports the maximum video resolution you use on the video adapter and does so in noninterlaced mode. If you can't afford a noninterlaced display, make sure that the monitor matches the capabilities of the video adapter you use. Ask the salesperson if you're not sure.

✔ **Interlaced/noninterlaced.** Monitors that support the higher resolution modes using noninterlaced display are more expensive, but a noninterlaced display generates less image flicker and helps keep eyestrain to a minimum with extended use of the PC.

✔ **Dot pitch.** The smaller the value for the monitor's dot pitch, the better. Look for a monitor with a dot pitch of .28mm or less.

✔ **Screen.** Look for a monitor with as flat a screen as possible. An antiglare coating on the screen also is a benefit.

Monitors generate EMF (electromagnetic frequency) emissions. Extended exposure to EMF emissions might cause cancer and other health problems. Look for a monitor that meets the Swedish MPR-II specification for reduced emissions, or purchase a filter screen that reduces EMF emissions from the monitor.

Installing a Video Adapter

Video adapters generally require little or no configuration before installation, although a few adapters sometimes require that you set switches on the adapter to control a few options. You also might need to configure one or more switches or jumpers on your system's motherboard. The following procedures explain these tasks.

Installing RAM on Your Video Adapter

To install RAM on your video adapter, follow these steps:

1. If your video adapter doesn't have the full amount of RAM possible, and you want to add additional RAM to it, first check the adapter's manual to determine the type of RAM required (usually DRAMs or SIMMs).

2. Locate the RAM sockets on the video adapter.

3. DRAM: Orient the chip correctly with its socket. Line up the pins on one edge of the DRAM with the socket (see fig. 29.3). Rotate the DRAM down and insert the other row of pins into the socket. After you verify that all pins are aligned properly with the socket, press the chip firmly into place. Repeat this procedure for the other DRAMs.

Figure 29.3
Installing video DRAM on a video adapter.

4. SIMMs: Determine the correct orientation of the SIMM to the socket (check the adapter's manual). Slip the edge connector of the SIMM into the socket; then carefully rotate the SIMM in the socket until the tabs on each end of the socket snap into place to hold the SIMM.

Configuring the Adapter and Motherboard

After you install RAM on the adapter (if required), check the adapter's manual to determine whether you need to set any switches or jumpers on the adapter to suit your installation. Set the jumpers or DIP switches as necessary. Check the following section of this chapter for tips on specific video adapters.

Check the system manual for your system's motherboard. Determine whether a DIP switch or jumper setting specifies either monochrome or color display. Set the switch or jumper accordingly (many newer motherboards don't have this setting).

Installing the Adapter

To install the adapter, follow these steps:

1. Choose an appropriate bus slot. You should install 16-bit video adapters in 16-bit bus slots. Some 16-bit adapters function in 8-bit slots, but with a loss of performance. You should install 8-bit video adapters in 8-bit slots, but you can install them in 16-bit slots if no 8-bit slot is available.

2. Install the adapter in the selected slot. Make sure you align the edge connector properly in the slot before you press the adapter into place. With full-length adapters, make sure the adapter is aligned in the correct guide at the front of the PC.

3. Secure the adapter with a screw.

Connecting the Adapter

Most video adapters require only that you connect a standard video cable between the adapter and the monitor. Some adapters, however, require special cables. These cables connect the video adapter to other devices in the system by way of the adapter's feature connector.

Check the adapter's manual to determine whether the adapter requires special cable connections. If it doesn't require special connections, attach the video cable supplied with the monitor to the rear of the adapter. Secure it in place with the screws provided with the cable. Attach the other end of the cable to the monitor.

Some video adapter installations require passthrough cabling. A passthrough cable connects the video adapter to another adapter in the system, and a cable then connects from the secondary adapter to the monitor. These connections usually are required only with video capture boards and other special-purpose video adapters.

Configuring Memory Usage

Video adapters require the use of some of the memory in the UMA. If your video adapter uses more memory than a standard EGA or VGA adapter, you should make sure that all the memory that is used by the video adapter is excluded from use by other applications.

1. Check your video adapter's manual to determine the range of memory the adapter uses in the UMA.

2. EMM386 users: Edit CONFIG.SYS to make sure that the EMM386.EXE command line includes an X switch to exclude the range of memory used by the video adapter.

3. Third-party memory managers: If you're using a UMA memory manager other than EMM386, check your memory manager's manual to determine how to exclude the video adapter's memory range from the memory manager's use.

4. Save your changes to CONFIG.SYS and reboot the system.

Installing Drivers

Video adapters don't require any special device drivers for general operation in the DOS environment. Many adapters do, however, require special drivers for applications, including Windows. The adapter generally comes with one or more disks that contain drivers to support the adapter with various applications.

The software disks provided with some adapters include an installation program that installs the drivers for you automatically. Others require that you use the application's setup or configuration program to install the driver.

Check the video adapter's manual and disks to determine which drivers are supplied with the adapter.

Decide which applications require the use of a special driver that is included with the adapter (for example, AutoCAD and other CAD programs, and Windows).

Installation program: If your video adapter software includes an automated installation program, run it to install the drivers for your applications. It may install only some of the drivers, leaving you to install the rest manually.

Application installation: Install drivers for any applications for which the installation program did not install the drivers. This procedure varies from application to application. Check your programs' manuals to determine how to install the driver. If you don't need to configure Windows for your adapter, this is the last step in the procedure.

Windows: To install a new driver for Windows, run the Setup program. You can run Setup from DOS by changing to the Windows directory and typing **SETUP**, or you can run Setup in Windows by double-clicking on the Setup icon in the Main program group. The following steps describe Windows-based Setup.

The following steps describe how to install a third-party video driver for Windows. Your video adapter may be compatible with the SuperVGA or other standard drivers supplied with Windows. Third-party drivers generally provide more options for resolution or color support but sometimes do not support all the features included with the standard Windows drivers, such as the use of the mouse in a windowed DOS program.

To install a third-party video driver, follow these steps:

1. Select the Setup icon from the Main program group.

2. From the Options menu in the Windows Setup dialog box, select Change System Settings.

3. Click on the Display drop-down list and then scroll to the bottom of the list to locate the option labeled "Other display (requires disk from OEM)." Select that option.

4. Setup prompts you to insert a disk. Insert the disk supplied with the video adapter that contains the Windows device drivers. Check your video adapter's manual if you're not sure which disk to use. After you insert the disk, click on OK.

5. If Setup displays a list of different video options from which to choose, select the options you want. Then follow the dialog box's directions to install the driver. Setup also might prompt you to insert some of your Windows distribution disks in order to copy font files for the display.

6. Setup prompts you to either continue working with the current setup or restart Windows. You must restart Windows for the new driver to be used.

Testing

The only way to test the video adapter is to start the PC and run your applications. If you turn on the PC and get only a black display, the monitor is probably turned off, or else you have a loose connection between the adapter and the monitor. Check the monitor and the connections first.

If you start Windows and see multiple images on the display, your monitor and adapter aren't using the same video modes. You might be able to set an option (a switch, for example) on the monitor to make it match the video adapter modes. Check the monitor manual and video adapter manual for instructions on how to set options.

The alternative is to switch to a video mode that is supported by both the video adapter and the monitor. Some monitors don't support 800×600 mode with some adapters, for example, but they do support 1024×768 with the same adapter.

If a problem persists in Windows, try running Setup and select either the VGA or Super VGA drivers. If neither of these options works with your video adapter and monitor combination, contact technical support for the video adapter.

Installing a New Monitor

Installing a new monitor is usually just a matter of unpacking the monitor, connecting the power cord, and connecting the video cable between the video adapter and the monitor. Instead of giving you a procedure for installing the monitor, this chapter just gives you some pointers to keep in mind when connecting it.

✔ **Compatibility.** The monitor must match the video mode that your video adapter uses. If you experience problems, the monitor might be unable to match the video mode being used by the video adapter. Check the manual for the monitor to see whether you can set its switches to make it match the adapter's video mode.

✔ **Cables.** If you have a tower system and the video cable isn't long enough to reach from the PC to the monitor, you can get a monitor extension cable to double the effective length of the video cable. Also think about getting a monitor power cord that plugs into the back of the PC instead of the wall outlet. A monitor power cord enables you to turn on the monitor automatically when you turn on the PC.

✔ **EMF filters.** If you're installing an EMF filter on your display, it probably includes a ground cable that plugs into a wall outlet. Make sure you plug it in to ground the filter.

Windows Video Tips

You can use a handful of tips to improve the video performance of Windows and make Windows more usable. The following sections explain these video-related Windows tips.

Optimum Speed and Performance

Because it is a graphical operating environment, Windows relies heavily on the capability of your PC's video adapter. Aside from disk access speed, video speed is one of the most important factors in determining how well a system performs under Windows.

Following is a list of tasks you can do to improve your system's video performance in Windows and troubleshoot video problems in Windows:

✔ **Use 16-color mode.** The 16-color display mode is generally faster than the 256-color mode (or higher). Use 16-color display mode if you don't use applications that make use of 256-color (or better) capability.

✔ **Eliminate wallpaper.** Windows wallpaper is a novelty and doesn't add any productivity to your PC or to Windows. Wallpaper takes up valuable memory that your applications can use to better advantage. Unless you've fallen in love with your wallpaper, I suggest that you eliminate it.

✔ **Use a different resolution.** If you're using a relatively high video resolution and can get by adequately with a lower resolution, switch to the lower resolution. You will speed up your PC's video performance under Windows.

✔ **Troubleshoot.** If strange messages appear on-screen when you try to run Windows, you might have a memory conflict between your video adapter and Windows (or another program). To troubleshoot the problem, try starting Windows by using the WIN /D:X switch. The WIN /D:X switch prevents Windows from using any of the memory in the UMA. If this switch clears up the problem, make sure you exclude *all* the video adapter's memory from use by Windows.

Changing Icon Font

When you're using a high-resolution display on a smaller monitor (14-inch or 15-inch, for example), you might find it difficult to read the descriptions under icons. You can change the font and appearance of the text that Windows uses for icon descriptions by adding a few settings to the WIN.INI file. Following are the settings you can use:

- ✔ **IconTitleFaceName.** This setting specifies the name of the font Windows uses for icon text.

- ✔ **IconTitleStyle.** This setting specifies whether the font is displayed normal or bold.

- ✔ **IconTitleSize.** This setting specifies the size of the font used for icon text.

- ✔ **IconTitleWrap.** This setting specifies whether icon descriptions are contained on one line or word-wrap to a total of three lines. Set this setting to 1 to make the titles wrap.

To change the way icon text appears, open Notepad or SysEdit and edit the WIN.INI file. Look for the [Desktop] section and add the settings you like. The following example specifies a 12-point Times New Roman font in bold as the icon text:

```
[Desktop]
IconTitleFaceName=Times New Roman
IconTitleSize=12
IconTitleStyle=1
```

For the change to take effect, you must save the changes to WIN.INI and then restart Windows.

Changing the System Font

In the [boot] section of SYSTEM.INI are three settings that control the font files that Windows uses for various components of the Windows display. The fonts.fon setting specifies the Windows system font. The system font is used for title bar text, menu bar text, and other standard Windows components. If you're using a video resolution that makes it difficult to read the menus in your applications, you can use a larger font.

The system font must be a proportional system font. These files contain SYS in the file name. Examples are VGASYS.FON, 8514SYS.FON, and so on. If your system is using VGASYS.FON, for example, you can specify the 8514SYS.FON instead and make menu text larger and easier to read. Or you may want to make the text smaller by using a smaller font.

To change the system font, follow these steps:

1. Decide which font file you want to use. For a listing of fonts, check the Windows distribution disks for any font files containing the string "SYS" and the file extension FO_ or FN_.

2. At the DOS prompt, use the EXPAND command to expand the font file from the Windows disks to the Windows System directory. The following example expands the file 8514SYS.FO_ from the disk in drive A and copies it to the Windows System directory:

```
EXPAND  -R  A:8514FON.FO_  C:\WINDOWS\SYSTEM
```

The -R switch directs EXPAND to rename the file automatically according to its original file name. In the preceding example, EXPAND creates a file called 8514SYS.FON in the Windows System directory.

3. After you expand the font file from the distribution disk to the Windows System directory, edit SYSTEM.INI using Notepad or SysEdit. Look for the fonts.fon= setting in the [boot] section. After the "equals" sign, specify the name of the font file you want to use. Following is an example using the 8514FON.FON file:

```
fonts.fon=8514SYS.FON
```

4. Save the changes to SYSTEM.INI and restart Windows for the change to take effect.

If you want to change the font used by Notepad, use a different font file for the fixedfon.fon= setting. To change the font used by DOS programs that run in a window, change the oemfonts.fon font setting. Use the same guidelines outlined in the preceding procedure.

Chapter Snapshot

One of the fastest growing markets in PC hardware today is the audio adapter (more commonly known as the sound card). *Sound cards* are adapters that give your PC the capability to play high-fidelity sounds, and they can be used for everything from playing audio CDs to embedding a voice note in a document.

The chapter covers the following topics:

✔ Uses for a sound card

✔ Tips for buying a sound card

✔ Configuring and installing a sound card

✔ Integrating sound with Windows programs

This chapter offers an explanation of some of the things you can do with a sound card, tips on what to look for when shopping for a sound card, and procedures for configuring and installing a sound card,

30

CHAPTER

Audio Adapters

The speaker in your PC was never intended to reproduce sound with any degree of fidelity. The PC's speaker is good for making beeping noises, but that's about it. The speaker and sound support circuitry can't play back a Bach concerto from CD. Even if you just want to hear the great sound effects from your favorite game, the PC's speaker leaves a lot to be desired.

Using Audio Adapters

Sound cards not only enable you to play back audio CDs on your PC, but they also open up a lot of new possibilities for using sound. If you have a sound card, you can do the following:

✔ Play audio CDs on the PC, which enables you to control contrast, treble, bass, and other parameters, just as you could with a conventional stereo

✔ Play various types of sound files

✔ Enjoy realistic sound effects in games and simulation programs

✔ Digitize and store sounds in files from CD, stereo, microphone, or other audio sources for playback, editing, or use in documents

✔ Assign sound effects to various Windows events (for example, an obnoxious noise whenever a warning or error dialog box appears)

✔ Embed digitized sound clips in documents that you create with Windows programs

✔ Embed your own digitized voice messages in electronic mail that you send to other people, and play back voice messages received in e-mail from other users (see fig. 30.1)

✔ Create complex musical compositions with your PC

✔ Mix and edit sounds and musical compositions

✔ Experience the full range of sounds and sound effects provided by multimedia CDs and programs

✔ When a sound card is combined with a video-grabber board, you can capture and edit video and audio sequences to create your own video presentations

Of all the gadgets that are available for the PC, a sound card probably can add the most enjoyment. But sound cards aren't just for fun; they're great for the business world as well.

As a matter of fact, the capability to embed a voice annotation in a spreadsheet can be very valuable as a management tool. There's no better way to check a spreadsheet's figures than to have the PC read the numbers back to you as you check them. What's more, sound capability can be a big asset when you're using tutorial and training applications that make use of sound.

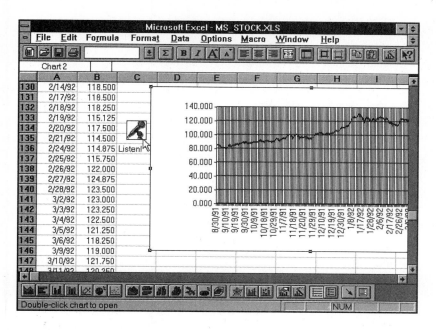

Figure 30.1
A voice annotation embedded in an Excel spreadsheet.

Whether you're looking for a little more enjoyment from your PC as you work, or you want to integrate sound into your business documents, a sound card is a good investment.

Shopping for a Sound Card

You need to think about several features when you're considering buying a sound card. Consider not only the technical features of the card, but also whether it includes the right software to fit your needs. The following is a list of features to keep in mind when shopping for a sound card:

✔ **Support for Windows multimedia extensions.** Make sure the sound card supports the Windows multimedia extensions and works with the sound capabilities built into Windows 3.1. That way, you can take full advantage of sound in Windows, including integrating sound in your Windows documents and using Windows-based multimedia titles.

✔ **MPC compatibility.** The MPC (Multimedia PC) specifications define the minimum recommended requirements for multimedia hardware. Sound cards that are compliant with the MPC Level 2 standard (currently the latest revision of the standard) support sampling in 8 bits and 16 bits with sample rates of 11 KHz, 22 KHz, and 44 KHz. The card also should support input mixing, MIDI in, MIDI out, and MIDI pass-through, and should use no more than 10 percent of the CPU's time. You don't have to knock yourself out researching all this—hardware meeting MPC requirements is marked with a logo or statement saying so.

✔ **Compression.** Sound files can be enormous. Shop for a card that supports on-the-fly compression of sound. Look for a compression ratio of at least 3:1 or 4:1.

✔ **Voice recognition.** Many sound cards support voice recognition, which means you can connect a microphone to the sound card, speak commands into the microphone, and have the sound card recognize and act on those commands. If you're interested in controlling your software with voice commands, look for a sound card that supports voice recognition.

✔ **Voice synthesis.** This feature enables the sound card to convert text into spoken words. If you want your PC to be able to read your e-mail or other documents to you, look for a sound card that supports voice synthesis.

✔ **MIDI support.** MIDI (Musical Instrument Digital Interface) is a standard for interfacing electronic instruments such as keyboards to a PC. MIDI sound files store sound as individual notes, rather than as digitized waveforms, saving a tremendous amount of disk space to store sound files. If you want to compose or edit music on your PC, shop for a sound card that includes a MIDI port and can play MIDI files.

✔ **Maximum number of stereo voices.** The more stereo voices supported by the card, the more complex the MIDI compositions the sound card can render. Think of this as having more musicians in your electronic orchestra.

✔ **Maximum sample rate.** The sample rate determines the playback quality of a digitized sound. For CD-quality reproduction, shop for a card that supports at least 44 KHz sampling.

✔ **Maximum playback rate.** The higher the playback rate, the better the sound will be. If you want to play audio CDs on your system, shop for a sound card that supports a playback rate of 44 KHz or higher.

✔ **Stereo.** Shop for a sound card that supports stereo playback to get the best possible sound quality.

✔ **Supports Windows OLE.** If you intend to use sound in your Windows documents, make sure the sound card supports OLE (Object Linking and Embedding).

✔ **Ad Lib and Sound Blaster compatibility.** If you plan to use your sound card with a wide selection of games, look for a sound card that is compatible with the Ad Lib and Sound Blaster cards. If you're not interested in sound effects for games, this isn't important.

✔ **Built-in amplifier.** A built-in amplifier on the sound card enables you to use unamplified speakers and deliver more "sound power" to the speakers.

✔ **CD-ROM interface.** If you buy a multimedia upgrade kit that includes a CD-ROM drive, this isn't as important an issue as if you are buying the CD-ROM separately. If you plan to add other SCSI devices to your system, shop for a sound card that includes a standard SCSI-2 interface. As an alternative, buy a separate SCSI host adapter and use it instead of the sound card to connect your SCSI devices to the PC.

✔ **Bundled software.** A sound card isn't much good without software to run it. Look for sound cards that include programs for mixing, CD playback, sound recording and playback, and, where applicable, voice recognition and synthesis.

If you can't make sense of the specifications in a sound card's advertisement, call the manufacturer for more information. It's also a good idea to listen to a particular sound card before you buy it. Check out your friends' or business associates' sound cards or shop at a retail dealer where you can listen to the card. Evaluate the sound just as you would when buying a new stereo system.

Sound for Notebooks and Portables

If you want to add sound to your notebook or portable PC, there are some parallel port sound devices you should check out. These devices connect to the PC's parallel port and include audio input and output connections. Two such products are VocalTec's CAT and Logitech's AudioMan. Figure 30.2 shows the Logitech AudioMan.

These devices enable you to continue to use your printer while you play back or record sound. You can connect a set of small speakers to the device or use a set of headphones for playback. The AudioMan includes a built-in microphone, while the CAT uses a plug-in microphone or can use a telephone headset (it includes a standard modular phone jack for plugging in the handset). These devices have the benefit of not requiring configuration for DMA or IRQ settings, so if you've run out of IRQ lines on your desktop PC, these types of sound adapters are an alternative to internal sound cards.

Figure 30.2
The Logitech
AudioMan
parallel-port
sound adapter.

Don't Forget Input and Output

A sound card is absolutely useless if you don't have some type of output device connected to it. At the least, the sound card you buy will have an output jack for a set of headphones.

Using headphones is fine when you're working in an office with someone else, or are using a parallel-port sound adapter connected to your notebook. For the best sound reproduction, though, you may want to connect your sound card to a set of speakers or to a stereo system.

Buying Desktop Speakers

Desktop speakers (also called bookshelf speakers) range from inexpensive to expensive, with price dictating performance up to a point. You can buy a relatively inexpensive set of speakers for about $30, but the sound reproduction won't be as good as with some of the more expensive models. I have a set of Sony SRS-38 speakers that sell for about $60, and which provide a good level of sound quality and volume range.

Some desktop speakers are unamplified, relying on the strength of the signal coming from the sound card to drive the speakers. Others contain their own amplifiers that require battery power or an AC adapter. The Sony speakers that I use are amplified, although they can be used in either amplified or unamplified mode. When amplified, the speakers provide a much broader volume range.

Some of the more expensive speakers also include their own subwoofers, either as separate modules, built into the speaker units, or with all components mounted in an under-the-monitor unit. Whether you buy speakers with these added features depends on the type of fidelity you want from the speakers, but don't expect a speaker system with a subwoofer to necessarily sound better than one without. Test the speakers by listening to them before you buy them.

Look for speakers that are magnetically shielded if you plan to place the speakers next to your monitor. The magnetic field generated by the speakers can affect the display, and the field generated by the monitor can affect the sound quality.

Positioning the Speakers

How you position your speakers relative to your PC and yourself has almost as great an impact on how they sound as the speakers' design. By experimenting with the positioning of your speakers you can potentially coax much better sound from them.

Start with the speakers positioned on your desktop as far apart as possible, and aim the speakers so that their axes converge a few inches in front of you. You also might want to try moving the speakers up to ear level, placing them on a bookshelf on the wall behind your desk or actually mounting them to the wall. Placing the speakers on the wall also will generally improve the speakers' bass output.

Using Your Stereo for Playback

For even better sound control and fidelity, you may want to connect your sound card to a stereo system. This isn't something you'd do if you share an office with someone, but it's great for a home office.

If your stereo has auxiliary jacks, you can connect the sound card to these jacks. The auxiliary jacks probably are RCA-type jacks, while the sound card probably uses a miniature phono-plug, so you need an adapter. You can get the necessary cables and adapters at stereo shops and most stores that sell audio components (Radio Shack, for example).

Keep in mind that your sound card probably uses a single stereo output jack, with output lines for both left and right channels. Your stereo probably uses separate left and right inputs, so shop for a Y-cable that has a stereo connector at one end and two individual channel connectors at the other end. If you're not sure what to get, tell the salesperson you need the cables and adapters necessary to go from a single stereo mini-jack to separate left and right auxiliary jacks on your stereo.

Tip Your stereo may have an auxiliary CD-ROM jack for connecting an external CD-ROM drive to the stereo system. If you don't have an external CD-ROM drive connected to your stereo, you can connect your sound card to the CD-ROM jack.

If there are no auxiliary jacks (common with less expensive, single-unit stereo systems), you still should be able to connect the sound card to the stereo system, but it requires a little more work. Check the components in your stereo system to determine how they connect to the system's amplifier.

In particular, check the connections from the turntable and tape deck. Either one probably will be connected inside the system by RCA connectors (which simplifies the assembly process when the unit is manufactured). You'll probably have to open the system in order to check it, so make sure you turn it off and unplug it before doing so.

If either component connects to the amplifier with RCA plugs, you can disconnect the component, install splitter cables (Y-cables) in the line, then reconnect it. You then can connect your sound card to these splitter cables.

When you're using the sound card connected to the stereo system in this way, the stereo device selection will have to be set to the device to which the Y-cables are connected. If you have the Y-cables connected between the turntable and the amplifier, for example, select the turntable on the front panel of the stereo system whenever you want to use your sound card.

Input to the Sound Card

If you will be using your sound card to digitize or mix voice annotation or music, you need to connect one or more input devices to the sound card. In the case of voice annotation, you need to connect a microphone to the sound card. The sound card will provide a microphone input jack. Check the sound card's manual to determine which type of microphone is best.

If you will be capturing audio from a CD-ROM drive, you need a connection between the sound card and the CD-ROM drive. Check the card's manual to determine where its line-in connectors are located. There may be only one, or there may be two. Generally, the line-in connectors are located on the board rather than on the connector bracket that attaches at the back of the PC's chassis (where the MIDI connector and output jacks usually are located).

If there is a primary line-in and an auxiliary line-in connector on the sound card, the CD-ROM drive should be connected to the primary line-in connector. You can connect other devices (including a second CD-ROM drive) to the auxiliary input, but you may have to make a cable for it.

Adding a Sound Card

Like many devices, sound cards require a free IRQ, and usually, a free DMA channel. In addition to configuring these options on the card, you also might need to make speaker and CD-ROM connections when installing a sound card. Then, finish the installation by installing any required drivers and other software to enable you to use the card.

Adapter Configuration and Installation

Use MSD and your system logs to determine a free IRQ and DMA for your sound card. You may need to shuffle the IRQ and DMA settings for other devices to allocate settings for your sound card. Then follow these steps:

1. Turn off and open the system.

2. Configure the sound card's IRQ line. Make sure you assign an IRQ to the card that isn't used by any other device. If necessary, you may have to disable an unused COM port. An alternative is to use the same IRQ allocated to LPT1 or LPT2, although you may experience problems using the sound card while printing, and possibly at other times as well. If you have no other options, however, sharing an LPT port IRQ with the sound card is worth trying. Most sound cards provide jumpers or switches on the card to set the IRQ, but some use a configuration program instead.

3. Configure the sound card's DMA channel, making sure to assign a DMA channel that isn't used by any other device in the system. You may have to assign a DMA channel from a specific range of channels in order to use all the capabilities of your sound card. Read the section in the sound card's manual carefully to see if this is the case. As with IRQ settings, most sound cards use jumpers or switches to set the DMA channel, but some use a configuration program instead.

4. Depending on where the connectors are located on your sound card, it may be easier to connect the cables to it before installing the card in the PC. Examine the card to locate any connectors you will be using. If you think it will be easier to connect the cables now, skip forward to the procedure on connecting cables to the card, then return to this procedure.

5. Locate an appropriate slot for the adapter. Choose an 8-bit slot or 16-bit slot for an 8-bit adapter, and choose a 16-bit slot for a 16-bit adapter.

6. Carefully install the sound card in the slot, securing it with a screw.

Connecting Cables

The number of connections you need to make to your sound card depends on the optional equipment you'll be using with the sound card. Adding a CD-ROM may require connecting the drive to the sound card's CD-ROM port. Adding speakers and a microphone or connecting the sound card to your stereo are other possibilities.

✔ **CD-ROM drives:** Unless you're using a separate SCSI host adapter for the CD-ROM drive, connect the interface cable of the CD-ROM drive to the sound card's interface connector. Connect the cable from the line-out connector on the CD-ROM drive to the primary line-in connector on the sound card. Or, connect the CD-ROM drive to the sound card's stereo line-in connector (there might be a stereo line-in connection on the card itself, as well as a stereo line-in connector at the back of the sound card). See figures 30.3 and 30.4.

✔ **Microphone:** Connect the microphone to the sound card's microphone line-in at the back of the adapter (probably a monaural, rather than stereo, connection).

Figure 30.3
Connect the CD-ROM drive to the sound card's interface connector.

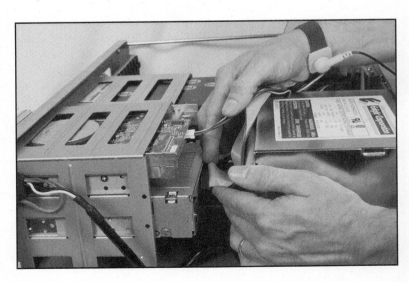

Figure 30.4

Connect the audio cable from the line-out connector on the CD-ROM to the line-in connector on the sound card.

V

Hardware Concerns

✔ **Speaker output:** Connect the speakers to the sound card's stereo line-out connector (see fig. 30.5). Most desktop speakers require a single stereo cable connection between the sound card and one speaker, and another stereo line connection between the two speakers. Set up the speakers as described in the section "Positioning the Speakers" earlier in this chapter.

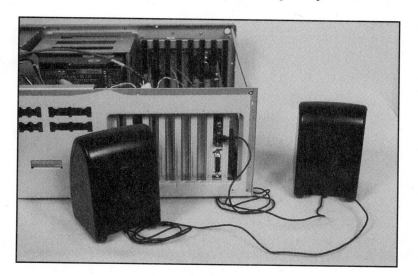

Figure 30.5

Connect the speakers to one another and to the sound card.

✔ **Stereo system output:** If you want to connect the sound card to your stereo system instead of to bookshelf speakers, read the section earlier in this chapter titled "Using Your Stereo for Playback." Then, with the stereo turned off, make a connection from your sound card's stereo line-out connection to the auxiliary input on your stereo (or to the Y-adapters you have installed between one of the stereo system's components and its amplifier).

✔ **Auxiliary input:** If you have other, non-MIDI devices to connect to the sound card, make a connection between the device and the sound card's auxiliary line-in connector.

Your sound card may not support direct connection to the CD-ROM drive's line-out connector, even if the sound card has the appropriate connector. Some sound cards require that you connect the CD-ROM to a small additional adapter (supplied with the sound card), and then connect a patch cable between this additional adapter and the sound card. Figure 30.6 shows this type of patch cable on a Gateway 2000 system with a vendor-supplied CD-ROM and sound card.

Figure 30.6
External patch cable for CD audio output to sound card.

Completing the Installation

If you are using the sound card to drive a CD-ROM drive, you need to install a CD-ROM driver for the card. The driver will be included with the sound card if you purchased the CD-ROM drive and sound card as a multimedia kit. If you purchased the sound card and CD-ROM drive separately, you may have to buy the driver and cable kit separately.

The software for your sound card probably includes an installation program that will install the driver for you. If not, you'll have to install the driver manually by adding an entry for the driver to CONFIG.SYS and copying the driver file to the appropriate directory. In addition to this CD-ROM driver, you need to install MSCDEX.EXE. Read Chapter 31, "CD-ROM Drives," for more information on installing and configuring your CD-ROM drive and MSCDEX.

In addition to installing a CD-ROM driver and MSCDEX, you also need to install the software included with your sound card that enables you to use the card. These applications typically include a sound mixer, recorder, CD playback, and possibly other programs. The installation process for your sound card might also install one or more drivers for Windows. Otherwise, the manual may direct you to install the drivers yourself using the Windows Control Panel.

Installing Device Drivers for Windows

If you will be using your sound card in Windows, you will have to install some sound drivers with Control Panel, unless the software installation program for the sound card takes care of this step for you. To install sound drivers, follow these steps:

1. In Windows, open the Control Panel and choose the Drivers icon.

2. In the **D**rivers dialog box, choose the **A**dd button.

3. From the Add dialog box, choose the driver required by your sound card. Check the manual to determine which drivers to install. It's probable that your sound card disks include updated drivers. Choose the option titled Unlisted or Updated Driver to install drivers from your sound card disks. You might need to install more than one driver, which will require that you repeat this step for each driver.

4. When you have finished installing all of the necessary drivers, close the Drivers dialog box and close Control Panel. Then, restart Windows.

You can assign sounds to various events so that when the event occurs, the assigned sound plays on your sound card. This is covered in the next section, "Integrating Sound with Windows."

Integrating Sound with Windows

There are a number of ways you can integrate sound with the Windows environment and with Windows programs. Some are purely for fun, while others apply to the everyday use of your PC for business. This section covers ways you can use sound in Windows, starting with assigning sounds to general Windows events.

Assigning Sounds to Windows Events

There are a number of standard events that occur in Windows. These events include starting and exiting Windows, opening various types of dialog boxes, and more. By default, you can assign sounds to seven standard Windows events through the Windows Control Panel. You can assign the TADA.WAV file ("Tah Dah!"), for example, to play when Windows starts.

Your sound card may include software that enables you to assign sounds to other Windows events. There also are some third-party programs that enable you to assign sounds to other Windows events not supported through the standard Control Panel.

Assigning Sounds to Windows Events

To assign sounds to Windows events, follow these steps:

1. In Windows, open the Control Panel and choose the Sound icon.

2. Verify that the E<u>n</u>able System Sounds check box is checked.

3. In the Sound dialog box, select the event from the <u>E</u>vents list to which you want to assign a WAV file.

4. In the <u>F</u>ile list, select the WAV file you want to assign to the event. If you want to listen to a WAV file before you assign it, click on the <u>T</u>est button. Whichever WAV file is selected will be played.

5. Repeat steps 3 and 4 for any other events to which you want to assign sounds.

6. Click on OK to store your selections.

If the selections in the <u>E</u>vents and <u>F</u>iles lists are dimmed, your sound drivers are not properly installed. Windows is not recognizing that you have a valid sound device installed in the system. Run through your driver installation steps again to make sure the drivers are properly installed, and make sure you restart Windows after installing the drivers for the changes to take effect.

Using Sound in Documents

If your sound card supports Windows 3.1's OLE, you can embed sound objects in your Windows documents—you can embed a voice notation in a Word or Excel document, for example. Someone else who views the document can double-click on the object to hear your note played back (assuming there's a sound card in his system). Or, you may want to embed a short voice note in an e-mail message.

Recording and Embedding a Sound Object in a Document

The steps in this procedure are geared toward Word for Windows, but the general procedure applies to most applications that support OLE. The only differences will be in menu names and options—some programs may use slightly different menu names and commands, but the general procedure still is the same. Follow these steps:

1. From the application's **I**nsert menu, choose **O**bject. The Object dialog box appears, as shown in figure 30.7.

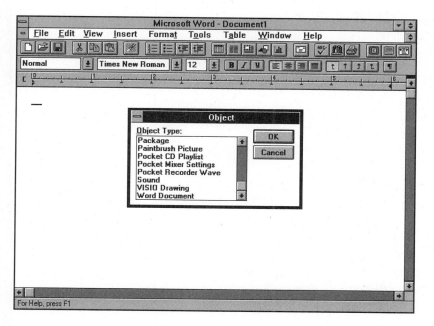

Figure 30.7

The Object dialog box in Word for Windows.

2. Scroll through the list of objects in the Object dialog box and locate the Sound entry.

3. Click on the Sound entry, then choose the OK button. The Sound Recorder appears on the desktop.

4. When you are ready to record your note, click on the microphone button. The screen pointer changes to an hourglass as the Sound Recorder sets up the recording.

5. When the arrow pointer reappears, the Sound Recorder is recording. Speak your message into the microphone, then click on the Stop button when you are finished. (The Stop button has a solid rectangle on it.)

6. From the Sound Recorder's File menu, choose Exit. Sound Recorder asks whether you want to update the object in the document. Choose Yes to embed the sound in the document.

Embedding an Existing Sound File in a Document

Use this procedure if you want to embed an existing WAV file in a document.

1. Open the document in which you want to embed the file and position the cursor where you want the sound file to be inserted.

2. Open File Manager and locate the WAV file to be inserted.

3. Drag the file from File Manager to the document and release the mouse button. A Sound Recorder icon will appear in the document with the title of the WAV file listed underneath it. If you don't want to change the text under the icon, skip the remaining steps.

4. To edit the description under the WAV file object, click once on the object's icon. Then from the Edit menu, choose Package Object. This opens the Object Packager.

5. From the Object Packager's Edit menu, choose Label, then type the label you want to appear under the icon. Click on the OK button when you've finished editing the label.

6. From the Object Packager's File menu, choose Exit. Click on Yes when you're prompted to update the document.

There are a number of other ways to embed a sound object in a document. If you're interested in learning more about OLE, pick up a copy of *Maximizing Windows 3.1*, from New Riders Publishing.

Embedding a Voice Note in an Electronic-Mail Message

If you want to embed a sound recording in an e-mail message, you first need to record the message in a WAV file using the Sound Recorder or the recording program that is included with your sound card. You then attach the WAV file to the message, just as you would attach any other binary file to a text message.

With most mail programs, you begin by composing the text of the note, if any. A short explanation of what the voice message is about might be useful. Then, position the cursor where you want the voice note object to be inserted in the message. Next, choose the mail program's Attach menu, or whatever menu option is required in the program to attach a file to a message.

When you're sending voice notes to other users, remember that the recipient must have a sound card in her system in order to play back the recorded note.

Chapter Snapshot

CD-ROM technology is becoming more of a necessity than a novelty. This chapter covers CD-ROM basics and explains how to buy, install, use, and troubleshoot a CD-ROM drive. In this chapter, you learn:

- ✔ The history of CD-ROM technology

- ✔ Tips for purchasing a CD-ROM

- ✔ How to install a CD-ROM drive

- ✔ How to share a CD-ROM across a network

This chapter answers all of your basic questions about CD-ROM drives so that you can quickly get up to speed on this popular technology.

CD-ROM Drives

CD-ROM drives are fast becoming a popular addition to PCs. They offer a cheap and easy means for developers to distribute their applications, and are essential for using multimedia applications on your PC. You even can play audio CDs on your PC if you want to. Given the popularity of CDs, it's a good bet that you'll soon want to add a CD-ROM drive to your system.

With release 5, owning a CD-ROM drive is even more important. Corel Systems offers a price break for the CD-ROM version of release 5. You also get an extensive collection of clip art and fonts with the CD-ROM version.

Understanding CD-ROM Drives

CD-ROM stands for *Compact Disc Read-Only Memory.* CD-ROM discs and drives used in PCs are a lot like audio CDs and CD drives. The only difference in the discs is the type of information stored on the disc and the way that information is encoded. The only difference in the drives is that CD-ROM drives for PCs generally are a little more ruggedly built to withstand the more exacting requirements of data retrieval. That's the primary reason why PC CD-ROM drives are more expensive than audio CD-ROM drives. Figure 31.1 shows a CD-ROM drive and a data CD.

Figure 31.1

A CD-ROM drive and disc cartridge, and a data CD.

What's so great about CD-ROMs? Primarily, the storage capacity. Each CD can hold 680 MB of data. As application size steadily increases, many developers are turning to CDs to distribute their software.

Developers are turning to PCs for a couple of reasons. First, duplicating a single CD is much cheaper than duplicating 10 or 12 disks. After you've installed software from a CD, you'll also know why they're great for users—no more swapping disks in and out of the drive during installation.

CD-ROMs also can free up valuable hard disk space. Many applications enable you to leave peripheral files on the CD until you need them. You can leave a large Help file on the disc, for example, then pop the CD into the drive when you need to access the Help file. Clip art and other support files you don't use regularly also can often be left on the CD instead of installed on the hard disk.

The large storage capacity of CDs also is a big asset, bringing the capability to maintain and search large amounts of data very quickly. You can search the entire encyclopedia on CD for the word *freedom*, and almost instantly have a list of all the articles that include that one word.

Can you imagine thumbing through an entire set of hardcover encyclopedia volumes to find all the occurrences of a single word? If you're looking for a piece of information, there is no better way today than to search for it on one of the rapidly growing number of specialty data CDs.

What's Available on CD?

You might be amazed at the wide variety of data you can find on CD. Many applications now are available on CD instead of disk, often offering more features and a lower price than their disk-based versions. Microsoft Word on CD, for example, is less expensive than the disk version. It also includes a copy of Microsoft Bookshelf, which gives you the ability to access, right from within Word, *Roget's Thesaurus*, *Bartlett's Familiar Quotations*, *The Concise Columbia Dictionary of Quotations*, the *World Almanac*, and *The American Heritage Dictionary*.

Many images, which include illustrations, photos, and textures, are available to the computer artist to expand his or her design capabilities.

Aside from applications you'll find a wealth of incredible data, from literary collections to reference works, to fact collections on every subject from animals to geopolitical information compiled by the CIA and KGB. Figure 31.2 shows a clip from Microsoft's Encarta CD, a multimedia encyclopedia.

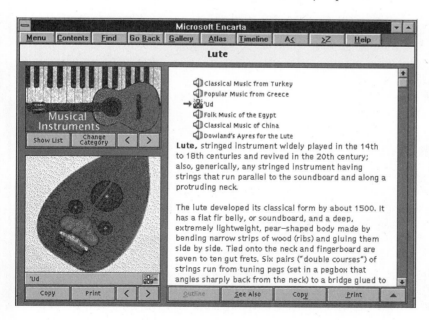

Figure 31.2
A clip from Microsoft's Encarta encyclopedia CD.

A good multimedia CD also can give you new ways to learn. You can view how a particular piece of machinery works by watching an animation of the device in action. Clicking on a musical term can give you a musical example of what the term means. If you don't know how to pronounce a word, clicking on the word might cause it to be spoken (assuming you have a sound card in your PC).

The Pros and Cons of CDs

Aside from the fact that you can find a CD title that covers nearly any subject imaginable, CDs offer practical benefits. In addition to providing a quick and easy means to install software and freeing valuable hard disk space, CDs are nearly indestructible. Unlike floppy disks, CDs are not susceptible to damage from dust, dirt, scratches, temperature changes, and magnetic fields.

Currently, CDs also have a few disadvantages. CD-ROM access is relatively slow when compared to hard disk access. A typical CD-ROM drive provides an access time between 265ms (milliseconds) to 300ms or more, which is nearly 20 times as slow as a good hard disk. You also can't save files to a CD because they are read-only devices. Within a few years, however, writable CDs will be available for the average user, giving you an almost unlimited amount of storage space for your data and applications.

A Buyer's Guide to CD-ROM

You should consider several issues when deciding which CD-ROM drive to buy. Higher-priced units often offer better performance, but you should check the specifications of the drive before deciding which one fits both your use requirements and your budget.

Performance

The first issue to consider when evaluating CD-ROM drives is performance. Average access time is one specification to check. Many drives on the market today offer an access speed of around 300ms. Some offer better access times (indicated by a lower value), and some offer poorer performance—sometimes 600ms or more. Shop for a fast access time (lower numbers), but temper your selection by how much you can afford to spend on the drive.

You also need to check the drive's *data transfer rate*, which is the rate at which the drive can transfer data from the disc to the PC. Most drives today offer a transfer rate of 150 KB/sec (kilobytes per second), but some drives offer better transfer rates of 300 KB/sec or more. Shop for a drive that gives you the highest possible transfer rate.

Also look for drives that include a built-in disc cache of 64 KB or more. As it can for a hard disk, a cache on the CD-ROM drive will improve the drive's performance by holding frequently accessed data in memory rather than having to retrieve it from the disc each time it's needed.

Photo CDs

One of the newest additions to CD-ROM technology is the photo CD. Developed by Kodak, *Photo CD technology* enables photographs to be scanned and placed on a CD. There's nothing novel about the technology—you can scan photos from slides and store them on a writable CD if you have the equipment to do so. Kodak's Photo CD technology simply imposes a proprietary standard format on the discs.

To get a photo CD, you can take your film to a photography shop that has the necessary equipment, and the shop transfers your photos onto CD. Most photo finishing shops that don't have the equipment will send your film to a service bureau that does have the necessary equipment.

When you get the photo CD back, you can load those pictures of Aunt Agnes into Paintbrush on your computer and draw a mustache on her if you want to. Figure 31.3 shows a photo CD image displayed in a Windows application, Collage Complete.

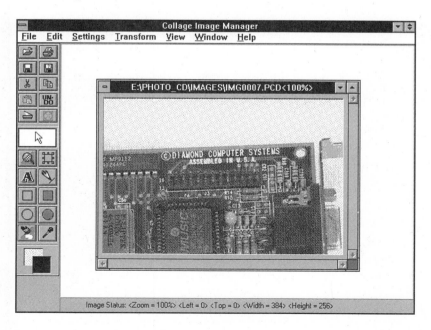

Figure 31.3
A photo CD image displayed in Windows-based Collage Complete.

Corel Systems offers several collections of photo CDs, ranging from airplanes to sunsets.

There are single-session photo CDs and multisession photo CDs. A single-session photo CD has had all its photographic images placed on the CD at the same time (in one recording session). Multisession photo CDs have been recorded in multiple sessions. Some CD-ROM drives are capable of reading only single-session photo CDs, and can read only the first set of images on a multisession CD.

If you plan to view only your own photo CDs, a single-session drive may be fine. If you will be swapping photo CDs with other users, shop for a drive that supports multisession photo CDs.

CD-ROM/XA Capability

Also consider whether a drive is XA-compatible. CD-ROM/XA drives offer two benefits: they provide interleaved audio and video, and highly compressed digital audio. The interleaved audio/video capability offers two advantages.

Interleaved audio and video portions of a video clip require less space on the disc to store the clip, making more room available for other data. Interleaving also provides faster performance for a more realistic and jitter-free playback. XA's capability to compress digital audio increases its audio storage capacity from the standard 72 minutes in audio CDs to up to 16 hours.

When you're shopping for a CD-ROM drive, look for a drive that not only offers multisession photo CD capability, but also XA-compatibility.

Audio Capability

You probably will want to play audio CDs on your PC at some point. You also want the best possible audio reproduction possible from the drive. Shop for a drive that provides a sampling frequency of 44.1 MHz, which is the sampling rate used in audio CDs.

Multimedia upgrade kits that include a sound card (as well as stand-alone sound cards) generally include software to play audio CDs. Figure 31.4 shows the Pocket CD program that's included with Mediavision's Pro Audio Spectrum card.

Figure 31.4
The Pocket CD program from Mediavision gives you software to play audio CDs on your PC.

Internal or External CD Drives?

CD-ROM drives are available as internal units that mount inside your PC, just like a floppy drive. You also can get external CD-ROM drives that sit on your desk (or on top of your PC) and connect to the back of the PC by an interface cable.

The only benefit internal CD-ROM drives offer over external drives is that they take up less desk space and eliminate one more cable that has to connect to the back of your PC. If you like an uncluttered desk and don't need to move the drive from one system to another, buy an internal drive.

If your system is on a network and you want to be able to access the CD-ROM drive from other nodes on the network, you can do so. If you want the option of being able to move the drive from one system to another, buy an external drive.

Which Interface To Choose?

Some CD-ROM drives use a proprietary data interface and controller to connect the CD-ROM drive to the PC. These proprietary interfaces usually are based on a variation of a standard IDE or SCSI interface. These types of drives naturally include their own controllers.

Other CD-ROM drives use a parallel interface, connecting to the PC through one of its parallel (LPT) ports. CD drives often offer slower performance than other types, primarily because the system's parallel ports are not designed for high-speed data transfer. These types of drives are great, though, for systems that don't offer the possibility of any other type of interface.

Most notebook PCs, for example, don't include built-in SCSI support, and parallel port CD-ROM drives are one solution for these types of systems. You also can buy SCSI adapters that plug into your parallel port, however, so a portable SCSI CD-ROM drive may also be a solution for your notebook PC.

SCSI drives generally are the best choice, although you may have to buy a SCSI host adapter for your system in addition to the CD-ROM drive (read the next section for more information on requirements for a SCSI host adapter).

The benefit to the SCSI interface is that you can connect other devices—such as scanners, hard disks, and tape drives—to the same adapter.

Multimedia Kits

A good way to buy a CD-ROM drive is to get it as part of a multimedia upgrade package that includes an audio adapter (a sound card). If you intend to use your CD-ROM drive for audio, either for listening to the audio portion of a multimedia CD or when playing audio CDs in the drive, you'll probably want a sound card.

The only other option (if you want to be able to listen to your CDs) is to plug a set of headphones into the front of the drive. A sound card will give you better sound quality and more options for controlling options such as treble, bass, and fade.

There are lots of different multimedia upgrade packages available that include a CD-ROM drive, a sound card, and software. When you evaluate a multimedia kit, choose a kit that uses a standard SCSI-2 interface if you plan to connect other SCSI devices to the SCSI host adapter built into the sound card.

If you want to buy a stand-alone SCSI host adapter to get the best possible performance from your SCSI devices, the interface that the sound card uses doesn't matter quite as much, as long as it provides good performance. If the kit includes a SCSI CD-ROM drive, you don't have to connect it to the sound card if you have a dedicated SCSI host adapter. You can connect it to the host adapter rather than to the sound card.

Adding an Internal CD-ROM Drive

The installation procedure for an internal CD-ROM drive is a little more complex than for an external drive because you have to open the PC to install the drive. (You also might have to open the PC to install an external hard drive, but that's for a different procedure.) Even so, the installation procedure is fairly simple. In fact, it's a lot like the installation procedure for a floppy drive, but with a few extra steps.

Termination and Configuration

To set the drive ID, follow these steps:

1. On SCSI devices, set the SCSI ID for the drive to a higher number than any SCSI hard drives that also are installed in the system. If there are no other SCSI devices in the system, set the drive's ID to 1, leaving ID 0 available for future installation of a hard disk. Make sure to use a unique ID number that isn't shared by any other SCSI device in the system.

Usually, the SCSI ID is configured by setting DIP switches on the drive. Figure 31.5 shows the SCSI ID configuration switches on the NEC CDR-84 drive.

If you're installing a parallel-port device, you probably won't need to set a drive ID or other configuration options, but check the drive's manual to be sure. If you're installing a drive that uses a proprietary interface, it's more likely—but not a certainty—that you'll have to set one or more configuration options on the drive. Check the manual to be sure.

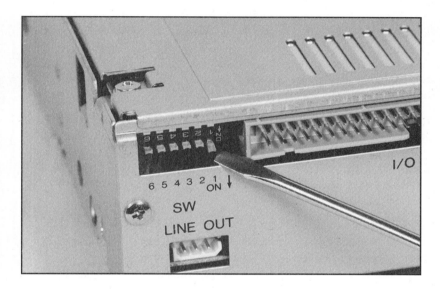

Figure 31.5
The ID configuration switches on the NEC CDR-84 CD-ROM drive.

2. If the drive will be the last device on the bus, it may have to be terminated, which usually involves adding a terminating resistor pack to the drive. Check the drive's manual to determine how to terminate the drive. Some drives, such as the NEC internal drive, require a special terminating adapter that plugs into the drive's data cable.

    If you can't figure out how to terminate the drive, or don't want the added expense of a terminating adapter, consider connecting the drive so that it isn't the last device on the bus (assuming there are other devices on the same bus). The last device currently on the bus probably is already terminated, which solves the problem.

Installing the Drive

Installing the drive is not difficult. Just follow these steps:

1. Turn off, unplug, and open the PC.

2. Choose a drive bay for the CD-ROM drive. If you don't have a drive bay available, you may have to eliminate a floppy drive to install the CD-ROM drive. But first, check your system to see if you can relocate the hard drive to another bay. Many tower systems, for example, include a drive bay at the top of the unit above the bay that normally is used for drive A.

    If you can relocate your hard disk and make a bay available for the CD-ROM drive, do that as an alternative to eliminating a floppy drive. Another option is to replace your two floppy drives with a single, dual-drive unit that takes only one drive bay but gives your system a 3 1/2-inch drive and a 5 1/4-inch drive.

3. After checking your drive's configuration, install mounting rails on either side of the drive if your PC's chassis requires them (usually only required on AT-style cases). If there is only enough room in the drive bay for the CD-ROM drive, you don't need the rails. If you need rails and they didn't come with the drive, you can buy a set from a PC component dealer like JDR Microdevices or your local PC shop.

4. Carefully slide the CD-ROM drive into the drive bay (see figure 31.6) until the front of the drive is aligned with the front of the floppy drive(s), then secure the drive in the bay with screws.

Connecting Cables

There are either two or three cable connections to make, depending on whether your system contains a sound card. In either situation, you need to connect a power cable to the drive, as well as a data cable. If your system contains a sound card, you also need to make a connection between your CD-ROM drive and the sound card.

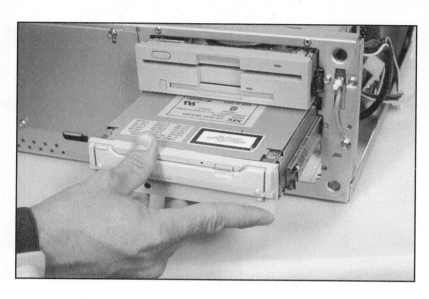

Figure 31.6
Slide the CD-ROM drive into the bay until the front lines up with the floppy drive(s).

You might already have run out of power cables if you have two floppy drives, a hard drive, and another device connected to the power supply. If you don't have an available power supply connection for the CD-ROM drive, you can get a power splitter cable that connects to one of your existing power connectors and provides two connectors for the cable harness on which it's installed.

If you need to use one of these power cable splitters, connect it to the power connector for the floppy drive that you use the least, and connect the CD-ROM drive and the floppy drive to the same power cable.

To make the cable connections, follow these steps:

1. Connect a power cable to the CD-ROM drive (see the previous Note if you don't have an available power cable).

2. Connect the interface cable between the host adapter (or sound card) and the CD-ROM drive. Make sure to align pin 1 on each end of the cable with the proper pin on the CD-ROM drive and on the adapter (see fig. 31.7). You might find it easiest to remove the sound card or host adapter, connect the interface cable to it, and then reinstall the adapter.

Figure 31.7
Connecting the data interface cable between the CD-ROM drive and the host adapter.

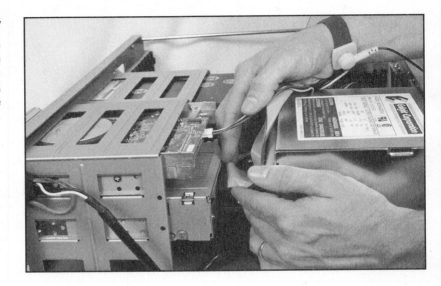

3. If your system contains a sound card, connect the CD-ROM drive to the sound card by the necessary cable (see fig. 31.8). If the cable didn't come as part of a kit, you'll have to buy the cable separately. Check with the sound card manufacturer or dealer for the right cable. If you don't want to get the cable right away, you can connect a pair of headphones to the front of the CD-ROM drive.

Figure 31.8
Connecting the audio cable between the drive and the sound card.

If you can't see paying extra money for a cable to connect your CD-ROM drive to your sound card, and if you're the adventurous sort, you might be able to make your own cable. The line-out connector on the CD-ROM drive probably will have only three pins: left, right, and ground. If you can locate the right type of connectors at your local electronics supply store, you should be able to put together a cable that will work.

Check the manual for your sound card and for your CD-ROM drive to determine the pin connections for the audio connectors. Then, make a cable that connects the two left outputs to one another, the two right outputs to one another, and the ground pin(s).

Hardware Concerns

After you've finished connecting all of the necessary cables to the drive, skip to the section in this chapter titled "Completing the Installation" to install drivers and test your drive.

Adding an External CD-ROM Drive

The process required to install an external CD-ROM drive is similar, though slightly different, from the procedure for installing an internal drive. Aside from the fact that you don't have to install the drive in one of the PC's drive bays, the connections for the drive are a little different. Even though the drive is external, you still might need to open up the PC. This section covers installation of SCSI-based CD-ROM drives.

The CD-ROM drive requires a connection to whichever device in the PC will be controlling it, whether that device is the sound card or a host adapter. Unless you already have installed the host adapter or sound card and have the necessary connector available at the back of the PC, you'll have to open the PC as part of the installation procedure. SCSI host adapters generally have a connector for external SCSI devices, which sticks out the back of the PC like all the other connectors on the system's adapters.

Many sound cards don't provide the CD-ROM connection on the back of the adapter because the space is taken up by audio connectors. Instead, the CD-ROM data connector is on the adapter, and a short cable connects the adapter to a special bracket that is installed in back of a free bus slot. An external cable then connects the drive to a connector installed on the bracket. This special bracket is supplied with the sound card, not with the CD-ROM drive. Unless the card is supplied in a kit with an external CD-ROM drive, the adapter bracket will be optional.

Termination and Configuration

Follow these steps to set termination and configuration:

1. Set the drive's ID. On SCSI devices, set the SCSI ID for the drive to a higher number than any other SCSI hard drives that are installed in the system. If there are no other SCSI devices in the system, set the drive's ID to 1, leaving ID 0 available for future installation of a hard disk. Usually, the SCSI ID is configured by setting DIP switches on the drive.

Make sure to use a unique ID number that isn't shared by any other SCSI device in the system.

2. If the drive will be the last device on the bus, that drive might have to be terminated, which usually involves adding a terminating resistor pack to the drive. Check the drive's manual to determine how to terminate the drive if it isn't already terminated.

   If you have another external SCSI device already attached to the system, and you're adding an external SCSI CD-ROM drive, you can avoid the termination issue altogether by attaching the CD-ROM drive between the PC and the other SCSI device. The CD-ROM then no longer will be the last device on the bus and won't require termination. If the CD-ROM drive is terminated and you install it in the middle of the bus instead of as the last device, you must remove its termination.

Installing and Connecting the Drive

To install and connect the drive, do the following:

1. Choose a good spot for the CD-ROM drive on your desk or on top of your PC if you have a tower case.

2. Connect the power cord from the back of the CD-ROM drive to an outlet.

3. Connect the interface cable from the drive to the host adapter or special bracket adapter (sound cards only).

4. If your system includes a sound card, connect the audio cable between the CD-ROM drive and the sound card. If you don't have the necessary cable, you can get a small stereo cable and connect one end to the headphone jack of the CD-ROM drive, then connect the other end of the cable to the input jack on the sound card. You also can buy some connectors and make your own cable.

Completing the Installation

The PC's BIOS doesn't include direct support for CD-ROM drives, so your system requires a special CD-ROM driver to enable the CD-ROM drive to communicate with the PC. The required driver will be included with whichever device is controlling the CD-ROM drive, and not with the drive itself.

If you want to connect your CD-ROM drive to a SCSI host adapter, for example, you'll need a CD-ROM device driver specifically written for your SCSI host adapter. Some SCSI host adapter manufacturers include a CD-ROM driver with the adapter, while others make you pay for it as an option. Multimedia kits in which the CD-ROM drive can connect to the sound card include a driver to enable the sound card to control the CD-ROM drive.

Installing the CD-ROM Driver

The procedure you use to install the CD-ROM driver varies according to the type of adapter or sound card you're using. Check the adapter's manual and disks to determine how to install the driver. Most adapters include an installation program that will install the driver for you automatically.

Installing and Configuring MSCDEX

In addition to the device driver that enables your adapter to control the CD-ROM drive, you also need MSCDEX.EXE, which is the Microsoft CD-ROM extension for DOS. MSCDEX that enables DOS to recognize the CD-ROM drive as a logical DOS storage device represented by a drive ID letter, just like a floppy drive or hard drive.

Usually, the CD-ROM or sound card software will include a copy of MSCDEX.EXE, but it might not be the latest revision. MS-DOS 6 includes an update to MSCDEX, so if you've upgraded to the latest copy of DOS, you should have a recent copy of MSCDEX also.

Typically, the installation program for your CD-ROM or sound card software will install MSCDEX for you, but you need to make sure it installs the right copy. Check the copy of MSCDEX provided with your software and the copy provided with MS-DOS. If your DOS copy has a later file date than the one supplied with your CD-ROM software, copy the later copy of MSCDEX to the CD-ROM software disk that contains a copy of MSCDEX. This enables you to let the software install MSCDEX for you and still have the latest version of MSCDEX installed.

Although your CD-ROM software probably will install MSCDEX for you, you might have to install it or change parameters for it manually. MSCDEX can be started from the DOS command line, but usually you should add it to AUTOEXEC.BAT so that it starts automatically whenever you boot the system. Here's the syntax of the MSCDEX command line:

```
MSCDEX.EXE /D:CD_driver_ID /L:drive_ID /M:sector_buffers
```

The `CD_driver_ID` parameter is taken from the /D parameter specified on the line in CONFIG.SYS that loads your CD-ROM device driver. Here's an example of a line that might appear in CONFIG.SYS (using a Future Domain driver as an example):

```
DEVICE=C:\FDOMAIN\FDCD.SYS /D:MSCD0000
```

The parameter `MSCD0000` in the previous example is the logical device name associated with the CD-ROM drive. The line in AUTOEXEC.BAT for MSCDEX would then appear as follows:

```
MSCDEX.EXE /D:MSCD0000 /L:E /M:20
```

What are those other parameters for? The /L parameter specifies that the CD-ROM drive will be recognized as drive E. Specify whichever drive letter you want to use for the CD-ROM drive. The /M:20 parameter specifies 20 sector buffers for the CD-ROM drive, which will improve performance (sort of a disc cache).

The higher the number, the more memory that is used for the buffers. Use 10 or 20 as a rule of thumb. If you want information on MSCDEX's other possible command-line switches, type **HELP MSCDEX** at the DOS prompt.

Sharing a CD-ROM

If you're on an MS-NET (LAN Manager, NT, or MS-NET compatible) or Windows for Workgroups network and want to share a CD-ROM drive with other users on the network, add the /S switch to the MSCDEX command line on the machine that contains the CD-ROM drive.

The switch is not necessary on the remote nodes that are accessing the CD-ROM drive. If there are no CD-ROM drives installed on the remote nodes, those nodes do not require that MSCDEX be loaded. MSCDEX is required only at the node where the CD-ROM is physically located. It then appears as a logical DOS disk to the other nodes.

Here's an example of the MSCDEX command line to use:

```
MSCDEX.EXE /D:MSCD0000 /L:E /M:20 /S
```

Installing Other Software

After installing your CD-ROM device driver and MSCDEX, you're ready to start using your CD-ROM drive to read data CDs. If you also want to play audio CDs, you need to install some additional software.

If your sound card included an installation program that installed software on your system, the installation program might already have installed the necessary software. Mediavision's software, for example, includes a program for playing audio CDs, called Pocket CD, which is installed by the Mediavision setup program.

If you don't have a sound card, or if it didn't include software for playing CDs, you can use the Windows Media Player application to play audio CDs. To use Media Player for audio CDs, though, you first must install the Media Control Interface (MCI) CD Audio driver (covered in the next procedure).

If you want to view photo CDs, your CD-ROM driver must be capable of reading photo CDs (your CD-ROM drive also must be capable of reading photo CDs). In addition, you'll need software to view the images on your PC. Collage Complete, CorelDRAW!, and many other graphics programs include support for photo CD image formats.

Installing the MCI CD Audio Driver

The MCI CD audio driver must be installed for the Windows Media Player to play audio CDs. If you're using a different program to play audio CDs, you might not need the MCI CD audio driver, depending on how the program accesses the CD-ROM drive.

To install this driver, follow these steps:

1. Open the Windows Control Panel and click on the Drivers icon.

2. In the Drivers dialog box, choose Add.

3. From the List of Drivers, select [MCI] CD Audio, then choose OK.

4. Control Panel will prompt you to insert one of your Windows distribution disks. Insert the requested disk, then choose OK.

5. Control Panel will display an informational dialog box indicating that the driver was installed. Select OK, then choose Close to close the Drivers dialog box. Exit Control Panel.

Testing and Troubleshooting

You should test all the aspects of your CD-ROM drive to make sure all your software is configured properly. You should test the drive's capability to read a data CD, play an audio CD, and, if appropriate, share a CD across the network.

Reading a Data CD

Many data CDs include their own viewer/reader programs that display the information contained on the CD. Even so, the data CD still should be recognized by DOS as a logical disk device, which means you should be able to display a directory of the CD. Follow these steps.

1. Insert a data CD into the CD-ROM drive.

2. **DOS method:** At the DOS prompt, enter **DIR *E:*,** substituting the correct drive ID letter for your CD-ROM drive in place of the E: in this example. You should see a directory listing of the drive.

3. **Windows method:** In Windows, open File Manager and select the drive icon for the CD-ROM drive. A directory listing should appear for the CD-ROM drive.

4. If you see a directory listing, your CD-ROM drive is working properly. If you don't see a directory listing, or if you receive an error message that the disk does not exist or is not ready, verify that you have inserted the CD properly. The printed side of the CD faces up, and the data side (with no printing on it) faces down. If the CD is inserted properly and you can't read the CD, verify the installation of your CD-ROM driver and MSCDEX.EXE.

After verifying that you can read the CD's directory structure, follow the directions provided with the CD to install any necessary viewer or application software to enable you to use the CD.

Testing Audio CDs

Make sure that your CD-ROM drive is connected to your sound card, or that you have headphones connected to the CD-ROM drive, and follow these steps.

1. Place an audio CD in the CD-ROM drive.

2. From the Accessories group in Windows, open the Media Player program.

3. From the Device menu, choose CD Audio. The Media Player program window changes to appear as shown in figure 31.9. (If CD Audio is not one of the choices in your menu, your driver hasn't been installed correctly.)

Figure 31.9
The Media Player program window configured for CD Audio.

4. If you don't have the CD Audio menu option, close the Media Player, erase the file MPLAYER.INI from your Windows directory, and then try running Media Player again.

5. Click on the Play button (the left-most button in the button bar).

Viewing a Photo CD

Insert the photo CD into the CD-ROM drive and follow these steps:

1. Open the program you use to view photo CDs. This program may have been included with your CD-ROM drive, or you might have purchased it separately.

2. Use the commands provided in the program to view the images on the CD. If you receive an error message to the effect that there is no CD in the drive or the drive is not ready, your CD-ROM driver probably is not capable of reading photo CDs. Contact technical support for the CD-ROM manufacturer or the place where you bought the CD-ROM drive.

Part Six

Appendixes

APPENDIX

Installing
CorelDRAW! 5

Before you begin your excursion into the world of CorelDRAW!, you must first install the program on your system. You'll want to read this appendix thoroughly before you begin the installation process because Corel offers you several installation options. By understanding the various options, you can choose the type of installation that best fits your needs. This appendix also discusses the basic hardware requirements you need to effectively use CorelDRAW! 5.

System Requirements

As software packages mature and expand in scope, especially graphics packages, a more powerful computer system on which to install the package is needed. The complete package of CorelDRAW! 5, for example, takes more than 60 MB of hard disk space. Along with this large amount of hard disk space, you also need an ever-increasing amount of system memory.

Although Corel Systems recommends that you have a 386 computer that runs Windows 3.1 or higher and has at least 4 MB of RAM with an 80 MB hard drive, you should have at least 8MB of RAM and a 240 MB hard drive. Anything less causes problems. CorelDRAW! is a memory-intensive program that creates large files. You also need a VGA monitor and a mouse. A CD-ROM drive is highly recommended.

Corel ships version 5 on CD-ROM or on floppy disks. You pay an additional fee for the disks; therefore, now may be a good time to invest in that CD-ROM you have always wanted. Besides offering a much faster installation time, the CD version also offers more fonts and clip art.

Making a Backup Copy

The first step you should take before you begin the installation process is to make a backup copy of version 5. Although you may be tempted to dive right in, don't! Always make backups of your original program disks and store them in a safe place.

If you have the CD version of CorelDRAW! 5, you don't need to make a backup copy of the program. Just make sure that you guard your CD with care. Place it in its jewel case and store in a safe place away from heat.

Whether you plan on installing CorelDRAW! from floppy disk or CD, write your registration number down on an index card and place it in your Rolodex or tape it to the software box. You won't get very far in the installation process unless you have this number handy.

You need at least 20 blank, formatted 3 ½-inch high-density disks to make a backup copy of version 5. Have enough labels to place on the disks and label them sequentially.

Close any other applications that you might have running. From Windows Program Manager, open File Manager and choose **C**opy Disk from the **D**isk menu. The Copy Disk dialog box appears on-screen (see fig. A.1).

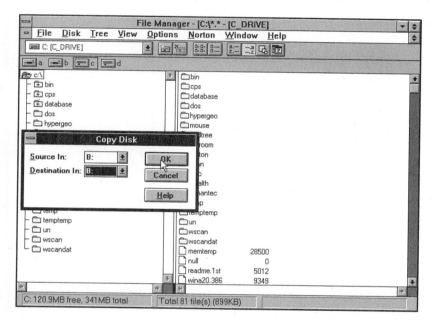

Figure A.1
The Copy Disk dialog box.

You are prompted to enter the source drive and the destination drive. The *source* drive is the drive that contains the original Corel disk. The *destination* drive contains the disk to which you are copying. Clicking on the down arrows changes the drive letters within the boxes. Click on OK after the drive letters are correct.

The Confirm Copy Disk dialog box appears to advise you that the operation will erase all the data from the destination disk and be replaced by the data from the source disk. You must click **Y**es to continue.

Place the version 5 disk labeled Disk 1 in the source drive. Click on OK. Windows begins the copying process. As the disk is copied, you see a percentage displayed in the Copying Disk dialog box. After Windows has copied the contents of the disk into memory, you are prompted to insert the destination disk. Insert the destination disk in the drive and click on OK.

After the copying process is complete, Windows asks you if you want to copy another disk. Remove the disk and label it accordingly. Then click Yes to continue copying the original Corel disks.

Always position the write-protection notch into the locked position by sliding the notch up. Write protecting your backup set of disks ensures that you, or someone else, cannot accidentally erase your set of program disks.

Choosing the Installation Procedure

Before you continue installing CorelDRAW!, consider how you will use the package. CorelDRAW! 5 offers two types of installation. The full installation option installs all of the CorelDRAW! package, including example files, help files, and templates. The full installation takes up to 50 MB of hard disk space. The custom installation enables you to choose which applications you want to install. To perform the custom installation, you need at least 38 MB of hard disk space. This installation provides all of the applications, but does not install examples, help, or templates.

Checking the amount of available hard disk space you have on your system is quite easy. From Windows Program Manager, choose File Manager. Make sure that the highlight appears on the letter of the drive to which you want to install. At the bottom of the File Manager window, you should see the amount of available disk space.

You can choose to run CorelDRAW! from your CD-ROM drive. This option may seem tempting, especially if your hard disk space is at a premium, but the software runs slowly this way.

Beginning the Installation

No matter if you are installing CorelDRAW! from floppy disks or CD, the procedure is similar. Place Disk 1 of the floppy disks or CD 1 in the appropriate drive. Choose **F**ile, **R**un and type **A:\SETUP.EXE,** where A is the letter of your disk drive. If you are not installing from drive A, substitute the correct drive letter, then click on OK. After a few moments, you should see the opening installation screen (see fig. A.2). Click on the **C**ontinue button to proceed with the installation.

The CorelDRAW! 5 Setup screen is displayed. You must enter your name and product serial number. You can locate your serial number in volume 1 of the user manual. The number appears on the top right of the Technical Support card.

Tip You may enter any name that you choose in the Name field, but you must enter your official serial number. You cannot continue the installation process until you enter this number and choose Continue.

Choosing the Full Install Option

The CorelDRAW! Installation Options dialog box provides you with two installation options (see fig. A.3). Choosing Full Install installs all of the CorelDRAW! modules and data files. Choosing Custom Install installs the minimum files required for each CorelDRAW! module.

Figure A.3
The
CorelDRAW!
Installation
Options dialog
box.

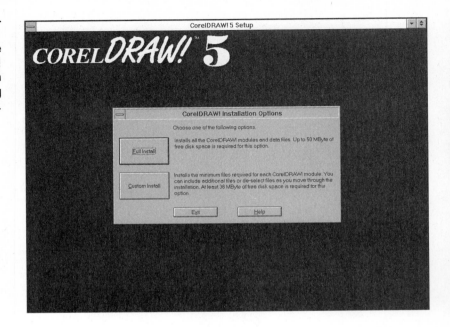

To select the **F**ull Install option, simply click on the button and the installation begins. A dialog box is displayed to show the percentage of the program that has been installed. After installation is complete, you are notified.

Choosing the Custom Install Option

The basic custom installation installs the minimum files needed to run all of the Corel modules. You can customize this installation further by picking the modules that you use and deselecting those that you don't use. If hard disk space is at a premium or you find that you use only certain modules, this option is for you. If you never create charts and graphs, for example, you may choose not to install CorelCHART!.

To begin the custom installation, click on the Custom Install button. Figure A.4 shows the opening custom installation screen. All of the Corel modules are pictured on the left side of the screen.

You can see just how much hard disk space each module consumes by looking at the box that appears to the right of the directory path locations.

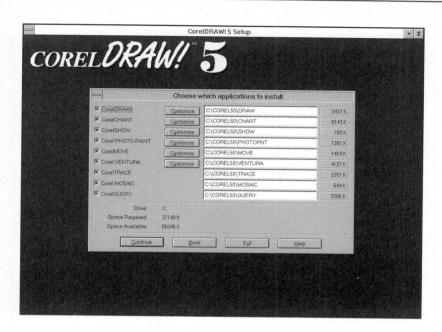

V

Appendixes

Figure A.4
The opening custom installation screen displays all of Corel's modules.

The following list provides a brief overview of each module so that you can make installation decisions:

✔ CorelDRAW! is the premiere drawing package and is the meat of version 5.

✔ CorelCHART! is a program that creates all types of charts and graphs. If you create statistical data on a regular basis, then choose to install this module.

✔ CorelSHOW! enables you to create presentations that include charts, sound clips, and animation sequences. If you need to prepare multimedia presentations, install this module.

✔ CorelPHOTO-PAINT! enables you to take scanned photographs and bitmap graphics into CorelDRAW! and edit them or add special effects.

✔ CorelMOVE! is an animation application that you can use with CorelSHOW! to make multimedia presentations.

✔ The remaining modules—CorelTRACE!, CorelMOSAIC!, and CorelQUERY!—must be installed entirely or not at all. CorelTRACE! enables you to convert bitmapped images into a file format that CorelDRAW! can use. CorelMOSAIC! is a file management utility that enables you to view thumbnails of your illustrations. CorelQUERY! is used to retrieve data from large databases.

If you know that you do not need to install all of the modules, click on the check box to the left of those modules that you want to remove. Notice at the bottom of the dialog box that Corel displays the amount of space required to load the modules you have checked and the amount of available space you have on your drive.

Tip

If you decide that you do not want to perform the custom installation, you can click on the **B**ack button, which appears at the bottom of the screen, to return to the installation option window.

Customizing Specific Modules

Corel provides the option for you to further customize the installation of CorelDRAW!. By further customizing each module, you can add more or fewer options. This capability assures that you can build your applications around the way that you work.

The procedure for further customizing a module is simple. Follow these steps:

1. Click on the **C**ustomize button that appears to the right of the module you want to customize. Figure A.5 shows the dialog box that appears when you want to customize CorelDRAW!.

Figure A.5
The CorelDRAW! Options dialog box.

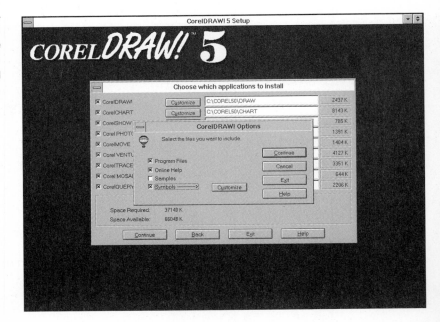

Within the CorelDRAW! Options dialog box, you find options for installing the Program Files, Online Help, Samples, and Symbols.

2. Make sure that an X appears in the box to the left of Program Files and Online Help. You may not want to add the Samples because they do take up a substantial amount of space on your hard drive.

3. You can further personalize the Symbols library by clicking on the Customize button. The Symbols Selection Window appears (see fig. A.6).

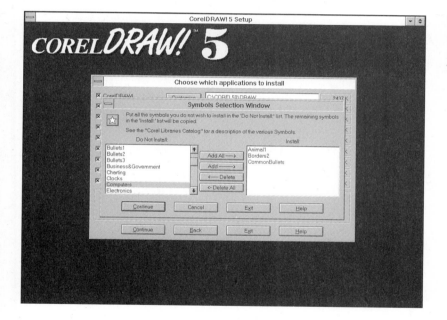

Figure A.6
The Symbols Selection Window.

CorelDRAW! provides this library of illustrations so that you can use them in conjunction with your own creations. You can view the collection of illustrations in the Corel Libraries Catalog, which comes with your documentation material.

4. Click on the names of the symbols you don't want to install and choose the Delete button.

5. After you choose your symbols, click **C**ontinue.

You can continue this customization process for CorelCHART!, CorelSHOW!, CorelPHOTO-PAINT!, and CorelMOVE!. You can always check your available disk space against the space required. Also of note is your ability to change the drive onto which you load a specific module. After you finish the applications customization, click <u>C</u>ontinue.

Corel then displays the Choose which files to install dialog box (see fig. A.7). Here you can customize the filters setting to suit your importing and exporting needs. You also have a choice of several hundred fonts, scanner drivers, and animation drivers.

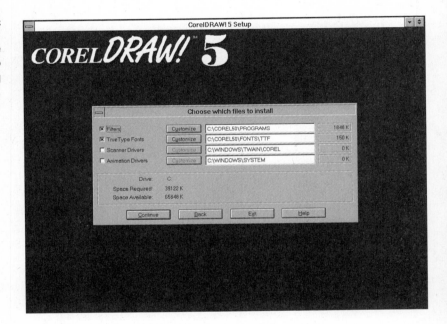

Figure A.7
The Choose which files to install dialog box.

Setting Up Filters

If you are a true graphics professional or want to be, you will want to take advantage of all the import and export filters that CorelDRAW! has to offer. The more filters you have on your system, the more capacity you will have for reading and dealing with different graphics file formats.

Choosing filters is easy; just follow these steps:

1. Click on the <u>C</u>ustomize button next to the Filters option. The Filter Selection dialog box is displayed (see fig. A.8).

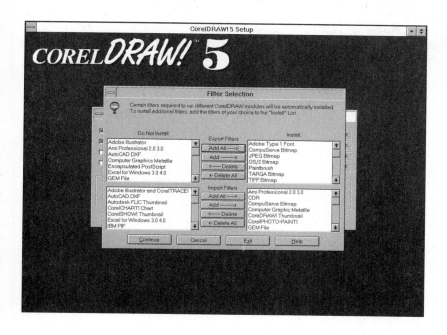

Figure A.8
The Filter
Selection dialog
box.

2. In the scroll box on the left side of the box are the filters that will not be installed. You can choose to add all of the filters or select only the filters you know that you use. After you select the filters, they appear in the box on the right side of the screen.

   If you know for certain that you will never use certain filters, click on them and choose the Delete button.

3. Click on the <u>C</u>ontinue button to proceed with the installation.

Installing Fonts

The CorelDRAW! 5.0 CD-ROM comes with 825 TrueType fonts. The disk version comes with fewer fonts. Even so, don't be tempted to install too many fonts. Installing more fonts that you need just slows down Windows and CorelDRAW!. Besides, you can always install a specific font when you need it.

Don't install more fonts than you need. Each TrueType font that you install adds to your WIN.INI file. If this file exceeds its 64 KB size, Windows will crash. You can find information on installing and removing TrueType fonts in Chapter 24, "Building Your Own Font."

You may find it helpful to make a list of the fonts that you want to install before you actually begin the installation process. All the fonts are illustrated in the Corel documentation.

To begin the installation, click on the Customize button that appears next to the TrueType Fonts check box. The TrueType Fonts Selection dialog box appears (see fig. A.9).

Figure A.9
The TrueType
Fonts Selection
dialog box.

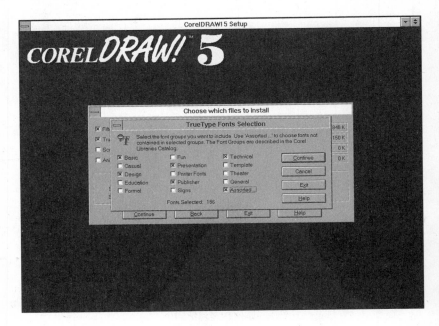

5.0

With version 5, Corel has divided TrueType fonts into various categories. The categories are Basic, Casual, Design, Education, Formal, Fun, Presentation, Printer Fonts, Publisher, Signs, Technical, Template, Theater, General, and Assorted. Appendix E contains illustrations of these various categories.

You can choose various categories, or, if you truly want to have control over font selection, choose the Assorted category. All the fonts, except for Avant Garde, appear in the Do Not Install box that appears on the left side of the screen. You are now ready to begin your font selections.

Scroll through the fonts list until you find a font you want to install. Then click on the font name and click on the Add button. Continue this process to install all of the fonts you want added to your system. You can change your mind any time and decide to delete any font you previously added to the installation list. After you select all the fonts you want to add, click on <u>C</u>ontinue.

Adding Scanner Drivers

If you have a scanner that Corel supports or is TWAIN compliant, you can scan your source image or document straight into CorelPHOTO-PAINT!. PhotoPaint is the only Corel module that can handle bitmap images. If you plan to use a scanner with Photo-Paint, you may need to install one of Corel's scanner drivers.

To install a scanner driver, follow these steps:

1. Click on the Scanner Drivers check box. The Scanner Selection dialog box is displayed (see fig. A.10).

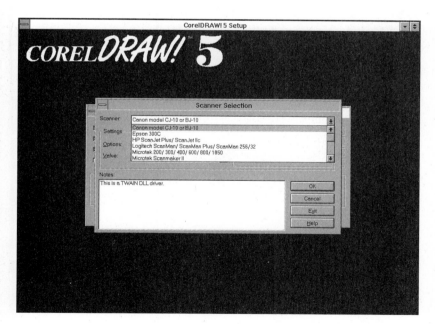

Figure A.10
The Scanner Selection dialog box.

VI

Appendixes

2. To choose your scanner, click on the down arrow on the Scanner drop-down list box.

3. Click on the name of your scanner and make any changes to the Options or Value settings.

If your scanner does not require special settings, the Options and Value settings appear dimmed and cannot be changed.

4. Click on OK to add the scanner settings.

Installing Animation Modules

The last thing to install with version 5 is third-party animation drivers. Animation drivers enable you to play animation and motion picture clips from your screen. These drivers are run-time modules.

Corel provides three choices of animation drivers. The choices are AVI Runtime Player driver, Quicktime Runtime Player driver, and Autodesk Animator Runtime Player. Of the three drivers, the Autodesk driver is the oldest and most well known. The Quicktime for Windows and AVI formats can be used to export animations created with CorelMOVE!.

Click on the check boxes of the drivers you want to install and then click on Continue.

Finishing Up the Installation

After you select the files to install, click on Continue. Corel informs you that the program is ready to install (see fig. A.11). You can choose to return to the former screen by clicking on **B**ack. You also can choose to exit from the installation process. To continue with installation, click on **I**nstall.

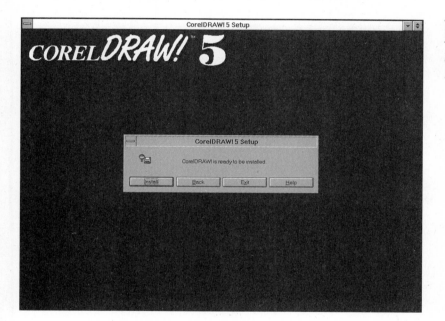

Figure A.11
The CorelDRAW! 5 Setup box.

Corel then provides a status box that tells you the percentage of the program that has been installed on your system (see fig. A.12). This box also provides information on the drive that contains the source disk and the destination drive.

Figure A.12
Corel updates
you on the
installation
process.

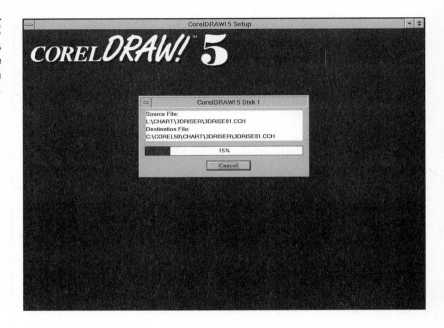

If you are installing from floppy disks, Corel prompts you to insert the appropriate disks. Do not be alarmed if you are prompted to skip certain disks. If you customized your installation, you may not need all of the Corel installation disks.

Figure A.13 shows the CorelDRAW! Setup window, which appears when installation is complete. You can choose to restart Windows now and dive right into CorelDRAW! or choose to continue with other work.

 The artwork pictured on the Setup screen won first place in last year's Corel annual World Design Contest.

The Corel group appears in Program Manager. Resize the group and position it where you want it to appear. Fill out your registration card and send it in. You now have one of the most powerful drawing packages installed on your system.

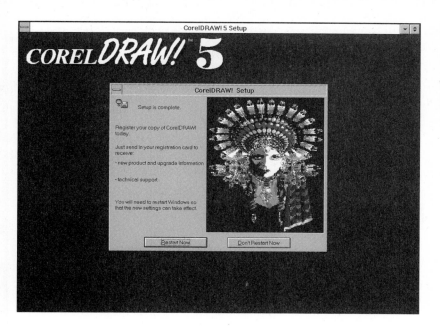

Figure A.13
The CorelDRAW! Setup window that shows installation is complete.

V

Appendixes

APPENDIX

Glossary

A

Anamorphic scaling. Stretching. Reducing or increasing one dimension (height or width) of an object without changing the other dimension.

Artistic text. CorelDRAW!'s display text mode, used for headlines and the like.

Ascender. The part of a lowercase letter that extends above the x-height. See also *descender, x-height*.

B

Baseline. The implied boundary on which a line of type sits.

Bézier curve. A mathematical formula for the description of a curve drawn between two anchor points (or nodes, in Corel terms). Each curve has a set of tangent (control) points to delineate the curve's path. The curve was developed in the early 1970s by French mathematician Pierre Bézier.

Bitmap. A dot-by-dot method of rendering images. Common file formats include BMP, GIF, JPG, PCX, TGA, and TIFF.

Bleed. The illusion of printing to the edge of the paper. Accomplished by printing on an oversized piece of paper and then trimming to size.

Blend. The metamorphosis between two objects. An interpolation of colorized shape.

C

Caps. Uppercase or capital letters.

Clone. A copy style that enables you to copy and link a blend, extrude, contour, or power liner. When you change the first, the second changes along with it.

Color correction. A method of calibrating the monitor and output to achieve consistent, predictable, and reliable results.

Color separation. Separating a color original (photograph or illustration) into the four process colors—cyan, magenta, yellow, and black. See also *process color*.

Color trade shop. A firm that specializes in printing prepress, specifically process color work, with a higher craft orientation than the common service bureau. Usually employs a combination of traditional stripping techniques along with high-end graphics systems, such as Scitex, DS, Linotype-Hell, or Crosfield. See also *stripping*.

Comp. Abbreviation for *comprehensive*. The designer's term for a mock-up of a finished job. Used for presentation rather than production purposes.

Condensed. A narrow version of a font with a high character-per-line-count. CorelDRAW! can produce a pseudo-condensed version of any font through the use of anamorphic scaling. Use with caution, however—readability can be affected. See also *anamorphic scaling, extended*.

Continuous tone. Refers to an image with a smooth transition in tone, as in original photographs, charcoal drawings, or watercolor paintings. Cannot be rendered through any printing process. See also *halftone*.

Contour. A CorelDRAW! effect that blends an object unto itself. Great for creating glowing objects.

D

Decorative. An overdone typeface with a distinctive look. Used mainly for headlines; not normally used for text.

Descender. The part of a lowercase letter that extends below the baseline. See also *Ascender, x-height.*

Desktop publishing (DTP). The use of a personal computer as a system for producing typeset-quality text and graphics. The term reportedly was coined by Aldus chief Paul Brainerd.

Dot-matrix. An inexpensive printer that uses a print head commonly consisting of nine to 24 pins. Typically an office printer, a dot-matrix printer does not have a high enough resolution to be used for computer graphics work.

DPI. *Dots per inch.* Used in reference to the resolution of an output device or scanner. The higher the device's dpi, the higher the quality of the image.

Dropout (or Knockout) type. White type that "drops out" of a black or darkly colored background. Often referred to as *reverse type.*

E

Em dash. A dash approximately as wide as the letter M (most often used in text).

Envelope. A CorelDRAW! effect that enables you to radically alter the shape of objects or type.

En dash. A dash as wide as the letter N (most often used with dates or numbers).

Extended. A wide version of a font. CorelDRAW! can produce a pseudo-extended version of any font through the use of anamorphic scaling. See also *condensed.*

Extrude. CorelDRAW!'s effect for creating pseudo-three-dimensional objects.

F

Family. All the fonts of the same typeface in various sizes and weights. Typically includes Roman, italic, bold, and bold-italic.

Flush. A term (as in *flush-right* and *flush-left*) referring to type set with an even margin on the right or left side. Also commonly referred to as *quad left* or *quad right*, alluding to the metal-type days when such lines were filled out with blanks known as quads.

Fill. The color, tint, pattern, or texture inside an object's outline. An object must be a closed path to be filled.

Font. A set of characters of one typeface, weight, and size. In the hot-metal days (before cold type), the term referred to a particular font of a particular size and style, such as 10-point Times Roman. With the advent of digital composition, a font is thought of as the style throughout its complete range of sizes.

H

Hairline. A fine rule or line of one-half point or less.

Halftone. A halftone image fools the eye into thinking that black and white can produce gray by breaking down the tones into a series of noncontiguous dots. Dark shades are produced by dense patterns of thick dots. Lighter shades are produced by less-dense patterns of smaller dots. Can be produced photographically or electronically. See also *continuous tone.*

High-res. Slang for *high resolution.* Refers to an output device's capability of rendering images at 1,270 dpi or higher.

I

Inferior figures. Small numbers, letters, or special characters set below the baseline.

Intersection. One of CorelDRAW! 5.0's cookie cutter tools; it creates a new object from the overlap of two selected objects, but the original objects remain untouched.

J

Justified type. Type set with even left and right margins. High-end composition programs hyphenate and justify (H&J) copy by using both dictionary and algorithm methods.

K

Kerning. Reducing or increasing space between character pairs to compensate for character shape. Some examples of character pairs commonly kerned are *AW, LY, Te,* and *Ve.*

L

Leading. The amount of space between lines of type. Pronounced "ledding," the term comes from the actual strips of lead placed between lines in the hot-metal era.

Lens. A transparent fill effect introduced in CorelDRAW! 5.0.

Letterspacing. Increasing or decreasing the space between all characters. Current use of the term commonly refers to the act of opening up space, as opposed to *tracking,* which refers to the tightening up of space.

Ligatures. Character pairs, such as *ae, fi, fl, ff, ffi,* and *ffl,* combined to form one character for aesthetic reasons.

Line length. The column width of a block of type, normally measured in picas.

Low-res. Slang for *low resolution.* Refers to an output device's limitation of rendering at 400 dpi or less.

O

Oblique. A variation of italic.

OLE. Object linking and embedding.

Overprint type. Black or dark-colored type printed over a lighter underlying color, halftone, or light-gray tint.

Overprinting. Printing over an area that has already been printed with a color. (The only way to trap with CorelDRAW!.) See also *trapping.*

P

PANTONE Matching System (PMS). The printing industry's standard method of mixing inks and describing spot colors.

Paragraph text. CorelDRAW!'s body text mode.

Pica. The printer's basic unit of measurement. An inch contains approximately six picas.

Point. There are 12 points to one pica; approximately 72 points to one inch.

Point size. The measurement used to describe type height. Refers to the approximate distance between the top of the ascenders and the bottom of the descenders.

PostScript. The de facto standard page-description language used in laser printers and other output devices. This Adobe Systems product revolutionized the typesetting and graphics art worlds.

PowerClip. CorelDRAW! 5.0's version of "paste inside." An automated method for creating clipping paths.

PowerLine. Tool that emulates traditional illustration techniques, such as woodcutting. Continued from version 4.0.

Pre-flight. Test printing a file to a laser printer (as separations) before going to a high resolution output.

Process color. The process used to produce the illusion of "full-color" printed pages. The image is produced using four printing plates, with one color (cyan, magenta, yellow, or black) on each plate. See also *spot color*.

R

Ragged. A term (as in *ragged-left* or *ragged-right*) that refers to type set with an uneven margin on one side. Depending on client preference, ragged type can be set with or without hyphenation.

Registration marks. The bull's-eyes (or cross hairs) used by printers to align multicolor jobs when stripping negatives.

S

Sans serif. A typeface without serifs, such as Helvetica. See also *Serif*.

Script. A typeface rendered with a calligraphic style, such as Zapf Chancery. Commonly used for wedding invitations.

Serif. A typeface with end strokes, such as Times Roman. See also *sans serif.*

Service bureau. A firm that specializes in high-resolution output of PostScript files. Commonly equipped with a combination of imagesetters, color printers, and other proofing equipment.

Set solid. Type set with a leading equal to the point size. Best used in larger display sizes with all caps.

Small caps. Type set in all caps smaller than the standard uppercase capital letters of the font. Small caps are drawn to synchronize with the normal x-height.

Spot color. Printing with more than one color, but not process. Ink is mixed to attain the precise color. See also *Process color.*

Spreads and chokes. Swelling and shrinking negatives to compensate for press variations. Commonly referred to as *trapping.*

Standing head. A "department head" that identifies a standard feature column in a periodical.

Stripping. The craft of assembling film negatives prior to printing. This is best left to the professional.

Subscript. Small numbers, letters, or special characters set below the baseline.

Superior figures. Small numbers, letters, or special characters, such as the dollar sign, aligned with (or higher than) the top of the caps. Also known as *superscript.*

Superscript. Small numbers, letters, or special characters, such as the dollar sign, aligned with (or higher than) the top of the caps. Commonly referred to as *superior figures* in typographic terms.

T

Texture fill. A fill that uses fractal algorithms to generate unique bitmap fills. Continued from version 4.0.

Thumbnail sketches. The first stages of a project. These are simple scribbles, often done on whatever paper might be available at the time—including coffee-stained restaurant napkins.

Tracking. Tightening the space between all characters, as opposed to *kerning,* which affects only the space between two characters.

Trapping. Slightly overlapping adjoining colors to prevent gaps when printing.

Trim. One of CorelDRAW!'s cookie cutters. Unlike Intersection, Trim cuts away the overlap between two objects. Trim affects the bottom object, leaving the top object untouched.

TrueType. An attempt by Apple and Microsoft to quash the Adobe Type 1 font format standard. Pretty much a dead issue on the Mac, it's alive and well on the PC market. Many Service Bureaus shun jobs that contain TrueType fonts (see Chapters 11 or 27 for further information).

TruMatch. A system for defining process color.

Typography. The craft of designing with type.

U

U&lc. Type set in uppercase and lowercase. Also, an excellent magazine published by the International Typeface Corporation.

V

Vector-based art. Drawings based on mathematical equations rather than bit-by-bit representations. This genre of electronic art can be scaled at will without loss of resolution.

W

Weld. A feature introduced in CorelDRAW! 4.0 that joins two overlapping objects by fusing them together.

X

x-height. The height of a lowercase letter *x*. Two typefaces can be the same point size, but have different x-heights.

CorelDRAW! Keyboard Shortcuts

+ (on the numeric keypad). Leaves the original object in place when moving, stretching, mirroring, rotating, or scaling. Also places a duplicate object behind the selected object, without any other actions.

Alt+F1. Accesses the CorelMOSAIC! Roll-Up menu.

Alt+F2. Accesses the Dimension Roll-Up menu.

Alt+F3. Accesses the Lens Roll-Up menu.

Alt+F4. Quits CorelDRAW!.

Alt+F5. Accesses the Presets Roll-Up menu.

Alt+F7. Accesses the Move mode of the Transform Roll-Up menu.

Alt+F8. Accesses the Rotate mode of the Transform Roll-Up menu.

Alt+F9. Accesses the Scale mode of the Transform Roll-Up menu.

Alt+F10. Aligns to baseline.

Alt+F11. Accesses the Size mode of the Transform Roll-Up menu.

Alt+F12. Accesses the Skew mode of the Transform Roll-Up menu.

Alt+A. Drops down the Arrange menu.

Alt+Backspace (also Ctrl+Z). Accesses the Undo command.

Alt+C. Drops down the Effects menu.

Alt+E. Drops down the Edit menu.

Alt+Enter. Accesses the Redo command.

Alt+F. Drops down the File menu.

Alt+H. Drops down the Help menu.

Alt+L. Drops down the Layout menu.

Alt+S. Drops down the Special menu.

Alt+T. Drops down the Text menu.

Alt+Tab. Switches between active programs.

Alt+V. Drops down the View menu.

Click the right mouse button on the selected object. Accesses the Object menu (if another function has been assigned to that button, you must hold the button down for a few moments on the object to open the Object menu).

Click the right mouse button as you drag an object. Leaves the original object.

Ctrl+F1. Accesses Help on the current command.

Ctrl+F2. Accesses the Text Roll-Up menu.

Ctrl+F3. Accesses the Layers Roll-Up menu.

Ctrl+F5. Accesses the Styles Roll-Up menu.

Ctrl+F7. Accesses the Envelope Roll-Up menu.

Ctrl+F8. Accesses the PowerLine Roll-Up menu.

Ctrl+F9. Accesses the Contour Roll-Up menu.

Ctrl+F10. Accesses the Node Edit Roll-Up menu.

Ctrl+F11. Accesses the Symbol Roll-Up menu.

Ctrl+F12. Accesses the Object Data Roll-Up menu.

Ctrl+A. Accesses the Align dialog box.

Ctrl+B. Accesses the Blend Roll-Up menu.

Ctrl+C (also Ctrl+Ins). Copies to the Clipboard.

Ctrl+D. Duplicates an object.

Ctrl+E. Accesses the Extrude Roll-Up menu.

Ctrl+Esc. Accesses the Windows Task Manager.

Ctrl+F. Accesses the Fit Text To Path Roll-Up menu.

Ctrl+G. Groups objects with objects selected.

Ctrl+Ins (also Ctrl+C). Copies to the Clipboard.

Ctrl+J. Accesses the Preferences dialog box.

Ctrl+K. Breaks apart combined objects.

Ctrl+L. Combines objects with objects selected.

Ctrl+N. Opens a new CorelDRAW! file.

Ctrl+O. Opens an existing CorelDRAW! file.

Ctrl+P. Accesses the Print dialog box.

Ctrl+PgUp. Moves selected object forward one.

Ctrl+PgDn. Moves selected object backward one.

Ctrl+Q. Converts an object into curves.

Ctrl+R. Repeats the last command or function.

Ctrl+S. Saves the current drawing to disk.

Ctrl+spacebar. Enables the Pick tool.

Ctrl+T. Accesses the Character Attributes dialog box.

Ctrl+Shift+T. Accesses the Edit Text dialog box.

Ctrl+U. Ungroups objects.

Ctrl+V (also Shift+Ins). Pastes from the Clipboard.

Ctrl+W. Refreshes the screen.

Ctrl+X (also Shift+Del). Cuts to the Clipboard.

Ctrl+Y. Turns Snap to Grid on and off.

Ctrl+Z (also Alt+Backspace). Access the Undo command.

Ctrl while drawing an ellipse or rectangle. Constructs a perfect circle or square.

Ctrl+Shift while drawing an ellipse or rectangle. Constructs a perfect circle or square from its center.

Ctrl while moving. Constrains movement to horizontal or vertical.

Ctrl while rotating or skewing. Constrains movement to preset increments (program default is 15 percent).

Ctrl while stretching, scaling, or mirroring. Constrains movement to 100-percent increments.

Del. Deletes a selected object or node.

Double-clicking a character node. Accesses the Character Attributes dialog box.

Double-clicking the page border. Accesses the Page Setup dialog box.

Double-clicking the ruler. Accesses the Grid & Scale Setup dialog box.

Double-clicking a guideline. Accesses the Guideline Setup dialog box.

Double-clicking the Pick tool. Selects all objects in the drawing.

Double-clicking the Node Edit tool. Accesses the Node Edit Roll-Up menu.

Double-clicking the Rectangle toll. Creates a page frame.

Double-clicking the Text tool. Accesses the Text Roll-Up menu.

F1. Accesses Help on a currently selected command.

F2. Zooms in.

F3. Zooms out.

F4. Zooms to fit all objects in window.

F5. Enables the Pencil tool.

F6. Enables the Rectangle tool.

F7. Enables the Ellipse tool.

F8. Enables the Text tool.

F9. Switches between full-screen Preview and Wireframe mode.

F10. Enables the Shape tool.

F11. Accesses the Fountain Fill dialog box.

F12. Accesses the Outline Pen dialog box.

Shift+F1. Accesses Help on screen or menu item.

Shift+F2. Zooms to selected object.

Shift+F4. Zooms to fit page in window.

Shift+F6. Accesses the Fill Roll-Up menu.

Shift+F7. Accesses the Outline Pen Roll-Up menu.

Shift+F8. Enables the Paragraph text tool.

Shift+F9. Switches between Full-Color and Wireframe mode.

Shift+F11. Accesses the Uniform Fill dialog box.

Shift+F12. Accesses the Outline Color dialog box.

Shift+Del (also Ctrl+X). Cuts the selected object to the Clipboard.

Shift+Ins (also Ctrl+V). Pastes the selected object from the Clipboard.

Shift+PgDn. Moves object to back.

Shift+PgUp. Moves object to front.

Shift+Tab. Selects the previous object.

Shift while drawing. Erases when the mouse moves backward along a curve.

Shift while drawing an ellipse or rectangle. Stretches or scales from the middle of the object.

Spacebar. Switches between the currently selected tool and the Pick tool.

Tab. Selects the next object.

Clip-Art Compendium

This appendix presents a brief list of electronic clip-art vendors. You might recognize some of the names from the collection that accompanies CorelDRAW!. Before you buy any clip art, make sure that you know what you are getting. Feel free to request brochures and samples from the manufacturers.

To get the most value for your clip-art dollar, install a CD-ROM drive. Every copy of CorelDRAW! 5.0 includes a CD-ROM that contains thousands of clip-art images from such vendors as Corel, Image Club, Cartesia, One Mile Up, TechPool, and Totem. The money you spend to install the drive is far outweighed by the wealth of high-quality artwork—not to mention the abundance of additional fonts!

21st Century Media PhotoDisc™

Volume 1: Business & Industry
Volume 2: People and Lifestyles
Volume 3: Backgrounds and Textures
Volume 4: Science, Technology, and Medicine
Volume 5: World Commerce and Travel
Volume 6: Nature, Wildlife, and Environment
Volume 7: Business and Occupations
Volume 8: Backgrounds and Objects
Volume 9: Holidays and Celebrations
Volume 10: Sports and Recreation
Volume 11: Retro Americana
Volume 12: Food & Dining

Now you can afford to design in full color by using professional digital stock photos. 21st Century Media's PhotoDisc™ collections consist of high-quality images on CD-ROM. Every photo is model-released and ready to use for advertising, promotions, newsletters, presentations, and multimedia. These images are award-winning stock photographs that have been scanned from transparencies and are provided in high-resolution TIFF format for desktop applications. Each volume includes a browsing utility that manipulates on-screen images to search, retrieve, store, view, copy, and paste.

PhotoDisc, Inc.
2013 4th Ave.
Seattle, WA 98121
800/528-3472

Allegro New Media

InPrint Art Library Volume 1
InPrint Art Library Volume 2

Allegro New Media offers two different double CD-ROM sets, each consisting of 202 color and grayscale TIFF images. Both of these collections come with screen shows that provide photo usage tips. "InPrint Art Library Volume 1" focuses on graphics textures and cartoon idioms, and "InPrint Art Library Volume 2" contains both graphics photos and scenic photos.

Graphics textures are designed to be used as backgrounds, borders, and accents. The disc includes: marble, granite, wood, high-tech, natural, marbleized paper, textile, jungle, leather & lace, and tie dye textures. Cartoon Idioms are rendered by cartoonist Peter Bernard in both color and grayscale versions. The 101 retouched images on the Graphics Photo disc include such subjects as: celebrations, frames, globes, hands, plaques, music, sculpture, sports, and trophies. The like number of images on the Scenic Photo disc are categorized as: still life, plant life, textures, landscapes, water bodies, architecture, and doorways.

> Allegro New Media
> 387 Passaic Avenue
> Fairfield, NJ 07004
> 201/808-1992
> 201/808-2645 (fax)

Arroglyphs

> *ARROglyphs: Environment Volume 1*
> *ARROglyphs: Energy*
> *ARROglyphs: Living Planet*
> *ARROglyphs: Pollution*
> *ARROglyphs: Recycling*
> *ARROglyphs: Wildlife*
> *ARROglyphs: Wildlife Accents*

This is artwork for the environmentally aware. Through its original hand-drawn images, Arro focuses on mankind and its relationship with our planet. Each of the collections is available in EPS (AI 1.1), TIFF, WMF, PICT, and CGM formats. The illustrations are beautifully rendered in such diverse styles as woodcuts, marker sketches, and fine brush. The original collection, "Environment Volume I," has been upgraded and now consists of 200 black-and-white images, along with 92 color images covering environmental issues such as pollution, recycling, and life on Earth. Subject matter includes acid rain, global warming, ozone depletion, and so on.

Arro's six new offerings are smaller, more focused collections. "Energy" includes 50 color and black-and-white images of energy production, use, waste, and pollutants. "Living Planet" contains 30 color and 35 black-and-white images, with subject matter that includes the greenhouse effect, ozone depletion, forests, water, and fire. "Pollution" focuses on acid rain, garbage, batteries, fuel tanks, and factories, with 30 color and 33 black-and-white images. "Recycling" consists of 32 color and 40 black-and-white images related to recycling issues. "Wildlife-Accents" includes just under 100 color and black-and-white images of plants and animals, along with a Wildbits font (available as either PostScript Type 1 or TrueType) that features an array of ornate capitals. "Wildlife" contains 50 color and black-and-white images

VI

Appendixes

that illustrate a variety of creatures, including 20 that are listed on protected or endangered species lists.

ARRO International
P.O. Box 167
Montclair, NJ 07042
201/746-9620
Fax: 201/509-0728

Artbeats

Marbled Paper Textures
Backgrounds for Multimedia, Volumes 1 and 2
Marble and Granite Collection
Full-Page Images

Artbeats offers beautiful vector-based and bitmapped background art for multimedia and desktop-publishing applications. Artbeats' newest release, "Marbled Paper Textures," is a double CD-ROM set of carefully digitized images of hand-marbled papers, created by internationally recognized artists. This collection includes 40 high-resolution images, 120 multimedia images, 225 buttons and mortices, 160 seamless tiles, metallic attributes, and more in TIFF format. "Backgrounds for Multimedia" are 8-bit and 24-bit images specifically designed for video, slide, animation, and texture mapping. The "Marble and Granite Collection" is an awesome, two-disc CD-ROM set of bitmapped images in TIFF format. It includes 40 high-resolution images for prepress work; 120 multimedia backgrounds that you can use in slides and presentations; and 160 seamless tiles and floor tiles, which are ideal for three-dimensional renderings. The high-resolution TIFFs are highly recommended for four-color process printing. All high-resolution images are suitable for full bleeds because they measure 8.7" by 11.2".

The "Full-Page Images" collection (available on disk or CD-ROM) consists of a six-volume set (including Dimensions, Potpourri, and Natural Images) of CDR or EPS files, available as individual volumes or as a complete set. Each set consists of 10 images. The majority of these images are provided in black-and-white format, with high- and low-contrast (or light and dark) versions of each design.

Artbeats
2611 S. Myrtle Road
Myrtle Creek, OR 97457
503/863-4429
Fax: 503/863-4547

ArtMaker

ArtMaker has a four-volume disc art library that has over 250 illustrations to round out your collection of 300 dpi PCX files. You get an antistatic disc storage sleeve, a pictorial index guidebook, and a free disc of your choice with your purchase.

> The ArtMaker Company
> 500 N. Claremont Blvd.
> Claremont, CA 91711
> 714/626-8065
> Fax: 714/621-1323

BBL Typographic

Volume 1: Westminster Abbey
Volume 2: Pontificale of John I
Volume 3: The Golden Bible
Volume 4: St. Mary of Soest
Volume 5: Paris Book of Hours
Volume 6: Musica Antiqua
Volume 7: Cardinal Mazarine
Medieval & Renaissance Library (Volume 1-6 bundle)

From the Land Down Under comes a series of well-rendered medieval and renaissance letter forms and ornaments. Volumes one through six each contain a full alphabet of initial caps, in addition to decoratives, borders, and other period artworks. More than 70 images per volume, these volumes are available in CDR and EPS formats. These collections now ship with CorelDRAW! 5.0, so you can find BBL's images on your CD-ROM!

> BBL Typographic
> 137 Narrow Neck Road
> Katoomba, NSW 2780
> Australia
> 011-61-47-826111
> Fax: 011-61-47-826144

VI

Appendixes

Casady & Greene

One of the more popular small electronic type foundries, Casady & Greene specializes in calligraphic, classic, and continental-flair typefaces. Their latest type collection, "Fluent Laser Font Library 2," contains 120 fonts in your choice of PostScript or TrueType format. The company also produces a limited amount of clip art. "Special Events" is a charming little collection containing Dorothea Casady's Meow Cat Alphabet along with a variety of electronic art files suitable for holiday use. Perfect for calendars, lighter newsletters, and so on.

> Casady & Greene
> 22734 Portola Drive
> Salinas, CA 93908
> 408/484-9228
> Fax: 408/484-9218

Church Mouse Electronic Illustration

ArtSource: The Ultimate Youth Ministry Clip Art Series
Volume 1: Fantastic Activities
Volume 2: Borders, Symbols, Holidays, and Attention Getters
Volume 3: Sports
Volume 4: Phrases and Verses
Volume 5: Amazing Oddities and Appalling Images
Volume 6: Spiritual Topics

As you might guess, these collections are ideal for churches or organizations. "Fantastic Activities," for example, is more than just clip art: it's an inspiration for fun events, such as pizza parties, food drives, summer safaris, and more! Capture kids' attention with the whimsical and cartoony renderings in the "Sports" and "Amazing Oddities" collections. "Spiritual Topics" is filled with topical and thematic clip art. All images are digitized 300 dpi TIFF files.

> The Church Art Works
> 875 High Street NE
> Salem, OR 97301
> 503/370-9377
> Fax: 503/362-5231
> To order, call: 800/776-8008

Clipables

Clipables
Statements
Travel and Vacation

"Clipables" contains more than 1,400 professionally drawn black-and-white EPS files. This particularly versatile collection spans some of the following topics: animals, borders and ornaments, computers and business machines, children, construction, dingbats and symbols, display banners, drop cap toolbox, expressions, famous people, holidays, humor, maps and flags, medical, music, portfolio, sports, and transportation. Fortunately, this extensive library comes with a user's manual featuring a pictorial index that includes every image in the library. Available on disk and CD-ROM, this product is a good value when you consider the excellent cost-per-image ratio.

"Statements," along with the "Travel and Vacation" collection, are the two latest releases from C.A.R. The "Statements" collection consists of 150 skillfully rendered and emotional illustrations, ranging in content from humorous to serious. The "Travel and Vacation" collection contains 80 travel- and leisure-oriented illustrations.

C.A.R., Inc.
7009 Kingsbury
St. Louis, MO 63130
800/288-7585
314/721-6305

Clip-Art Connection (Subscription)

Clip-Art Connection is an electronic catalog, ordering, and fulfillment software package that runs under Windows. This subscription service provides modem access to over 29,000 clip-art images from 17 top vendors. Users can quickly locate and preview images using the keyword search feature. Within minutes, individual images can be purchased by credit card and downloaded for use.

Connect Software
A Division of Adonis Corporation
6742 185th Ave. NE, Ste. 150
Redmond, WA 98052
800/234-9497

VI

Appendixes

Clipatures

Clipatures Volume 1: Business Images
Clipatures Volume 2: Business Images 2
Clipatures Volume 3: Sports
Clipatures Volume 4: World Flags
Clipatures Volume 5: Borders

Clipatures offers five collections of EPS artwork targeted specifically for the business user and desktop publisher. Each volume contains hundreds of images, each hand-drawn by a professional artist. The business collections are populated with many people in office settings. "Volume 1" includes credit cards, icons, and a number of business-specific cartoons. "Volume 2" includes silhouettes, computers, and airplanes. "Volume 3" contains many male and female athletes, as well as sports icons, graphics, and symbols. "Volume 4" features over 300 flags (national, territorial, organizational, and code flags). "Volume 5" contains a wide variety of border styles, from Art Deco to Contemporary.

Dream Maker Software
925 West Kenyon Avenue, Suite 16
Englewood, CO 80110
303/762-1001
Fax: 303/762-0762

Dana Publishing

The Balthis Collection
The California Coast
Around the World

Dana Publishing offers three CD-ROM collections of 72 dpi, 24-bit TIFF images from professional photographer Frank Balthis. Each collection consists of 500 images. These images are sold as royalty free for desktop presentations, comps, and limited press runs. For larger press runs, you may purchase high-resolution versions of these images for a reasonable royalty fee. This arrangement assures that the designer receives high-quality stock photography without the high costs of dealing with a conventional stock photo house. By working in this manner, Dana Publishing helps to guard against overuse of an image, saving you from the embarrassment of "your" photo showing up in a competitor's advertisement or marketing materials.

Frank Balthis' photos have appeared in publications by National Geographic, Time/Life, and Popular Photography. The Balthis Collection is a wide-ranging survey of work by the noted photographer, with images from American park lands, ocean views, mountains, deserts, forests, cities, and other environments. "The California Coast" is a ride along the glorious Pacific, with everything from Californian architecture to coastal recreation and abundant wildlife, both at sea and on land. "Around The World" is a whirlwind tour of landmarks and images from Africa, Asia, the Caribbean, Europe, and the Americas, with a healthy dollop of landscapes.

> Dana Publishing
> P.O. Box 112
> Boulder Creek, CA 95006
> 408/338-0108
> 408/338-3723 (fax)

DataTech

Federal Logos
Symbols & Seals

Doing work with the Fed? "Federal Logos, Symbols & Seals" contains almost 700 logos and other images that pertain to the United States government. You will find logos for all your favorite government agencies, such as the Internal Revenue Service, the Veterans Administration, and the United States Postal Service. These images are 300 dpi PCX files.

> DataTech Distributors
> 55 South Progress Avenue
> Harrisburg, PA 17109
> 800/788-2068 or 717/652-4344
> Fax: 717/652-3222

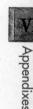

Deniart Systems

Alchemy Symbols Font
Castles & Shields Font
Egyptian Hieroglyphics Font Set

Deniart Systems asks, "Have you written to your mummy lately?" If not, they have the perfect picture font for you! Deniart offers a selection of picture fonts in both Postscript and TrueType formats. The "Egyptian Hieroglyphics Font Set" includes over 270 unique Phonogram and Ideograph characters. The accompanying user manual includes a comprehensive keyboard layout diagram and interpretation guide.

If a Medieval look is what you are after, take a look at Deniart's other offerings. The "Alchemy Symbols Font" consists of over 130 characters and includes a comprehensive interpretation guide. The "Castles & Shields Font" features each uppercase character embossed in a unique castle silhouette, lowercase characters in shields, and numbers sporting armor. Deniart also includes castle silhouettes sans letters.

Deniart Systems
Box 1074, Adelaide Station
Toronto, Ontario
M5C 2K5 Canada
416/941-0919

DesignClips Natural Environment Series

DesignClips is a thorough, well-planned library of black-and-white graphics symbols perfect for use as design elements. The "Fish" collection, for example, includes (from A to D): Albacore, Anchovy, Angelfish, Bandtail Puffer, Barracuda, Bluefin Tuna, Blue Marlin, Bonito, Butterflyfish, Cod, and Dolphin. Each collection consists of 50 files, along with a comprehensive pictorial index. These images were originally designed as object-oriented art, and therefore, the collection is available as EPS files. TIFF and PCX files are also available. LetterSpace is a subsidiary of David Curry Design, a New York-based graphics design firm.

LetterSpace
338 East 53rd Street #2C
New York, NY 10022-5254
212/935-8130

Digital Stock

Babies & Children
Men, Women & Romance
Indigenous Peoples
Animals
Business & Industry
Buildings & Structures
Sunsets, Skies & Weather

Undersea Life
Transportation
Space & Spaceflight
Textures & Backgrounds
Trees
Landscapes
Flowers
Mountains & Waterfalls
Active Lifestyles

Digital Stock prides itself as being image conscious. The company sells Photo CD collections containing the finest work of award-winning professional photographers. While these images are of the quality of conventional stock photographs, they are sold with no additional usage fees. Once you buy the disc, you own the rights to reproduce all the photographs on the disc. Each Digital Stock collection consists of 100 photographs, and is accompanied by a high-resolution color proof sheet illustrating each image.

The collections are well-suited to professional design and publishing work. In particular, the "Business & Industry," "Transportation," and "Buildings & Structures" collections are ideal for corporate marketing collateral such as brochures and direct mail pieces. For a quick vacation, try the "Active Lifestyles," "Sunsets, Skies & Weather," "Undersea Life," and "Mountains & Waterfalls" collections; these four packages are great for travel- or leisure-based advertising. For family-focused materials, look into the "Babies & Children," as well as the "Men, Women & Romance" collection.

Digital Stock is constantly adding to its library. If you need a collection that is not listed above, it would be worth your while to check to see if they've added any new collections.

> Digital Stock Professional
> 7163 Construction Court
> San Diego, CA 92121
> 800/545-4514
> 619/794-4040
> 619/794-4041 (fax)

Digital Wisdom

Mountain High Maps
Mountain High Map Frontiers
BodyShots—Business

Digital Wisdom offers maps in two delicious flavors—grayscale relief and editable outline—for those who are serious about their geographic info-graphics.

The company's first package, "Mountain High Maps," is a two-disc CD-ROM set of relief images that provides a truely unique resource. The maps accurately portray the world's continents and ocean floors, and give graphic designers the resource they need to produce geographic images of the highest caliber. The relief maps are in TIFF format, ready for your specific coloration and customization requirements.

Digital Wisdom's second package, "Mountain High Map Frontiers," consists of geopolitical boundaries, including coastlines, and state and country borders. The package, available in editable EPS and TIFF formats, is offered both bundled with the relief maps and as a stand-alone package.

Digital Wisdom Inc.
Box 2070
Tappahannock, VA 22560
800/800-8560
804/758-0670
Fax: 804/758-4512

DS Designs

KidBAG—Art by Kids
KidBAG—Environmental Art by Kids
KidBAG—DingBRATS
KidsAT
KidTOONS
KidTYPE
KidTYPE Block
KidTYPE Ruled
FunTYPE

DS Designs refers to its wares as "Alternative Art and Fonts from Fascinating Folks." You can think of it as the quickest way to add a charming, childlike touch to your printed piece. KidBAGs are electronic collections (EPS or TIFF) of authentic children's artwork. Art by Kids contains over 130 illustrations, originally created by children in crayon, paint, marker, watercolor, pastel, and pencil. Environmental Art by Kids, created by 5- to 11- year- olds, includes over 100 images with recycling, nature, and endangered species themes.

The company also offers KidTYPE, a nice collection of genuine children's handwriting (4) and instructional (5) fonts in both PostScript Type 1 and TrueType formats. DingBRATS is a cool collection of 100 children's illustrations in font format. FunTYPE is a package of 20 spunky font designs with such great names as BlockHeadJam, CobraCreep, HorribleSquish, Pasta Aldente, PizzaMunch, and Snake. Just the thing to liven up an annual report!

KidsAT and KidTOONS fill out the product line and were created by professional artists. KidsAT includes over 100 images of children, ranging in age from preschoolers through high-schoolers, in a variety of settings, such as the classroom or at play. KidTOONS consists of humorous caricatures of animals and children. DS Design has an admirable social conscience, and contributes 2 percent of all KidBAG products' gross sales to schools and other nonprofit organizations dedicated to improving the quality of education.

> DS Design
> 2440 SW Cary Parkway, Suite 210
> Cary, NC 27513
> 800/745-4037
> 919/319-1770
> 919/460-5983 (fax)

Dynamic Graphics

By Subscription:

Electronic Clipper
Electronic Print Media Service
Designer's Club

"Electronic Clipper" is Dynamic Graphics' premier all-purpose electronic art and idea service. Each month, subscribers receive over 70 TIFF and EPS files through floppy and CD-ROM. This service also includes *Options*, a monthly magazine filled with electronic design tips and layout ideas. "Electronic Print Media Service" is a monthly CD-ROM targeted for retail advertising and promotion. Each disc includes over 100 TIFF and EPS files per month in seasonal and topical themes. "Designer's Club" provides over 55 general-purpose EPS images (10 are also in color) per month on floppy and CD-ROM. Many of the images are layered. Subscribers also receive *Ideas & Images*, a monthly magazine offering design ideas and how-tos.

Non-subscription:

ArtAbout
Designer's Club Annual CD-ROM
Electronic Clipper Annual CD-ROM

"ArtAbout" is a series of themed clip-art collections made available on a single-purchase, non-subscription basis. Each collection includes over 100 TIFF and EPS images. Subjects include sports, healthcare, food, seasons, business, education, graphics and symbols, and dining. The Designer's Club and Electronic Clipper Annual CD-ROMs offer previously released Dynamic Graphics artwork in convenient CD-ROM format. Each Designer's Club CD-ROM contains over 500 EPS images covering assorted subjects in a variety of styles. The Electronic Clipper Annual CD-ROM contains over 800 images (60 percent TIFF and 40 percent EPS) in a wide variety of contemporary styles and themes.

> Dynamic Graphics, Inc.
> 6000 N. Forest Park Drive
> Peoria, IL 61614-3592
> 800/255-8800
> Fax: 309/688-5873

Federal Clip Art

Federal Clip Art I:	*A Congress of Artwork*
Federal Clip Art II:	*Air Combat*
Federal Clip Art III:	*Naval Combat*
Federal Clip Art IV:	*Ground Combat*
Federal Clip Art V:	*Army Insignia*
Federal Clip Art VI:	*Diplomatic Art*
Federal Clip Art VII:	*State Art*
Federal Clip Art VIII:	*European Art*
Federal Clip Art IX:	*NASA Art*
Federal Clip Art X:	*Book of Seals*
Federal Clip Art XI:	*Naval Insignia*
Federal Clip Art XII:	*Air Force Insignia*
National Archives CD-ROM	

Serious newspaper publishers, along with government and defense contractor DTPers, will be very pleased with these 12 packages. Each collection contains over 300 meticulous illustrations of various military hardware, insignia, and other U.S. government-specific items, including aircraft, missiles, and naval vessels. You will find lots of great One Mile Up clip art on the CorelDRAW! 5.0 CD-ROM discs. This art is black-and-white EPS, but packages also include Pantone and CMYK settings for exact government colors. The packages demonstrate an impressive attention to detail. The international and state flags found in the "Diplomatic Art" and "State Art" collections, for example, are trapped for accurate color printing.

One Mile Up, Inc.
7011 Evergreen Court
Annandale, VA 22003
703/642-1177
Fax: 703/642-9088

Fine Art Impressions

Fine Art Impressions Art Library

A highly stylized package of hand-created illustrations, these 177 black-and-white detailed illustrations are available in CDR, EPS, CGM (for PC PageMaker users), and GEM (for Ventura Publisher users) formats. The package includes "Image Extras" (hardcopy illustrations not found on the discs), The "Designer's Desktop" (a step-by-step layout and design guide), The "Illustrator's Portfolio" (large, printed samples of each image), a "Troubleshooting Guide," and even a full-color, three-ring binder to store it all in! Titles in the library include "Money & More Money," "Making Headlines," "Professional Workforce," "Borders & Boxes," and "Occupational Themes."

Best Impressions
3844 W. Channel Islands Blvd. #234
Oxnard, CA 93035

Letraset

FONTEK Design Fonts

Attitudes
Calligraphic Ornaments
Celebrations
Commercials
Delectables
Incidentals
Industrials
Journeys
Mo' Funky Fresh
Moderns

Naturals
Organics
Primatives
Radicals
Wildlifes

FONTEK Backgrounds & Borders

Abstractions
Geometrix
Impressions
Realities
Spatials
Synthetix

From the company responsible for those wonderful display fonts now comes two new lines that are bound to make your designs sizzle! Letraset took great care in choosing talented graphics designers and illustrators to create each of these products. The FONTEK "DesignFont" series features 15 fabulous PostScript picture fonts, while the FONTEK "Backgrounds & Borders" series consists of six cutting edge collections of textures, patterns, and shapes.

"DesignFonts" are the perfect illustration solution for projects from brochures to newsletters to magazines. You can achieve consistency throughout a brochure (or spread) by using a number of illustrations created by the same talented hand. For example, illustrator Debbie Hanley rendered the Organics font in a whimsical woodcut style. For even more fun, check out Mo' Funky Fresh, which was designed by David Sagorski, a New York-based graphics designer. This one is a personal favorite of Joe DeLook, because it looks so great at the beach!

"Backgrounds & Borders" collections each contain from 12 to 15 grayscale images, conveniently provided in both 72 dpi and 266 dpi formats. You can use the low-res files for design comps and proofing, then pop in the high-res files when you are ready to go to print. These images print well in gray, PANTONE colors, or you can use Photoshop to create duotones from the images. Spatials, created by photographer Jenny Lynn, is a collection of mysterious, floating collages. Realities contains 15 natural textures, such as River Pebbles, Water Drops, Linen, Cork, and Rice Noodles.

Letraset USA
40 Eisenhower Drive
P.O. Box 281
Paramus, NJ 07653-9951
800/343-TYPE

FontHaus Picture Fonts

Set No. 1: Transportation & Travel
Set No. 2: Commerce & Communication
Set No. 3: Holidays & Celebrations
Set No. 4: Food & Drink
Set No. 5: Household Items
Set No. 6: Animals

FontHaus calls its picture fonts "pictures you wouldn't expect from your keyboard," and that's quite an accurate description. As scalable, PostScript fonts, the first two sets in the series offer nice collections of symbols and borders. You can build your own train set (each car is a character) and create wonderful coupons and advertisements. Borders are created directly from the keyboard, using an old typesetter's trick. FontHaus Picture Fonts are thoughtfully designed, whimsical, and of high quality.

FontHaus, Inc.
1375 Kings Highway East, Suite 240
Fairfield, CT 06850
800/942-9110

Image Club

DigitArt Volumes 1-3, 8: Miscellaneous
DigitArt Volumes 4-5: Cartoon People
DigitArt Volume 6: Business & Industry
DigitArt Volume 7: World Maps
DigitArt Volume 9: Design Elements
DigitArt Volumes 10-11: Design Letters
DigitArt Volume 12: Symbols & Headings
DigitArt Volume 13: Food & Entertainment
DigitArt Volume 14: Occasions
DigitArt Volume 15: Lifestyles
DigitArt Volume 16: Office & Education
DigitArt Volume 17: Universal Symbols
DigitArt Volume 18: Celebrity Caricatures
DigitArt Volume 19: Silhouettes
DigitArt Volume 20: Design Backgrounds
DigitArt Volume 21: Fabulous Fifties
DigitArt Volume 22: Business Cartoons
DigitArt Volume 23: Borders & Ornaments

V

Appendixes

DigitArt Volume 24: Science & Medicine
DigitArt Volume 25: Wood Cuts
DarkRoom Clip Photography
PhotoGear, Volume 1: Backgrounds & Textures CD
PhotoGear, Volume 2: Images of Business CD
PhotoGear, Volume 3: ndustrial Backgrounds CD
PhotoGear, Volume 4: Snackgrounds CD
Art & Type Vendor 2.0, 3.0

DigitArt is a collection of 25 volumes of EPS art, available by volume or in combination. The volumes are also available as a complete collection, the ArtRoom CD-ROM, which contains over 9,000 images. The work ranges from slick and stylized to fanciful cartoons; for example, the "Wood Cuts" collection is designer-chic, and the "Fabulous Fifties" collection is sheer camp.

"DarkRoom Clip Photography" is a stock photo library for CD-ROM. This collection consists of over 500 ready-to-use grayscale TIFFs. Subjects include business, lifestyle, sports, and travel. You can use the photos in black and white without paying additional royalties—provided the photographer is credited. Color photos can be requested for a royalty fee.

"PhotoGear" is a CD-ROM disc filled with 30 RGB TIFF files for high-quality, full-page offset printing. Image Club is also known for its massive collection of over 720 PostScript fonts, with an unabashed focus on display faces. The "Art & Type Vendor" is the original unlocking font and clip art CD-ROM, and it is a great choice for DTPers on a budget.

> Image Club Graphics, Inc.
> #5, 1902 11th Street S.E.
> Calgary, Alberta, Canada T2G 3G2
> 800/661-9410 or 403/262-8008
> Fax: 403/261-7013

Images With Impact

Accents & Borders 1 & 2
Business 1
Graphics & Symbols 1
People 1
Places & Faces 1
Images With Impact! CD-ROM v2.0

The award-winning "Accents & Borders 1" contains 270 design elements, including seasonal, geometric, historical, and contemporary designs. "Accents & Borders 2"

contains 300 decorative and representational images. "Graphics & Symbols 1" covers a broad range of subjects. The same goes for "Business 1," which includes people, computers, financial success, and hands at work. "Places & Faces 1" includes illustrations of people of many ages and cultures, along with the world's top travel destinations and high-contrast recreational graphics. The CD-ROM contains all six Images With Impact! titles on one disc. Available in EPS, WMF, and 75 dpi BMP file formats.

> 3G Graphics
> 114 Second Avenue South, #104
> Edmonds, WA 98020
> 206/774-3518 or 800/456-0234

Innovation Advertising & Design

AdArt Logos & Trademarks, Volumes 1-12
AdArt Logos & Trademarks, Automotive Edition
AdArt Logos & Trademarks, Real Estate Edition
AdArt Logos & Trademarks, 500 Volume 1, Vinyl Edition
AdArt Logos & Trademarks, 500 Volume 2, Vinyl Edition
Weddings
Women
Animal Silhouettes
Patriotic Art
Astrology
Fraternal Symbols
Cars & Light Trucks
Real Estate Art
International Symbols & Icons, Volumes 1 and 2
Flags of the World
Medical Symbols
Transportation
Credit Card Art
Business Symbols Collection
Vinyl Cutters Collection
Safety & Packaging Collection
Recycled Art—Environmentally Safe Clip Art
Accents & Attention Getters
AdArt: Clip Art for Advertising CD-ROM 3.0
AdArt: Logos & Trademarks, Volumes 1-12 CD-ROM 3.0

Appendixes

This clip art should be standard issue for those who build advertisements or signage. AdArt is a superb idea: EPS logos for every company that you can think of!

If you have ever spent hours searching for a logo for use in a newspaper ad, you will find this series indispensable. It includes graphics appropriate for businesses that sell or use autos, credit cards, insurance, real estate, and so on. "International Symbols & Icons" includes over 300 EPS files perfect for business charts, maps, and packaging. This collection is bread-and-butter electronic clip art. The CD-ROM package offers exceptional value—everything on one disc!

> Innovation Advertising & Design
> 41 Mansfield Avenue
> Essex Junction, VT 05452
> 800/255-0562 or 802/879-1164
> Fax: 802/878-1768

Logo SuperPower

This collection is not clip art, but a set of over 2,000 electronic EPS design elements developed with logo and publication creation in mind. You can combine and tweak design elements for an infinite number of combinations. What formerly took days for an artist to render with pen and ink can be executed in a few minutes. An excellent choice for electronic designers who need to crank out logos at a moment's notice. You can find a number of Logo SuperPower images on the *Inside CorelDRAW! 5, Fifth Edition CD-ROM*.

> Decathlon Corporation
> 4100 Executive Park Drive #16
> Cincinnati, OH 45241
> 800/648-5646
> Order Fax: 606/324-6038

MapArt

MapArt Volume 1: Countries and Continents
MapArt Volume 2: U.S. States
MapArt Volume 3: Global Perspective Maps
MapArt Volume 4: Metro Areas US
MapArt Bundle

These versatile, comprehensive map collections are essential for many business situations. In fact, you might find that these packages pay for themselves the first time you use them. They might not quicken the pulse, but they will pay the rent. Excellent for creating everything from simple line art to complex information graphics. "Countries and Continents" includes 4 world maps, 15 world regions, and 31 countries with states or provinces and major city locations. "US States" includes all 50 U.S. states with counties, highways, rivers, ZIP codes, and major cities. Neighboring states fit together exactly, so you can cut and paste adjacent states together. "Global Perspective Maps" features over 40 world maps, including standard projections such as Mercator and unusual ones such as Armadillo and Heart. "Metro Areas US" includes maps of 25 key metropolitan areas, with major roads, coastlines, city boundaries, parks, airports, universities, and stadiums.

You can find a nice selection of Cartesia's maps on the CD-ROM that accompanies this book, as well as on the *Inside CorelDRAW! 5, Fifth Edition CD-ROM* disc.

> Cartesia Software, Inc.
> P.O. Box 757
> Lambertville, NJ 08530
> 609/397-1611

[metal]

> *General Collection*
> *General Collection II*
> *General Collection III*
> *Animal Collection*
> *Pattern Collection*
> *Background Collection*
> *Holiday Collection*
> *Illustration Collection*

Designed by designers for designers, [metal] Studio offers eight intriguing visual element collections. The "General Collection" contains 144 unique EPS images, covering subjects such as food, travel, animals, architecture, the oil industry, tools, and special events. The "General Collection II" contains 92 EPS files including cubist elements and line drawings with an emphasis on fun, travel, entertainment, and holidays. The "General Collection III" and "Holiday Collection" each contain 72 EPS images. The "Animal Collection" consists of 72 EPS images rendered with a distinctive line-and-curve style. The "Pattern Collection" and "Background Collection" are each made up of 15 TIFF images in a variety of stylistic and abstract patterns and backgrounds. The "Illustration Collection" contains 18 TIFF images.

> [metal] Studio, Inc.
> 13164 Memorial Drive #222
> Houston, TX 77079
> Info: 713/523-5177
> Fax: 713/523-5176

Metro ImageBase

Metro, one of the leaders in printed clip art, has published a large body of quality bitmapped images. Over 23 collections are available. A new package just released, "ARTrageous!™ Beyond the Border," contains 100 full-color EPS borders that yield 500 art elements (when ungrouped). ImageBase also has two collections on CD-ROM. "Metro ImageBase on CD" contains 2000 images covering 11 categories. "Metro ImageBase Food on CD" contains 440 highly detailed images. Other collections include "People," "Business Graphics," "Team Sports," "The Four Seasons," and many others. These files are in 300-dpi PCX or TIFF format.

> Metro ImageBase
> 18623 Ventura Boulevard
> Suite 210
> Tarzana, CA 91356
> 800/525-1552 or 818/881-1997
> Fax: 818/881-4557

MileStone Graphics

Golf Collection 1
Golf Collection 2

Are you a country club golf pro or just a golf fanatic? Do you need to prepare printed materials, silk-screen shirts or hats? If so, the MileStone Graphics Golf Collections are perfect for your needs. These collections include 24 images each, in either Adobe Illustrator or PCX file format. The artwork is black-and-white, but can be tinted or colorized to your specifications.

The collections include plenty of male and female golfers in mid-swing, post-swing, at the tee, and on the green. There are dramatic silhouettes, stylistic line drawings, whimsical cartoons, and graphic type treatments. You'll also find plenty of golf clubs, balls, tees, bags, flags, and even a golf shoe (which is great for the "no spikes" sign at the 19th hole). Whether you are running a golf club or organizing a company outing, the MileStone Golf Collections could be just what you need.

> MileStone Graphics
> 1093 A1A Beach Boulevard, #388
> Saint Augustine, FL 32084
> 800/932-5404
> 904/823-9962
> Fax: 904/824-6209

Planet Art

Book of Hours/Jean de Berry
Albrecht Durer/Selected Works
Gustave Doré/Doré Bible
Arabic Tiles/Navoi
William Morris/Selected Works
Charles Gibson/Selected Works
French Posters/Featuring Toulouse-Lautrec
Handbook of Medieval Alphabets and Devices
Japanese Art
Iconographic Encyclopedia of Science
Literature and Art
1851 Architecture

Michelangelo may have slaved for years on the Sistine Chapel, but now you can place his imagery into your work with just a click of the mouse. These Photo CDs of classic artwork quickly put some class into your designs, with a wide range of work from a host of great artists in a variety of media. In addition to Michelangelo's famous frescos and sculpture, you might choose from among Albrecht Durer's many woodcuts and engravings, which show his theory of proportion, or you might prefer the wood engravings of Gustave Doré.

These classic artworks provide countless design possibilities. A four-color magazine advertisement might benefit from the dramatic chiaroscuro of Leonardo Da Vinci's famous oil paintings, whereas a black-and-white advertisement may call for the technical precision of his drawings. You might long to use one of William Morris's distinctive fabrics, tapestries, wallpapers, and embroideries as an intriguing background. By adding the crisp linework of Charles Gibson, you can provide a turn-of-the-century elegance to a two-color printed piece. Planet Art CDs are more affordable than an art history class and more durable than a coffee table book. Quite simply, these are art collections, not clip art.

Planet Art collections have obvious uses for everyone from high-end designers to nonprofit art association newsletter editors. Each volume contains 100 royalty- and license-free images and is accompanied by a full color index reference. Planet Art offers these collections as individual titles or in groups of three. In addition, they offer economical monthly and bimonthly subscription plans.

Planet Art
505 South Beverly Drive #242
Beverly Hills, CA 90212
800/200-3405

V

Appendixes

PolyType

Volume 1: Ornaments
Volume 2: Corners
Volume 3: ArtDeco
Volume 4: Images

PolyType images are in font format so that you can access ornaments or objects from your keyboard instead of by importing a file. Each volume contains 130 images (in five fonts). All fonts are supplied in Adobe Type 1 format, along with character outlines in EPS format.

PolyType
P.O. Box 25976
Los Angeles, CA 90025
310/444-9934
800/998-9934

Presentation Task Force

A collection of over 3,500 files in object-oriented CGM format from one of the ground-breakers in electronic imagery. As the name implies, these images are perfect for presentation work, including 35mm slides. Almost half the images are color. Subject matter centers on business. The latest version (4.0) comes with a conversion utility that converts color artwork into black and white.

New Vision Technologies, Inc.
Box 5468, Station F
Ottawa, Ontario, Canada K2C 3M1
613/727-8184

ProArt

Multi-Ad Services, Inc. is a 46-year veteran in the clip-art industry. The electronic ProArt collections contain over 100 images. The 13 collections available are "Holiday," "Business," "Sports," "Food," "People," "Borders & Headings," "Health & Medical," "Educational," "Religious Images," "Christmas," "Animals," "Generic Products," and "Business 2." These EPS files are available on floppy disk or CD-ROM.

Multi-Ad Services, Inc.
1720 W. Detweiller Drive
Peoria, IL 61615-1695
800/447-1950 or 309/692-1530
Fax: 309/692-5444

Quick Art

Quick Art Deluxe: Volume 1 CD-ROM
Quick Art Deluxe: Volume 2 CD-ROM
Quick Art Lite: Volume 1 CD-ROM

"Quick Art Lite" consists of over 1,600 black-and-white images in a wide variety of subjects including animals, borders, flowers, food, holidays, mail, maps, money, numbers, office/media, people, science/energy, sports/exercise, and travel. "Quick Art Deluxe: Volume 1" contains over 3,200 images (including all the images in the "Lite" collection) with buildings/landscapes, celebrations, clothing/sewing, education, entertainment, farm, gardening, health/medicine, insects, mail, maps, music, mystery, plants, religion, tools, toys/games, transportation, and weather. "Quick Art Deluxe: Volume 2" contains over 3,200 images and is great as a stand-alone volume or as an addition to Volume 1. All collections come with an illustrated user's manual. Individual subjects are available on floppy disk. The majority of images are in 300 dpi TIFF, IMG, and PCX formats.

Wheeler Arts
66 Lake Park
Champaign, IL 61821-7101
217/359-6816
Fax: 217/359-8716

Santa Fe Collection

Designers and desktop publishers in search of Native American and Southwestern art will be pleased by the quality and value of the Santa Fe Collection. Originally developed on the Macintosh and now available in PC EPS format, this collection is one of the most complete and affordable genre libraries around. The many designs—including birds, bugs, fish, lizards, and motifs (over 100!)—show care, research, and sensitivity to Native American culture. An excellent value with almost 35 MB of art, especially considering the low cost. The Santa Fe Collection Professional Version in EPS includes over 500 images and 125 preconstructed borders.

As a bonus, the collection ships with RT's Santa Fe Font (a display typeface in both TrueType and Type 1 formats) as well as LOOKaRT, RT Graphics' EPS file viewer. Look forward to other indigenous art collections from RT Graphics in the near future.

RT Computer Graphics
602 San Juan de Rio
Rio Rancho, NM 87124
800/891-1600 or 505/891-1600
Fax: 505/891-1350

Steven & Associates

One thousand images are found in this volume. Topics include architecture, birds, holidays, insects, mythology and fantasy, religion, semiconductors, symbols and signs, and many more. All images are 300 dpi PCX files.

Steven & Associates
5205 Kearny Villa Way, #104
San Diego, CA 92123

Studio Productions

Electronic Preview, The Multimedia Edition, Volume 1

"Electronic Preview, Desktop Publishing and Multimedia Edition," is a CD-ROM containing over 250 royalty-free background images suitable for print and multimedia. The collection features images in a number of categories, such as special effects, natural effects, skies, advertising concepts, fabrics, and papers. Most notably, you will find a large number of cool photographic backdrops and marbleized textures. The professional quality images are arranged with coordinating title pages and borders, accent objects, bullets, and buttons. Studio Productions even offers printed (four-color) laser paper to match.

The background images are non-compressed, 24-bit TIFF files. These are provided in both 72 dpi, 640×480 and 4 MB files, the latter suitable for slides or film. For magazine-quality printing, higher-resolution files and transparencies are also available. In addition, Studio Productions includes a number of tiles for three-dimensional modeling. In short, the Electronic Preview CD-ROM is ideal for the CorelDRAW! user who needs to do sophisticated presentation work.

Studio Productions
18000 East 400 South
Elizabethtown, IN 47232
800/359-2964
Fax: 812/579-5063

SunShine

Visual Delights

SunShine's "Visual Delights" is a large collection of over 60 affordable sets of black-and-white, 300-dpi TIFF images. Each set covers one topic and contains approximately 68 pictures. Topics include men, women, children, designs, humor, borders, music, dance, mythology, Native Americans, Africa, the Middle East, American West, China, Japan, knighthood, royalty, angels, landscapes, fantasy, decorative letters, silhouettes, flowers, trees, plants, and other hard-to-find subjects. Animal sets include realistic and stylized mammals, birds, reptiles, insects, and sea life. Besides separate Jewish, Catholic, and Christian sets, plus Valentine's Day, Christmas, and Easter, many elaborate borders, cartouches, friezes, and other decorative elements are included.

Most images are line art, although some are delicate halftone images. Rights to use the images are granted for almost all purposes. Each set comes with a printed catalog that shows all the images along with a listing of their physical.dimensions and file size.

There are 38 sample images from Sunshine on the *Inside CorelDRAW! 5, Fifth Edition CD-ROM.*

SunShine
Box 4351
Austin, TX 78765
512/453-2334

Taco Clipart Company

Animals Collection
Aquaculture and Fish Collection
Background Collection

Business Collection
Cellular Industry Collection
CompuServe "You asked for it, you got it" Collection
Court Related Collection
Ethnic Collection
Ethnic Business Collection 1-3
European Landmark Collection
Factory Collection
Food Collection
Hands Doing Things Collection
Holiday Collection
Icon Collection
International Finance Collection
Misc Collection
Money Collection
Pizza Collection
Relaxation Collection

Need a specific custom image, but can't afford to spend thousands of dollars? Or perhaps you are designing a program and need special buttons? Your prayers have been answered. Taco Clipart Company is a professional art-generating and archiving company that specializes in custom artwork, delivered in your choice of formats. Taco's clip art is available in standard PC formats such as AI, EPS, GIF, TIF, DRW, CDR, TGA, WPG, GRF, and PIC (among others), as well as programming bitmap formats like BMP, ICO, and DIB.

Most of the images offered by Taco have been paid for by commissioning companies, but each company paid a lesser price than standard by allowing Taco to retain the rights to the images. In return, Taco promises each company exclusive use of the image (usually six months) and then offers the images to their subscribers for use in their publications. Some of the original images were billed at $4,000. Many of Taco's images are copyright free.

Whenever possible, the company tries to deliver its images by modem. This method also facilitates delivery to European countries without wasting time waiting for mail delivery. In addition to custom artwork, Taco offers pre-made collections. Many collections can be put together for specific needs. At this writing, Taco has over 10,000 images (all from this decade, with the exception of a collection of 1800s art).

Taco Clipart Company
1208 Howard Street
Omaha, NE 68102
402/344-7191 or 800/233-TACO
CompuServe ID: 74140,1110

TechPool Studios

The LifeART Super Anatomy Collection
Atmospheres Background Systems

Do you need anatomically correct illustrations? The "LifeART Super Anatomy Collection" provides "the best in anatomic exactness and visual clarity." An excellent resource for those involved in medical, legal, and educational presentations or publications. Topics covered include external views of the body, musculoskeletal, cardiovascular; reproductive; endocrine; gastrointestinal, nervous, and urinary systems; the special senses; joints; and more. Color images can be ungrouped to show underlying structures, or layered and cut away. Other collections include Emergency, HealthCare, and Dental. All collections ship with Transverter to convert EPS to other formats and to provide several color-treatment options. Check out the CorelDRAW! CD-ROM for a nice selection of TechPool art.

TechPool's "Atmospheres Background Systems" consists of a number of full-page, full-color and graytone collections of background vector clip art. They include the Watermark special effects tool to provide a professional look to any publication or presentation. Collections include "CityScapes," "Habitats," "Patterns," "Classics," and "Geometrics." Watermark allows color ghosting and graytone contrast controls for any EPS file.

TechPool Studios
1463 Warrensville Center
Suite 200
Cleveland, OH 44121
216/382-1234

Three D Graphics

CD-ROM PixelLoom Sampler

Do you need unique presentation backgrounds, pattern fills, or texture maps? Three D Graphics' "PixelLoom Sampler" is a "way cool" CD-ROM containing 64 textures in four different resolutions (320×240, 640×480, 1280×960, and 300×300 horizontal strip tiles). The larger images are great for use as slide backgrounds in CorelSHOW!, or you can use the 300×300 strip tiles as fills in CorelPHOTO-PAINT!. The disc also contains 11 QuickTime movies that can be imported into CorelSHOW!. All the images are 24-bit, 72 dpi files.

Three D Graphics' PixelLoom images are computer generated through chaos theory algorithms. This PixelLoom technology produces a huge variety of amazingly realistic textures. The disc includes a wonderful collection of textures, including bumps, embosses, granites, irridescents, marbles, minerals, natural wonders, stones, and woods. These photo-realistic renderings are hard to tell from the real thing! The stones are awesome, with eight different granites, four different marbles, and 12 other stone or mineral textures. The woods are equally impressive, with cherry, cocobolo, curly maple, violin, oak floor, driftwood, mahogany, and grained wood patterns. The shimmering iridescent abalone and pearl textures will take you right to the beach!

PixelLoom chaos technology delivers far more realism than you may have seen in other (fractally) generated images. The Sampler disc is the first in a series of texture CD-ROM discs from the original developers of CorelCHART!. Look for more PixelLoom CD-ROMs in the near future.

> Three D Graphics
> 860 Via de la Paz
> Pacific Palisades, CA 90272
> 310/459-7949
> 310/459-5822
> CIS: 72210,2700

Totem Graphics

Birds
Borders
Deluxe Business Images #1
Deluxe Business Images #2
Domestic Animals
Education
Fish
Food
Flowers
Healthcare
Holidays
Insects
Nautical
Sports
Tools & Hardware
Travel
Wild Animals
Women

These files are gorgeous, full-color EPS images. You might have seen several of Totem Graphics files in the CorelDRAW! version 5.0 CD-ROM discs. Totem's artists have an excellent feel for wildlife illustration. The "Fish" and "Insects" collections are particularly well-executed. Each package includes 96 files and is available in CorelDRAW!, EPSF, and PCX formats.

> Totem Graphics, Inc.
> 6200-F Capitol Blvd.
> Tumwater, WA 98501-5288
> 206/352-1851

U-Design Type Foundry

Bill's American Ornaments
Bill's Barnhart Ornaments 3.0
Bill's Cast O' Characters
Bill's Classic Ornaments
Bill's DECOrations
Bill's Broadway DECOrations
Bill's Tropical DECOrations
Bill's Modern Diner
Bill's Peculiars
Bill's Printers Pals
Bill's Victorian Ornaments
Buddy's Things

Lots of cool stuff from Bill! U-Design specializes in picture fonts with a period feel (as well as unique display fonts). These wonderful decoratives are worth owning. All are value-priced, and many come with bonus fonts such as Bill's Dingbats (which was named by MacUser Magazine as one of its favorite 50 shareware products, as well as one of the 200 best products for the Mac). A catalogue is available.

> U-Design Type Foundry
> 270 Farmington Avenue
> Hartford, CT 06105
> 203/278-3648

Visatex Corporation

The "US Presidents" collection contains portraits of 41 U.S. presidents. These files come in manually dithered grayscale PCX format.

Visatex Corporation
1745 Dell Avenue
Campbell, CA 95008
800/PC2-DRAW or 408/866-6562

Wide Open Images

Action & Adventure
Nature & Views

Wide Open Images sells high-quality Photo CD collections that have unlimited usage rights and carry no usage fees. Each image is included in five resolutions: 128×193 pixels, 256×384 pixels, 512×768 pixels, 1024×1536 pixels, and 2048×3072 pixels. This allows you to choose the right size image for your application, whether it is a small-sized image for a multimedia presentation or the largest image for reproduction-quality printing. Photo CD files can be imported into CorelDRAW! or edited in CorelPHOTO-PAINT!.

The Action & Adventure collection consists of 71 images of people working hard at having a good time. While you will find excellent depictions of traditional winter sports such as downhill and cross-country skiing, as well as some radical snowboard shots, summer sports are the mainstay of the collection. A number of cycling shots, including competitive and mountain biking, are found, along with activities such as fishing, golf, and tennis. Watersports are well represented, and the collection includes waterskiing, swimming, sailing, sailboarding, canoeing, rafting, and kayaking.

Nature & Views includes 83 images depicting a wide variety of locations from Las Vegas, to the farm fields, to the beaches. There are many pictures of flora and fauna, including palm trees, evergreens, autumn leaves, seagulls, horses, and a hippopotamus. A nice assortment of sunsets and snowy peaks rounds out the collection.

Wide Open Images
1139 Wing Point Way NE
Bainbridge Island, WA 98110
800/334-9433
206/780-2747

Work For Hire

ClassicPhoto CD Volume 1
ClassicPhoto CD Volume 2
ClassicPhoto CD Volume 3

Work For Hire has a great niche. ClassicPhoto CDs are royalty-free photographic collections of frequently used objects, from marbles to plumb bobs. These objects have been carefully lit and photographed on neutral backgrounds so that you can easily incorporate them into your projects. Each collection contains 100 different 24-bit color images, and each image can be found in five different resolutions (from 128×192 to 2048×3072). A full-color photo reference chart accompanies each collection.

The company promises that "Classic Photo CDs haven't been around before." All of the images are brand new; they are not recycled stock photos. "ClassicPhoto Volume 1" contains such images as a combination lock, a cap pistol, a seltzer bottle, a lit light bulb, a rubber duck, marbles, and a pocket watch. "ClassicPhoto Volume 2" includes an old telephone, a plumb bob, a spark plug, a chewed pencil stub, a vise, and a piggy bank. "ClassicPhoto Volume 3" features a lemon, a glass of champagne, a tennis ball, a baby pacifier, a cue ball, dominos, and a bunch of bananas, as well as over a dozen sunset and cloud shots.

These images provide a multitude of possibilities for print and multimedia projects. You can use them to create montages in such paint programs as Adobe Photoshop and CorelPHOTO-PAINT!, or you can bring in individual images into CorelDRAW!, CorelMOVE!, or Ventura.

Work For Hire
P.O. Box 121
Pleasantville, NY 10570
914/769-3776 (phone/fax)

VI
Appendixes

CorelDRAW! Fonts

The following are samples of the Basic category of CorelDRAW! fonts:

This is your Basic Bodoni Book BT, *and Italic*

This is your Basic Calligraphic 421 BT

THIS IS YOUR BASIC CANCUN

THIS IS YOUR BASIC CARLETON

This is your Basic Charter BT, *Italic,* **Black,**
and Black Italic

This is your Basic Charter Bold BT, *and*
Bold Italic

This is your Basic Dom Bold BT

This is your Basic Dom Diagonal Bold BT

THIS IS YOUR BASIC EKLEKTIC

This is your Basic Futura Bold Italic BT

This is your Basic Futura Light Condensed BT

This is your Basic 415 Black BT, *and*
Black Italic

This is your Basic 415 Lite, *and Lite Italic*

This is your Basic 415 Medium BT, *and*
Medium Italic

This is your Basic Geometric 706 Black

This is your Basic Humanist 777 Light BT, *and*
Light Italic

THIS IS YOUR BASIC LITHOGRAPH
THIS IS YOUR BASIC LITHOGRAPH BOLD
This is your Basic Oranda BT, and Bold Italic
This is your Basic Original Garamond BT,
Bold, *Italic,* *and Bold Italic*

The following are samples of the Casual category of CorelDRAW! fonts:

This is your Casual Ad Lib BT
This is your Casual Allegro BT
THIS IS YOUR CASUAL BALLOON LIGHT BT
This is your Casual Brisk
This is your Casual Brush 445 BT
This is your Casual Brush Script BT
This is your Casual Cooper Black Italic Headline BT
This is your Casual Cooper Black Outline BT
THIS IS YOUR CASUAL COPPERPLATE GOTHIC BOLD CONDENSED BT
This is your Casual Della Robbia BT
THIS IS YOUR CASUAL ENGRAVERS' GOTHIC BT
This is your Casual Engravers' Old English BT
This is your Casual Freehand 575 BT
This is your Casual Freehand 591 BT
This is your Casual Gando BT
This is your Casual Goudy Sans Light BT, and *Italic*
This is your Casual Goudy Sans Medium BT, and *Italic*
THIS IS YOUR CASUAL HUXLEY VERTICAL BT
This is your Casual Impress BT
This is your Casual Lapidary 333 Black BT
This is your Casual Lapidary 333 BT, **Bold,** *Bold Italic,* and *Italic*
This is your Casual Mister Earl BT
This is your Casual Parisian BT
This is your Casual Seagull Heavy BT
This is your Casual Seagull Light BT, **and Bold**
This is your Casual Seagull Medium BT
This is your Casual Zapf Calligraphic 801

The following are samples of the Design category of CorelDRAW! fonts:

This is your Design Aldine 401 BT, *Italic, **and*
    Bold Italic

This is your Design Bedrock

This is your Design Belwe Light BT

This is your Design Belwe Medium BT

This is your Design Benguiat Bold BT,
    and Bold Italic

This is your Design Benguiat Book BT,
    and Book Italic

This is your Design Bernhard Bold Condensed BT

This is your Design Bodoni BT

This is your Design Caslon 540 BT, *and Italic*

This is your Design Caslon No.224 Bold
    BT, ***and Bold Italic***

This is your Design Caslon No.224 Book BT,
    and Book Italic

This is your Design Cheltenham Bold BT,
    and Bold Italic

This is your Design Cheltenham BT, *and Italic*

This is your Design Classical Garamond BT,
    Bold, *and Italic*

This is your Design Dutch 801 Italic Headline BT

This is your Design Dutch 801 Roman BT

This is your Design Dutch 801 Roman
    Headline BT

This is your Design Fry's Baskerville BT

This is your Design Futura Bold BT

This is your Design Futura Light BT,
    and Light Italic

This is your Design Futura Medium BT,
    and Medium Italic

This is your Design Geometric 706
    Medium BT

This is your Design Goudy Catalogue BT

This is your Design Goudy Handtooled BT

This is your Design Goudy
    Heavyface BT

This is your Design Goudy Heavyface
    Condensed BT

This is your Design Humanist 777 BT,
    and Italic

This is your Design Humanist
    970 BT, and Bold

This is your Design Kabel Book BT

This is your Design Kabel Medium BT

This is your Design Kis BT, *and Italic*

This is your Design Square 721 Bold BT

This is your Design Swiss 721 Black BT

This is your Design Swiss 721 Black Outline BT

This is your Design Swiss 721 Bold BT, *Italic*, **and Bold Italic**

This is your Design Swiss 721 Extended BT

This is your Design Swiss 721 BT

This is your Design Swiss 721 Medium BT

This is your Design Zurich Extra Black BT

This is your Design Zurich Light Italic BT

The following are samples of the Formal category of CorelDRAW! fonts:

This is your Formal Amazone BT

This is your Formal American Text BT

This is your Formal Bernhard Tango BT

This is your Formal Caslon Openface BT

This is your Formal Commercial Script BT

This is your Formal Elegant Garamond BT, **Bold,** *and Italic*

This is your Formal Embassy BT

This is your Formal Engravers' Old English Bold BT

This is your Formal Flemish Script BT

This is your Formal Kunstlerschreibsch D Bol

This is your Formal Kunstlerschreibsch D Med

This is your Formal Lucia BT

This is your Formal Modern No.20 BT, *and Italic*

This is your Formal Nuptial BT

This is your Formal Revival 565 BT, *Italic,* **Bold,** *and Bold Italic*

This is your Formal Snell Black BT

This is your Formal Snell BT

This is your Formal Snell Bold BT

This is your Formal Stuyvesant BT

This is your Formal Zapf Chancery Demi BT

This is your Formal Zurich Black BT, *and Black Italic*

This is your Formal Zurich Condensed BT, *Condensed Italic,* **and Bold Condensed Italic**

This is your Formal Zurich BT

This is your Formal Zurich Light Condensed Italic BT

The following are samples of the Fun category of CorelDRAW! fonts:

This is your Fun ArnoldBoeD
THIS IS YOUR FUN BALLOON BOLD BT
THIS IS YOUR FUN BEEGIVE
This is your Fun Blippo Black BT
THIS IS YOUR FUN DAVIDA BOLD BT
This is your Fun Formal Script 421 BT
This is your Fun Fraktur BT
This is your Fun Freeform 710 BT
This is your Fun Freeform 721 Bold BT
This is your Fun Geographic Symbols,

THIS IS YOUR FUN GLACIER,
AND ITALIC
This is your Fun Goudy Old Style
Extra Bold BT
This is your Fun Grizzly BT
this is your fun harpoon
This is your Fun Hobo BT
THIS IS YOUR FUN INFORMAL 011 BT
THIS IS YOUR FUN KEYPUNCH
This is your Fun Lucian BT, and Bold
This is your Fun MusicalSymbols
This is your Fun P.T. Barnum BT
THIS IS YOUR FUN SHOTGUN BT
This is your Fun Slogan
This is your Fun Square Slabserif 711 Light BT
This is your Fun Square Slabserif 711 Medium BT
THUNDERBIRD BT
This is your Fun Tiffany Heavy
Italic BT

The following are samples of the General category of CorelDRAW! fonts:

This is your General American
Typewriter Bold BT
THIS IS YOUR GENERAL ATLANTIC
INLINE-NORMAL
This is your General Bauhaus Bold BT
This is your General Bauhaus Light BT
This is your General Century Oldstyle
Bold BT
This is your General Century Oldstyle Italic BT
This is your General Century
Schoolbook BT
This is your General CroissantD

This is your General Dom Casual BT

This is your General Emboss-Normal

This is your General Eras ContourITC-Normal

This is your General FirenzeITC-Normal

THIS IS YOUR GENERAL FRANKFURTERHIGD

This is your General Franklin Gothic ITC Book Italic BT, **Demi,** *and* ***Demi Italic***

This is your General Freestyle Script ITC-Bold

This is your General FreestyleScrD

This is your General Futura Bold Condensed BT and *Bold Condensed Italic*

This is your General Futura Medium Condensed BT

This is your General Garamond ITC Book BT, *Book Italic,* **Bold,** *and **Bold Italic***

This is your General Harlow D

This is your General Honda ITC

This is your General Kabel Bd-Normal

THIS IS YOUR GENERAL LCDD

This is your General Letter Gothic 12 Pitch BT, *Italic,* **Bold,** *and **Bold Italic***

This is your General Mona Lisa RecutITC-Normal

This is your General Mona Lisa SolidITC-Normal

This is your General Park Avenue BT

THIS IS YOUR GENERAL PLAZADREG

THIS IS YOUR GENERAL PRINCETOWN SOLID-NORMAL

THIS IS YOUR GENERAL PRINCETOWND

This is your General ProseAntique and **Bold**

This is your General PumpTriD

THIS IS YOUR GENERAL QUICKSILVERITC-NORMAL

This is your General QuillScript-Normal

This is your General SquireD and Bold

This is your General Swiss 721 BT

This is your General Swiss 721 Condensed BT, *Condensed Italic,* **Condensed Bold,** *and **Condensed Bold Italic***

This is your General Tiffany Heavy BT

This is your General Tiffany Light BT, *Light Italic,* **Demi,** *and **Demi Italic***

this is your general trafficite-normal

This is your General University Roman Bold BT

This is your General Upright NeonITC-Normal

𝔗𝔥𝔦𝔰 𝔦𝔰 𝔶𝔬𝔲𝔯 𝔊𝔢𝔫𝔢𝔯𝔞𝔩 𝔚𝔢𝔡𝔡𝔦𝔫𝔤 𝔗𝔢𝔵𝔱 𝔅𝔗

This is your General Zapf Calligraphic Italic 801 BT

This is your General Zapf Chancery Medium BT

This is your General Zapf Humanist 601 Italic BT, **and Bold Italic**

The following are samples of the Presentation category of CorelDRAW! fonts:

This is your Presentation Aachen Bold BT

This is your Presentation Aldine 721 Bold Italic BT

This is your Presentation Bauhaus Medium BT

This is your Presentation Belwe Bold BT

This is your Presentation Belwe Condensed BT

This is your Presentation Bitstream Arrus Black BT, *and Black Italic*

This is your Presentation Bodoni Bold BT, *and Bold Italic*

This is your Presentation Bodoni Bold Condensed BT

This is your Presentation Bodoni BT

THIS IS YOUR PRESENTATION BREMEN BLACK BT

THIS IS YOUR PRESENTATION BREMEN BOLD BT

This is your Presentation Brochure

This is your Presentation BrodyD

This is your Presentation Cooper Black BT

This is your Presentation Cooper Black Italic BT

V

Appendixes

This is your Presentation Eras Bold BT

This is your Presentation Eras Book BT

This is your Presentation Eras Demi BT

This is your Presentation Eras Medium BT

This is your Presentation Eras Ultra BT

This is your Presentation Friz Quadrata BT, **and Bold**

This is your Presentation Garamond ITC Book Condensed BT, *and Book Condensed Italic*

This is your Presentation Humanist 521 Extra Bold BT

THIS IS YOUR PRESENTATION STENCIL BT

ꓔꓧꓲꓢ ꓲꓢ ꓜOꓴꓣ ꓑꓣꓱꓢꓱꓠꓔꓮꓔꓲOꓠ ꓢꓔOꓑꓒ

This is your Presentation Swiss 721 Black Italic BT

This is your Presentation Swiss 721 Light BT

This is your Presentation Tango BT

The following are samples of the Printer category of CorelDRAW! fonts:

This is your Printer Bookman ITC Demi BT, *and Demi Italic*

This is your Printer Bookman ITC Light BT, *and Light Italic*

This is your Printer Century Schoolbook Bold BT, *Italic,* **and Bold Italic**

This is your Printer Dutch 801 Bold BT, *Italic,* **and Bold Italic**

This is your Printer Symbol Proportional BT ΑΒΧΔΕΦΓΗΙ

This is your Printer Zapf Calligraphic 801 Italic BT, and Bold Italic

This is your Printer Zapf Chancery Medium Italic BT

This is your Printer Zapf Dingbats BT
✧❑ ▼○ ✺⑥ ♥ ✗ 🙰 ☛

The following are samples of the Publisher category of CorelDRAW! fonts:

This is your Publisher Americana BT, *Italic,* and Bold

This is your Publisher Americana Extra Bold BT

This is your Publisher Americana Extra Bold Condensed BT

This is your Publisher Bauer Bodoni Black Condensed BT

This is your Publisher Bauer Bodoni Bold Condensed BT

This is your Publisher Bauer Bodoni BT, *Italic,* **and Bold Italic**

This is your Publisher Cooper Black Headline BT

This is your Publisher Cooper Medium BT, *and Medium Italic*

This is your Publisher Exotic 350 Bold BT

This is your Publisher Exotic 350 Demi-Bold BT

This is your Publisher Exotic 350 Light BT

This is your Publisher Franklin Gothic ITC Book BT

This is your Publisher Franklin Gothic ITC Heavy BT

This is your Publisher Franklin Gothic ITC Heavy Italic BT

This is your Publisher Futura Book Italic BT

This is your Publisher Futura Heavy Italic BT

This is your Publisher Geometric Slabserif 703 Extra Bold Italic BT

This is your Publisher New Baskerville BT, *Italic,* **Bold,** *and Bold Italic*

This is your Publisher Normande BT

This is your Publisher Poster Bodoni BT

This is your Publisher Schneidler BT, *Italic,* **Bold,** *and Bold Italic*

This is your Publisher Swiss 721 Light Condensed BT

This is your Publisher Swiss 721 Light Italic BT

V

Appendixes

The following are samples of the Signs category of CorelDRAW! fonts:

THIS IS YOUR SIGNS BALLOON EXTRA BOLD BT

This is your Signs Bauer Bodoni Bold BT

This is your Signs Bauer Bodoni Black BT, *and Black Italic*

This is your Signs Bauhaus Heavy BT

This is your Signs Benguiat Gothic Bold BT, *and Bold Italic*

This is your Signs Bitstream Iowan Old Style Black BT, *and Black Italic*

This is your Signs Brush 738 BT

This is your Signs Caslon Bold BT, *and Bold Italic*

THIS IS YOUR SIGNS DECORATED 035 BT

This is your Signs Incised 901 Nord BT

This is your Signs Incised 901 Nord Italic BT

THIS IS YOUR SIGNS INFORMAL 011 BLACK BT

THIS IS YOUR SIGNS MACHINE BT

THIS IS YOUR SIGNS PIONEER BT

This is your Signs Poster Bodoni Italic BT

This is your Signs Revue BT

This is your Signs Swiss 721 Black Extended BT

This is your Signs Swiss 921 BT

THIS IS YOUR SIGNS UMBRA BT

The following are samples of the Technical category of CorelDRAW! fonts:

This is your Technical Architecture

THIS IS YOUR TECHNICAL ENGRAVERS' ROMAN
BOLD BT

This is your Technical Eras Light BT

This is your Technical Geometric Slabserif 712
Light BT, *and Light Italic*

**This is your Technical Gothic 725
Black BT**

This is your Technical Humanist 521 Condensed BT,
and Bold Condensed

This is your Technical Humanist 521 Light BT,
and Light Italic

THIS IS YOUR TECHNICAL
KEYSTROKE

THIS IS YOUR TECHNICAL
LITHOGRAPHLIGHT

This is your Technical OCR-A BT

This is your Technical OCR-B
10 Pitch BT

This is your Technical Orator
10 Pitch BT

This is your Technical Orator 15 Pitch BT

This is your Technical Orbit-B BT

This is your Technical Square 721 BT

This is your Technical Square
721 Extended BT

This is your Technical Swiss 721 Bold Condensed
Outline BT

This is your Technical SwitzerlandNarrow, *Italic,* **Bold,
and Bold Italic**

This is your Technical Technical *and
Technical Italic*

This is your Technical Van DijkITC-Normal

Appendixes

The following are samples of the Template category of CorelDRAW! fonts:

This is your Template American Typewriter Medium BT

THIS IS YOUR TEMPLATEBANK GOTHIC LIGHT BT

THIS IS YOUR TEMPLATEBANK GOTHIC MEDIUM BT

This is your Template Bernhard Fashion BT

This is your Template Bernhard Modern BT, *Italic,* **Bold,** *and Bold Italic*

This is your Template Cheltenham ITC Book BT, *Book Italic,* **Bold,** *and Bold Italic*

THIS IS YOUR TEMPLATE COPPERPLATE GOTHIC BT

THIS IS YOUR TEMPLATE COPPERPLATE GOTHIC HEAVY BT

This is your Template EnviroD

This is your Template Futura Book BT

This is your Template Futura Extra Black BT

This is your Template Futura Heavy BT

This is your Template Galliard BT, *Italic,* **Bold,** *and Bold Italic*

This is your Template Geometric 231 BT, **and Bold**

This is your Template Geometric 231 Heavy BT

This is your Template Geometric 231 Light BT

This is your Template Geometric Slabserif 703 Extra Bold BT

This is your Template Geometric Slabserif 703 Extra Bold Condensed BT

This is your Template Geometric Slabserif 703 Medium BT, *Medium Italic,* **Bold,** *and Bold Italic*

This is your Template Geometric Slabserif 703 Medium Condensed BT, **and Bold Condensed**

This is your Template Goudy Old Style BT, *Italic,*
and Bold
This is your Template Humanist 521 BT, *Italic,*
Bold, *and Bold Italic*
This is a Template Kaufmann BT
This is your Template Korinna Regular BT
and Bold
This is your Template Oz Handicraft BT
This is your Template Shelley Allegro BT
This is your Template Souvenir Light BT, *Light*
Italic, **Demi,** *and Demi Italic*
This is your Template Staccato 222 BT
This is your Template Typo Upright BT
This is your Template Zapf Elliptical 711
BT, *Italic,* **Bold,** *and Bold Italic*
This is your Template Zapf Humanist 601 BT
and Bold
This is your Template Zurich Bold Condensed BT
This is your Template Zurich BT
This is your Template Zurich
Extended BT
This is your Template Zurich Extra Condensed BT
This is your Template Zurich Light BT
This is your Template Zurich Light Condensed BT
This is your Template Zurich Ultra Black
Extended BT

Appendixes

Design Tips

Although CorelDRAW! is not a desktop publishing program, you can use it to create documents in a way that is similar to those kinds of programs. Naturally, you want to create all your artwork, logos, and display type in CorelDRAW!. You also can create many complete documents in CorelDRAW!.

Because you can enter, edit, and format text in CorelDRAW!'s, producing some documents is actually easier than exporting to another program. CorelDRAW! also offers several type control features: kerning, alignment, column guides, and text wrap.

Understanding Consistency and Emphasis

Probably the two most important design elements you can incorporate into artwork or page layout are consistency and emphasis. Consistency, or unity, is created in any page design by repetition of elements. Emphasis, on the other hand, is produced by accenting one important characteristic or feature of the page. A design that incorporates both consistency and emphasis is well-organized, impressive, and eye-catching.

Consistency in Page Layout

Create consistency in a design by repeating elements within the design. For example, duplicate a color, shape, or path in an artwork or a font, type size, or column width in a page design. The following is a list of elements that you can repeat to create consistency in a document:

- ✔ **Fonts.** Use no more than two or three different fonts in any one document, no matter how many pages in the document.

- ✔ **Type Size.** Use no more than four or five type sizes in any one document.

- ✔ **Attributes.** Choose one or two attributes and stick with them throughout the document. Do not apply bold in one paragraph, italic in another, and underlining in yet another. In addition, apply attributes sparingly. Do not use bold, italic, all caps, and so on more than a word or two at a time.

- ✔ **Spacing.** If you add an extra line of space below each heading or after each paragraph of text, continue to add that same spacing throughout the document. Furthermore, keep kerning, letter, word, and especially line spacing (leading) consistent throughout.

- ✔ **Columns.** Keep the number of columns consistent throughout the document. Do not change from one column on page one to three columns on page two. Additionally, keep the same column widths you specify on page one, throughout the document.

- ✔ **Alignment.** If you choose to center one heading, center them all. If the body text is left-aligned, left-align all body text in the document.

✔ **Graphics.** Repeat graphic elements, such as horizontal lines, frames around pictures, illustrations, or callouts, use the same color or screened fill, and so on. In addition, use the same thickness for all lines and no more than two colors or screens for fills. If you plan to use a pattern for fill, use only one pattern throughout the document.

Figure F.1 illustrates all the preceding consistency guidelines in the first page of a newsletter.

World Travel News, Inc.
A Newsletter for Our Customers

Broderick & Associates Offer Travel Package

As the first promotion of the new year, Broderick & Associates offer a travel package that is sure to make your heart leap with joy. Our new package includes a walking tour of Ireland, a trip to the Aran Islands, and ten days and nights at local guest houses in and around County Clare.

This is a trip you cannot afford to miss! We leave at the beginning of March so you absolutely must make your reservations now. We only have room for forty people and spots are filling fast.

Traditional Irish Music in County Clare

If you love traditional Irish music--jigs, reels, polkas, hornpipes, and waltzes--then you are in for a treat! Great musicians are found playing in pubs, fleadhs, and even on the streets in County Clare. For our trip to Ireland, we have an evening scheduled at the County Fleadh, or music festival, and we're sure you will enjoy the fiddle, banjo, and tin whistle players.

In addition, ceili band tryouts are scheduled that same day. You will have some free time, so if you want to schedule some of your day at the fleadh, let us know and we will get you tickets.

Castle ruins cover the countryside.

Pubs -- Not Just for Drinking

If the thought of going to a pub in Ireland doesn't excite you, remember, pubs are not just for drinking. Aye, tis true, the Irish like to drink a bit. However, the real purpose of the pubs of Ireland is for social gathering.

Men, women, and children meet at the pub Sundays, after mass, for a pint and village news. Men discuss the local sports of the season and the weather; whereas the women talk about what's for dinner and why Siobhan wore that same dress to church this morning. The children run about, playing with their friends and watching the adults.

At least one night of the week is set aside in most pubs for music of some sort. Musicians may gather to share a new tune and talk about their instruments while the rest of the patronage enjoy the show. In other pubs, singers stand and perform while enticing the pub customers to join them in a rousing song or two.

During rainy afternoons, men often gather in the pub to discuss the crops or watch a soccer game. Often, women pop into a pub for a quick pint after they do their shopping. And everyone enjoys stopping by the pub for some pub grub, or lunch, now and then.

As you can see, the pub is not just for those who drink, it's for everyone who is friendly and wants to meet people.

Figure F.1
Consistency and emphasis in a document.

Appendixes

Emphasis in Page Layout

Emphasis is also important in any design. Emphasize, or accent, one feature or characteristic in a design to maintain interest, catch the eye, and relieve monotony.

You must be careful to avoid overemphasizing in a design; too many emphasized features is self-defeating—nothing stands out.

You can emphasize any one part of a document to attract attention to that part. Obviously, you should choose an element that is interesting or important to emphasize. Emphasize an element by making it larger, more colorful, a different color, fancier, and so on. Make the emphasized part of the document stand out from the rest.

In figure F.2, a filled rectangle around one article emphasizes that article. You could, alternatively, emphasize the picture in the article by painting it with color while everything else remains in black and white.

Planning the Page Design

If you are an artist, you most likely know many design guidelines that help you create an artwork that is attractive, refined, and professional-looking. Use these same guidelines when you design a document. Whether your document consists of many pages, or only a small part of one page, you should always consider the design guidelines when planning the page.

The following sections include descriptions of page design guidelines that you should keep in mind as you lay out any document.

Orientation

You can choose portrait or landscape orientation for your document. Choose the page orientation that is most consistent with your document or design. For example, if your artwork is wider than it is tall, that artwork suggests a landscape orientation, as shown in figure F.3.

World Travel News, Inc.

A Newsletter for Our Customers

Broderick & Associates Offer Travel Package

As the first promotion of the new year, Broderick & Associates offer a travel package that is sure to make your heart leap with joy. Our new package includes a walking tour of Ireland, a trip to the Aran Islands, and ten days and nights at local guest houses in and around County Clare.

This is a trip you cannot afford to miss! We leave at the beginning of March so you absolutely must make your reservations now. We only have room for forty people and spots are filling fast.

Traditional Irish Music in County Clare

If you love traditional Irish music--jigs, reels, polkas, hornpipes, and waltzes--then you are in for a treat! Great musicians are found playing in pubs, fleadhs, and even on the streets in County Clare. For our trip to Ireland, we have an evening scheduled at the County Fleadh, or music festival, and we're sure you will enjoy the fiddle, banjo, and tin whistle players.

In addition, ceili band tryouts are scheduled that same day. You will have some free time, so if you want to schedule some of your day at the fleadh, let us know and we will get you tickets.

Castle ruins cover the countryside.

Pubs -- Not Just for Drinking

If the thought of going to a pub in Ireland doesn't excite you, remember, pubs are not just for drinking. Aye, tis true, the Irish like to drink a bit. However, the real purpose of the pubs of Ireland is for social gathering.

Men, women, and children meet at the pub Sundays, after mass, for a pint and village news. Men discuss the local sports of the season and the weather; whereas the women talk about what's for dinner and why Siobhan wore that same dress to church this morning. The children run about, playing with their friends and watching the adults.

At least one night of the week is set aside in most pubs for music of some sort. Musicians may gather to share a new tune and talk about their instruments while the rest of the patronage enjoy the show. In other pubs, singers stand and perform while enticing the pub customers to join them in a rousing song or two.

During rainy afternoons, men often gather in the pub to discuss the crops or watch a soccer game. Often, women pop into a pub for a quick pint after they do their shopping. And everyone enjoys stopping by the pub for some pub grub, or lunch, now and then.

As you can see, the pub is not just for those who drink, it's for everyone who is friendly and wants to meet people.

Figure F.2
Emphasis added to document.

V

Appendixes

Figure F.3
Landscape-oriented magazine ad.

Note In the preceding figure, consistency is created through the use of color variance and repeated shapes.

In addition to the shape of the artwork, you can also determine orientation by other factors. Headings or subheadings that are long phrases suggest a landscape orientation. Bulleted and numbered lists that contain short phrases or words are better suited for portrait orientation. Additionally, large amounts of body text often look better in portrait orientation; large amounts of body text are hard to read if the line length is too long (as it would be in landscape orientation).

Balance

Balancing elements on the page means to even the distribution of text and graphics so that no one item overpowers another. Because you cannot actually weigh the elements on the page, you must visually judge the balance. Figure F.4 illustrates balance in an advertisement. The walking stick divides the space and the type balances on either side of the stick. The type to the left consists of only three short lines of text; however the type is 30-point and bold. The type to the right of the stick consists of more lines and words, but is 22-point, regular. The differences in the type sizes balances on either side of the stick.

Figure F.4
Asymmetrical balance.

Blackthorn
Walking
Stick

Now
Available
at all
Byrne
Department
Stores

Three common types of balance are used in page design: symmetrical, asymmetrical, and module. Figure F.4 illustrates asymmetrical balance. Asymmetrical balance depends on the visual weight of the elements on the page. You can balance a large dark shape, for example, with several small dark shapes or one large headline with a paragraph of body text.

Asymmetrical balance creates an interesting and often exciting page design; but it is not always easy. Try to think of it as balancing quantities and mass. One large shape balances many small ones; one dark area balances many light areas, and so on.

Alternatively, you can use symmetrical balance to compose a page. Symmetrical balance distributes text and graphics equally on either side of a center point: top to bottom, left to right, or both top to bottom and left to right. Symmetrical balance is easy to create, but it doesn't always fit with the elements of the page and it is not extremely interesting.

Figure F.5 illustrates the same ad using symmetrical balance (left) and module balance. This example to the right emphasizes the walking stick through repetition, thus making it the eye-catching part of the ad.

Blackthorn Walking Stick

Now Available at all Byrne Department Stores

Blackthorn Walking Stick

Now Available at all Byrne Department Stores

Figure F.5
Symmetrical and modular balance.

Modular balance is similar to symmetrical in that it is a uniform and constant balance. Modular balance uses intersecting guidelines to form boxes across the page. There can be one horizontal line, four horizontal lines, four horizontal lines and two vertical lines, and so on; the combinations are endless. After creating the grid, the text and graphics are placed in the boxes, forming an ordered, systematic layout.

In the following figure, two horizontal lines were used to divide the space in the ad. As you can see, modular balance can be symmetrical or asymmetrical.

White Space

White space, areas that have no text or graphics, provides contrast, emphasis, and a rest for the reader's eyes. Any message in your document has more impact when it is surrounded by white space. As a general rule, balance white space with text and graphics (gray space) on a 50:50 ratio. Although this might sound like too much white space, you can apply the white space in many ways.

Margins provide an excellent source for white space, and all margins do not necessarily need to be 1/2 or 1/4 inch. The possibilities (for use of white space) are many.

Why not make the top and left margins 2 inches and the right and bottom margins 1/2 inch? Or try a bottom margin of 2 1/2 inches and side and top margins of 1 inch. Experiment with the margins of your documents to add interest and variety to your documents.

Other sources for white space include areas around graphic lines, shapes, artwork, and illustrations. Also, add extra space in the gutters (the space between columns). Spacing between paragraphs of text, above or below headings, around center-aligned text, or to the right of left-aligned text, adds valuable white space to your documents.

Figure F.6 illustrates interesting use of white space in a magazine advertisement. The text is wrapped to fit the shape of the bird and twig on the left. White space fills the area to the left of the bird. The balance of the text and white space adds more impact to the picture and the text is more interesting to read. In that figure, the large shape of the bird balances the wrapped text. Additionally, the twig the bird is resting on leads your eye to the text.

Figure F.6
Interesting use of
white space.

Margins and Gutters

Use plenty of margin space and gutter space so that the text does not overwhelm the page. Margin space serves as breathing room for the reader and as a contrast to the gray of a page filled with text and graphics.

Additionally, use margins and gutters to provide consistency from page to page in a document. For example, a newsletter or report should use the same margins on every page.

You can leave margins as white space or you can block the margins off with graphic lines. If you use graphic lines, however, add extra margins inside the lines so that you fill the white space quota. Figure F.7 illustrates ample margin space for a flyer using a border to help define the page. In addition, the figure illustrates sufficient gutter space between the two columns of text. Make sure to leave extra gutter space when using any type of graphic line in a column.

Columns

Use columns to divide and organize text and graphics in your documents. Placing text in columns enables the reader to quickly understand the text flow and the page layout. In addition, shorter lines of text—such as those in columns—are easier to read than longer lines of text—as when you have only one column to a page.

Orientation

When you use portrait orientation, use no more than three columns. You can use two even columns or two uneven ones (such as the columns used in figure F.1) or you can use three even columns. You could try three uneven columns—such as 1 1/2-inches, 2 1/2-inches, and 3 1/2-inches—but be certain your text and graphics fit the design and that the design does not distract the reader.

In landscape orientation, you can use three, four, or five columns, depending on the text and the graphics you plan to use. Just remember to make the text easy to read and to not get overly artistic with the layout. For example, don't vary the column widths too much, or place the columns at odd angles, otherwise you risk losing your reader.

Line Length

If you make sure the type size is easy to read in columns, you should have no problem getting your message across. For example, 10-point type on a page with no columns may afford too great a line length for comfortable reading. When the line length is too long, the reader's eye misses the beginning of the next line or wanders over the page.

Figure F.7
Margin space
outside and
inside the page
border and
between
columns.

Accounting Program

FREE

We are so sure you'll love our new
accounting program that we'll let you
try it FREE for 30 days.

Try our new ACCOUNT IT! free for 30 days.
If you don't like it, return it to us for a full refund.
Take advantage of this offer during the month
of May, and we'll also send you a free disk containing fourteen fonts you can use with any Windows
program. Additionally, we will send a sales
representative to your place of business to install
and train you and your staff in the use of our
accounting program.* What more could you ask for?

CALL TODAY--800-555-9019

* At a minimal charge of just $375 per hour.

ACCOUNT IT!

Accounting Software

Full Package $169.95
Separately, Modules cost $49.95

This offer good only during the month of May, 1994. Offer
limited to one package per customer. Package must be
paid for in advance; if customer is not satisfied after 30
days, we guarantee a full refund of purchase price.

Tip

The optimum length of a line is usually 2 1/2 full alphabets wide,
about 65 to 70 characters. If you're unsure of the best size of type for
a space or the space for size of type, for example, this formula works
well.

In general, 10-point type is good for two or more columns; 12-point type is good
for one column or two columns. Be careful with larger type, 24- or 36-point type in
columns, because the narrower the column, the harder large type is to read.

Gutter Space

Another important factor in column creation is gutter space. Make sure you leave adequate gutters—at least 1/4-inch and as much as 1/2-inch. If you use left-aligned text, you can use 1/4-inch gutters because you have extra white space on the ragged right of the text. If you use justified text, however, you need the extra gutter space; use 3/8-inch or 1/2-inch to ensure comfortable reading.

Planning the Type Design

Typography, the style, arrangement, and appearance of the type elements on the page, is one of the most important elements of design. Because the type in a document contains the message, you must make sure the type is attractive and easy to read. You can ornament, decorate, paint, transform, or mold type to a shape, but the text must remain easy to read. You must not only attract the reader's attention, but maintain it as well.

To that end, there are several type guidelines to follow when you lay out the page. By following these guidelines, you make the type consistent, attractive, and effortless to read. This section covers the type guidelines.

Fonts

Fonts, such as Helvetica or Times Roman, are plentiful in most Windows programs. CorelDRAW! comes with 825 fonts but there's no reason to install all of them because you will never use all 825. Limit the number of fonts you use in any one document to two or three. There may be an occasion to use four different fonts, but any more than that can confuse and distract the reader.

Additionally, some fonts are better suited to use with others; for example, use serif or Roman and sans serif fonts together. Use Helvetica (sans serif) with Times Roman (serif) or Gill Sans (sans serif) with Garamond (serif). Often, a sans serif type is used for headings, subheadings, captions, and headers, whereas a serif font is used for body text.

Another font characteristic is ornamentation. Texts and script fonts are more ornamented than, say, sans serif fonts. Text fonts are Old English, German, and in Illustrator, Goudy Text; whereas, script fonts are Park Avenue, Chancery, and in Illustrator, Bellevue. Never use a text and script together in the same document. Furthermore, if you use a script or text font, use a simple, sans serif font for additional type in the document.

Attributes

Type attributes, such as bold and italic, are useful for adding emphasis to specific text. By adding bold or italic to text, you make the text stand out; however, when you apply too much or too many attributes, the text is no longer emphasized.

Apply attributes to a word or short phrase, never to entire sentences or paragraphs. The reader does not know what part of the text is the most important if all of it is accented. Additionally, a sentence or paragraph of bold or italic type is difficult to read.

Another common mistake is to use uppercase letters in more than one word or a short phrase. Although uppercase headings and subheadings are appropriate in some cases, sentences or paragraphs are difficult to read set in uppercase. Our eyes are accustomed to seeing upper and lowercase letters when reading. Moreover, lowercase letter pairs, such as th, er, ch, ly, and so on, are easier to recognize and thus make our reading faster and easier.

No matter the font or type size you use, a paragraph of all bold text is difficult for the reader to continue to read. Additionally, if you want text to stand out from the rest, applying bold to one or two words is more efficient than applying bold to all of the text in a paragraph.

The same is true for italic type. Although a large amount of italic text may be easier to read than bold, it does not make sense to emphasize entire sentences or paragraphs using the italic attributes.

Never use uppercase for more than a word or short phrase. When all uppercase letters are used, reading is a struggle and the reader may, therefore, quit reading before the end of the message.

Figure F.8 illustrates examples of which attributes you should not use in specific situations. The first paragraph is tagged all bold, the second is tagged all italic, the third is tagged all caps, and the last two are tagged all caps in ornamental font styles.

No matter the font or type size you use, a paragraph of all bold text is difficult for the reader to continue to read. Additionally, if you want text to stand out from the rest, applying bold to one or two words is more efficient than applying bold to all of the text in a paragraph.

The same is true for italic type. Although a large amount of italic text may be easier to read than bold, it does not make sense to emphasize entire sentences or paragraphs using the italic attribute.

NEVER USE UPPERCASE FOR MORE THAN A WORD OR SHORT PHRASE. WHEN ALL UPPERCASE LETTERS ARE USED, READING IS A STRUGGLE AND THE READER MAY, THEREFORE, QUIT READING BEFORE THE END OF THE MESSAGE. AS INDICATED IN THE FOLLOWING TWO SENTENCES, NEVER USE UPPERCASE TEXT OR SCRIPT.

𝔑𝔈𝔙𝔈ℜ 𝔘𝔖𝔈 𝔘𝔓𝔓𝔈ℜ𝔆𝔄𝔖𝔈 𝔗𝔈𝔛𝔗.

𝒩ℰ𝒱ℰℛ 𝒰𝒮ℰ 𝒰𝒫𝒫ℰℛ𝒞𝒜𝒮ℰ 𝒮𝒞ℛℐ𝒫𝒯.

Figure F.8
Examples of inappropriate type attribute use.

Appendixes

Type Size

In addition to limiting the number of fonts and attributes you use in a document, limit the number of type sizes. Some documents can require several type sizes— outlined documents or some reports, for example. For the most part, however, limit the number of type sizes you use to four or five. When you use less text, use fewer type sizes. Too many type sizes can distract the reader and make the piece look busy and crowded.

Additionally, use proportion when you work with type sizes. For example, if you use 10-point body text, use 14- and 18-point headings. When you use 12-point body text, headings can be 18-, 24-, and 36-point. Larger text, like you might use in a flyer, can be proportioned with larger body text; for example, if the headings are 60-point, the smallest type, proportionally, would be 24-point.

Figure F.9 illustrates a poster that applies proportion and limitations to type sizes. There are only three type sizes used in the poster: 64-, 42-, and 24-point type.

One exception to the proportion rule is display type. Display type is very large— 60-, 72-point, or larger—ornamental type used to attract attention in an ad, brochure, announcement, and so on. When you use display type in an ad, the proportion is thrown off. You can, however, apply proportionate sizing to the rest of the text in the document, as shown in figure F.10.

Figure F.9
Limit type sizes within a document and gauge them proportionally.

Figure F.10
Display type in an advertisement.

Spacing

Correct spacing between letters, words, and lines of text is critical for ease of reading. When there is too little space between words or letters, the page is too gray and uninviting to the reader. On the other hand, if there is too much space between words or letters, gaps in the text make it hard to read.

Word and Letter Spacing

Justified text, which is aligned with a flush left and flush right edge, causes problems with letter and word spacing. When text is justified, the program inserts space between letters and words to force the text to the right and left edges. Sometimes those spaces become too large and cause gaps, or "rivers" of white space.

You can alleviate the problem by inserting hyphens in justified text. You also can adjust the word and letter spacing options.

If you insert hyphens, you must use the hyphen (-) key on the keyboard. The problem with this method is that if you edit the text, the hyphen could appear in the middle of a sentence. If you do insert hyphens, make sure you do so at the end of text formatting and editing. Additionally, try not to use more than two consecutive hyphens; more than two hyphens at the end of consecutive lines can distract the reader.

Figure F.11 illustrates the same paragraph of justified text. The first example (left) illustrates the text as it normally appears, with some very large gaps of white space. The second example uses hyphens to alleviate the gaps of space; and the third example uses word spacing and two hyphens.

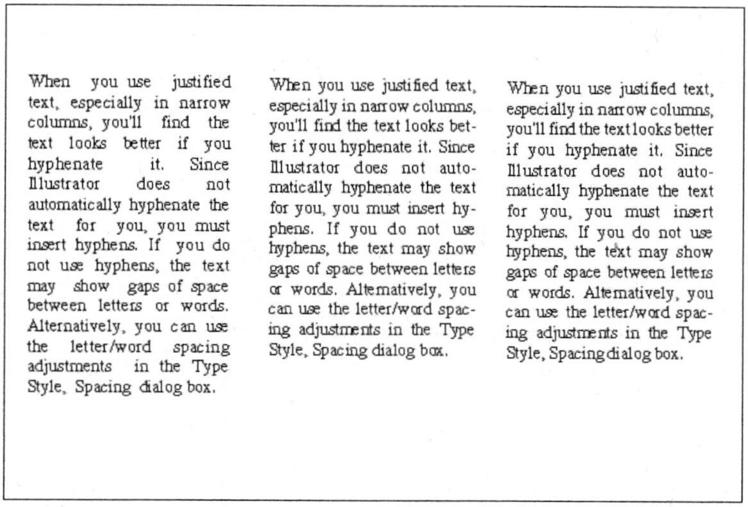

When you use justified text, especially in narrow columns, you'll find the text looks better if you hyphenate it. Since Illustrator does not automatically hyphenate the text for you, you must insert hyphens. If you do not use hyphens, the text may show gaps of space between letters or words. Alternatively, you can use the letter/word spacing adjustments in the Type Style, Spacing dialog box.

When you use justified text, especially in narrow columns, you'll find the text looks better if you hyphenate it. Since Illustrator does not automatically hyphenate the text for you, you must insert hyphens. If you do not use hyphens, the text may show gaps of space between letters or words. Alternatively, you can use the letter/word spacing adjustments in the Type Style, Spacing dialog box.

When you use justified text, especially in narrow columns, you'll find the text looks better if you hyphenate it. Since Illustrator does not automatically hyphenate the text for you, you must insert hyphens. If you do not use hyphens, the text may show gaps of space between letters or words. Alternatively, you can use the letter/word spacing adjustments in the Type Style, Spacing dialog box.

Figure F.11
Justified text with adjusted word spacing and hyphenation.

Line and Paragraph Spacing

Spacing between lines of text (also called *leading*) and between paragraphs of text is a personal preference. There are only a couple of guidelines of which you should be aware.

If you create a numbered or bulleted list, headings, subheads, and so on, feel free to adjust the line spacing to suit the design.

Text Alignment

You can choose to arrange the text on the page using any of four alignments: left-aligned, right-aligned, center-aligned, or justified. Naturally, each type of alignment has its own particular guidelines to consider.

For consistency's sake, choose one alignment for body text and one alignment for headings and subheadings, and stick to it. Constant changes in text alignment within a document can be disconcerting to the reader.

Left-Aligned Text

Left-aligned text is the most common text alignment. Left-aligned text, flush left and ragged right, is perfect for body text, lists, headings, subheadings, almost any text in any document.

If you use left-aligned text as body text, the ragged-right edge adds white space and there's little need for hyphenation or adjusted word spacing. Left-aligned headings also add valuable white space. Additionally, left-aligned text is easy and comfortable to read.

Right-Aligned Text

Right-aligned text, flush right edge and ragged left, is a good alignment to use for short phrases or one-word headings. Never use right-aligned text for body text; it's too hard for the reader to find the beginning of the next line.

In addition, it is best to use upper- and lowercase characters with right-aligned text; all uppercase makes the text harder to read.

Center-Aligned Text

Centered text, ragged right and left edges, is perfect for short phrases. Use centered text for headings, subheadings, captions, datelines, and so on. In addition, you might want to use centered text for lists, names, announcements, invitations, and short lines of text in a flyer, document, or newsletter.

Figure F.12 illustrates the same text and logo for a letterhead. The top example is aligned left, the middle example aligned right, and the bottom example is centered.

Figure F.12
Various alignments provide a different look to the same letterhead.

Justified Text

Justified text, flush left and right edges, is perfect for documents with a great deal of body text: books, reports, articles, and so on. A page of justified text is organized and easy to read. In addition, you can fit more text on a page if you use justified alignment.

If you use page after page of justified text, consider using interparagraph spacing to add white space to the page. If you use justified text in columns, add extra gutter space (3/8 or 1/2-inch) so the page isn't so gray.

Additionally, watch for uneven word or letter spacing with justified text. Add hyphens or adjust the word spacing in the text.

Finally, never use justified text for a heading; large text (18-, 24-point, and so on) does not justify well. Center headings used with justified body text for an elegant look.

Text for Emphasis

You can use text and graphics for emphasis or ornamentation in your documents. Callouts (pulled quotes), large first characters, and bulleted and numbered lists are ways to make the text more interesting and to attract the reader.

Callouts

A callout is a short, pithy statement taken from the body text to entice the reader into reading the article, story, or page. A callout (sometimes called a "pulled quote") is normally set off from the rest of the text by a rectangle, filled space, or horizontal lines above and below. In addition, callouts are usually set in 12- or 14-point italic text, and centered between the left and right edges of the column.

Large First Characters

A large first character or initial cap is the first letter of a paragraph enlarged so that it stands out from the rest of the text and breaks up the text on the page a bit. Use a large first character, for example, in the first paragraph of every chapter of a book or of every section in a report. Don't overuse the large first character, however; it can be distracting to the reader.

Large first characters pulled out of text are often referred to as drop caps. Drop caps either drop down into the text—with the text wrapping around it—or extend one to three lines above the text.

Figure F.13 illustrates two types of large first characters. The example on the left was created by enlarging the letter "A" to 36-point and changing the font to Gill Sans bold. In the second example, the letter was created as a graphic image, grouped, placed on top of the text, and the text was wrapped around the image.

Figure F.13
Two types of
large first
characters.

As the first promotion of the new year, Broderick & Associates offer a travel package that is sure to make your heart leap with joy. Our new package includes a walking tour of Ireland, a trip to the Aran Islands, and ten days and nights at local guest houses in and around County Clare.

The days will be filled with shopping excursions, visits to castles and other tourist attractions, and lunches at pubs. The evenings will be spent either individually or with the group, your choice. We have several activities planned, including traditional music and dance.

In addition, the tour includes a day trip to the Aran Islands, where you will see rock walls stretching for miles and miles. Purchase that special

As the first promotion of the new year, Broderick & Associates offer a travel package that is sure to make your heart leap with joy. Our new package includes a walking tour of Ireland, a trip to the Aran Islands, and ten days and nights at local guest houses in and around County Clare.

The days will be filled with shopping excursions, visits to castles and other tourist attractions, and lunches at pubs. The evenings will be spent either individually or with the group, your choice. We have several activities planned, including traditional music and dance.

In addition, the tour includes a day trip to the Aran Islands, where you will see rock walls stretching for miles and miles. Purchase that special

Lists

You can precede every item in a list with a bullet or a number to attract attention to the items in the list. Bullets signify that no one item on a list is any more important than another. Numbers signify that there is an order of importance to the items on the list or that there is a sequential significance, as in steps of an activity.

A *bullet* is a dot, asterisk, or other symbol that organizes and attracts attention to each item on a list. Bullets attract attention to a list and make it easier to read.

You can, alternatively, number the items on a list. Numbering a list signifies that each item is recorded in order of importance. When you number a list, be sure to indent the number and the list to set it off from the rest of the text. In addition, separate the number from the text in each item with two spaces or so. Finally, if an item in a list overflows to the next line, indent it as well.

Figure F.14 illustrates the same list with bullets (left) and numbers.

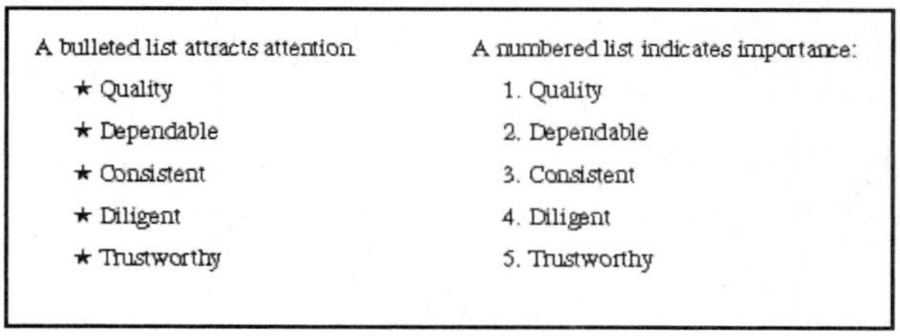

A bulleted list attracts attention.	A numbered list indicates importance:
★ Quality	1. Quality
★ Dependable	2. Dependable
★ Consistent	3. Consistent
★ Diligent	4. Diligent
★ Trustworthy	5. Trustworthy

Figure F.14
Bulleted and numbered lists.

Using Color

If you use color in page layout, consider all the design guidelines discussed in this chapter. Following is a list of how to apply color effectively to your documents:

✔ **Consistency.** Use one, two, or three colors when you design the page and use those same colors throughout the entire document. Use, for example, red for all graphic lines and headlines and dark blue for all body text.

✔ **Emphasis.** Add a splash of one bright color somewhere for emphasis. In the example of red lines and blue body text, add a bright yellow fill over one announcement or heading to make it stand out.

✔ **Balance.** Balance the colors so that there is an equal distribution of each color on the page.

✔ **Paper/Ink.** Consider and use the color of the paper when you choose colors for the type and graphics. If, for example, you have light green paper, that light green shows through when you print a hollow rectangle, outlined text, and so on.

✔ **Contrasting Colors.** Consider choosing contrasting colors, such as red and blue, black and yellow, green and yellow, and so on, instead of two closely related colors, like light blue and dark blue. Make the color count.

✔ **Light Colors.** Be careful if you use light colors—yellow, for example— for text. Make sure there is enough contrast to read the text comfortably.

Integrating Text and Graphics

When you design a document or page using both text and graphics, you must rely heavily on the design guidelines previously discussed in this chapter. If you apply all the design elements to the page, then your document should be attractive, professional, and easy to read.

The following sections show you a few guidelines for integrating text and graphics, followed by several document examples of successful text and graphic integration.

Lines

Graphic lines can help divide and organize a document. A line can extend from margin to margin, border a column, or extend an inch or two. Lines can add emphasis to a word or headline or separate text. Additionally, a line can be thick or thin and of varying colors. Following are a few line guidelines:

✔ Make sure you are consistent with your use of lines when you lay out the page. Keep the lines the same thickness and color throughout.

✔ Do not use a line in place of white space. For example, when you have very little gutter space between two columns, do not add a vertical line to further separate the columns. All that does is crowd the text. Instead, make more room between the columns, even if you have to cut some text.

✔ Be careful how you place thick, dark lines. A line such as this can signal the reader to stop rather than invite the reader to continue.

✔ Never use vertical lines where a fold will go, in the gutters between brochure panels, for example. The line and the fold never line up, and the result looks messy.

✔ Use a line to divide lists, numbers in columns, a callout from the rest of the text, and so on.

Figure F.15 illustrates a newsletter that has vertical and horizontal lines dividing the text and adding to the organization of the page. The lines, as well as the nameplate and headings on the page, are red and the body text and drawing are black. The lines could be overwhelming if they were all black.

Figure F.15
Vertical and horizontal rules divide and organize the text.

Appendixes

Rectangles

Use rectangles on the page to surround text or images. Rectangles direct the reader's attention to whatever it contains. Following are a few guidelines for using rectangles in page layout:

✔ Do not overuse rectangles on the page; try to limit rectangles to no more than two or three, unless the design specifically calls for more.

✔ Leave plenty of margin space around the outside and the inside of all rectangles; do not crowd the text.

✔ Use a rectangle to isolate and call attention to specific text within a document, to several related items in a document, or to encompass the entire page.

✔ Keep line thickness and fill consistent between the rectangles. If you use a rectangle to encompass the entire page, it can use slightly thicker lines than the smaller rectangles on the page.

Figure F.16 illustrates a flyer that uses a 2-point line around the entire page and a 1-point line around the specific accounting program information.

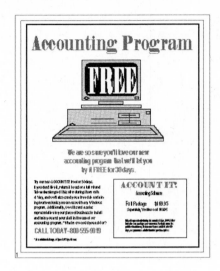

Fill

Adding fill to rectangles can emphasize their contents and make your document more attractive. Follow all design guidelines, such as using the same color throughout the document, balancing filled areas with non-filled areas, and so on.

In addition, if you use a shade of black—40%, 50%, and so on—or if you use some other dark color, make sure you can still read the text in the filled area. If you use a shade darker than 50%, you might want to use light—white or yellow—type to guarantee that the type shows up.

Finally, a fill does not have to have a border (stroke surrounding the rectangle); but any fill should conform to the text edges and margins. For example, if you place a fill in a column, do not overlap the fill into the gutters; instead, indent the text within the filled shape a little on either side.

Figure F.17 illustrates the same flyer used in the preceding example using a light yellow fill in the page rectangle and a white fill in the smaller rectangle. The smaller rectangle stands out from the rest of the flyer.

Figure F.17
Creative use of
fill in rectangles.

APPENDIX

What's On the CD-ROM?

The *Inside CorelDRAW! 5, Fifth Edition CD-ROM* has been assembled with you in mind. Items were chosen that would add value to the book, without adding a whole bunch of shovelware to the disk. In addition to the exercise files used throughout the book, the CD features electronic images from a wide variety of vendors—from black-and-white line art through carefully constructed artwork and gorgeous full-color TIFFs. It also provides awesome textures, stunning patterns, wild shapes, fun wallpaper, wacky sounds, cool animations, quality programs, and the Visual Reality Demo.

Exercises

The EXERCISE directory contains a number of subdirectories, broken down on a chapter-by-chapter basis. Each subdirectory contains the corresponding exercise files for the chapter.

Vendors

The VENDORS directory contains a wide variety of commercially available images from 12 different sources. See Appendix D, "Clip-Art Compendium," for more information about the contributing vendors. The following is a list of vendors, along with the directory structure, number of files, and file types.

Vendor	# of Files	Type
Arro		
\VENDORS\ARRO\ENERGY	4	EPS
\VENDORS\ARRO\LIVEPLNT	3	EPS
\VENDORS\ARRO\POLLUTE	3	EPS
\VENDORS\ARRO\RECYCLE	3	EPS
\VENDORS\ARRO\WILDACCS	4	EPS
\VENDORS\ARRO\WILDLIFE	4	EPS
Artbeats		
\VENDORS\ARTBEATS\BACK4MM\HI-RES	2	GIF
\VENDORS\ARTBEATS\BACK4MM\LO-RES	1	GIF
\VENDORS\ARTBEATS\DEMO	5	EPS
\VENDORS\ARTBEATS\MARBGRAN\FLOORS	2	TIFF
\VENDORS\ARTBEATS\MARBGRAN\IMAGES	2	TIFF
\VENDORS\ARTBEATS\MARBGRAN\SEAMLESS	2	TIFF
\VENDORS\ARTBEATS\PAPERTEX	5	TIFF

Vendor	# of Files	Type
Cartesia		
\VENDORS\CARTESIA\VOL_1	2	CDR
\VENDORS\CARTESIA\VOL_2\MN	4	CDR
\VENDORS\CARTESIA\VOL_2\WI	4	CDR
\VENDORS\CARTESIA\VOL_3	2	CDR
\VENDORS\CARTESIA\VOL_4	1	CDR
\VENDORS\CARTESIA\WDB	2	AI
Deniart		
\VENDORS\DENIART\TRUETYPE	3	TTF
\VENDORS\DENIART\TYPE1	3	PFB
DS Design		
\VENDORS\DSDESIGN	14	EPS
\VENDORS\DSDESIGN	6	TIFF
Logopower		
\VENDORS\LOGOPOWR\60-99	5	EPS
\VENDORS\LOGOPOWR\BASE	3	EPS
Planet Art		
\VENDORS\PLANETAR	12	TIFF
ProArt		
\VENDORS\PROART	8	EPS
Sunshine		
\VENDORS\SUNSHINE	38	TIFF

V

Appendixes

continues

continued

Vendor	# of Files	Type
Taco Clipart Company		
\VENDORS\TACO	262	GIF

(These 262 GIF images have been exported from the ICONS.BIF (burrito) file. There are a total of 486 WPG images in ICONS.BIF. In addition, there are 15 TIFF images in COFFEE.BIF and 7 assorted files in SAMPLE.BIF.

Vendor	# of Files	Type
Three-D Graphics		
\VENDORS\THREE-D	10	TIFF
Work For Hire		
\VENDORS\WORK4HIR	7	TIFF

Goodies!

The goodies directory contains a variety of interesting multimedia files, such as animations, original WAV sounds, CorelDRAW! pattern files, Windows wallpaper, wild shapes, and some basic objects.

Animations

In the \GOODIES\ANIMATE\CRYSTAL directory, you'll find a dozen FLC animations courtesy of, and created by, Crystal Graphics. These files were created with Crystal Flying Fonts. In addition, you'll find some original animations in the \GOODIES\ANIMATE\QUICKEES directory (which were also created with Crystal Flying Fonts).

Directory	# of Files	Type
\GOODIES\ANIMATE\CRYSTAL	12	FLC
\GOODIES\ANIMATE\QUICKEES	4	FLC

Lovely Illusions—Custom Full-Color Pattern Fills

The \GOODIES\PATTERNS directory contains 116 wonderful shareware color pattern (PAT) files, created by Virginia Schmitz. These are only a fraction of her complete collection. Virginia offers 400 more fills for a reasonable $35 registration fee. The CD-ROM also contains 30 of her awesome shape files, which were created in CorelDRAW! 4.0.

Directory	# of Files	Type
\GOODIES\PATTERNS	116	PAT
\GOODIES\SHAPES	30	CDR

Wild & Crazy Wallpapers

You'll have plenty of Windows wallpaper choices with Virginia Schmitz's Wild & Crazy Wallpapers. The CD-ROM contains 105 shareware BMP files to personalize your electronic workplace. A $20 registration fee will bring you 200 more wallpaper designs, along with a shareware copy of WWPlus (a wallpaper changer and screen saver).

Directory	# of Files	Type
\GOODIES\WALLPAPER	105	BMP

Silly Sounds

One late night, during the production of this book, this assortment of 68 freeware sounds came to life. Blame it on the hour. Blame it on too much sugar and caffeine, or blame it on sleep deprivation. Whatever you blame it on, you are bound to find at least one of these silly sounds worth playing for your buddies!

Directory	# of Files	Type
\GOODIES\SOUNDS	68	WAV

V

Appendixes

Some Basic AI Objects

This is a collection of some basic objects in Adobe Illustrator format. You will find 120 different stars (open and filled), spirals, polygons, spokes, and wheels. They were created with Deneba Canvas and saved as AI88 files. These files illustrate a variety of the powerful object creation tools in Canvas. Some of the files (SSTAR*.AI) were opened and saved in Adobe Illustrator for Windows.

Directory	# of Files	Type
\GOODIES\CANVASAI	120	AI

Grayscale TIFF Textures

Here's a bunch of original freeware full-page grayscale TIFF textures, suitable for use with printed materials at up to a 150 lpi screen. The file sizes are quite large, but that's what's necessary for high-resolution images intended for print. The \GSTEXTUR directory contains fifteen images at high resolution along with five images that have been sampled down (for lower resolution printing). These textures were created with a combination of programs, including Adobe Photoshop, Fractal Sketcher, Kai's PowerTools, and Fauve Matisse.

Directory	# of Files	Type
\GSTEXTUR	20	TIFF

Programs

We were very selective in choosing the programs to include on the *Inside CorelDRAW! 5, Fifth Edition CD-ROM*. Hence, you'll find just a handful of entries. Check the README file in each directory for information on installation.

Burrito

The Burrito (\PROGRAMS\TACO) is a tasty treat—a full version of the multimedia database/viewer/player/translator (with compression) file utility—from the Omaha, Nebraska-based Taco Clipart Company. The Burrito is designed to compress clip art files, sounds, and avi files. The program also will convert artwork into different file formats and annotate files with text, which allows for cross-relational database searches. This is the full version of the Burrito, which you can register for $29. You can read more about Taco in Appendix D.

Cubit Meister

The \PROGRAMS\CUBIT directory contains a shareware copy of Cubit Meister, version 1.04. Cubit Meister performs several functions specifically designed for the Windows DTP professional. Cubit Meister converts decimal and fractional inches, millimeters/centimeters, picas/points and points into all the other formats simultaneously. CM also provides an electronic Proportional Scale that calculates proportions even when different measurement systems are entered for the "Original" and "Target" sizes. This latest version features an improved interface, a highly accurate and configurable proportional scale, as well as the ability to handle large numbers.

Fauve Matisse in Gray

The \PROGRAMS\FAUVE directory features a free copy of Fauve Matisse in Gray, a grayscale version of the exciting Windows-based paint program. This is one hot application! A capsule review of the full version of Fauve Matisse can be found in Chapter 10, "You're the Designer."

The Visual Reality Demo

This interactive demo introduces you to the world of Visual Reality (\VSOFT), with lots of really cool photorealistic images and animations. The demo installs a few files to your hard disk, but runs from the CD-ROM (it's over 130 MB!). Check out Chapter 10 for more information on Visual Reality, "the Suite of Tools for 3D Graphics and Animation," from Visual Software.

INDEX

Inside CorelDRAW! Fifth Edition
REGISTRATION CARD

Fill out this card to receive information about future CorelDRAW! books and other New Riders titles!

Name _____ **Title** _____

Company _____

Address _____

City/State/ZIP _____

I bought this book because: _____

_____

I purchased this book from:

☐ A bookstore (Name _____)

☐ A software or electronics store (Name _____)

☐ A mail order (Name of Catalog _____)

I purchase this many computer books each year:

☐ 1–5   ☐ 6 or more

I currently use these applications: _____

_____

_____

_____

I found these chapters to be the most informative: _____

_____

I found these chapters to be the least informative: _____

_____

Additional comments: _____

_____

☐ I would like to see my name in print! You may use my name and quote me in future New Riders products and promotions. My daytime phone number is:_____

New Riders Publishing 201 West 103rd Street • Indianapolis, Indiana 46290 USA

Fold Here

- -

New Riders Publishing
201 West 103rd Street
Indianapolis, Indiana 46290
USA

WANT MORE INFORMATION?

CHECK OUT THESE RELATED TITLES:

	QTY	PRICE	TOTAL

Inside Adobe Photoshop for Windows. Users uncover the secrets of Adobe Photoshop with this illuminating tutorial and reference written by award-winning artist Gary Bouton—plus a bonus CD-ROM with images, exercise art, and shareware—this book is everything Photoshop users need. ISBN: 1-56205-259-4   ____ $42.00   _____

Adobe Photoshop NOW! Master the complexities of Adobe Photoshop—fast! Realistic 4-color images, complete with expert tips and techniques—plus a bonus CD-ROM that is loaded with images, textures, and fonts—this is the end-all book for easily mastering high-end Photoshop imaging tricks now! ISBN: 1-56205-200-4.   ____ $35.00   _____

CorelDRAW! Special Effects. Learn award-winning techniques from professional CorelDRAW! designers with this comprehensive collection of the hottest tips and techniques! This full-color book provides step-by-step instructions for creating over 30 stunning special effects. An excellent book for those who want to take their CorelDRAW! documents a couple of notches higher. ISBN: 1-56205-123-7.   ____ $39.95   _____

CorelDRAW! Now. Users who want fast access to thorough information, people upgrading to CorelDRAW! 4.0 from a previous edition, new CorelDRAW! users—all of these groups will want to tap into this guide to great graphics—now! Developed by CorelDRAW! experts, this book provides answers on everything from common questions to advanced inquiries. ISBN: 1-56205-131-8.   ____ $21.95   _____

Name _____

Company _____

Address _____

City _____ State ____ ZIP _____

Phone _____ Fax _____

☐ Check Enclosed   ☐ VISA   ☐ MasterCard

Card #_____Exp. Date_____

Signature _____

Prices are subject to change. Call for availability and pricing information on latest editions.

Subtotal   _____

Shipping   _____

$4.00 for the first book and $1.75 for each additional book.

Total   _____
Indiana residents add 5% sales tax.

New Riders Publishing 201 West 103rd Street • Indianapolis, Indiana 46290 USA

Orders/Customer Service: 1-800-428-5331

Fold Here

- -

New Riders Publishing
201 West 103rd Street
Indianapolis, Indiana 46290
USA

GO AHEAD. PLUG YOURSELF INTO
MACMILLAN COMPUTER PUBLISHING.

Introducing the Macmillan Computer Publishing Forum on CompuServe®

Yes, it's true. Now, you can have CompuServe access to the same professional, friendly folks who have made computers easier for years. On the Macmillan Computer Publishing Forum, you'll find additional information on the topics covered by every Macmillan Computer Publishing imprint—including Que, Sams Publishing, New Riders Publishing, Alpha Books, Brady Books, Hayden Books, and Adobe Press. In addition, you'll be able to receive technical support and disk updates for the software produced by Que Software and Paramount Interactive, a division of the Paramount Technology Group. It's a great way to supplement the best information in the business.

WHAT CAN YOU DO ON THE MACMILLAN COMPUTER PUBLISHING FORUM?

Play an important role in the publishing process—and make our books better while you make your work easier:

- Leave messages and ask questions about Macmillan Computer Publishing books and software—you're guaranteed a response within 24 hours
- Download helpful tips and software to help you get the most out of your computer
- Contact authors of your favorite Macmillan Computer Publishing books through electronic mail
- Present your own book ideas
- Keep up to date on all the latest books available from each of Macmillan Computer Publishing's exciting imprints

JOIN NOW AND GET A FREE COMPUSERVE STARTER KIT!

To receive your free CompuServe Introductory Membership, call toll-free, **1-800-848-8199** and ask for representative **#597**. The Starter Kit Includes:

- Personal ID number and password
- $15 credit on the system
- Subscription to CompuServe Magazine

HERE'S HOW TO PLUG INTO MACMILLAN COMPUTER PUBLISHING:

Once on the CompuServe System, type any of these phrases to access the Macmillan Computer Publishing Forum:

GO MACMILLAN   **GO BRADY**
GO QUEBOOKS   **GO HAYDEN**
GO SAMS   **GO QUESOFT**
GO NEWRIDERS   **GO ALPHA**

Once you're on the CompuServe Information Service, be sure to take advantage of all of CompuServe's resources. CompuServe is home to more than 1,700 products and services—plus it has over 1.5 million members worldwide. You'll find valuable online reference materials, travel and investor services, electronic mail, weather updates, leisure-time games and hassle-free shopping (no jam-packed parking lots or crowded stores).

Seek out the hundreds of other forums that populate CompuServe. Covering diverse topics such as pet care, rock music, cooking, and political issues, you're sure to find others with the same concerns as you—and expand your knowledge at the same time.

GRAPHICS TITLES

INSIDE CORELDRAW! 4.0, SPECIAL EDITION

DANIEL GRAY

An updated version of the #1 best-selling tutorial on CorelDRAW!

CorelDRAW! 4.0

ISBN: 1-56205-164-4

$34.95 USA

CORELDRAW! SPECIAL EFFECTS

NEW RIDERS PUBLISHING

An inside look at award-winning techniques from professional CorelDRAW! designers!

CorelDRAW! 4.0

ISBN: 1-56205-123-7

$39.95 USA

CORELDRAW! NOW!

RICHARD FELDMAN

The hands-on tutorial for users who want practical information now!

CorelDRAW! 4.0

ISBN: 1-56205-131-8

$21.95 USA

INSIDE CORELDRAW! FOURTH EDITION

DANIEL GRAY

The popular tutorial approach to learning CorelDRAW!...with complete coverage of version 3.0!

CorelDRAW! 3.0

ISBN: 1-56205-106-7

$24.95 USA

WINDOWS TITLES

ULTIMATE WINDOWS 3.1

FORREST HOULETTE, JIM BOYCE,
RICH WAGNER, & THE BSU
RESEARCH STAFF

The most up-to-date reference for
Windows available!

Covers 3.1 and related products

ISBN: 1-56205-125-3

$39.95 USA

WINDOWS FOR NON-NERDS

JIM BOYCE & ROB TIDROW

This helpful tutorial for Windows
provides novice users with what they
need to know to gain computer
proficiency…and confidence!

Windows 3.1

ISBN: 1-56205-152-0

$18.95 USA

INSIDE WINDOWS NT

FORREST HOULETTE, RICHARD WAGNER,
GEORGE ECKEL, & JOHN STODDARD

A complete tutorial and reference to
organize and manage multiple tasks and
multiple programs in Windows NT.

Windows NT

ISBN: 1-56205-124-5

$34.95 USA

INTEGRATING WINDOWS APPLICATIONS

ELLEN DANA NAGLER, FORREST HOULETTE,
MICHAEL GROH, RICHARD WAGNER, &
VALDA HILLEY

This book is a no-nonsense, practical
approach for intermediate- and
advanced-level Windows users!

Windows 3.1

ISBN: 1-56205-083-4

$34.95 USA

Installing the CD-ROM

Portions of the companion CD-ROM must be installed to your hard drive. The installation program runs from within Windows. (Note: To install the files from the CD-ROM, you'll need at least 12 MB of free space on your hard drive.)

1. From File Manager or Program Manager, choose **Run** from the File menu.

2. Type *<drive>*INSTALL and press Enter, where *<drive>* is the letter of the CD-ROM drive that contains the installation disc. For example, if the disc is in drive D:, type D:INSTALL and press Enter.

Follow the on-screen instructions in the installation program. Be sure to look at README.TXT file in the root directory of the disc and the file displayed at th of the installation process; they contain information on the files and progra were installed.